INDIAN WARS

AND

FAMOUS FRONTIERSMEN

TRUMBULL
WHITE

AUGUSTUS
LYNCH
MASON L L D

JOHN
CLARK
RIDPATH LLD

EMINENT AMERICAN HISTORIANS
(THE AUTHORS OF THIS BOOK)

INDIAN WARS

AND

FAMOUS FRONTIERSMEN

THE THRILLING STORY OF PIONEER LIFE
IN AMERICA

EXCITING EXPERIENCES WITH THE INDIANS WHILE
PUSHING BACK THE WILDERNESS

EMBRACING THE PRINCIPAL EPISODES

IN THE STRUGGLE OF THE WHITE RACE WITH THE RED
MEN FOR THE POSSESSION OF THE
NEW WORLD

A TRUE AND VIVID ACCOUNT OF THE

DARK CAPTIVITIES AND THE UNCONQUERABLE COURAGE OF THE MEN AND
WOMEN WHO WRESTED THE AMERICAN FORESTS FROM THE ABORIGINES
AND GAVE THEM TO THE PLOW AND THE SICKLE

BY

AUGUSTUS LYNCH MASON, LL.D.

DEAN OF THE LAW SCHOOL OF DE PAUW UNIVERSITY

WITH INTRODUCTION AND SPECIAL CONTRIBUTIONS

BY

JOHN CLARK RIDPATH, LL.D.

AUTHOR OF "A CYCLOPÆDIA OF UNIVERSAL HISTORY," "THE GREAT RACES OF
MANKIND," "HISTORY OF THE UNITED STATES," ETC.

PROFUSELY ILLUSTRATED WITH RARE AND THRILLING PICTURES. THE ORIGI-
NAL ENGRAVINGS AND REPRODUCTIONS OF CHOICE PHOTOGRAPHS
COMBINE TO MAKE IT A BEAUTIFULLY ILLUSTRATED WORK.

Fredonia Books
Amsterdam, The Netherlands

Indian Wars and Famous Frontiersmen:
The Thrilling Story of Pioneer Life in America

by
Augustus Lynch Mason

ISBN: 1-58963-785-2

PREFACE.

CIVILIZATION is a war—a war of light with dark-ness; of truth with falsehood; of the illuminated intellect and the rectified heart with the barbarism of ignorance and the animalism of the savage.

The present work portrays a single phase of this sublime conflict. It recounts one of the thousand campaigns of this war. It is an attempt to condense into a single volume, and give an adequate literary expression to, the thrilling history of the struggle between the White man and the Red man for the possession of this continent. It is also intended to be a memorial to a race of heroes. Other countries have esteemed their earliest heroes as worthy of the song of the poet and the praise of the historian. With us the deeds of our fathers are as yet unsung, and their very names are fading from our memory.

The author has aimed to make this book not only historical, but realistic. It is a truthful account of actual events, gathered from a vast mass of authorities. Yet the design has been pictorial rather than geometrical. The author has sought rather to paint a picture than to make a map. In the execution of this purpose he has been nobly seconded by the PUBLISHERS, who have spared neither trouble nor expense to procure for

7

him rare and valuable authorities. The large collections of
the public libraries of the country were found inadequate,
and booksellers from Boston to San Antonio have been called
upon for books difficult of access.

To the vast number of painstaking and truthful writers
from whom the author has thus drawn his facts, and perchance
even the expression of them, an obligation exists for which
no adequate return can be made. The author also takes this
opportunity to express his deep obligations to PROFESSOR
JOHN CLARK RIDPATH, the eminent historian, to whose
generous aid he is indebted for suggestions, as well as for
additions to the narrative. A similar recognition is due to
HON. HENRY A. RATTERMANN, whose unequaled library of
rare books on American Pioneer History—especially that
part relating to the settlement of the Ohio Valley,—has
furnished valuable data for this volume, without which much
that is interesting would have been lost to these pages.

The liberality of the PUBLISHERS has extended not merely
to the procurement of literary materials, but has also enriched
the book with a collection of artistic engravings in every way
worthy of the topic. Supplemented as his own efforts have
been by these powerful and generous aids, it is not without
confidence that the work is submitted to the public.

A. L. M.

DEER PARK, MARYLAND.

PUBLISHERS' PREFACE

This book is presented to fill a long felt want on the part of the public, for what may be called "Pioneer History."

Its educational qualities are instantly recognized by all readers who seek definite information and facts concerning the early settlement and first development of America. It is intended to serve and DOES serve all readers with that important part of American history not found in the numerous Histories of the United States. The question arises, "Who were the mothers and fathers of America?" Generally, they were small bodies of men and women, of sturdy and resolute character and sterling qualities. This volume tells you who they were and what part of our great country they originally settled, what they had to contend with —in many cases sacrificed their lives for the true principles involved.

To the teacher or student, this volume WILL TEACH American history and perhaps the most important part of American history, and furthermore that part which is not to be found elsewhere. To the parents its great value cannot be estimated. It paints for their children, character, courage, resolute endurance and firmness of mind. The stories are thrilling, yet true, and intensely interesting. It cultivates a desire for a closer acquaint-

PUBLISHERS' PREFACE

ance with these men and women of the noblest and grandest period of pioneer history. It is a storehouse of essential information to young or old in any vocation of life.

To the foregoing facts must be added a mention of the illustrations. These were drawn and engraved on wood at an enormous expense. There never were any photographs of these scenes from which to make half tone or photographic pictures. Each one of these rare and renowned illustrations tells a story in itself. They make a lasting impression on the reader. We are proud to be able to present this excellent volume to all readers.

THE PUBLISHERS.

ROBERT SIEUR DE LA SALLE.

BY LOUIS GUDEBROD.

The name of LaSalle is ever present in the early history of the Mississippi Valley from the Great Lakes to the Gulf of Mexico. His wonderful voyages, his perils, his achievements, are all related in earlier chapters of this volume.

PERE MARQUETTE.

Father Marquette's fame is immortal as one of the greatest of the early French explorers of this continent, traversing its forests and rivers year after year, laboring for the conversion of the Indians, and finally laying down his life among them in Northern Michigan where much of his noble work had been done.

WILLIAM CLARKE   THOMAS JEFFERSON   MERRIWETHER LEWIS

President Jefferson and the men sent by him under his administration to explore the great Northwest—known in history as the Lewis and Clarke expedition.

PIERRE LACLEDE, FIRST SETTLER OF ST. LOUIS.
BY J SCOTT HARTLEY.

THE DESTINY OF THE RED MAN.
BY A. A. WEINMANN.

STATUE OF CAPTAIN
WILLIAM CLARKE

STATUE OF SACAGAWEA,
THE INDIAN WOMAN
WHO LED LEWIS AND
CLARKE THROUGH THE
INDIAN TRAIL OVER THE
MOUNTAINS

STATUE OF CAPTAIN
MERRIWETHER LEWIS

Lewis and Clarke's expedition, covering nearly two years and a half, gave the people of this country their first information concerning the immense extent, vast wealth and natural wonders and resources of the Northwest.

CONTENTS

CHAPTER I.

THE LEGEND OF POWHATAN.

CHAPTER II.

THE TRIALS OF LA SALLE.

CHAPTER III.

ROGERS' RANGERS.

CHAPTER IV.

THE AMBITION OF PONTIAC.

CHAPTER V.

JOSEPH BRANT AND THE MOHAWKS.

CHAPTER VI.

THE CONFLICT IN THE OHIO VALLEY.

CHAPTER VII.

THE COURAGE OF KENTON.

CHAPTER VIII.

BRADY THE BACKWOODSMAN.

CHAPTER IX.

THE DAYS OF DANIEL BOONE.

CHAPTER X.

THE CRUELTIES OF GIRTY.

CHAPTER XI.

THE DOOM OF CRAWFORD.

12   *CONTENTS.*

CHAPTER XII.

THE ROMANCE OF RED EAGLE.

The Emperor Alexander—Red Eagle as a boy—A rich man's home—The idol of the people—Tecumseh—A false prophet—Red Eagle's sweetheart—Love and War—The massacre of Fort Mims—Card playing and drinking among the garrison—The growing sand-heap—The attack—The hopeless defense—"To the bastion!"—Red Eagle's nobility—Searching the heaps of corpses—The dog charge—Jackson's campaigns—Dale's famous canoe fight—Mutinies—The battle of the Horseshoe—Surrender of Red Eagle ....Pages 421-450

CHAPTER XIII.

THE TRUE STORY OF THE PROPHET.

The change of name—Mythical ancestry—The good elder brother—White scoundrels—Red villains—The great conspiracy—The rogue of a prophet—His miracles—The sun darkened—Tecumseh's love for his sister—His ambition—The nigh-before the battle—Tippecanoe—Harrison's victory—Tecumseh's rage—Battle of the Thames—Who killed Tecumseh?.............................Pages 451-484

CHAPTER XIV.

THE SORROWS OF THE SEMINOLES.

The Seminole's curse—Blood-money—Exile or war—Massacred among the Palmetto trees—Reign of terror on the plantations—The "House of Blood"—Scalped in a parlor—The tragedy in the flower garden—Thirty skeletons in a row—Fever, flood, famine—The conspirators in the chief's wigwam—Knives glistening in the starlight—The flight—Osceola betrayed—"I feel choked; you must talk"—The caged eagle—The squeeze through the embrasure—A fifty-foot leap—Osceola's dungeon—Despair—Death—Bloodhounds used in the war—Killed in a cupola—Horrors of the Florida war—Coacoochee's capture—The departure into perpetual exile..Pages 485-520

CHAPTER XV.

BLACK HAWK'S HUMILIATION.

First chapter of an Indian Genesis—Battles of the gods—Tricked into a treaty—Willing to die for his brother—"Move"—Who is Black Hawk?—Stealing roasting-ears from one's own fields—A dog banquet—A squaw swims the Mississippi, carrying her child in her teeth—"Paint me as I am"—The princely Keokuk—Gall and wormwood..Pages 521-536

INTRODUCTION.

THE PIONEER was a rugged seer
  As he crossed the Western river,
Where the Copper Man called the INDIAN
  Lay hid with his bow and quiver.

As for the pioneer, his days are numbered. As for the Indian, there he stands, a specter on the horizon!

The conflict has been irrepressible. There could be no compromise; the races were too unlike. The red man had no beauty that our spirits could desire him. The verdict of civilization has been, that his room is better than his company. It is an edict issued from the court of Progress—that ferocious Titan who strides from East to West—that the Indian shall disappear, shall be remanded to the past, shall evanish.

In those great movements by which the populations of the world are transformed, History is blind, cruel, remorseless. She is the least sentimental of all the divinities. She neither smiles at human happiness, nor weeps at human sorrow; she merely attends to her syllogism. When she finds a tribe of nomads living in a valley adapted to the cultivation of corn, she sends the news to some corn-raising race, and leaves the rest to cupidity and the casuists.

And the casuists make a muck of the whole business. They seek a design. They find it in this—that the soil is intended for those who will cultivate it. They fix on this correlation. The hint of nature is, that the clover-field and the orchard must take the place of the brake and the wilderness. It is all very beautiful. The designated race comes in; and the gray squirrel, after gibing at the business for a season, goes over the horizon followed by a bullet.

But how about the other side of the question? It is well for the supplanters—but the supplanted? The red deer is designed for the cane-brake, and the cane-brake for him. Both are designed for the hunter. Is Nature not as well pleased to be tracked by a buck of ten spikes, as to be wounded in the breast with a hoe?

In this world there is one law: *the weakest goes to the wall.* Men may as well expect a weight on the shorter arm of a lever to lift a greater weight on the longer, as to suppose a reversal of this law. There is such a thing as a science of *Historical Physics*, which it is time for thinkers to consider. The fundamental maxim in the dynamics of progress is, that the greater force overcomes the less. They who will, may complain of the result and try to explain it.

The movement of civilization westward, from Babylon to Rome, from Rome to London, from London to San Francisco, has furnished a succession of eras in which the stronger, more highly developed races, have flung themselves in heavy masses upon the aboriginal populations. The latter have yielded, have perished, are perishing. In Greece, the Hellenes came upon the Pelasgians, and the latter were either exterminated or absorbed. Again, in Southern Italy, the Œnotrians were overwhelmed by the aggressive colonists of Magna Græcia. The Gaulish and British Celts sank into the earth under the tremendous pressure of the Roman and the Saxon. The American aborigines, forced back from the seaboard through the passes of the Alleghanies, are swept across the great valley of the Mississippi, and thrown up like pebbles on the plains of the West.

In the great march which has thus substituted the wheat-field for the cane-brake, and made the White man the exterminator of the Red barbarian, there is this that is peculiar: in America the work has been done by a class of men unknown

Ysa Kit Carson

The famous American trapper. He served as guide to Fremont in
his Rocky Mountain explorations and was an officer in the
United States service in both the Mexican and Civil Wars.
The tombstone at top is at Taos, New Mexico.

UPPER—COW BOYS, NORTH DAKOTA.
LOWER—EXHIBIT OF GAME.

DAVID CROCKETT.

GENERAL SAM HOUSTON.

UPPER—BEN HUR ROOM.

it was in this room that General Lew Wallace wrote his famous book "Ben Hur." The room is in the Governor's Palace, Santa Fe, New Mexico.

LOWER—TIPPECANOE AND TYLER TOO.

When General William Henry Harrison was elected President in 1840, the watchwords "Log Cabin" and "Hard Cider" were effectively used in winning votes.

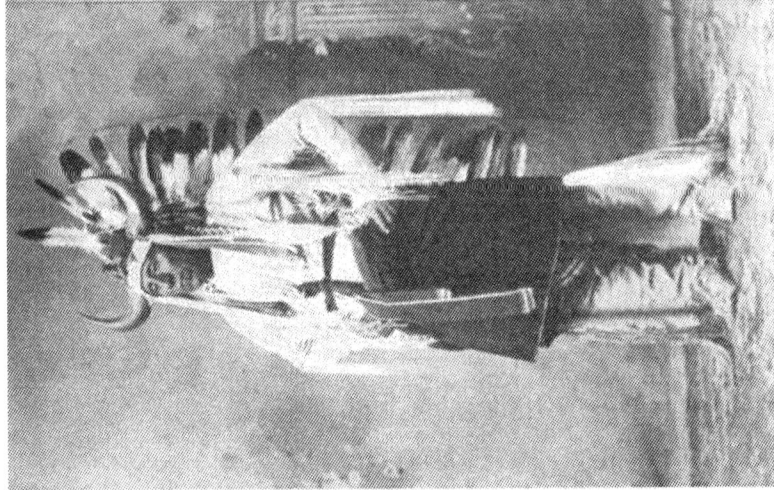

TINNEY TONE.
Kiowa Indian in war costume.

CAPT. JACK CRAWFORD, THE POET-SCOUT, AND
E. S. PAXSON, WITH CAMP PARAPHERNALIA.

SIOUX INDIANS, SUN DANCE.

INDIAN CAMP, OKLAMOMA.
PRAIRIE SCHOONERS, SOUTH DAKOTA.
SIOUX INDIAN TEPEES, SOUTH DAKOTA.

KIOWA INDIANS DRAWING RATIONS, ANADARKO, OKLAHOMA.
CREE INDIANS, MONTANA.

GERTRUDE THREE FINGERS AND PAPOOSE. OKLAHOMA.

ASSINABOINE INDIAN MOTHER AND CHILDREN. MONTANA.

COW-BOYS, TEXAS.

Man with hat off is Clay McGonigle, who in a test in 1903, lassoed three and tied a steer in 28¾ seconds. Next to him is Miss Lucille Mulhall.

NAVAJO INDIAN WEAVING.　　　**INDIAN GRAVES, DEADWOOD, SOUTH DAKOTA.**

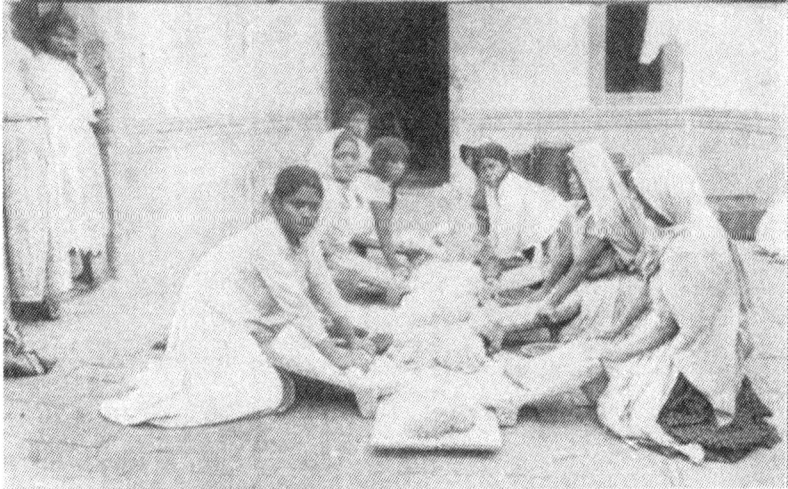

INDIAN LAUNDRY GIRLS, ANADARKA, OKLAHOMA.
INDIAN BREAD MAKERS, ARIZONA.

BUFFALO ON THE RANGE.
MOUNTAIN SHEEP, COLORADO.

UPPER--OUTFIT WAGON, INDIAN TERRITORY.
LOWER--SOD HOUSE, NORTH-WEST NEBRASKA.
Former home of a now wealthy Alliance resident.

STATUE FORT DEARBORN MASSACRE, CHICAGO.
Black Partridge rescuing Mrs. Helm.

FT. DEARBORN TABLET, CHICAGO, ILL.

ZUNI INDIAN VILLAGE, ARIZONA.

in Europe—THE PIONEERS. Europe was peopled by large bodies of men moving from one country to another. In many regions the antiquarian finds the Age of Stone suddenly cut off by the Age of Bronze, without any intervening Age of Copper. This means that a bronze-bearing soldiery overwhelmed the people of the Stone Age before the latter had developed into a capability of working the metals. The Hellenes came from the east as migrating tribes. The original peoples of the peninsula were extinguished by the invaders. The Gaulish nations were trodden under foot by Cæsar's armies. The followers of Hengist and Horsa, before whom the Celts of Britain perished, were an innumerable horde. Everywhere, except in our own country, the movement has been *en masse*. But in America the work has been accomplished by a different process. Here we have had the gradual approach of civilization, and the gradual recession of barbarism. Population has been flung westward in a spray, which has fallen far out beyond the actual line of the column. Hence the pioneers.

It is surprising that no State of the great sisterhood, west of the influence of the Atlantic tides, has been *colonized*. Every commonwealth has been peopled by the scattered scouts of progress—the pioneers. They have come by twos and threes. The individual, unable longer to endure the hardships of civilization, has moved out to find the comforts and conveniences of the wilderness. At the first he consisted of himself, his dog, and his gun. A little later he consisted of himself, several dogs, one wife, and many children. Afterwards he consisted of himself, with the concomitants last mentioned, and a neighbor of precisely the same definitions.

We have thus had in America a race of men, *sui generis*—the pioneers—the hardiest breed of adventurers that ever foreran the columns of civilization. They belonged, like other heroes, to the Epoch of the Dawn. The Old World knew them not. They are our own—or were; for the pioneer type is in process of extinction. Like the red tribes, pressed back

2

by their energies, the rugged adventurers who made ourselves possible, are seen only in the glow of sun-down. The line of pioneer life has swept westward from the Connecticut to the Hudson; from the Delaware to the Ohio; from the Ohio to the Wabash, the Wisconsin, and the Illinois; from the Father of Waters to the Rockies and the Plains. In a few more years there will be no place on the continent, or any continent, that can properly be called THE WEST. The pioneer has always lived in the West. He will disappear with his habitat, and never be seen more.

The pioneers were a people of heroic virtues—and no literature. The situation forbade it. The actual life of the men who made civilization possible in the larger part of the United States was remanded at their death to tradition. The pioneer bard starved. The pioneer annalist left his note-book to his son, who lost it while moving further west. The next generation repeated the story of frontier life as it had been received from the fathers. A few wrote. From Canada to the lagoons of Louisiana a traditional lore grew up and was perpetuated. Then came books, most of them written with little skill and no dramatic quality, often garrulous, sometimes dull. In them, however, were portrayed the incidents and accidents of that daring life which was soon to sink behind the horison.

A few of these frontier books were written by the actors; others, by those who had not participated in the scenes described; most, by persons of little scholarship or wit. Until the present time few works on pioneer life and adventure have been produced which have exhibited artistic merit and literary ability. The flash of life through the cumbrous drama has been obscured by dull conception, coarse diction, ungainly style, and unnatural arrangement. It is important at the present epoch, when the sun of our heroes' fame is setting, but has not set, that a true and vivid picture should be preserved of the life which they led, and the deeds which they performed.

As it respects this preservation for posterity of the annals of our Pioneer Age—the story of our great adventurers and heroes—there is thus presented an alternative between the *now* and the *never*. What is not presently accomplished in the way of an authentic record of the daring exploits of the fathers will never be accomplished at all. It is a question of immediate photography. The pioneer may still be sketched ere the sunlight fades into darkness; but the evening cometh, when no instrument, however delicate its lenses, can supply the want of a living subject for the picture. In another generation the sketch of the American adventurer will be but the reproduction of a wood-cut, instead of a photograph from nature. Whoever by genius and industry contributes to fix in our literature an adequate conception of the lives and deeds of our heroes will make himself a favorite of the present and a friend of the coming generation.

Such a work requires the skill of a dramatist. It is not enough that the story of the men, "who by their valor and warcraft beat back the savages from the borders of civilization, and gave the American forests to the plow and the sickle," should be told even passably well; it must be told with the fervor and living power of the drama. Shakespeare is now recognized as the prince of historians. If we would study the story of the struggles of York and Lancaster, we shall do better in the three *Henrys* and the two *Richards* than in the flat and lifeless pages of Hall and Hollinshed. It has remained for our times to discover that the historical imagination is better than the historical microscope. The former discovers men; the latter, insects. The former composes the Drama of Life; the latter the Farce of Particulars.

The present work is a series of dramas in prose. It gathers and relates the exploits of our national heroes. The characters live and act. The material is gathered from the wild, but not extravagant, annals of frontier life. Every scene in this book is a true photograph from Man and Nature. The incidents are real. They are sketched with a dramatic power which can be paralleled in no other book devoted to the romance and tragedy of American adventure. The author has precisely that kind of fervor which is requisite to make alive the very pages whereon his characters are marshaled for our interest. The book conforms emphatically to the prime conditions of narrative: it is *interestiny* and *true*. The interest is maintained by the vigor and enthusiasm of the treatment; the truth has been elicited by a careful culling and comparison of the various traditions, which are thus given a new lease of life.

The book is a work of art. It is composed with a skill worthy of the highest species of literary effort. The arrangement of the several parts, and the adaptation of style to subject, show on the part of the author a rare combination of brilliant fancy and artistic taste. Mr. Mason has made the happy discovery that dullness in a book is never commended, except in the columns of a magazine called the *Owls' Own Quarterly*.

To all classes of people THE STORY OF THE PIONEERS will recommend itself. The book will be read carefully—which is an important consideration in the premises. The American boy will take fire as he turns these pages. The mild-eyed youth in the bubble-stage of sentiment will wonder that such things could be and not o'ercome the actors. He who has reached the zone of apathy in the Middle Age of Man will find in these thrilling stories of the life that is setting a-west food to revive the adventurous spirit; and the nonagenarian may chance to be re-warmed to hear again so graphically related the traditions that hovered about the fountains of his youth.

A book so well conceived and admirably executed—so vivid in its delineations of the lives and deeds of our national heroes, and so picturesque in its contrasts and surprises—can hardly fail of a hearty reception by the public.

JOHN CLARK RIDPATH.

INDIAN WARS

AND

FAMOUS FRONTIERSMEN

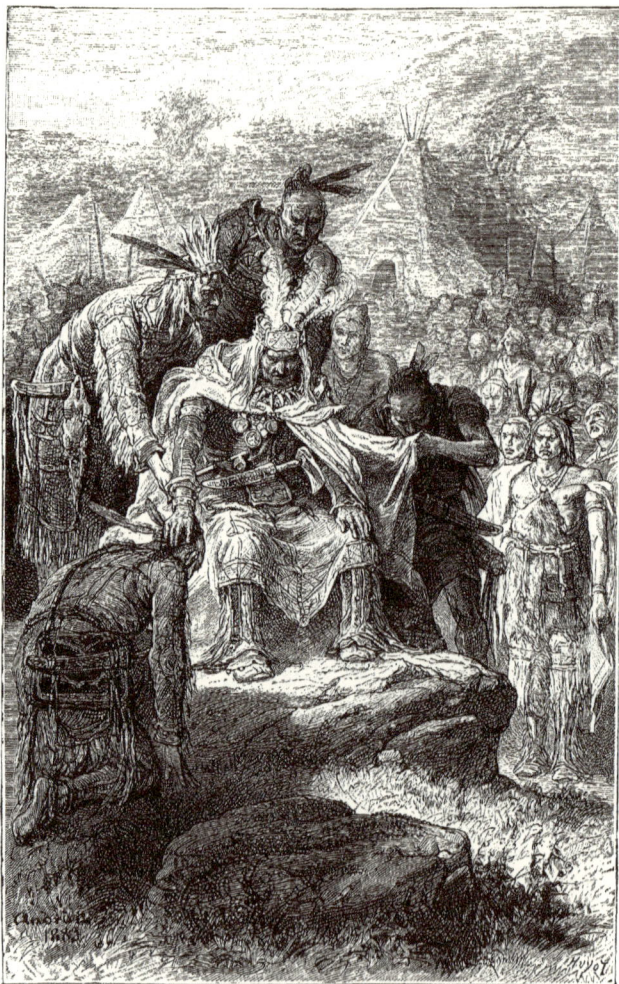

THE GREAT POWHATAN.

SUFFERINGS OF THE VROOMAN FAMILY.

PIONEER WOMEN INCITING INDIANS TO VIOLENCE

ALICE THOMPSON'S APPEAL FOR MERCY.

RED JACKET PLEADING FOR PEACE.

JOHN ELIOT PREACHING TO THE INDIANS

CARSON PARLEYING WITH CHEYENNE SCOUTS.

CHEYENNE BRAVES ON THE WAR PARTH.

PEQUOT INDIANS IN COSTUME.

INDIANS HUNTING WILD BUFFALOES.

CHAPTER I.

THE LEGEND OF POWHATAN

HE age of Elizabeth was an age of wonders. The extension of commerce and the revival of learning, the reformation of religion and the revolution of science, the rise of civil liberty and the invention of negro slavery, the theory of the planets, the proof of the circulation of the blood, and the discoveries in the New World, all combined, at once, by their variety and oppositeness, to stimulate and astonish the minds of men. It was a dozen epochs crowded into one. The wildest romances were seriously believed, and the soberest facts laughed at as chimeras. Every thing which was simple and matter of fact was rejected. The more improbable a thing was, the more willingly men received it as truth. At such a time the stories of the traveler found a ready audience.

Captain John Smith, the historian of Powhatan and Pocahontas, was a traveler who narrated his own adventures. As a story-teller he was a success. What he tells us of Powhatan and his amiable daughter, is told as an aside to the stirring drama of his own life, Left an orphan, in England, at fifteen, but with competent means, he was apprenticed to a trade, while his guardians appropriated his fortune to themselves. He had read books of romance and adventure enough to inspire him to

3

run away. But he was no ordinary boy. He rambled around over Europe, meeting with various adventures, taking part in the Continental wars until the peace of 1598. Being nineteen years old and eager for adventure, he enlisted in an army of mercenaries, employed in the war of the Netherlands. After a year or two of hacking at his fellow-men, he fell in with three rogues for companions, who robbed him and escaped. One of these gallants he afterward met, and ran through with his sword.

Our hero next appears on a ship bound for Italy. Getting into a quarrel with the passengers over religion and politics, they settled the argument by pitching him overboard. But "God got him ashore on an island." He was picked up by a trading vessel, the *Britaine*, which seemed to have no particular destination, but lingered around for freight. The "freight" wanted was a Venetian merchant vessel, which no sooner "spoke" than the *Britaine* fired a broadside. A lively fight followed, but the merchant surrendered to the pirate. Of the spoils, Smith got "five hundred sequins, and a little box God sent him, worth as much more." His acknowledgments of Providence are touching.

Having wandered around Italy till he was tired, Smith went to Vienna, and enlisted in the army of the Emperor Rudolph, in the war against the Turks. The Turks had shut up Lord Ebersbraught in the besieged town of Olumpagh. Smith had invented a system of signals, which he had once providentially explained to Ebersbraught. Letters from A to L were represented by one torch displayed as many times as the letter was removed from A; letters from M to Z were represented by two torches, similarly displayed. Three torches signified the end of a word. Going upon a hill, Smith flashed his torches to the besieged, signaling that they would attack at midnight on the east. The garrison were to make a sortie at the same time. On the side opposite to that of the intended attack, Smith set up some stakes in the plain, and strung them with long lines of powder strings. At the moment of the attack these were touched off, resembling the flash of musketry, and the Turks prepared, in force, to resist the attack from this quarter. Their mistake was discovered too late to prevent the rescue of the garrison. From this time on, Smith bore the rank of captain.

Still more chivalric are his performances in another siege. During the slow toil of the besieging Christians in making trenches and fortifications, the Turks would frequently yell at them, and ridicule their work. In order to pass away the time and "delight the ladies," the Turkish bashaw sent a challenge for single combat with any Christian. John Smith, aged twenty-three, accepted it. A theater was built, the armies drawn up, and the bashaw appeared to the sound of music. His caparisoned horse was led by two janizaries, and his lance was borne by a third. On his shoulders were a pair of silver wings, and his costume was ornamented with jeweled plumes. "This gorgeous being Smith did not keep long in waiting. Accompanied by a single page, he took position, made a courteous salute, charged at the signal, and, before the bashaw could say 'Jack Robinson,' thrust his lance through the sight of his beaver, face, head, and all, threw him to the ground, and cut off his head." A friend of the bashaw's then challenged Smith. The fight was with pistols, the Englishman winning another head. Smith then became challenger. The combat was long and doubtful. The weapons were battle-axes. Once Smith dropped his, and the Turks set up a great cheer, but "by his judgment and dexterity in such a business, by God's assistance, having drawn his fanchion, he pierced the Turk so under the culets, thorow backe and body."

Smith was eventually taken prisoner, but only to meet with a new adventure. He was sent to be the slave of the beautiful Charatza Tragabigzanda at Constantinople. He was by no means ill-favored, and the tender passion soon inflamed the heart of the young mistress. But controlling herself, she sent him away to her brother Tymor, "to learn the language, till time made her mistress of herself." Smith thought he would, ere long, become her husband, but in an hour after his arrival the brother stripped him naked, forged a great iron ring about his neck, with a bent stick attached to it, and set him about the vilest tasks. One day Tymor was alone with him in a field. Mad with rage, Smith sprang on him, beat out his brains, dressed himself in the dead man's clothes, and made his escape. After wandering several days in a desert, he found a kind-hearted man, who knocked off the iron, and helped him to a ship homeward bound.

Such was the man who, in 1605, returned to smoky, pestilential, and filthy London, a city without sidewalks or lighted streets, its houses, built of wood, vilely constructed and ventilated, one-half of its people religious bigots, the other half abandoned debauchees. The town was feverish with excitement over the stories of the great Virginia, where gold was as common as iron, where copper was dipped out of the rivers by the bowl full, where the inhabitants decked out in pearls as large as peas, supplied all visitors with the rarest fish and game and the finest fruits, " four times bigger than those in England." So, in 1606, when a charter was granted for a colony in Virginia, notwithstanding several previous ones had utterly failed, and left no monument but the story of their fate, Smith joined the expedition. Edward Wingfield was president. It is not wonderful that this crowd of seventy-one persons soon fell to quarreling. They were from the slums of London—thieves, plugs, cut-throats, idlers—in search, not of glory, but of a country where money could be had without labor, men, as Smith said, "more fit to mar a state than to make one." Their settlement in Virginia was called Jamestown. Here they had a rough time.

The engraving on the opposite page gives a faithful view of the first day's work in the wilderness. It was a struggle for existence rather than for wealth. Discipline there was none. The president was accused of keeping the choicest stores for himself. The men would not work, supplies ran low, disease and famine alike attacked the unhappy adventurers. One night they had an ugly row, in which all took part. Their preacher, Mr. Hunt, a good man, pacified them, and the next

THE FIRST DAY AT JAMESTOWN.

day the crowd partook of the holy communion. All these
colonial undertakings, no matter how abandoned the men, wore
a cloak of religion. The ostensible aim, as expressed in the
Jamestown charter was, "by the grace of Almighty God, to
propagate the Christian religion to such people as yet live in
darkness and miseráble ignorance of all true knowledge, and
worship of God."

But the quarrel was ever breaking out anew. Conspiracies
to kill Smith, depose Wingfield, and escape to England in the
pinnace were as thick as hops. Sometimes one faction had
the upper hand, sometimes the other. The intelligent directors,
safe at home, had instructed the colonists to search for a passage to the North Sea, and in exploring rivers, when they
reached a fork to take the branch leading to the north-west as
most likely to come out right. In obedience to this, Captain
Newport, Smith, and others shortly ascended the river which
the savages called POWHATAN. The country, too, bore the name,
and the various tribes of Indians, whatever else they called
themselves, were continually mentioning the same mysterious
word. On their journey the explorers were hospitably treated,
receiving presents of fruit, game, and vegetables, as well as a
roast deer and baked cakes. They reached a wigwam village,
governed by a king, the name of town and ruler both being
Powhatan. This chief is supposed to have been a son of the
great Powhatan. The natives made elaborate feasts, and in
return their chief was entertained on the ship, where the English pork and peas and the liquors quite enraptured him.
When the latter grew suspicious of a cross erected as a sign of
English dominion, Newport told him the arms represented Powhatan and himself, and the middle their united league.

On the morning after the feast on shipboard, the noble red
man found himself too sick to get up ; no doubt, the result
of the hot drinks he had taken to so kindly. After a multitude of feastings from other chiefs, the explorers returned to find
that the colony had suffered a severe attack from savages. The

president was cursed to his face for his failure to erect fortifications. He was accused " of ingrissing to his private use oat-meale, sacke, oyle, aqua vitæ, beef, and egges;" while the others had only " a half pint of wheat, and as much barley boyled with water for a man a day, and this being fryed some twenty-six weeks in the ship's hold, contained as many wormes as graines." As a result of the quarrels, Wingfield was deposed and imprisoned. Wingfield denies embezzling the delicacies. "I never had but one squirrel roasted!"

The colonists hung one of the council, and Smith himself came near it. The pious frauds had a church, however, with " Common Prayer morning and evening, every day two sermons, with an Homily on Sundaies." Smith seems to have been almost alone in his efforts to build up the colony. Every one else was crazy about gold. He made several short voyages, securing small amounts of corn from the Indians, which, with the swans, geese, and ducks on the rivers, wild " pumpkins and persimmons," made life quite tolerable, so that for a while the " tuftaffety " gentlemen of the colony quit wanting to return to England. Necessity, however, again drove Smith to make a more extended voyage up the Chickahominy.

They proceeded up the river as far as possible with the pinnace. Then Smith took two of the crew, Robinson and Emry, ashore with him, where two Indians were hired to take them further in a canoe. The crowd in this canoe paddled some twenty miles. For convenience in getting supper, they pulled ashore. Leaving one Indian and the two Englishmen to " boyle the pott," Smith took the other Indian with him to look around in the neighborhood for game. He had gone some distance when cries and yells were heard from the canoe, and then all grew still. Smith rightly conjectured that the men had been attacked and killed. Seizing his guide, he bound him fast to his own arm with a garter, and made ready to fight. No Indians were yet in sight, but an arrow, winged by a hidden hand, struck Smith's thigh. Shortly a score of savages jumped from their cover. Holding his terrified guide before him as a shield, Smith began a retreat to the boat. His pistol he fired as often as he could, and at every shot the savages fled. When the sound died away they would again appear and discharge their arrows, but the unlucky Indian tied to Smith's arm protected him well. But for an accident, the retreat would have been successful, and the story of Powhatan never have been set afloat in the current of history. While walking backwards, intent on his enemies, Smith fell into a quagmire, both his guide and himself sinking up to their breasts. To escape was out of the question. Almost dead with the cold, Smith threw away his weapons. The Indians then ran to him and pulled him out of the mud, built a fire, rubbed his benumbed limbs, and took him before their king, Opechancanough, a brother, as it transpired, of the great Powhatan.

Smith was a man of resources. He drew out a compass, which greatly interested the savage, and then proceeded to "demonstrate by that globe-like Jewell, the roundness of the Earth and Skies the Spheare of the Sunne, Moone, and Starres, and how the Sunne did chase the night round about the world continually; the greatness of the Land and See, the diversitie of Nations, varietie of Complexions, and how we are to them Antipodes." These wonderful qualities of a compass have, probably, never been made use of by any but our own Smith.

The secret of his demonstration is lost to science. At any rate, it evidently impressed the savage, as it must the reader, with the ingenious intellect of the lecturer. The king saw his captive was an extraordinary man. Smith was placed under guard, and the Indians formed in procession to conduct him to Orapaka, a "Town and Seat much frequented by Powhatan and the Imperial Family." The king walked first, followed by poor Smith, held by three lusty savages. On either side walked a file of six more, with their arrows notched. The remainder followed in single file. The village celebrated the strange capture with games, dances, and feastings. Smith was placed in a long house, with forty savages for a guard. For supper he had a quarter of venison and ten pounds of bread. Each morning three women brought him three great platters of fine bread and more venison than a dozen men could devour. In spite of the plenty, Smith's appetite was poor, as he thought they fed him highly in order to eat him. His captors were preparing to attack Jamestown, and Smith exerted himself to explain the terrible cannon, the mines with which the fort was, he said, surrounded, and the certain failure which would result from an attack. To prove it, and to procure some presents for the Indians, he asked the king to send messengers to the fort. This request was granted. Three naked savages set out through the snow and ice of winter on the trip. Smith took care to send a letter, scratched on some bark, telling the colonists that he was safe, and how to both treat the messengers well, yet to frighten them with the cannon, and to send him certain trinkets. When the messengers returned, great was the astonishment of the village that Smith had been able to talk so far to his friends, and that the messengers had brought what he predicted they would bring.

After many days of delay and ceremony, the Indians decided to take Smith before their emperor, Powhatan, the Indian Cæsar, who had conquered the entire region, to whom innumerable chiefs and tribes were subject. Such was the extent of his name that the English, understanding little of the language but hearing the word often repeated, by turns regarded it as we have seen, as the name of a river, of the country, of the people, of a town, and of the chief whom they met in their first voyage. This man had extended his dominions till they were many times the size of his original inheritance. The hereditary chiefs or "kings" of the subject tribes were permitted to rule their own tribes as before the conquest, and their local laws and customs were not interfered with, on condition of their paying annual tribute to Powhatan of "Skins, Beades, Copper, Pearl, Deare, Turkies, wild Beastes, and Corn," a system of government strangely similar to that of the Roman Empire. His subjects

regarded him as half man and half God, a rather intimate union
of church and state.

When the dauntless Smith was presented to this important
personage, he seemed about sixty years old, his hair was gray,
his figure tall and majestic. He was reclining at the end of a
long apartment, on a chair or couch of state, covered with great
robes of furs, with a coronet of immense, gayly colored plumes
on his head. At his head and feet sat two shapely young
Indian girls, in scanty attire, his youngest and favorite wives.
Behind him were grouped the rest of his wives, adorned with
beads and decorated with the most gaudy paints. Around the
room were arranged fifty of the tallest warriors in his dominions. This "palace guard" was increased to two hundred from
this time on account of the English. He is said to have lived
"in great barbaric state and magnificence." At night a sentinel
was posted on each corner of the house, who was required at certain intervals to give a signal to the guard in the house. If he
slept or omitted the signal he received terrible punishment.
Powhatan had a large number of towns or seats in which he,
from time to time, made his residence, according to the season
or the character of the game which each place afforded.

On Smith's entrance into the dusky emperor's hall of state,
a terrific shout was set up. The Queen of Appomattox (a name
now familiar to every American), brought a copper basin of
water, while her companion attended with a bunch of feathers
on which to dry Smith's hands. The emperor, having assured
himself that Smith's hands were clean, proceeded to ask him
innumerable questions as to where he was from, where he was
going, what brought the whites to his kingdom, what were their
intentions, what kind of a country they lived in, and how many
warriors they had. No doubt, the slayer of three Turkish
bashaws, and the pet of the princess, Tragabigzanda, was equal
to his opportunities. It is possible that the old savage regarded
him as a liar, for after his questionings were over, Smith says,
"a long consultation was held, but the conclusion was, two

great stones were brought before Powhatan; then as many savages as could, layd hands on him, dragged him to them, and theron laid his head," preparatory to beating out his precious brains with their war-clubs. By lucky accident Smith escaped the doom through the famous intercession of Pocahontas, " the king's dearest daughter, whom no entreaty could prevaile, but gat his head in her arms, and laid her own upon his to save him from death," an incident which has been expanded, moralized upon, and applauded in turn by a hundred historians.

No doubt poor Smith received the caresses of the Indian maiden with a sensation rarely the lot of mortals to enjoy, for the stern old emperor looked at the scene for a moment, muttered a few words in his strange tongue, and, with his own hand lifted the girl and Smith from the ground. Smith was still doubtful of his fate for a day or two. During this time he busied himself carving wooden toys for Pocahontas, who had saved him by her intercession. These filled the childish hearts of herself and her companions with delight. While making himself popular with the young girls, Smith noticed with satisfaction that the chiefs still admired and wondered at the compass as much as ever. In the picture on the opposite page the wily Englishman is presenting Pocahontas with a wooden doll, which he has just manufactured.

One day, old Powhatan laid aside his dignity, as most kings do at times, and disguising himself in the most horrible manner, with two hundred others, " as blacke as himselfe," hid behind a curtain in a large house, to which Smith was presently brought. He sat down by the fire, thinking the apartment otherwise unoccupied, when with unearthly shrieks and a "hellishe noise," the savages jumped from their hiding-place, brandishing weapons, and making horrible contortions as they circled around him. He supposed his end was at hand. The affair was only a joke, though he was well-nigh dead with apprehension. There are still savages, white enough, who enjoy such jokes. Powhatan explained the matter with many grins, furnished him with

CAPTAIN SMITH AMUSES POCAHONTAS WITH TOYS.

guides, and sent him back to Jamestown. Smith promised to
send his liberator "two gunnes and a gryndestone." This
promise he fulfilled by offering his guides two culverins and a
mill-stone, which they could not possibly transport. He took
care both to frighten by firing the culverins and to pacify them
with many presents for Powhatan and his wives.

Smith's life, however, was scarcely safer among the ruffians
at the fort than among the savages. On the day of his return,
his enemies, headed by Ratcliffe, the president, arrested him
on the charge of murdering his two companions, Robinson and
Emry, found him guilty, and sentenced him to be hung the next
morning, a sentence of which the fulfillment was only prevented
by the arrival of Newport, from England, the same evening.
The affectionate Pocahontas and her father did not forget Smith.
Two or three days after his return a fire broke out, destroying
their buildings and supplies at the fort. Shortly afterward,
Pocahontas, a perfectly nude maiden, appeared at the fort with
a train of attendants such as herself, bringing presents of corn
and game to Smith and his friends. This visit was only the
first of a long series, in which Pocahontas came to the fort regularly, at least twice a week, with abundant gifts. She was only
eleven or twelve years old, evidently of a kind and generous
nature, but full of the fun which belongs to youth. On the
occasions of her visits to the fort, she became well acquainted
with the men. Her sportiveness was manifested by "making
cart wheels," falling on her hands, "heeles upwards," and turning over and over around the fort.

During Smith's seven weeks' captivity, which had been a
great advantage in gaining the confidence and learning the language of the Indians, he, in order to awe them, greatly bragged
of the immense power and skill of Captain Newport. Though
he secretly despised the man, Smith, priest-like, set up the
bogus image before the worshiping multitude, and called it
divine. Powhatan naturally had a great desire to see Newport, and he was promised the pleasure. The new-comers on

the ship **completely** demoralized the prices in trade with the Indians. The sailors were foolishly granted the privilege of trading, and it soon took a pound of copper to buy the quantity of corn for which only an ounce of the metal had previously been required. Only such Indians as had his special license were allowed by Powhatan to visit the fort and trade. One poor redskin slipped in one day without license, and furtively sold a little basket of corn. For this offense the emperor had him killed. Newport sent forward to Powhatan presents, much too rich to be wise, and followed himself with Smith and forty men.

When they arrived at Werowocomoco, the wary Newport declined going ashore, for fear of treachery, till Smith first examined the situation. Even Smith, before crossing the crazy traps, which bridged a network of creeks, required a large number of Indians to precede him, and retained others as hostages, lest the affairs should be pitfalls. The village wore a holiday look. Fifty great platters of fine bread stood in front of Powhatan's lodge. The emperor received Smith with great state and display, caused him to sit on the right hand of his throne, and renewed the old acquaintance with friendly conversation, in which Smith's joke about the "gunnes and gryndestone" drew much loud laughter. Smith presented Powhatan with a suit of red cloth, a white greyhound, and a hat. He was lodged with Powhatan, and served by a young Indian woman, who was appointed to attend him, with an abundance of rich and various food. In the evening there was a feast, with songs, dances, and speeches. Next morning Newport came ashore, and was royally entertained for four days. Powhatan spared no effort to elaborate his hospitality, proclaiming death to any subject who offered any discourtesy to his guests. Newport gave him a white boy, Thomas Savage, as a present.

When they came to trade, Powhatan was much too crafty for Newport. He affected great dignity, said the great Powhatan could not enter into a dicker. "Let Captain Newport lay down all his commodities. Such as Powhatan wants he will

take and then make such recompense as is right." Such was
his speech. Newport fell into the trap. He received four
bushels of corn when he should have had two hundred. Smith
seeing this failure, apparently by accident glanced some blue
beads, so that their glint caught the eye of the Indian, who at
once became eager to see them. Smith denied having them,
then protested he could not sell them, that they were made of
the same stuff as the sky, and were only to be worn by the
greatest kings on earth. All this inflamed the savage's anxiety to the highest pitch, and he offered twenty, fifty, a hundred,
two hundred, three hundred bushels of corn. Smith yielded
to this last offer with great show of reluctance, took his corn,
" and yet," he says, " parted good friends."

The presence of Newport's ship at the colony was a constant
demoralization. Such of the shoremen as had any thing of
value whatever traded it to the sailors for liquor or ship stores,
which were wasted in excesses. Smith wanted Newport to
leave, but he caught the "gold fever," and remained fourteen
weeks, diligently loading his vessel with river sand, in which
were shining particles of mica, which he insisted were gold.
The idle colonists gave up regular work, in spite of Smith's
expostulations, and dreamed of fabulous wealth. The ship
remained so long that its stores were exhausted, and instead
of the colony receiving supplies from Newport, actually had to
divide its meager store to revictual the ship for the return.
Newport sailed proudly away with his cargo of dirt, but not
without doing a mischief to the colony. Powhatan, with a
motive clear as day to Smith, sent Newport twenty turkeys,
asking for twenty swords in return, which the goose at once
sent him. Soon afterward he sent a like present and message
to Smith, but obtained no swords for his trouble, which angered
him. Though professing friendship, the Indians began to give
trouble with their thieving. Several men from the fort were
waylaid in the forest and stripped of their weapons. Thus
matters went on till Smith took several of the Indians prisoners,

and by dint of threats and promises learned from them that the crafty Powhatan, seeing the superiority of English weapons, and designing to massacre the colony, had undertaken to trade for weapons with Newport and Smith, and, failing with the latter, to take them from the colonists whenever caught out alone. Another sign of hostility was the return of the boy Savage, with bag and baggage, to the fort. Learning that some of his people were prisoners, the emperor of Virginia sent the lovely Pocahontas, "who not only for feature, countenance, and proportion, much exceedeth any of the rest of his people, but for wit and spirit the only nonpareil of his country," to Smith to deny hostile intentions and ask for the release of his men. Any favor asked by Pocahontas was certain to be granted, and after prayers, and a hearty meal, the warriors were given back their bows and arrows, and restored to liberty.

Smith, who was never idle, one day went on an exploring trip around the Chesapeake Bay, on which he met with many adventures. Once he caught a fish on his sword, which in being taken off thrust its "poysonne sting of two or three inches long, bearded like a saw," into his wrist. The arm quickly swelled to an enormous size, and the torment was so great that he gave up hope, and his friends prepared a grave under his directions. Luckily "it pleased God, by a precious oyle Dr. Russell applied to it, that his tormenting paine was so assuaged that he ate of that fish to his supper." Once he met the Susquehannock Indians, distinguished by their friendly disposition and enormous stature. Their tobacco pipes were three feet long, their voices "sounded from them as they were a great noyse in a vault or cave, as an ecco." The calf of the chief's leg "was three-quarters of a yard about," and his body of similar proportions.

On September 10, 1608, Smith was made president of the colony. He at once stopped the erection of a pleasure house, which Ratcliffe, who had succeeded Wingfield in the presidency, was having built for his own use, and set the men about useful labor. Things had barely begun to run smoothly when the marplot Newport returned with several wild schemes. He brought with him orders for a coronation of Powhatan as emperor, together with elaborate presents for the old Indian.

A more foolish thing was never perpetrated. The effect of the coronation was to increase Powhatan's notion of his own importance, and make it impossible to maintain friendly relations with him. Smith's hard sense protested against the folly, but finally he insisted on at least trying to get Powhatan to come to Jamestown for the ceremony. With this object he went to Powhatan's residence, but finding him away from home, was compelled to wait a day for his return. In the meantime Pocahontas had some more of her fun. Smith and his men were sitting around a fire in the open air, when they were alarmed by the most frightful uproar in the surrounding woods. They seized their arms and thought they were betrayed. In a moment Pocahontas came running up to Smith, and told him he might kill her if any hurt was intended, and explained that it was only sport. At the head of her thirty young women, attired as we have intimated was their fashion, she led them in a wonderful "anticke," dancing, singing, crying, leaping, casting themselves in circles around the visitors, and "falling into their infernal passions." An hour was spent in this "mascarade." Then "they solemnly invited Smith to their lodgings, where he was no sooner in the house, but all these nymphs more tormented him than ever, with crowding, pressing, hanging about him, most tediously crying, "Love you not me? Love you not me?" After this he was seated at the most elaborate banquet of savage dainties which the ingenuity of Pocahontas and her nymphs could devise. The feast at last broke up, and his dusky tormentors escorted him to his lodging with a fire-brand procession.

In the morning, Smith, his head no doubt a little thick from the frolic, stated his wish to Powhatan, agreeing to assist him in a war against his enemies, the Monacans, if he would come

4

to Jamestown. But this proud representative in the American forest of the divine rights of kings, haughtily replied: "If your king has sent me a present, I also am a king, and this is my land; eight days I will stay to receive them. Your father is to come to me, not I to him, nor yet to your fort; neither will I bite at such a bait; as for the Monacans, I can revenge my own injuries."

"This was the lofty potentate," says a charming writer, "whom Smith could have tickled out of his senses with a glass bead, and who would infinitely have preferred a big shining copper kettle to the misplaced honor intended to be thrust upon him, but the offer of which puffed him up beyond the reach of negotiation."

Smith returned with his message. If the mountain would not come to Mahomet, then Mahomet must go to the mountain. Smith describes with rare humor the ridiculous ceremony of the coronation, the last act of which shows that Powhatan himself must have seen the size of the joke. "The presents were brought him, his bason and ewer, bed and furniture set up, his scarlet cloke and apparel with much adoe put on him, being assured they would not hurt him. But a foule trouble there was to make him kneel to receive his crown; he not knowing the majesty, nor wearing of a crown, nor bending of the knee, endured so many persuasions, examples, and instructions as tyred them all. At last, by bearing hard on his shoulders, he, a little stooped, and three having the crown in their hands, put it on his head, when by the warning of a pistoll the boats were prepared with such a volley of shot, that the king started up in a horrible feare, till he saw all was well. Then remembering himself to congratulate their kindness, *he gave his old shoes and his mantell to Capt. Newport!*" The mountain labored, and brought forth a mouse.

This magnificent failure to get two ship loads of corn which Newport had promised, reduced the colonists almost to starvation. Smith, finding no corn was to be procured peaceably from the Indians, began a more radical policy. Taking a strong force with him, he again sailed up the Chickahominy, and declaring his purpose to be to avenge his captivity and the murder of his men, he made war. It was not long before the Indians sued for peace, and paid one hundred bushels of corn, a serious inroad on a small harvest, for their crops had failed.

Things went on poorly enough at the fort. Out of three hundred axes, hoes and pick-axes, only twenty could be found, the thievish colonists having secretly traded them off to the Indians. The hundred bushels of corn were soon gone. In their extremity Powhatan sent word to Smith to visit him, send him men to build him a house, give him a grindstone, fifty swords, some big guns, a cock and hen, much copper and beads, and he would in return load Smith's ship with corn. Unwilling to miss an opportunity, however slight, to procure supplies, Smith resolved to humor Powhatan by sending some workmen, among whom were two knavish Dutchmen, to build the house, and to follow with a force strong enough to take old Powhatan's corn by force if it could not be had peaceably.

It was midwinter. A severe storm detained Smith and his men on the way, and compelled them to celebrate their Christmas among some friendly Indians. While the winter storm raged without, the men were warmly lodged among the savages, and feasted around the roaring fires on splendid bread, fish, oysters, game, and wild fowl.

Proceeding on their journey, their landing at Powhatan's residence had to be made by wading breast deep through the half frozen shallows and mire for a half mile. Powhatan sent down provisions for them, but pretended not to have sent for them at all. Smith reproached him with deceit and hostility. Powhatan replied by wordy evasions, and seemed coolly indifferent about his new house. He demanded guns and swords in exchange for corn, which Smith refused. The old emperor then said he doubted the intentions of the English, for he had heard that they came not so much for trade as to invade and possess his country. For what good purpose did Smith and his men carry arms, if they really came on an errand of peace? Let them leave their weapons in their vessel, in order that his people might not be afraid to bring in their corn, and as a proof that their intentions were peaceful. "Let us all be friends together and forever Powhatans." The secret of Powhatan's conduct lay in the fact, not entirely discovered by Smith for some months, that the two Dutchmen, yielding to the seductive influence of Powhatan's abundant table and comfortable quarters, had betrayed the destitute condition of the colonists to him.

At an interval in the dispute Smith managed to trade an old copper kettle to the emperor for eighty bushels of corn. Then the debate was renewed with the same vigor. Powhatan, liar that he was, said that he had lived to see the death of three generations of his people, and his experience taught him that peace was better than war. Why then would the English try to take by force what they could quickly have by love? Why would they destroy Powhatan and his people who provided them food? What could be gained by war? Powhatan in his old age could take his people, hide their corn, burn their lodges, fly to the forest, and live there in the cold, subsisting on acorns and roots. But this would not only make him and his people bitterly unhappy; the English themselves must starve if they destroyed the people who furnished them food. Powhatan and Captain Smith would alike end their lives in misery. He concluded with an earnest appeal to Smith to have his men lay aside their guns and swords.

But Smith was proof against this eloquence. Believing that Powhatan's purpose was to disarm the English and then massacre them, he ordered his men to break the ice and bring the vessel nearer shore. Then more men were to land and an attack was to be made. The intellect of the Indian and the white man were well matched in their insight into character and in craftiness. No diplomacy inferior to that of the Indian emperor could have so long retained the upper hand of Smith.

No leader of less courage and resources than John Smith could so long have maintained a starving colony in the hostile dominions of the great Powhatan. In order to consummate the movement by which his entire force should become available for action, Smith kept Powhatan engaged in a lengthy conversation. But the Indian outwitted him. Suspecting his motive, Powhatan, skillfully excused himself for a moment, leaving three of his most entertaining wives to occupy Smith's attention, and passing through the rear of his bark dwelling, escaped to the forest, while the house was silently surrounded by his warriors.

When Smith discovered his danger, he rushed boldly out, fired at the nearest Indian, and made his way unhurt to the shore. The English, then, with leveled muskets, forced the Indians to load the boat with corn. Night came on; the work was done, but the vessel could not sail till high tide. Smith and his men had to pass the night ashore. Powhatan designed to surprise them by an attack while at their supper. Once more the gentle Pocahontas saved Smith. Slipping into the camp, she took Smith aside, hurriedly told him that her father would shortly send down an abundant supper for the English, but, that while the latter were engaged in the meal, an attack would be made by her father with all his warriors. Smith offered her handsome presents and rewards, but with tears running down her cheeks, she refused them all, saying, that if she were seen to have them, it would cost her her life. Once more urging Smith to depart, the affectionate girl turned from him and fled into the forest, the gloom of which was deepened by the thickening shadows of a winter twilight. Presently ten huge savages came, bearing a hot supper for the English, and urged them to eat. But Smith compelled the cooks first to taste their own broth as an assurance that it was not poisoned.

The night was one of anxiety. Large numbers of savages could be seen lurking around. No one was permitted to sleep, but all were required to be prepared for a fight at any moment. Their vigilance saved them, and in the morning the homeward trip was commenced. It was a dark prospect for the colonists. They had escaped this time, but could they always do as well? Where were their supplies to come from, if not from the Indians? Meanwhile, the Dutch traitors made a trip overland to the fort, represented that Smith had sent them, and procured guns, ammunition, fifty swords, tools, and clothing. They also induced six "expert thieves" to desert with them to Powhatan.

On the way back Smith had a thrilling adventure with Opechancanough, the savage to whom Smith had delivered his lecture on astronomy. In the hope of securing corn, Smith took fifteen men and went up to the chief's house, where he found himself betrayed and surrounded by seven hundred armed savages. Smith spoke to his men, told them to follow his example and die fighting. He then openly accused Opechancanough of an intent to murder him, and challenged him to single combat, the Indian to choose the weapons, and the victor to cut off the other's head and be lord over the countrymen of the vanquished. This the Indian refused, denied his hostile intention, and laid a handsome present just outside the door. Had Smith gone outside, he would have fallen, pierced by a hundred arrows. Seizing an opportunity, he rushed up to the king, grabbed him by the hair, placed a loaded pistol at his head, and marched him around, half dead with fright, before all his warriors. Looking on Smith as a god, the people threw down their arms. It was not long till they were trading in good style. Here Smith was overtaken by a messenger from the fort, who had gone to Powhatan's residence, seen great preparations for war, and only escaped alive through being concealed by Pocahontas in her lodge, and, having been furnished by her with provisions for his journey, safely conducted away at night.

New disasters at the fort required Smith's presence. Beset by hostile savages along the river, he at last reached home, with five hundred bushels of corn as the result of this exhausting campaign in the dead of winter. New hardships beset the colony, but were met with renewed energy on the part of Smith.

FRENCH AND INDIAN HUNTERS OF THE BLUE JUNIATA.

AN INDIAN SCOUT RECONNOITERING.

BATTLE OF CAPTAIN SMITH AND THE INDIAN CHIEF.

The renegade Dutchmen managed through confederates in the gang of ruffians within the fort to continue the thefts of arms and ammunition.

One day, Smith, while walking in the forest, encountered the gigantic king of Paspahey, and a terrible combat ensued. The savage, of great strength and stature, slowly forced Smith into the water, intending to drown him. But the Indian stumbled over a stone. To regain his balance he threw up his hands. At the same instant Smith's iron hand grasped his throat; with the other hand the Englishman whipped out his sword to kill his foe. But the Indian pleaded for his life. Smith was a kind-hearted fellow, and besides, full of vanity. The notion struck him that it would be a fine thing to take the big Indian prisoner to the fort as proof of his prowess. This he at once proceeded to do. Our artist has given us a vivid picture of the scene of the combat, just at the moment when Smith, clutching his adversary's throat, paused with sword in air. The Indian was taken safely to the fort and put in chains. He subsequently managed to escape, probably through the help of Smith's enemies.

Shortly afterward, on a trip up the Pamunkey (now York) River, Smith was attacked by this king's people, but when they knew their foe, they threw down their arms, and their best orator addressed Smith, telling him that his ex-captive was there and proceeding to justify the escape. "Do you blame the fish for swimming, or the bird for flying? Then you should not blame my master for obeying the instinct of his nature to escape to the freedom of his forests. Why do you pursue us and force us at too great loss to avenge the injuries we receive at your hands? The red man is a savage; he knows not the white man's God. But these are his rivers and forests. Here his people have hunted and fished, planted seed and gathered harvests, for many generations. Yet the white man seeks to take what is not his. If you succeed in conquering us, we will simply abandon the country of our fathers, and remove to a place where we will be beyond the white man's reach. If that were done the English would gain nothing, but would lose the corn and fruit we are willing to sell them. Why not, then, let us enjoy our houses, and plant our fields in peace and security, seeing that you as well as we will be benefited by our toil?" The result of this speech was a friendship which lasted for many years.

A singular incident at this time raised Smith's reputation to the highest pitch among the savages. Two of Powhatan's people had stolen a pistol. Smith arrested them, threw one in the dungeon, and gave the other a certain time to produce the pistol, in default of which the prisoner should die. Smith, pitying the fellow in the dungeon, sent him some food and some charcoal for a fire. At midnight the other returned with the pistol, but his friend was found badly burned, and smothered to death with charcoal fumes. The grief of the poor fellow was so great that Smith said, if he would be quiet he would restore his companion to life. Little thinking a recovery would take place, Smith applied stimulants and rubbed the Indian's body, when suddenly he sat up! To the great sorrow of his friend the "dead" Indian was crazy. Smith, catching the spirit of the thing, told the other to be quiet, and he would restore reason to his friend also. The patient was laid by the fire and allowed to sleep till morning. He awoke in his right senses. Thenceforth the Indians believed Smith could restore the dead to life. For three months, the colonists, through the iron discipline of Smith, enjoyed peace and prosperity. Twenty cabins were built at the fort; a blockhouse erected for defense, through which lay the only entrance; a good well was dug, and a considerable quantity of tar and soap ashes manufactured.

One day the unlucky colonists found that their abundant store of corn was eaten up by the rats, which, from the few brought over in the ship, had increased to thousands. Without corn for bread work had to be stopped. No provision, except wild roots and herbs, could be procured at that time of year. Eighty men were sent down the bay to live on oysters;

twenty went up the river to subsist on fish. The Indians, to show their friendship, brought to the fort what game they could find. Sturgeon were abundant. Those of the colony who were not too lazy, dried the fish, pounded it to powder, mixed it with herbs, and made a very tolerable bread. The majority, however, would rather starve than work. They importuned and abused Smith because he refused to trade guns, swords, and ammunition for corn. He, at last, issued an order, reciting that every man able to work who failed to gather each day as much provision in a day as he himself did, should be taken across the river, and left as a drone. Some of the vagabonds preferred to desert to the Indians, where they could partake of the abundance without labor. But Powhatan and his tributary chieftains imitated Smith, and all whites who refused to work were flogged and sent back to the fort.

Meanwhile treachery was at work without and within. The villians at the fort plotted with Powhatan to betray it. The Indians were being taught that King James would kill Smith for his ill-treatment of them. Besides these obstacles, the Virginia Company was greatly dissatisfied. A considerable investment of money in the colony had brought no return. The North Sea was undiscovered. This was without excuse, argued the London magistrates, when only a little longer trip, twenty, thirty, or forty miles would, doubtless, have brought the colonists to the other ocean. What want of courage and common sense was shown by not pushing the matter! Besides, there were yet no cargoes of gold pigs or even copper pigs sent home. There must be gold there. Every one said there was. Probably Smith was amassing a fortune, and his colony rolling in a life of wealth and luxury, while he left the Honorable Board of Directors to hold the bag. No doubt there were mountain ranges of solid gold in Virginia, but the directors were not fault-finding. A certain report of one single mountain, or even hill, of gold would be satisfactory. Even a very little hill, say two hundred feet high and two thousand feet in circumference, if it

were not full of caves, would be quite comforting. Such a
modest demand, they argued, ought to be complied with.

Thus, at war with the Indians, betrayed by his own men,
and misrepresented and abused by the English capitalists,
Smith, no doubt, felt that, after all his hardships, his fall was
at hand. Lord De La Ware and others obtained a new charter
and commission from the English king. Preparations, more
elaborate than for any previous expedition, were made. Several ships in the fleet were wrecked in a storm. Those which
reached Jamestown brought many enemies of Smith, and a
great crowd of the London riff-raff. Smith, not yet formally
superseded, continued to exert his authority.

To relieve the Jamestown settlement somewhat of its unruly
elements, Smith planned two new settlements, one under Captain West and one under Martin. Each, with its proportion
of provisions, set out in high glee. Martin and his men went
to Nausemon. The poor savages received him kindly, but the
novice mistook their noisy mirth, as they celebrated his arrival,
for hostility, and falling on the wretched Indians, captured their
poor, naked king and his houses. The work of fortification was
begun, and the savages, divining Martin's fear, attacked him,
released their king, killed several men and captured a thousand
bushels of corn which Martin had traded for.

The other expedition pitched its settlement in low, swampy
ground, liable to inundation, and well suited to breed fevers
among the men. To remedy this mistake Smith, still the
president, sent to Powhatan proposing to buy the town called
Powhatan, for the new settlement. A treaty was at last made
between them, by the terms of which Powhatan agreed to
resign the town, its forts and houses, with the entire region
thereabouts to the English. The latter, in return, were to
defend him and his dominions from the Monacans, and to pay
annually a certain proportion of copper. All thieves were to
be promptly returned to their own people for punishment. Each
house of Powhatan's was to annually furnish one bushel of corn

in exchange for a cubic inch of copper. When this treaty of trade and friendship was completed, the swaggerers and roustabouts of the settlement denied Smith's authority, and refused to stir an inch from their swamp. In attempting to quell the mutiny Smith barely escaped with his life. Well knowing the importance of keeping faith with Powhatan, he exerted all his skill to induce the men to take advantage of the treaty. But the settlement had the notion that the Monacan country was full of gold, that they could prevent any one else than themselves from visiting it, and that Smith's desire to remove them was prompted by his wish to secure access to the gold fields for himself.

Meanwhile, Powhatan's people began to complain bitterly to Smith. The old emperor sent messengers, saying that those whom he had brought for their protectors were worse enemies than the Monacans themselves; that these "protectors stole their corn, robbed their gardens, broke open their houses, beat them, and put many in prison; that, heretofore, out of love for him, they had borne these wrongs, but after this they must defend themselves." The shrewd old diplomate also offered to fight with Smith against the settlement and quell the mutiny, which he was keen enough to perceive and understand.

Failing in his well-meant efforts, Smith sailed away. Accidents are sometimes fortunate. His ship ran aground. Messengers came running, begging him to return. In the brief interval since his departure, Powhatan's enraged people had made an attack, killing many of the settlement. Smith returned, restored order, removed the colony to the town Powhatan, where they found a fort capable of defense against all the savages in Virginia, good warm and dry houses to live in, and two hundred acres of land ready for planting corn. This comfortable and secure place was called Non-such. Hardly were they well settled, when the old infatuation seized them. Mutiny broke out. Smith, seeing the mutineers bent on their own destruction, gave up in despair and left them forever.

They at once abandoned the eligible lodges and fort at Non-
such to return to the open air, and poisoned at that, of the
old swamp.

Misfortunes come not singly but in whole battalions. As
Smith was returning to Jamestown, disgusted at the folly he
had witnessed, a bag of powder in the boat was accidentally fired,
tearing the flesh from his body and thighs and inflicting terrible
burns. In his agony he leaped into the river, and was barely
saved from drowning. Lacking both doctor and nurse, flat on
his back at the fort, suffering untold torments from the wounds,
poor Smith succumbed at last. His enemies deposed him; a
plot to murder him in his bed was almost consummated, an elaborate indictment for his misdeeds was drawn up, and on September 29, 1609, he sailed away from the inhospitable shores of
Virginia to return no more—

> "Ingratitude, more strong than traitor's arms,
>   O'ercame him quite."

Powhatan at once commenced active hostilities.

Henry Spelman was an English boy whom Smith had given
to Powhatan in the trade for the town of the same name. He
had afterwards left Powhatan and returned to the fort. Powhatan sent Thomas Savage, the other boy whom Newport had
given him, to Jamestown on an errand. Savage complained
of loneliness, and easily persuaded Spelman to return with him.
Powhatan now made use of him by sending word to the fort
that he would sell them corn if they would come up for it. It
may be easily believed that supplies were running low, now that
Smith was no longer there to plan and execute methods for
their procurement. An expedition of thirty-eight men set out
at once. No suspicion of treachery was felt. As the boat
landed, the Indians, who lay in ambush, sprang forth in overpowering numbers and killed every man in the party except
Spelman, who was returning with them. He fled through the
woods, made known his distress to Pocahontas, whose tender

heart seems to have been ever responsive to misfortune. Through her help he was hidden for a while, furnished with provisions by her own hand, and then assisted to secret flight.

Powhatan henceforth haughtily refused all trade. The forests were filled with lurking savages. Many a man went out from the fort to hunt game who never returned. Such food as they had on hand was consumed and wasted by the officers. The colonists bartered away their very swords and guns, with which alone corn could be procured. Of the five hundred colonists at the time of Smith's departure there remained, at the end of six months, only sixty, and these subsisted chiefly on "roots, herbs, acorns, walnuts, and berries, and now and then a little fish." It is almost impossible to believe the stories of this "starving time." The corpses of two savages who had been killed, were seized by the poorer colonists, boiled with roots and herbs, and greedily devoured. *" One among the rest did kill his wife, powdered her, and had eaten part of her before it was known."* This man was burned alive for his crime. Strange as this story is, it was reaffirmed in most particulars in the published report of an official investigation into the affairs of the colony by the London directors in the year 1610. These extremities were the result of sloth, vice, and crime as much as of the natural hardships of the situation. The colony was composed of the very offscourings of London. All planting and gathering of crops was abandoned, the houses decayed, the church became a tumbling ruin. They ate their fish raw rather than build a fire and cook it. When Somers and Gates, after terrible adventures, arrived with re-enforcements, they said the colony would have been extinct in ten days had not succor arrived.

With wavering fortunes the colony continued to exist. We have little account of Powhatan, owing to the fact that his remorseless hostility cut off all intercourse with him. In 1613 the princess, Pocahontas, had developed into the maturer beauty of eighteen years. Captain Argall, Smith's ancient enemy, was making a voyage in search of supplies, when he learned that Pocahontas, instead of being with her father, the emperor, was living with the King Potowomek's people. It is not certainly known why she was away from home. There are reasons for thinking that she went to Potowomek, partly because her father suspected her of friendship to the English, and desired to remove her from their vicinity, and partly, because she herself was glad to escape from the scenes of torture and butchery which took place on the occasion of every capture of an Englishman.

Another account is, that she was making a friendly visit on the occasion of an Indian fair. Argall resolved to capture her if possible, and force Powhatan to ransom her by the release of his prisoners, the restoration of stolen property, and abundant gifts of corn. He resorted to a mean stratagem. Among the tribe whose guest she was, Argall found a low savage, named Jabazaws, to whom he offered the bribe of a copper kettle, to decoy her on board his ship. The scoundrel had a keen insight into his victim's character. Having no chance to play upon her curiosity, because Pocahontas had seen many larger vessels, he instructed his wife to pretend her great desire to see one.

Carefully planning for Pocahontas to overhear them, the savage proceeded to beat his wife for her mock importunities. She cried lustily, and at last he told her that if Pocahontas would go aboard with her, she might go. The amiable girl, always glad to oblige others, fell into the snare. Once on board the ship, Argall decoyed her into the gun room, and locked her up, in order to conceal from her the treachery of her own people. Jabazaws and his wife gleefully received their reward. Then Argall told Pocahontas she was his prisoner, and must be the means of making peace between the English and her father. At this announcement the cheat, Jabazaws, and his wife, cried louder than poor Pocahontas herself, finally, with many tears and embracings, taking leave of her. The meanness of the man Argall, who could thus take advantage of a young girl, a *barbarian*, forsooth, whose very life she had risked again and again to help the English, is almost beneath the whip of scorn.

This gallant gentleman took his prize to Jamestown, which she looked upon for the first time since Smith's departure, four years before. Messengers were dispatched to Powhatan, announcing the capture of his daughter and the requisite ransom set on her head. English captives, stolen tools, captured guns, were to be restored, with much corn. Powhatan was greatly disturbed by this news. Pocahontas was still his favorite daughter. But it was a great sacrifice to give up the English weapons. Besides she had always inclined to aid the English, which was wrong. Whatever were the thoughts of the white-haired emperor, as this new sorrow burdened his heart, it was three months before he responded to the message. This delay was singular, and is hard to account for. It may have been caused by the struggle between private affection for his daughter and public duty to his country and people. At the end of three months, he sent back seven of his English captives, each armed with an unserviceable musket, and promised, on the release of his daughter, to give five hundred bushels of corn. This was promptly declined, and a demand made for the return of every captive, gun, and sword. Powhatan was so angered at this reply that he was not heard from for a long time.

In the following Spring, an expedition of one hundred and fifty men took Pocahontas, and went up to Powhatan's seat. The emperor refused to see their messengers. The English then told bis people they had come to receive a ransom for Pocahontas and restore her to liberty. To this the Indians replied with showers of arrows. A fight ensued. Forty houses were burned. Then a palaver was had, and a truce arranged till the following day. Meanwhile Pocahontas went ashore, and two of her brothers and some friends were permitted to see her. She welcomed them, but in a rather frigid way. She spoke little to any but her brothers, and told them plainly, that if her father loved her, he would not value her less than old

5

swords, axes, and guns; that for her part, she preferred to remain with her captors, who treated her more kindly than her father, unless he manifested his affection more actively. Her brothers were fond of her, and were glad to find her gently treated. They promised to persuade the emperor to make a peace. Two Englishmen, John Rolfe and one Sparkes, at once started to Powhatan's court to arrange a treaty. He haughtily refused to see them, but his brother, Opechancanough, intimated that a peace might be effected.

But while these elaborate negotiations were working to patch up a cumbrous and probably short-lived treaty, another power, with more skillful hands, was knitting a surer alliance. Pocahontas, whose gentle and refined nature from the first seemed to yearn toward the civilization of the English, had changed greatly during her residence with them. Her tears and entreaties to be set free, at the time of her capture, are in marked contrast with her indifference, at the interview with her brothers, toward her own people, and her willingness to remain with the English. The real reason for this was known only to a single one of her captors, Mr. John Rolfe, a steady, industrious, and enterprising man, one of the best of the colony. He was a widower, his young wife having died. When he came in contact with Pocahontas, her charms of person and graces of character filled him with an admiration tinged with emotion.

Rolfe was a very religious fellow, and he made his Christian duty to the untutored maiden the excuse for frequent calls, long conversations, and earnest persuasions to renounce her idolatry, and adopt the true Christian religion. Love is a cunning fellow. He knows the foibles of human nature. He delights to masquerade long in the characters of duty, friendship, mutual improvement, pleasure, or religion, and then suddenly to throw aside his masque and startle his victims with the sight of his own true self. Thus it was that Master Rolfe kept assuring himself that his talks and persuasions with Pocahontas were merely done from a sense of duty; and, as the girl slowly yielded to his influence, until at last, just before her wedding, she renounced the religion of her fathers, and formally professing her adoption of Christianity, was baptized and re-christened by the name of Rebecca, she too persuaded herself that she was animated wholly by the strength of Master Rolfe's arguments and the truth of his cause.

When the expedition set out, of which the object was to restore Pocahontas to her people, Rolfe must have undergone great inward torment. He resolved to ask the governor, Sir Thomas Dale, for permission to marry Pocahontas. Instead of speaking to Dale, whom he saw every day, Rolfe drew up a long letter, a sort of theological treatise, to him, and when he set out to interview Powhatan on the subject of the peace, left this curious document with a faithful friend, who was to deliver it to the governor in the author's absence. The letter is a glorious illustration of the perfection of love's masquerade, his deft concealment of his real character from his victim.

It began with solemn assertions that the writer was moved only by the Spirit of God; that he sought only to obey his conscience, as a preparation for the "dreadful day of judgment, when the secrets of all men's hearts shall be opened;" that he was in no way led by "carnall affection," and that he sought only "for the good of this plantation, for the honor of our countrie, for the glory of God, for my owne salvation, and for the converting to the true knowledge of God and Jesus Christ, an unbelieving creature, namely Pokahuntas." He went on to describe how long the subject had borne on his mind, how he had set before his mind the proneness of mankind to evil desires, how he had studied the rebukes of the Bible against marrying strange wives; how the fearful struggle had kept up day and night between the powers of light and darkness; how "besides the weary passions and suffering, he had daiely, hourely, yea, and in his sleep indured; even awaking him to astonishment, taxing him with remissnesse, and carelessnesse, refusing and neglecting to perform the duteie of a good Christian, pulling

him by the eare and crying; why dost thou not indeavor to
make her a Christian?" Still he proceeded with his foolish
delusion. He said that the Holy Spirit often demanded why
he was created, if not to labor in the Lord's vineyard. Here
was a good chance for him. Besides all which were her
apparent love for him, her intelligence and desire to be taught,
her willingness to receive good impressions, "and also the
spirituall, besides her owne incitements stirring me up hereunto."
That these "incitements" and the rest had great influence over
the writer of this remarkable love-letter is plain. "Shall I be
of so untoward a disposition as to refuse to lead the blind in
the right way? Shall I be so unnatural as not to give bread
to the hungrie, or uncharitable as not to cover the naked?"

Such horrible wickedness was not to be thought of. He
determined to sacrifice himself on the altar of duty. He could
not close, however, without renewed protests that he was not
influenced by his own desires or affections. In fact, one thinks
he doth protest too much. He finishes, saying, "I will heartily
accept of it as a godly taxe appointed me, and I will never
cease (God assissting me) untill I have accomplished and brought
to perfection so holy a worke, in which I will daily pray God
to bless me, to mine and her eternal happiness."

Governor Dale read this tedious missive, and no doubt saw
the size of the joke. But, nevertheless, he could see the marriage would be a good thing for the colony, and lay the foundation for a lasting peace. He approved of it heartily, humoring
Rolfe by giving his assent in the same style in which the letter was written, and, so far as we are informed, without wounding the susceptible heart of the widower by any facetious
reflection on his cant and self-delusion.

Word was sent to Powhatan, and he, too, seemed to approve
of it. He was growing conservative in his old age, and he saw
in the marriage a career suited to the tastes of his daughter as
well as an assurance of long continued peace for his weary
people. The expedition returned to Jamestown, where Poca-

hontas, as before remarked, formally announced her conversion to Christianity. This was really a good joke on Rolfe, for it demolished at one blow the entire fabric of mock reasoning, by which he justified his desire to marry Pocahontas. However, the question was not sprung. Preparations for the wedding went on merrily. Powhatan shortly sent down an old uncle of Pocahontas to represent him at the wedding and give the bride away. The ceremony was performed in the Jamestown Church, about the 5th of April, 1614. This marriage is justly celebrated as being the basis for a peace with the Powhatans as long as Pocahontas lived. Other tribes, among them the Chickahominies, who are said to have had no king, but a rude sort of republican government, sent in their submission to this colony, which no longer had occasion for war.

It is instructive to notice that the colony at this time abandoned the communal system of property, because while all were fed out of the common store, some would shirk the labor, and even the most industrious would " scarcely work in a week so much as they would for themselves in a single day." The prosperity of the colony was assured. Communism is the very soul of barbarism; individual property the earliest sign of civilization.

The first time a thing occurs it is remarkable. The wedding of Rolfe and Pocahontas, famous as the first marriage of a white man with an Indian woman on this continent, recalls an incident which had transpired twenty-seven years before. This was the birth of a little waif known to history as Virginia Dare, the first white child born in America. It took place in 1587, in the unhappy colony at Roanoke, Virginia, founded under the auspices of Sir Walter Raleigh, whose transcendent genius more nearly apprehended the glorious destiny of America than that of any other man of the age. This little maiden was baptized when she was a week or two old. The scene was one of thrilling interest to the anxious group of spectators. That ceremony performed over the unconscious babe has been described with touching interest by every historian of America.

Well might it be. What a world drama has been and will be enacted on the new continent between the births of the first white child and of the last white child in America! But the history of little Virginia Dare closes with her baptism. Shortly after, her father, leaving his wife and child behind, went to England for food and help. When he returned no trace was to be found of the colony, save the single word "CROATAN" carved on a tree. Historians have speculated upon the fate of the lost colony of Roanoke and of Virginia Dare, but no satisfactory solution has ever been given of the mystery.

Such benefits had flowed from the marriage of Pocahontas that good Governor Dale piously ascribing it to the Divine approval which rested on the conversion of the heathen, and reflecting that another daughter of Powhatan would form an additional pledge of peace, sent Hamor and the interpreter, Thomas Savage, to Powhatan, for the purpose of securing another daughter for himself. At the town of Matchcat, farther up the river than Werowocomoco, from which the emperor had removed on account of the proximity of the English, the visitors were received. The emperor seemed glad to see Savage, and invited him to his house. After a pipe of tobacco had been passed around, Powhatan inquired anxiously about his daughter's welfare, " her marriage, his unknown son, and how they liked, lived, and loved together." Hamor answered that Rolfe was very well, and " his daughter so well content that she would not change her life to return and live with him, whereat he laughed heartily, and said he was very glad of it."

Powhatan then desired to know the reason of the unexpected visit. Hamor said his message was private, and he desired no one to be present. The emperor at once ordered the room cleared of all except the inevitable pair of queens who sat on either side of the monarch. As a propitiatory introduction to the subject, Hamor delivered a message of " love and peace," supplementing it with presents of coffee, beads, combs, fish-hooks, and knives, and a promise of the long-wished-for grindstone, whenever Powhatan would send for it. Hamor then proceeded to speak of the great reputation for beauty and attractiveness which Powhatan's youngest daughter bore, of the desire of Pocahontas to have her sister's companionship, of Governor Dale's intention to remain permanently in Virginia, and his desire, in case the young lady proved to be all that was reported of her, to make her his "nearest companion, wife, and bedfellow." Such an alliance, Hamor represented, would be an honor to all concerned, and would form a new bond of alliance and friendship.

When Hamor had finished, the emperor gracefully acknowledged the compliment, but protested that his daughter had been three days married to a certain one of his kings. Hamor replied that this was nothing, that the groom would readily relinquish her for the ample presents which Governor Dale would make, and further, that the emperor might easily exert his authority to reclaim his daughter on some pretext. To this base proposition the old monarch made an answer, of which the nobility and purity might have put to shame the brazen Hamor. He confessed that his real objection was the love he bore to his daughter, who was dearer to him than his own life; that though he had many children, none delighted him as much as she; that he could not live unless he saw her every day during the few remaining years of his life, which he could not do if she went to live with the English, as he was resolved never to put himself in their power by visiting them. He desired no other pledge of friendship than the one already existing in the marriage of his Pocahontas, unless she should die, in which case he would give up another child. Finally, he urged with vehement and pathetic eloquence, "I hold it not a brotherly part for your king to endeavor to bereave me of my two darling children at once. Give him to understand that, if he had no pledge at all, he need not distrust any injury from me or my people. There hath been already too much of blood and war. Too many of my people and of his, have already fallen in our strife, and by my occasion there shall never be any more.   I, who have power to perform it, have said it; no, not though I should have just occasion offered, for I am now grown old and would gladly end my few remaining days in peace and quiet.   Even if the English should offer me injury, I would not resent it.   My country is large enough, and I would remove myself farther from you.   I hope this will give satisfaction to your king. He can not have my daughter.   If he is not satisfied, I will move three days' journey farther from him, and never see Englishmen more."

His speech was ended.   The barbarian's hall of state was silent.   The council fire, unreplenished, had burned low during the interview, and the great, crackling logs lay reduced to a dull heap of embers, fit symbol of the aged monarch who had just spoken; within their midst still burned the glowing heart of fire, but more and more feebly, while over all the white and feathery ashes were weaving the shroud of death.   Call him a savage, but remember that his shining love for his daughter only throws into darker shadow the infamous proposition of the civilized Englishman to tear away the three days' bride from the arms of her Indian lover, and give her to a man who had already a wife in England.   Call him a barbarian, but forget not that, when his enemies hungered he had given them food.   When his people were robbed, whipped, and imprisoned by the invaders of his country, he had only retaliated, and had never failed to buy the peace, to which he was entitled without money and without price.   Call him a heathen, but do not deny that when he said that, if the English should do him an injury, he would not resent it, but only move farther from them, he more nearly followed the rule of the Master, of whom he was ignorant, than did the faithless, pilfering adventurers at the fort, who rolled their eyes heavenward and called themselves CHRISTIANS.

In 1616 John Rolfe and Pocahontas went to England, taking several Indians with them.   Here Rolfe well-nigh got into trouble over his marriage. The intelligent King James, the same who wanted his minister to procure him a flying-squirrel, because he was "so well affected to such toys," took it into his limited head that Rolfe, a private gentleman, by marrying into the imperial family of Powhatan, had committed high treason. The "anointed" pedant was deeply offended, and insisted that Rolfe meant to claim the Virginia dominion as his wife's heritage, and have the crown descend to his posterity. His counselors succeeded with difficulty in showing him how far-fetched the notion was. The Lady Rebecca, as Pocahontas was called in England, received, for a little while, considerable attention. The aristocracy ventured to patronize her slightly on account of her rank. She was received by the king and queen, taken to the theaters, and called on by several of the nobility. Captain Smith, busy with other matters, did not see her for some time, but either to help Pocahontas or draw attention to himself, wrote the queen a letter, in which he gave a brief and spirited account of the many kindnesses which Pocahontas had bestowed on the colony, and earnestly requesting that she receive the royal favor and attention while in England.

In a little while, however, Pocahontas seems to have been neglected. The novelty wore off. After the first weeks of her visit she was no longer spoken of as the wife of Rolfe at all. Either on account of the London smoke or the neglect of the Virginia company, she was staying at Branford. Smith relates the story of a singular interview which he had with her here. After a modest salutation, she, without a word, turned her back to him, and passionately buried her face in her hands. At length she broke forth with pathetic reproaches, recalling the old scenes at the colony, and her sacrifices for the English, how he had called Powhatan "father" when he was a stranger in a strange land, yet how, now that their positions were reversed, he neglected her and objected to her calling him "father." She said that after his departure the English always told her he was dead, yet Powhatan had commanded those of her people that were with her to search for Smith, and find out whether he was living, "because your countriemen will lie much." The reason of her conduct is obscure. Many have thought that Rolfe had told her Smith was dead, because she was resolved never to marry to any one as long as he was alive. It is not impossible that she had loved him, and was deeply grieved to find the trick which had been played upon her. More likely she was

CAPTAIN JOHN SMITH.

homesick, and, grieved to find the English no longer paid her any attention, was deeply sensitive to Smith's neglect, in not visiting her earlier and renewing their old acquaintance.

Among the Indians who accompanied Pocahontas was Tocomoco, her brother-in-law, who was sent by Powhatan to take the number of people in England, and bring an account of their strength and resources. When he arrived at Plymouth he got him a long stick, and began to cut a notch in it for every person he met. But he soon wearied of the endless task, and threw away the stick. When he was asked by Powhatan on his return, how many Englishmen there were, he said: "Count the stars in the sky, the leaves on the trees, and the sand on the sea-shore; for such is the number of people in England."

This same savage accidentally met Captain Smith in London, where their old acquaintance was renewed. He at once begged Smith to show him his God, king, queen, and prince, about whom Smith had told him so much. Smith put him off the best he could about showing his God, but told him he had already seen the king, and the others he should see when he liked. The Indian stoutly denied having seen the king, James not coming up to his notion of the ruler of such a people. When convinced that he had really seen the king, he said, with a melancholy countenance: "You gave Powhatan a white dog, which he fed as himself; but your king has given me not a mouthful nor a present; yet I am better than your white dog."

In May, 1617, Rolfe, who had been appointed secretary of Virginia, with his wife and child, prepared to return to America. They were on board their ship, which was detained a few days in the Thames by contrary winds. During this delay the lovely Pocahontas was taken ill, and, after an illness of three days, died, in a stranger's land.

Thus ends one of the briefest and loveliest romances to be found in all literature. Amid the darkness of barbarism and savagery, bloomed the rare and delicate nature of Pocahontas, a wild rose in the rocky cleft of black precipices and gloomy mountains. She seemed born for a different sphere than that in which she was placed. The brutality of her people was wholly absent from her affectionate heart. She took naturally to the civilization which she so little understood. Whatever motives may have influenced her in her adoption of Christianity, it is on record that she "lived civilly and lovingly" with her husband. From the first she had no fear of the English, going freely to their fort and on board their ships. Nearly every one in the colony had some favor, bestowed in the days of her frolicsome visits to Jamestown, for which to remember her. On all occasions she was their friend, supplying them with provisions, concealing them from her father, and aiding them to escape. Her influence over her father was unceasingly exerted in behalf of the strangers. Modern criticism has regarded some of the stories told of her as romances. But after disentangling the flower from all the weeds and mosses of legend which may have sprung up around it, the beautiful, affectionate nature, the refined manners, and apt intelligence of the Indian princess, remain in all their lily-like freshness and fragrance. Her early death, though sad enough, was perhaps fortunate, both for her and for her history. As to herself, had she lived, her keen intelligence would have learned to understand more and more fully the difference between her people and the English, a knowledge which would have brought only pain and sorrow to her loving heart. And as for her history, her early death has left us only her portrait in the perfect bloom of youth, a youth which has been made immortal by the pens of countless historians.

POCAHONTAS.

In 1618 died the great Powhatan, "full of years and satiated with fightings and the delights of savage life." He is a prominent character in the early history of our country, and well does he deserve it. In his prime he had been proportionally to his surroundings, as ambitious as Julius Cæsar, and not less successful. He had enlarged his dominions by conquest to many times their original size, and had spread the terror of his arms over a vast extent of country. He had many towns and residences, and over a hundred wives. In his government he was despotic and cruel. Offenders were beaten to death before him, or tied to trees and torn limb from limb, or broiled to death on red-hot coals.

His people had a sort of religion, with priests, temples, and images, but "the ceremonies seemed not worship, but propitiations against evil," and they appear to have had no conception of an overruling power or of an immortal life. Their notions of personal adornment were very decided, if not pleasing. Oil and paints were daubed all over the person. Their ears had large holes bored in them, in which were hung bones, claws, beads, "and some of their men there be who will weare in these holes a small greene-and-yellow coloured live snake, neere half a yard in length, which crawling and lapping itself about his neck, oftentimes familiarly he suffreeth to kiss his lips. Others wear a dead ratt tyed by the tayle."

In his last days Powhatan much feared a conspiracy, between his brother Opechancanough and the English, to overthrow his government, to prevent which his diplomacy was carefully exercised. There is much that is pathetic in the close of his career, his dominions overrun with strangers, his well-beloved daughter sleeping her last sleep in a foreign land, and himself, no longer opposing armed resistance to the English, which he was shrewd enough to see must in the long run result in the extermination of his people, but simply "moving farther from them."

It would be unjust to the man, to whom we are indebted for the story of Powhatan and his lovely daughter, to close this account without referring briefly to his career after leaving Virginia. He was forever after a hobbyist on America. He was always laboring to get up new expeditions, of which he should have command. Once he did go to New England, and as usual, met with thrilling adventures. But he was pursued by the same ill luck which had been his evil star. His ambitious plans were never fulfilled, or, if he did get men to invest in his enterprises, they always met with disaster and ruin. Smith had the great good fortune to be his own historian. He took care to tell his own story, and he told it well, making himself the center of every scene. He was a graphic writer, full of wit, and his pages, though crude in style and bungled in arrangement, are the most interesting chronicles of his time.

Smith was a prolific author.   His first work was "The True Relation," written by him, while in America, narrating the history and condition of the colony, published in London, 1608.   In 1612 he published his "Map of Virginia and Description of the Country."   This map shows that he had a fine eye for topographical outline.   Other works were "A Description of New England," 1616; "New England's Trials," 1620; "The General Historie," 1624, with three later editions.   He wrote also "A Sea Grammar" and several other books, which went over the same ground of his own adventures and the history of the Jamestown colony. These books were written and published by him at his own expense.   He distributed them gratuitously in large numbers, solely with a view to exciting interest about America, and helping him in working up his plans.

Reading between the lines, we see a man of strong nature, full of conceit, of manners disagreeable because egotistical, impatient of opposition, and insufferably fond of talking about and magnifying his own adventures.   Yet he was no ordinary character.   The very rashness and impulsiveness which he manifested in England made him fertile in expedients in fighting Powhatan.   The very strength of his dictator-like intellect, which gained him the hate of the Jamestown colonists, whether of lower or equal rank, caused him to achieve success with the savages and keep the storehouse of the fort full of corn.   His great energy expending itself on the one hobby of working up expeditions to America, no doubt, made him to some extent a nuisance in England, after he was discountenanced and insulted by the Virginia company.   But that Smith was a smart man, of rare force and ingenuity, far ahead of his age in foreseeing the future greatness of America, and possessing executive ability of a high order, must be conceded.   He came, in time, to regard himself as the originator of all the discoveries and colonizations of his busy age, mentioning the Virginia colony as "my colony," and in relating the story of an expedition, of which he was only a private in the rear rank, saying, "*I* took ten men and

BAPTISM OF VIRGINIA DARE.

MARRIAGE OF ROLFE AND POCAHONTAS

went ashore," "*I* ordered the boats to be lowered," and so forth. His swaggering rhetoric brings a smile to the face of the reader. His latest and best biographer says : " If Shakespeare had known him, as he might have done, he would have had a character ready to his hand that would have added one of the most amusing and interesting portraits to his gallery. He faintly suggests a moral Falstaff, if we can imagine a Falstaff without vices." Smith was not only a good Churchman, but a good man. His private life, passed amid the roughest characters and surroundings, was upright and pure. He was never heard to use an oath.

In spite of his incessant efforts, by writing books, making speeches, and addressing letters with offers of his services, to colonization societies, Smith was compelled to remain a mere spectator of the rapid settlement of the New World. Though out of money and out of reputation, his buoyant spirits never sunk. He was a Micawber, always expecting something to turn up. or better yet, a Colonel Mulberry Sellers, who was never without a scheme with " millions in it." Hardship and disappointment made him prematurely old, if it did not make him unhappy. His last years were spent in poverty-stricken seclusion, a " prince's mind imprisoned in a pauper's purse," as was said of him by a friend. Fed by his " great expectations," he held up his head to the end. Almost his last act was to make his will in due form, pompously disposing to Thomas Parker, Esq., of " all my houses, lands, tenements, and hereditaments whatsoever." They were located only in his fancy. When the instrument was duly drawn, he, who had written so many books, could only make his mark. The end had come. On June 21, 1631, being fifty-two years old, he passed away. He lived and died a bachelor. He was wedded to his love of adventure. While there is much about him at which to laugh, there is more which begets admiration and sympathy for him who called himself, on the title-pages of his books, the " sometime Governor of Virginia and Admiral of New England."

6

CHAPTER II.

THE TRIALS OF LA SALLE.

OBERT CAVALIER DE LA SALLE is one of the loneliest characters of history. His life was a struggle between Will and Fate. He was a Frenchman, the descendant of a wealthy family of Rouen. While but a child his love of study, his dislike of amusements, his serious energy, caused his family to select for him a career in the Church. His education was carefully attended to by the great "Society of Jesus," of which he became a member. But while La Salle was at first attracted to the Jesuits by their marvelous discipline, their concentrated power, their unequaled organization, his strong nature, as he approached manhood, rebelled at the vast machine of which he was only a part. He found himself, not at the center, but at the circumference of power. He left them. By the laws of the order, the fortune left him by his father had become the property of the "Society." Impoverished, but ambitious, La Salle, a young man of twenty-three years, in 1666, turned his back on the splendors and achievements of France in the reign of *Le Grand Monarque*, to seek his fortune among the wildernesses of America.

His destination was Montreal. An association of priests called the Seminary of St. Sulpice, were the feudal proprietors of the entire region. The priests were granting out their lands on easy terms to any who would form a settlement. La Salle at once arranged for a large tract of land, eight miles above

Montreal, at the place now called La Chine. The location was exposed and dangerous, but eligible for the fur trade. Here he marked out a palisaded village, platted the land within the palisade into lots containing a third of an acre each, and without the palisade into forty-acre fields. These tracts he rented out for a small, annual rent to tenants. He built a comfortable house for himself, and a small fort. The little settlement of which he was the feudal lord grew and flourished. At evening La Salle would look out over the tranquil waters of Lake St. Louis, and as his imagination dwelt on the lonely world stretching ever toward the sunset, the great purpose of its exploration took shape in his mind. The Indians who came to trade with him told him of a great river in the West, but of its destination they were ignorant. The dream of the age, a passage to the South Sea, was realized, if this river emptied into the Southern or Pacific Ocean. So the restless La Salle sold his seignory back to the priests of St. Sulpice, and with the money bought canoes and supplies for an expedition.

The Sulpitians were envious of their more famous rivals, the Jesuits. The latter had long excluded every rival from missionary labors among the Indians. They threaded forests, swam rivers, endured hunger, cold, and disease to follow the Indian to his wigwam. With deathless pertinacity, they learned hideous languages, lived on nauseous food, and dared the flames of torture, to tell the story of their religion. No sacrifice was too great, no enterprise too hazardous, no suffering too severe to deter them from their great object—the conversion of the savages. Everywhere these heroic priests had preceded the march of civilization. Twenty years before the saintly Marquette floated down the Mississippi, a Jesuit establishment was located on its banks. When the Hurons, among which they labored so long, were driven from their homes by the resistless arms of the Five Nations, the priests shared their sufferings and exile. Long before any other white men, they had traversed the great lakes and unfurled the banner of the cross on their farthest shores.

For all this wasted heroism the rewards seem meager enough. Now and then a savage, attracted by some beads, would allow himself to be baptized; but, as one chronicler says, "an Indian would be baptized ten times a day for a pint of brandy." Sometimes the priests were edified by seeing a warrior throw a piece of tobacco at the foot of the cross as a symbol of worship. "I have been amply rewarded," says one of these fathers, after being fed by his hosts for six days on some nauseous, boiled lichen and a piece of old moccasin, "for all my sufferings. I have this day rescued from the burning a dying infant, to whom its mother allowed me to administer the sacred rites of baptism, and who is now, thank God, safe from that dreadful destiny which befalls those who die without the pale of our most holy Church."

The Sulpitians, envying the Jesuits, aided La Salle in his efforts, and also fitted out an expedition of their own to join him, hoping to find fields for their own missionary zeal. This double-headed expedition was ill-suited to the imperious will of La Salle. After weeks of travel the priests resolved to direct their course to Lake Superior. La Salle warned them that they would find the field preoccupied by the Jesuits. La Salle's goal was the Ohio, which his Indian friends had confounded with the Mississippi. The two expeditions separated. The priests traversed the great lakes, and met with many hardships, only to find La Salle's prediction true. One night a storm swept their baggage, containing their altar service, into the lake. This they took to be the work of the Devil, to prevent their having mass. Soon afterward they found a stone idol in the forest, which inspired their highest resentment. Hungry and petulant, they attacked the thing with fury, broke it up, and dumped the fragments in the lake. This pious exploit was, as they said, divinely rewarded by a bear and a deer, killed the same day. They returned to Montreal without having made a convert or a discovery.

La Salle's men had mostly deserted him, and returning to

his old settlement, called it La Chine in derision of his phantom idea of a passage to China. With one companion, he pushed on to the south, discovered the Ohio River, and descended it to the falls at Louisville, Kentucky. Here his guide deserted him, and La Salle made his way back to Montreal alone. In the following year he made a similar trip to Lake Michigan, and discovered the Illinois River.

The information gained on these trips and from the Indians, together with vague rumors among the Jesuits, gradually created a belief by La Salle, that the Mississippi flowed into the Gulf of Mexico. His fertile mind mapped out the vast scheme of discovery and conquest, to the accomplishment of which he devoted the remainder of his life. History has no parallel for his labors. His idea was to explore the Mississippi, build a chain of French forts from the Lakes to the Gulf, command the mouth of the Mississippi with a fortress which should be the key to the continent. The great river should be open only to the navies of France. The vast interior domain of the continent should become a new empire for Louis XIV to govern.

England should be confined to the strip of sea coast east of the Alleghanies; Spain to Florida, Mexico, and South America. The trade with Indians for furs and hides, opened up through the whole interior of the continent, from the base line of the Mississippi and the chain of forts, would enrich France beyond the scope of the imagination; and this was but the prelude to the great empire which La Salle foresaw was destined to flourish between the Alleghanies and the Rockies, the Lakes and the Gulf. The Jesuits might hold undisputed sway in frozen Canada. It was for him to discover and control the rich and beautiful Mississippi valley.

In 1672 the Count de Frontenac became governor of New France. He was a bold and ambitious man, with many points of resemblance to La Salle. The latter, nursing his mighty dream in the secrecy of his own brain, saw that Canada must be the basis for the fabric. From there he must start, from there receive supplies and men.   Nor could he stir without the permission of the government.   Frontenac became the friend of the youthful, but stern, and self-poised adventurer.

A plan was formed between them, to build a fort at the spot now occupied by Kingston, near the junction of Lake Ontario and the St. Lawrence River.   The ostensible reason was defense against the Iroquois.   But Frontenac saw in it a monopoly of trade and La Salle regarded it as the first link in the chain which was to bind America to the throne of France.

The location chosen was the territory of the Iroquois, the dreaded Five Nations.   This league of Indians, the Mohawks, Oneidas, Onondagas, Cayugas, and Senecas, embraced the most intelligent, powerful, and warlike races on the continent.   Originally occupying about what is now New York State, they had extended their all-conquering arms over Pennsylvania, Ohio, Michigan, Indiana, and Illinois, and much of Canada.   A thousand miles from their council fires were brave but subjugated peoples, who held their lands at the pleasure of their conquerors, paid annual tribute, and prostrated themselves before embassies of Iroquois, who called them dogs and spat in the faces of their proudest chieftains.

The Iroquois hated the French, who had helped their Canadian neighbors to defend themselves from the scourge.   Moreover, the English and Dutch furnished them arms, and made them a sort of police over other tribes.   Many a party of Indians from the Lake Superior region, with its fleet of fur-laden canoes, was waylaid by the Iroquois on the way to Montreal, and either plundered or forced to trade with the English and Dutch.

La Salle was dispatched to Onondaga, where the council-house of the confederacy was located, to invite them to a conference at the site of the proposed fort.   On the appointed day, Frontenac, in glittering armor, with a brilliant and formidable force of French soldiery, met the assembled hosts of the Iroquois.   By means of alternate threats, persuasions, and presents, he obtained their consent to build the fort, which was named in honor of himself.

The next step in La Salle's course was to erect a fort at the mouth of the Niagara River. But it was indispensable to obtain the sanction of the French Government. Fort Frontenac had been built without any authority. Already strong influences were at work to have Louis XIV order it to be torn down. First, was the political party in Canada, who had supported the former governor, and who became the mortal enemies of Frontenac when he supplanted his predecessor. The political animosities of Frenchmen are the most bitter and far reaching of any people. When they hate, they hate. Another group of formidable enemies were the merchants of Montreal and Quebec. They saw that Frontenac and La Salle, with their fort so much nearer the lakes, the great avenue of Indian traffic, would have a practical monopoly of the fur trade. The last, but by no means least, of the enemies of the governor and the dauntless La Salle, were the Jesuits. La Salle was a zealous Catholic, but he despised the Jesuits. The latter, who had long had a monopoly of New France, were already losing it in Lower Canada. They therefore watched their western missions with the greatest jealousy, and resented every movement which tended to open up the great lakes to their rivals.

The first attack of these dangerous enemies on La Salle was an attempt to secure the destruction of Fort Frontenac. La Salle was arranging to return to France in the fall of 1674, in order to lay his projects before the king, and resist these intrigues, when his ambition received a powerful stimulus from the report of Joliet, who in the spring of 1673 had set out with Father Marquette, and five boatmen, to explore the Mississippi, and carry the Gospel to the countless tribes along its banks.

Marquette was the child of an illustrious family of the French nobility. Inspired solely by a sense of religious duty, he had bidden farewell to the splendors of the baronial castle in which he was born, to dwell among the Indians. Slowly the little party made their way through the lakes, up Green Bay and Fox River, thence by many weary portages on to the Mississippi. The simple and inoffensive savages, perhaps drawn more by the gentle and saint-like spirit of Marquette than by his explanations of the atonement, received the strangers kindly, pressed on them their best hospitality, and after many solicitations for them to remain, helped them on their weary way. At the village of the Illinois the two unarmed Frenchmen were treated to a great feast. The first course was Indian meal, boiled in grease, which their host fed them with a spoon. This was followed by a vast platter of fish. The host carefully picked the bones from each mouthful, cooled it by blowing, and tucked it in their mouths with his fingers. This excessive politeness seemed to destroy the Frenchmen's appetites, either from embarrassment or other causes, as the remaining courses of baked dog and buffalo were hardly tasted.

Day after day the voyagers floated down the majestic river, into the ever-opening landscape. Now their eye swept over boundless prairies; now they peered into the perennial gloom of mighty forests; now they shuddered with alarm at the imaginary dangers of red and green dragons and scaly monsters, painted by some Indian artist on the dark background of the overhanging bluffs; now they struggled with a more real danger in the mighty torrent from the Missouri River, which hurled its masses of mud and uprooted trees far out into the transparent depths of the Mississippi. As they proceeded southward the sun became warmer, the vegetation denser, the flowers more luxuriant. Every evening, after hauling their canoes ashore, Marquette, with clasped hands, would kneel before the "Father of Waters," and pour out his soul in prayer to the Infinite. As he prayed, a mild supernatural radiance would illumine his delicate and scholarly features. The spoken words would often cease, but still the slender black-gowned figure, with hands lifted, and face turned toward the crimson glories of the dying day, con-

ESCAPING FROM BRANT'S INDIANS,

LA SALLE AND HIS COMPANIONS.

tinued kneeling till the black bannered armies of night darkened all the air.

Seven hundred miles from the mouth of the Mississippi the voyagers commenced to retrace their lonely way. After weeks of toil, they made their way back to the Green Bay mission. Here Marquette, sick and exhausted from the toils of the expedition, was compelled to stop, while Joliet carried to Montreal the news of the discovery, and of their firm belief that the Mississippi flowed, not into the Pacific Ocean, but the Gulf of Mexico.

Marquette, though feeble in health, after a long repose, determined to return to the Illinois Indians, among whom he had promised to found a mission. Taking two boatmen, Pierre and Jaques, he started on the slow journey. Overtaken by winter and renewed sickness, the gentle father was compelled to pass the winter in a rude hut on the shores of Lake Michigan. Some branches from the trees formed his bed, a log his pillow. His earthly companions were filthy savages, but he had constantly present with him a divine Companion. Urged on by love and pity, he set out amid the sleet and rain of early spring toward his destination. He was received by the Illinois at their great village, near the site of the present town of Utica, La Salle County, Illinois. Here, every morning, in a vast wigwam, he told his breathless auditors the story of the cross.

At last his failing health forced him to leave his sorrowful Indian friends. Slowly and wearily, he set out with his two faithful boatmen on the return trip. During the day he reclined on a rude pallet in the canoe, his face turned toward the skies he was so soon to inhabit. At night his two companions would hastily build a shelter, gently lift and carry him from the boat, and then prepare the rough dish of Indian meal, so ill suited to the sufferer. One evening Marquette pointed to a lonely eminence on the lake shore: "That is the spot for my last repose." The encampment was made earlier than usual. It was well. In the darkness of the night, with a crucifix in his hand and a prayer on his lips, the gentle spirit of Marquette exhaled to the skies, amid the sobs of his heart-broken companions. There in the wilderness they laid him to rest. Though always called Father Marquette, he was just thirty-eight years old.

We turn abruptly from this angelic nature to the iron figure of La Salle. When Joliet arrived at Montreal with the news of his discovery, La Salle found all of his beliefs as to the course of the Mississippi confirmed. He at once sailed for France, it being the fall of 1674. His tireless energy and address secured him an audience with the great French monarch himself. In strong, clear statements he explained the necessity of the forts. His effort was successful. The king granted him the fort and a large tract of land. He was to pay back what the fort had cost the king, and rebuild it in stone. His friends, anxious to share his prosperity, loaned him money to pay the king.

La Salle returned to Canada with his grant in his pocket. From this moment he was encircled by enemies who shadowed him to his grave. The merchants and traders of Canada organized into a league to oppose him. The country became a hornet-nest for him. Every weapon which malice could wield or ingenuity invent was employed to strike him. The Jesuits procured an order from France forbidding his traders to go out among the Indians. La Salle formed an Iroquois settlement around his fort, so that the Indians thereafter came to him. When he was at Quebec, the wife of his host undertook to play the part of Potiphar's wife. La Salle quickly left the room to find the hall filled with spies, who had expected to catch him in the baited trap. Reports were sent to his brother, the Abbé Cavalier, a Sulpitian priest, to the effect that La Salle had seduced a young girl, and was living in gross immorality. His excommunication might have taken place, had not his brother visited him, only to find him presiding over a most exemplary household. A servant was hired to put poison in his food.

La Salle ate of the dish, and was taken dangerously ill, but finally recovered. Emissaries were sent out among the bloody Iroquois, telling them that the fort was designed to aid in making war on them. On the other hand, word was sent through many channels to La Salle that the Iroquois intended a massacre, and Frontenac was urged to raise a force and attack them. It was with great difficulty that the Indians were quieted.

In spite of these villainous machinations, La Salle's inflexible will was victorious. By the help of Indians, Fort Frontenac was rebuilt of stone. Within its walls were substantial barracks, a guard house, an officer's house, a forge, a well, a mill, and a bakery. Nine small cannon peeped through the walls. A dozen soldiers formed the garrison, and three times as many laborers and canoe men were also inhabitants of the fort. Outside were a French settlement, an Iroquois village, a chapel and priest's house, a hundred acres of cleared land, and a comfortable lot of live stock. Four forty-ton vessels and a fleet of canoes were built for navigating the lakes.

Here in this solitude, a week's journey from the nearest settlement, La Salle reigned with absolute power and rapidly increasing wealth. But La Salle's ambition was not gain, but glory. In the autumn of 1677 he again sailed for France His enemies, growing more numerous and bitter all the time, were ahead of him, and denounced him to the government as a fool and madman. This was embarrassing. The scheme he was about to propose was so vast as to inspire distrust of his sanity. In his memorial to the king, La Salle recited his discoveries, described the great Mississippi valley, predicted its future, unfolded its immense value to France, enumerated the enormous difficulties which would attend its conquest, pointed out the anxiety of the English to possess it, outlined the plan of securing it by a vast chain of forts, artfully hinted at a chance to wrest Mexico from Spain, declared that it was as a basis for this enterprise that he had built Fort Frontenac, and asked similar privileges for another fort at the mouth of the Niagara—the

key to Lake Erie. The statesmen of France gave La Salle
an attentive audience. They granted him a royal patent allowing him to build as many forts as he chose on the same terms
as Fort Frontenac, gave him a monopoly of the trade in buffalo
hides, and as a crumb of comfort for the Jesuits, forbade him
to trade in Upper Canada or the great lakes. This patent says
nothing of colonies. Louis XIV was always opposed to them.
But a military dominion over the wilderness, and a path for the
invasion of Mexico, suited him well. For the accomplishment
of this Titanic labor he gave La Salle five years !

La Salle's imperative need was money. This he borrowed
in large sums at ruinous interest. These creditors lived to
change from wealthy friends to bankrupted enemies. The
exploration of America cost untold fortunes, thousands of
heroic lives, and centuries of unrequited toil and hardships.
Our debt to the past is beyond computation. La Salle was
joined by the valued and trusted Henri de Tonty, a son of an
Italian banker, who invented Tontine insurance. Tonty had
lost a hand in battle. He was the only one of all his followers
in whom La Salle could place complete confidence.

On his arrival in Canada, although it was in the dead of
winter, La Salle pushed forward his enterprise. Father Hennepin, a Ricollet friar, and La Motte, another ally, who had joined
La Salle in France, with sixteen men were dispatched from Fort
Frontenac across the chopping waves of Erie as an advance
party. After breasting the fierce December storms, they disembarked in the snow at the mouth of the Niagara River, and
commenced to erect a fortified house. The ground was thawed
with hot water. Little progress was made before it became
evident that the consent of the Iroquois must be obtained. La
Motte failed in this, but La Salle, following with supplies and
re-enforcements, appeared before the solemn council of the Five
Nations. Forty-two stately chiefs, arrayed in robes of black
squirrel skin, listened to him and received his presents. " The
senators of Venice," wrote Hennepin, " do not look more grave

or speak more deliberately than the counselors of the Iroquois." La Salle's dexterity won their permission to erect a fortified warehouse at the mouth of the Niagara River and to build a ship above the Falls. This was a triumph over the Jesuits, two of whom he found at the Iroquois capital, who spared no effort to thwart his proceeding.

But La Salle's enemies were just beginning to show their hand. He made his way to the camp on the Niagara River, only to find that the pilot, to whom he had intrusted the navigation of his vessel, laden with costly supplies, tools, and materials for building the ship above the Falls, had wrecked her on the rocks, and of all her precious cargo nothing but the anchors and cables for the new vessel had been saved. This disaster was appalling and irreparable, and, as Hennepin says, "would have made any one but La Salle give up the enterprise." It became evident, too, that others of his party, besides the pilot, had been tampered with. They were a motley crew of French, Flemings, and Italians, quarrelsome, discontented, and insubordinate.

La Salle, inflexible and silent, ordered an advance. Formed in single file, every man heavily burdened with materials and supplies for the new ship, the priest, Hennepin, with his altar on his back, the procession stumbled through the deep snow, and up the steep heights above Lewiston. Six miles above the Falls, in spite of the terrible cold, the ship was begun. Food was scarce. The Iroquois acted suspiciously. A squaw told the French that they intended to burn the vessel on the stocks. No corn could be bought. Leaving the energetic Tonty in command, La Salle returned to the mouth of the river, marked out the foundations for the new fort, and then set out on foot, with two companions, for Fort Frontenac, two hundred and fifty miles away, a trip made necessary by the loss of his supply vessel. It was a bitter February. His path lay through the country of the treacherous Iroquois, among whom the Jesuits were intriguing for his destruction. For food he had a small bag of parched

corn. Though a long way from the fort, the bag was growing
very light. Their rations were reduced one-half. This did not
suffice. They again reduced them one-half. One night they ate
the last handful. Then they did without eating.

La Salle arrived at the fort to find himself ruined. His
enemies had circulated reports that he was gone on a hare-
brained adventure. Though his property at Fort Frontenac was
ample security for his Canada creditors, they had seized all
his property of furs, ships, and corn, wherever found. The
blow was terrific and beyond remedy. La Salle simply hardened himself to the shock. If any thing, his step was more
haughty, and his mouth more stern. But he could not allow
his foes to triumph by giving up his enterprise.

In August he reappeared on the Niagara River. He had
contrived to get a few supplies in spite of the vigilance of his
creditors, and he brought three more friars. Though he hated
Jesuitism, he was zealous for the faith. Tonty had long since
completed the *Griffin*, as the new ship was called. It swung
easily at anchor, so near the shore that Hennepin preached from
its deck to the Indians.

On the seventh day of August, 1679, amid the chant of Te
Deums and the booming of cannon, the *Griffin* spread her snowy
canvas, and sped out over the blue depths of Lake Erie. The
first few days were lovely. The rippling water sparkled in the
sunlight; the distant shore seemed like a delicate blue penciling
upon the cloudless horizon; the bulwarks of the *Griffin* were
decorated with splendid game. On up the Detroit River and
Lake St. Clair into Lake Huron, which spread before them like
a sea, the voyagers held their way. Suddenly a terrific storm
arose. The vessel shook like a leaf before the fury of the billows. La Salle and his company cried aloud to all the saints,
some one of whom it is presumed heard their cries, as the storm
passed away and the vessel found refuge behind Point St.
Ignace. La Salle lingered here at the Jesuit mission to find
his ever present enemies still bent on his destruction. He had

expected to have the expedition proceed from this point in canoes, while he returned in the *Griffin* with a cargo of furs to appease his creditors. Such signs of disloyalty appeared that he sent the *Griffin* back without him. It proved to be a most disastrous determination.

The fleet of deep-laden canoes were soon caught in another storm. With great difficulty and danger the explorers reached the shore, where they remained a week, drenched by incessant sleet and rain. As the tempest raged on the lake, La Salle trembled for the *Griffin*. Though sorely pressed for food, he dared not camp near Indians, for fear some of his men would steal his goods and desert to them. The hardships were intolerable. Overhead great rain clouds swept across the sky; beneath raged an angry turmoil of tossing waves. At night the heavy canoes had to be dragged by the exhausted and hungry men through the breakers and up the steep shores. One morning foot-prints were seen in the soft mud and a coat was missing. La Salle knew that the theft must be punished. A stray Indian was made prisoner, and La Salle went to his people and told them he would be killed unless the coat was returned. This was embarrassing. The coat had been cut up and divided among the Indians. It was a fight or a compromise. The latter was effected by paying for the coat in corn.

La Salle made his way to the mouth of the St. Joseph River. Here he was to meet Tonty, coming along the east shore of the lake from Michillimackinac. The spot was wrapped in its primeval solitude. To wait for Tonty was dangerous. Winter was setting in; the men were restless; yet La Salle said he would wait, if it was by himself. In three weeks Tonty arrived. One of his canoes with guns, baggage and provisions had been swamped. Part of his men had deserted. For many days their only food had been acorns. It was time for the *Griffin* to have made her trip to Niagara and back again. Day after day La Salle scanned the horizon, with anxious eye. No sail appeared. To delay longer was impossible. Two men were sent to

7

meet it, while the remainder, thirty-three in all, began to force their canoes up the St. Joseph River. They looked eagerly for the trail which led to the great village of the Illinois. Nowhere could it be found. La Salle went ashore to search for it. Night came with thick falling snow, but La Salle returned not. The suspense of the party was intolerable. It was four o'clock the next day before he came in sight. He had lost his way. In the night he saw the gleam of a fire through the forest. Hastening to it, he found, not his camp, but a spot warm from the body of a man who had evidently fled. Calling loudly and getting no answer, La Salle coolly lay down and slept till morning. On his return he was greatly exhausted from his exposure, and slept in a hut close to the camp-fire. During the night the hut caught fire, and he narrowly escaped the flames.

When at last the Illinois trail was found, the party shouldered canoes and baggage for the tramp. One of the men, enraged at his hardships, raised his gun to shoot La Salle through the back, but was prevented from doing so. The great Indian town of five hundred enormous lodges was reached, but every wigwam was silent and empty; and the ashes of every camp-fire cold. The people were absent on their great hunt. Abundant stores of corn were found, but it was a terrible offense to touch it. La Salle felt that he must have the friendship of the Indians at any cost. The Jesuit emissaries were busy among the Iroquois, inciting them to make war on the distant Illinois, hoping by this means that La Salle and his forlorn companions might be massacred, or at least forced to abandon their enterprise. One morning, as the little flotilla of canoes drifted down the Illinois River, the Indians of the deserted village came in sight. They received the strangers as friends, providing food, and rubbing their feet with bear's grease. La Salle made them a speech, told them he came to protect them against the Iroquois, and intended to build a great wooden canoe with which to descend the Mississippi and bring them the merchandise they so much wanted.

INDIANS MAKING A MIDNIGHT ATTACK UPON SETTLERS.

One would think that La Salle, in this wilderness, far remote
from the dwellings of men, would have been free from the pursuit of his enemies. Not so. Hate, like love, laughs at distance and difficulties. That very night a Jesuit emissary
reached the Indian camp. A secret nocturnal council was held.
The stranger warned the Illinois that La Salle was their enemy,
an Iroquois spy, soon to be followed by the Iroquois themselves
in all their blood-thirstiness. After this speech he disappeared
in the forest. In the morning La Salle noticed the change in
his hosts. Distrust and malignity were depicted on every
savage face. Adroitly learning the facts from an Indian to whom
he had given a hatchet, he made a bold speech, denying the
slander, and challenging them to set him face to face with his
traducer. The speech restored general confidence. If oratory
is the art of persuading men and swaying an audience, La
Salle was a great orator.

One morning, La Salle found six of his men, including two
of his best shipbuilders, had deserted. It cut him to the
quick. But this was not all. A treacherous hand again placed
poison in his food. His life hung in the balance for hours, but
an antidote given by the faithful Tonty turned the wavering
scale. Worse than all, it was evident that the *Griffin,* the main
stay of the whole enterprise, was lost. Nothing was ever heard
of her again. Two men sent to search for her, reported that
they had made the circuit of the lakes and found her not. La
Salle afterwards found evidence of her having been deliberately
sunk by the pilot, at the instance of his enemies. The loss of
the *Griffin* was the severest blow yet. She carried anchors,
cables, and equipment for the new boat he was to build on the
Mississippi, as well as costly supplies. The mountain of disasters was enough to break a heart of stone.

Did La Salle give up? No! He mocked at despair, and
instead of yielding, built a strong permanent fort, which he
called Fort Crevecœur, or "Broken-hearted," in very irony at
his misfortunes. He also commenced the great task of building

a forty-ton ship for the river. Trees had to be felled and laboriously sawed into plank by hand. Yet in six weeks the hull was completed by men who were not carpenters. La Salle induced Father Hennepin to give up his preaching, and render some reluctant service by exploring the Illinois River to its mouth. Hennepin, who was a great boaster but poor worker, tried to shirk the enterprise, but at last, with two companions and a canoe well filled with hatchets, beads, and other presents for the Indians, supplied at La Salle's own cost, started on his trip. He descended the Illinois to its mouth, and then ascended the Mississippi, was taken prisoner by the Sioux, and after many adventures made his way back to Montreal, and thence to Europe. He at once published an account of his travels, laying no claim to having discovered the mouth of the Mississippi. Fifteen years later, La Salle being long since dead, Hennepin rivaled our friend Captain John Smith by publishing a new story of his travels, in which he claims to have traversed the entire Mississippi, and thus anticipated La Salle in his chief work. The falsehoods and exaggerations of the book have long since been exposed.

La Salle's exploration could advance no farther until the precious articles for the new ship, lost in the *Griffin,* could be replaced. The expedition was eating itself up with expense. Its chief determined to make his way on foot through the vast and gloomy wildernesses which lay between him and Montreal, in one last effort to replace the loss. It was equal to one of the labors of Hercules—a journey of twelve hundred miles, through a country which was the perpetual battle-ground of hostile and cruel savages, without food, sleeping on the open ground, watching by night and marching by day, carrying a heavy load of blanket, gun, ammunition, hatchet, kettle and a sack of parched corn. Sometimes pushing through thickets, sometimes climbing rocks covered with ice and snow, with clothing constantly wet from swimming a dozen rivers a day, and wading for hours at a time waist or even neck deep in marshes, exposed continually to attack from ravenous beasts, and to a thousand other hardships, toils, and dangers. In all the journey there was not a gleam of light from a single cabin window to welcome the weary travelers at night-fall, not a white man's face to cheer them amid the frightful and gloomy solitudes of unending forests.

La Salle's companions were a Mohegan hunter, who had followed him with ceaseless fidelity, and four Frenchmen. Two of the latter left the party at the point nearest Michillimackinac. The terrible exposures impaired the health of the party. The Mohegan and one Frenchmen were taken ill, and were spitting blood. This left La Salle and one man in health. They had to provide for the additional burden of the sick men.

But we may not linger over the tragic story. After sixty-five days of unparalleled sufferings, the stone bastions of Fort Frontenac rose before their weary eyes. The unconquerable will and iron frame of La Salle, who had been reared in delicate luxury, a scholar, whose career had been marked out to be that of a gentle parish priest for some rural flock in France, had achieved the impossible.

Poor La Salle had reached his goal, but his long journey had but brought him to new grief. It is almost too cruel to record. Within a week he had, by extraordinary effort, in spite of his bankruptcy and misfortunes, collected the needed supplies. He was on the point of setting out on the return trip to his forlorn colony on the Illinois, when two messengers from Fort Crèvecœur arrived with a letter from Tonty. He reported to his stricken chief that, after his departure, the men had mutinied, blown up the fort, plundered its stores, throwing into the river all they could not carry off, and then deserted. All was lost. His mighty effort was spent. Yet he gave not an hour to his grief. Whatever was the inward conflict, no human eye could pierce beneath the iron mask of his features. He chose nine trusty and well-armed men and went to meet the mutineers. Two canoes surrendered at once. The third showed fight. Two of the villains were killed. The remainder were safely lodged in the dungeon of the fort, to await the coming of Count Frontenac. La Salle's enemies used the killing of the two mutineers as a basis for a charge of murder.

After all his toil, the mighty dream of the interior empire seemed wrecked forever. But La Salle was incapable of retreat. He seemed impelled by an inward force, as resistless as his fate was remorseless. On the 10th of August, 1680, he embarked again with his succor for Tonty. If the latter could keep his foothold on the Illinois, success might yet be wrested from adversity. Through Lakes Ontario, Erie, Huron, and Michigan, up the St. Joseph River, and down the Kankakee, he once more took his way. At every step he found the Indians prejudiced against him by the Jesuits.

When, at last, they drew near the meadows on which had stood the great village of the Illinois, with its population of eight thousand souls, their horror-stricken gaze met a scene of utter desolation. Where once was heard the busy hum of human life, no sound, save their own footsteps, broke a silence as of the grave. The plain was covered with heaps of ashes and charred poles. Hundreds of human bodies, hideous souvenirs of battle, half-eaten by wolves and birds of prey, filled the air with pollution. With but one thought, La Salle searched the blackened and bloody field of death, with sleepless anxiety, for traces of the fate of Tonty. That the Iroquois had wrought the work of ruin was clear. That Tonty had been burned alive, or taken prisoner, he thought he read in some charcoal drawings on some stakes. Taking four men with him, La Salle pushed on to Fort Crèvecœur. Hope was dead in his breast, and dark despair floated on raven plume, like a bird of ill-omen, in ever-narrowing circles above his dauntless form.

The fort was destroyed. On the stocks stood the hull of the half-finished vessel, with every nail and spike withdrawn. In charcoal letters La Salle read, " *Nous sommes tous sauvages :* *ce* 15, 1680," inscription by the mutineers. Even here he found bodies lashed to stakes and half-consumed by the torturing flames. Down the Illinois he floated, till he saw before his eyes the mighty river of the Mississippi. It was the source and object of all his vast ambitions and incomparable efforts. But its charms were unheeded by his anxious eye. No trace of Tonty could be found.

Tonty, after the mutiny, lived in the Illinois village, a weak, one-handed soldier of fortune, yet, withal, a courtly gentleman, amid his savage companions; one who would have graced any court in Europe. One evening word was brought that the Iroquois were coming. The same messenger said La Salle was with them; hence, Tonty must be a traitor. The excited savages threw his precious forge and tools into the river. He was in the utmost peril. All night the warriors sang, danced, painted their bodies, and worked themselves into a frenzy to raise their courage. Tonty resorted to a desperate expedient. He went unarmed into the Iroquois camp, bearing a belt of wampum.

By exaggerating the numbers of the Illinois and threatening future vengeance from the French, he patched up a peace. Scarcely was it made before being broken. In six days the Iroquois chieftains summoned Tonty to meet them. An orator presented him with six packs of beaver skins. The first two, he said, signified that the children of Frontenac, that is, the Illinois, should not be eaten; the next was a plaster to heal Tonty's wound; the next was oil to anoint himself, that he might not be fatigued in traveling; the fifth signified that the sun was bright; the sixth required him to pack up and go back to Canada forthwith. Sadly he called his five faithful companions together and started on foot for Green Bay Mission.

La Salle, failing to find his friend, retraced his steps to the fort on the St. Joseph River. Here he located for the winter. Instead of being crushed by the cruel aggregation of disasters and defeats, he modified his plans and mapped out in his own secretive mind a new plan for the pursuit of the great enterprise, from which he never took his eye. His notion was to induce the Western tribes of Indians to unite in a defensive league against the Iroquois, with himself at its head. He worked incessantly, traveling far and near. As has been said, he was a great orator with the Indians. He punctuated his sentences with presents of hatchets and kettles, and emphasized his words with red blankets. Such eloquence was irresistible. Besides, the Indian knows a hero by instinct. He recognizes a true leader at sight. Everywhere the Indians from innumerable tribes lent their aid to the enterprise. La Salle was to protect them against the Iroquois, and French traders were to bring to them all the articles they needed, in ships which would sail up the Mississippi.

Things looked promising. To discover the mouth of the Mississippi was of the first importance. For this a trip to Canada was again necessary. On his way back, La Salle, to his infinite joy, found Tonty at Michillimackinac. Each told his tale of disaster. The new scheme and its signs of promise were laid before Tonty. Arrived at Montreal, La Salle made a last effort to appease his creditors and procure a new equipment. Once more he set out for the Illinois, by the same dreary route, so full of suggestions of wasted wealth, disappointed ambitions, and fruitless toil. The past was a failure. Would the future prove brighter?

The plan of building a large vessel for the journey down the Mississippi, if consummated, would have enabled La Salle to gather quantities of furs, and pay the cost of the expedition. Disaster had forced him to abandon the plan and the trip was made in canoes. The Indians along the river proved to be friendly, intelligent, and polite. Concerning the Arkansas tribe, one of the party writes: "They are gay, civil, and free-hearted. The young men, though alert and spirited, are so modest that not one of them would take the liberty to enter our hut, but all stood quietly at the door. We greatly admired their form and beauty. We did not lose the value of a pin while among them." At the principal town of the Taensas, the travelers were dum-

LA SALLE PROCLAIMING THE FRENCH EMPIRE IN AMERICA.

founded to find large square dwellings, built of mud, straw, and cane, arched over with dome-shaped roofs.

In one of these buildings, in a room forty feet square, sat the king on a chair of state; three wives were at his side, and ranged around him sat sixty old men, wrapped in white cloaks, woven of mulberry bark. When he spoke his wives howled. His death would be celebrated with the death of one hundred victims. Another building formed the temple. In the center was an altar on which burned a perpetual fire. Around the room were ranged long rows of grinning skulls from the victims sacrificed to the Sun. The king was frightfully solemn. No smile had ever flitted across his cast-iron countenance. But if he failed to appreciate a joke, he liked presents and visited La Salle at his camp. On this important occasion the solemn old savage advanced in his white robes, preceded by two men with large white fans, while a third bore an enormous disc of burnished copper, representing the Sun, which was the king's ancestor. At each spot that he visited, La Salle erected a cross with the arms of France, as an emblem of her dominion.

On the 6th of April they reached a point where the river divided into three channels. It was the Delta. It was not long till the heavy current bore the voyagers out into the lonely gulf. For a thousand years its tossing waves had in that mighty solitude striven to rise above themselves; for a thousand years they had fallen back, broken and sullen, to their own level—fit emblems of human ambition. Gathering on the shore, the little group of weather-beaten men erected a column and a cross, with the insignia of the French people. Then La Salle proclaimed aloud the French dominion.

"On that day," says Francis Parkman, "the realm of France received on parchment a stupendous accession. The fertile plains of Texas; the vast basin of the Mississippi, from its frozen northern springs to the sultry borders of the gulf; from the woody ridges of the Alleghanies to the bare peaks of the Rocky Mountains—a region of savannahs and forests, sun-

erts, and grassy prairies, watered by a thousand rivers, ranged by a thousand warlike tribes, passed beneath the scepter of the sultan of Versailles; and all by virtue of a feeble human voice inaudible at half a mile."

The new domain was called Louisiana, in honor of its king. Henceforth the name of La Salle was a part of history. But his labors were only begun. Impatiently he urged his little fleet of canoes upward against the heavy current. His way seemed clear now for the execution of his original plan, to aban- don the difficult and roundabout route through frozen Canada, the great lakes and the Kankakee swamps, to plant a fort at the mouth of the Mississippi, and thus monopolize the magnificent natural pathway to the interior of the continent. On his way back, La Salle was stricken down with a deadly fever. Against this foe his stubborn will was powerless. He could not proceed to Canada to announce his discovery, nor to France to raise means for carrying out his splendid plans, nor even to the Illinois to commence his fort. While La Salle lay in a hut on the banks of the Mississippi the fever of ambition and impatience uniting with that of disease, Tonty pressed on to Canada with the glorious news of the discovery.

By December Tonty and La Salle were once more together on the Illinois River, busy with perfecting the great Indian league. Overhanging the river, La Salle had previously noticed a great rock, one hundred and twenty-five feet high, inaccessible on all sides except by a difficult footpath in the rear. Its top was about an acre in extent. This rock, properly fortified, could be defended by a score of men against hosts of savages. It is now called "Starved Rock." It is six miles below the town of Ottawa, Illinois. On the top of this rock La Salle and Tonty made a clearing, and built a palisade, lodges, storehouses. It was named Fort St. Louis.

The league grew and strengthened. Every day brought re-enforcements. Around the fort a hundred tribes took up their dwelling, inspired with the idea of being protected by La Salle from the terrible Iroquois. They came from the Kankakee, from the Ohio, even from Maine. Among the promiscuous throng of lodges were those of some discomfited warriors of Philip of Mount Hope, who had for a while spread terror and despair through the Puritan settlements of New England. La Salle's diplomacy had achieved a wonderful success. Twenty thousand savages planted their wigwams upon the plains, over which he looked from his castle in the air.

Of all men the Indian is the most unstable. La Salle understood the Indian character thoroughly. His mushroom colony could only live by his fulfilling his promises to protect it from the Iroquois, and bring Frenchmen to exchange commodities for their furs. To achieve these things he needed help. Frontenac was no longer governor of Canada. His successor, La Barre, belonged to the political faction composed of La Salle's enemies. These last were not asleep. The news of his discovery and his mammoth Indian town teased their jealousy and hate into a perfect frenzy. Their emissaries worked incessantly to induce the Iroquois to make war and destroy La Salle, who, they said, was combining the western Indians against the Five Nations. On the other hand, they spread rumors through the excitable throngs around Fort St. Louis that La Salle was keeping them there for the Iroquois to destroy them all at once. Reports were frequent that the Iroquois were coming.

La Salle's situation was full of peril. He dared not leave Fort St. Louis to carry out his plans for traffic on the Mississippi, for if an attack should be made in his absence he would be denounced as the instigator of the Iroquois war. Yet the necessity for his departure grew stronger each day. No one but he could arrange to build the fort at the mouth of the Mississippi, and bring vessels from France laden with articles of traffic for his savage allies. To meet the emergency, he sent letters to France, imploring assistance. They were never heard from. He begged La Barre to send him supplies and re-enforcements. No answers were ever received. He weakened his little colony by sending messengers to Montreal to procure supplies and bring them by canoes. The messengers were plundered of their cargoes by the Canadian governor and thrown into prison. La Salle, in the depths of the wilderness, was unaware of the governor's enmity. Again and again he wrote, describing the situation, and imploring that his men might be allowed to return with supplies. The only response was angry letters from his creditors, accusing him of every crime under heaven. There remained but a hundred pounds of powder in the fort. Should the Iroquois come, strong resistance was impossible.

On receipt of La Salle's letters, La Barre wrote to the government of France that La Salle was a crack-brained adventurer, bent on involving the Canadian colonies in a war with the Iroquois; that he had set himself up as king; that he had robbed his creditors only to waste the ill-gotten gain in riotous living and in debauching the Indians; that so far from serving the king, his sole object was private gain. These slanders reached the mark. The king wrote back that "the discovery of La Salle is utterly useless, and such enterprises should, in the future, be prevented." What a prophet was Louis XIV concerning the future of America! Had he but known better, his " New " France was most speedily to far surpass his " Old " France. La Barre, emboldened by the king's letter, seized all of La Salle's property, declared his privileges forfeited, and dispatched an officer to supersede him at Fort St. Louis. He found only Tonty. La Salle had started for France.

It was an opportune moment for La Salle when he appeared before the gold and ivory chair of state in which sat the small specimen of humanity, in high-heeled shoes and gaudy attire, who represented the sovereignty of France. A war with Spain was in progress. La Salle was smart. His great object was to get a fort and colony on the Mississippi. Instead of dwelling on its use in controlling and developing traffic with the vast interior, he held out the more glittering, but far less substantial, allurement that such a fort would be a basis for a descent on Mexico and the Spanish dominion. His geographical notions were wrong. Mexico was much farther off than he thought. But the king knew no better. The idea of wresting Mexico, with its rich mines of silver and gold from the indolent Spaniards who guarded it, caught his eye. Feeling exerts a powerful influence on conduct. He hated Spain. Any plan to hurt her was grateful to him.

So La Salle was granted more than he asked. La Forest, La Salle's lieutenant, was dispatched to Canada with a royal reprimand for La Barre. He was also to resume possession of Fort Frontenac and Fort St. Louis. He was further ordered to march the four thousand warriors at the latter place, to the mouth of the Mississippi, to co-operate with La Salle in an invasion of Mexico. When his lieutenant received this latter order from La Salle, the latter must have nearly burst with inward laughter. It is the solitary joke in his stern career. It gives him a rank among the funny men of all ages. Gulliver's exploits are nothing in comparison with marching four thousand wild Indians, as unstable as water, belonging to a hundred wandering tribes, two thousand miles from their hunting-grounds; their women and children left behind at the mercy of savage foes; their numbers so great that, without any provision for supplies, they must starve on the way; with no arms but bows and arrows, and no object but to invade a country of which they had never heard. But the wise simpleton of Versailles saw nothing of the joke. What could be more natural? The idea delighted him. He gave La Salle four ships instead of one. Of these the *Joly* was the largest.

A hundred soldiers, thirty gentlemen, a number of mechanics, besides the wives of some and a few girls who saw a certain prospect of matrimony, embarked on this last expedition of Robert Cavalier De La Salle. The command was divided. Beaujeu, a high-tempered, but old and experienced naval officer,

was to command the ships at sea; La Salle was to have entire
control on land. This two-headed arrangement gave rise to no
end of trouble. La Salle, always suspicious and secretive,
found out that Beaujeu's wife was devoted to the Jesuits.
His cold, impenetrable manner, confiding in none, counseling
with none, haughty and reserved, would have exasperated a
far less testy and excitable man than old Beaujeu. As it
was, La Salle's colleague sputtered over with fury. Before
they were out of the harbor, La Salle believed that Beaujeu
was a traitor, in connivance with his enemies to ruin the expedition. Old Beaujeu, on his part, was furious that he, an
experienced naval officer of high rank, should divide command
with a man " who has no experience of war except with savages, who has no rank, and *never commanded any body but school-
boys*"—a thrust at La Salle's school-teaching days, when he was
with the Jesuits. Beaujeu wrote letters continually to the
government, complaining of his ignominy. To these ebullitions
of age, vanity, and temper the answers were curt enough.

The two leaders quarreled—about the stowage of the cargo,
about the amount of provision to be taken on board, about the
destination of the expedition. Beaujeu believed that La Salle
was not a sane man. It is not impossible that his terrible
exposures and sufferings, his ceaseless struggles with his creditors and enemies, his crushing disappointments had affected
the poise of La Salle's mind. His universal distrust included
even the faithful Tonty. On July 24, 1684, the little fleet
spread its canvas. On the fourth day out the *Joly* broke
a bowsprit. La Salle believed it to have happened by design.
The ships put back to Rochelle to repair the damage.

The wretched voyage lasted two months. La Salle was in
miserable health. The disagreements between him and Beaujeu grew continually worse. La Salle desired to put in at Port
de Paix. Here he was to receive supplies and information from
the French governor, who had orders to render all possible assistance to the expedition. Beaujeu, boiling with rage, managed to

run by the place at night and insisted on landing at a different place, Petit Gouare. No supplies were to be had here. Many of the men were sick from the intense heat and close confinement on shipboard. The smallest vessel, the one laden with stores, tools, and ammunition, had fallen behind. Two days passed, and instead of her arrival, word was brought that she had been captured by pirates. The blow was terrific, and could not have fallen, had Beaujeu put in at Port de Paix. La Salle, eaten up with anxiety, became dangerously ill and delirious. In the extremity, Joutel, a gardener, who had joined the expedition, was his main reliance, and continued so till the end. He became the historian of the enterprise. While lying at this port, freed from the restraint of their leader's eye, the men engaged in the worst debauchery, contracting diseases which brought many to their graves.

The captain of the *Aimable* gave La Salle great uneasiness. To prevent treachery, he went on board the vessel himself. It was near New Year's, when, having entered the Gulf of Mexico, they discovered land. Every eye was strained to detect the mouth of the great river.

At this point La Salle committed a fatal blunder. Having heard that the currents of the gulf set strongly to the eastward, he supposed he had not reached the Mississippi. *In fact he had passed it.* Day after day they sailed slowly to the west. No sign of the river appeared. A halt was called. The weather was stormy ; the coast unknown and dangerous. The men were rapidly consuming the provisions. Beaujeu was irritable. Joutel says La Salle requested him to sail back in search of the river and that the naval commander refused to do it. Impatient of the restraint and anxious to assume the sole command, La Salle determined to land his soldiers on the swampy shores and send them to search for the river by land. Joutel was placed in command.

For three days the detachment pushed their way northeastward through tropical forests and across lagoons. The men were constructing a raft to cross Matagorda Bay, when they dis-

8

covered the ships which had been following along the coast.
La Salle came ashore, and announced that this was the western
mouth of the Mississippi. He ordered the ships to enter the
narrow harbor. The *Aimable* came first. La Salle was watching her. Suddenly some men came running in from the forest
reporting that two of their number had been carried off by the
Indians. La Salle ordered instant pursuit. With a last anxious
look at the *Aimable,* which was steering in the wrong direction
to be safe, he started after the Indians. He had just come in
sight of them when the report of a cannon was heard from the
bay. The savages fell prostrate with fright. But the chill of
a more deadly fear froze the blood in La Salle's veins. The
gun was a signal of distress. The *Aimable,* with her cargo of
stores and utensils for the colony, had struck the cruel reef.

Securing his men from the Indians, La Salle hastened back
to the scene of either accident or treachery to save, if possible,
the cargo. The small boat of the vessel was found to have been
staved in. This looked suspicious and caused delay. A boat
was sent from the *Joly.* Some gunpowder and flour had been
landed, when the wind rose. The breakers came rolling in,
lifting the doomed vessel and hurling her, again and again, upon
the rocks. The greedy waves were strewn with her treasures.

La Salle's heart must have been broken. The circumstantial
evidence that the captain of the *Aimable* had wrecked his vessel
on purpose was of the strongest character. The wretched company encamped near the wreck behind a rough pile of boxes,
bales, driftwood, and spars. The Indians were unmistakably
hostile. They plundered the camp, fired the woods, and even
killed two men. The colonists were nearly all sick. Five or
six were dying every day. Beaujeu having accomplished his
mission and landed La Salle at what he declared was the mouth
of the Mississippi, set sail for France. Toward the last, the
testy old sea-captain sympathized with La Salle. He, at least,
had not proved treacherous, and they parted friends. The colonists were left to their misery. It is to be remembered that

MURDER OF LA SALLE IN TEXAS.

in the unhappy company were women and girls. The colony
lived in constant fear of the Spanish, who were patrolling the
gulf in search of them.   Two of the men deserted.   Another
was hung for crime.   One of the best of the company was bitten
by a snake and died.

The most serious thing, however, which befell the colony
was the discovery by La Salle that he was not at the mouth
of the Mississippi.   He knew not where he was, only not on
the river which was the source and object of all his Titanic
toil.   Unless the river could be found, and that speedily, his
mighty undertaking was utterly and forever ruined.   If it could
be found, a good fort built, and communications established with
Fort St. Louis, on the Illinois, something might yet be accomplished.   Unless this was done, La Salle felt that all his Herculean labors were wasted, his life a ruin, and his dream of empire a bitter folly.

The future was as black as midnight.   A single star beam
shone through the darkness.   The little frigate *Belle,* a gift from
the king to La Salle, was still safe.   If the Mississippi could be
found, this vessel might convey the colony and such stores as
they had left to its banks.   A spot was sought where protection
could be had from the scorching sun.   The industrious toiled.
The friars got out their battered altar and crosses.   A fort
was built.   The stoutest sank under this labor.   Numbers also
were being slowly consumed by diseases brought with them.
La Salle's company was not the "flower of France."   Many
of his men had been professional street beggars.   On the walls
of the new "Fort St. Louis," as La Salle called it, were planted
eight cannon.   In the absence of balls, they were loaded with
stones and bags of bullets.

When the wretched colonists were thus located, La Salle
started on a journey of exploration.   He was still dauntless,
self-contained, energetic.   His mighty sorrows may have shattered him.   In his extremity his fierce temper only became
more fractious, his suspicion more dark.   He treated his men

with more and more rigor and hauteur. He kept his own counsel more obstinately than ever. He was made of iron. He bent not one inch to the storm. His invincible intellect refused to bow to defeat. It insulted Fate, and hurled defiance at all the powers of destiny and hell.

The day of his departure was the last of October, 1685. His brother, Abbe Cavalier, just recovered from a long illness, accompanied him with fifty men. It was March before they returned. They told a tale of suffering and disappointment. Some of the men had deserted, some were drowned, some snake bitten, some killed by Indians. The Mississippi had not been found. This was not the worst. The *Belle* had been ordered to follow them along the coast. At a certain point in the journey La Salle lost sight of her. Men were sent to search. They brought back no tidings. The day after La Salle reached the fort the last one of these detachments arrived. They had been more successful. The pilot of the *Belle,* while on shore, had been killed by Indians. Soon after this the crew got drunk. A wind arose; the vessel was clumsily handled; in five minutes all that was left of her was a mass of spars and splinters hanging on the rock-bound coast.

In all his troubled career, the unfortunate La Salle had never met with a disaster so utterly overwhelming and irretrievable as this. With the loss of the *Belle* was lost the only means of returning to France, or of planting a colony on the Mississippi.

There was no longer any use to hunt for the river. If it were found the colony could never get there. To transport their cannon, forges, tools, and stores by land was preposterous. A man could not carry enough food to take him half-way. La Salle broke down. He was taken with another terrible attack of fever.

For months he fought this foe as he had every other. His sublime will rose superior to difficulty. His mind once more cleared. He determined to make his way to the Mississippi, force his canoe upward against its current to the Illinois; thence from Fort St. Louis again to Canada and to France, where he would obtain succor. It was a journey of seven thousand miles. The imagination fails to compass the immensity of the undertaking. It surpassed the labors of Hercules.

One April day, after mass and prayer, a little handful of men, with hatchets, kettles, guns, corn, and presents for the Indians, strapped to their backs, set out over the prairie on the mighty undertaking. La Salle alone knew its extent. He kept the secret locked in his own breast, or not a man would have accompanied him. The trusty Joutel remained in command at the fort. The strictest discipline was enforced. This was to divert the minds of the colonists from their terrible situation. Every one was compelled to work. Joutel says: "We did what we could to amuse ourselves, and drive away care. I encouraged our people to dance and sing in the evenings, for when M. de La Salle was among us pleasure was often banished. I tried to keep the people as busy as possible. I set them to making a small cellar to keep meat fresh in hot weather; but when M. de La Salle came back he said it was too small. As he always wanted to do every thing on a large scale, he prepared to make a large one, and marked out the plan." Like poor La Salle's other plans, the one for this cellar proved too large to be practicable. So it was never built at all.

The situation of the colonists was practically hopeless. There was not one chance in a thousand that La Salle could really make his way across the wilderness of a continent inhabited by sleepless and bloodthirsty savages, to Montreal, and thence to France. Even if he reached France, from what resources could the disappointed and ruined adventurer draw the large sums necessary to equip a vessel and come to their relief? It was now nearly two years since they left Rochelle. La Salle had promised to conquer Mexico in a year! Yet La Salle's trip to France was their only hope. Located at the mouth of a Texan river, no ship would ever pass that way, unless some Spanish cruiser, seeking whom it might destroy.

Still, that the colonists were not overwhelmed with despair, is shown by one Barbiers, who asked leave to marry one of the girls. Joutel held a solemn consultation with the friars, and the two lovers were united. Shortly afterward a marquis begged the same privilege concerning another girl. Joutel, the young gardener, concerned at such an abasement of nobility, refused, and deprived the lovers of all communication with each other. Meanwhile great discontent became manifest. Duhant, the greatest villain in the company, declared that La Salle had left them to their fate, and would never return.

One night a knocking was heard at the gate. It was La Salle. Out of twenty men only eight had lived to return. They had journeyed far, incurring almost every peril and disaster of which one can conceive. At last La Salle took sick. This delayed them two months, and by exhausting their ammunition and strength, forced them to return to the fort. The colonists, of whom only forty-five remained, murmured loudly. La Salle had a heavy task to make them contented with the dreary weather-beaten palisade and fort. He was about to renew his effort to reach Canada, when he was attacked with hernia. His constitution seemed badly shattered.

It was in January, 1687, before the start could be made. Joutel this time was to accompany his chief. La Salle made a farewell address, in an unusually kind, winning and hopeful manner. With heavy hearts, both of those going and those remaining, the little band took up its slow march, followed by straining eyes, until it disappeared from view forever. The company was full of discord. Liotal, the surgeon, had sworn revenge on La Salle for having on one occasion sent his brother on a trip, during which he was killed by Indians. Duhaut had long hated La Salle, and both men alike despised Moranget, La Salle's nephew. Several quarrels took place. One day Duhaut, Liotal, Hiens, a buccaneer, Teissier, l'Archevêque, and Nika and Saget, two Indian servants of La Salle, were out hunting buffalo. Having killed some, they sent word to the camp. Moranget and DeMarle were dispatched with horses, which had been bought of Indians, to bring in the meat. When Moranget arrived he abused the men violently because the meat was not smoked properly, and quarreled fiercely with Duhaut because he claimed the marrow bones. Moranget ended by seizing them.

It was too much. The men who might in France have lived and died respected citizens, embittered by disappointment, and crushed by disaster, were no longer men. They were wild beasts. That evening Duhaut and Liotal took counsel with Hiens, Teissier, and l'Archevêque. A bloody plot was laid. The supper over, the pipes smoked, each man rolled himself in his blanket. Then the conspirators arose. Duhaut and Hiens stood with guns cocked, to shoot any who might resist. The surgeon stole forward, and, with hurried blows from an axe, clove the skulls of the sleeping Moranget, Nika, and Saget, the nephew, the friend, and the servant of La Salle.

It was quickly done. Their victims lay weltering in pools of blood, while the night wind sighed through the lonely forest. The red demon of murder, which had entered the hearts of the conspirators, pointed with bloody finger at La Salle, six miles away. Hatred and self-preservation alike demanded his death.

That evening Moranget had not returned, and La Salle seemed to have a presentiment of evil. He questioned Joutel closely as to whether Duhaut had any bad designs. Joutel knew nothing except that he had complained about being found fault with so much. La Salle passed an uneasy night. In the morning he borrowed the best gun in the party, and taking a friar for a companion and an Indian for his guide, started in search of the missing men. As he walked, he talked with the good friar, only "of piety, grace, and predestination; enlarging on the debt he owed God, who had saved him from so many perils, during more than twenty years of travel in America." "Suddenly," says the friar, "I saw him overwhelmed with a profound sadness, for which himself could not account. He was so moved I scarcely knew him." His approach was perceived by the murderers. Duhaut and the surgeon, crouched in the long grass, with guns cocked. L'Archevêque remained in sight. La Salle called to him, asking where was Moranget. The man replied in a tone agitated but insolent, that he was strolling around somewhere. La Salle rebuked him, and continued to advance. At that moment two shots were fired from the grass, and the great La Salle, the hero of a thousand exploits, dropped dead with a bullet in his brain.

The toiler had found rest at last. The toilworn body was rudely thrown into the bushes, and became the food of vultures and of wolves.

Thus, at forty-three years of age, fell one of the greatest explorers of all time. That he had grave faults is most true. He was often impractical. His movements seem sometimes the result of hasty and inconsiderate resolve. His fierce temper, and gloomy, unsocial nature brought on him the dislike of his men. He attempted too much. Yet, it is clear that he far surpassed his age in his foresight of the future of the Mississippi valley. His dream of the interior empire was to what has really come to pass, as the first faint blush of dawn in eastern skies is to the blazing radiance of noon. If his material resources were too small for his vast undertaking, he possessed a will like that of a god. The vast and continuous stream of energy, proceeding for twenty years from the brain of La Salle, was superhuman. His sensibilities were weak or wholly wanting. His intellect and will place his name above that of every other explorer.

It is impossible to find anywhere an equal for La Salle's undertakings and efforts, his sufferings and toils. Yet for it all he received no reward save the bullet of an assassin. Like many another hero, La Salle was ignored and cast out by mankind. Unfortunate in life, he was still unfortunate in death. His countless throng of enemies each made a stab at his memory. The only thing we, who enjoy the fruits of his terrific toil, can do for La Salle, is to accord him the praise of history.

We have said he was one of history's loneliest characters. It is true. He was and is a solitary of the solitaries. In life his lonely, retiring, secretive nature forced him, as he himself said, to abandon various employments in which, without it, he would have succeeded, and to choose a life more suited to his solitary disposition. We see him driven to the wilderness by his own solitariness. Still he was not enough alone. He shut out from his confidence even the handful of men with whom he traversed the silent and uninhabited forests of America. His was the solitude of genius. "Buzzing insects fly in swarms; the lion stalks alone." He was separated from his nearest friend by fathomless abysses. Solitary in life, he is also solitary in history. He can not be classed with nor compared to any other. His name is a star which belongs to no constellation. The Chevalier de La Salle is like no one but himself. His very greatness makes it so.

After the murders, Joutel, and one or two companions, who had been faithful to their leader, expected nothing but death. The conspirators would never allow the witnesses of their crime to reach the settlements alive. But the way was strangely cleared. The murderers fell out among themselves, and Hiens and his friends deliberately shot and killed Duhaut and Liotal. Thus these heralds of civilization instructed the savages in its lessons. Joutel and his friends were allowed to depart on condition of giving the murderers certificates of their innocence of the crime. They made their way to Fort St. Louis, on the Illinois, where the brave Tonty still held his own, and thence to Canada and France. When Tonty had learned that La Salle had landed on the shores of the gulf, he had gone to meet him. But though he explored the coast for sixty miles from the mouth, failed to find him. La Salle, at that moment, was seeking the fatal river in the plains of Texas. The brave Tonty remained for some years at Fort St. Louis trading in furs. The king finally ordered the post to be abandoned, and his subsequent career is unknown.

The colony on the gulf was left to its fate by Louis XIV. In his gorgeous palaces at Versailles, he turned an ear of stone to the account of Joutel concerning the unfortunates left behind. One day a Spanish ship, guided by one of La Salle's deserters, sought out the spot where the colony had been, intent on its destruction. But the destroyers found the place as silent as death. The weather-beaten palisade was out of repair. The roof of the store-house had tumbled in. The dismounted cannon lay scattered around in the mire. The whole place had fallen into decay. Looking a little farther, the fierce Spaniards found a cluster of human skeletons, lying as if they had fallen there in death. Around the bony finger of one was a little ring. Its possessor had been a woman. Awed by the mystery of the place, the strangers were about leaving, when two men, apparently Indians, came up. They said the colony had been attacked by small-pox. Many had died. The rest were murdered by the Indians. The speakers were l'Archevêque and Grallet. They alone remained to tell the tale. They were made prisoners of war, and sentenced to a life imprisonment in a Spanish dungeon. The last of La Salle's colonies had disappeared from the face of the earth!

TORTURE OF A PRISONER BY THE IROQUOIS.

DEATH OF BRADDOCK.

CHAPTER III.

ROGERS'S RANGERS.

MONG the colonial recruits raised for the British army in the year 1755, after the awful defeat of Braddock, was Captain Robert Rogers, who was at the head of a small company of rough fellows from New Hampshire. He was over six feet high, physically the most powerful man in the army. He had been virtually brought up in a hunter's camp. From boyhood he had, with gun, blanket, and kettle, some ammunition, and a little sack of parched corn, ranged the untrodden forests of New England and Canada in search of furs and game. He had slept with the savages in their wigwams, wrestled and gambled with their warriors, ogled their squaws, shot the rapids with them in their frail bark canoes, until the Indian character and methods hid no secret from him. When the recruits assembled at Albany, New York, General Johnson, knowing Rogers by reputation, employed him from time to time on important scouts. His head-quarters were at Fort William Henry, a new fort erected by the British at the southern extremity of Lake George.

Taking four or five trusty men with him, he would proceed up the lake to a convenient point, hide the canoe in the rushes, and push his way through the forest, penetrating the sentry lines to the very camp of the enemy. At Crown Point, one of the French forts, his men, under cover of night, concealed themselves in the willows only three hundred yards from the fort. When morning dawned, Rogers, holding some bushes in his hand, crawled nearer. While making his reconnoissance, numbers of soldiers and Indians came out of the fort and engaged in drilling or shooting at marks so near that Rogers could not rejoin his men, nor could the latter retreat without discovery. As he lay behind a small log, a Frenchman left his companions and walked directly toward the spot of concealment. Rogers sprang at him with his gun, offering quarter. The stranger, instead of submitting, whipped out a dirk, and made a quick lunge at Rogers, but the latter shot him dead. The report instantly gave the alarm. The Frenchmen ran to the spot where lay the bleeding corpse, but no sign was there of the hand which had done the deed. If Rogers and his men had suddenly evaporated, the mystery, understood only by themselves, could not have been more perfect.

Soon after their safe return, with information of the enemy gained on the above scout, Rogers took thirty men and two small cannon in four bateaux, and, pushing down the lake, discovered the enemy in an open camp in the forest. Runners bore the information to Fort Henry asking for re-enforcements. The delay caused them to be discovered. The British moved forward to surprise the French, when they perceived a fleet of hostile canoes coming down the lake. No doubt a similar force was advancing by land to catch the British between two fires. Rogers at once threw fifteen men into canoes to decoy the French within range of the two cannon. He steered as if meaning to escape. The French at once headed diagonally toward the shore, to cut him off. The stratagem succeeded. Two cannon shots sunk as many canoes, and the remainder fled, pursued unsuccessfully by the entire force of British, who had swiftly embarked for the chase.

In another scout, toward Fort Ticonderoga, Rogers and two companions were discovered on the lake by the enemy. Determined not to retreat, the scouts quickly assumed the guise of

fishermen. All day they coolly floated within gunshot of the
French, dropping hook and line into the placid lake, and at evening actually sold their catch to the French. When night came
on the adventurers pushed on toward their destination. Their

reconnoissance at Ticonderoga, rendered difficult by the intense cold, was about completed,
except as to capturing a prisoner, when a snow
began to fall. No art could conceal their
trail, if they lingered till the snowfall ceased.
So the return trip was hastily begun. By
Christmas Lake George was entirely frozen
from shore to shore. But Rogers and his
tireless woodsmen, instead of remaining idly
in the warm quarters at the fort, equipped
themselves with skates, and braved the win-
try tempest in many an expedition. Their

VICINITY OF LAKE
GEORGE.

success was unvarying. Taking a force of from ten to fifty
men, on skates, Rogers would skim along the icy floor of the
lake surface to a point opposite Ticonderoga or Crown Point,
order his men to change their skates for snow-shoes, and move
swiftly to some ambush along the roads leading to the fort. Here
they would lie in the snow, exposed to the bitter cold, sometimes
for two or three days, with no shelter but a few pine boughs hastily thrown together, and without a spark of fire, the smoke
of which would instantly reveal them to the neigboring fort.
Here they intercepted the sledges carrying fresh beef, venison,
and corn to the fort, captured the drivers, and appropriated
the provision. When they had caught several prisoners, they
would glide into the French settlement, cut the throats of the
cattle, set fire to the barns full of grain and to the houses
of the villagers, and just as the red flames shot upward into
the winter night, throwing their angry glare far across the
whitened landscape, the mysterious and deadly Rangers would
disappear in the forest as suddenly as they came.

So valuable were the services of Rogers and his hardy

woodsmen, that, in the spring of 1756, he received a special commission from the commander-in-chief to raise an independent corps of experienced foresters, men whom he was to choose himself, of the most approved courage and fidelity, and of the greatest physical inurement to exposure. The corps was to be known as ROGERS'S RANGERS, the men receiving the pay of regular soldiers, but carrying on warfare as scouts in their own brave fashion. This famous corps became the right arm of the British troops. Their official instructions were " to use their best endeavors to distress the French and their allies, by sacking, burning, and destroying their houses, barns, barracks, canoes, bateaux, etc., and by killing their cattle of every kind; and at all times to endeavor to destroy their convoys of provision, by land and water, in every part of the country."

On the way to Fort Henry, with his new Rangers, Rogers made an elaborate scout around Crown Point. After killing large numbers of cattle, the tongues of which were carefully removed for the Rangers' use, they were discovered and closely pursued by an overwhelming force of French and Indians. In this emergency, Rogers executed a masterly maneuver. Appointing a rendezvous at a distant point on the lake shore, the Rangers suddenly separated, every man taking his own course. Where there had been five minutes before a stout body of men, the enemy found no one. The Rangers had dispersed and left only thin air. From this point on, their history is a succession of thrilling and successful exploits, of which we may only take an occasional glimpse. Not a week passed without some daring scout or victory. The Rangers only had to go out in order to catch a net full of birds, as they called their prisoners. These Rogers would examine separately and with great care, to see if their stories agreed, concerning the strength, movements, plans, supplies, and situation of the enemy. Keen and sagacious in these examinations, able at a glance to separate the truth from falsehood, and wonderfully skillful in reading character, Rogers kept the British head-quarters more accurately posted

9

with regard to the enemy than were the French and Indian
commanders themselves. From time to time, during the war,
the "Rangers" were gradually increased from their original
strength of sixty-two men, to more than a thousand.

One night in July, 1756, while on a lengthy scout, the
Rangers prepared to attack a French schooner, lying one mile
from the lake shore. Just then two lighters, laden with provision and strongly guarded, came in sight, and made for the
shore as if to encamp, it being about ten o'clock at night. As
they drew close to land, the Rangers fired from the forest,
and Rogers offered quarter to the enemy. The latter, however,
put about, and made every effort to reach the opposite shore.
Before they reached it the terrible Rangers had made prisoners
of the entire party, and sunk and destroyed both cargoes, consisting of wheat, flour, wine and brandy. At this time the
French were offering the Indians sixty francs for every English
scalp, and prisoners were sold in Canada for sixty crowns.
Rogers's first-lieutenant was John Stark, afterwards major-general of the American army in the Revolution.

The fall and winter of 1756 were busily employed in harassing the enemy in the neighborhood of Lake George. On the
21st of January, 1757, Rogers had a company of eighty men
with him, equipped with skates and snow-shoes. They were
encamped three miles from the lake, on elevated ground, near
Ticonderoga, from which they commanded a view of the snowy
landscape for many miles. Far off on the glittering ice, they
saw a small object moving across the lake. The keen eye of
Rogers pronounced it to be a sled laden with provision. Lieutenant Stark set out with ten men to head it off, while Rogers
and the others moved swiftly to intercept the retreat.

Soon after Stark had departed, Rogers detected ten other
sleds following the first. It was too late to warn Stark of
the fact. The latter struck out for the first sled, and the
other sleds, still at a distance, discovering him, instantly put
about. Pursuit was the only thing possible. The sleds were

made of a long board, turned up in front, and with high racks at the side and end to hold the load. They were as light as egg-shells, and drawn each by two horses, rough shod, and, urged to the top of their speed by relentless drivers, sped over the ice with the velocity of the wind. Quick as thought, Rogers's men clapped on their skates and began the chase. The nearest sleds were a half a mile away. It was a race between swift and powerful horses and the swiftest skaters in the world. On flew the foaming horses, their manes flying and eyeballs strained, scattering showers of ice as their ponderous feet dug into the glittering surface. Wildly the hoarse drivers shouted and plied their rawhide lashes upon the reeking steeds. Behind them came the shaggy and powerful Rangers, seeming as they whirled over the ringing ice like superhuman creatures. The pursuers had the shorter path. The sleds must cross it. Whoever reached the intersection first would win the deadly race.

As the steel of the pursuers' skates flashed in the sunlight, it could be seen that they were gaining. Stark and his men had overtaken the rear sled, but the other Rangers paused not in their impetuous career. Still, it was evident, that some of the sleds would escape. One after another of those farthest in advance crossed the point where met the paths of pursuer and pursued. All but two of the sleds had passed the line of safety Suddenly Rogers, who was six yards ahead of the nearest Ranger, was seen to unsling his gun. Without slackening his terrific speed, or removing his eye from the enemy for a moment, just as the second sled from the rear crossed his path he threw his gun to his shoulder and fired.

The nearest horse was seen to lunge forward and fall, thrown by his momentum, a hundred feet along the ice. His mate, frightened and entangled, lost her footing. In a moment the Rangers were upon their foes. The last sled fell an easy victim. The race between man and brute had been won by man.

It was evident that the sleds which had escaped would carry the news to the fort, and rouse instant pursuit. Rogers ordered his men to take the seven prisoners, and return at once to the camp fires they had left three hours before. So sudden had been their departure, that the men had not removed the priming in their guns since the previous day. Every thing was made ready for a fight, and a retreat commenced. They had just crossed a little valley, and were nearing the opposite ridge, when the woods blazed with a deadly volley of bullets. Several Rangers fell dead, Rogers himself being wounded in the head. The Rangers retreated to the opposite ridge, where, sheltered by trees, they were enabled to fight to advantage. From two o'clock till sunset the battle raged. Three times the French and Indians tried to flank the British, but as many times were driven back. Rogers received a wound in his wrist, and many of his brave men, scorning the idea of a surrender, lay helpless and bleeding in the snow. At dark the enemy withdrew.

Worn out with the exciting events of the day, many of their number badly wounded, the exhausted Rangers still felt it necessary to retreat farther from the enemy's neighboring fort. For six weary miles they groped their way through the forest. Once they caught sight of a camp fire, and made a wide detour for fear of Indians. At last, a comfortless camp was pitched for the night. In the morning the wounded were unable to proceed farther without assistance. Lieutenant Stark offered to go to the fort on snow-shoes, a distance of forty long miles, and procure sleighs for them.

In spite of the many difficulties and hardships of the way, he traversed the entire forty miles by sundown, and dispatched a relief party with sleighs for the wounded, so that they reached the suffering men before morning. Just as the sleighs arrived the Rangers perceived a black object, at a great distance, crawling over the ice. Supposing it to be one of their stragglers, a sleigh was sent to investigate. It proved to be Joshua Martin, who had been shot through the hips. He had been left for dead on the field of battle, but managed to crawl back into the woods and build the fire which his companions saw and avoided.

Feebly and with great pain, crawling through the snow, he followed their track to the lake, and then moved along the ice. When relief reached him he fainted away, but afterward recovered and fought all through the war.

The French made several attempts to capture Fort Henry, but as long as the Rangers were there these efforts failed. Rogers, suffering greatly from his wounds, had gone to Albany for surgical aid, soon after the events last recorded. While there he was attacked with the small-pox, that scourge alike of the wilderness and of the city. So it happened that on the 16th of March, 1757, Stark was acting commander of the Rangers at Fort Henry. On that evening, as he made his round of inspection, he noticed the men standing in little knots, engaged in busy conversation, interrupted with many laughs. It was the eve of St. Patrick's day. These lonely fellows were planning their celebration. Stark at once gave orders to the sutler to issue no rum to his men without written permission from him. The men, not to be foiled, at once applied to him for it, but Stark put them off, on the ground that his hand was lame and he could not write. The Rangers were not in the best of humors, when they saw the Irish troops, who composed the remainder of the garrison, freely filling their bumpers with fiery draughts in honor of St. Patrick's wife, and making the fort ring with their hilarious songs and carousals. That night the French, knowing the habit of the Irishmen, to celebrate the occasion, made a terrific attack on the fort. But instead of surprising a set of intoxicated fellows, they were met at the first onslaught by the cool and invincible Rangers. These men bravely fought the enemy hand to hand, repelling assault after assault, until their drunken companions could come to their senses. The Rangers had saved the fort.

In May the Rangers were ordered to Halifax, to join in an expedition against Louisburg. Their versatile talents were employed during harvest, while the preparations for the expedition were going on, in making hay for the horses. The expe-

dition was afterwards abandoned and the Rangers ordered to
Fort Edward.

On the 18th of December, 1757, Rogers led his men on a
lengthy scout. On their way, they for the first time since their
previous departure in April looked on Fort William Henry.
Then it had been a solid log structure, occupied by a large garrison, and supplied, as Rogers says, "with every thing they
could desire for their comfort and convenience."

We smile at a rough Ranger's notion of "comfort and convenience." It was filled by a rude frontier fort, with its long
barrack rooms, the walls of logs, the floor of puncheon; no ceiling but a smoky thatch, the cracks stuffed with mud and straw
to keep out the winter; no windows except openings, closed with
heavy shutters; no light or fire except from an immense fire-place
at one end, from which the heat was dissipated long before it
reached the frosty region at the opposite end; no fare but salt
pork, soup, and black bread, eaten at greasy log tables, twenty
inches wide, set with a gloomy array of battered iron plates and
cups. Yet to the Ranger, accustomed as he was to sleep often
in the snow, and pass days and nights without fire or shelter,
the rough fort, with its rougher company, was "every thing
he could desire for comfort and convenience." Looking back
to the luxury of their life in Fort William Henry, it was with
keen regrets that the Rangers now beheld it, a deserted ruin,
covered with half-burnt rafters and fragments of exploded cannon.

With a British army of six thousand men only fifteen miles
away, the French had, in the previous August, while the Rangers
were away, been allowed to besiege Fort Henry. After a
brave defense of six days, during which time the steady cannonade from the besiegers' batteries had dismounted their guns
and rendered the place no longer tenable, its defenders had surrendered on condition of quarter. Whatever may have been
the wishes of the French commander, the Indian allies, of whom
was composed the principal part of his army, could not be
restrained from violating the condition. Many prisoners were

massacred outright. Others were led away to suffer the exquisite agonies of the stake. Worse and more horrible still, an Indian tribe called the Cold Country Cannibals, who were present at the siege, roasted their prisoners and ate them. For this statement there is unquestionable authority.

In spite of these terrible associations, the sturdy Rangers entered the ruin, scraped away the heavy snow, and built fires in the partial shelter of a corner which was yet standing, and passed the night "comfortably," as Rogers says. As they continued their scout, the Rangers met with fine success, and on their return to Fort Edward, December 27th, they were enabled to present the commandant with a fine Christmas gift of several prisoners, who gave full and accurate information of the enemy. During this winter a company of regular soldiers were placed in Rogers's hands to learn Ranger tactics. For their benefit he drew up a written code, which was published with his memoirs.

On the 10th of March, 1758, Rogers received orders to march with one hundred and eighty Rangers to the neighborhood of Ticonderoga. He protested that the force was too small, and asked to be allowed to take four hundred men, but his requests were refused. The march was made along the solid ice of the lake, the party lying concealed on shore during the day and marching by night. Since the capture of Fort Henry, the enemy had been exceedingly active, strong forces of Indians scouring the country in every direction.

The nights were as dark as pitch, and while fifteen Rangers on skates acted as an advance guard, the main body marched as closely together as possible, to avoid separation. When within eight miles of the French army, an advanced guardsman skated swiftly to the rear with word to halt. The men were instantly ordered to sit down on the ice. Rogers went forward. The advance guard were called in, and thought they had seen a fire on the east shore. The sleighs and baggage were hastily pulled ashore, guards posted, and the main body marched swiftly forward to attack the supposed camp. No light was to be seen.

At last, concluding that the guard had mistaken a patch of snow or some rotten wood, which in the night has a phosphorescent glow, for a hostile camp fire, the Rangers returned to their packs, and passed the night on shore, without fire. The truth was, the guard had seen a real camp fire, which had been extinguished on the approach of the Rangers, and a hasty message sent to the fort of their presence. In the morning it was thought best to push on by land with snow-shoes, the snow being now four feet deep.

Toward night word was brought that a band of ninety-six Indians was approaching. On the left of the line of march was a small rivulet, and on the right a steep mountain. The Rangers extended their line, and at the first fire killed fifty Indians. Supposing this to be the entire force of the enemy, the Rangers pressed on in pursuit, when suddenly they were attacked by over six hundred well armed Indians and Canadians, who on receipt of the news of the Rangers' approach had set out to attack them. Rogers shouted to his men to fall back quickly to their former ground, but before they reached it the life-blood of fifty gallant Rangers reddened the snow where they had fallen.

With cool desperation they continued to fight for an hour, against the overwhelming numbers of the foe. Small detachments were thrown out on the right and left to prevent flanking. But the contest was too unequal. One hundred and eight out of the one hundred and eighty Rangers were killed on the spot. Of these, ten men under Lieutenant Phillips, on the left flank, had been surrounded and captured. They were tied to trees in sight of their friends, and deliberately hacked to pieces by the savages.

At last, Rogers cried to his men to fly, every one for himself. Rogers himself, with twenty men, rushed to an icy precipice, over a hundred feet high, which sloped abruptly down to the lake. Turning and firing on their pursuers, Rogers and his followers deliberately jumped over the perilous precipice and slid down to the lake with terrific force. The spot is still pointed out as "Rogers's Leap." By this exploit, these men, though severely injured, escaped alive, one of their number making his way to Fort Edward, and sending out a relief party with sleighs and blankets.

But others were not so fortunate. Accompanying the Rangers had been two British officers, Captains Creed and Kent, who had gone out to study their mode of warfare. At the beginning of the fight Rogers had advised them to retire, but being unused to travel on snow-shoes, ignorant of the country, and seeing their friends attacked by such a multitude of yelling savages, painted in the most gaudy colors, they chose like brave men to remain and fight. At the retreat, Rogers shouted to them to fly with him, but in their efforts to escape their snow-shoes came off, and the poor fellows sunk breast deep in the soft surface. By the strangest good fortune the savages overlooked them in the fury of their pursuit after Rogers. Not till the moon arose did they venture to stir. Then with fluttering hearts they stole through the forest, knowing nothing of their course, but hoping that it took them farther from the Indians. When morning dawned, it found them still struggling on through the snow, along the shore of some body of water.

As the fear of savages departed, another dreadful apprehension laid hold of them. Which way was the fort? The dangers of death from exposure or starvation stared them in the face. Suddenly they saw a man. He came towards them. He proved to be a servant of Rogers, and claimed to know their whereabouts and the way to the fort. He affirmed that they were on South Bay and not Lake George. All day they followed their guide, at first on the ice and then on foot, through the slavish snow.

At night they halted. Creed and Kent had thrown off their coats and fur caps in the battle, and had on only their vests. Over their heads they tied handkerchiefs. For a single blanket they would have given worlds. The third day the guide promised that the fort would be reached. But at sunset their weary eyes beheld nothing but the same vast expanse of whiteness. The fourth day he said it would be impossible to fail, but the day passed with the prophecy unfulfilled. Again and again their snow-shoes broke. Again and again, with benumbed fingers they tried to tie and patch them up. Every few paces they sank up to the breast in the snow. The hardships were intolerable. They scrambled up mountains full of dangerous chasms and hidden holes. They made detours to avoid impassable forests of fallen timber, prostrated by some tornado.

At the outset their entire stock of food had been a link of bologna sausage and a little ginger. This had long since been exhausted, and for two days they had lived on some frozen berries and water. Their nights had been passed without cover, and with the scantiest fires; for without a hatchet, by their utmost efforts, they could only wrench a few twigs from the frozen trees for fuel. During the fifth day they struggled along a dreadful road in the mountains, with only one snowshoe apiece.

Towards noon on the sixth day they came once more to the ice. *At a single glance the unfortunate men perceived it to be the same spot which they had left four days before.* This terrible discovery paralyzed them with horror. Their only chance was to throw themselves into the hands of the French at Fort Carillon. All day and night the wind blew hard, and a freezing rain incrusted their clothes with ice. The remainder of the sad story we give in Captain Creed's own words.

"We traveled a few miles, but the snow driving full in our faces, made every thing appear as dark as the fog upon the banks of Newfoundland. As the storm cleared up we looked in vain for the fort. Proceeding onward by land we came to a large waterfall. I attempted to ford the stream above it, and had almost gained the opposite shore where the water reached my breast, when the rapidity of the stream hurried me off the slippery rocks and plunged me under water. I lost my fusee, and narrowly escaped being carried over the fall. Mr. Kent and the guide fared no better, but the hopes of reaching a fire made us think lightly of the matter.

"As night approached we labored through the snow, being now certain that the fort was near; but our guide now confessed for the first time that he was at a loss. We plainly perceived that his brain was affected; he saw Indians all around him, and, though we have since learned that we had every thing to fear from them, yet that was a danger we did not think of. We even shouted to give notice where we were, but could neither see nor hear of any one to lead us right. If we halted we became pillars of ice. We therefore resolved to make a fire, though the danger was apparent. We had one dry cartridge on hand, but in trying to catch a fire with a little of it, by means of my pistol, Mr. Kent held the cartridge so near as to have it blow up in our faces, almost blinding him and causing great pain. This appeared to be the last stroke of fortune.

" We had now no hopes of fire and were not anxious for life, but wished to carry the scene out in a manner becoming to soldiers. We made a path round a tree and there exercised all night, though scarcely able to stand or to prevent each other from sleeping. Our guide, notwithstanding repeated cautions, strayed from us, sat down, and died immediately. On the morning of the 20th we saw the fort, and approached it with a white flag. The officers ran violently toward us, and we were saved from a danger we did not apprehend, for we were informed that if the Indians, who were close after them, had seized us first, it would not have been in the power of the French to have prevented our being hurried to the camp, and perhaps the next day to Montreal, or killed for not being able to march."

The prisoners were afterwards exchanged by the French.

From this time on in the war the Rangers operated in larger bodies and in more important movements. All the companies were concentrated at Fort Edward. Rogers was raised to the rank of major. Their history during the years of 1758 and 1759 is

full of romance, adventure, and excitement. When we pass it
over, we leave out their heroic service in the fatal attack of the
British on Fort Ticonderoga, from which the army retreated,
leaving two thousand of their number slain. We omit, too, the
thrilling story of their exploits in the triumphant expedition
against Crown Point. In these movements the Rangers formed
a part of the general army, whose defeats and victories are a
part of history.

When the British occupied Crown Point, they dispatched a
messenger with a flag of truce and proposals of peace to the
St. Fràncis Indians. They dwelt in the heart of Canada, midway between Montreal and Quebec, at a point three miles from
the St. Lawrence River. They were notoriously attached to
the French, and no other six tribes of Indians combined had
done the English more injury than the single one of St. Francis. Their unspeakable ferocity, their exhaustless hatred and
malicious industry, had resulted in the murder of over six hundred colonists during the years of the war. On the 13th of
September the commandant of Crown Point learned that his
messenger, bearing the flag of truce, had been coolly taken
prisoner and subjected to insult and indignity. Shortly after
receipt of this news an orderly handed Major Rogers the
following :

"You are this night to take a detachment of two hundred
picked Rangers and proceed to Missisqui Bay, from which you
will proceed to attack the enemy at the settlements of the St.
Francis Indians, on the south side of the St. Lawrence River,
in such a manner as shall most effectually disgrace and injure
the enemy and redound to the honor and success of his majesty's arms. Remember the barbarities committed by the
enemy's Indian scoundrels on every occasion where they have
had opportunities of showing their infamous cruelties toward
his majesty's subjects. Take your revenge, but remember
that, although the villains have promiscuously murdered women
and children of all ages, it is my order that no women or chil-

dren should be killed or hurt. When you have performed
this service, you will again join the army, wherever it may be

"Yours, etc.,

"JEFF. AMHERST.

" *Camp at Crown Point, Sept.* 13, 1759.
"To MAJOR ROGERS."

What a commission! Two hundred men ordered to make
a journey of more than three hundred miles, through a country
barren of provisions, and occupied by the whole French and
Indian army of fifteen thousand men; when at that distance
from support and their base of supplies, to attack and destroy
by stealth a powerful tribe of Indians, which had been a terror
through the whole war, and after all this to effect a retreat
by the same tremendous journey, only through a hostile
country aroused by a knowledge of their presence, and exerting
every effort to destroy them.

That night as the moon arose the little band sallied from
the fort, and, with firm tread and rigid countenances, swiftly
embarked in a fleet of canoes. Their progress down the lake
was itself one of difficulty and danger. Its waters were
patrolled incessantly by hostile schooners, armed with cannon,
and other mischievous engines of war, for the discovery and
destruction of the English. By night only did the Rangers
advance.

On the fifth day a keg of gunpowder exploded in their
camp, injuring a number of men, who, together with some
sick, were forced to return to Crown Point, making a defection
of forty-four men, one fourth of the entire company. At the
end of ten days, Rogers, having successfully eluded the enemy,
landed at Missisqui Bay. Here he stored the boats and provisions enough to take the Rangers back to Crown Point. Two
trusty Indians were left in charge, with orders to remain until
their return, unless the enemy should discover the boats and
strike the trail of the Rangers. In this case the two guards
were to follow the Rangers at the top of their speed, bringing
the fatal news.

On the evening of the second day, as the Rangers went into camp, the two Indians left behind came running in, breathless and excited. Four hundred French and Indians had discovered the boats and destroyed them, and two hundred of them were now in pursuit of the Rangers. "This," says the dauntless Rogers, "caused us some uneasiness. Should the enemy overtake us, and we have the advantage in an encounter, they would be immediately re-enforced, while we could éxpect no assistance, being so far advanced beyond our military posts; and our boats and provision likewise being taken, cut off all hope of retreat by the route we came."

A hurried council of war was held. The situation was desperate. But the motto of Rogers was, "In boldness lies safety." It was determined to push on to their destination, at the highest possible speed, avoiding an encounter, simply by out-marching their pursuers, strike their blow at the St. Francis settlements, and retreat quickly. The survivors were to make their way back by the roundabout route of the Connecticut River. Lieutenant McMullen was dispatched to Crown Point, to inform General Amherst of the disaster, and have him send relief and provisions at the Ammonoosuck River, "that being the way we should return, if we ever did return at all."

These arrangements were quickly made. McMullen, with a small sack of food, started back on his lonely journey to Crown Point; the others hurriedly prepared for the race with their pursuers. No sleep that night; the sunrise must find them many a mile on their way. Much of the time they advanced in double quick time, the hardy Rangers being able to run for hours in a sort of dog-trot. After the first night's march they uniformly began their day's advance one hour before dawn, and continued it without halt, their meals being eaten as they marched, until one hour after dark.

Nine days they marched through a spruce bog, where the ground was low and swampy, the greater part being covered with water a foot deep. Wher the weary Rangers encamped at night, it was necessary to go into the darkened forest and cut boughs from the trees and construct a kind of hammock to protect themselves from the water. The day before their destination was reached, they came upon the St. Francis River, with its swift current. Placing the tallest men up stream, and joining hands in a single line, the entire company passed the ford in safety. Their only loss was a few guns, which were recovered by diving to the bottom of the river. Towards evening of the twenty-second day from their departure from Crown Point, when the scout, as usual, climbed a tall tree for reconnoissance, he saw at a distance of three miles the unconscious village of the St. Francis Indians, over which hung the lightning-charged clouds of doom.

The Rangers were ordered to refresh themselves, and prepare for action on the following morning. Every gun was carefully dried and freshly loaded; ammunition bags were replenished, and such readjustment of clothing made as was possible. While the men rolled themselves in their blankets for a sound sleep, Rogers and two trusty companions stole out under the starry sky towards the fated settlement. As they drew softly near, wild shouts of merriment issued from the wigwams. Around enormous fires were dancing in frantic glee hilarious circles of warriors and maidens. It was a wedding dance. These wild Indians had turned aside, for tho moment, from thoughts of war and bloodshed to the mild gentleness of love. A noble brave had chosen to himself a dusky bride. The chord of sentiment touched at the incident still trembled responsive in the savage breasts. Their festivities were bright, innocent, and happy, shining like a star in the midst of all the gloom and blackness of their lives.

All unconscious of their danger, the dance went on, each moment with madder, merrier glee. The squaws ran about, serving to all who wished the rare bounties of the wedding feast. The old men stood apart from the revelers, smoking their pipes. Ever and anon their stately dignity gave way to unwonted outbursts of hideous laughter. Within the wigwam of the bride and groom, was dispensed with careless hand the blazing draughts of rum to the happy throng.

At last these potations began to have their effect. One after another of the braves staggered to his wigwam, and sunk into drunken slumber. The fires burned lower. The circle of dancers grew smaller, until only a handful of uproarious fellows and their girls kept up their shrieking orgies. At two o'clock in the morning Rogers and his companions returned quickly to their camp. A shake of the shoulder and a whispered command roused each sleeping Ranger to his feet. Blankets were hastily rolled up, packs adjusted, and guns examined. A frugal meal was eaten standing.

By three o'clock the Rangers were in motion for the village. With stealthy step they advanced to within a quarter of a mile. Another halt was made. Rogers crawled forward to make another reconnoissance. Meanwhile the men lay flat on their faces. At five o'clock Rogers returned. The feast had ended. The last reveler was wrapped in oblivion, and the entire settlement was asleep. The Rangers were disencumbered of all their packs. Weapons formed their only load. The men were formed in three columns. They were to fall on the settlement on three sides at once.

The first faint flush of dawn reddening the east had only obscured a few stars as the men moved rapidly forward through the frosty air. When the settlement was reached each man knew his work. The nearest wigwams were entered. In a moment the throat of every sleeping warrior was cut from ear to ear. The knife only was used as yet. No guns were fired. In this way the deadly Rangers had massacred two-thirds of the warriors in the settlement before a single note of alarm. Many children and squaws, who slept soundly, were left undisturbed. Such was the case with the new bride, whom they found locked in her husband's arms. Poor sleeper; too soon, alas, too soon, would she awaken to find all joy, all light, all

10   ROGER'S RANGERS ON LAKE GEORGE.

love, gone out from life. If, perchance, a child's wide wondering eyes opened as the glittering knife swept across its father's throat, it was the work of an instant to gag its mouth and hand it over as a prisoner.

At last, the groans of some dying brave, or the screams of an awakened squaw, gave the alarm. Small time was there for the warriors to reach for weapons. Their only safety lay in flight. Only one side lay open; that was the river. But as the canoes of the frightened savages pushed out into the current, the swift messengers of lead sped from the gun of the destroyers and stilled every noble form in death. Five English captives were found and rescued. The scalps of more than six hundred murdered white men hung from the wigwam poles. These sights were not unnoticed by the Rangers. Snatching brands from the smouldering embers of the wedding fires, the wigwams were ignited. Black volumes of smoke, pierced by forked tongues of flame, rolled upward to the peaceful sky of the morning, and draped its blue canopy with the mournful color which all the world has chosen for the sign of sorrow.

By seven o'clock, with the exception of three wigwams, preserved for their own shelter, the Rangers had utterly destroyed the village and its inhabitants. Two hundred wariors had been slain, while of their own number but one had been killed and two or three wounded. From their prisoners, who, excepting two Indian boys and three girls, were shortly set at liberty, Rogers learned that his pursuers had missed him; but that their messengers had sent word of his approach; that only four miles down the river were a force of five hundred French and Indians, waiting at a settlement which was supposed to be Rogers's destination, instead of the St. Francis settlement. While this examination took place, the Rangers supplied themselves with corn from the granaries of the village. A council of war determined that instant retreat by way of the Connecticut River and Number Four must be begun.

The hardships of the retreat far exceeded those of the

advance. The way led over barren mountains and through endless swamps. In one of these morasses, trusting an Indian squaw for guidance, they were led about three days, and brought back to their own tracks, to gain time for their pursuers. After eight days' travel, provisions gave out, and the Rangers divided into small companies of eight or ten each, for procuring sub- sistence from roots and berries.

One of these detachments, lingering behind the rest, was surprised by the enemy, and seven of their men taken prisoner. Two other detachments, similarly attacked, had nearly all their number slain. Some of the men, being still in fair condition, preferred to make their way directly to Crown Point. The bulk of the company, however, was to rendezvous at the mouth of the Ammonoosuck River, a hundred miles above Number Four (now Charleston, New Hampshire), where Rogers con- fidently expected provisions and relief, in accordance with the message sent to Crown Point by McMullen, after the news of the destruction of their boats.

When at last the straggling companies of wretched men reached the rendezvous, they found camp fires still burning, but no succor. They fired their guns, and shouted for help, but only the mocking echoes of the forest answered them. Not till some time later did they learn that in accordance with McMullen's message provisions had been sent to this spot in charge of a Lieutenant Stevens. Arriving there and not find- ing Rogers, the fellow thought proper, after waiting only two days, to return, taking his provisions with him. His departure took place just two hours before the exhausted and famished Rangers arrived. The signal guns fired by the latter were heard by Stevens, but only served to hasten his march, as he believed them to be fired by Indians.

The disappointment was cruel. It was evident that the men who, nerved by the hope of succor, had exhausted all their little remaining strength to reach this point, could proceed no farther. Relief must be had, or the whole party die in the wilderness. "In this emergency," says Rogers, "I resolved to make the best of my way to Number Four, leaving the remainder of the party, now unable to proceed any farther, to obtain such wretched subsistence as the wilderness afforded, until I could relieve them, which I promised to do in ten days. Captain Ogden, myself, and a captive Indian boy, embarked upon a raft of dry pine trees. The current carried us down the stream in the middle of the river, where we kept our miserable vessel with such paddles as could be split and hewn with small hatchets.

"The second day we reached White River Falls, and very narrowly escaped running over them. The raft went over, and was lost, but our remaining strength enabled us to land and march by the falls. At the foot of them Captain Ogden and the Ranger killed some red squirrels, and also a partridge, while I attempted to construct another raft. Not being able to cut the trees, I burnt them down, and burnt them at proper lengths. This was our third day's work after leaving our companions.

"The next day we floated down to Nattoquichie Falls, which are about fifty yards in length. Here we landed, and Captain Ogden held the raft by a withe of hazel bushes, while I went below the falls to swim in, board, and paddle it ashore; this being our only hope for life, as we had not strength sufficient to make a new raft should this be lost. I succeeded in securing it, and next morning we floated down within a short distance of Number Four. Here we found several men cutting timber, who relieved and assisted us to the fort. A canoe was immediatly dispatched up the river with provisions, which reached the men at Coos in four days after, which, according to my agreement, was the tenth after I left them. Two days afterwards I went up the river with two other canoes to relieve others of my party who might be coming that way."

Relief parties were also sent out in other directions to hunt up stragglers. Slowly the haggard men were gathered at the fort at Number Four. It was two months before they had recovered sufficiently to proceed to Crown Point.

With this story of the unfortunate expedition against the St. Francis Indians, a military exploit which, for boldness and dexterity, is hardly equaled in the history of our country, our recital of the story of Rogers's Rangers must close. They continued their operations until the close of the war in 1760, when they were directed to take formal possession of all the French forts west of the Alleghanies, in accordance with their surrender by France.

After performing this duty with approved success, Major Rogers went to England, where he resided till the opening of the Revolutionary War. He then returned to America, and visited the American camp, but was refused admission by General Washington, who suspected him as a British spy. Rogers was, however, visited by Colonel Stark, and other old Rangers, who had since enlisted in the cause of the colonies. He seemed greatly chagrined by Washington's treatment, and soon after joined Lord Howe, who commanded the British army. In a short time, however, he returned to England, and never again visited the land in which he had won undying fame. It was the opinion of General Stark, and other friends, that Washington misjudged Rogers, and that he would have proved a true and valuable soldier in the American army had he not been mistrusted. He was denounced as a Tory before he had declared his principles.

CHAPTER IV.

THE AMBITION OF PONTIAC.

THE web of history is woven from the countless threads of individual lives. Its pattern is controlled by the genius of great men.

Pontiac was the chief of the mighty confederacy of the Ottowas, the Ojibwas, and the Pottawotamies, which had its center of power in what is now the State of Michigan. But the genius of the mighty chief had spread his fame and influence, not merely through the confederacy, nor yet alone to the surrounding tribes, but over the greater part of the continent.

On the east his name was respectfully mentioned among the Indians of the Mohawk Valley as that of their greatest foe. Far to the South, the wandering tribes of Florida and Louisiana, had heard of the unapproachable prowess of Pontiac. and looked up to him as the greatest of all the Algonquin chiefs. His intellect was broad, powerful, and far-seeing. In him were combined the qualities of a great leader, a great warrior, and a great statesman. His plans continually reached out beyond the narrow limits of his tribe. His ambitions vaulted far beyond the scope of those of common chieftains. His understanding rose to higher generalizations, broader comprehensions, than those of any other Indian mind. In 1760 he was fifty years old, just at the meridian of all his splendid powers.

Great minds require great opportunities. The world is full of wasted genius. "Hands that the rod of empire might have swayed," are to be found holding the plow-handle and the plane. Cromwell without the English Revolution, Washington without the Revolutionary war, Grant without the Civil war, would have been indistinguishable from the common throng of men.

Pontiac was great. He also had great opportunities. Let us take a survey.

The English had conquered America. The French, the idols of the Indian heart, to support whose cause the remotest tribes of the north and west had furnished quotas of warriors, traveling hundreds upon hundreds of miles to strike a blow at the English, were humiliated, driven from the continent.

From the small and widely separated forts along the lakes and in the interior the red men had, with sorrow and anger, seen the *fleur-de-lis* disappear and the cross of St. George take its place. This took place, although the Indian power was unbroken. Toward the intruders, victors over their friends, patrons, and allies, the Indians maintained a stubborn resentment and hostility.

We have already noticed the difference in the policies of the French and English. The abundant supplies of rifles, blankets, gunpowder, beads, pipes, and brandy, which had for so many years been dispensed from the forts with lavish hand, were abruptly stopped. When the Indians visited the forts, instead of being treated with politic attention and politeness, they were received gruffly, subjected to indignities, and not infrequently helped out of the fort with the butt of a sentry's musket or a vigorous kick from an officer.

In addition to these things the wilderness was overrun with brutal English traders, who plundered, cheated and cursed the warriors, dishonored their squaws, and indulged in every form of profligacy. The best settlers tried to break this up, sometimes stopping a mad revel by force of arms. Such a scene is presented in the opposite picture. Meanwhile France, still smarting under her defeats, dispatched emissaries to almost every council house and wigwam from the lakes to the gulf, saying that French armies were already on their way to drive out the English, and inciting the Indians to inflict swift and bloody revenge upon the foes of France.

Lashed almost into frenzy by these agencies, still another disturbing influence appeared in a great Indian prophet, who arose among the Delawares, preaching the recovery of the Indian's hunting grounds from the white man, and claiming to have received a revelation from God. Vast throngs listened to his wild eloquence, his audience containing hearers who had come from distant regions to hear him. The white man was driving the Indians from their country, he said, and unless the Indians obeyed the Great Spirit, and destroyed the white man, then the latter would destroy them.

This was the state of affairs among the Indians in 1761 and 1762. Everywhere was discontent, sullen hatred, and explosive passion. The shadows of the forest were not blacker than the ominous darkness which pervaded the Indian breast. This was not local, but was far more nearly universal, spreading from the lakes to the gulf, than any other Indian disturbance before or since.

It is impossible to say how much of this state of affairs was due to Pontiac's designing intrigue and instigation, and how much of it arose spontaneously. We can not tell whether Pontiac made it, or whether it made Pontiac. Certain it is that Pontiac maintained close relations with the great Shawanese prophet. However this may be, we are certain of two things, that it constituted Pontiac's opportunity, and that but for his genius the whole mighty ferment would have evaporated in a few scattering Indian raids.

While these things moved the common Indian, the vision of the great and wise Pontiac took a wider scope, and was inspired by loftier notions than a mere resentment at the failure of the presents and the summary treatment of idle loungers about the forts. He saw that as long as France and England had been opposed to each other in America, the Indians had held the balance of power, and received the treatment which their importance merited. But now that England had no longer a rival, the Indians were spurned and crowded to the wall. This he saw must result in the destruction of the race, unless France could regain her foothold on the continent. This became his ambition. To this end he conceived and concerted the most wonderful conspiracy, taking into view the surroundings and circumstances, upon which the historian's toil has shed the light of day.

Toward the close of 1762, dark messengers from Pontiac, bearing the war belt of wampum, broad and long as the importance of the occasion demanded, threaded their way through the forest to the farthest shores of Lake Superior, and the distant delta of the Mississippi. On the arrival of these ambassadors among a tribe, the chief warriors would assemble in the council house. Then the orator, flinging down the red-stained tomahawk before his audience, would deliver, with energetic emphasis and action, the message from his lord. The keynote was WAR! On a certain day in May, after so many moons, the Indians from lakes to gulf, were to take the war-path simultaneously, destroy the English fort nearest them, and then throw themselves on the unprotected frontier.

The bugle call of such a mighty leader as Pontiac roused the remotest tribes. Everywhere they joined the conspiracy, and sent lofty messages to Pontiac of the deeds they would perform. The ordinary pursuits of life were given up. The warriors danced the war-dance for weeks at a time. Squaws were set to sharpening knives, moulding bullets, and mixing war-paint. Children caught the fever, and practiced incessantly with bows and arrows.

For the one time in their history, a thousand wild and restless tribes were animated by a single inspiration and purpose. That which was incapable of union, united. Conjurors practiced their arts. Magicians consulted their oracles. Prophets avowed revelations from the Most High. Warriors withdrew to caves and fastnesses, where, with fasting and self-torture, they wrought themselves into more fearful excitement and mania. Young men sought to raise their courage by eating raw flesh and drinking hot blood. Tall chieftains, crowned with nodding plumes, harangued their followers nightly, striking every chord of revenge, glory, avarice, pride, patriotism, and love, which trembled in the savage breast.

As the orator approached his climax, he would leap into the air, brandishing his hatchet as if rushing upon an enemy, yelling the war-whoop, throwing himself into a thousand postures, his eyes aflame, his muscles strained and knotted, his face a thunderstorm of passion, as if in the actual struggle. At last, with a triumphant shout, he brandishes aloft the scalp of the imaginary victim. His eloquence is irresistible. His audience is convulsed with passionate interest, and sways like trees tossed in the tempest. At last, the whole assembly, fired with uncontrollable frenzy, rush together in the ring, leaping, stamping, yelling, brandishing knives and hatchets in the firelight, hacking and stabbing the air, until the lonely midnight forest is transformed into a howling pandemonium of devils, from whose fearful uproar the startled animals, miles away, flee frightened into remoter lairs.

The time for the bursting of the storm drew near. Yet at only one place on the frontier was there the least suspicion of Indian disturbance. The garrisons of the exposed forts reposed in fancied security. The arch conspirator, Pontiac, had breathed the breath of life into a vast conspiracy, whose ramifications spread their network over a region of country of which the north-western and south-eastern extremities were nearly two thousand miles apart. Yet the traders, hunters, scouts, and trappers who were right among the Indians, and were versed in the signs of approaching trouble, suspected nothing wrong. Colossal conspiracy! Stupendous deceit!

On the 27th of April, 1763, Pontiac met the chiefs of the

allied tribes, from far and near, in a grand war council, on the banks of the little river, Etorces, not far from Detroit. Parkman gives a vivid picture of the assembly, as band after band came straggling in before the appointed time. "Here were idle warriors, smoking and laughing in groups, or beguiling the lazy hours with gambling, with feasting, or with doubtful stories of their own exploits in war. Here were youthful gallants, bedizened with all the foppery of beads, feathers, and hawks' bills, but held, as yet, in light esteem, since they had slain no enemy, and taken no scalp. Here also were young damsels, radiant with bears' oil, ruddy with vermilion, and versed in all the arts of forest coquetry; shriveled hags, with limbs of wire, and voices like those of the screech owls; and troops of naked children, with small, black, mischievous eyes, roaming the outskirts of the woods.

"On the long expected morning, heralds passed from one group of lodges to another, calling the warriors in loud voice to attend the great council before Pontiac. In accordance with the summons they came issuing from their wigwams—the tall, naked figures of the wild Ojibwas, with quivers slung at their backs, and light war-clubs resting in the hollow of their arms; Ottawas, wrapped close in their gaudy blankets; Wyandots, fluttering in painted shirts, their heads adorned with feathers, and their leggins garnished with bells. All were soon seated in a wide circle upon the grass, row within row, a grave and silent assembly. Each savage countenance seemed carved in wood, and none could have detected the deep and fiery passions hidden beneath that immovable exterior.

"Then Pontiac rose. According to tradition, not above middle height, his muscular figure was cast in a mould of remarkable symmetry and vigor. His complexion was darker than is usual with his race, and his features, though by no means regular, had a bold and stern expression, while his habitual bearing was imperious and peremptory, like that of a man accustomed to sweep away all opposition by the force of his impetuous will.   His ordinary attire was that of the primitive savage, a scanty cincture girt about his loins, and his long black hair flowing loosely at his back; but on occasions like this he was wont to appear as befitted his power and character, and he stood before the council, plumed and painted in the full costume of war.   Looking round upon his wild auditors, he began to speak, with fierce gesture and loud impassioned voice."

Parkman's story of the council reminds one of the council of infernal peers in Pandemonium, as described by Milton. One naturally expects Pontiac, this Moloch of the forest, to begin, "My sentence is for open war," and the expectation is fulfilled. He inveighed against the arrogance, rapacity, and injustice of the English, and contrasted them with the French, whom they had driven from the soil.   He recounted the neglect, the insults, the outrages, which he and his braves had suffered at their hands. He pointed out how the English, no longer having the French to contend with, had not only ceased to treat the Indians with respect, but had stolen their hunting-grounds, and awaited only a chance to destroy them.   Next he showed them an immense belt of wampum, saying that he had received it from the French king, whose armies and war-canoes were already on the way to sail up the St. Lawrence, and retake the forts from the English. The Indians and their French brothers would again fight side by side against the common foe, whose waving banners had long, long ago been trailed in the bloody mire of defeat on the Monongahela.

The orator having lashed his audience into fury, quickly soothed them with the story of a Delaware Indian, probably the prophet before mentioned, who had had a dream, in which it was revealed to him that, by traveling in a certain direction, he would at length reach the abode of the Great Spirit.

After many days of journeying, full of strange incidents, he saw before him a vast mountain of dazzling whiteness, so precipitous that he was about to turn back in despair when a beautiful woman, arrayed in white, appeared to him, and told him that, in order to proceed he must throw away his gun, ammunition, provision and clothing, and wash in a stream of crystalline purity, flowing near by. He obeyed, but again failed to climb the mountain, when the vision reappeared and told him he must climb with one hand and foot. So doing, he succeeded, and at last came to a city of splendid dwellings. Hesitating which to enter, a man, gorgeously attired, took him by the hand, and led him into the largest one, where, astonished by the unspeakable splendor which surrounded him, the poor Delaware found himself in the presence of the Great Spirit.

The Great Spirit bade him to be seated, and addressed him, saying that he was the Maker of heaven and earth, that he had made this country for the Indian, and not for the white man; that as for the English, " these dogs dressed in red," the Indians must lift the hatchet against them, and destroy them from the face of the earth. Many other things did the Great Spirit say to the Delaware before the latter found his way back to his brothers. Pontiac next told the wide-laid plans for the outbreak during the next moon, urged his auditors to go to war, and, finally, laid before the vast council a stratagem for the capture of Detroit.

He ended. A deep roar of applause burst forth. No one was hardy enough to venture opposition to the proposal of their great leader. Chief after chief arose, and with solemn emphasis, entered his approval of the great Pontiac's conspiracy.

> " The bold design
> Pleased highly those infernal states, and joy
> Sparkled in all their eyes. With full assent
> They vote."

" With this conclusion the assembly dissolved, and all the evening the women were busily employed in loading the canoes, which were drawn up on the bank of the stream. The encampments broke up at so early an hour, that when the sun rose, the swarm had melted away, the secluded scene was restored to its wonted silence and solitude, and nothing remained but the slender frame-work of several hundred cabins, with fragments of broken utensils, pieces of cloth, and scraps of hide, scattered over the trampled grass, while the smoldering embers of numberless fires mingled their dark smoke with the white mist which rose from the little river."

In 1763, the site of the city of Detroit, Michigan, was occupied by a settlement of some twenty-five hundred people. In the center of the long line of dwellings, with their little gardens, straggling along the river shore for several miles, stood what was known as the Fort. It was, in fact, a fortified part of the town. It consisted of a palisade twenty-five feet high, with a bastion at each corner, and block-houses over the gates. Within this palisade were crowded a hundred small, wooden, straw-thatched dwellings, crowded closely together, along narrow streets. Besides these incommodious dwellings, there was a little church, a council-house, and a well-built range of barracks. A wide roadway separated the houses from the palisade.

The garrison of the fort consisted of one hundred and twenty English soldiers, under Major Gladwyn. Besides these, were forty fur-traders, and the ordinary Canadian residents of the fort. Several light pieces of artillery peeped out from the bastions, and two armed schooners, the *Beaver* and the *Gladwyn*, stood motionless in the stream. The settlement outside the fort, stretching out more than eight miles along both sides of the river, consisted of the dwellings of Canadians, and three Indian villages.

It was the afternoon of the 5th of May. A Canadian woman from the fort crossed the river to the Ottawa village, to buy some maple sugar and venison. She noticed some warriors in a strange occupation. They were filing off their gun-barrels. This left the entire weapon, stock and all, only a yard in length. Such a weapon could easily be hid under a blanket. That night the woman mentioned it to a neighbor. "Oh," said he, "that explains it." "Explains what?" "The reason why so many Indians have lately wanted to borrow my files."

He was a blacksmith. No more attention was paid to either circumstance.

The next afternoon a plump and pretty Ojibwa maid came to the fort. She was Gladwyn's mistress. But this time Catherine's eyes no longer sparkled with pleasure and excitement. Her face was anxious, and her look furtive. She lingered long at the gate till she could speak to Gladwyn alone.

The major at once saw that the girl knew something which she feared, yet longed to tell. He caressed her, and sought to

CATHERINE REVEALS THE CONSPIRACY TO GLADWYN.

win her secret, but it was not for a long while, and under solemn promises that she should not be betrayed, that the dusky sweetheart spoke. She said that on the morrow Pontiac would come to the fort with sixty chiefs, and demand a council. Each would be armed with a gun, cut short and hidden under his blanket. When all were assembled in the council-house, at a given signal from Pontiac, the chiefs would fire on the officers, then rush out and massacre the garrison. Gladwyn believed the maid.

She went back to her people. The guards that night were doubled. At times the watchers on the walls heard unwonted sounds, borne to them on the night wind from the distant villages of the Indians. They were the steady beat of the Indian drum, and the shrill choruses of the war-dance.

At the expected hour, Pontiac came, followed in single file by his sixty chiefs. Each was wrapped to the throat in his gaudy blanket, his face smeared with paint, and his head adorned with nodding plumes. The leader started as he saw the soldiers drawn up in line, and heard the ominous tap of the drum.

The council took place, but under the encircling guns of the soldiers. Pontiac saw that the plot was discovered. The signal for attack was not given. After a short and uneasy sitting, he and his chiefs withdrew with marked discomfiture and apprehension. Better far had it been if Gladwyn had made prisoners of the chiefs of the conspiracy. But he knew nothing of the extent of the plot. He supposed it to be a fit of bad temper. He allowed his enemies, and the arch-conspirator, Pontiac, to slip through his fingers. Enraged at his defeat, and shrewdly perceiving Gladwyn's ignorance of the real situation, Pontiac returned the next day, to remove the suspicions of the garrison by smoking the pipe of peace.

On the 9th of May a great throng of Indians appeared before the fort. Pontiac was told that he might enter, but his company must be excluded. Instantly the savage threw off the mask of deceit he had worn so long, and, casting one look of unspeakable rage and hate at the fort, he strode away across the plain. At his approach, the whole horde of savages rushed to an exposed cabin, where lived an old English woman and her family. The doors were beaten in, and the inmates tomahawked. On a neighboring island lived an Englishman named Fisher. In a few moments he, too, was murdered.

That night, while the garrison watched with sleepless apprehension, the whole Ottawa village was removed to that side of the river on which stood the fort. "We will be nearer them," said Pontiac. A messenger arrived at the fort with news. Two

Englishmen had been murdered on Lake St. Clair, and Pontiac had been re-enforced by the whole war strength of the Ojibwas.

The garrison passed the night in feverish anxiety. Not till the blush of dawn tinged the eastern sky did the fierce Indians, yelling with infernal power, come bounding naked to the assault; but when they came it was not the Ottawas alone, but the Wyandots, the Pottawattamies and Ojibwas as well. For six hours the cautious Indians, from behind trees, logs, and cabins, showered their rifle-balls upon the fort with slight effect; and for the same time the garrison ineffectually returned the compliment. When the disappointed savages withdrew, Gladwyn, believing the affair ended, dispatched La Butte, a neutral interpreter, accompanied by two old Canadians, to open negotiations. Numbers of the Canadian inhabitants took this opportunity of leaving the place.

Pontiac received the three ambassadors politely, and heard their offers of peace with apparent acquiescence. La Butte hastened back to the fort, reporting that a few presents would fix up the difficulty, but when he returned to Pontiac he found the negotiation had made no progress. After a consultation with his chiefs, the treacherous Pontiac said that he desired Major Campbell, the veteran soldier, second in command at the fort, to come. When the word reached Campbell, he prepared at once to go, in spite of Gladwyn's fear of treachery. The officer's companion was Lieutenant McDougal. A Canadian met them, and warned them that they were advancing into the lion's jaws, but the brave officers refused to turn back.

As they entered the camp, a howling mob, armed with clubs and rocks, surrounded them, but Pontiac quelled the tumult, and conducted them to the council-house, where they were surrounded by sinister faces. Campbell made his speech. There was no reply. For an hour he waited in dead silence before the steady gaze of his dark-browed enemies. Not a chief deigned to open his mouth.

At last Campbell rose to go. Pontiac made an imperious

11

gesture for him to resume his seat. "My father," said the wily traitor, "will sleep to-night in the lodges of his red children." Campbell expostulated, he argued the matter to Pontiac with enforced calmness. Useless—he was a captive. Late that night La Butte returned with anxious face to the fort. Some of the officers suspected him, no doubt unjustly, of a share in the treachery. Feeling the suspicion, he stood in the narrow street, gloomy and silent, refusing all efforts at conversation.

Pontiac proceeded to redistribute his forces. One band hid in ambush along the river below the fort. Others surrounded the fort on the land side. The garrison had only three weeks' provisions. The Indians intended that this stock should not be replenished. Every house in the fort was searched for grease, tallow, or whatever would serve for food. Whatever was found was placed in the public storehouse.

The Indians, unused to protracted sieges, also suffered from want of provisions. The Canadian settlers were ruthlessly despoiled of their stores. Aggravated beyond endurance, they complained to Pontiac. He heard them. After that, each settler was required to contribute a certain quantity of food daily to the Indians, but it was to be deposited in a certain place. If any Indian entered a Canadian's premises, he was shot.

These dispositions on the part of Pontiac reveal his genius for command. He was an Indian Napoleon. He did another thing. After he had visited the house of each Canadian, examined the property, and assigned the amount of provision to be furnished by the owner, he found he had nothing with which to pay for it. In this emergency he hit upon a remarkable expedient. He issued promissory notes, drawn upon birch bark, and signed with the figure of an otter, the totem to which he belonged. These notes were afterwards faithfully redeemed. This incident is wonderful. The whole principle of paper money, the great resource of modern statesmanship, was utilized by this savage. It was an issue of greenbacks—a war measure.

Pontiac kept two secretaries, one to write letters, one to read

ROGER WILLIAMS OPPOSING THE PEQUOT EMISSARIES

those received. Neither secretary knew what the other trans-
acted. It is to be remembered that Pontiac maintained his
ascendancy among the Indians by the sheer force of his genius.
Accident, birth, fortune, laws, institutions, the power of the
government—all these things which make and help the leaders
in a civilized country, were wanting. One day a bottle of
whisky was sent Pontiac as a present by our old friend, Rogers,
of Rogers's Rangers, who was in the fort. His counselors
urged him to let it alone, for fear of poison. As usual, he
listened respectfully to them. Then he at once drank a large
cupful, saying the man had no power to kill him.

Weeks rolled by with no change in the situation. Unawares
of any trouble at Detroit, the British commander-in-chief at
New York, had, as usual in the spring, sent a detachment up
the lakes with food, ammunition, and re-enforcements for the
forts along the lakes. In order to hasten this flotilla the
schooner *Gladwyn* was dispatched down the river. On the
30th of May some faint specks appeared on the watery horizon.
They grew larger and blacker. The sentry in the bastion called
aloud to the officers, who eagerly ran to look with spy-glasses.
They recognized the banner of St. George, under cover of which
advanced the expected fleet of canoes. Quick, joyous commands were given for a salute of welcome.

When the sound of the booming cannon of the fort died
away, every ear was strained to catch the response. It came,
faint but unmistakable—a war-whoop, and not a salvo of
artillery. The faces of the watchers grew pale. The approaching flotilla was watched with breathless anxiety. When it was
well in view, a number of dark and savage forms rose up in the
leading canoe. The truth was manifest. The flotilla was in
the hands of the Indians. In the foremost of the eighteen
canoes, there were four prisoners and only three Indians. In
each of the others there were more savages than white men.
These latter were forced to row.

Just as the leading canoe was opposite the small schooner.

which lay at anchor before the fort, one of the white men was seen to seize the first savage by the hair and throw him overboard. The Indian clutched his adversary's clothes, and stabbing him again and again, dragged him into the river, and locked in a death embrace, the two floated down the stream. The two remaining Indians jumped overboard, while the prisoners pulled desperately toward the schooner, which they succeded in reaching, amid showers of bullets from the pursuing canoes.

The poor fellows told the story of their misfortune. After coasting for days, without seeing a sign of life, the soldiers had landed for a night encampment, when they were surrounded by savages, and, after a desperate fight, overpowered. As was afterwards discovered, only three, including the commander, Lieutenant Cuyler, escaped.

The Indians besieging Detroit now had two causes for rejoicing. One was the whisky of which the canoes, among other supplies, of course, brought large quantities for the garrisons. The other source of pleasure was the captives. Every Indian took his choice, either to become drunk with liquor or intoxicated with the fiercer frenzy of massacre. It was a puzzling alternative. Many chose the latter. After every species of torture and butchery, the poor, mutilated corpses were thrown into the river, with knives sticking in their hearts. Floating past the fort, they were seen by its defenders. The gloom of despair settled upon them. At any time the slender palisade might be cut or burned through, and then ——!

Throngs of Indians, having proceeded to get blindly drunk on whisky, sought consolation for their sorrow at not being participants in the massacre. This they found in biting off each other's noses, a cheerful and amusing sport. But even this hilarious fun grew monotonous. Then they organized a massacre of their own. Having no captives to kill, they killed each other.

One afternoon the famished and anxious garrison heard the dismal death-cry. A line of naked warriors extended across the

plain. Each savage was painted black, and carried a pole. At
the end of the poles were small, fluttering pennants. An officer
ran for a spy-glass. The pennants were discovered to be the
scalps of white men. What had happened?

That night a Canadian crossed the river to the fort, bearing
the tidings. Fort Sandusky was about seventy miles south-
east of Detroit. Its garrison was commanded by Ensign Paully.
About dark, on the evening of May 16th, there had been a
knocking at the gates. It proved to be a few Indians. It was
a time of peace. The Indians were well known to Paully.
What was more natural than to admit them? The dark visitors
were seated in a circle in the council-house. The pipe of peace
was being handed from mouth to mouth. Suddenly the guests
sprang up, and in a hand to hand conflict butchered or overpowered the garrison. As the commander was hurried away
in a canoe, he saw the fort wrapped in flames, where he had,
fifteen minutes before, commanded in as he supposed monotonous
security.

Twenty-five miles south of the present town of Erie, then
Presqu 'Isle, stood a heavy block-house, known as Fort Le Bœuf.
Simultaneously with the treachery at Sandusky, a multitude of
howling savages surrounded the little post. By means of blazing arrows the roof was fired. As the flames swept through
the structure, the savages poured in a continuous storm of balls,
expecting each moment that the garrison must be driven from
the building.

The brave men, however, chopped a hole through the heavy
logs in the rear of the building, and escaped, while the Indians
were still covering the doors and windows with their guns. The
refugees made their way to Fort Venango, to find only a heap
of red-hot coals. Of this post, not a single white man survived
to tell the story of its fate. Overcome with suffering and starvation, most of the desolate band from Le Bœuf perished. Only
seven haggard and weary men succeeded in reaching Fort Pitt.

The magnitude of the Pontiac conspiracy and the powers

of combination which its creator possessed are demonstrated by the widely separated points at which the smoldering flames of Indian hostility simultaneously burst through the thin crust of peace. Fort St. Joseph stood on the river of that name near the southern shore of Lake Michigan. Here the priests of the Roman Catholic Church had, for many years, maintained a rude temple of worship. Here, in the solitude of the wilderness, the toil-worn fathers labored, without recompense, to plant in the savage heart the germ of Christian faith.

One May morning a crowd of Indians pushed their way into the fort under various pretexts. At a sudden signal, they ran to the gates, tomahawked the sentinels, and threw them open to a host of savages without. The little band of fourteen soldiers made a fluttering attempt to rally, but in less than two minutes, as an eye-witness says, eleven of them were corpses, and the remaining three made captives.

Everywhere the Indian attack was made by stratagem and treachery. Everywhere their devilish ingenuity was successful. Fort Ouatanon, situated on the Wabash river, a short distance below the present flourishing and aristocratic city of Lafayette, was captured in this way. The, Indians, however, did not massacre the garrison. They were merely made captives. About midway between Sandusky, St. Joseph, and Ouatanon, that is, about one hundred and twenty-five or fifty miles from each of them, on the Maumee river, stood another one of these lonely and isolated wilderness posts—Fort Miami.

One morning an Indian girl, a favorite of the commanding officer, Holmes, came to the fort. Unlike the Ojibwa maid at Detroit, this girl came to lure her lover into a trap. An old squaw, she said, was lying sick in a wigwam, a short distance from the fort, and she begged Holmes to come and see if he could do any thing for her. The unsuspecting officer yielded to the request. As he entered the lodge where the sick squaw was supposed to lie, a dozen rifles were discharged, and he fell dead. A sergeant, hearing the shots, ran out of the fort to see what was the matter, and met a similar fate. The panic-stricken garrison, possessing no longer a leader, threw open the gates and surrendered.

The news of these disasters poured in thick and fast upon the horror-stricken garrison at Detroit. It seemed to them that the whole fabric of English supremacy in the wilderness was falling around them. In the great San Domingo insurrection of slaves, Toussaint L'Ouverture, their great leader, took a cup full of gunpowder, and placed a few grains of rice on top. Showing it to his officers, he said: "The black grains of powder are the multitudes of negroes on the island. The few white grains of rice on top are the few white men who are our masters." Shaking the cup, the rice was quickly overwhelmed and covered by the powder. "This," said he, "is the negro rebellion." The illustration applies equally to the situation of the defenders of Detroit at the time of which we write. But the worst news was yet to come.

Fort Presqu 'Isle, standing near the present site of Erie, was constructed on the lake shore, at the mouth of a small brook. At one angle of the fort was a heavy block-house. Its roof was of bark, and easily fired, but on the comb was an opening, with a small bulwark of plank, where the guard could, from behind this partial protection, pour water on the flames. One lovely June morning, just as the rising sun shot his horizontal rays far across the blue expanse of Erie, tipping each wave with gold, hideous yells broke the silence of the lonely spot. The soldiers, catching the alarm, ran to the block-house.

Two hundred Indians had surrounded the post, and from behind some neighboring ridges of land discharged their guns at every opening visible in the walls of the block-house. In a short time fire arrows were showered on the roof. Again and again it burst into flames. Again and again they were extinguished. The tireless savages rolled logs to the summit of the ridges, and from these loftier barricades were enabled to command every point in the parade ground. Hour after hour the soldiers returned the shots of the savages. About two o'clock the besiegers could be seen throwing up vast heaps of earth and stone behind their breastworks. What did it mean? A mine?

The garrison had no time to speculate on this problem. A more pressing danger was at hand. It was no longer possible to procure water from the well in the parade ground. The water barrels in the block-house were almost empty. Yet almost every moment the flames curled upward from the bark roof. The only resource was to dig a well in the block-house. While a part of the men discharged their heated muskets from the port-holes, the rest, with a strength inspired by the emergency, dug a hole in the ground. Before the well was finished the last drop of water was poured on the roof. It caught again. A soldier said, "I will put it out." He crawled out on the roof, amid a storm of balls, and tore the blazing shingle from its place.

Night came, but it brought little respite for the worn men. Some slept, while the others watched. All night long the flash of the enemy's guns startled the darkness. By morning the well was finished. It was fortunate! The savages had dug a mine to the commandant's cabin, which stood in the parade-ground. The building was fired. So close did it stand to the block-house, that the walls of the latter scorched, blackened, then burst into flames. Still the men passed water up from the well, and choked and blinded with the hot, sulphurous air of their wooden redoubt, fought with all the fury of the first repulse.

All day the storm raged, and nightfall brought no interruption. At midnight there was a sudden lull in the Indian fire. In a moment a voice was heard from the breastworks, calling for a surrender, saying that the speaker was an Englishman, who had been taken captive in childhood, and had espoused the Indian cause; that the besiegers had now completed a mine to the block-house itself, making its destruction certain; that a surrender would save the garrison's lives, while further resistance

would result in certain death.   At daybreak, the pale and haggard defenders of the block-house looking, after their fiery
ordeal, almost like blackened specters, marched out and surrendered.   They were made captive, but not massacred.

The news at Detroit of the fall of Presqu 'Isle was only
surpassed in tragic importance by that of the fall of Michillimackinac.

The pleasure seeker who spends a summer on the lovely
Island of Mackinaw, with its white cliffs, its piny woods, its
" Tower Rock," and " Devil's Kitchen," its old fort and venerable hotels, its meandering drives, and all the quiet scenes which
go to make up the Mackinaw of to-day, is impressed with a
sense of its antiquity.   The prevailing air of decay, the old-
time buildings of the Old Mission and Island House hotels, the
quaint manners of the resident population, the rotting sail boats,
which lie at abandoned wharves, all tend to make this impression.

The old fort looks as if it had been built in some remote
age.   Every thing is antique, quiet, un-American.   Our summer
traveler is completely shut in from the roar and bustle of the
busy world.   Mails come twice a week, or rather did a year or
two ago, when the writer spent a summer there.   The only
event of the day is the arrival of some steamer.   One feels as
if the clock had been turned back a hundred years.

Drinking in the pure and bracing atmosphere, indulging in
such quiet sports as the place affords, he soon learns to love
the island.   Sometimes he spends a day in fishing.   More often
he wanders with some friends through the woods.   Now he
joins his lady friends, and visiting the few little stores, inspects
the stocks of Indian ware.   Birch bark canoes, from six inches
to three feet long, pipes, bows and arrows, birch baskets, all
these he finds in immense quantities.

Lower down on the island he will find the shanties of the
Indians who manufacture these articles.   Stolid, copper-colored
men, with straight, black hair, everlastingly smoking tobacco
pipes, lounge around on benches in the open air on a summer

day. Now and then a grunt or a guttural ejaculation breaks the silence. That is all. They look sullen and sad. Too infinitely lazy to do any work, they seem simply to be waiting, waiting the extinction of their race. Yet these are the descendants of the fierce Ojibwas, whose principal village occupied the Island of Mackinaw in the year 1763.

So the air of antiquity which hangs about Mackinaw is an illusion. In 1763 no white man resided on the island. It was the home of the terrible Ojibwa chief. Fifteen miles to the south, across the beautiful straits, in which the blue waters of Michigan meet and mingle with the fresh tides of Huron, near the site of old Mackinaw, stood the fort of Michillimackinac, at the time of which we write.

This post was in 1763 nearly a hundred years old, while the Island of Mackinaw was yet only the seat of an Indian town. Parkman describes the post as it was on the eventful morning of June 4, 1763. The houses and barracks, containing thirty families, and a garrison of thirty-five men, were arranged in a square, inclosing a considerable area. Outside of this square was a larger one, formed by the high palisades. "In the vacant space inclosed by the houses, appeared the red uniforms of British soldiers, the gray coats of Canadians, and the gaudy blankets of Indians, mingled in picturesque confusion. Women and children were moving about the doors; knots of Canadian voyagers reclined on the ground, smoking and conversing; soldiers were lounging listlessly at the doors and windows of the barracks, or strolling in undress about the area."

There was absolutely no suspicion of danger. Yet the garrison had had warnings plain enough to put the British on their guard. Several Canadians had warned them that the Indians were plotting their destruction. The commander of the fort, Captain Etherington, did not overlook these warnings. He threatened to send the next alarmist in chains to Detroit! Only the day before the tragic fourth of June an Indian named Wawatam, who had taken a fancy to Alexander Henry, a trader, who was in the fort, came over and first advised, then urged, and finally begged Henry, on his knees, to leave the fort that night. In vain!

All that day unusual throngs of Indians had visited the fort. Their special demand was for guns, hatchets, and knives. Valuable articles of jewelry were also called for, the place of their keeping carefully marked, and then the treacherous customers would leave, saying, "We will call to-morrow." This remark was deeply significant. What was the real state of affairs?

The news of Pontiac's attack on Detroit, at the head of the Ottawas and their neighbors, had inflamed the Ojibwas of Mackinaw. With the exception of the tribes around Detroit, the State of Michigan was occupied by the Ottawas and Ojibwas. Their territory was separated about equally by a line running south from Michillimackinac. The western, or Ottawa, tribe had their principal village, L'Arbre Croche, on what is now Little Traverse Bay. At the head of this lovely inlet now stands the bustling town of Petosky, while a pocket in the shore of the bay forms a quiet harbor which the wildest storm scarcely ripples. The spot where now stands the microscopic settlement of Harbor Springs was once occupied by the populous lodges of the Ottawas.

The original plan was for the warriors of L'Arbre Croche to unite with the Ojibwas of Mackinaw in the attack on the fort. But so jealous were the latter that they resolved on carrying out the plot without telling their neighbors.

The scene outside the fort on the morning of June 4, 1763, was quite different from that we have described within the palisade. The plain in front was covered by throngs of Indians engaged in ball playing. The gates of the palisade were wide open. Groups of soldiers stood in the shade of the palisade looking at the sport. Most of them were without their arms. Sober Indian chiefs stood as if intently watching the fortunes of the game. In fact, however, their thoughts were far otherwise employed. Large numbers of squaws also mingled in the throng, collecting chiefly near the open gates. In spite of the warm day they were wrapped to the throat in blankets. The game of ball or baggattaway was between the Ojibwas and the neighboring Sacs. At either extremity of the open ground stood a post, which constituted the station of one of the parties. Except that the ball was smaller and that a bat much like those used in lawn tennis served instead of the kick, the game was identical with our well known foot-ball.

The ball was started from the middle of the ground, and the game was for each side to keep it from touching their own post, and drive it against that of their adversaries. The game was played on this morning with unprecedented fury and abandon. Hundreds of naked Indians were running, jumping, bounding over each other, turning hand-springs, executing aerial somer-saults, striking with the bats, tripping each other up, every way, any way, to get at the ball and foil the adversary. Now they surged together in a knotted mass, struggling furiously for the ball; now the sphere rose high in air, with the players bounding after it like hounds, with hilarious uproar.

Suddenly the ball rose high, and descending in a wide curve, fell near the gate. It was no chance stroke. The players instantly bounded toward the ball, but just as they reached the neighborhood of the gates the shouts of sport changed suddenly to the ominous war-whoop. The squaws threw open their blankets, and withdrawing therefrom guns, hatchets, and knives, the players instantly flung away their bats, seized the weapons, and fell upon the defenseless garrison and traders. Fifteen of the garrison were butchered outright.

The story of Alexander Henry, the trader, is full of interest. At the time the war-whoop was raised, he was in his room writing letters.

"Going instantly to my window, I saw a crowd of Indians within the fort, furiously cutting down and scalping every Englishman they found.

"I had in the room in which I was a fowling-piece, loaded

with swan-shot. This I immediately seized, and held it for a few minutes, waiting to hear the drum beat to arms. In this dreadful interval I saw several of my countrymen fall, and more than one struggling between the knees of an Indian, who, holding him in this manner, scalped him while yet living.

"At length, disappointed in the hope of seeing resistance made to the enemy, and sensible, of course, that no effort of my own unassisted arm could avail against four hundred Indians, I thought only of seeking shelter. Amid the slaughter which was raging, I observed many of the Canadian inhabitants of the fort calmly looking on, neither opposing the Indians, nor suffering injury; and from this circumstance I conceived a hope of finding security in their houses.

"Between the yard-door of my own house and that of M. Langlade, my next neighbor, there was only a low fence, over which I easily climbed. At my entrance I found the whole family at the windows, gazing at the scene of blood before them. I addressed myself immediately to M. Langlade, begging that he would put me into some place of safety, until the heat of the affair should be over, an act of charity by which he might perhaps preserve me from the general massacre; but while I uttered my petition, M. Langlade, who had looked for a moment at me, turned again to the window, shrugging his shoulders, and intimating that he could do nothing for me,—'*Que voudriez-vous que j'en ferais?*'

"This was a moment for despair; but the next, a Pani woman,* a slave of M. Langlade's, beckoned to me to follow her. She brought me to a door, which she opened, desiring me to enter, and telling me that it led to the garret, where I must go and conceal myself. I joyfully obeyed her directions; and she, having followed me up to the garret-door, locked it after me, and with great presence of mind took away the key.

"This shelter obtained, if shelter I could hope to find it, I

---

* Usually written Pawnee. This tribe lived west of the Mississippi, and was frequently at war with the northern nations. This woman was a captive of war.

was naturally anxious to know what might still be passing without. Through an aperture, which afforded me a view of the area of the fort, I beheld, in shapes the foulest and most terrible, the ferocious triumphs of barbarian conquerors.

"The dead were scalped and mangled; the dying were writhing and shrieking under the unsatiated knife and tomahawk; and from the bodies of some, ripped open, their butchers were drinking the blood, scooped up in the hollow of joined hands, and quaffed amid shouts of rage and victory. I was shaken not only with horror, but with fear. The sufferings which I witnessed, I seemed on the point of experiencing. No long time elapsed before, every one being destroyed who could be found, there was a general cry of 'All is finished!' At the same instant I heard some of the Indians enter the house in which I was.

"The garret was separated from the room below only by a layer of single boards, at once the flooring of the one and the ceiling of the other. I could therefore hear every thing that passed; and the Indians no sooner came in than they inquired whether or not any Englishmen were in the house. M. Langlade replied that 'he could not say; he did not know of any;' answers in which he did not exceed the truth; for the Pani woman had not only hidden me by stealth, but kept my secret and her own. M. Langlade was therefore, as I presume, as far from a wish to destroy me as he was careless about saving me, when he added to these answers, that 'they might examine for themselves, and would soon be satisfied as to the object of their question.' Saying this, he brought them to the garret-door.

"The state of my mind will be imagined. Arrived at the door, some delay was occasioned by the absence of the key, and a few moments were thus allowed me in which to look around for a hiding-place. In one corner of the garret was a heap of those vessels of birch-bark, used in maple-sugar making, as I have recently described.

"The door was unlocked and opening, and the Indians

ascending the stairs, before I had completely crept into a small opening which presented itself at one end of the heap. An instant after, four Indians entered the room, all armed with tomahawks, and all besmeared with blood upon every part of their bodies.

"The die appeared to be cast. I could scarcely breathe; but I thought that the throbbing of my heart occasioned a noise loud enough to betray me. The Indians walked in every direction about the garret, and one of them approached me so closely that at a particular moment, had he put forth his hand, he must have touched me. Still I remained undiscovered; a circumstance to which the dark color of my clothes, and the want of light in a room which had no window, and in the corner in which I was, must have contributed. In a word, after taking several turns in the room, during which they told M. Langlade how many they had killed, and how many scalps they had taken, they returned down stairs, and I, with sensations not to be expressed, heard the door, which was the barrier between me and my fate, locked for the second time.

"There was a feather-bed on the floor; and on this, exhausted as I was by the agitation of my mind, I threw myself down and fell asleep. In this state I remained till the dusk of the evening, when I was awakened by a second opening of the door. The person that now entered was M. Langlade's wife, who was much surprised at finding me, but advised me not to be uneasy, observing that the Indians had killed most of the English, but that she hoped I might myself escape. A shower of rain having begun to fall, she had come to stop a hole in the roof. On her going away, I begged her to send me a little water to drink, which she did.

"As night was now advancing, I continued to lie on the bed, ruminating on my condition, but unable to discover a resource from which I could hope for life. A flight to Detroit had no probable chance of success. The distance from Michillimacki-nac was four hundred miles: I was without provisions: and the whole length of the road lay through Indian countries, countries of an enemy in arms, where the first man whom I should meet would kill me. To stay where I was, threatened nearly the same issue. As before, fatigue of mind, and not tranquillity, suspended my cares, and procured me further sleep.

"The respite which sleep afforded me during the night was put an end to by the return of morning. I was again on the rack of apprehension. At sunrise I heard the family stirring, and presently after Indian voices, informing M. Langlade that they had not found my hapless self among the dead, and that they supposed me to be somewhere concealed. M. Langlade appeared, from what followed, to be by this time acquainted with the place of my retreat, of which, no doubt, he had been informed by his wife. The poor woman, as soon as the Indians mentioned me, declared to her husband, in the French tongue, that he should no longer keep me in his house, but deliver me up to my pursuers; giving as a reason for this measure, that, should the Indians discover his instrumentality in my concealment, they might revenge it on her children, and that it was better that I should die than they.

"M. Langlade resisted at first this sentence of his wife's, but soon suffered her to prevail, informing the Indians that he had been told I was in his house, that I had come there without his knowledge, and that he would put me into their hands. This was no sooner expressed than he began to ascend the stairs, the Indians following upon his heels.

"I now resigned myself to the fate with which I was menaced, and regarding every attempt at concealment as vain, I arose from the bed, and presented myself full in view to the Indians who were entering the room. They were all in a state of intoxication, and entirely naked, except about the middle.

"One of them, named Wenniway, whom I had previously known, and who was upward of six feet in height, had his entire face and body entirely covered with charcoal and grease,

12

only that a white spot, of two inches in diameter, encircled
either eye. This man, walking up to me, seized me with one
hand by the collar of the coat, while, in the other, he held a
large carving-knife, as if to plunge it into my breast. His eyes,
meanwhile, were fixed steadfastly on mine. At length, after
some seconds of the most anxious suspense, he dropped his arm,
saying, 'I won't kill you!' To this he added that he had been
frequently engaged in wars against the English, and had brought
away many scalps; that on a certain occasion he had lost a
brother, whose name was Musinigon, and that I should be called
after him.

"A reprieve upon any terms placed me among the living,
and gave me back the sustaining voice of hope; but Wenniway
ordered me down stairs, and there informing me that I was to
be taken to his cabin, where, and indeed everywhere else, the
Indians were all mad with liquor, death again was threatened,
and not as possible only, but as certain. I mentioned my fears
on this subject to M. Langlade, begging him to represent the
danger to my master. M. Langlade, in this instance, did not
withhold his compassion, and Wenniway immediately consented
that I should remain where I was, until he found another opportunity to take me away. Thus far secure, I re-ascended my
garret-stairs, in order to place myself the farthest possible out
of the reach of drunken Indians."

In an hour a rough voice again summoned Henry from his
hiding-place. The savage ordered him to strip, and then follow
him. The fellow owed Henry for some goods, and as he
carried a dangerous knife, Henry feared that he was to be
murdered. The Indian conducted his prisoner some distance,
when Henry, finding that their way led to a lonely and hidden
spot behind some sandhills, stopped and told the Indian he
believed it was a plot to murder him. The savage coolly replied
that it was, and raising his knife, was about to suit the action
to the word, when Henry turned and ran with all his might to
the fort. The savage followed with uplifted knife, but the

trader regained the house from which he had been taken, and the pursuit was abandoned.

The next morning Henry, with two other prisoners, was placed in a canoe, to be taken by several Indians to the Isles du Castor. When well out of the straits and into Lake Michigan, a heavy fog and stormy weather caused them to hug the gloomy coast. When within twenty miles of L'Arbre Croche, a hundred Indians suddenly jumped out of the woods into the surf, dragged the canoe ashore, and while making captives of the guards, explained to the three Englishmen that their lives had been saved by the Ottawas, as the Ojibwas were going to eat them. In a short time the Ottawas embarked for the fort, and Henry started back, arriving at Michillimackinac, the Ottawas coolly took possession of the fort and proceeded to abuse the Ojibwas for springing the trap without notifying their brothers. Henry hoped to be freed, but the two tribes patched up the quarrel, and he again found himself a prisoner of the Ojibwas.

The latter removed the disappointed man to a neighbor town. Here, by strange good fortune, the trader met his friend Wawatam, who had given the unheeded warning. The Indian possessed more than the ordinary nobility of the human heart. He at once asked the council to set his friend free, and his eloquent appeal was emphasized at every pause by presents, which literally impoverished the savage. His request was granted, and Henry found himself established in an Indian family, on the footing of a brother of Wawatam.

On the morning following his release, Henry, whose fears were by no means quieted, was alarmed by a noise in the prison lodge from which he had been removed. "Looking through the openings of the lodge in which I was, I saw seven dead bodies of white men dragged forth. Upon my inquiry into the occasion, I was informed that a certain chief, called by the Canadians Le Grand Sable, had not long before arrived from his winter's hunt; and that he, having been apsent when the war began, and being now desirous of manifesting to the Indians at large his hearty concurrence in what they had done, had gone into the prison-lodge, and there with his knife put the seven men whose bodies I had seen, to death.

"Shortly after, two of the Indians took one of the dead bodies, which they chose as being the fattest, cut off the head, and divided the whole into five parts, one of which was put into each of five kettles, hung over as many fires, kindled for this purpose, at the door of the prison-lodge. Soon after things were so far prepared, a message came to our lodge, with an invitation to Wawatam to assist at the feast. An invitation to a feast is given by him who is the master of it. Small cuttings of cedar wood, of about four inches in length, supply the place of cards; and the bearer by word of mouth states the particulars.

"Wawatam obeyed the summons, taking with him, as is usual, to the place of entertainment, his dish and spoon.

"After an absence of about half an hour, he returned, bringing in his dish a human hand, and a large piece of flesh. He did not appear to relish the repast, but told me that it was then and always had been the custom among all the Indian nations, when returning from war, or on overcoming their enemies, to make a war-feast from among the slain. This he said inspired the warrior with courage in attack, and bred him to meet death with fearlessness."

Soon after this agreeable information, Henry learned that the Indians were going to remove to the Island of Mackinaw, which was accordingly done. One day the Indians captured a couple of canoes from Montreal, carrying a quantity of liquor. The savages began to drink heavily, a proceeding full of danger to every one near. Wawatam told Henry that he was bound to get drunk, and that it would not be safe for the Englishman to remain where he was during the debauch. Wawatam therefor conducted him to a cave in the center of the island, where he was to hide himself until the liquor was all gone.

Henry broke some branches from the trees, and spreading

them down in a corner of the cave for a bed, went to sleep. During the night he felt some hard substance under him, and groping for it, seized some kind of a bone, and threw it away. Not till morning did he discover that "he was lying on nothing less than a heap of human bones and skulls, which covered all the floor." He remained in this cheerful apartment a day or two without food, until Mr. Wawatam, with swollen eyes and thick utterance, staggered up to the cave, and told him the drunk was over. For more than a year Henry lived with his protector, Wawatam, hunting through the gloomy forests of Michigan, before he finally succeeded in making his way to Montreal.

When Henry had met with his friend Wawatam, and been adopted into his family, the other survivors of the massacre were still kept by the Ottawas at Fort Michillimackinac, whence they were removed to L'Arbre Croche. Captain Etherington dispatched a letter to Lieutenant Gorell, the commander of the little post of Green Bay. The latter was requested to bring all his force to the relief of the prisoners. Gorell was on the point of obeying and abandoning his post, when the neighboring Indians intimated that his departure would be prevented. The threat might have been carried out had not a messenger from the terrible Dakota nation, with its thirty thousand braves, arrived with words of loyalty to the English, and denouncing with threatenings and slaughter, every tribe which was unfaithful to them. This sentiment must be attributed to no loftier source than the ancient hostility of the Dakotas to the Ojibwas. Gorell was now allowed to depart, and making his way to the Ottawa village, negotiated the release of the prisoners.

On July 18, 1763, they embarked in their canoes for Montreal, reaching there more than a year sooner than Henry. With the fall of Michillimackinac, and the abandonment of Green Bay, the Detroit garrison found itself left alone in the wilderness. There was not a British soldier west of Fort Niagara, except those behind the palisades of Detroit.

We have wandered far from the story of the defenders of
Detroit.   The news of the disasters which we have related
was received by the despairing garrison with sad punctuality.
Meanwhile, though we have neglected to follow their fortunes or
misfortunes, events crowded each other in this remarkable siege.

One night some friendly Canadians, from the other side of
the river, reported at the fort that there were rumors among
the Indians that the schooner *Gladwyn* was coming up the river.
This vessel had gone down to hasten Cuyler's ill-fated expedition.   Having passed the flotilla, which was yet voyaging pros-
perously, she held on her way to Niagara.   She was still riding
at anchor in the smooth river above the falls, at the time when
Cuyler and two companions, haggard and exhausted, reached
the fort with the story of the disaster, and of themselves alone
being left to tell the tale.

A force of sixty men was at once placed on board the
schooner, with such ammunition and supplies as could be spared
from the fort.   She had made her way up the river, and was
about to undertake the few dangerous miles which separated her
from the fort.   The garrison fired two guns to let the crew
know that the fort still held out.   This done, they waited.

The schooner, meanwhile, weighed anchor and started up
the narrow channel between the shore and Fighting Island.
Just as she reached the narrowest part, the afternoon breeze
grew more and more gentle, and at last died away, leaving the
white sails drooping idly in the air.   Nothing is so absolutely
helpless as a sail-vessel without a favoring wind.   It is hardly
possible to understand how the commerce of the globe was car
ried on entirely by means of them until within the present century.   The anchor chain rattled off rapidly from the capstan.
The great iron fluke disappeared in the water, and energetically
grabbed the bottom of the river.   The vessel was standing still,
within gunshot of an Indian ambush.

As the sun sank to rest in his couch of flame, the guards
on board the vessel were doubled.   Hour after hour their

strained eyes sought to penetrate the darkness. At last, the plash of muffled oars was heard. Dark objects came moving swiftly down the river toward the vessel. Every man was silently summoned on deck. A blow of a hammer on the mast was to be the signal for firing. The long black canoes approached the dark and silent schooner. The Indians thought the prize was theirs. At last the hammer struck the mast. The slumbering vessel burst into a blaze of cannon and musketry. The hostile fleet was demoralized. Many Indians were killed. Some canoes were sunk outright. As the enemy opened fire from their barricade, the schooner weighed anchor, and, drifting with the river's tide, floated down out of danger.

The following day the passage was again attempted, this time with success. The beleaguered garrison received the much-needed supplies of men, ammunition, and provision.

Pontiac was disappointed. Everywhere success had crowned the conspiracy except that part of it which he superintended himself. For forty days his genius and resolution had held his restless followers to the dull monotony of the siege. How much longer could he do it? His uneasiness manifested itself. One thing which showed it was his attempt to force the neighboring Canadians to lend active assistance. He called them together in council, made a long speech, told them that he fought for the king of France, their sovereign; that if they were loyal Frenchmen they must lend their help; that if they were friendly to the English, and would not join in the war against them, then he would make war on them as enemies of France.

All men can, on occasion, be hypocrites. Some of the Canadians pretended to take up the hatchet and join in the siege. This accession required a celebration. Pontiac ordered a feast— of dogs. In every one of all the numberless wigwams which formed the besieging lines, a dog was slain, and the flesh eaten. If an Indian happened to dislike the dish, it was so much the worse for him. An enormous piece of the delicacy was placed before him. By all the laws of Indian society and etiquette.

he was not allowed to rise from the repast till he had eaten every bit of the meat.

Another incident revealed Pontiac's rage. It is hard even for a great leader to hide his real feelings from his followers. At first he had protected Major Campbell from Indian cruelty. But his red retainers now read a new lesson in his imperious eye. The captive was murdered in his prison.

The two schooners in the bay were regarded by the Indians with mingled rage and superstition. The broadsides with which their camps were bombarded, the white wings which they spread, the mysterious control of their movements by the sailors, the knowledge that the schooners served to connect the otherwise isolated garrison with the rest of the world, inspired the savages with apprehension and fury.

One night in July, the lookout on one of the schooners saw a glowing speck of flame far up the river. It came nearer, growing brighter and brighter as it approached. The white beach along the river front, the dark pine trees in the background, were lit up by the illumination, revealing dense throngs of Indians crowded along the water's edge. The palisades of the fort, and the spars and rigging of the vessels, glowed like fire itself. Far across the harbor the waves were reddened with the light. The anxious soldiers of the garrison could be seen, watching with anxiety the singular apparition. As the flaming object came nearer, it was discovered to be a fire-raft. The inventive genius of Pontiac had caused a number of canoes to be lashed together, and a vast quantity of combustibles to be piled on the structure. A torch was applied, and the thing of destruction was pushed off into the current.

But fortune or providence protected the schooners. The blazing monster, sending up vast volumes of roaring flames, missed them by a hundred feet, and floated harmlessly down the river, consuming nothing but itself. As the relieved soldiers and sailors watched it receding into the night, the light grew fainter and fainter, until, at last, with a mighty hiss, the demon of fire plunged into the watery depths, as if to drown its sorrow at the wretched failure. This attempt was made again and again, but the crews of the vessel arranged a barricade of boats and chains, which foiled every effort.

Unknown to the garrison, Captain Dalzell was on his way to Detroit with two barges, two hundred and eighty men, several small cannon, and a fresh supply of provision and ammunition. Under cover of night and fog, they reached the fort in safety, having been attacked only once, a conflict which, however, resulted in the loss of fifteen men. Boat after boat discharged its loads on shore amid the cheers of the soldiers and the booming of cannon. Among the arrivals was Major Rogers, of Rogers's Rangers, with twenty of his old followers.

Captain Dalzell, on the day of his arrival, much against Gladwyn's advice, insisted on attacking the Indians. These had been forced, by the cannonading from the schooners, to remove their camp to the rear of a great marsh, several miles from the fort.

At two o'clock on the morning of July 31st, the gates of the palisades were noiselessly opened, and two hundred and fifty men marched down the road along the river shore. Not a sound was heard in the still night but the muffled footfalls of the soldiery and the occasional rattle of an officer's sword. Close to the river shore, keeping pace with the troops, two bateaux, each carrying a swivel gun, were rowed with stealthy stroke. The starlit sky was moonless. But for the fresh lake breeze, which sighed among the foliage of the overhanging forest, the midsummer night would have been intolerably sultry. On the right of the winding road lay the river, with its dark and restless tide; on the left, the houses and farms of Canadian settlers.

A mile and a half from the fort the road wound over a narrow, wooden bridge which spanned a small stream, and then crossed a succession of ridges lying parallel with the rivulet. These ridges were crowned with low barricades. The spot had

ARRIVAL OF DALZELL WITH SUPPLIES.

been Pontiac's old camp. On either side of the road were vast piles of firewood, cut by the Canadians, and stumps of trees from which the fuel had been cut. Here was a long line of heavy picket fence, inclosing several orchards. There, on rising ground, stood the house of a Canadian named Meloche. Over it all hung the pall of darkness and mist from the river which made the various objects indistinct.

The soldiers supposed their attack would be a complete surprise to Pontiac. Yet, in spite of this, the men shuddered as they filed down the descent which led across the narrow, wooden bridge. The ravine looked lonely and suspicious. The spot seemed fit for a massacre.

The advance guard had proceeded half-way across the bridge. Suddenly there was a wild war-whoop in the darkness, and the ridges, the intrenchments, the orchard fence, the black wood-piles, the half-chopped logs, whatever could afford a shelter to a savage, burst into flame. Half the advanced guard fell at the first fire. The unhurt men fled to the rear, and in a moment the whole column wavered. Dalzell dashed to the front. His clear voice rang out above the infernal din. The men rallied, and in a spasm of rage, charged across the bridge and up the opposite slope. It was sad folly. Before one-third of the way up the slope, every howling Indian had fled to another spot, from which he could fire upon the English. The latter pushed on with the courage of insanity. The charge which they maintained so stubbornly was a bloody mockery. The lines were broken and entangled in a labyrinth of fences, outhouses, trees, and woodpiles, from behind which the red foes kept up a murderous fire.

To advance was madness. To halt was folly. To retreat was a necessity. One company, under Captain Grant, hurried back across the bridge, and taking possession of the road prepared to cover the retreat. The two bateaux had been rowed up the creek to the bridge, and the dead and wounded were hurriedly placed on board. A heavy fire was poured in upon

the English during this last office of friendship. All at once
a concentrated volley was received from another direction.
The men of Grant's company turned to find a body of Indians
strongly posted on their left flank about the house of Meloche
and the neighboring orchards. To stop the deadly cross-fire,
Grant's men charged up the hill, and, at the point of the bayonet, drove the savages from the orchards and house. In the
latter were two Canadians. They said the English should
retreat at once to the fort, as large numbers of Indians had
posted themselves on the road in the rear.

The situation was critical. The men retreated rapidly and
without serious opposition for a half mile. At this spot the
road again ran through a region thickly planted with houses
and fences. Here, also, was a newly dug cellar for a house.
This pit was near the road. It was full of Indians. As the
center of the column arrived opposite the ambuscade, a heavy
volley of balls was discharged at the soldiers.

Already unnerved by the disaster at the bridge, the men
were well-nigh panic-stricken at this new surprise. They
started down the road in wild confusion, breaking ranks, tram-
pling on each other, throwing away their weapons, any way,
every way, to fly from the storm of bullets. Dalzell, with
drawn sword, shouted at the men, and forced some to stop.
Others he seized by the shoulders and held. He was twice
wounded, but paused not till his panic-stricken command was
rallied.

It was almost daybreak. But a dense fog from the river,
illuminated by incessant flashes from the enemy's guns, nevertheless concealed the enemy. Finally it grew light enough to
discern the shadowy outline of a house, of which the Indians
had taken possession, and from the windows of which they
poured murderous volleys upon the little band of Englishmen.
This house commanded the road along which the men must
pass to reach the fort. Major Rogers, with his handful of
Rangers, burst in the door of the house with an ax, and, in a

fearful hand-to-hand conflict, killed every Indian in the house who did not fly. Another detachment charged a line of fences behind which the savages were concealed. This, too, was in the main successful.

In the lull that ensued after these two advantages, Dalzell at once ordered the retreat to recommence. The column had not moved twenty feet when the Indians came running from every direction with wild yells, and fell upon their rear and flank. Dalzell was shot and killed. The loss of their leader threatened the battered and unnerved command with total destruction.

In the crisis Major Rogers and his Rangers took possession of another house which commanded the road. Some of the terrified regulars followed him, in frantic eagerness to gain shelter from the tempest of destruction without. The building was large and strong. The Canadian women and children of the neighborhood had already fled to it for refuge. They were crowded into the cellar.

As the Rangers entered the building, its owner, an old man named Campan, resolutely planted himself on the trap-door leading to the cellar, and thrust back every soldier who sought to lift it. No time was to be lost. Rogers's stentorian voice shouted to the men to barricade the windows. In a moment the yells of two hundred Indians, surrounding the house, mingled with the shrieks and cries of the half-stifled women and children in the cellar. With skilled hands, the Rangers piled the windows full of furs, bedding, clothes, whatever would serve to shelter them from the bullets of the savages, which now rattled against the building like the roar of a hailstorm.

While Rogers and his men boldly risked their lives to cover the retreat of the others, Captain Grant hurried forward for another half mile, and posted a squad of men in a strong situation, from which base of operations he sent forward other detachments, as they came up, to occupy other points along the road within supporting distance of each other, until by these tactics he had a complete line of communication with the fort. Each squad in turn, commencing with the farthest, then guardedly retreated to the fort, till all were in.

The gallant Rogers and his handful of Rangers, who had by their courage saved the command from complete destruction, were yet defending themselves in Campan's house against a vast multitude of savages, who had concentrated their force upon this isolated band of heroes. To relieve these brave fellows from their imminent peril, Grant ordered the bateaux to ascend the river to a point opposite the house. The swivel-guns were brought to bear, and in a short time the assailants were driven to the rear of the house. Rogers and his men seized the opportunity to rush out, just as the savages burst in at the rear door. Under cover of the cannonade, the Rangers made their way to the fort. At eight o'clock in the morning, after six hours of fighting, the last man entered the sheltering palisade. The fight at Bloody Run, as the creek was known from that time, had cost the English a loss of fifty-nine men.

The news of the Indian victory spread far and wide through the north, and bands of painted warriors arrived daily to re-enforce the besiegers. The siege resumed its old monotony, which was at last disturbed by a thrilling attack on the schooner *Gladwyn*. This vessel, the smaller of the two, was returning from a trip to Niagara. She had on board ten sailors and six Iroquois, who were supposed to support the cause of the English. One morning these wily children of the forest asked to be put ashore. In a moment of folly the request was complied with. That they repaired at once to Pontiac with reports of the weakness of the crew, there can be no doubt.

That night the schooner attempted the narrow river channel below the fort, but was caught midway in a dead calm. The pitchy darkness concealed from the eyes of the anxious lookouts a fleet of canoes, with three hundred and fifty Indians, which floated unobserved to within a few yards of the schooner. One cannon-shot was fired, but before its echoes had ceased the

savages swarmed over the sides of the vessel by scores. A
fearful hand to hand conflict ensued.

But resistance was useless. Ten or fifteen savages surrounded each sailor. Just as all was about over the mate
shouted, "Boys, fire the magazine, and blow her up!" A moment more and the vessel would have been a dismantled wreck.
But some Wyandots understood the words. With a wild cry
of alarm the Indians leaped from the vessel into the water,
swimming away at the top of their speed. The deck was
cleared instantaneously. The astonished crew found not an Indian on board, where a minute before they had been by scores.
The savages ventured no more near the vessel. The next morning a stiff breeze filled the languid sails, and the plucky little
schooner made her way safely to the fort.

We can not follow the detailed story of the siege further,
but turn to view other fields which the ambition of Pontiac
desolated with the horrors of war. When the weak line of
frontier forts was overwhelmed, the news of the successive disasters was carried, not alone to the starving garrison of Detroit,
and the great chieftain who sat watching it like an Evil Genius,
but the same tidings spread like wild-fire along the defenseless
frontiers, and among the wild Indians of the west, who yet
hesitated to take up the hatchet. Venango, Sandusky, Le Bœuf,
St. Joseph, Miami, Ouatanon, Michillimackinac, Presqu' Isle,
these were the fated names which flashed over the frontiers,
carrying dread and terror to every cabin.

It is to be remembered that the defenseless frontiers of Virginia and Pennsylvania bore the recent scars of the fearful
desolation of the French and Indian War, which ensued after
Braddock's defeat. Their sufferings were recent. The memory
of the mighty panic which desolated vast stretches of settled
country, and of the awful fate of hundreds and thousands of
settlers, who, with dogged courage, faced the savage hordes,
was fresh and vivid.

The imaginations of the terror-stricken pioneers dilated with horror as the black-winged rumors flew from cabin to cabin, and from settlement to settlement. Nor were these apprehensions untimely. The very worst came to pass. The most exaggerated fears were those which most nearly foretold the truth. The war-parties of savages, with reddened tomahawk and flaming torch, followed swiftly after the tidings of the fall of the forts.

It was the French and Indian war over again. This statement must be received with some qualifications. It was more extended. It was bloodier. It was more sudden. It was more fearful in its details. In these respects the war of Pontiac was worse than that of the French and Indians. From the tall Creeks, who dwelt among the palms and magnolias of the sunny south, to the wiry savages who shivered around frosty Halifax, the war-cry resounded through the unending forests, and the tomahawk was uplifted by cruel hands.

The details of the fearful conflict may not be followed in this place. Only a few of the most striking incidents can be mentioned. In three months more than two thousand families were driven from their homes in Pennsylvania and Virginia to the settlements and cities of the east, and more than a thousand persons were massacred or taken captive. As in the former war, vast sweeps of settled country were absolutely abandoned by the flying inhabitants. As before, the multitudes of unhappy refugees were crowded together in the towns to which they had hurried, seeking shelter in barns, hovels, and temporary huts of bark, where they were confronted by all the horrors of penury and famine. As before, the Quaker government sat with folded hands, extending to the bleeding frontiers no comfort but counsels to non-resistance, and no aid but pious maxims. From every valley of the Alleghanies rose black columns of smoke from burning cabins and blazing hay-stacks.

The commander-in-chief of the British army was reluctantly forced to believe in a wide-spread Indian insurrection. From the meager resources at his command, two relief expeditions were organized for the two posts, which were thought to be in imminent peril. The story of the one designed for Detroit, under the brave but incautious Dalzell, we have already traced. The other expedition, under Henry Bouquet, consisting of five hundred emaciated and feeble regulars from the West Indias, was designed for Fort Pitt.

Day after day the weak, little band pressed on their errand of succor. Now they passed the charred ruins of desolated settlements in some lovely valley; now they came to some lonely little block-house, from which a swarm of beleaguering Indians fled at their first approach; now suffering from the heat of the July sun, they toiled, panting up the long slopes of the Alleghanies; now from the crest of some range they looked out over the landscape, with its purple mountain ranges, its shimmering rivers, and its deep valleys, embowered in all the luxuriance of midsummer foliage.

The fate of Braddock's army, of more than ten times the strength of this little command of regulars, already wasted by disease contracted in the burning atmosphere of the Indias, and wholly unused to Indian warfare, hung constantly before the eyes of the men. Every possible precaution against ambuscade was taken. They were within twenty-five miles of Fort Pitt, descending a hill through a dense forest, when a volley of shots at the head of the column announced to every startled soldier that they were attacked. A command to charge was given, and company after company dashed down the hill. Before the impetuous onset the Indians fled.

Just at the moment of victory, a heavy fire in the flank and rear announced that the enemy were by no means all in the front, and that the provision wagons, carrying the precious stores for Fort Pitt, as well as the supplies for the troops, had been attacked. No time was to be lost. The men turned and hurried back up the hill to the relief of the convoy. A circle was formed about the wagons right on the hill-side. It was none too soon, for the Indians at once flung themselves on this

13

protecting ring of soldiers. The forest rang with the war-whoops of the savages. Every tree and log served as a shelter from which they peppered the British regulars, who were wholly unused to bush fighting. The fight was kept up for seven hours, until night hid the combatants from each other.

The English were forced to encamp on the hill where they were. To attempt a remove was certain destruction. Yet not a drop of water could be had in their camp. After seven hours of fighting in a scorching midsummer sun, the men were almost insane with thirst. The gloom of the night could hardly darken the prospect which confronted the command. Sixty of their number had been killed and wounded. The latter were placed behind a low barricade of sacks of flour from the wagons. Fever lent its flames to intensify the fearful sufferings from thirst.

Bouquet, cool, competent commander, saw so little hope for the morrow, that he wrote a concise report of the engagement to his commander-in-chief, that the latter might be informed concerning it, "whatever our fate may be." The dream-haunted slumbers of the restless men were broken as the first gray light came stealing through the damp forest. It was the struggle of the previous day renewed. Yet some changes could be noticed. The Indians, confident of victory, dashed more openly and boldly upon the lines. The soldiers, on the other hand, fought with less hope, and some demoralization from their sufferings.

At ten o'clock in the morning there was no further altera-tion in the situation. Bouquet saw that it was only a question of time until his men were overpowered, unless a change came soon. The savages pressed harder and harder upon the dis-tressed soldiery. The horses picketed in the circle near the barricade for the wounded, received many shots, and maddened with pain, added to the uproar of battle their own wild and unearthly cries, or sometimes breaking loose they would bound through the lines of friends and foes, and run up and down the mountains screaming with agony.

One thing was true. If the Indians could be collected into a body and stand long enough to fight it out, Bouquet might yet achieve a victory. He resolved on a desperate stratagem. Two companies, forming a part of the line hotly pressed, were ordered to fall back quickly, while the troops on either side were to rapidly cover the gap by a thin extension of their own lines, as if to cover the retreat.

The maneuver was executed successfully. The savages, as Bouquet had foreseen, mistook the movement for retreat. They sprang forward at the gap from all directions, and throwing themselves on the slender line, were on the point of breaking into the very heart of the camp, when the aspect of affairs underwent a sudden change. The two companies which had withdrawn made a quick flank movement, hidden by the forest, and just as the Indians were on the point of victory, discharged a fearful volley into their flank at point-blank range.

The astonished savages turned at bay, and fought like tigers to extricate themselves from the trap. Before they could do so, and break out of the circle which they had fought so long to break into, two other companies were precipitated upon the Indians. At this new onslaught they broke and fled, pursued by the English and overwhelmingly routed. The exhausted troops collected their wounded, and, by the following evening, reached Fort Pitt.

This place had been in peril, but on the report of the defeat of their warriors at Bushy Run, near which the battle had been fought, the besiegers fled. The defenders of the fort had taken every precaution possible. They had cleared the land around it so that the savages might have no shelter. They had raised the palisade, strengthened the barracks, and even constructed a rude fire-engine to be used in case the savages succeeded in firing the buildings.

On the other hand, the Indians had displayed equal ingenuity. Under cover of night, they had crawled up the open river banks, under the ramparts, and by incredible industry had dug out innumerable rifle-pits with their knives. Each one of these burrows held one or two warriors, whose deadly aim was certain to bring down every exposed soldier. The peril of the fort, thus closely invested, arose from famine. The arrival of Bouquet, however, happily averted it.

Bouquet's victory caused only a temporary lull in the desolation of the frontiers in its immediate neighborhood. The history of the time is full of fearful incidents. A party of twenty-four soldiers, in charge of a train of provision wagons, was ambuscaded three miles below Niagara Falls, where the narrow road ran close to the brink of the gloomy precipices and black abysses of Devil's Hole. Such as were not killed on the spot were thrown over the cliff, and were shattered beyond recognition far below upon the rocks. A relief party started out from Fort Niagara on hearing the sound of rifles, but fell into an ambuscade not less terrible than the first, leaving over fifty of their number slain.

In the war on the Pennsylvania border one incident stands out unmatched in its cruelty. In the center of a lonely forest stood a small school-house. This building was attacked by Indians just as the master was about to begin the daily round of study with prayer. He was killed with the open Bible in his hand, and an agonized plea for the safety of his scholars on his lips. At nightfall, when the little fellows who attended the school failed to return home, anxious searchers made their way to the school-house, where they found the lifeless remains of the teacher, surrounded by the corpses of his nine scholars.

Before the winter closed in, another attempt was made to relieve Detroit. Major Wilkins, with a force of six hundred regulars, collected with painful effort from the colonies, started up the Niagara River. Before proceeding far they were attacked by Indians and driven back in confusion to Fort Schlosser.

A second time the ill-fated expedition set out, and succeeded in reaching Lake Erie. The inland lake of azure, as deceitful as a coquette, had been almost traversed. The broad mouth of the Detroit River was already in sight. The tired garrison were just on the point of being relieved. But the sailors in the flotilla shook their heads with misgiving, and talked in low voices, as they saw rising in the north-western sky the dark battalions of the Storm King. With inconceivable rapidity, the little line of blue vapor which hung lazily on the horizon expanded and dilated until the blue canopy was obscured with dark and thunderous clouds. The ragged rain line advanced swiftly. A heavy gale of wind arose. The helpless bateaux were rocked more and more uneasily on the rising waves.

The surface of the lake grew black as ink, and was flecked with angry white-caps. The bright day was succeeded by the greenish darkness of the tempest. Every muscle was strained by the crew of each canoe to make the shore. It had been four miles away when the first signs of the approaching storm were detected. For fifteen minutes they had been headed for land. Yet it was still two miles and a half away.

The gale rose higher and higher. Now a rolling wave lifted the prow of a canoe five feet in the air, now plunged it as far below the surface of the lake, and broke athwart the bow, deluging the rowers with spray and water. Red lightnings shot zigzag across the angry sky, and terrific peals of thunder exploded like the trumps of doom. As the tempest grew heavier and wrought the mobile lake into more perfect reflection of its own fury and violence, the bateaux heaviest laden began to fill and sink. Some of the crew would be taken on board other boats; others, with white faces upturned, and piercing screams for help, sank out of sight forever in the raging depths. Great drops of water began to fall. The oarsmen pulled with swollen arteries and knotted sinews.

At last, as the flood-gates of the sky were opened, the flotilla attempted to land. The frail vessels were caught in the arms of giant breakers and flung again and again with remorseless violence against the beach. The men jumped overboard, and abandoning provisions, weapons, and ammunition to the greedy waves, fought their way through the seething surf to the land so many had failed to reach. The equipment of the expedition was utterly lost. To proceed to Detroit was only to treble the number behind the palisade which must be fed, without replenishing the scanty supply of provision. With misery and hardship the men struggled back to Niagara. Detroit was still left alone.

Before the news of this disaster reached the garrison, information of a very different kind had filled the spirit of the mighty Pontiac with bitterness and rage. While Pontiac had been maturing the far-reaching plans of his ambitious conspiracy in the winter of 1762–1763, to overtl row the English, re-establish France in the military dominion of the west, and seat the Indians, the aboriginal lords, upon the throne of the balance of power between the two European nations, these latter had been maturing a counter movement, culminating on the 10th of February, 1763, in the treaty of Paris, by which France resigned all claim to the territory east of the Mississippi.

The news of this treaty reached Pontiac when the siege of Detroit was but a month old. But with iron-headed skepticism the dark-browed king of the forest refused to believe it, and threatened death to every person who ventured to bring such news. As the summer rolled away, with Detroit still unsubdued, and the expected war canoes of the French king, which he had promised his followers months before were already on their way to strike the English, were yet as far off as ever, Pontiac stamped his foot with rage, and dispatched a fierce, haughty demand for weapons, provisions, and re-enforcements to the French commandant of Fort Chartres, in the Illinois country.

The reply to this demand reached the haughty Pontiac about the time of the Lake Erie disaster. It was to the effect that the French king had made peace and resigned all claim to her territory in America; that instead of expecting help for war, Pontiac should himself lay down the hatchet.

On receipt of this message, of which the authenticity could

not be doubted, Pontiac's fierce spirit was wrought into unspeakable fury. For hours no man or woman dared go near him, so terrible was his rage. He sat raving and cursing, like an "archangel fallen." There are fiercer storms than those of wind and wave. This was one. It was a tempest in a brain. At last he rose, and with imperious gesture ordered the frightened squaws to take down the wigwams. That night the dark conspirator withdrew to the tribes along the Maumee River. The siege of Detroit, however, though practically suspended during the winter, was renewed the following spring, but with less pertinacity and zeal. The eye of the master was no longer there to oversee it.

Though Detroit still baffled the fierce tribes of the north, the defenseless borders of Pennsylvania and Virginia ceased not to be desolated with fire and blood. Farther and farther to the east the savages pushed their depredations. Nearer and nearer to the quick of the nation did the assassin's knife cut its way. To these things the Quaker Assembly of Philadelphia refused to make any resistance. With placid obstinacy and undisturbed countenances, they heard the horrible tales of border massacre and bloodshed, and then declared that resistance would be sinful! The poor frontier people flooded the assembly with memorials, pleas, petitions, prayers, and supplications, imploring, begging, demanding protection. To these things the good Quakers turned an ear of stone.

So the frontiersmen, as is always the case where the government fails to discharge its duty and enforce the law, took the law and its execution into their own hands. Bands of maddened and desperate men organized for protection and revenge. As the report of their telling blows against the savages reached Philadelphia, the Quakers raised a fearful clamor of denunciation. As the majority of the frontiersmen were Presbyterians, the gall of sectarianism was added to the wormwood of political strife over the issue of resistance or non-resistance—which?

The bold borderers fought well, shouting their notes of defi-

ance to the citizens of the Quaker capital. Among them, our
old friend James Smith, whose fortunes in captivity we traced
in a former chapter, was one of the most notorious and successful leaders. Of course this irregular warfare, a sort of unli-
censed murdering, led to excesses. One of these has become
historic. It illustrates the stormy time.

Near the broad and mirror-like Susquehanna, and at no great
distance from the town of Lancaster, at a spot known as the
Manor of Conestoga, lived a small band of Indians. The settlement was old, and in former years had been prosperous,
but at the time of which we write had dwindled, till nothing
remained of it but a cluster of squalid hovels, inhabited by
twenty wretched Indians, regarded in the neighborhood simply
as lazy, but harmless vagabonds. On the east bank of the Susquehanna, and some distance farther up, stood the town of Paxton. It had been burnt by the Indians in the French war. Of
this burning and the massacre which followed, the inhabitants
carried in their hearts the memory. For the Indians they had
no mercy, but only black hate and an undying thirst for
revenge. For some time, as the horrors of Indian warfare again
swept along the frontiers, they had watched the poor vagabonds
of Conestoga with an eye of fierce suspicion. The verdict of
history is that one or two of the Conestoga Indians were guilty;
the rest innocent.

One night word was brought to Paxton that an Indian,
known to have committed depredations, had been tracked to
Conestoga. The Paxton blood was fired. Fifty men, athirst
for blood, mounted on horses, proceeded to the Indian settlement and surrounded it just before daybreak. As they drew
near to the hovels, an Indian overheard them and looked out.
One of the men thought or pretended that he recognized him.
" Curse him! he is the one that killed my mother," he shouted,
and firing at the instant, the poor wretch fell dead. With wild
shouts, the ruffians burst into the cabins, and shot, stabbed, and
butchered the inmates. As it happened, there were only six

Indians in the settlement, the rest, vagabonds that they were, being scattered over the surrounding country. After firing the cabins, the fierce Paxtonians rode rapidly away, freely scattering the news.

In an hour or two the sheriff of Lancaster arrived on the ground. He at once proceeded to collect the fourteen other Indians who had escaped the massacre by being absent, and lodged them in the Lancaster jail for safety. On receipt of the news at Philadelphia, the government at once offered a reward for the apprehension of the murderers. This measure inflamed the Paxton men beyond all control. On December 27, 1763, they started to Lancaster, against the protests of the cooler-headed people of the community, with the purpose, more or less understood among them, of breaking into the jail and killing the Indians who had escaped the first massacre.

About three o'clock in the afternoon the rioters, all heavily armed, galloped into the little town and up to the jail, quickly burst in the door, and made their way to the Indians. The latter gathered billets of wood for self-defense. At sight of resistance the rioters fired into the crowd. " In a moment more," says Parkman, " the yard was filled with the ruffians, cursing and firing upon the cowering wretches, holding the muzzles of their pieces, in some instances, so near their victims' heads that the brains were scattered by the explosion. The work was soon finished. The bodies of men, women, and children, mangled with outrageous brutality, lay scattered about the yard, and the rioters were gone."

The whole country was thrown into an uproar by this event. On the one hand, the government was offering rewards for the apprehension of the murderers; on the other hand, the hardy frontiersmen threatened to destroy a government which left them to their fate, and branded them as murderers if they but defended themselves. The sectarian quarrel, and political disputes concerning inadequate representation, and taxation without protection, filled the country with agitation and clamor.

To Philadelphia there had been removed, a few weeks before the Lancaster affair, a community of Moravian Indians from Bethlehem, in order to save them from the fate which afterwards befell the Conestogas. All along the line of march the refugees had been insulted, and a howling mob assaulted them in the streets of Philadelphia. They were protected by the Quakers, and afforded shelter and food. This thing was remembered as the agitation over the Paxton matter grew greater and greater. Far and wide through the frontier borders, the notion sprang up of proceeding to Philadelphia, destroying these poor savages, and overturning the government.

Towards the close of January, a force of from five hundred to fifteen hundred desperate borderers started on this mission to Philadelphia. They expected co-operation from the city mob. Rumor had anticipated their movement by several days, and thrown the city of Philadelphia into a panic of fear.

The first resolution was to send the Indians away to New York. The execution of the timid plan was hastily begun. Before daybreak, one bitter cold January morning, the half-clad Indians filed mournfully through the streets of the City of Brotherly Love. The report of their removal had filled the streets with a howling mob, even at that hour. Under the protection of soldiers little less hostile than the mob itself, the unfortunate and shivering Indians commenced their march on foot to New York.

Greeted everywhere by the curses of the people, the sad children of the forest proceeded as far as Amboy, where they were notified by the governor of New York that they would not be allowed to enter that province, and that an attempt to do so would be resisted by force. For some days the poor Indian converts remained in the barracks at Amboy, engaged almost constantly in singing and praying. But there seemed to be no resting-place for them in the land of their fathers. The governor of New Jersey sent a message requiring them to leave

PANIC OF THE PHILADELPHIANS AT THE APPROACH OF THE PAXTONS.

that province forthwith. Beaten from pillar to post, the unhappy Indians again turned their faces to Philadelphia.

The return of the Indians, together with the news of the approach of the Paxton men, again convulsed the city with apprehension, discord, and fright. A large element in the city openly declared that they would espouse the cause of the borderers if it came to an armed conflict. The rest of the inhabitants took active measures for defense. The Quakers said no more about non-resistance. Barricades were thrown up in the streets, cannon were mounted, patrol guards posted, and a citizen soldiery hastily organized.

At two o'clock one morning the wild clangor of the alarm bells sent a shudder to every heart. By previous arrangement, every window was filled with candles. A vast multitude of armed citizens surged up and down the streets of the city. The alarm proved groundless. The rioters, learning the reception prepared for them, advanced no nearer than Germantown. Here they were visited in camp by many citizens.

A compromise treaty was drawn up. The Paxton men contented themselves with presenting elaborate memorials to the assembly, which were never acted on. They withdrew to their homes without having accomplished any thing further than to demonstrate the weakness of the provincial government, and the folly of all doctrines of non-resistance. As for the city, as soon as the external danger was removed, the rival factions engaged in a war of pamphlets and newspapers, which at the time was one of the most serious, but now appears as one of the most laughable, disputes in American history.

With this outline of the border wars of the time we must be content. The year 1764 witnessed serious military efforts commensurate with the undertaking to crush the Indian power. Bradstreet in August of this year effected the relief of Detroit. The weary garrison, after a siege of fifteen months, during which they had been cut off from communication with the rest of their race, had been pent up in rigorous and wearisome confinement, had contended with a sleepless and powerful foe, had subsisted on scanty and wretched food, and had worn their clothes threadbare, were at last relieved, and permitted to step outside the worn and hard beaten inclosure of the palisade, and return to a world from which they had been so long banished.

In the south, Bouquet, at the head of a strong army, pushed westward from Fort Pitt, compelled the Indian tribes everywhere to submit, make treaties of peace and surrender their captives.

On a certain day the Indians from far and near brought their captives, taken during many years of warfare, to an appointed rendezvous for their surrender. Thither also repaired anxious throngs of settlers, whose relatives and friends had long been missing. The scene was tragical. The long lost were restored. Friend recognized friend; mothers clasped their children to their eager breasts. There was great joy. There was also great grief. Many persons failed to find the faces of the loved ones sought. Some of the captives had their hopes crushed, their hearts broken by failing to meet a single familiar face.

As his gigantic conspiracy crumbled into ruins, Pontiac, furious as a lion at bay, unconquered, because in spirit unconquerable, placed himself in person among the Indians of what are now the States of Indiana and Illinois, rousing them by his individual influence into a state of frenzy and warlike wrath. To defend this region, over which still waved the flag of France, into which no English foot had dared to penetrate, he resolved to devote all of his great and desperate energies. French traders, hostile to the advance of the English which would destroy their occupation, practiced on his ignorance and favorite belief. By means of forged letters, purporting to be written by the king of France, they again inspired in him that belief which was the corner-stone of his conspiracy, namely, that France would lend him her powerful aid and re-enforcement.

Bent on this idea, Pontiac presented himself to the French commander at St. Louis. and demanded arms and ammunition.

The Frenchman tried to soften his refusal by presents of a less warlike character. But Pontiac had one absorbing, overmastering ambition. Whatever ministered to that ambition he desired and demanded. Whatever did not minister to it he flung aside as unworthy his attention. So he refused the presents with angry scorn and bitter words.

Still the resources of this Napoleon of the forest were not exhausted. He dispatched an embassy all the way to New Orleans to demand help from the French Government. These ambassadors also carried war-belts to the distant warriors of Louisiana, to whom the name and fame of the mighty Pontiac were as the sun at noon. These tribes were urged at every cost to prevent the English from ascending the Mississippi, which Pontiac's military genius foresaw they would attempt. In this he was right, and their attempts to ascend the river were completely foiled.

The principal mission of the ambassadors was, however, a complete failure. The French rule was just about to give way to that of Spain, to whom France had by the treaty of Paris resigned Louisiana. The governor interviewed them and explained the true situation. From France no help was to be expected.

To this announcement the Indian orator made a reply full of the most cutting sarcasm. " Since we last sat on these seats, our ears have heard strange words. When the English told us they had conquered you, we always thought they lied ; but now we have learned that they spoke the truth. We have learned that you, whom we have loved and served so well, have given the lands that we dwell upon to your enemies and ours. We have learned that the English have forbidden you to send traders to our villages to supply our wants, and that you, whom we thought so great and brave, have obeyed their commands like women, leaving us to starve and die in misery. We now tell you once for all that our lands are our own ; and we tell you, moreover, that we can live without your aid, and hunt, and fish, and fight as our fathers did before us. All that we ask of you, is this, that you give us back the guns, the powder, the hatchets, and the knives which we have worn out in fighting your battles. As for you," hissed the orator, shaking his long forefinger at some English officers who were present,—"as for you, our hearts burn with rage, when we think of the ruin you have brought on us."

When the report of this embassy reached Pontiac, he saw that all was lost. The foundation of all his ambitious schemes was French interference. He had rested on a delusion. He had believed in a lie. His solitary will, which had controlled and combined into co-operation a thousand restless tribes, had breathed life into a conspiracy continental in its proportions, and had exploded a mine ramifying to forts, isolated by hundreds of miles of unbroken wilderness, could no longer uphold the crumbling fabric. His stormy spirit had warred with destiny, and had been conquered.

For the proud Pontiac there remained but two alternatives, destruction or submission. With a hell of hate in his heart, he chose the latter. Near the site of Lafayette, Indiana, he met an English officer and formally tendered the traditional calumet of peace. He proceeded to Detroit with his diminished retinue, and, in the old council-hall, where he and his blanketed chiefs had attempted to destroy the garrison, the terms of the peace were arranged. The following spring he visited Sir William Johnson, at his castle in the Mohawk valley, and finally concluded the peace, renouncing forever the bold ambition by which he expected to avert or retard the ruin of his race.

From this time he disappears from the historic page, only to reappear in the last scene in the eventful drama of his life. Of his movements during the intervening years no record exists. He is known to have planted his lodge, and to have hunted and fished like a common warrior, through the region which now forms the great States of Indiana and Illinois.

In April, 1769, he appeared at St. Louis, and made a two

days' visit on his old friend, St. Ange, who was still commandant, though by that time his command was in the interest of
Spain.   On the second day, word came that the Indians of an
Illinois town, across the river, were having a dance and carousal,
and Pontiac announced his intention of going over.   He drank
deeply, and, marching down the street into the forest, sang the
medicine song.

An English trader named Williamson, apprehensive of the
proximity of such a mighty chieftain and conspirator as Pontiac,
and especially suspicious on account of his visit to the French
at St. Louis, resolved to dispatch him while he was in his power.
A drunken Illinois Indian was bribed with liquor to watch Pontiac as he left the place, and stealing after him through the
forest, to kill him.   The assassin carried out the plan, and buried
a tomahawk in the mighty brain in which all ambitions were
dead forever.

Parkman, the great chieftain's biographer, thus closes his
work : " The dead body was soon discovered, and startled cries
and wild howlings announced the event.   The word was caught
up from mouth to mouth, and the place resounded with infernal
yells.   The warriors snatched their weapons.   The Illinois took
part with their guilty countryman, and the few followers of
Pontiac, driven from the village, fled to spread the tidings and
call the nations to revenge.   Meanwhile, the murdered chief lay
in the spot where he had fallen, until St. Ange, mindful of
former friendship, sent to claim the body, and buried it with
warlike honors near his fort of St. Louis.

" Thus basely perished this champion of a ruined race.   But
could his shade have revisited the scene of murder, his savage
spirit would have exulted in the vengeance which overwhelmed
the abettors of the crime.   Whole tribes were rooted out to ex-
piate it.   Chiefs and sachems whose veins had thrilled with his
eloquence, young warriors whose aspiring hearts had caught the
inspiration of his greatness, mustered to revenge his fate; and,
from the north and east, their united bands descended on the

villages of the Illinois. Tradition has but faintly preserved the memory of the event; and its only annalists, men who held the intestine feuds of the savage tribes in no more account than the quarrels of panthers or wildcats, have left but a meagre record. Yet enough remains to tell us that over the grave of Pontiac more blood was poured out in atonement than flowed from the hecatombs of slaughtered heroes on the corpse of Patroclus; and the remnant of the Illinois who survived the carnage remained forever after sunk into utter insignificance.

"Neither mound nor tablet marked the burial-place of Pontiac. For a mausoleum, a city has risen above the forest hero; and the race whom he hated with such burning rancor trample with unceasing footsteps over his forgotten grave."

CHAPTER V.

JOSEPH BRANT AND THE MOHAWKS.

HE traveler along the New York Central railroad may have pointed out to him, near the town of Amsterdam, a heavy stone mansion, half hidden from view by a grove of locust trees. The building is "Johnson Castle," a name which its owner gave it one hundred and forty years ago. Its walls are thick and massive, its windows small and deep-set. Though extremely odd in its architecture, its size and durability still give it just rank as a fine residence. A century and a half sit lightly on its shoulders, and, barring accidents, it will survive two or three times that period. A few miles away, in the edge of Johnstown, the curious visitor will find "Johnson Hall." It is twenty years younger than the castle.

A visitor describes the place as follows: "Although both house and grounds have been greatly altered and modernized, we can even now judge well what they must have been originally. The hall is a two-storied double mansion, built of wood, in the most substantial, conscientious manner, with raised panels on the outside in imitation of stone. It was, without doubt, in its day the most spacious and elegant edifice in the colony outside of New York City. The hall is fully fifteen feet wide, and the ceilings over twelve feet high, surrounded with massive wooden cornices of carved work. The sides of the rooms are elegantly wainscoted with pine panels and heavy carved work. A broad staircase, of easy ascent, leads from the lower to the upper hall, ornamented with massive mahogany balustrades, which still, at every foot, bear the marks of the tomahawk's hacking, said by tradition to have been notched there by Chief Brant himself, when he fled the valley with Sir John Johnson, in 1776, "to protect the house from the torch of Indians, who would understand and respect these signs."

"Of the garden and nursery, situated to the south of the hall, and which in the olden times were the delight of their owner, and the pride of the surrounding country, no vestige remains. Some of the poplars, however, which he planted, still stand, green and vigorous. The hall was formerly flanked by two stone block-houses, with sundry loop-holes for musketry cut directly under the eaves. But one of these—now converted into a servants' dwelling—yet stands, the other having been burned down many years ago. Of the stone wall which surrounded the whole place as a protection against attack, but little now remains.

"A subterranean passage formerly led from the main building to the block-house on the left, and thence another communicated with the block-house on the right flank. These passages, however, as well as the port-holes in the remaining block-house, have been filled up. Although the building never experienced a siege, yet it was twice fortified; once, as stated, by a strong stone rampart in 1763, and again in 1776."

The builder and original proprietor of these singular and romantic looking mansions was Sir William Johnson, Baronet. He came to this country when a young man, without title or fortune. Engaging in traffic with the Indians, Johnson, by dint of great natural abilities, which were assisted rather than retarded by a coarse nature, made money in large quantities. In 1742 he bought from the Mohawk Indians a large tract of the richest land in the world, lying in the very heart of the far-famed Mohawk valley. To this he added by yearly purchases, until he became the wealthiest man, and, next to the Penns, the largest landed proprietor in America. The "castle" was his residence throughout the year, until he built the "hall,"

in 1763, which he occupied as a summer residence, using the
older mansion only in winter.

Four or five years after he built the castle, the wife of Colonel
Johnson, as he was then called, a plain, fair-haired German girl, of
humble lineage, died, leaving her husband one boy, John, and two
baby daughters. One day the widower attended a muster of
the county militia. As an officer came riding by on a prancing
steed, a bright-eyed, red-cheeked Indian girl of sixteen, a real
beauty, with her white teeth, long, flowing, black hair, and a
form of rare symmetry and grace, laughingly bantered him for
a ride. The officer told her she might jump on if she could.
Quick as flash the agile girl leaped on the horse behind the
gallant rider, and clinging to him, her hair and ribbons blowing
wildly in the breeze, rode round and round on the flying steed
before the applauding crowd. One man took more than ordinary
interest in the incident. It was the susceptible and lonely widower. That night Mollie Brant, for such was the name of the
dusky beauty, went home with the baronet to Johnson Castle,
becoming thenceforth the mistress alike of it and its proprietor.

The two motherless daughters were assigned apartments
of their own, where they lived in complete seclusion under the
care of a devoted friend of their mother, an officer's widow.
Their time was occupied with needle-work or study. Their
library consisted of the Bible and prayer-book, a lot of the
ponderous romances, which mark the beginning of the English
novel, and Rollin's "Ancient History." A game of chess, a
walk in the park or a drive up the valley, constituted their only
amusements. At the age of sixteen they had never seen a lady
other than their governess. Occasionally some gentleman visitor found his way to Johnson Hall. This was a rare treat to
the lonely girls, to whom such a guest was always presented.
They married early, and their father built for them two elegant
stone residences a few miles from the castle.

Far different from this conventual life of the two sisters
was that led below stairs by the baronet. From the first, Sir

William, as we will call him, though the title was not conferred by the king until the French and Indian War, acquired great influence over the warriors of the far-famed Six Nations. He had located himself in the heart of the territory of the Mohawks, the most easterly of the Iroquois nations. Thoroughly understanding the Indian character, he won their confidence and attained an ascendancy in their councils which no other white man ever approximated. The negotiations of the British Government with the Iroquois were all carried on through him. The castle was his store-house, where all the wonderful supplies of guns, ammunition, and trinkets were kept for trade. Around the castle were clusters of cabins for the accommodation of Indians who came to trade.

Sir William kept a bounteous table, open to every comer, and dispensed his hospitality in lord-like style. The Indians would visit him day and night, sleeping in the halls, on the steps, or in the cabins, as suited their fancy, and faring on their host's sumptuous provision for days at a time. The natural genius· of the man for controlling the restless red men, and bending their rigid natures to his will, was powerfully supplemented by his rather questionable alliance with Mollie Brant. She was immensely popular, possessed a shrewd intelligence, and herself acquired great influence over her people.

The baronet, moreover, by this connection, for it was not a marriage, won the hearts of the warriors. His castle, to which they were always delighted to come, was looked up to as the splendid establishment of one of their own people. As they exchanged their valuable furs for the wares of the baronet, the heavy profit which went into his pocket was, they felt, well earned by the free and easy manner with which he treated them. In winter, the baronet often humored them by arraying himself in Indian disguise—war-paint, feathers, and tomahawk, complete—and living with them for weeks at a time as one of their own braves. His word once given them, whether a threat or a promise, was kept inviolate.

His vast landed estate was parceled out among Dutch and Highland tenantry, who were as devoted to his interests as the Indians themselves. "Nature had well fitted him," says a writer, " for the position in which his propitious stars had cast his lot. His person was tall, erect, and strong; his features, grave and manly. His direct and upright dealings, his courage, eloquence, and address were sure passports to favor in Indian eyes.

"He had a singular facility of adaptation. In the camp or at the council-board, in spite of his defective education, he bore himself as became his station; but at home he was seen drinking flip and smoking tobacco with the Dutch boors, his neighbors, talking of improvements or the price of beaver-skins; and in the Indian villages he would feast on dog's flesh, dance with the warriors, and harangue his attentive auditors with all the dignity of an Iroquois sachem. His temper was genial, he encouraged rustic sports, and was respected and beloved alike by whites and Indians.

"His good qualities, however, were alloyed with defects. His mind was as coarse as it was vigorous; he was vain of his rank and influence, without any scruples of delicacy as to proclaiming them. Eager and ambitious in pushing his own resistless way, he trampled beneath his iron heel whomsoever might cross his pathway."

Before proceeding to the story which forms the more immediate subject of this chapter, it may be well to speak more at length than we have heretofore done of the far-famed Iroquois, among whom Sir William Johnson lived, and over whom he exerted such a commanding influence. Francis Parkman gives the following eloquent summary of their tragic history:

"Foremost in war, foremost in eloquence, foremost in their savage arts of policy, stood the fierce people called by themselves the Hodenosaunee, and by the French the Iroquois, a name which has since been applied to the entire family, of which they formed the dominant member. They extended their conquests and their depredations from Quebec to the Carolinas, and from the western prairies to the forests of Maine. On the south, they forced tribute from the subjugated Delawares, and pierced the mountain fastnesses of the Cherokees with incessant forays. On the north, they uprooted the ancient settlements of the Wyandots. On the west, they exterminated the Eries and the Andastes, and spread havoc and dismay among the tribes of the Illinois; and on the east, the Indians of New England fled at the first peal of the Mohawk war-cry.

"Nor was it the Indian race alone who quailed before their ferocious valor. All Canada shook with the desolating fury of their onset; the people fled to the forts for refuge; the blood-besmeared conquerors roamed like wolves among the burning settlements, and the youthful colony trembled on the brink of ruin.

"The Iroquois, in some measure, owed their triumphs to the position of their country; for they dwelt within the present limits of the State of New York, whence several great rivers and the inland oceans of the northern lakes opened ready thoroughfarès to their roving warriors through all the adjacent wilderness. But the true fountain of their success is to be sought in their own inherent energies, wrought to the most effective action under a political fabric well suited to the Indian life; in their mental and moral organization; in their insatiable ambition and restless ferocity.

"In their scheme of government, as in their social customs and religious observances, the Iroquois displayed, in full symmetry and matured strength, the same characteristics which in other tribes are found distorted, withered, decayed to the root, or, perhaps, faintly visible in an imperfect germ. They consisted of five tribes or nations, the Mohawks, the Oneidas, the Onondagas, the Cayugas, and the Senecas, to whom a sixth, the Tuscaroras, was afterwards added.

"To each of these tribes belonged an organization of its own. Each had several sachems, who, with the subordinate

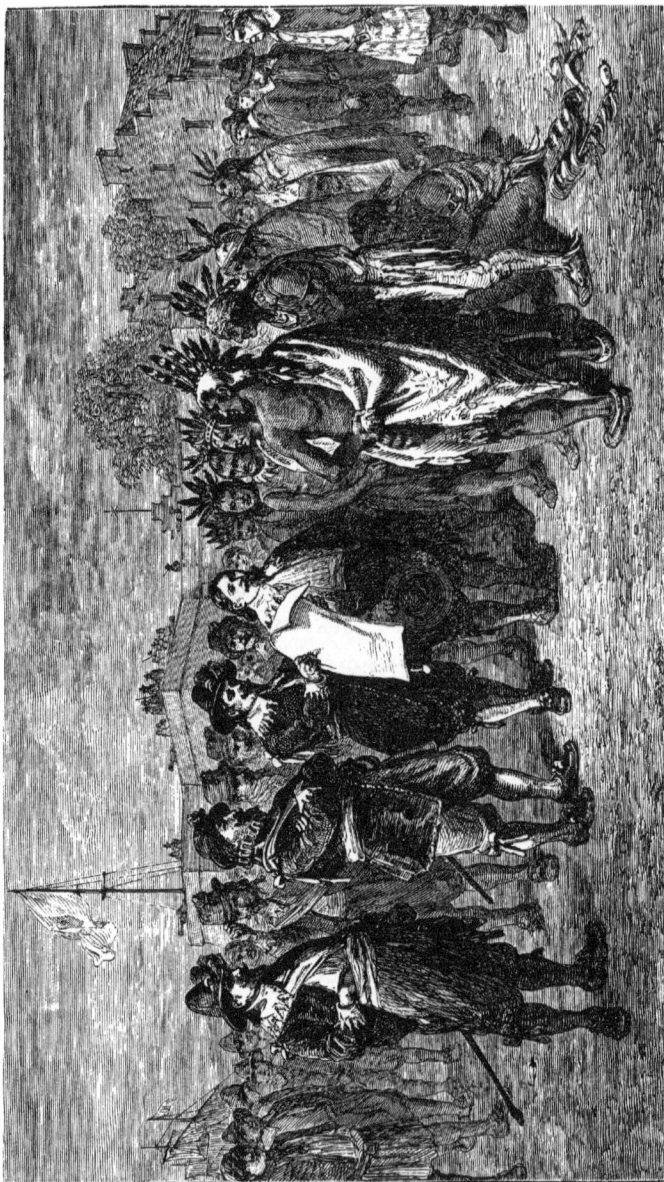

THE BARONET IN COUNCIL WITH THE MOHAWKS.

chiefs and principal men, regulated all its internal affairs; but when foreign powers were to be treated with, or matters involving the whole confederacy required deliberation, all the sachems of the several tribes convened in general assembly at the great council-house in the valley of Onondaga. Here ambassadors were received, alliances were adjusted, and all subjects of general interest discussed with exemplary harmony. The order of debate was prescribed by time-honored customs; and, in the fiercest heat of controversy, the assembly maintained its iron self-control.

"But the main stay of Iroquois polity was the system of totemship. It was this which gave the structure its elastic strength; and but for this, a mere confederacy of jealous and warlike tribes must soon have been rent asunder by shocks from without or discord from within. At some early period, the Iroquois must have formed an individual nation, for the whole people, irrespective of their separation into tribes, consisted of eight totemic clans; and the members of each clan, to what nation soever they belonged, were mutually bound to one another by those close ties of fraternity which mark this singular institution.

"Thus the five nations of the confederacy were laced together by an eight-fold band; and to this hour their slender remnants cling to one another with invincible tenacity. The Iroquois had no laws, but they had ancient customs, which took the place of laws. Each man, or rather each clan, was the avenger of its own wrongs; but the manner of the retaliation was fixed by established usage. The tribal sachems, and even the great council at Onondaga, had no power to compel the execution of their decrees; yet they were looked up to with a respect which the soldier's bayonet or the sheriff's staff would never have commanded; and it is highly to the honor of the Indian character that they could exact so great an authority where there was nothing to enforce it but the weight of moral power.

"The superiority of the intellect of the Iroquois was as

marked as that of their political organization. The energy of
their fancy displayed itself in that peculiar eloquence which
their wild democracy tended to call forth, and to which the
mountain and the forest, the torrent and the storm, lent their
stores of noble imagery. That to this imaginative vigor was
joined mental power of a different stamp, is witnessed by the
caustic irony of Garangula and Sagoyewatha, and no less by the
subtle policy, sagacious as it was treacherous, which marked the
dealings of the Iroquois with surrounding tribes.

"Their dwellings and works of defense were far from con-
temptible, either in their dimensions or in their structure; and
though by the several attacks of the French, and especially by
the invasion of De Nonville, in 1687, and of Frontenac, nine
years later, their fortified towns were leveled to the earth, never
again to reappear; yet in the works of Champlain and other
early writers, we find abundant evidence of their pristine condition. Along the banks of the Mohawk, among the hills and
hollows of Onondaga, in the forests of Oneida and Cayuga, on
the romantic shores of Seneca Lake, and the rich borders of
the Genesee, surrounded by waving maize fields, and encircled
from afar by the green margin of the forest, stood the ancient
strongholds of the confederacy. The clustering dwellings were
encompassed by palisades, in single, double, or triple rows,
pierced with loop-holes, furnished with platforms within, for the
convenience of the defenders, with magazines of stones, to hurl
upon the heads of the enemy, and with water conductors to
extinguish any fire which might be kindled from without.

"The area which these defenses inclosed was often several
acres in extent, and the dwellings, ranged in order within, were
sometimes more than a hundred feet in length. Posts, firmly
driven into the ground, with an intervening frame-work of poles,
formed the basis of the structure; and its sides and arched roof
were closely covered with layers of elm bark. Each of the
larger dwellings contained several distinct families, whose separate fires were built along the central space, while compart-

ments on each side, like the stalls of a stable, afforded some degree of privacy. Here rude couches were prepared, and bear and deer skins spread ; while above, the ripened ears of maize, suspended in rows, formed a golden tapestry.

"In the long evenings of midwinter, when in the wilderness without the trees cracked with biting cold, and the forest paths were clogged with snow, then, around the lodge-fires of the Iroquois, warriors, squaws, and restless, naked children were clustered in social groups, each dark face brightening in the fickle firelight, while, with jest and laugh, the pipe passed round from hand to hand. Perhaps some shriveled old warrior, the storyteller of the tribe, recounted to attentive ears the deeds of ancient heroism, legends of spirits and monsters, or tales of witches and vampires—superstitions not less rife among this all-believing race than among the nations of the transatlantic world.

"The life of the Iroquois, though void of those multiplying phases which vary the routine of civilized existence, was one of sharp excitement and sudden contrast. The chase, the war-path, the dance, the festival, the game of hazard, the race of political ambition, all had their votaries. When the assembled sachems had resolved on war against some foreign tribe, and when, from their great council-house of bark, in the Valley of Onondaga, their messengers had gone forth to invite the warriors to arms, then from east to west, through the farthest bounds of the confederacy, a thousand warlike hearts caught up the summons with glad alacrity. With fasting and praying, and consulting dreams and omens ; with invoking the war-god, and dancing the frantic war-dance, the warriors sought to insure the triumph of their arms; and, these strange rites concluded, they began their stealthy progress, full of confidence, through the devious pathways of the forest.

"For days and weeks, in anxious expectation, the villagers await the result. And now, as evening closes, a shrill, wild cry, pealing from afar, over the darkening forest, proclaims the return of the victorious warriors. The village is alive with sudden commotion; and snatching sticks and stones, knives and hatchets, men, women, and children, yelling like fiends let loose, swarm out of the narrow portal, to visit upon the miserable captives a foretaste of the deadlier torments in store for them. And now, the black arches of the forest glow with the fires of death; and with brandished torch and firebrand the frenzied multitude close around their victim. The pen shrinks to write, the heart sickens to conceive, the fierceness of his agony; yet still, amid the din of his tormentors, rises his clear voice of scorn and defiance. The work is done; the blackened trunk is flung to the dogs, and, with clamorous shouts and hootings, the murderers seek to drive away the spirit of their victim.

"The Iroquois reckoned these barbarities among their most exquisite enjoyments; and yet they had other sources of pleasure, which made up in frequency and in innocence all that they lacked in intensity. Each passing season had its feasts and dances, often mingling religion with social pastime. The young had their frolics and merry-makings; and the old had their no less frequent councils, where conversation and laughter alternated with grave deliberations for the public weal. There were also stated periods, marked by the recurrence of momentous ceremonies, in which the whole community took part—the mystic sacrifice of the dogs, the wild orgies of the dream-feast, and the loathsome festival of the exhumation of the dead. Yet, in the intervals of war and hunting, these multiform occupations would often fail; and, while the women were toiling in the cornfields, the lazy warriors vainly sought relief from the scanty resources of their own minds, and beguiled the hours with smoking or sleeping, with gambling or gallantry.

"If we seek for a single trait pre-eminently characteristic of the Iroquois, we shall find it in that boundless pride which impelled them to style themselves, not inaptly as regards their own race, 'the men surpassing all others.' 'Must I,' exclaimed one of their great warriors, as he fell wounded among a crowd

JOSEPH BRANT AND THE MOHAWKS.

of Algonquins,—'must I, who have made the whole earth trem-
ble, now die by the hands of children?' Their power kept pace
with their pride. Their war-parties roamed over half America,
and their name was a terror from the Atlantic to the Mississippi ; but, when we ask the numerical strength of the dreaded
confederacy, when we discover that, in the days of their greatest triumphs, their united cantons could not have mustered four
thousand warriors, we stand amazed at the folly and dissension
which left so vast a region the prey of a handful of bold
marauders. Of the cities and villages now so thickly scattered
over the lost domain of the Iroquois, a single one might boast
a more numerous population than all the five united tribes."

Before leaving the history of the Iroquois, it is possible to
give the account of their terrible destruction of the Eries, which
is said to have been handed down by their traditions. This
mighty tribe, which, prior to their subjugation, far exceeded in
strength any other single tribe of Indians, lived at the lower
end of the lake which bears their name. Their chief town,
Tushuway, occupied the site of the modern city of Buffalo.
Jealous of the great confederacy to the eastward of them, the
proud Eries sent a challenge to the Senecas, their nearest neighbors, for a game of ball between one hundred young men from
each tribe. The great council of the Five Nations deliberated
upon the challenge, and decided to decline it.

The next year the " Lords of the Lake " renewed the challenge. It was again declined. A repetition of it the third year
so inflamed the younger warriors of the Five Nations, that the
challenge was reluctantly accepted. One hundred braves, the
very flower of the confederacy, armed with nothing but the
small bat, used in ball-playing, and commanded by a chief of
approved experience, marched away through the forest to the
city of the Eries. A vast pile of furs, bracelets, beads, silver,
and copper was to be the stake.

The eventful day arrived. The great Eries far excelled the
more timid young men from the Five Nations in their self-con-

fidence. But the superiority went no farther. After a desperate contest the Iroquois bore off the prizes. The chief of the
chagrined Eries at once challenged the visitors to a foot-race,
with ten runners on a side. The Iroquois accommodated him,
and were again victorious. As a last trial of skill, the Erie
chieftain proposed to select ten wrestlers to be matched against
an equal number from the ranks of the visitors, the victorious
antagonist, in each case, to dispatch his adversary on the spot,
by braining him with a tomahawk and scalping him. This
bloody proposal was assented to by the Iroquois with altered
countenances.

The first pair of wrestlers struggled furiously. The Iroquois finally threw his opponent on the ground, but refused to
kill him. In a moment the angry chief of the Eries flung his
own tomahawk revolving through the air and with unerring aim
scattered the brains of his defeated kinsman on the soil of the
arena. Another pair of champions from the rival sides then
grappled for the conflict. Again victory was achieved by the
strangers. Again the victor refused to strike his fallen foe.
Again the Erie chieftain, black and choking with a tempest of
rage, killed the vanquished brave with his own hand. A third
time the singular scene took place. This was the last. At a
signal from their leader, the well-disciplined Iroquois suddenly
withdrew from the field, and, taking their canoes, returned
home to relate their victories and the strange customs of their
hosts.

The Eries at once resolved on war. The confederacy, on
the other hand, prepared for defense. Three thousand warriors and a thousand reserves rode with nodding plumes into
the forest to meet their foes. The two armies met half-way
between Canandaigua Lake and the Genesee River. The battle
raged with indescribable fury. The Eries saw too late that
their enemies, too weak to cope with them single-handed, had
combined against them, and that it was no longer a fight for
glory, but a struggle for existence. Hour after hour, far into

nightfall, the awful carnage proceeded. With unyielding courage and invincible obstinacy the doomed Eries, like the Spartans
of old, refused to fly, but fought to the bitter end, preferring
death on the battle-field to survival of defeat. The battle
was lost.

The victors, like avenging demons, pushed on to the Erie
strongholds. Using their canoes for scaling ladders, the maddened Iroquois, insane with the delirium of victory, leaped
down like tigers, and butchered the defenders without mercy.
For the Eries it was not merely defeat. It was destruction.
The proud people were literally destroyed from the face of the
earth. To-day nothing remains to tell us that they ever existed,
except the name of ERIE, which the generations of men still
give to the blue inland sea along whose shores they flourished
and then fell forever.

Such also was the fate of the noble Hurons, the Neutral
Nation, and the Wyandots.

Thus, within less than a quarter of a century, four nations,
the most brave and powerful of the North American savages,
sank before the arms of the confederates. Nor did their triumphs end here. Within the same short space they subdued
their southern neighbors, the Lenape or Delawares, the leading
members of the Algonquin family, and expelled the Ottawas, a
numerous people of the same lineage, from the borders of the
river which bears their name. In the north, the west, and the
south, their conquests embraced every adjacent tribe; and meanwhile, their war-parties were harassing the French of Canada
with reiterated inroads, and yelling the war-whoop under the
very walls of Quebec.

They were the worst of conquerors. Inordinate pride, the
lust of blood and dominion, were the mainsprings of their warfare, and their victories were stained with every excess of savage
passion. That their triumphs must have cost them dear; that,
in spite of their cautious tactics, these multiplied conflicts must
have greatly abridged their strength, would appear inevitable.

Their losses were, in fact, considerable; but every breach was repaired by means of a practice which they, in common with other tribes, constantly adhered to.

When their vengeance was glutted by the sacrifice of a sufficient number of captives, they spared the lives of the remainder and adopted them as members of their confederated tribes, separating wives from husbands and children from parents, and distributing them among different villages, in order that old ties and associations might be more completely broken up. This policy, as Schoolcraft informs us, was designated among them by a name which signifies "flesh cut into pieces and scattered among the tribes."

With two explanations, we resume the thread of the story, interrupted to relate the history and character of the Iroquois. A southern tribe, the Tuscaroras, having been expelled from their former home, came north, upon the invitation of their old allies, the Five Nations, and were received into the confederacy, which, from that time, became the "Six Nations." Although the Iroquois had been such as we have related, it is to be remembered that they had been greatly weakened by successive wars, and at the time of Sir William Johnson, though still powerful, the "Six Nations" were very far from being what they had once been.

From early times the Iroquois were allies of the English and Dutch colonists of the coast. Through them the confederacy procured fire-arms and ammunition far earlier than other nations, and by this means their power was infinitely increased. In return they constituted themselves a sort of police for the colonies against other tribes of Indians. They had early come in conflict with the French, as we have seen in the story of La Salle, and their prejudices were for the English. But the latter, by long years of neglect and aggression, lost their advantage.

When the French and Indian war broke out, the Six Nations were strongly disposed to join their red brethren in a war which was to drive the white man out of the country which he had wrongfully invaded. That they did not do so was solely owing to the ascendancy and influence, the earnest eloquence, the tireless efforts, the superb diplomacy of Sir William Johnson. For his sake they buried the hatchet. Such an important figure did the British Government find him, that he was appointed Indian commissioner for the North, a position which he held for twenty years, rendering heroic and invaluable service to England. He was further made baronet, and received vast grants of land, as a reward for his work during the war. When Pontiac, "the archangel fallen," planned his gigantic conspiracy, the baronet again needed all his influence and resources to hold the confederacy to its alliance with England. Indeed, the Senecas, farthest removed from his influence, did get away from him and join the conspiracy.

From 1763 Sir William lived in ease, his immense possessions multiplying year by year. But a struggle was coming, in which it would have been as difficult for him to choose his own side as for his Indian allies themselves. The volcanic fires of the AMERICAN REVOLUTION were, at the time of which we write, shooting their forks of flame upward through the fissures in the political and social crust. Which side should he take? Should he, on the one hand, turn traitor to the government which he had served so long, and from which he had received such abundant favors? Or should he, on the other hand, let loose the thunderbolts of savage warfare which he held within his grasp, upon the struggling colonists, his neighbors, friends, and countrymen, who were so clearly in the right? He never gave his final decision.

Deeply disturbed at the approaching crisis, and perhaps lacking the nerve which had belonged to the earlier years of his strange life, the great baronet gave way to his anxieties, and died suddenly in the summer of 1774. The belief was widespread at the time that his sudden death was the work of his own hand.

The zeal of Sir William Johnson for the improvement of his
15

Mohawk neighbors had planted churches and sent missionaries among them. More than this, he selected promising youths from the Mohawk nation, and sent them to be educated at a school in Lebanon, Connecticut.

Women are often designing, and use their influence over men for their own purposes. It is natural to find that Mistress Mollie Brant made use of her influence with the baronet to further the interests of her brother Joseph. He was born about 1742, and became a lad of unusual precocity. Of course he became the recipient of Sir William's bounty. He was sent to the school at Lebanon. He was employed by the baronet in the discharge of his multitudinous duties as Indian commissioner. He acted as interpreter, he labored to carry out his master's notions concerning his people, and he was often sent on long journeys to the wild Indians of the west. In this work he early exhibited rare diplomatic ability.

Nor was this all. His precociousness and talent were turned to the assistance of the missionaries. The smart heathen helped to prepare translations of portions of the Bible, and of the prayer book and ritual, into the Mohawk tongue. With a readiness which is suspicious, he joined the Episcopal Church. So zealous was Joseph in the observance of the forms of worship, and in partaking of the sacraments of the Church, that enthusiastic friends pointed him out as a model Christian.

As he took the rank which his lineage and his native abilities alike insured him, these good missionaries predicted that he would absolutely lift his people out of their savage state and transform them into solid citizens. No doubt they expected the wild Mohawk warriors to lay aside their filthy blankets, and don knee-breeches, silk stockings, knee-buckles, and powdered wigs, all on account of Joseph. He lived much of the time with Sir William, and was devotedly attached to him. His Indian name was Thayendanegea, of which "Brant" was a translation.

At the time of the baronet's death, Brant was a powerful Mohawk sachem. The title and much of the property of Sir

William went to Sir John Johnson, the only son of the dead baronet. Guy Johnson, the son-in-law, became Indian commissioner. To him Joseph Brant became private secretary. By means of their great wealth and family prestige, Sir John and Guy Johnson naturally inherited much of the influence of Sir William over the Six Nations. This influence was greatly strengthened by the attachment of Brant.

Meanwhile, the colonies were hurrying forward to a crisis. The spirit of patriotism entered into and possessed the people. Resistance to tyranny, free-trade, and self-government became the catch-words of the hour. The struggling colonies, hitherto a mere outlying and uninfluential province of a great empire, suddenly felt themselves assuming a vast and startling importance before the eyes of mankind.

Political discussion became loud and heated. The people found themselves ranged into two hostile parties. The great majority were patriots. They believed in the colonies having justice, though the heavens fell. These were the Whigs. There was also another party, a minority, who retained their old attachment to England. They justified the home government. They abused the Whigs. They were opposed to revolution and even to agitation. They were the Conservatives, or Tories. The lines between these two parties were very clearly marked out. The warfare was bitter. The same party lines exist in every epoch of progress. They are the Radicals and Conservatives. The one demands a change, a reform, a revolution. The latter cries out, " Let be ; let well enough alone ; peace ! peace !" when there is no peace.

These party dissensions extended to the Mohawk valley. As elsewhere, there were Whigs and Tories. The majority of the people were enthusiastic Whigs. They wished to better their condition. They were therefore Radicals.

The Johnsons, however, were Tories. Property and aristocracy are conservative. The wealthy few who are on top are comfortable. They are averse to change. They desire only that things remain as they are. If you touch them they scream. This is natural, but it is selfish. On the other hand, the many who are underneath, want to take the risk and make a change. They have nothing to lose and every thing to gain. This also is natural, but selfish.

Sir John Johnson held a title of nobility under the British crown. Guy Johnson held the lucrative office of Indian commissioner under the same government. They had vast possessions. They lived in baronial splendor in magnificent stone castles, from whose turrets the eye swept over an estate, stretching many miles along the lovely valley, and supporting a vast tenant population. These gentlemen, therefore, were strongly conservative. What cared they for a tax of a few cents on tea? Their dinner table would not be thereby deprived of the steaming tea-pot. What was it to them if troops were quartered in Boston? It cost them nothing. So they wanted things to continue as they were.

As the times became more violent and explosive, the colonists instinctively felt, rather than foresaw, that war was inevitable. In case this should come to pass, the leading men also rightly foresaw that the western tribes of Indians, always ready to strike a blow at the white invaders, would seize the opportunity to assail the colonies on the west, while England would levy war on the Canada frontier and along the coast. While the attitude of the western Indian was thus certainly hostile and dangerous, that of the Six Nations was more a matter of doubt. From the earliest times, the Iroquois, with the single exception of the Senecas, during the war of Pontiac, had been allies of the colonies and therefore of England. To which would the Indian allies incline if the colonies engaged in war with England?

Both parties to the contest saw that the alliance of the Six Nations was a strategic point. The powerful influence of the Johnsons and of Brant might be confidently counted on by England. The colonies relied mainly on the old friendship, and the influence of the patriotic missionaries. They hoped simply that the Iroquois would remain neutral. The Oneidas early took this position. In May, 1775, their chiefs wrote to the governor of New York, "You are two brothers of one blood. We are unwilling to join on either side in such a contest, for we bear an equal affection to both Old and New England. Should the great king of England apply to us for aid, we shall deny him; if the colonies apply we shall refuse. The present situation of you two brothers is new and strange to us. We Indians can not find, nor recollect, in the traditions of our ancestors, the like case or a similar instance."

Both British and Americans were busily engaged in feverish preparations for war. Sir John Johnson constructed heavy fortifications around his castle. Guy Johnson, alarmed at the popular threatenings, raised a band of several hundred Mohawk warriors, headed by Brant, and re-enforced by the leading chiefs of the Senecas, Cayugas, and Onondagas. With this force he fled to Oswego and then to Canada, leaving his splendid mansion desolate and unoccupied.

The colonies, on the other hand, issued a call for a grand council at Albany, in August. The meeting was attended very thinly, except by the Oneidas, and the Lower clan of the Mohawks. However, the representatives of the colonial congress made speeches, urging the Six Nations to remain neutral. A treaty to that affect was made, but it amounted to little.

On their return home, a plague broke out among the Mohawks. Like all ignorant people, they regarded it as a visitation from the Great Spirit. They believed that he was angry for their desertion of the cause of the king. Superstition is both blind and deaf. It has neither eyes to look at facts, nor ears to listen to argument. It transforms a man into a mummy. The Mohawks were superstitious. Many of them at once joined Brant's forces. A few, however, of the Lower clan still remained neutral. Probably they were not much troubled with the plague.

As a price of their neutrality they demanded one thing, that Sir John Johnson be left at his house in peace. This gentleman on his part bound himself by agreement to remain neutral. This promise was a sham. He remained in his fortified castle with a strong force of Indians and tenantry. He intrigued incessantly to excite the remaining Iroquois to a revolt. He carried on constant correspondence with leading Tories. In other words, he was a spy.

The colonies resolved to arrest him. Troops were dispatched up the Mohawk Valley for that purpose. A messenger was sent in advance to quiet the nerves of the excitable Iroquois. In this way Sir John heard of the plan for the seizure of his person. He hurriedly buried his treasure in the garden, and, regretfully leaving his splendid home, plunged into the wilderness with a band of retainers, to make his way to Canada. After nineteen days of hardship and suffering the proud baronet, ragged, footsore, and starved, with such remnant of his famished followers as had not fallen by the weary wayside, arrived at Montreal. Such are the vicissitudes of war!

Meanwhile, Joseph Brant had been advanced to the position of principal war-chief of the Six Nations. Around his standard rallied the dark warriors of the great confederacy, in whose veins ran the blood of the most terrible fighters among the American Indians. Thayendanegea was a fit leader for them. He was tall, erect, and majestic, with the manners and bearing of a king of men. He was distinguished alike for his courage and his intelligence, for his prowess as a warrior and his skill as a diplomate. His name was a tower of strength among the nations of the confederacy. While in native genius and originality of intellect he was inferior to Powhatan, Philip, and Pontiac, he knew more of the world than either of his great predecessors. If he was not inspired by the burning loyalty to his race, by the lofty ambitions and purposes of the two latter, he at least had a much wider education and range of ideas. If he was less of an Indian, he was more of a white man.

Although Thayendanegea had pledged himself to the cause of the king, he still hesitated to take up the hatchet. The Americans opened the campaign in Canada with a brilliant victory. Our Indian friend had an eye to the main chance. He sailed for England in the winter of 1775–6 to interview the king, and, no doubt, with a view to forming an estimate of the war strength of the English. The wily war-chief wanted to be on the winning side.

On his arrival in London he was conducted to a rather obscure inn, called " The Swan with the Two Necks." Statelier lodgings were soon provided for the great " Indian king," as the Englishmen called him. But Brant politely declined, declaring that the kind treatment of his host at " The Swan" had won his heart, so that he could not think of leaving him.

In this Joseph showed his innocence. He mistook the broad smile and hearty handshake, which forms such an important part of the landlord's stock in trade, for the genuine article. If he was taken in by the patronizing airs of the shrewd tavern-keeper, Brant showed no other sings of verdancy. He dressed in European clothing. His courtly manners and clear-cut English caused the throng of titled men and jeweled women who sought his company and pressed upon him the honors of the capital to lose sight of the fact that this lordly gentleman of foreign accent and distinguished air was, in fact, a red-fisted savage, accustomed to lead his yelling band of braves to midnight massacres, a man whose flashing tomahawk eagerly brained the fallen foe, and whose nervous fingers had often clutched the bloody scalps of his victims.

When he appeared at court on visits of business or ceremony, he laid aside his European habit, and wore a gorgeous costume of the fashion of his own people. Bands of silver encircled his sinewy arms. Tall plumes adorned his head-dress, and highly colored fabrics, hung with copper pendants, formed his clothing. A glittering tomahawk and a scalping-knife dangled carelessly from his belt. On such occasions he attracted the greatest attention.

Of course, the magnificent entertainments and presents which were pressed upon the war-chief of the Six Nations, together with the material splendor of England, the dazzling pageantry of the court, and the soldiery, with their equipment of cannon, small arms, ammunition, uniforms, and all the accoutrements of war, made a profound impression on his mind. When he sailed for America in April, he had pledged himself and his people to the cause of England in her conflict with the colonies.

He and his six hundred warriors in Canada at once joined the British army, and commenced vigorous hostilities. The great majority of the Iroquois still remained in their ancient seats in the Mohawk valley, and seemed peaceably inclined to the colonists. The people of the frontier built block-houses and organized parties of rangers for self-defense. They kept scouts constantly on the watch for an Indian outbreak. The isolated settlers moved into towns. At Cherry Valley, the most exposed point, the inhabitants, daily excited by the news of the battles of the Revolution, were deeply anxious about the Indians. But month after month rolled by, and the Iroquois still lingered idly in their wigwams.

In the spring of 1777 Brant reappeared in the Mohawk valley. The influence of the great war-chief at once made itself felt in the remotest wigwam. Carefully concealing his plans, he commenced collecting an enormous war-party at the Indian town of Oghkwaga. There were further indications, as the excited and patriotic Whig settlers thought, of a Tory uprising in connection with Brant's movement. On June 15th, General Herkimer reached Cherry Valley with a force of three hundred local militia. He was an old acquaintance of Brant, and determined to have an interview with him. The meeting was near Unadillo.

On the first day Brant threw off the mask, and declared himself as a soldier of the king. By agreement, the conference was to be resumed in the morning. That night Herkimer laid a dark plot to massacre the chief and his few attendants when they returned to his camp the following day. Brant, however, was up to such tricks. At the appointed hour he appeared in Herkimer's camp with five hundred picked warriors, plumed and painted for war. The raw recruits with Herkimer were completely in the power of the Indians. With a haughty gesture Brant said, "You may go." The colonists took the hint, and went—at the highest possible speed.

At Cherry Valley the people selected the strongest house for a fort, surrounding it with embankments. Near this place the road ran along the edge of a precipice. A hundred and fifty feet below lay a gloomy glen, filled with a dense growth of evergreens. In this lonely spot, Brant and a half-dozen braves hid in ambush. Late one afternoon, a gallant young colonial officer, "well-mounted, and clad in a suit of ash-colored velvet," spurred out of the settlement along the road by the glen on some errand of war. A few moments after the gentleman had left the village, the sharp crack of rifles was heard from the direction of the glen, and shortly the young officer's horse came galloping back, riderless, and the saddle crimsoned with blood.

A party of armed men at once started out to solve the mystery. Not till the following day, however, did they find the lifeless body of the gay lieutenant, gay no longer, but rather pale, mangled, and bloody. Brant, however, withdrew after this murder, without attacking Cherry Valley. He was deceived as to the strength of the place by some false dispatches found by him on the person of a captive whom he secured near the settlement. The man carried double dispatches, and, when captured, was smart enough to destroy the genuine and surrender the bogus documents.

While the settlers were being daily horrified by these and a hundred other isolated deeds of violence, information was brought them by friendly Indians and scouts of an impending danger of much greater magnitude. As Burgoyne descended from the north along Lakes Champlain and George, Colonel Barry St. Leger, with Thayendanegea's wild warriors was to rendezvous at Oswego, and then sweep down the Mohawk valley from the west, conquering and destroying, and form a junction with Burgoyne at Albany, whence the united armies would descend the Hudson. At the upper end of the valley, on a strategic spot on the carrying path which led from the Mohawk River to Wood Creek, stood Fort Schuyler. Wood Creek flowed into Oneida Lake, from which the Oswego River led into Lake Ontario. The carrying path between the Mohawk and Wood Creek was thus the only interruption which the war canoes of the Iroquois would meet in their voyage from Oswego to Albany. The carrying path was the door to the Mohawk valley. Fort Schuyler was the lock on the door. To unlock that door was the first task of Colonel Barry St. Leger and Thayendanegea.

Fort Schuyler was an old fortification, originally built by the British during the French and Indian War, at an enormous expense. It was not a mere block-house, nor a stockade, but, as originally laid out, was a regular fort, costing over a quarter of a million of dollars. It was square, with a bastion at each corner. It had had the traditional moat or ditch, the glacis or earth embankment, and the draw-bridge. A covered way led to a spring. In the center of the ditch had been planted rows of pickets. In the interior was constructed what was supposed to be a bomb-proof citadel. On one side, the fortification was further protected by a swamp. But at the outbreak of the Revolution the old fort was a miserable ruin. The ditch was filled up. The draw-bridge had fallen to pieces. The rows of pickets consisted of nothing but rotten stumps, projecting a foot or so from the ground. The ground about the fort, which had been cleared with infinite trouble of every obstruction which might afford a cover to the enemy, was once more overgrown with a dense forest, which flung its shadows over the decaying fortification.

In the spring of 1777, Colonel Gansevoort took command of the feeble and sickly garrison. Such men as were able to work were employed in placing the fort in a defensible state. But their feeble labors made slight impression on the old ruin. The commandant ceased not to write for re-enforcements and supplies. On the 4th of July, when St. Leger's plan was already made known, the place was still in a deplorable condition. Cannon there were, but not a ball in the magazine. The rifle balls on hand were too large for the fire-locks, and there were no moulds to make others. The supply of powder was dangerously small. As for provision, a quantity of spoiled beef, sufficient, perhaps, for six weeks, formed the larger part of the supplies.

From time to time, small re-enforcements had reached the fort, until the garrison was something over five hundred men. Of these, a hundred and fifty were employed in cutting and hauling timber to repair the fort and to build an obstruction in the channel of Wood Creek. As many more were required to keep guard over the workmen, for the woods were infested by hostile Indians. Others still were out on scouting and foraging parties, so that the fort proper was left with scarcely a man behind the ramparts.

One morning two officers went gunning, to secure, if possible, some untainted meat. A mile and a half from the fort they were fired upon. Madison was killed outright, but Gregg was only wounded. The Indians sprang forward to secure the scalp. Gregg, with incomparable grit, feigned death, and endured the horrible pain of being scalped, without the quiver of a muscle, or the utterance of a groan.

Some fishermen, a quarter of a mile distant, were that afternoon disturbed by a dog, who bounded toward them, and by lamentable howls, and every sign of distress, attracted their attention. The poor animal would run a short distance into the forest, and seeing they did not follow, would return and pull at their clothing, as if asking them to come with him. The men's suspicions were aroused, and they started to follow the dog,

18

who at once gave a yelp of joy.   Every time the men stopped he would resume his supplications.

At last the men reached the spot where lay the dog's fallen master, Captain Gregg, still breathing, but stupefied from pain and loss of blood.   They bore him to the fort, with the corpse of his companion, followed by the faithful dog, who had seen his master's need.   Gregg afterwards recovered.

On another day sixteen of the garrison were out cutting turf, about three-quarters of a mile away.   All at once they discovered a party of thirty or forty Indians coming toward them at a rapid run.   The men turned to fly.   Only nine men reached the fort.   Of these, two were badly wounded; a third was dying in the arms of his companions.

This was not all.   On the 3d of July, a little girl ran screaming toward the fort, with a basket in her hand, and her calico frock stained with blood.   She and two others of her age had been picking berries in the neighborhood.   The other children had been killed, while she herself was wounded, though slightly.

While the garrison of Fort Schuyler were thus preparing, as well as they could, for the coming storm, of which the indications were so clear, the friendly Oneidas looked on the approach of Brant with as much uneasiness as the whites themselves.   Their neutrality had incurred the wrath of the other tribes, and they feared, not without reason, that the indiscriminate fury of the invaders might involve them in destruction. They ceased not to urge the colonies to send prompt and powerful succor to Fort Schuyler.   Ticonderoga had fallen before Burgoyne without the firing of a shot.   "The chiefs" wrote the Oneidas, with cutting directness, "desire the commanding officers of Fort Schuyler not to make a Ticonderoga of it."

On the 2d of August, a re-enforcement of two hundred men, with two bateaux of provision, reached Fort Schuyler. The supplies were hurried into the fort as fast as possible, for the enemy was expected at any moment.   All scouting and repairing parties had been called into the fort. The time for further strengthening their defenses was gone. The siege was about to begin. As the boats were just emptied of their cargoes, and the last armfuls were being hurried into the fort, the savages burst from the forest with loud yells. The captain of the expedition, with drawn sword, hurried his men forward. Too brave to enter the fort before his men, he remained to the last, and was unfortunately made prisoner.

The siege was begun. Inside the fort were seven hundred and fifty men, with supplies and ammunition for six weeks, and no longer. But the garrison was without a flag! In this emergency stripes of white from officer's shirts, of blue from a cloak captured from the enemy, and of red from some ragged sashes, were sewed together, and the patchwork run up on the flag-staff. The besieging army numbered some seventeen hundred, composed of one thousand warriors under Thayendanegea, together with some Hessian and Canadian troops. They at once threw up redoubts for their batteries and commenced active hostilities.

Meanwhile, General Herkimer was marching to the relief of the defenders of Fort Schuyler, at the head of eight hundred militia-men, from the anxious settlements farther down the valley. Thayendanegea was kept constantly informed of Herkimer's movements. He repeated the stratagem which had resulted in the destruction of Braddock's army and brought Bouquet's entire command so near to death.

A few miles below the fort, the Albany road, along which Herkimer was advancing, crossed a low marsh by means of a causeway. Just at this point the road was intersected by an immense lateral ravine, or depression. Here, with devilish sagacity, Thayendanegea ambushed his dark followers. They were arranged in a circle, in which a narrow segment was left open at the bridge, for the militia-men to enter the trap. As soon as the main body had crossed the bridge, a band of warriors rushed in to close the gap of the circle, completely inclosing the colonists, with the exception of the rear guard, consisting of about sixty men, and the supply train, which had not entered the causeway.

A frightful struggle ensued. Herkimer was wounded at the first fire. Propped against the foot of a tree, with a pipe in his mouth, the brave old man continued to command his men. From

THE BATTLE NEAR FORT SCHUYLER.

every side the savages poured in the most galling fire. Everywhere that the men attempted, like wild beasts at bay, to break through the fatal lines which encircled them, they were beaten back with fearful slaughter. The men got stuck in the mire, and the vast boa-constrictor, which had wound its fearful coils about them, began to tighten. Yet many of the men fought bravely.

Observing that a savage, waiting till a colonist had discharged his gun from behind some tree, would rush forward and tomahawk him before he could reload, they placed two men behind each tree, one reserving his fire. Finding themselves pressed on all sides, the militia-men disposed themselves in a circle. It was a small wheel within a larger one.

Just as the Indians charged on their foes with desperate valor, to conquer them at the point of the murderous bayonet, a fearful thunder-storm broke over the dark field of battle. The trees of the forest writhed in the fury of the tempest. Unearthly bolts of lightning, followed by peal after peal of sky-splitting thunder, lent horror to the scene. In a moment a mighty flood of waters burst forth from the surcharged clouds. The conflict of men became puny in comparison with the conflict of the elements. The noise of battle was but a stillness contrasted with the awful roar of the storm. The awed combatants desisted. The dark clans of Thayendanegea withdrew in sullen rage to the sheltering distance.

The tempest, however, gradually subsided. Not so the fierce passions of the men. The Indians renewed the onset, re-enforced by a detachment of Johnson's "Greens." These were American Tories. Many of them were friends, or even relatives of the members of the colonial militia. In the close hand to hand fighting these foes recognized each other. With the fiercest rage these enemies flew at each others' throats like tigers.

War is horrible. Civil war is awful. These neighbors and acquaintances grappled each other, kicking, biting, stabbing, each refusing to let go of his antagonist until, at last, some fatal thrust opened the ruddy door through which the spirit took its flight. As a *ruse de guerre*, another detachment of Greens hurried forward to the front with hats disguised as Americans. The men were about to receive them as friends from the fort, when the counterfeit was at the last moment discovered.

A militia-man ran forward to give his eager hand to an acquaintance. The hand was grasped, but not in friendship. The Tory sought to make his verdant friend a prisoner. In the struggle, Captain Gardenier, of the colonial forces, sprang forward and felled the would-be captor to the ground. Several Greens set on him, the first falling dead, the second severely wounded. His spur catching in the clothes of one, threw Gardenier to the ground. A bayonet was just entering his breast, when the brave man seized it, and, with a terrific effort, dragged his opponent down, and used him as a shield from the blows of two other assailants. One of the militia-men now ran to his relief. As his foes turned on the new enemy, Gardenier sprang to his feet, and buried his sword in the body of the man whom he had dragged down. This was but one of a thousand individual combats.

The militia-men fought hand to hand with the Indians and Greens. "Let me recall, gentlemen, to your recollection," said the eloquent Gouverneur Morris at a later time, "that bloody field in which Herkimer fell. There was found the Indian and the white man, born on the banks of the Mohawk, their left hand clenched in each other's hair, the right grasping in a gripe of death the knife plunged in each other's heart. Thus they lay frowning."

At last Thayendanegea reluctantly called off his braves, of whom so many were falling. The colonists could not be driven from the field. They had determined to die in their tracks rather than yield. Two hundred of the Americans had been killed, and twice as many more wounded or taken prisoner. Hardly a cabin in the valley was there from which some father or son had not gone forth to return no more. Many of the unfortunate captives were tortured and put to death by the Indians. The direct reason for the withdrawal of the enemy was a spirited sally by the garrison of Fort Schuyler. So well conducted was the sortie that nearly the entire camp equipage of St. Leger fell into their hands.

Thus ended one of the bloodiest battles of the Revolution. Thayendanegea had commanded the enemy in person. Heavy as was the loss of the Americans, that of the enemy was still heavier. Two or three days afterward a solitary scout chanced to come upon the field of battle. "There I beheld the most shocking sight I had ever witnessed. The Indians and white men were mingled with one another just as they had been left when death had first completed his work. Many bodies had also been torn to pieces by wild beasts."

General Herkimer did not long survive the battle. His wounded limb was unskillfully amputated. The flow of blood was not properly staunched. As the hemorrhage renewed again and again, the hero calmly called his friends about him. With mind unclouded, and a body almost free from pain, he read the thirty-eighth Psalm aloud, while the red tide ebbed fast away. "Make haste to help me, O Lord, my salvation." As the closing words of the psalm died away on his pallid lips, the light of an unseen morning momentarily lit up his eye, and then it closed in eternal sleep.

Meanwhile the siege was resumed. One day an Indian entered St. Leger's camp. His clothes were riddled with shot. He was a half-crazy fellow, regarded by the Iroquois with considerable awe and superstition. With knowing looks and a few significant words, he led them to believe that a vast army of Americans was on the way to Fort Schuyler. He had, he said, been informed in a dream. A panic seized the Indian camp. Wigwams were hastily taken down and preparations made to decamp. St. Leger persuaded, threatened, and expostulated. In vain. The whole Indian army abandoned the siege, and fled in precipitation before nightfall. For St. Leger no alternative was left but retreat. As it turned out, the dreamer was a liar. Having been captured by the Americans and condemned to death, he was offered his liberty if he could frighten the Indians away from Fort Schuyler. His brother stood as hostage while the knave went on his errand, and, as we have seen, achieved success.

During the winter of 1777–78 Brant kept his head-quarters at Niagara, from which point he maintained constant communication with the western Indians, inciting them to co-operate with the Iroquois. As the spring advanced, he again returned suddenly to his old haunts at Unadillo on the Susquehanna.

16

This was sufficient to cause innumerable patriotic hearts to pop into their owners' mouths. Brant, with a large force of warriors, secure enough behind his fortifications, forthwith inspired and directed incessant raids up and down the defenseless valley.

Besides their Indian foes, the people were also torn by political animosities. In one locality the male settlers capable of bearing arms were summoned from far and wide to meet the king's commissioners at the house of Captain Mann, a wealthy loyalist. At the appointed day a large assemblage met. Numbers of Indians came, impressed by the warlike preparations. Each man was required to take the oath of allegiance to the king, and wear a scarlet badge on the hat. Earnest loyalists wore red caps. Less zealous ones pinned on a small piece of red cloth. Others, who were at heart Whigs, through fear of confiscation and arrest, contented themselves with a bit of red yarn. Two men refused absolutely to take the oath. Just as they were about to be arrested, a thick cloud of dust down the road betokened the approach of horsemen. In a moment a strong body of American cavalry, with drawn swords flashing in the sunlight, dashed up, and ordered the loyalist gathering to disperse.

Captain Mann made his escape. The orders were to take him alive, if possible, but dead, if not. Late at night, a young patriot, a neighbor lad, found him in a wheat-stack. He summoned Mann to surrender on pain of instant death. The latter answered with entreaties to be spared. The country boy hesitated to shoot down the richest man in the locality. He wavered. It was midnight. A heavy rain was falling. Perhaps, in the pitchy darkness, he did not see Mann edging away. Perhaps his heart softened, and at the crisis his nerve became weak. The loyalist got away.

The whole country turned out to hound him down. In the search a party ran across a stray Indian. He wore a bit of scarlet cloth in his hat. Unstrung by excitement, the whites

THE SUMMONS AT CAPTAIN MANN S.

absolutely butchered the poor fellow. The badge may have been that of a loyalist. More likely the bright color had caught the barbarian's eye, and he wore it as an ornament. After fifteen days' search, Mann was captured in the mountains. He was thrown into a prison at Albany, and detained until the war was over.

During the year 1778 the valley was filled with a thousand frightful rumors. Many of these were true. Innumerable lonely farm-houses were plundered and burned, and their occupants massacred. Rage is often near-sighted. In their indiscriminate fury the Indians massacred a woman and six children. She was the wife of a Tory.

But a greater enterprise was at hand. The valley of Wyoming, in North-eastern Pennsylvania, is one of the loveliest spots of earth. It is a second Eden. It has been the burden of the poet's song and of the historian's admiration. Yet from the earliest time this paradise had been the scene of the bloodiest contentions. Indian tribes had warred over it, until both of the contending parties were extinct. A civil war had broken out there between rival settlers from Connecticut and Pennsylvania, and again drenched its soil with blood. But in the year 1778, the sounds of violence had long since died away in this sequestered vale, and the crimson foot-prints of war had been effaced. From many a rude cabin chimney the blue smoke curled peacefully upward toward the sky. Around many a fireside sat happy families.

Towards this lovely spot the English commanders at Niagara turned their cruel eyes. A large force of whites and Indians pushed across the country on their mission of destruction. Two or three days before the 1st of July wild reports of their approach were carried down the valley by galloping horsemen. These reports were followed by others even more dreadful. Nine men at work in a field had been murdered. Two forts near the upper end of the valley had been captured and burnt. Colonel Zebulon Butler at once toiled day and night to collect a force of settlers to resist the enemy. The country was already drained of its men to fill the ragged, but heroic, ranks of the American army. Still, from far and near, they came, with their fire-locks and ammunition, until about three hundred men assembled in Fort Forty.

The name of this fort is a history in itself. At one time, in the earlier border wars, it had been defended by forty men against fearful odds. Hence its name. The enemy took possession of Fort Wintermoot, farther up the valley. The impatient and undisciplined militia-men, roused by the unusual occasion to a fever of martial excitement, demanded that they advance to attack the foe. Of course, the attempt at a surprise failed. The whites, under Colonel John Butler, fought the settlers from the front. In this engagement the militia gained a slight advantage. They were pressing forward to pursue it.

Suddenly a terrific yell from hundreds of savage throats, just in their rear, thrilled every patriot with horror. The Indians, under their leader, for a long time supposed to have been Brant himself, had passed around to the rear of the Americans. The latter fought with boldness. But it was useless. They were being crushed between the two forces. Besides this, some one blundered. The drummer beat a retreat when the order was an advance. They broke and ran—ran for life. The Indians leaped after them, flinging down their rifles, and using only the tomahawk. They pursued every straggling runner. Only sixty out of the noble three hundred escaped unhurt. Some of these did so by swimming the river, others by fleeing to the mountains.

This was not a battle. History calls it a MASSACRE. An eye-witness, an Englishman, slightly changes these figures. He says there were three hundred and forty Americans, and that *forty only escaped.* The other statement was frightful enough. But for this latter unquestionable testimony, the former report would have been regarded as an exaggeration.

As the news of the defeat was carried down the valley by

the hunted fugitives, the women and children fled panic-stricken into the wilderness. Colonel Zebulon Butler managed to make a stand in Fort Wyoming, where large numbers of settlers were huddled together. Concerning what followed, there is a bitter historical dispute. The earliest writers relate the following: On the morning of July 4th, the invaders demanded surrender of the fort. A parley was proposed. A large body of Americans marched to the appointed place. Instead of the truce being respected, the Indians suddenly sprang, howling, upon them from the shadowy recesses in the forest, and commenced a second and more horrible massacre, slaughtering nearly all in cold blood. "A remnant only regained the fort. A demand was sent in for surrender, accompanied by one hundred and ninety-six bloody scalps, taken from those who had just been slain. When the best terms were asked, the infamous Butler replied, *the hatchet.*" It will be observed that the hostile commanders bore the same name. They were cousins and old friends.

Some of the occupants of the fort, including Colonel Zebulon Butler, managed to escape to the wilderness. The rest, with those who were found in the settlement—men, women, and children—were locked up in the houses, which were set on fire, and "the whole consumed together." This was not all. Another fort was near by with seventy soldiers. They surrendered, under solemn promises that their lives would be spared. They were butchered to a man. Some details have been handed down to us. "One of the prisoners, a Captain Badlock, was committed to torture, by having his body stuck full of splinters of pine knots, and a fire of dry wood made around him, when his two companions, Captains Rauson and Durkee were thrown into the same fire and held down with pitchforks until consumed. One Partial Terry, the son of a man of respectable character, having joined the Indian cause, with his own hands, murdered his father, mother, brothers, and sisters, stripped off their scalps, and cut off his father's head!"

These were the earliest reports of the Wyoming tragedy. Later and more critical authorities deny them. It is creditable to human nature to disbelieve them. Whether the particular incidents recorded took place or not is of no importance. All agree that a Reign of Terror was inaugurated in the peaceful valley. At the best, history is only approximately true. Froude, Gibbon, Macaulay, Bancroft, have alike drawn on their imagination for details. The outline of history only is correct. The "historical imagination" is what makes history readable. It furnishes one a picture of the past.

Whether the particular details are true is immaterial. The scene, as a whole, may be true, nevertheless. Who doubts that one of Dickens's novels presents us with a better view of English life and manners than any history can do? Yet the whole book is a tissue of fiction. The truth or falsity of history is not to be determined merely by the pictorial and graphic details, which give life and animation to the scene. The real test is, whether the general outline, the perspective, the tone, proportion, and coloring is true to the original. Any thing else is impossible. No two witnesses will ever agree as to the exact details of a street brawl. Yet a hundred will substantiate each other as to the general and obvious facts.

One of the disputes over the Wyoming tragedy was, the leadership of the Indians. Early reports charged it to Brant. The poet Campbell, acting on this authority, gave him an immortality of shame in his "Gertrude of Wyoming." In his later years, however, Brant's son went to England and charged the poet with traducing his father. Indeed, the proofs strongly indicate that Brant was not present at the invasion of Wyoming.

If Brant was not at Wyoming, there were enough raids, burnings, ambushes, fights, and massacres which did take place during this summer under his leadership. One incident must suffice. German Flatts was the very flower of the Mohawk valley. A settlement of some sixty-five houses, was distributed equally on either side of the river. On one side stood the massive stone residence of the Herkimer family, used as a fort. One evening, half an hour before sunset, a scout brought word that Brant and several hundred warriors was on his way to this settlement. There had been four in the scout's party. The other three were killed. As the great and solemn sunset flung its dying splendors across the evening sky, there was alarm and terror in every household, for ten miles along the valley. The poor people piled their most valuable furniture into canoes, and hurriedly made their way to Fort Herkimer, and Fort Dayton, on the opposite side of the river. All night the fugitives continued to arrive. Their houses and flocks had been abandoned. A heavy rainstorm occurred after midnight, adding to the misery of the unhappy people, who were dragging their things up the river bank to the forts.

Brant arrived, and halted in a neighboring ravine, little suspecting that his approach was known. Anxious eyes kept watch from the fort. At the first flush of dawn, the Indians could be seen swarming through the settlement. The black smoke and flames from the incendiary torch rolled up at nearly the same moment from every house in the place. The Indians waited, in the morning air, with drawn tomahawks, impatient for the roasting inmates to rush forth. But they were disappointed. Not a scalp graced their victory. The unhappy settlers were forced to see every house and barn, one hundred and twenty in number, with the contents, and five mills burnt, and nearly a thousand head of live stock driven away.

Linked by a common fate with the melancholy Wyoming, is Cherry Valley. On the 10th of November, 1778, Brant and Walter N. Butler appeared suddenly before the place. No alarm had reached the settlement. For this there was a reason. All the scouts had been taken prisoners. The settlers were sleeping quietly in their houses. Even the officers of the fort were staying at the houses of the neighbors.

Just before daybreak the savages, a name which belongs equally to the Tory rangers and to Brant's Indians, dashed into the settlement. The house of Mr. Wells was first surrounded. The family was awakened by the bursting in of the door. Mr. Wells, his mother, his wife, three sons, and a daughter, were butchered in their beds. His sister Jane, a lovely girl, managed to get out of the house. She sought refuge in a woodpile, but was killed in the act of reaching it. The guards in the house were either killed or taken. Here too, was Captain Alden, commandant of the fort. He fled down the hill, pursued by an Indian. Refusing to stop, the savage hurled his tomahawk, with fatal accuracy. This was but a specimen of the horrid scenes.

Every house in the settlement was burnt. Thirty-two inhabitants, largely women and children, were slain, besides sixteen soldiers. In addition to this, some forty persons were taken prisoners. Most of the women and children were set free, but the rest were taken to Niagara.

For the atrocities at Cherry Valley, Brant's biographer claims, with much plausibility, that he was not responsible, that Walter N. Butler had entire command of the expedition. Indeed, there are many authentic instances where Brant interposed to save women and children from outrage. In this regard he differed from nearly all of the great Indian chiefs. He was always sensitive to any charge of cruelty.

There were other raids by Brant during this season. But they hardly deserve mention. Not more than twelve or fifteen firesides were desolated by each attack. What place can such small massacres find in history? One with fifty victims will do, but five hundred is better.

The whites managed to extract some sport out of affairs themselves. About this time the Onondagas were suspected by the Americans of infidelity. An expedition, under Colonel Van Schaick, fell upon their principal village, the capital of the confederacy, destroying it and numbers of the inhabitants. The immemorial council-fire was extinguished. The faithful Oneidas trembled in their moccasins at the fearful vengeance wreaked upon their neighbors. They at once sent an embassy to ask what it meant. " Was it done by mistake or design," they asked. " If our brethren, the Americans, mean to destroy us also, we will not fly—we will wait here and receive our death." " They were cut off by design. I was ordered to do it—it is done," was the reply. For the injury the Onondagas took ample revenge. Three hundred of their warriors fell upon the settlement of Schoharie, and destroyed it.

Another of Brant's exploits was the destruction of Minisink. In the massacre large numbers of whites suffered death. One man, Major Wood, was about to be killed when, either by accident or design, he made a Masonic signal, though he did not belong to the order. Brant was an enthusiastic Freemason, and at once rescued him. When the Indian leader found out the deception, he boiled over with rage, cursing the man terribly, but yet sparing his life.

In the summer of 1779, the colonies resolved on a united effort to crush the power of the Six Nations by an invasion of their country. The army for that purpose was strong and well equipped. Brant, on the other hand, rallied all his forces for the defense of his country. The battle took place on the site of the present city of Elmira, New York. It raged all day. The Americans gradually forced the enemy back. So many Indians were killed, that " the sides of the rocks next the river appeared as though blood had been poured on them by pailfuls."

All was lost. The Indian warriors fled, taking women and children with them, and leaving their smiling country, with its populous and regularly laid out villages, its vast acreage of waving grain, its numerous orchards, in which the ruddy fruit was already peeping from among the clustering leaves, open to the destroyers' advance. Town after town was laid in ashes. Of Kanadaseagea, the capital of the Senecas, not one wigwam was left standing. Genesee, the principal western town, containing all the winter stores of the confederacy, was completely obliterated. The fields of grain were burnt. The very gardens were uprooted, and the harmless apple trees hewn down.

Yet the wrath of the invaders wreaked itself alone upon these inanimate objects. The Indians fled at their approach, leaving their villages silent and deserted. Fires were still burning in the wigwams. Iron pots, with their noonday meal, were still simmering away over the coals. The rude cradle was still warm from the babe which had lain there. But no human being could be found. The hand which built the fire was invisible. The cook who had prepared the pot of broth was nowhere to be seen. The mother of the babe was out of sight. All were gone. The women and children were sent to Niagara. The warriors remained lurking in the forest, insane with wrath at the destruction of their lovely country, sometimes venting their rage in nameless tortures upon unfortunate stragglers whom they captured, but otherwise offering no resistance to the invaders.

The flight of the Iroquois on this occasion reminds one of the flight of the Russians on Napoleon's march to Moscow. But in one regard it is different. Napoleon found himself in a frozen wilderness. These invaders found themselves in a blooming garden. A soldier took the trouble to measure an ear of corn which he plucked from the rustling stalk. He found it to be twenty-two inches long. Another soldier made a rough count of the number of apple trees in a single orchard which was on the point of destruction. He estimated that there were fifteen hundred bearing trees. This was not unusually large. Of the number of orchards, the men said they were " innumerable." This, probably, included those of peach and pear trees. They were the product of the toil and care of countless generations of Iroquois. " A wigwam can be rebuilt in two or three days,"the Indians sadly said; " but a tree takes many years to grow again."

Their sorrows became the source of dissension. There arose a peace party. Among the Senecas was a young orator named Red Jacket. He had the gift of eloquence. He became the leader of the peace party. He spoke with thrilling earnestness of the folly of a war which was driving them forever from the lovely valley which they had inherited from their fathers; a war, too, in which they fought, not for themselves, but for the English. "What have the English done for us," he exclaimed, drawing his proud form to its fullest height, and pointing with the zeal of despair toward the winding Mohawk, "that we should become homeless and helpless wanderers for their sakes?" His burning words sank deep into the hearts of his passionate hearers. It was secretly resolved by his party to send a runner to the American army, and ask them to offer peace on any terms.

Brant was the leader of the war party. All his tremendous prejudices and masterful abilities were enlisted in behalf of England. He hated the young and eloquent Red Jacket. Moreover, Brant was no orator. He could not contend with his gifted rival in mere words. He was rather a man of action, a Cromwell of great executive ability and possessing a will of iron. He heard of the plot to make peace. He kept his own council. The runner left the camp. Two confidential warriors were summoned by Brant. In a few stern words he explained to them that the American flag of truce must never reach the Indian camp. Its bearers must be murdered on the way, yet with such secrecy that their fate should not be known. The expectant peace party, waiting for the message in vain, were to believe that the Americans had scornfully refused to hear their prayer for peace. The plot was carried out. The man of words was vanquished. The man of deeds triumphed. The flag of truce never arrived.

General Sullivan had now destroyed the home of the proud Iroquois, and driven their families abroad to strange and inhospitable regions. More than forty populous towns had been literally blotted out from the map of the country. The landscape was no longer variegated with fields of golden grain, with burdened orchards, staggering beneath their tinted fruitage, with verdant pastures, dotted over with sleek and peaceful herds, nor with waving forests of ancient trees, whose emerald foliage formed such a rich contrast with the sunny sky and the winding river. As far as the eye could stretch, the prospect presented a single ominous color. That color was black. It was a landscape of charcoal! The American general was happy.

Instead of pressing on to Niagara, and destroying the military head-quarters of the north-west, he turned about. Only one ambition remained unfulfilled. He had no captives. Casting about in his mind, he remembered a few families of the Lower clan of the Mohawks, who, as will be recollected, had refused to follow Brant. They had remained peacefully at home in their wigwams and fields. They were neutral. They expected no danger. As General Sullivan thought of them his eye brightened. He would add the missing plume to his hat. He would take these Mohawks prisoners. Happy thought! Brilliant idea! It was carried into execution. The peaceful tillers of the soil were rudely torn from their homes. It is hardly necessary to add that they were soon released, by order of Sullivan's superiors. The general himself soon found it convenient to resign on account of ill-health.

The winter of 1779–80, was one of unprecedented rigor. The shivering Iroquois, at Niagara, suffered severely. But the fire of hate burnt in the heart of Brant as hot as ever. Long had he been meditating a terrible revenge upon the Oneidas, who had refused to follow his leadership, but had persisted in neutrality. Upon them he laid the blame of all his disasters. That winter he led his warriors across frozen rivers, and through snowy forests, to the home of the unsuspecting Oneidas. Of what followed we have no detailed history. The Oneidas had no historian. Their sufferings have passed, like the sufferers themselves, into the unremembered past. It is only known that Brant fell upon them without mercy, that their villages and wigwams, their storehouses, and castles, were suddenly destroyed, that vast numbers of them were slain, and that the survivors fled to the white men for protection.

STRUGGLE OF A FRONTIER MILITIAMAN WITH A MOHAWK BRAVE.

The poor refugees, stricken for a fault which was not their own, were allotted rude and comfortless quarters near Schenectady, where they were supported by the government till the close of the war. Their misfortunes did not end with their dispersion. Driven from their homes, reduced to want, dependence, and abject poverty, they lapsed from their regular and industrious habits. They became intemperate and idle. Of the proud and loyal Oneidas, a few lazy drunkards came in time to be the only representatives.

In pursuing Brant's larger enterprises we omit wild fields of incident and individual adventure. One brave man, Solomon Woodworth, lived all alone, in a block-house, eight miles from Johnstown. He was repeatedly attacked in his lonely stronghold, and managed not only to repulse such small bands as came that way, but on one occasion, at least, pursued the Indians, and killed several. Another dramatic incident was the burning of Ellis's mills. They were located at the wild waterfall, where the foaming Mohawk plunges through a rocky gorge into the lower valley. Since the burning of the mills at Fort Herkimer, these were resorted to by the settlers from miles around, with their bags of grain carried on horseback. The mill was garrisoned by twelve men. The Indians attacked it at dead of night. The building was in flames before its defenders knew their danger. A brief and hopeless resistance was made, and then every man sought safety by flight. Six or seven were quickly captured.

Two of the men plunged into the race above the mill, leaving only their faces above water, and hoping to escape discovery in the darkness. Before long, however, the red tongues of flame were thrust out through the windows. The glare became brighter and brighter. Glowing seams appeared between the logs, through which shone the fierce fires within the doomed building. The roar grew louder and louder. The yells of the shrieking savages mingled with the crackling of the flames. Snatching brands in their hands, they ran up and down the shore, eagerly watching for lurking whites. At last, the roof tree fell in with an infernal crash. Millions of sparks flitted upward, followed by dense volumes of smoke. The surroundings grew darker for a moment. But suddenly the pall lifted. Mighty billows of seething fire burst upwards into the heavens, as if furious at their confinement. In a moment the race became as light as day. The poor fellows were discovered, and put to death.

Two others, Cox and Skinner, had sought a more dangerous and yet a safer hiding place. They were under the great water wheel, nearly choked with the dashing spray. The great embers from the conflagration above them dropped down, but were knocked off by the revolving water wheel. The savages sought for them in vain. When at last the mill was a smoking ruin, the Indians rode away with hideous yells. Then the poor fellows came out. They were severely burnt where coals had fallen on them. But they were safe.

From the beginning of 1780 the sufferings of the settlers of the lower Mohawk Valley steadily increased. It will be remembered that at the time of Sir John Johnson's hasty flight to Canada, he had secretly buried his papers and treasure. His estates were confiscated, and his splendid mansion passed into the possession of another. One morning, a year or so previous to the time of which we are writing, the owner was disturbed to find a hole dug in his garden walk, the marks of many footprints, and a number of papers scattered through the garden. A small band of Johnson's followers had recovered his chest of papers.

In the spring of '80, Sir John, incredible as it seems, made his way with five hundred men from Montreal to Johnstown, without his approach being discovered. His avowed object was the recovery of his treasure, which was still buried in the cellar. This expedition was one of the most impudent as well as brutal occurrences of the war. Entering Johnstown at dead of night, the ruffians proceeded to murder large numbers of the old acquaintances, neighbors, and friends of Sir John, and apply the torch to their homes. The treasure was recovered, the outrages consummated, and the strangers coolly made their retreat without a straw of opposition from the terrified people. On this occasion Jacob and Frederick Sammons were taken prisoners, of whose adventures more hereafter.

On the 2d of August harvesters in the fields around Johnstown noticed dark columns of smoke from the direction of Canajoharie. A company was at once collected to march to the relief of the settlers, who were undoubtedly attacked by Indians. The place had, for defense, a block-house, called Fort Plain, but on this occasion the fort was without a garrison.

For some time the valley had been filled with rumors to the effect that Brant intended to attack a convoy of boats, carrying supplies to Fort Schuyler. To prevent this the militia from the lower part of the valley were withdrawn and dispatched up the river. As soon as this was done, the wily Brant led his warriors by swift marches to Canajoharie, which, in common with the rest, had let her garrison go up the river. The scenes of slaughter and destruction which took place on this raid of Brant's were almost a duplicate, though, perhaps, covering a smaller territory, of those which had marked General Sullivan's great invasion of the Indian country during the previous year. In one regard it was much worse. The settlers were taken by surprise and had no time for flight. Great numbers of them were killed, and immensely more taken prisoner.

But still Brant's appetite for vengeance was unabated. Again he raised a force for a third invasion of the Mohawk Valley within a year. It was not enough to have equaled the work of Sullivan. It must be surpassed. To this end he and Sir John Johnson united their savages. To be sure, Johnson's men were white. History's verdict is that they were more savage and brutal and cruel in their warfare than the wild children of the forest by whose side they fought. The summer had brought a rich harvest to the glad settlers. When the

season of the sere and yellow leaf approached it found granaries almost bursting with their golden treasures, and barns
stuffed to the rafters with the sweetest hay and oats.

On the morning of October 16, 1780, the occupants of the
little mud fort at Middleburg, far down the Mohawk Valley,
and the settlers of the lovely region looked out at sunrise on a
startling sight. In every direction barns, hay-stacks, granaries,
and many houses were on fire. The product of the summer's
toil was mounting to the skies in chariots of flame. Everywhere
the people fled, abandoning all their effects, in the madness of
fear. Their alarm was justifiable. Brant's army of fifteen
hundred warriors and Tories was upon them without a single
note of warning. At first, the enemy mounted their little cannon, and prepared to besiege the fort. But the little mud
redoubt held plucky men.

Finding that the siege would delay them, Brant, a true master of guerrilla warfare, gave up the notion of taking the fort,
and swept on down the valley with his terrible band of destroyers. In their course the whole valley was laid in ruins. Houses
and barns were burned, the horses and cattle killed or taken,
and those of the inhabitants who were not safely within the
walls of their little fortifications were either killed or taken
captive. The very churches were fired.

But the torch of war was not applied to the property of
Tories. Wherever lived a loyalist to England, the horde of
destroyers stayed its ruthless hands. They passed by, leaving
the property untouched. Then one of the strange sides of human
nature displayed itself. The settlers, furious at their own wrongs,
and aflame with passion at the sight of their disloyal neighbors'
immunity from harm, issued from the forts, and, with their own
hands, completed the desolation of the valley, destroying every
bit of Tory property.

As the invading army hurried on, transforming, with its
greath of flame, the verdant valley into a mighty cinder, many
a cabin became the scene of a tragedy, more thrilling than those

performed behind the flashing footlights of any theater. The humble pioneers and their clinging families were enrolled in the terrible *dramatis personœ.*

John Vraoman was on a scout some miles from his home. An Indian jumped out of a bush. Vraoman killed him. A second Indian bounded forward, his long and sinewy fingers reaching to clutch the white man's throat, but a lightning blow with the clubbed musket stretched the savage senseless on the sod. At that moment a swarm of savages started up in the forest. Vraoman fled. By great skill and marvelous endurance he eluded his pursuers. After hours of strenuous exertion, he neared his cabin. His heart leaped for joy at the thought that his wife and children were saved from the lonely, unprotected, and poverty-stricken life of the widow and the fatherless. Nearing the spot, he caught a smell of burning. His tired steps were quickened with anxiety. Too late! The cabin was a heap of glowing coals, the wife and children captives. He suffered but a few days of anguish. Brant sent back the captives, with a note on birch bark, giving them sweet liberty.

A farmer was unloading a wagon of corn at his granary. Hearing a shriek from the house, he looked about to fin da swarm of Indians and Tories surrounding it on all sides. " The enemy, my boys!" shouted the father, but, as he leaped down from the wagon, a rifle ball pierced his patriotic breast. The shriek came from his wife, who was tomahawked. Her five-year old boy ran screaming to his fallen mother, his childish heart bursting with the frantic agony of sorrow. He knelt down in the crimson pool about the form he loved so well. In a moment a tomakawk ended his grief and life together.

An aged man in the fort at Middleburg owned a mill two miles away. His son had passed the night there alone. At the first discovery of the Indians, the white-haired father, knowing they would speedily attack the mill, started, regardless of earnest remonstrances on account of the danger of the attempt, to warn his son of his peril. He hoped to reach the mill before the savages, and succeeded. The father and son then hurried back to the fort, to find it already attacked. By a bold move they managed to get inside of the sheltering redoubt. Of the havoc wrought by Brant, one instance was the suffering of the large and prominent Vrooman family, three of whom were killed and nine carried captive to Canada.

These incidents are but a few drops from the bloody deluge. The invaders divided into two parties. One marched down one side of the Mohawk. The other division kept pace on the opposite side. In this way the country was laid waste in every direction. The goal of the expedition was Schenectady. It was never reached. Flying horsemen had long since carried the news of the invasion to Albany. Too much time had been taken up in the advance. General Van Rensselaer, with a strong army, was on the way to meet the enemy. Brant and Johnson began a retreat. It was too late. A heavy battle was fought. At sunset the advantage was with the Americans, but they failed to push it, and fell back to encamp. That night the enemy fled, without the rustle of a leaf or the rattle of a bayonet.

Some funny things occur in a forced retreat. Nine Tories were hurrying through the forest, each trying to outdo the other in the speed of retreat. Suddenly a stern voice cried out in the darkness, "Lay down your arms." They obeyed with precipitation, and were made prisoners. They could not see their hand before them. Of the number of their captors they had no idea. Every Tory was securely pinioned and led away. In the morning they found themselves in a little block-house. Their captors were seven militia-men. The nine had surrendered to the seven!

An incident of the invasion is worth relating. The Senecas were led by a half-Indian named Corn Planter. His father was a white trader, who had, many years before, on one of his trips, been enamored of a pretty Seneca maiden. Corn Planter became one of the living evidences of his affection.

The son was not ignorant of his father's name and whereabouts. With a dozen trusty followers, he sought the old man's cabin, where he lived in peace with his family, and took him prisoner. After proceeding a few miles the proud Seneca stepped up, and said : " I am your son. You are my father. I am a warrior. Many scalps have I taken. Many a captive have I tortured. Yet you have nothing to fear. If you will come with me to the distant lodges of my people, I will cherish you in your old age, and give you plenty of venison. If you scorn the simple life of the children of the forest, and prefer to return to the arms of your pale-face squaw and the caresses of your pale-face children, my brothers, it is well. You are free to choose."

It may be imagined that the old man, who was or wished to be ignorant of his near relationship to the stalwart savage, chose pretty quickly, and scampered off home as fast as he could. The young chief bowed to his wishes, and sorrowfully turned to hide himself in the forest.

The common name of John Shell, a Dutch settler who lived with his family in a lonely block-house four miles from Fort Herkimer, has been embalmed in an incident which comes down to us. A band of sixty or seventy Mohawks suddenly surrounded the little fortress one day, and laid siege. Mrs. Shell loaded the rifles, while her husband and sons fired them. The attack lasted from two o'clock until sunset. McDonald, the leader of the enemy, made repeated efforts to break in the door of the structure. He was in the act of using a heavy iron crowbar when he received a shot in his leg. He fell. None of his men were just at hand. The bold Dutchman, Shell, flung open the door and dragged him in—a prisoner. The cartridges found on him were greedily seized by the defenders, whose stock of ammunition was dangerously low.

Enraged at the capture of their leader, the enemy made a furious assault. Five guns were stuck through the port-holes. Quick as flash, Mrs. Shell seized an ax and ruined every gun by bending the barrels. As the Indians fell back, Shell ran up to the second story and calling out to his wife told her Captain Small was at hand from Fort Dayton with re-enforcements. Then, in a loud voice, he shouted to the imaginary Small to march his men around by the left side. It was a ruse, and it succeeded. The Indians fled, supposing that a heavy force was at hand. Shell hastily collected his family, and placing such food as they had, within reach of their wounded prisoner, set out for Fort Dayton, leaving McDonald in solitary possession of

JOSEPH BRANT.

the block-house. He was removed the following day, but died from an unskillful amputation.

The war of the American Revolution at last came to an end. For Brant's wonderful raids there was no longer opportunity. He received from the British government for his tribe a new home on the Grand River, Canada. Here he devoted himself to the work of civilizing and improving his people. He made another trip to England, being received with more splendor and ceremony than before. This was in consideration of his eminent services in the Mohawk valley.

During the Indian wars of the west, his prejudices were all against the United States, though he never actually took the field. He translated a number of devotional books into English, and sought to induce his people to give up the uncertainties and demoralizations of the chase and substitute agriculture. His own opinion, as expressed at a dinner party given him by the distinguished Aaron Burr, was that the civilization of the Indians must take place through their intermarriage and mingling of blood with the whites. His correspondence, of which much is yet extant, reveals a rugged and powerful intellect, on which his associations with white men had exerted a marked influence. He encouraged missionaries to come among his people, and renewed his Christian professions, which had, perhaps, been suspended or eclipsed while he was hurling his warriors like destroying lightnings upon the defenseless inhabitants of the Mohawk valley. His letters reveal a proud, sensitive spirit, jealous of its dignity, and which could not brook the slightest imputation of dishonor. Nothing escaped the attention of his eminently diplomatic mind, whether it transpired in the cabinets of ministers or around the council fires of the distant tribes of western Indians. He erected for himself a fine mansion on the western shore of Lake Ontario, where he lived in unprecedented splendor. Here he held his barbaric court, " with a retinue of thirty negro servants, and surrounded by gay soldiers, cavaliers in powdered wigs and scarlet coats, and all the motley assemblage of that picturesque era."

Two or three times Brant condescended to visit the eastern cities, receiving every attention from the great men of the day. That "uneasy lies the head which wears a crown" was freshly demonstrated by his career. On one of his trips east, he was followed by an assassin, a Dutchman, from the Mohawk valley, whose entire family had been murdered by Brant's warriors. The man shadowed him day and night, seeking a convenient opportunity to kill him. Brant knew his danger, and took unusual precautions. One day the assassin had well-nigh accomplished his purpose. Brant had taken a room in a New York hotel, which fronted on Broadway. Looking out of the window, he saw his enemy on the opposite side of the street, aiming a gun at him. The alarm was given, and the Dutchman taken care of.

On the way home, after this or a similar trip, Brant wanted to go by way of the Mohawk valley, a region so dear to him by reason of its associations, older than the dreadful scenes of the war. There as a boy he had been employed at the baronial hall of his friend and patron, Sir William Johnson. There, too, his people had from time immemorial lived, and loved, and died. But the people of the valley confronted this sentiment of Brant with a widely different one. If any man was ever hated with all the abhorrence of which human nature is capable, such was the feeling with which Brant was regarded throughout the length and breadth of the Mohawk valley. When word came that the monster was to pass through the country, the settlers prepared, with exultant curses, to kill him. A rumor of the danger reached Brant in time for him to change his route and escape secretly by another way.

Brant's ascendancy among the Iroquois was not maintained without some heart-burnings. His old enemy, Red Jacket, gathered a number of malcontents around his standard, and at a pretended meeting of the sachems of the confederacy, during Brant's absence, he was impeached and formally deposed from the head chieftancy of the Six Nations. When the old warrior returned he confronted his enemies in public council, boldly defied and denied their calumnies and charges, and demanded a fair hearing before his people. For reasons which Americans of the present generation will readily understand, the military fame and prestige of the great war chief overcame even the burning invectives of Red Jacket, and Brant triumphed over all opposition.

One unfortunate affair made a terrible impression on his mind, and he was never really himself again. One of his sons

was in the habit of getting drunk. While on one of his sprees
he entered his father's room and commenced a storm of cursing
and abuse. The exact circumstances are unknown, but Brant,
in a sudden heat, stabbed his son, from the effects of which he
died. The old man never ceased to lament the deed, and it is
said would lie awake at night and cry by the hour.

On November 24, 1807, as the shrill winds of winter
began to whistle through the forest, and the first light snow
spread a delicate mantle over the earth, the old chief looked out
upon the whitened landscape for the last time. He had been in
ill-health for quite awhile. That day a sudden change for the
worse took place. After several hours of suffering, Thayendanegea, Joseph Brant, turned his face to the wall, and died.
Among his latest words were those to his adopted nephew, in
which he uttered the burden of his heart. "Have pity on the
poor Indian; if you can get any influence with the great,
endeavor to do them all the good you can."

In 1876, William Cullen Bryant, the poet, whose lyre is
now attuned to celestial harmonies, visited the old house of
Brant. His description will form a pleasant conclusion to our
story.

"To visit this quaint old mansion and find it untenanted for
the moment, as chanced to the writer one sunny day last June,
is like stepping backward from the nineteenth century into the
last quarter of the eighteenth. You enter a spacious hall, and
turning to the right, find yourself in a large old-fashioned draw-
ing-room, whose front windows look out upon the blue expanse
of Burlington Bay.

"On the opposite side of the room is a grate, surmounted by
an absurdly tall mantel, and flanked on each side by a curious,
arched recess. Life-size oil portraits of Brant, in his paint and
war-dress; of John Brant, the ideal of an Indian hero; of Sir
William Johnson and members of his family, in stiff wigs and
scarlet coats, richly laced, stare down upon you from the walls.

"Upon the mantel lies Brant's dagger, which drank the blood

of his ruffianly son Isaac; carelessly disposed upon a table are
a pair of richly ornamented dueling pistols, the gift of the Duke
of Northumberland; there lies his tomahawk, yonder hangs the
queer conch-shell medal, which he wore, and in the corner is
flung his small sword, its ivory handle studded with gems, a tes-
timonial from his sacred majesty, George the Third, to his gallant and faithful ally.   So carelessly are these and other relics
strewn about the room as to lend encouragement to the fancy
that the old chief had hurriedly thrown them down, expecting
momentarily to return and claim them.   A dreamy atmosphere
pervades the apartment, disposing the mind to reverie and rendering it hospitable to visions of the past.

"The writer, on the occasion mentioned, instinctively cast a
look toward the door, expecting to hear the tread of moccasined
feet, to catch a glimpse of those swarthy features, and be trans-
fixed by a glance of the basilisk eyes which are reproduced in
the portrait over the mantel.   But the spell was broken by the
hum of approaching voices, and a peal of childish laughter, proceeding from three bright little elves, descendants in the fourth
generation from Joseph Brant.

"I can readily credit the rumor reported to me in good faith
by a neighboring farmer, that Brant house is haunted."

CHAPTER VI.

THE CONFLICT IN THE OHIO VALLEY.

HAT changes have been mirrored in the blue Ohio during the last hundred years! The waters of the river itself have not been more changing than the landscape. This is the true age of magic. Who is there that does not see that the Lamp of Civilization far surpasses the dull luminary of one Aladdin? Not a single palace, but whole cities have sprung into existence, as it were, in a single night. Instead of transforming towns into lakes, and their inhabitants into blue, green, and yellow fish, by our magic, swamps and reedy lakes are transformed into cities, and in the place of innumerable suckers, cats, and minnows, behold thronging populations of men. Unnumbered generations of wide-eyed children have wondered at the enchanted horse, which, by the turning of a peg, in a single day transported the Prince of Persia and his lady love to his distant dominions. But we have enchanted horses which travel at the rate of a mile a minute, able to carry, not merely two persons, but whole populations. Yet we do not wonder. The author of the "Arabian Nights' Entertainments" thought his fancy had transcended the bounds of all that was possible. But the creations of his imagination are tame and dull beside the marvelous handiwork of the real Genie, the Spirit of Civilization.

It is still possible to imagine the past. We can conjure up faint visions of the majestic river rolling on in everlasting solitude. The winding shores lie wrapped in the mantle of perennial forests. Not a sound is heard above the muffled roar of the flood.

It is evening. At points where the shore slopes gradually to the water, stand shadowy herds of mild-eyed deer, now drinking from the cooling current, now lifting their graceful necks, and watching with timid anxiety some spot along the shore, from which had come the suspicious sound of rustling leaves. Lying hid in the thicket is a phantom canoe. A dusky form steals cautiously through the underbrush toward the gentle denizens of the forest. He obtains a view of the lovely sight. His eye flashes, his nostril quivers, but not with admiration of the beautiful.

There is a whirring sound, as a light shaft whistles through the air. The startled deer leap toward the shadow of the forest. Too late. The arrow-head is buried in the heart of a noble buck. His leap was unto death. The crimson tide spurts forth in hot jets upon the brown leaves of the wild wood. His large and intelligent eye is slowly covered with a film which shuts out forever the view of his forest home. His slender form stiffens. The head is partially lifted, as if to look with mild reproachfulness upon the enemy whom he had never harmed. Then it sinks back upon the spreading antlers. The agony is ended.

The dim picture quickly fades. Where stood the shadowy outlines of the forest, now stately buildings and the stony expanse of a great city's public landing, covered with vast piles of merchandise, force themselves upon the vision. Along the shore stretches a mile of stately steamers. From some just landed, streams of busy passengers pour forth over the wharf-boat. Others are about to depart. Dozens of drays thunder down the stony slope with freight for the out-going vessels. Gangs of deck-hands are hurriedly carrying aboard the last of the cargo. The voice of the master is heard above the din, incessantly urging the hands to greater exertions, now cursing them for clumsiness or abusing them for laziness, now threatening them with discharge and no pay, now promising various glittering rewards for more speed.

At last the cargo is loaded. The last barrel is rolled aboard. The last consignment of brooms and wooden buckets is stowed away. The smoke, which has been rising from the steamer's chimneys in thin, idle currents, now rushes upward in black volumes. The gangway is hauled aboard, the hawser cast off. There is a hasty jingling of various signal bells. A heavy puff from the engines, and the roaring swash of the paddle-wheels is heard as the steamer slowly draws off from the dock.

If we turn from the din and confusion of the landing, we hear above us the roar of the Queen City. Miles upon miles of bowldered streets stretch on between tall rows of gloomy buildings. The air is heavy with the smell of groceries, and tremulous with the clangor of metropolitan activity. The street lamps are being lighted, and as we look up the long avenue their yellow flames on either side extend in a narrowing vista, until, far up the hill, the walls of the street seem to come together.

How came the change? Whence is the marvelous transformation? Few of us think of it. The cities are here—it is enough. What care we for the struggles of our fathers? No doubt they were gentlemen, loving quiet, and, following their tastes, they left the settled towns and cities of the east to build rude homes in the peaceful valley of the Ohio. Unmolested by any disturber, we think they quietly plowed the glebe, harvested crops, reared their children, and were gathered to their graves.

What a mistake! The peace we now enjoy is the offspring of war. Our fathers were not peaceful, timid men. They were bold adventurers. They were scouts. They were Indian fighters. The Ohio valley was won from the savages only after the longest, the bloodiest struggle on record. It was a war which raged without perceptible intermission from the breaking out of Lord Dunmore's war, in 1774, to the battle of Fallen

Timbers, in 1794, a period of twenty years. During that time the pioneers of the magnificent valley knew no peace. The battles of the Revolution were fought and won, but in the struggle with the savages there was no victory for the brave colonists. The independence of the New Republic was achieved by force of arms in spite of the greatest military nation on earth, but against the redskins of the Ohio the arms of the colonies prevailed not.

Peace was made with England, but with her Indian allies no armistice took place. Treaties were concluded with every European government, but the outraged red man still shook aloft the gory tomahawk. Years rolled by. Expedition after expedition was sent against the Indians of the west, only to end in rout and massacre. Children grew to be men and women, middle-aged men and women grew gray in the ceaseless conflict, yet they fought with all the zeal of the bygone years.

The prize was worth the struggle, and the combatants knew it. The region of Ohio, Indiana, Illinois, Kentucky, and Tennessee is the finest part of the American continent. The Indians of the west for unnumbered generations knew it as the best hunting-ground between the oceans. The white settlers saw in it a seat of empire for their posterity, unequaled in Europe or America. Midway between the extremes of temperature, with mild winters and cool summers, with the richest soil, moderate rain-fall, a rolling surface, and abundant forests, it is evident at this day that the pioneers did not overestimate the prospect. There is hardly any limit to the population which the region is capable of sustaining. Delightful for residence, it is also the natural home of trade, agriculture, and manufacture.

As a nursery of great men, the Ohio valley has long since distanced any other portion of the country. Henry Clay, Abraham Lincoln, Ulysses S. Grant, Joseph E. McDonald, John Sherman, James A. Garfield, Rutherford B. Hayes, Hugh McCulloch, Robert G. Ingersoll, Oliver P. Morton, Stephen A. Douglas, Thomas A. Hendricks, Allen G. Thurman, Benjamin Harrison,

Matthew Simpson, E. S. Ames, Tom Corwin, Thomas Marshall, George D. Prentice, Robert Dale Owen, Henry Ward Beecher, William T. Sherman, Henry Bascom, A. E. Burnsides, Stonewall Jackson—these are the men whom the valley of the Ohio has already furnished to the Republic. Where can be found any other portion of the country, which, within less than a hundred years after the first settlers found it a silent wilderness, has given to the world such a constellation of statesmen, orators, military commanders, and writers?

The Ohio valley then was won by war, by twenty years of conflict. Reserving for separate chapters the stories of the different expeditions and the most famous Indian fighters, in this chapter we will collect the crumbs which fall from the table of the feast.

The greater part of the romantic stories of Indian adventures have been buried with the daring actors in oblivion. Besides, the few tales which happened to be preserved in manuscript or print, there yet linger in certain old families shadowy traditions of their ancestors' struggles and adventures. Gray-haired men are yet to be found in warm chimney corners, who can repeat many romantic stories told them by their mothers. But in another generation these dim traditions will be gone, as will be the men who tell them. Even with a recountal of the feats of which the stories have been preserved, many volumes could be filled. Here we can only outline some representative deeds and dangers.

THE ESCAPE OF McCONNEL.

People will eat. Alexander McConnel, of Lexington, Kentucky, though no philosopher, had observed this. So it came to pass that he went hunting one spring morning in 1780, and killed a fine deer. It was necessary to procure a horse to transport the game. Five Indians happened to find the fallen buck, understood the situation, and, from a neighboring thicket prepared a reception for the hunter. Presently McConnel, careless of danger and chuckling over his good luck, appeared on his horse.   The Indians fired, killed the horse, but not the rider, and took the latter captive.

His captors turned out to be jolly fellows, in spite of the deep melancholy which is supposed to haunt the heart of the savage. They let McConnel have his gun, and he chimed in with the fun by killing game for them with fancy shots.   About the fourth evening the travelers encamped on the shore of the Ohio. McConnel concluded the fun had gone far enough.   He resolved to escape before they crossed the river.   He complained that the cords with which they tied him at night were painful. Being polite gentlemen, they tied him loosely, passed the ends of the buffalo tug around their own bodies, and went to sleep. McConnel lay quiet till midnight.

Then he made his right hand as small as possible, and tried to draw it out of the loop.   Impossible!   He tried the left hand with the same result.   He attempted to reach the knot with his mouth.   It could not be done.   Heretofore he had borne his light captivity with considerable resignation.   Now he became frantic.   His veins grew swollen with rage.   He strained and pulled with the energy of despair.   Useless!   He thought of his home, of perpetual captivity, of a death by torture, of suicide.

As he lay almost bursting with fury, something on the ground, glittering in the firelight, caught his eye.   He studied it attentively.   At last he made it out.   It was a knife.   How could he reach it?   He could not move his hands two inches without waking his sleeping guards.   It lay nearly two yards from his feet.   He commenced to slowly move his body toward the foot of his rude pallet, under the cover of buffalo skin.   As this singular movement continued, he gradually drew his hands upward, leaving them in the same relative position.   Now they were over his face, now above his head; now stretched at full length toward the head of the bed.   His head was covered with the buffalo robe.   It could no longer be lifted.   Unable to see the knife he sought it with his foot.   He felt everywhere for it. He could not find it. With his great toe he made a mark in the ground. Then he drew himself up. He raised his head. The knife was there. The mark made by his toe was eleven inches this side of it. Eleven inches between liberty and a death by torture!

McConnel thought. In a little while he commenced moving his head from side to side. At each movement he seized the edge of the buffalo skin in his teeth and dragged it a little. Presently the skin was partially pulled off the savage on the right. He got cold. He turned over in his sleep to warm his cold side. This threw him much nearer McConnel. But it also gave considerable play to the prisoner's hands. Again the latter cautiously wriggled toward the foot. Again he extended his hands above his head. Again the foot sought for the precious knife.

It was reached, grasped firmly between the toes, and drawn upward. In a moment McConnel had it in his hand and severed his bonds. He rose. Instead of fleeing, he deliberately sat down by the fire. Strange conduct for a fugitive! Too well he knew that to fly without killing his captors meant certain pursuit and recapture. The trail he would leave would be as plain to their eyes as a plow furrow. He might succeed in cutting the throats of one or two. But the death rattle must rouse the rest.

At last he took all but two of the guns of the savages and hid them in the forest. Of the two he carefully examined the loads. They appeared satisfactory, for he noiselessly laid the barrels across a log, and aimed each at a savage. The flickering light of the camp fire revealed his calm but determined face. Bang! Bang! The guns were fired almost simultaneously, killing two of the savages outright. At the report the other three sprang to their feet. McConnel rushed instantly to the spot where he had hid the guns. As his enemies bounded towards him, he fired again. The ball passed through the body of the foremost Indian and wounded the one behind him. The fifth
18

and last savage instantly fled. McConnel clubbed the wounded brave, shouldered his gun, and made his way home in safety.

The surviving Indian paused not till he reached his people. Among them was a white captive, Mrs. Dunlap. Afterward she escaped, and told McConnel of this Indian's account of the affair to his people. He related that he and his companions had captured a fine young hunter at Lexington, and had brought him as far as the Ohio; that, while there encamped, a large party of white men had fallen upon them in the night, and killed all his companions, together with the defenseless prisoner, who lay bound hand and foot, unable either to escape or resist.

A RACE FOR LIFE.

One July evening in 1781, as the tired harvesters of what is Hardin County, Kentucky, were trudging to their cabins, a war party of Indians burst into the settlement with wild yells, murdered no less than twelve persons, and withdrew as swiftly as they came. The stricken pioneers started in pursuit. In their party was Peter Kennedy, a young Indian fighter, known as the swiftest runner in Kentucky. This talent caused him to be looked on as a very brilliant fellow. In the fury of pursuit the settlers ran into an ambuscade. Better had it been for the anxious women and children, left behind in the cabins, if the brave ones had never gone from them. The savages fired from ambush, killing every white except Kennedy. He jumped behind a tree. As an Indian ran at him with uplifted tomahawk, the runner fired, killed the savage, and ran. Nine rifles were discharged. A ball in his leg disabled him. It also cost him two years' captivity in the wigwams along the Wabash River in Indiana.

The time came at last when his wound healed and his captors were off their guard. He made his way to the Ohio River, built a raft, and crossed it. He felt pretty safe. A fat deer was shot by him, and, building a fire, he proceeded to roast a delicious haunch of venison. The savory roast was just done, and the hungry man was putting the first rare morsel to his lips, when a rifle was fired from the thicket, and Kennedy felt a sharp sting on his leg. Hurt, but not disabled, he seized his gun and started at the top of his speed for the mountains. Thirty miles away was Gooden's Station. That point he must make.

The Indians started in hot pursuit. Now Kennedy summoned to his aid all the skill and endurance which had won his fame as a runner. Up-hill, down-hill, through underbrush, over fallen logs, across stony ground, and in the midst of quagmires, he sped like an arrow. He gained on his pursuers. At the end of five miles he was out of gun-shot. But still they followed. At the end of ten miles the perspiration streamed from his brow. His face and neck were swollen till the blood seemed ready to burst forth. Still he ran on without the least abatement of speed. Fifteen miles were accomplished. He found himself at the summit of a ridge of hills, near Rolling Fort. He paused for a moment. The pursuers were no longer in sight. He leaned against a tree for a whole minute. This seemed to refresh him immensely.

With redoubled speed he bounded down the rugged hillside, leaping from rock to rock, momentarily planting his flying feet on spots which seemed to furnish no foothold. A vast plain was before him. He was a mile from the ridge before he heard the yells of his pursuers. He looked over his shoulder. They had paused on the summit. At the moment Kennedy saw the Indians they caught sight of him. Far away on the hill-top he saw their gestures of rage outlined against the sky. Suddenly they leaped down the slope as he had done.

Kennedy redoubled his exertions. Mile after mile was accomplished. Hour after hour he maintained his terrific speed. At times he could see his pursuers crossing the open country two miles behind him. Once, losing sight of them, he thought the pursuit was abandoned. He threw himself on the ground. His limbs trembled violently. His chest heaved up and down in convulsive respiration. In a moment more stupor would have seized him. Just then the wind bore to his ears a faint yell. They were still after him, only much nearer. He had not been able for an hour to hear their voices.

Once more he started. The speed was no longer so great. His gate was stumbling and irregular. Twice he fell headlong over trifling obstacles. But he was nearing his goal. Twenty-five miles were completed. Kennedy again lost sight and sound of his pursuers. Twenty-six miles—they were hopelessly in the rear. Twenty-seven miles—the flaming disk of the afternoon sun sank behind the tree-tops. Twenty-eight miles—Kennedy felt he had won the race. Thirty miles—and he sank exhausted, but victorious, on the floor of the fort. He gasped out an explanation. A party was organized. Almost within gunshot of the fort lay the savages. When discovered, they tried to run. But their strength was exhausted. They had run their race only to meet death at the end.

It was several weeks before Kennedy recovered from the effects of his fearful exertions. His race is without parallel in frontier chronicles.

A FIGHT IN A FOG.

Bryant's Station was a fort. It was on the bank of the Elkhorn Creek, between Lexington and Maysville, Kentucky. Being exposed and liable to frequent attack, it was strongly built, containing forty cabins, in parallel rows, connected by heavy palisades. From this shelter no man dared to venture alone. The garrison of fifty men required food. But the hunting parties never went out with less than twenty men.

It was in May, 1781, that such a party sallied forth, under command of William Bryant. The men picked their way cautiously through the overhanging branches of the forest. No enemy was seen. A ravine, which had been the site of many a bloody ambuscade, was passed in peace. What reason was there for further caution? Why not divide the party, sweep a large tract of country, and gather a heavy supply of game while they had the opportunity? Ten men, under James Hogan, took the north bank of the creek and Bryant the south bank. They were to meet and join camps at night-fall. Hogan's men were proceeding on their way, when they were startled by a loud cry of " Stop !" in good English. In their rear a party of Indians was to be seen in rapid advance.

The whites at once turned loose a pack-horse, put spurs to their animals, and galloped into the forest at a break-neck speed. After a run of several miles they reined in, and held a hurried consultation. That their flight had been premature was evident. The strength of the attacking party was unknown. Bryant's men might be in great peril. To cross the creek, and lie in ambush till the Indians came along, learn their numbers, then either fight, join Bryant, or fly to the fort in case of overwhelming force, seemed the best way to remedy the mistake. It was three hours before the crunching of twigs across the creek announced the footsteps of the enemy.

It was already night. The starlight revealed an Indian starting to cross the stream. Hogan fired. There was a yell, and a mighty splash of waters. The bullet had made its home in his heart. At once all became still. After an hour's waiting, the hunters mounted and made their way to the fort. Bryant and his little company were still out. Long before daylight, Hogan and his men, ashamed at their flight and anxious about Bryant, started once more down the creek to join him. The morning was very foggy. Objects were invisible at a distance of ten feet.

While they were thus on their way, Bryant met with a sad disaster. He had gone into camp the night before at the appointed time, but Hogan came not. The men prepared and ate their supper. They sat around the camp fire, speculating anxiously on his absence. Usually, these hunting parties were jolly crowds. The evenings in camp were filled with rough fun and jokes. But on this evening the men were in no humor for levity. The horses were picketed more closely than usual.

The men grouped themselves in a narrower circle. They talked in anxious whispers. A dozen times Bryant left the circle and went out into the forest to listen for Hogan's approach. As many times he returned with his anxiety unallayed. It was far in the night before the men rolled themselves in their buffalo robes for sleep.

The night passed uneasily. In the morning the men rose, and were preparing breakfast. Just then the faint tinkle of a bell was heard through the fog. Every one listened. In a few moments it was heard again. This time Bryant recognized it. It was the bell of Hogan's pack-horse. Believing Hogan to have missed the camp and to be wandering in the fog, Bryant and Grant mounted their horses and rode to the spot where the bell was still giving irregular tinkles. Just as they had about reached it, a dozen Indians started up in the fog and fired. Both men were wounded, Bryant mortally. The bell was the bell from Hogan's pack-horse, which the Indians had captured. But instead of being on the horse's neck, the bell was held by a savage, and shaken slightly from time to time. Both men retained their seats and managed to make their way to the fort, where Bryant shortly expired.

The Indians at once charged on the camp, killed some, and dispersed the rest. They proceeded to occupy the camp, and lounged about the fire, smoking their tobacco. At this moment Hogan's party rode upon them, unseen in the fog. The surprise was equal. Each side sought shelter, and a sharp battle was fought, lasting half an hour, at the end of which time the Indians fled, leaving several dead behind them. The camp trappings of Bryant's party were found by Hogan in the camp. His suspicions were at once aroused concerning the fate of their owners. After a vain search for them, he and his men sadly returned to the fort, to find their worst apprehensions realized. Bryant, the leader of the fort, the man for whom it was named, the hero of a hundred fights, was lying cold in death amid the corpses of the men who fell in the same attack.

A SETTLER'S SELF-DEFENSE.

Not in Kentucky alone, but throughout the length of the Ohio valley, raged the conflict with the red man. David Morgan occupied a cabin on the Monongahela River, several miles from the nearest neighbor. He was seventy years of age, but still braved the dangers of his situation.

One morning two of his younger children went to plow a field a mile away from the cabin. Morgan became uneasy from some cause, and taking his trusty rifle, determined to go to them. He found the boys all right. Taking a seat on the top rail of the worm fence, he was giving some directions about the work, when he suddenly became aware of the fact that he and his children were not alone. In the edge of the forest he perceived two Indians gliding stealthily and rapidly upon the boys. Morgan called to the latter to fly to the house. For himself, he determined to cover their retreat. The children, having two hundred yards the start, and being fleet runners, were soon out of reach.

The old man also ran with considerable activity for a short distance, but as his strength failed, his pursuers gained on him. He turned at bay, to contend with the two powerful and well-armed savages. The woods were thin. Morgan planted himself behind the only large tree in the locality. His pursuers instantly sought cover behind some saplings, but old Morgan, seeing a little of the person of the nearest savage exposed, fired with unerring skill and killed him. The other Indian at once rushed on Morgan, whose gun was of course empty. The latter ran, but in a moment his pursuer, less than twenty steps behind him, fired. By great fortune, the ball missed its mark. Morgan again turned at bay, clubbing his musket, while the Indian raised his tomahawk. Both blows took effect, the gun stock being broken on the Indian's skull, and the tomahawk, shattered by striking the gun-barrel, having cut off two of Morgan's fingers. The savage reached for his knife, but the old man grappled with him, hurling him to the ground.

An awful struggle took place, but the youth and superior strength of the Indian availed to turn Morgan. The savage planted his knee on his opponent's breast, and again reached for his knife. Again his luck turned. He had lately stolen a woman's apron. It was tied around his waist, covering the knife handle, so he could not readily get at it. Old Morgan, however, was game to the last. He managed to get one of the savage's fingers between his teeth. This maneuver caused the Indian to howl with rage, and struggle furiously to get loose, but Morgan's jaws were locked on that finger with the grip of a steel vise.

Seizing his little advantage, Morgan reached for the Indian's knife himself. Both grasped it at the same instant, Morgan getting a small grip on the handle, the savage a better one on the blade. At this juncture, Morgan gave the finger a terrific bite, and with swift dexterity twitched the knife out of his adversary's hand. Quick as thought he plunged it into the Indian's side, then into his stomach, blade, handle, and all. The latter fell over on his side.

Old Morgan rose, greatly exhausted by the exertion and excitement of the struggle, and feebly made his way home. A party of neighbors was raised within an hour or two, who found that the old man's antagonist had crawled some little distance to a clump of bushes. When discovered, he held out his hand, and feebly uttered "Brothers!" The whites, however, failed to acknowledge this claim of relationship. He was killed, scalped, and skinned, the hide being tanned by the settlers for bullet-pouches.

AN AMERICAN MEG MERRILES.

The genius of Walter Scott has immortalized the character of old Meg Merriles throughout the world. Her character was drawn from life, the original being a certain Jean Gordon, a famous gypsy of the Scottish border. Great novelists must have appropriate subject-matter on which to base their stories. The border lore and legendry from which Scott drew his treasure, is popularly supposed to be unparalleled. Nowhere is the error of this notion, to which we have called attention in our preface, better shown than in the fact that in the conflict of the Ohio valley, there arose a woman, if such she might be called, more remarkable in career, more strange and wild in character, than Jean Gordon ever was. "Mad Ann Bailey," as she was known among the settlers, though of vastly different origin and surroundings, bears a general resemblance to the immortal Meg Merriles of "Guy Mannering."

The strange creature of whom we write was born in Liverpool, England, about 1750. Her maiden name was Hennis; her husband being Richard Trotter. Along with other adventurous spirits of the time, she and her husband emigrated to America, and, as if by instinct, sought the perils and excitement of border life. Trotter was an Indian fighter. He became a volunteer in Dunmore's war, and was killed in the bloody battle of Point Pleasant. From that day his widow lead that strange career which spread her name far and wide through the border settlements, and which will perpetuate it so long as the stories of the border struggles are read among men.

Thenceforth she followed but one pursuit—that of fighting the Indians. She unsexed herself, wore men's clothes, and instead of household tasks, she took upon herself the toilsome life of a scout. She became a dead-shot with a rifle. She learned to throw the tomahawk with all the accuracy and strength of an Indian warrior. As a hunter, she had no superior on the border. Wherever prizes were offered in contests in rifle shooting, tomahawk throwing, or other athletic sports, far or near along the border, this strange and solitary woman always appeared at the last moment as a contestant, and carried off the prize. She rode a powerful black horse, called "Liverpool," after her birthplace. It was the only living creature she loved. Her horse and rifle were her constant companions.

She spent her time as other scouts, roaming the forests in search of game, or stealthily watching in ambush for some wan-

CAPTURE OF DAVID MORGAN'S ASSAILANT.

THE END OF VENGEANCE.

dering Indian. Amid storms of rain and sleet, beset by the rigors of winter, followed by wild beasts, or pursued by Indians, her immense frame of iron strength knew no fatigue, her restless rancor no slumber. As she bestrode her horse, her male attire, her weather-beaten features, her black, wiry hair, cut short in men's fashion, her cold, gray eyes and grating voice, her rifle easily thrown over her shoulder, revealed the AMAZON. No service in behalf of the settlers was too arduous, no mode of injury to the savages too cruel or bloody for her fierce zeal.

The story of one incident has come down to us. She was making her head-quarters at Charleston Fort, in West Virginia, when the fort was besieged by an overwhelming force of Indians. Unable to subdue it by force, the besiegers undertook to reduce it by famine. The brave pioneers defended it resolutely until their hearts were chilled to find the supply of ammunition nearly exhausted. The nearest point from which supplies could be had was more than a hundred miles away. The way lay through dense forests, bottomless morasses, vast ranges of mountains, terrible precipices, and rushing rivers. Worse than all this, the whole country was overrun with war-parties of savages. Great as was the peril of the fort, great as was the peril of the journey, this bold woman alone would undertake the task of procuring supplies. Avoiding all trails, roads, and regular passes, she took her way directly across the mountains of West Virginia for more than a hundred miles.

Reaching her destination in safety, she procured lead and gunpowder, loaded it on a pack-horse, and commenced the fearful return journey. Followed by raving packs of wolves, at every step beset by hissing serpents which still infest the mountains of Virginia, discovered and pursued by Indians, hardly daring to sleep a moment, she recrossed the mountains by a different route, swam her two beasts across foaming mountain torrents, and, after exposure to every conceivable peril, and escape from all, delivered her precious load to the beleaguered garrison. This service became famous throughout the border.

On her return she again took her place among the resolute defenders of the fort, doing guard duty, or sharing in the fray of every attack.

At some period in her career, this strange, unsexed creature, with her disordered intellect, was actually wooed and won by a man named Bailey, but this marriage made no change in her life, except that, instead of being known as "Mad Ann," she was thereafter "Mad Ann Bailey." Her numerous services to the settlers caused her to be as much loved by the whites as she was feared and hated by the Indians. In the latter part of her life, when times had become more settled, she used at times to visit the families she had known and served in her earlier years. From such visits she never failed to return laden down with presents.

THE GREAT FIGHT OF POE AND BIG FOOT.

"No man ever took more satisfaction in hunting deer, bear, wolves, and buffalo than I have, but the greatest enjoyment I ever took was in hunting Indians." The speaker was an old man, of gigantic frame and shrunken muscles. He sat by an open fire-place, with its great andirons and blazing back-logs. Around him sat a group of younger people, his family and friends. A hush was upon the little circle. The old man was still quivering with excitement, as if he had gone through some violent exertion far beyond his strength. He had sat silent for a few moments, as if recovering his breath, and then uttered the sentence given above.

The old man was Andrew Poe, a man whose name was known in every cabin in the Ohio valley during the twenty years' conflict. His excitement and apparent exhaustion had a cause. He had just been relating to the company for the hundredth time the thrilling story of his fight with Big Foot. As he set himself afloat in the current of the story, he illustrated it by action. He went through all the fury and effort of a death-struggle with an imaginary adversary. Not a detail of the fight had been omitted. With flashing eye, tense and knotted muscles, almost choked with frothing rage, he had re-enacted the scene with all the spirit of the original conflict, for the benefit of the little group.

We have entered the room too late to hear the old man tell it himself, too late to see him reproduce the conflict in all its vividness. All we can do is to learn the story from others who heard old Poe relate it.

In 1781, there stood on Harmon's Creek, twelve miles back from the Ohio River, in what is Washington County, Pennsylvania, a small settlement of white people.

Among the settlers were two brothers, Andrew Poe, then thirty-nine years of age, and his brother Adam, six years younger. The elder was a man of large build and splendid muscular development. He and his brother were both Indian fighters, and were looked on as the chief defenders of the settlement. Andrew, especially, by reason of his great strength, his matchless agility, and rare courage, was the pride of the valley. In the spring of the year of which we write, the settlement, in common with the rest of the valley, had suffered heavily from Indian attacks. On one occasion, while the Poes and their nearest neighbor, Kennedy, were off on a scout, a party of Indians had burst into Kennedy's house, and murdered his young wife and child.

A short time afterwards, probably in June, a band of seven bloody Wyandots stole into the settlement at midnight, broke into a lonely cabin, in which lived William Jackson, all alone. He was an old man, sixty years of age. Having made Jackson a captive, they attempted to enter another house, but aroused the inmates, who gave the alarm. The seven Indians made off with their prisoner. The men of the settlement were quickly collected. Jackson was discovered to be missing.

Arrangements were made for pursuit. In the morning, as soon as it was light enough to see the trail of the marauders, which was tolerably distinct in the high dewy grass, the settlers set out to save their friend. Twelve of them rode at full speed toward the river. At the top of a steep descent to the river. down which the trail led, the horses were hitched, and the men pressed forward on foot. At the foot of the hill the trail turned down the river. It led across a shallow rivulet that entered the Ohio. The waters of the stream were muddied. They had been recently disturbed. Andrew Poe called the attention of the men to it, as a suggestion that the game was near. He had been convinced by the indications of the trail that the Indians were led by a person no less distinguished than the renowned "Big Foot," chief of the Wyandots, so called from the size of his feet, which, however, were not out of proportion to his immense stature and Herculean proportions.

Poe was not unwilling to measure his strength with such a famous adversary, should opportunity occur. For some reason, after crossing the rivulet, while the others followed the trail leading away from the river bank, Poe turned to his right, and kept on alone through some heavy willows along the shore. Suddenly he discovered, about twelve feet below him on the slope toward the water, two Indians, crouching behind a small bluff or elevation in the river bank. They had guns cocked and were looking intently towards a spot from which they had heard a noise. One Indian was of enormous size, and Poe at once conjectured that he was no other than Big Foot. The other, though smaller, was fully the equal of Poe, who was himself the boast of the settlements.

To take in the situation at a glance, to level his gun at the breast of Big Foot, and draw the trigger was the work of an instant. But the much vaunted weapons of the pioneers were clumsy affairs to those of to-day. The gun missed fire. The Indians yelled. Poe hastily drew back into the bushes. Just then the rest of the party had overtaken the other five Indians a hundred yards down the river. The shots momentarily attracted the attention of Poe's adversaries. He a second time attempted to fire.

A second time, as if reluctant for its task, the gun missed fire. Poe flung it down, boldly jumped over the bluff, throwing one arm around Big Foot's neck, and the other around his companion, throwing both to the ground by his weight and momentum. Big Foot fell on his back, with Poe on top of him, on his left side, his left arm around the Indian's neck. The smaller Indian fell to the right of the other two, but with his head caught in the vise-like grip of Poe's right upper arm and side. From this embarrassing situation the smaller savage struggled to withdraw his head, but in vain.

Poe felt that in order to save his life he must kill one of his opponents, before either disengaged himself from him. If one of them should get free while he still held down the other, he saw little hope. To kill Big Foot, however, he must get at his knife. This was in its scabbard, pressed tightly between his left side and Big Foot's body. Nor could he use more than his fore right arm in his effort to disengage it. He pulled and tugged frenziedly to get the knife out, but Big Foot's hand was also on it. While Poe and his larger antagonist tugged at the knife, the other lunged and twisted to free himself. At last Poe gave a furious wrench to the knife, and Big Foot suddenly letting go, the weapon came out suddenly. Poe's arm pulling at the knife, and unexpectedly released, jerked back, releasing the smaller Indian from its grip, the knife at the same time slipping from Poe's fingers, and flying into the river.

Almost at the same moment Big Foot threw his long arm about Poe, and hugged with all his strength. The latter struggled to free himself. The smaller Indian overlooking, or, perhaps, for fear of shooting Big Foot, afraid to use a cocked gun lying just at Poe's head, ran to a canoe, ten feet away, seized a tomahawk, and running back, gave a terrific hack at Poe's head. The latter, however, though still a prisoner in the iron embrace of Big Foot, managed, just as the Indian delivered the stroke, to give his wrist a terrific kick with his right foot, diverting the blow, and flinging the tomahawk into the river.

At this Big Foot bellowed furiously at his companion in his own tongue. The latter procured the other tomahawk, and, carefully avoiding Poe's heels, again struck at him. This time Poe threw up his right arm, received the blow in his wrist, one bone and the cords of three fingers being cut, and the hand practically disabled. Giving his arm a jerk, the tomahawk, which was caught in the sinews, was snatched from the Indian's hand, and Poe in turn threw it into the river.

At this moment Big Foot's embrace relaxed. Poe tore himself loose, snatching up the cocked gun with his left hand as he rose, and in a moment shot the smaller Indian through the body. Just as the bullet left the barrel, Big Foot, who had risen only less quickly than Poe, seized him by the neck and leg, and pitched him toward the river as if he were a chip. Poe, however, could not be excelled for activity. Though too late to prevent this, he threw his left hand back, caught the Indian's buckskin breech clout firmly, and, as he fell, dragged Big Foot with him over the bank into the river.

The water was deep. Each man struggled with unearthly fury to drown the other. The water was lashed into angry foam by their conflict. First one and then the other obtained the advantage. At last, Poe got his fingers on the Indian's scalp-lock, and held him under, as he supposed, till he was strangled. But the Indian had deceived him by keeping quiet. As Poe let go the scalp-lock to get his knife and end the contest, the latter seized Poe, and in turn put him under.

But Poe was still full of resources; though half strangled, he managed to struggle toward deeper water. The current seized them, carried both beyond their depth, and the Indian, as well as Poe, was obliged to let go his hold and swim for life. There was yet one loaded gun on shore. To get that weapon each adversary put forth every exertion. Poor Poe, however, having only one hand to swim with, saw Big Foot beating him in the race. He therefore turned again to mid-stream, intending to live. Big Foot gained the shore, picked up the loaded gun, but in cocking it broke the hammer. Throwing it down he snatched the empty rifle, and ran to the canoe for ammunition.

At this moment Adam Poe came running down the shore, to find out what was the matter. Andrew shouted to him to "shoot the big Indian on shore." Adam's gun was empty. Just as Big Foot was loading his gun, Adam began the same act with his. Each felt that his life depended on completing the charge first. Big Foot would inevitably have been ready to fire first, had not another mishap befallen him. In withdrawing his ramrod too hastily, it slipped from his hand. The time it took to pick it up gave Adam Poe the advantage. Just as Big Foot raised his gun, Poe fired, and killed him.

The fight was ended, but not its mishaps. Another white man following Adam Poe down the bank, seeing that the latter had shot an Indian on shore, and perceiving Andrew Poe, with bloody face, swimming rapidly from the shore, mistook him for an Indian, fired and shot him in the shoulder. Adam Poe, alarmed for his brother, started to swim to his help, but the latter shouted to him to let him alone, and "scalp the Indian." Adam, however, refused, thinking more of his brother's safety than of the trophy. Big Foot, mortally wounded, exerted his failing strength to roll himself into the river and keep his triumphant antagonist from winning the glory of taking Big Foot's scalp. As the two brothers started to the shore, the swift current of the Ohio swept the body of Big Foot, scalp and all, out of sight.

It may be easily understood how the story of this fight spread throughout the border settlements, and made Andrew Poe the most famous man in his part of the country.

FIVE KENTUCKY BOYS AND THEIR PLUCK.

It is easy to see what sort of men the pioneers were. But what about the children? Nothing is more interesting than the influence of border life upon boys. There is something in it which summons forth all the latent heroism of the youthful
19

heart. We yet see this trait in the boys of our Middle and Western States. Books of adventure, of pioneering, of Indian fights, of explorations, form their chosen literature. No matter how quiet and attentive they may be in school, one may be certain that stuffed away in some corner of their desk is a dog-eared book of adventure, a book in which scouts perform impossible exploits, in which one man whips a dozen red Indians, and rescues a pretty girl whom they have made a captive; in which abound hair-breadth escapes, and bold adventures of boys of their own age, who either by chance or by choice live in that mysterious and wonderful region known as THE BORDER.

Many of these books no doubt are vicious. We pause not to moralize. We simply call attention to the fact that this appetite for adventure is in a boy, in such strength, that no vigilance of parents, nor instruction of teachers can prevent him from gratifying it. He will have and will read books of adventure—the best, the worst. "The Last of the Mohicans," and "Long Haired Jack, the Mountain Avenger," alike. If there is a public library in the community, it is the books of this sort which are seized and read with appalling voracity. If not, then each boy furtively lends his treasure to every other boy, until the worn volume has gone the rounds, whereupon, if no other be at hand, the same book is read over again. Whence comes this appetite? Is it not an inheritance from our fathers who fought the wars of the real border, and which is only overwhelmed and destroyed by contact with the practical side of life?

Let it be remembered that America has been colonized and populated by the boldest spirits of every clime, men and women who spurned the quiet comfort of their homes in the "old country," and chose rather the excitement and dangers of the wilderness. Then we may understand how natural it is for the American boy to love books of adventure. Then we may see whence comes that restless longing, which, unsatisfied with the quiet life of home, and the rigid discipline of school—in short, finding no scope or outlet in real life—seeks vent and gratification in imaginary adventures and exploits.

The children of the pioneers were offspring worthy of their sires. It was about 1785 that a group of five Kentucky boys afforded a splendid illustration of this. Colonel Pope was a leading citizen in a settlement near Louisville, Kentucky. Feeling keenly the total absence of educational facilities for his two sons on the frontier, he employed a tutor for them. He generously invited several of the neighbor's lads to share the privileges of instruction. Among them were two sons of Colonel Linn, a famous scout, who had been killed by Indians. To them Colonel Pope sustained the relation of guardian.

The little school had no session on Saturdays. On these days the boys were accustomed to have their fun. One Saturday in February five of these school-boys went out for a hunt. In the party were the two Linns, William Wells, Brashear, and a fifth whose name is not preserved. They were little fellows, ranging from ten to fourteen years old. Yet they were marksmen who might well put to blush many of the best shots of the present day. They made a trip of several miles from home, to a region of ponds and swamps, in which abounded ducks, geese, and swans. They had a rare day, and, delaying until too late to return home, they decided to encamp for the night on the spot. As to the proper method of building a hut and spreading boughs for their beds, they were thoroughly posted. During the night a light snow covered the ground.

Rising early, they prepared their breakfast, and made ready to return home, when suddenly a party of Indians burst into their little camp with unearthly yells. Two of the boys attempted to run. Of these, the elder Linn being fat and clumsy, and encumbered with some game he had hung over his shoulder, stumbled and fell. For this the Indians called him "Fat Bear." Brashear, however, was fleet of foot, and came near escaping. He, however, like all the rest, was captured, but his agility won him the name of "Buck Elk."

Having secured their boy captives, the Indians demanded to know where they came from. "From Louisville," said Brashear. "You lie," was the gentle response of the leading Indian. But the boys stuck to the falsehood, and by their sagacity and firmness prevented the savages from advancing upon the defenseless settlement in which they lived.

When they found themselves prisoners the boys took it coolly enough. Their captors at once started on the journey to their distant wigwams. They crossed the Ohio River and moved northward through what is the State of Indiana. Every day took the five plucky little fellows farther from home, and decreased their chances for rescue. Yet they kept quiet, ate heartily of the game and other food provided by the Indians, and above all remained cheerful. Their journey did not end till they reached an Indian village on the Little Calumet River, near the present town of Valparaiso, in north-western Indiana.

On entering the village they were compelled to run the gauntlet. This, however, they knew exactly how to do, having heard about it all their lives, and having prepared themselves in mind for the ordeal. Two rows of Indian boys, some smaller, many larger than themselves, were drawn up. The young Indians had their hands full of clubs, tomahawks, dirt, salt, and stones.

At the word, away dashed the five spirited little Kentuckians at the top of their speed. They were met with showers of filth, missiles, and blows, but by rapid running and skillful dodging, they were in a fair way to get through all right. Just as the younger Linn, who was in front, was three-quarters down the ranks of howling redskins, an Indian boy, much larger than himself, hit him a stunning blow with his fist. Linn was a hot-blooded and fiery-tempered fellow at best. Resenting the insult with all the fury of his impetuous nature, he knocked the ruffian down by a left-handed stroke. At this clever feat, the assembled crowd of warriors gave vent to a huge uproar of laughter, but the squaws sympathized with their own blood.

CONFLICT OF THE LINN BOYS WITH THE INDIANS.

Young Linn quickly planted himself with his back to the council-house, and with clenched fists uplifted, and his eyes blazing with rage through his heavy, tangled hair, which in the melee had fallen over his forehead, awaited the onslaught which he knew was sure to come. A large and brawny young Indian, with a sinister countenance, ran at him. Linn received him with the same left-handed stroke which had been so effective before, and knocking him down, sprang on him with the ferocity of a panther, kicking, biting, pinching, and pounding till, in a moment, his formidable foe was completely demoralized.

The ring of warriors shouted and danced with delight at this sport, which was so much better than any gauntlet running. But the whole crowd of juvenile Indians, seeing their champions vanquished, now became pugnacious, and rushed upon him to demolish him. At this, the other four Kentuckians came to their friend's rescue, and fought the howling mass of Indian youth with the fury of tigers turned at bay. They fought against great odds, but being far superior to their enemies in athletic and pugilistic skill, they overthrew them one by one, until the rest were glad to run off.

The warriors here intervened, and proudly carried the boys into the council-house, to be adopted into the tribe as Indians. Four of the boys were adopted into the families of the leading warriors of the village. Poor Wells, however, fell to the lot of an Indian living in a remote village. With sad hearts the boys parted from him as he went from them, and they never saw him again. For many years he lived with the Indians, marrying a sister of Little Turtle, one of their celebrated chiefs, and fighting with his tribe against the whites. He afterwards rejoined the whites, and became a noted scout under General Wayne.

The other boys, becoming gradually accustomed to the loss of their friend, rapidly adapted themselves toward their new mode of life. They soon excelled in all Indian sports, and seemed so well satisfied with the pleasures of savage life, fishing and hunting, wrestling, racing, riding Indian ponies, and romping with the maidens, that their captors no longer entertained any suspicion of their disloyalty, and they were allowed to roam about as they pleased. The boys, however, were playing a deep game, and were only biding their time to escape.

The chance came at last. In the autumn after their capture the warriors went off on their annual hunt, roaming far and wide over the country in quest of game, leaving the village inhabited only by old men, squaws, and children. One day the four boys arranged to go fishing some miles from the village. An old Indian and his wife alone accompanied them.

The boys felt this to be their opportunity for escape. But a serious problem had first to be solved. Did they dare to leave the old Indian and his squaw alive? The struggle in their minds was painful. The old people were kind to them in their way. To kill them seemed terrible. Yet to leave them alive meant speedy discovery of their flight, pursuit, and probably recapture, as the long journey to their homes lay through a wilderness of which they were ignorant, while their pursuers were thoroughly familiar with it. These boys, it must be remembered, had been brought up to regard the Indians as their most abhorred enemies. Frontier life was a constant warfare with them. The father of two of them had been killed by savages only four years before. These things decided them.

At dead of night the boys rose stealthily, armed themselves with tomahawks, and two of them placed themselves at the head of each sleeping Indian. At a signal from Brashear, they all struck at the skulls of the sleepers, killing them instantly. Hastily collecting the little stock of provisions in the camp, the boys set out in the darkness for home. Happy thought! With the skill of a band of Indian warriors themselves, they pursued their flight, traveling by night, guiding their course by the north star, lying by, hid in bushes and deep grass by day. They subsisted on nuts, wild berries, roots, and occasionally a squirrel or rabbit, which they succeeded in killing with a stone.

Their journey lay through a vast wilderness of gloomy swamps, lonely forests, solitary rivers, and silent prairies, which is now thickly populated with the citizens of Indiana. Their journey must have taken them over the site of the present splendid city of Indianapolis, the capital of the State, a city of fine public buildings, of wide, well-paved and brilliantly lighted streets and avenues, lined with tall business blocks, a city with miles of elegant residences, with numerous churches, handsome theaters, large manufacturing establishments, modern school-houses, and more railways than any other strictly interior city on the globe. The site of all this was, at the time of the boys' journey, a bottomless marsh. Besides this, our young heroes' path led them through the sites of innumerable flourishing county towns, such as Logansport, Franklin, Columbus, Seymour, New Albany, and Jeffersonville. Yet, in all their journey, they saw not a white man's clearing, nor a single cabin, nor a settlement.

After a three weeks' journey, they reached the shores of the Ohio, opposite Louisville. Here they tried by shouts and gestures to induce their friends to come over for them. But the Indians had been very troublesome that summer, and moreover, the young pioneers were dressed and disguised until they looked for all the world like four young Indians. So the good people of Louisville remained on their own side.

Nothing disheartened the boys went up the river some distance, and, with no tool but a small knife, constructed a raft. Their haste to finish it was so great, and the thing was so rickety, that it would only bear the weight of three. The elder Linn, being a splendid swimmer, swam by its side while the others paddled. In this way they reached the Kentucky shore. Just as they landed, their pursuers appeared on the opposite shore, mad with rage at their escape. Linn was nearly exhausted by his long swim in the chilly waters. But they soon found Colonel Pope, who had been driven from his settlement by Indians, and was living in Louisville. He gave them a hearty welcome, supplied their wants, and listened to their thrilling story with the joy of a loving father. The only cloud in the sky was the absence of poor Wells, whose fate remained unknown to his companions.

WHO WAS HE?

It was one morning in 1780, that the inmates of a cabin in what is Bourbon County, Kentucky, were startled by strange yells from the outside. The door was slightly opened, and, while no person was in sight, the yells were discovered to proceed from a dense clump of underbrush. The bushes were violently shaken, and in a moment there stepped into view a man. His features were European, but his complexion, costume, and speech were Indian. He continued to jabber in a loud voice, rolling his eyes and gesticulating in a frightful manner. In a short time all the people in the little settlement had formed in a circle around him.

From his jargon, the settlers, who knew a little of the Indian language, made out that, when a little child, he had been captured by the Indians and had been reared by them; that of his home or parents he remembered nothing; that he had gone out on a hunt with his Indian father and brothers, and had accidentally come within sight of the white men's cabins. The view had acted like a magician's wand. In an instant all the associations and attachments of the long years of life in the wigwam had been swept away. He was seized with an overwhelming desire to rejoin the people of his birth, and now he begged them to receive him. His Indian father would miss him, but he wanted to rejoin the white people, and, if possible, learn something of his own birth and parentage.

The settlers conversed in a low tone among themselves, and, fearful lest he should be a decoy, asked him many questions. Among other things he said that he and his companions had ascended the Licking River in a canoe, and burying it, had struck into the woods. The cautious pioneers, therefore, as a test of the truth of his story, proposed that he conduct them to the spot where the canoe lay concealed.

As soon as he understood the request, the stranger protested most vehemently against it. He said, that while he desired to leave his Indian father and brother, yet they had raised him and been very kind to him for many years; that they were the only friends he could remember having ever had, and he would not on any account betray them. The suspicion of the group of listeners deepened at this answer. They demanded that he lead them to the canoe at once, or they would treat him as a prisoner. With the strongest reluctance he set out to guide the company of twenty mounted men to the buried canoe.

Perhaps, with the hope of giving his Indian friends time to escape, the wild stranger nervously explained that he would first lead the white men to a spot where he and his father and brother had encamped, and where he said they would find a kettle hidden in a hollow log. As they approached the spot from a distance they discovered two Indians in the camp, an old man and a boy, sitting by the fire, roasting some venison. At the sight the stranger burst into tears, and falling on his knees, begged and implored the white men in the most vehement and frenzied manner, to spare his Indian father and brother.

Moved by his entreaties, the pioneers formed a circle to surround the two Indians, with the notion, real or pretended, of taking them captive. The old man, however, fought with such desperation that they killed him, while the boy, with incredible agility, escaped into the forest. Seeing the old Indian fall, the stranger leaped from his horse, and running, threw his arms around the neck of the dying savage, begging his forgiveness for having unwittingly betrayed him to death. The aged Indian evidently recognized him, giving him a pressure of the hand, but he was too far gone to speak.

The settlers at once called loudly to the stranger to lead them at a gallop to the buried canoe. He wrung his hands in bitter agony, begging them to see that he had already given proof of his honesty at the cost of his father's death, and beseeching that they might spare his younger brother. The only response was a peremptory demand to lead them to the canoe without delay. They rightly surmised that the young Indian would hasten thither. Overwhelmed with grief, the stranger again mounted his horse. In two hours they reached the spot. No footprints were visible. The young Indian had not arrived.

The men at once hid themselves in the bushes to wait. In ten minutes the young savage came running to the spot, and commenced hastily to dig up the canoe. In a moment he fell, pierced by a dozen balls. With a mournful cry the strange white man hid his face in his hands. They took him back to the settlement, but he mourned all the day long, saying over and over to himself in the Indian tongue, "I betrayed my best friends. I killed my father. I killed my brother. Oh, me!"

One morning the strange and unhappy man was missing. He appears only for this single act in the drama of history. That act is tragedy. Whether he sought out the white settlements of the east, or returned to the smoky wigwam which he had deprived of both its support and its hope, or whether, maddened with grief, Judas like, he went out into the solitary wilderness, and there, alone with his God, expiated his crime with the act of self-destruction, will never be known.

THE FIRST CHICKAMAUGA.

Horse-stealing is in the frontier code the worst of all crimes. This is because it is the one against which there is the least protection. In the spring of 1784, a small Kentucky settlement suffered this depredation from Indians. The pursuing party failed to overtake the thieves. Three of the pursuers, all hotblooded fellows, named McClure, Davis, and Caffree, determined to push on south to some Indian village, make reprisals of other horses, and thus balance the account.

One day, traveling along a trail, the three white men fell in

with three Indians. It was in the vicinity of the Tennessee
River, probably south of it, and near an Indian village called
Chicacaugo, or Chicamaugo. It seems not improbable that this
was near the field of the great battle of Chickamauga, in the civil
war, to which the name was given from the creek near which it
was fought. The two parties were equal in numbers. After
a moment's thought each seemed to come to the same conclusion. Instead of fighting, they made signs of friendship, and
agreed to travel together. The three white men walked in single file on one side of the path; the three Indians walked in
single file on the opposite side of the path.

For a while this interesting procession held its way along
the forest trail without incident or delay. It was observed at the
end of a quarter of an hour that the Indians were marching very
close together. Moreover they were, without turning their
heads, whispering to one another. The white men saw danger.
Each selected his man. Caffree, the most powerful of the party,
leaped upon one Indian. Davis, at the same instant, fired at
the second Indian, but missed him. McClure, with better success, killed his man.

Leaving Caffree still wrestling with his foe, his two companions jumped behind trees. The other Indian fired at Caffree,
inflicting a mortal wound, and was in turn shot by the cool-
headed McClure, who had reloaded his weapon. Caffree, poor
fellow, struggling now not only with the Indian, but with
the arch-enemy Death himself, called for help. Davis ran
towards him, but when half-way to him, the Indian threw off
Caffree's weakening grasp, seized his gun, and took aim at
Davis. The latter dropped his gun, still unloaded, and ran off
into the forest.

McClure, the coolest man of the trio, having already killed
two Indians, shouldered Davis's gun, and ran after him. Strange
as it may seem, in the short instant of picking up the gun, he
lost sight of both pursuer and pursued. On he ran into the
thick shadows of the southern forest, but not a trace could he

discover of their flight. He stopped to listen. Not a sign was audible, but the steady plash of the little creek of Chicamaugo, or the twittering of the birds. He ran on a little farther, and called aloud. No answer came, but the mocking echo, which rang in thousand-voiced responses, each fainter than the last, from every direction in the forest. He shouted with all his power. It only seemed to wake a thousand fiends, who took up his words and hurled them back and forth. The fate of Davis is unknown to this day.

McClure, left alone in the Indian country, resolved to make his way home at once, if possible. No more fine notions in him about running off a whole herd of Indian ponies from their masters. Still carrying Davis's rifle as well as his own, our brave young friend set his face to the north. He had only pushed forward for a mile or two, when he discovered approaching him, an Indian warrior, on a horse with a bell around its neck, and a boy walking by his side. A ready wit is valuable anywhere. McClure dropped one of his rifles, lest it excite suspicion, and boldly advanced, making signs of peace. The fellow returned them, dismounted, seated himself on a fallen tree, and producing a pipe, drew a few puffs, then handed it, following true Indian etiquette, to McClure.

Just then another tinkle was heard in the forest, followed by quite a troop of gayly attired Indian horsemen. McClure's companion now informed him that the Indians intended to tie him on a horse, and carry him off as a prisoner. To illustrate the thing, Mr. Indian, in the excess of his politeness, bestrode the fallen tree, and locked his feet beneath. As the dusky gentleman twined his legs about the log, the white man raised his rifle, and shot him dead. The Indian boy jumped on the horse and rode away. McClure ran in the opposite direction. A lot of small Indian dogs took after him, harmless in themselves, but succeeding in tripping him up. He fell several times with terrific force, but scrambled to his feet and ran on, until an unlucky fall filled his eyes with dust.

Blinded and exhausted, he lay still, expecting each moment to be seized by savage hands. Several minutes passed. No foe more formidable than the snapping dogs appeared. The silence of the woods was unbroken by a single foot-fall. His path homeward was open. Still anxious, but inspired with hope, he regained his feet, and again commenced the journey which brought him safely to his Kentucky cabin.

A WIDOW'S CABIN.

The homely name of "Widow Scraggs" has survived the death of its obscure bearer only by reason of her fate. Her home was an isolated cabin in Bourbon County, Kentucky. The structure contained two rooms, separated by a porch or passage-way, which was covered by the same roof as the rooms. In summer months on this porch was spread the frugal meal of the widow's family. In winter, but little use was made of it except for piles of firewood. One room was occupied by the old lady, two grown sons, a widowed daughter and her infant child. The other room was used by two unmarried daughters, one twenty years old, the other just blooming with all the blushing beauty of sweet sixteen, a girl living with the family, and the children.

It was twelve o'clock, on the night of April 11, 1787. In one room the elder daughter was still spinning flax at the old-fashioned spinning-wheel; in the other, one of the young men still busied himself with the humble task of cobbling his shoes by the flickering firelight. The remainder of the family were asleep. From time to time, the young cobbler raised his head, and, with awl arrested in mid-air, seemed to listen with anxiety to some sounds in the forest, which now and then disturbed the silence of the cabin.

These noises, to the ordinary listener, were no reason for the apparent apprehensions of the young man. They were but the hooting of owls and the restless neighing of a couple of horses in the barnyard. The young spinner in the other room seemed not to notice them. Probably the noise of the spinning-wheel or the preoccupation of her mind explained this. The shoes were almost mended, when a footfall was heard from the porch, followed by a knock on the door. "Who keeps house?" the person knocking inquired in good English. The young man, supposing it to be some belated settler, rose to unbar the door. At that moment his mother, roused by the unusual disturbance, screamed, "Keep the door shut! They are Indians!"

The other young man, till then asleep, sprang from his bed, and the two prepared for defense. The Indians, of whose character there could now be no doubt, set up terrific yells, and attempted to batter down the heavy door. A shot from a porthole in the cabin caused them to fall back quickly, only to discover the door to the other room, in which were the three defenseless girls. This door was out of range of the rifles of the young men. The fence supplied the savages with heavy rails. Using these as battering rams against the door, the savages filled the air with wild yells and discordant clamor, mingled with the heavy thuds of the rams, and the sharp sound of splitting wood and breaking hinges as the door began to give way.

At last the frail defense fell inward, and the savages leaped with exultant cries toward the frightened girls. The eldest, pale and desperate, braced herself against the door, but a savage hand and arm, thrust through a breach, buried a knife in her back. The second girl was captured without a struggle. The youngest one, in the uproar, slipped under a bed and out of the door. Instead of escaping, however, the little girl ran to the door of the other room, screaming that her sisters were murdered. The young men were about to attempt her rescue, when the mother firmly interposed, declaring that she must be left to her fate, as to open the door would be the death of all. At that moment a piercing scream announced that she lived no longer.

But a new horror was at hand. The room filled with smoke,

THE DEFENSE OF THE SCRAGGS CABIN.

the crackling of flames was heard. The dreadful truth was plain. The cabin had been fired. The inmates were forced to flight. Their plans were quickly made. The door was flung open. The widow, supported by her eldest son, ran in one direction; the daughter, with her child and the younger son, ran in another direction. The mounting flames lighted up the yard with the brightness of day. The widow was shot as she reached the fence; her son, by strange fortune, escaped. The other party also reached the fence, but were attacked in the act of crossing, by several Indians.

The younger brother, careless of his own safety, and seeking only that his sister and her child might have time for escape, fought with all the fury of despair and the sublime courage which is inspired by a consciousness of self-sacrifice. He had placed one foot on the fence. A spring, and he would have been over. Instead, he withdrew his foot. He resolved to remain on the side where he was. The foremost Indian he shot dead. Then, with clubbed musket, he beat back his swarming foes, till his sister and her child were well out of the way.

But the unequal contest ended. Wounded unto death, he fell into the fence corner, where the ground was stained with the ebbing life tide. Four members of the family had been killed on the spot and one, the second daughter, taken prisoner. The fugitives carried the dark tidings to their neighbors. There were hurried preparations, eager inquiries, and dreadful maledictions among the settlers. By morning, a company of thirty men was raised for pursuit. They tracked the foe easily through the light snow. The latter, finding themselves hard pressed, tomahawked the young girl, taken captive. While the main band fled, two of their number posted themselves on a woody ridge, where, by terrific yells and incessant darting among the trees, they deluded the whites into thinking that a large force of Indians occupied the hill. Such is heroism—to die for others. The two dusky braves suffered death to aid their friends' escape.

20

A TYPICAL HEROINE.

John Merril was a white settler in Nelson County, Kentucky. One night, about the time of the last incident, he and his wife had retired to bed. The glow of coals from the fire-place alone illuminated the rude apartment, and the loud tick of an old-fashioned clock measured off the flight of time, while the sleepers dreamed of other days. Suddenly the dogs without the cabin set up a furious barking. Mr. Merril, but half awake, rose to see what was the matter. As he opened the door, he was shot dead, receiving seven bullets in his body. His wife sprang forward, and closed and barred the door, which the Indians at once began to chop down with their tomahawks. A breach was soon effected. But Mrs. Merril was of great strength and invincible courage. Her hard life on the frontier had done much to prepare her for this crisis. As the Indians sought to enter the breach, the daring woman, with fearful exertion, successively killed or disabled four of the enemy.

Foiled in this, the savages climbed on the roof and commenced to descend the chimney. Again the courage and address of the solitary woman confronted them. Snatching up a feather-bed, she flung it on the fire. In a moment the volumes of flame and stifling smoke overcame two of the Indians who fell helplessly down into the fire. Seizing an ax, the now widowed woman quickly dispatched them, and then, with a quick side stroke, inflicted a fearful gash upon the head of the last savage, who was again attempting an entrance by the breach. This fellow escaped. The story of the immense strength and valor of the "long knife squaw" agitated many a barbarous audience in the wigwams of his tribe.

THE SUFFERINGS OF MASSY HARBISON.

Two hundred yards from Reed's block-house, which was itself about twenty-five miles from Pittsburgh, stood, in the year 1792, the rude cabin of an Indian fighter, named Harbison. At sunrise, one morning, while Harbison was absent on a scout, the horn sounded at the block-house. Not thinking the bugle blast a danger signal, Mrs. Harbison fell asleep again. Dreaming of trouble, she awoke, to find a huge savage dragging her from the bed by her foot, and the house swarming with Indians. After ransacking the house, they forced her to come along with them. She carried in her arms her infant child, and led by the hand her little boy of five years.

There was yet a third child, three years old. For the little fellow the mother had no hand. To relieve her of this embarrassment, an Indian took him by the feet, whirled him through the air, and brained him against the cabin wall. To relate these details is sickening. The mother fainted at the awful sight. For this the murderers had a cure. It deserves the attention of medical men. In her story the mother describes it. " The savages gave me a blow across my head and face, and brought me to sight and recollection again."

With this delicate attention the procession marched on. In a few minutes the path led down a steep hill. The little five-year-old boy fell. It hurt him. He was but a child. With uplifted voice and face filled with liquid grief, he sought consolation from the mother's heart, which had never failed. As she put forth her hand in gentle caresses, such as only a mother can give, her arm was seized and she was jerked back. Instead of the soft maternal touch, an Indian's hand seized the little fellow. His crying was stopped forever. The toy which quieted him was a tomahawk. Her babe alone was left to the mother.

All day she marched with her captors. At night, they spread a blanket on the ground, and, tying her hand and foot, said " Go sleep." Two Indians lay down on each side of the poor woman. The next day the march was continued. This day she had food. It was a piece of dried venison, "about the bulk of an egg." One of the Indians went away for a few hours. In his absence another savage busied himself with making a small hoop. At first the captive watched him with languid curiosity. Then, full of wretchedness, she turned her head to look upward into the waving foliage of the forest, and the vast illimitable sky-dome.   When her eyes fell on the savage again, he had something in his hand.   A flash of horror-struck recognition flickered in the woman's eyes.   It was the scalp of her boy.   The savage was stretching it on the hoop.

The second night was passed like the first.   Towards morning one Indian rose and left the camp.   The wakeful mother managed to slip loose from her bonds.   With a step, noiseless as a spirit, she fled with her babe in arms on and on, pausing not to look behind, breathless, frantic, "over rocks, precipices, thorns, and briers, with bare feet and legs," as she says pathetically.

She was a pioneer woman, the wife of a scout.   At two o'clock in the afternoon she could no longer keep up her flight. She waited.   At night, when the north star appeared, she marked out the course for the next day.   Long before sunrise she was on her way, resting not.   It rained all day.   She had no food for herself or child.   Yet she bravely pushed on.   At dark she made a bed of leaves in the forest.   The child was hungry.   The little creature wept aloud.   "Fearful of the consequences," writes the mother, "I put him to my breast, and he became quiet.   I then listened, and distinctly heard footsteps. The ground over which I had traveled was soft, and my footprints had been followed.

"Greatly alarmed, I looked about for a place of safety, and providentially discovered a large tree which had fallen, into the top of which I crept.   The darkness greatly assisted me, and prevented detection.   The savage who followed me had heard the cry of the child, and came to the very spot where it had cried, and there he halted, put down his gun, and was at this time so near that I heard the wiping-stick strike against his gun distinctly.   My getting in under the tree and sheltering myself from the rain, and pressing my boy to my bosom, got him warm, and, most providentially, he fell asleep, and lay very still during that time of extreme danger.   All was still and quiet; the savage was listening to hear the cry again.   My own heart was

ANDREW POE'S FAMOUS COMBAT WITH BIG FOOT.

the only thing I feared, and that beat so loud that I was apprehensive it would betray me.

"After the savage had stood and listened with nearly the stillness of death for two hours, the sound of a bell and a cry like that of a night-owl, signals which were given to him by his companions, induced him to answer, and after he had given a most horrid yell, he started off to join them. After his retreat, I concluded it unsafe to remain there till morning.

"But by this time nature was so nearly exhausted that I found some difficulty in moving; yet, compelled by necessity, I threw my coat about my child and placed the end between my teeth, and with one arm and my teeth I carried him, and with the other groped my way between the trees and traveled on, as I supposed, a mile or two, and there sat down at the root of a tree till morning. The night was cold and wet, and thus terminated the fourth day and night's difficulties, trials, and dangers!"

After two days more of incredible suffering, the unfortunate woman made her way to a settlement. So changed was she by the six days of hardship, that her nearest neighbor failed to recognize her. "Two of the females, Sarah Carter and Mary Ann Crozier, took out the thorns from my feet and legs, which Mr. Felix Negley stood by and counted, to the number of one hundred and fifty, though they were not all extracted at that time, for the next evening there were many more taken out. The flesh was mangled dreadfully, and the skin and flesh were hanging in pieces on my feet and legs. The wounds were not healed for a considerable time. Some of the thorns went through my feet and came out at the top."

Thus the pioneers of the Ohio valley endured for the sake of the hope which was set before them. Forty years they wandered in the wilderness that their children might enter into and possess the land of promise. What honor is due them by the thoughtless thousands who eat the fruit of their toil! Yet the shores of the Ohio contain no monument to their memory!

MOREDOCK'S REVENGE.

Nature is full of compensations, of balances. **Light** and darkness; heat and cold; love and hate; positive and negative; more and less—these are but a few instances of a law running through the universe. Indian massacres made Indian fighters. In the shadow of the murderer skulks the avenger. There was a woman named Moredock, who lived about 1793, at Vincennes, Indiana, the oldest and, historically, the richest town in the State. She had had several husbands, all of whom had fallen victims of Indian hostility. She had lived for twenty years on the extreme frontier. Husbands, children, neighbors, all these she had seen slain by the red destroyers. Yet with calm heart, stony face, and tearless eye, she faced the danger. She did more. She resolved to move farther west, that her boys might have a chance to grow up with the country.

The party of twenty-five or thirty voyagers, of which she and her family were members, journeyed easily down the Ohio and up the Mississippi. One noon they went ashore at what is Grand Tower, to tow the boats around a high cliff, by which the foaming river rushed with furious current. It was their last landing before reaching their destination. Every one was cheered at the happy prospect. At that moment a dark and dreadful band of warriors burst upon the little company. The surprise was too great, the force too overwhelming for the emigrants to rally. Only one man escaped. John Moredock, the widow's son, more lucky than the others, hid in a fissure in the rock. When the murderers left, glutted with the feast of blood, he climbed down and found the corpses of his family and friends. He buried them. Looking out over the majestic river, he lifted his hand heavenward, and with dark and rigid countenance, hissed out between clenched teeth, " Before God, I will have revenge."

That night the lonely youth started for the Kaskaskia settlements. By daylight he reached them. He told his story. Bold frontiersmen, hardy scouts, appalled by the extent of the horror, inspired by the suppressed fury of Moredock, vowed to help him track the murderers. The flower of the frontier joined the expedition. They set out. It was days before they came within reach of the fleeing murderers.

At last they were discovered. Their camp was on the banks of the Missouri River. But Moredock refused to allow an attack. Why? Did his heart fail him? No. Were he and his companions, after all their tremendous pursuit, going to let the Indians escape? Yes, and no. Moredock's determination was to kill every Indian in the party. Their camp was so pitched that some might escape. He contained himself. Almost bursting with hatred, he was as calm and cool as a marble statue. He said to his men, "We will wait." For several days the avengers shadowed the band of warriors. Their patience was inexhaustible; their pertinacity tireless.

At last they were rewarded. At last, the Indians, unconscious of danger, stepped into a trap. They encamped on a little island in the middle of the Mississippi. Moredock said, "We have them." At midnight the white men landed on the island. They were as noiseless as specters. The canoes of the Indians were floating at the water's edge. These were cut adrift. This made escape for the Indians impossible. Moredock stepped to the canoes from which he and his men had disembarked. With a face of cast-iron, he cut them adrift also. What did this mean? *It meant that escape for the white men was also impossible.* "We will fight to the death!" said Moredock.

The struggle which followed on the island was terrible. The Indians, surprised, ran to their canoes. They were gone. With a howl of despair, the red sons of the forest turned to fight to the death. Out of thirty, twenty-seven were slain. Was not Moredock's revenge complete? No! Three had escaped, by swimming. His appetite for vengeance was unappeased. He dismissed his friends with thanks. They returned to their settlements. For himself, he struck out into the wilderness. For two years he followed the three Indians like shadows. Across mountains, down rivers, over prairies he pursued them, day and night. One by one they fell before the avenger.

At the end of two years he returned to Kaskaskia with their scalps. His revenge was complete. He settled down. He was known as a quiet, peaceable man, strongly domestic in his tastes. This was his true character. Such men, once roused, make the deadliest of all foes. Moredock lived to be not only a respected, but a leading, citizen. He was chosen to hold offices of honor and profit. With it all, he spoke but seldom of the past. Many of the people among whom he lived and moved little suspected him of being a blood avenger. Yet it was the case. Such is our ignorance of our neighbors!

THE WIZARD'S PUNISHMENT.

Early in this century, a strange Indian appeared in a white settlement, near what is now the capital of Ohio. He seemed to be continually apprehensive of some danger, but otherwise acted as any Indian of the better sort. Gradually the white men won his confidence. He explained why he was always so watchful to see that no pursuer was after him. He was a Wyandot. His tribe had taken up a notion that he was guilty of witchcraft. His life was in peril. He fled to the wilderness. For a long time he had eluded them. But his tribe ceased not to pursue him with undying malignity. He was growing old. He needed a more settled habitation as he advanced in years. He had thrown himself upon the mercy of the white man, his father's foe.

One June morning he was sitting in a chair in his cabin. Suddenly a band of Wyandots entered the room. They had tracked him to his retreat. He made no effort to escape. With calm disdain and unruffled courage, he submitted quietly to be bound and carried away. The settlers asked his captors what it meant. With dark and bigoted looks they replied that he was a bad Indian, that he had caused horses, dogs, and even the people of his tribe to fall sick. For this crime he must die. The settlers labored to convince them that their captive had no power to achieve such wonders. To this the savages obstinately shook their heads. The white men exhausted their powers of argument and persuasion. The victim could only be saved by force of arms. This was out of the question. The band of savages greatly outnumbered the population of the settlement.

Finding that he must die, the suspected wizard asked that he might be arrayed in his finest clothes and ornaments. Gorgeously decked out in his gay trappings of silver, gold, and scarlet cloth, he took his place in a ring, and asked that a paper, which he handed them, be read aloud, and then fastened to a tree. It was done. The document was only a recommendation from a prominent settler. With much emotion he bade farewell to his white friends, and then obediently took up his march to a lonely wood, chanting the while the Indian death-song. Arriving at his destination, he was made to kneel before a shallow grave. His relentless executioners formed a circle about him. There was a pause. Then a young warrior stepped briskly forward. His uplifted tomahawk glittered for a moment in the light of the afternoon sun, then sank to the heft in the skull of the victim.

Herein Indian haters may find a text. The barbarism, the cruelty, the blood-thirstiness, the ignorance, the superstition of the savage! Softly, friend, if you please. Yonder, on the stormy New England coast, sits an old town, with its single street and its queer old houses, which look as if they were haunted. In the town museum you may see the wooden pegs which witnesses swore had been suddenly and mysteriously thrust into the flesh of tender babes, without any visible agency, except it was through the black art of the culprit at the bar. Near by is Witches' Hill, where innocent women and men were executed, under sentences rendered on just such testimony. Not ignorant savages were the witnesses, the jury, the judge, the approving crowd; but intelligent, educated, New England Puritans, from whom is said to flow the best blood in America. When we remember the Reign of Superstition in Salem, when we open to the black pages of the witchcraft persecutions, let us withhold our obloquy from the wretched Indian.

Why do we look with such intense aversion, such anger, such disgust upon these crimes, which were committed in the name of justice? It is because it is a part of this age to abhor superstition. We know that the poison flower sheds a fatal perfume. We see that nothing so enervates the intellect, corrupts character, and demoralizes society as this denial of the laws of cause and effect, this belief in a lie, which we call superstition. We hate it. But the place for us to attack superstition is right here and now, and not in the past. There are historical reasons for the witchcraft persecutions of New England. There are reasons, too obvious to be named, for the rank superstition of the Indians. Those reasons do not exist for us. Let us tear from our hearts every cherished bit of superstition. Let us not merely not believe in witches. Let us also trample under our feet every vague belief in table-tipping spirits, in luck, in good and bad omens, in fortune-telling, in the infallibility of the past. This is our work. But it is not our work to abuse the Indians or the Salemites, or any other people under heaven because they believe or believed in superstitions at which we smile with scorn.

Let us pause. This chapter and others, both before and after it, deals with the massacres, the bloodshed, the midnight surprises, the deadly combats, the decoys, the ambushes of the Indian wars in the Ohio valley. These terrible records cover a period of twenty years, from 1774 to 1794. During all that time the frontier was a line of battle.

The history of the time is a history of murders, of cruelties, of tortures. It recites the slaughter of children, the tomahawking of women, the burning alive of men. It recites captivities,

WITCHCRAFT AT SALEM VILLAGE.

starvations, and wanderings. It tells of ruined homes, of desolated lives, of suffering hearts. The midnight sky is forever red with the glare of blazing cabins; the forest is forever filled with blood avengers; yelling Indians are forever battering down the doors of lonely dwellings. Little bands of devoted pioneers are constantly being shut up to starve in block-houses. Strong men, brave women, and tender girls are alike ever running the gauntlet of the encircling foes, to secure food, ammunition, and relief. Lion-hearted men, maddened by the outrages, the murders, the cruelties of the foe, are giving up their farms, their settlements, to roam the forests with the dark occupation of the Indian scout. This is but another name for Indian killer.

Young men, snatched away when children from the arms of agonized mothers, and reared in the squalid wigwams of the savage, remembering not the loving parents who bore them, but knowing only their filthy and ignorant captors, are ever returning, when they reach years of maturity, to the habitation of the white man. They feel themselves strangely moved. Faint memories of their real parents are pictured on their minds. They forever search, without success, to find that early home, and carry with them through life a dull sorrow in the heart. All this, and much more, enters into the story of the time. Seated in our comfortable homes, we read this history. The Indian hater says, "I told you so." Their baseness, their brutality, their wickedness made and makes it just that the red men should be destroyed from the face of the earth.

Let us take a wider view. Let us turn from the silent forests, the majestic rivers, the unpopulated landscapes of the wilderness during the years of this war, to the sunny cities of France, with their cathedrals and palaces, with their gay nobility, their thronging populations, their courts, their literature, their civilization. View them as they were during these same years which the wild Indians of the west marked out upon the historic calendar with the emblems of death and destruction. Need we to be reminded that these very years were the years

of the French Revolution; that at the very time when a few
half starved Indians were attacking some cabin in the beautiful
valley, infuriated thousands were thronging through the streets
of Paris, crying "Bread or Blood?"

The past rises before us. The red panorama of the Revolution, with its sacked cities, its burning chateaux, its wild orgies
of massacre, its streams of blood, its guillotine blades rising and
falling with the regularity of heart beats, severing the heads of
the bravest, the tenderest, the noblest, the loveliest, the truest
sons and daughters of France, all these move in lurid procession
before our startled eyes. Mirabeau, Danton, Robespierre, rise
before us now terrible phantoms, but once, more terrible reali-
ties. Charlotte Corday, the peasant girl, leaving her rural home,
seeking admittance to Marat's chamber, thrusting the dagger into
his guilty heart, and then calmly waiting for her own execution,
which came so soon; the awful tan-yard, where the skins of the
guillotine's victims were transformed into a "fine soft leather,
which made excellent breeches;" the Hall of the Jacobins; the
procession of black tumbrils winding daily through the streets
of Paris, bearing poets, nobles, statesmen, even the silly king
and the sorrowful queen, to the place of public execution; these
are but a few of the flame-lit scenes of the Reign of Terror.

Yet all this was civilization, progress, political birth-throes,
the regeneration of the French, the richest, the gayest, the most
brilliant, the most highly civilized people of Europe. How
much worse was the '92 of the Ohio valley than the '93 of
France? Upon the surface, the savages of the Revolution were
blacker, bloodier, than the red men of America. The Philosophy
of History steps in, and laying her hand alike upon the raging
madmen of France and the untutored savages of America, says
to us, JUDGE NOT!

KILLIG AN INDIAN SCOUT IN OHIO VALLEY

CHAPTER VII.

THE COURAGE OF KENTON.

AITHFUL, rugged, and bold, the character of Simon Kenton is rarely equaled among the pioneers of the Ohio valley. He was by birth a Virginian, born in 1755, the long-remembered year of Braddock's defeat. He was reared an ignorant farm boy. The doors of a school-house were never opened to him, and labor early marked him for her child. Beneath the rough youth's exterior throbbed a warm and affectionate heart.

In the neighborhood of Kenton's home lived a young lady, whose spirited manners, personal charms, and coquettish arts had fascinated many a less susceptible young man than Kenton. The maiden of the frontier, like others of her sex in gentler situations, is full of stratagems. This belle of the border pretended to be interested in Kenton, who was but sixteen years old, and in another young fellow named Leitchman, some years Kenton's senior. All her ingenuity was exerted to bring about a conflict between these two suitors. She succeeded. Kenton sent a challenge to his rival. He repaired to the appointed spot alone, and was surprised to find Leitchman accompanied by a number of his friends, who at once assailed him with a volley of insults. Kenton, burning with jealousy and wrath, stripped himself of all but his pants and prepared to fight. The combat had proceeded but a few moments when Kenton's superior skill became manifest. Seeing their friend about to be punished severely, Leitchman's companions jumped upon Kenton and pounded, beat, and kicked him until he was nearly dead.

Kenton recovered from his injuries, but not from the insult. In the following spring he went over to Leitchman's house, and announced that he was ready to fight it out. In the combat which followed, Leitchman, more wary than before, succeeded in throwing Kenton to the ground, and at once sprang on him with malignant fury. Kenton lay still, enduring this severe punishment till his eye caught sight of a bush growing near by. He at once conceived a terrible revenge. He managed to lure his rival, who had remarkably long hair, to the spot where the bush grew. Watching his opportunity, he made a sudden and violent effort, sprang to his feet, pushed his foe into the bush, and quickly wrapped his long hair around its thick, tangled branches. Leitchman gave an unearthly roar of pain.

In that moment the long-suppressed rage burst forth from Kenton's heart. He took revenge terrible and complete for all his injuries, and leaving Leitchman for dead, he cast a last glance at his gasping foe, and then fled. Fled, he knew not whither, but any place to escape the pursuers with which his imagination peopled the woods through which he sped. Day and night passed, and he paused not.

In time he reached a region where the settlers were talking about the wonderful country of Kantuckee. In their stories it was an earthly paradise, an Eden in the wilderness. He fell in with two explorers, Yager and Strader. Yager had been a captive among the Indians, and claimed to have visited this El Dorado of the west. Fired by his glowing descriptions, his two companions resolved to join him in his search for this wonderful region, where fruits blushed unseen on the branches of trees which the hand of man had never planted; where fields of golden grain sprang spontaneously from the fertile soil and ripened untended beneath the summer sun; where the forests were stocked with supplies of rare and noble game, exhaustless and unequaled.

A boat was built, provisions gathered, and the trio of excited adventurers commenced their journey down the Ohio. Days

21

went by, but the Land of Promise did not appear. For weary weeks they journeyed, but Yager, whose memory of the beauty and luxuriance of the region was so vivid, was unable to locate it. Worn out with searching for a country which was a myth, they turned their attention to hunting and trapping on the great Kanawha. This profitable occupation they followed for two years, exchanging their furs with the traders at Fort Pitt for such things as they needed.

One evening in March, 1773, they were lying around their camp-fire in the forest, when a dozen shots were fired at them from the darkness. Strader was shot dead. Kenton and Yager took to flight, leaving behind them guns, ammunition, and all the accumulation of the two years' work. For five days they wandered through the woods, tortured with hunger and benumbed with cold. At sunset on the last day, to their great joy, they fell in with a party of traders.

Kenton soon obtained another rifle, and again began his forest life. He took part in Dunmore's war in 1774, acting as a scout. In the summer of 1775 he determined to join a party of explorers and again make search for the country which Yager had described. By careful exploration of the country for miles on either side of the Ohio, they at length reached a region which indeed afforded some basis for Yager's tales. In the neighborhood of what is now Maysville, Kentucky, the soil was found to be of wonderful fertility, far exceeding any thing in the Ohio valley, a reputation which it bears to this day. Here too, the eyes of the hunters brightened at the sight of vast herds of buffalo. Elk of rare size, were found in great numbers. The explorers were beside themselves. On the site of what is now Washington, Mason County, Kentucky, they cleared an acre of ground, and planted it with Indian corn. Here, in comfortable cabins, they made their home. Such fortune in hunting as they had surpassed their wildest dreams.

One day Kenton, while roaming along the banks of the Licking River, heard moans from the direction of some bushes.

Curious and alarmed, the trapper made his way with caution to the spot. He was astonished to find two white men lying on the ground, almost destitute of clothing and emaciated by starvation. The hunter hurriedly prepared them some food, and then started to conduct them to his cabin. The journey proved too much for the exhausted men, and a camp had to be pitched in the woods.

The unfortunate strangers related their story. Some time previous they had been descending the Ohio, when their boat capsized. All their supplies were lost. They saved their lives by swimming. But the hardships of the wilderness, finding them without food, cover, or arms, "o'ercame them quite." They had given up all hope when found by Kenton. The hunter informed them of his station, and invited them to join him and his companions there. One of the men accepted the invitation, but the other declared his intention to abandon the forest life forever.

Leaving Hendricks in the camp at the Blue Licks, without a gun, but well supplied with provisions, Kenton and his two companions, who had been with him on the hunt, courteously accompanied Fitzpatrick, who was eager to commence his homeward journey, as far as the "Point," by which name the site of Maysville was known. Bidding him farewell, they retraced their steps to the camp to rejoin Hendricks. To their great concern it was found deserted. The tent was thrown down and its contents scattered about. A number of bullets were found lodged in the neighboring trees. At a little distance was a ravine. A cloud of thick, white smoke, as if from a newly kindled fire, hovered over it.

That Hendricks had been captured by Indians was plain. That they themselves were in danger was no less so, and a hasty retreat was at once begun. They were halted at a distance of a few miles by some stinging rebukes from Kenton, who declared that common humanity demanded that an effort be made to save Hendricks. Caution compelled them to wait till nightfall. Under Kenton's lead they then made their way back to the camp. The fire was still dimly glowing. No Indians were near.

As the men proceeded to reconnoiter the locality, one of them kicked a round object lying on the ground. It rolled nearer the fire. He stooped to pick it up. He saw what the object was. It was Hendricks's skull! The poor fellow had been roasted and eaten. Sadly enough Kenton and his comrades made their way to the cabin at Washington. Not for several months did they behold the face of a human being. One lazy September day, Kenton was startled to discover a man at some distance. The stranger came nearer. His complexion was white. He informed Kenton that there were other white men in Kentucky besides himself and his companions. Daniel Boone had already founded a settlement in the interior. Tired of solitude, Kenton and his companions broke up the settlement at Washington, and repaired to Boonsborough.

In 1778 Kenton met with a remarkable adventure. He was with an expedition led by Daniel Boone against an Indian town on Paint Creek. While scouting some distance ahead of the main force, he was startled by a loud laugh. To conceal himself in a thicket was the work of a moment. Two large Indians mounted on one small pony rode along the path, laughing and joking in high glee. Kenton fired at short range, killing not only the first Indian, through whose body the ball passed, but wounding the second.

The scout sprang forward to scalp the wounded Indian, when a noise from a thicket attracted his attention. He turned to find two guns aimed at him by a couple of stalwart savages. Kenton jumped to one side just in time to miss the deadly balls. Without delay he sought the best shelter the place afforded. Before his gun was reloaded a dozen Indians were on a dead run toward him. The result would in all probability have been fatal to Kenton, had not Boone's party, alarmed by the sight of the riderless pony, which had galloped toward them when relieved of its riders, hurried to the rescue. Several Indians fell dead at the first fire.

Knowing that his approach was now discovered at the Indian town, Boone resolved on instant retreat. Not so with Kenton. He and a friend named Montgomery left the party, and proceeded alone to a neighborhood of the village. All day they lay in ambush in a corn-field, hoping that some Indian would come out to gather roasting ears. Disappointed in this expectation, they entered the town after night, captured four good horses, made a rapid night ride to the Ohio, which they swam in safety, and on the second day reached Logan's Fort with their booty.

No sooner was the restless Kenton through with this adventure than he set out on a scout with Montgomery and a young man named Clark to an Indian town on the Little Maumee River, against which an expedition was contemplated by the whites. Under cover of night a thorough investigation of the place and the number of its warriors was made. Having accomplished this, the scouts might have returned in safety. But the temptation to steal some horses was too strong to be resisted. In their greed they determined to take every horse in the village. Unfortunately they had attempted too much, and were discovered. The scouts saw their peril and rode for their lives, but were unwilling to abandon a single horse. Two rode in front and led the horses, while the third plied his whip from behind.

They were checked in their furious career by a swamp, in an attempt to avoid which they occupied the whole night. On the morning of the second day they had reached the Ohio. The wind was high, the river rough, the crossing dangerous. Kenton resolved to swim the horses across, while his companions hurriedly framed a raft on which to transport their guns and baggage. Again and again Kenton forced the horses into the water, but as often the animals, frightened by the boisterous waves, turned about, and swam back to shore.

No time was to be lost. The Indians were in hot pursuit.

Instead of abandoning the horses, which could not be made to cross the river, the trio still clung to their plunder and started down the banks of the Ohio. When the setting sun flung his red radiance over the stormy river, tipping the waves with crimson splendor, the horse-thieves still found themselves unable to cross. Totally infatuated, the three men encamped for the night. At dawn they awoke, rejoiced to find the river as placid as the blue morning sky which arched above them. But horses have memories, and the captive equines, mindful of their former experience, stubbornly refused to enter the water. Blows and curses were unavailing. For the white men but one course remained. Each mounted a horse, determined to ride to a point opposite Louisville, where they could obtain transportation.

It was too late. Scarcely had they ridden a hundred yards when the furious pursuers were heard in their rear. The fortunes of the scouts were widely different. Clark escaped. Montgomery was killed. Kenton was taken prisoner. Among the stolen horses was a wild colt, a vicious and powerful animal. Kenton was placed astride this animal, his hands tied behind him, and his feet bound together under the horse's belly. The animal was then turned loose without rein or bridle. A terrible cut from a whip caused it to dash furiously into the forest. On, on it went, its defenseless rider being scratched, bruised, and torn by the overhanging limbs of the trees.

Though blinded by the blood which flowed down his lacerated face, Kenton escaped without fatal injury. He was taken to the famous Indian town of Old Chillicothe. For amusement his guards beat his naked back and shoulders with hickory switches. Of all the borderers of the time no one was better known, more greatly feared, and so bitterly hated as Simon Kenton.

At his appearance the inhabitants of the town were beside themselves with rage. Their fury found no words adequate to give it utterance. Foaming at the mouth, they gave it vent in inarticulate and blood-curdling howls and curses. A stake was driven in the ground. To this the captive was tied, with his hands extended above him and fastened to the top of the stake. He was painted black. Instead of the torture fires being applied at once, the savages, choked with speechless rage, danced and howled around him until midnight, pelting him with stones, lacerating him with switches, and searing his body with red-hot irons.

The rare pleasure of the occasion was prolonged by his grim captors. In the morning he was ordered to run the gauntlet. At the beat of a drum he started down the line of warriors, armed with clubs, hoe handles, tomahawks, and butcher knives. Again and again he was felled to the ground by his ferocious assailants. When the race was over, and he lay bloody and unconscious in the corner of a cabin, a council was held in the village. The assembled warriors were unanimous in their opinion that such fun had not been enjoyed for many a year. They generously resolved to share the sport with the other villages. Kenton was accordingly dragged about from town to town. Once the poor man attempted an escape. The pursuit was instant and keen.

Kenton put forth all his powers. At every step he remembered that he was flying from the stake and the red-hot irons. But he was retaken and carried back—back to beatings and bruising, back to searing irons and the cruel gauntlet, back to the dreadful stake and the torturing flames.

He was taken to Wapputomica, where his execution was to end his sufferings. He arrived there just as Simon Girty, the notorious renegade, returned from an unsuccessful expedition. When the angry monster saw Kenton, he saluted him by knocking him down with his brutal fist. Too weak to rise, Kenton called to Girty for protection. For once in his life a prayer for mercy was not unheard by Girty. He paused. He scanned the emaciated stranger closely. He asked his name. As the word "Kenton" was feebly murmured, Girty, with a start of surprise, seized the fallen man in his arms and lifted him to a couch. The savages looked on in wonder. Such a thing had never been known before. Bloodier than the bloodiest, crueler than the cruelest, had ever been Simon Girty, a savage born amid civilization, an Indian who was the child of white parents.

The white chief sent forth a summons for a council. The dark audience assembled. On the rows of faces ranged round the room, rigid as if carved in ebony, not a trace of curiosity could be seen. But beneath every blanket beat a heart filled with fierce and cynical wonder. For some moments there was silence in the council hall.

Then Girty arose. He strode forward to the center of the room. He recounted the story of his own life; of how he had renounced the cause of the white man, and become an Indian of Indians; of his enormous services to the Wyandots, and of the rows of white men's scalps which decorated his cabin. He asked if he had ever been accused of mercy to the race from which he sprang. Yet, for this single time, he had a favor to ask. That favor was the life of a friend. That friend was Simon Kenton, the wretched captive lying there on that blanket. Many years before, said the orator, in rugged and convulsive eloquence, he and that captive had been brothers. They had slept under the same blanket. They had hunted through the same forests. They had dwelt in the same wigwam. For his own sake he asked that the life of the captive be spared.

Girty's influence was great. But the Wyandots regarded Kenton as their arch-enemy. The debate raged long and loud. At length the vote was taken. The captive was saved. Girty took Kenton to his own wigwam. For three weeks he remained there, recovering from his injuries.

At the end of twenty-one days a new war party returned. Many of their number had been slain. The families of the dead demanded vengeance. A cry rang through the village for the life of Kenton. A council was called. Speaker after speaker arose, and with vehement gesture and heavy emphasis, argued that Kenton must be put to death. Girty again put forth all his powers to save his friend. But he was overwhelmed. The sentence of death was passed.

Kenton was bound and marched away to another village. An old Indian was sitting by the roadside. As he caught sight of Kenton a spasm of passionate hate convulsed his sullen features. He sprang forward, and with a blow from his tomahawk cut open Kenton's shoulder, breaking the bone, and almost severing the arm from the body. In this condition he was driven on to Sandusky, arriving there in the evening. Arrangements were at once made to burn him alive on the following morning.

By strange coincidence a British Indian agent was in the town. Learning of Kenton's arrival, he at once demanded the captive, in order that the commandant at Detroit might obtain from him information of the enemy. The Indians consented to give him up only on condition that he be returned to them. That condition was never kept. He remained at Detroit, under mild restraint, from October, 1777, to June, 1778. In the latter month he resolved upon an escape, taking into his confidence two young Kentuckians, captives like himself. By great adroitness Kenton managed to get possession of three guns and some ammunition. After a journey of thirty days through a wilderness infested by Indian war parties, the three refugees arrived at Louisville.

"Thus," says a writer, "terminated one of the most remarkable series of adventure in the whole realm of western history. Kenton was eight times exposed to the gauntlet, and three times tied to the stake for execution. For three weeks he vibrated between life and death. Yet, amid the changes of fickle fortune, he remained perfectly passive. No wisdom, foresight, or exertion could have saved him. Fortune, and fortune alone, fought his battle from first to last."

For many years, Kenton continued to be one of the most formidable Indian fighters of the valley. Through the details of his eventful career we may not follow him. One incident is worth mentioning. While at Detroit, an English officer observing his fondness for smoking, and the difficulty of lighting his pipe, presented him with a fine burning glass or lens, by which the tobacco could easily be kindled from the rays of the sun. Two or three years afterward Kenton was again taken prisoner. He was bound hand and foot, preparatory to an immediate execution. As his last request to his captors, he asked the privilege of smoking his pipe. He placed the long, wooden stem in his mouth. The chief handed him the customary flint, steel, and tinder for lighting the tobacco.

With a gesture of indifference, Kenton refused the implements, to the great astonishment of the savage. Extending his hand toward the midday sun, cleverly grasping the burning-glass, he adroitly focused the rays in the pipe bowl and was quickly puffing clouds of smoke from his lips. The Indians were dumfounded. Not having noticed the glass, they supposed he had lighted his pipe by letting the sunlight pass through the circle formed by his thumb and forefinger. Awe-stricken and amazed, they grouped together at a little distance, with mutterings and grunts of wonder.

In a little while, Kenton refilled his pipe, and repeated the trick, accompanying it with three or four cries, mysterious and startling to the Indians. No one understood better than Kenton the superstition of their minds. Seizing his advantage, he made a sweeping gesture, clasping his hands above his head, and transferring the glass to his left hand. In a moment he had kindled some dry leaves at his side into a flame.

Struggling to his feet, tied though they were, and giving a terrific leap, such as Kenton alone could make, he brought himself to the pile of fagots which had been gathered for his torture. In a moment a flame blazed up around the stake as if the victim were already fastened to it. Kenton then beckoned to the chief to unbind his ankles. The mystified Indian durst not disobey such a man. While fumbling at the thongs, Kenton raised his burning-glass, and in a moment raised a blister on the

A WESTERN MAZEPPA—SIMON KENTON A PRISONER.

red man's wrist. He jerked his hand away with a howl of pain only to feel a spot of fire on his head. This was too much. The chief and his companions hurriedly got behind the nearest trees. Kenton then unbound his own ankles. Waving his arms towards the sun, he withdrew the stopple from a powder-horn, dropped by the Indians, focused the sunbeams upon the powder within, and shook his fist at his foes. In an instant the powder-horn exploded with a flash and roar. Not only had the powder-horn disappeared. The Indians left at the same instant. Kenton was free.

The later career of Kenton is a strange illustration of the reverses in the fortunes of men. When the Indian wars were over, the brave and generous Kenton found himself without an occupation. The lands which he had bought were lost to him through technical flaws in the title. He had braved the tomahawk, the gauntlet, and the stake in vain. The people who now came in to occupy and possess the fair region, to redeem which from the savages he had devoted the best years of his life, found no use for the old scout. His very body was taken for debt. He was imprisoned for a year on the very spot where he had built the first cabin, planted the first corn, and fought the savages in a hundred fierce encounters.

Beggared by losses and law-suits, he moved to Ohio about the beginning of this century. He was elected brigadier-general of the State militia, and was a soldier of the war of 1812. In 1810 he joined the Methodist Episcopal Church, and ever after lived a consistent Christian life. After the war of 1812 he returned to his lonely cabin in the woods, near Urbana, Ohio. In 1820 he moved to Mad River, in sight of the old Indian town of Wappatomica, where he had once been tied to the stake. Even here he was pursued by judgments and executions from the courts of Kentucky. He still had some large tracts of mountain lands in Kentucky which were forfeited for taxes. He tried boring for salt on them, but failed. His last resource was an appeal to the Kentucky Legislature to release the forfeiture.

"So," says McClung, "in 1824, when about seventy years old, he mounted his sorry old horse, and, in his tattered garments, commenced his weary pilgrimage. The second night he stopped at the house of James Galloway, of Xenia, Ohio, an old friend and pioneer.

"Kenton at last reached Frankfort, now become a thrifty and flourishing city. Here he was utterly unknown. All his old friends had departed. His dilapidated appearance and the sorry condition of his horse and its wretched equipments only provoked mirth. The grizzled old pioneer was like Rip Van Winkle appearing after his long sleep. He wandered up and down the streets, 'the observed of all observers.' The very boys followed him. At length, the scarred old warrior was recognized by General Fletcher, an old companion-in-arms. He grasped him by the hand, led him to a tailor-shop, bought him a suit of clothes and hat, and, after he was dressed, took him to the State capitol.

"Here he was placed in the speaker's chair, and introduced to a crowded assembly of judges, citizens, and legislators, as the second pioneer of Kentucky. The simple-minded veteran used to say afterwards that 'it was the very proudest day of his life,' and ten years subsequently, his friend Hinde asserted, he was wearing the self-same hat and clothes. His lands were at once released, and shortly after, by the warm exertion of some of his friends, a pension from Congress of two hundred and fifty dollars was obtained, securing his old age from absolute want.

"Without any further marked notice, Kenton lived in his humble cabin until 1836, when, at the venerable old age of eighty-one, he breathed his last, surrounded by his family and neighbors, and supported by the consolations of the Gospel. He died in sight of the very spot where the savages, nearly sixty years previous, proposed to torture him to death.

"General Kenton was of fair complexion, six feet one inch in height. He stood and walked very erect, and, in the prime of life, weighed about a hundred and ninety pounds. He never was inclined to be corpulent, although of sufficient fullness to form a graceful person. He had a soft, tremulous voice, very pleasing to the hearer; auburn hair and laughing gray eyes, which appeared to fascinate the beholder. He was a pleasant, good-humored, and obliging companion. When excited, or provoked to anger, which was seldom the case, the fiery glance of his eye would almost curdle the blood of those with whom he came in contact. His wrath, when aroused, was a tornado. In his dealings he was perfectly honest. His confidence in man and his credulity were such, that the same man might cheat him twenty times—and, if he professed friendship, might still continue to cheat him."

Such was the man after whom was named the county of Kenton, Kentucky.

CHAPTER VIII.

BRADY, THE BACKWOODSMAN.

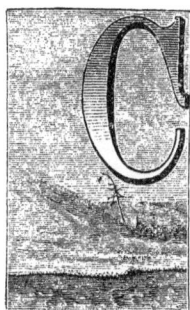

APTAIN SAMUEL BRADY, the hero of this narrative, was born in 1758, in the town of Shippensburg, Pennsylvania. John Brady, his father, had before him been a brave and adventurous man. On the eleventh day of April, 1779, this gentleman, being in command of an exposed post, set out for Fort Augusta, to procure supplies of provisions. He had loaded his wagon heavily, and with several guards started early in the afternoon to return.

At a certain point the road forked. Those in charge of the wagon went one way, while Brady and a companion named Smith, who were on horseback, took the shorter cut. The spot was lonely. As the two men rode slowly along, Brady related to his companion an incident in his life which had made a deep impression on his mind.

The story he told was as follows: In 1776, information had been received at Fort Augusta, of the approach of Indians. Runners were at once dispatched to the neighboring settlements. In the afternoon Brady remembered that they had forgotten to send word to a trading post, occupied by a Dutchman named Derr. He threw himself into his saddle to carry the message.

Arriving at his destination, Brady found the yard full of Indians, stretched out on the ground, brutally drunk, while Derr sat calmly by, smoking his pipe, as if nothing unusual had occurred. Brady rebuked him sternly. The Dutchman replied

that the Indians had come and informed him that they would
kill him unless he gave them liquor. Acting on the hint, he
had politely rolled out a barrel of rum for his guests' entertainment. As he spoke, a drunken Indian, with a long scar on

DEATH OF JAMES BRADY.

his left cheek, staggered toward the half-emptied barrel to take
another drink. Brady, however, interfered, and upset the barrel,
spilling its contents. The Indian broke out into curses, and,
with bitter emphasis, told Brady that the day would yet come
when he would regret that act.

Ever since that time, said the Captain to his companion, the memory of that threat had haunted him. Knowing the Indian character, he believed that if that savage should ever chance to meet him, the threat would be fulfilled by an attempt on his life. By this time the riders had reached a place of exceeding wildness. At that moment three rifles were fired in quick succession. Brady dropped lifeless on the road. Smith bounded away. Momentarily glancing back, he saw an Indian standing over his dead friend flourishing a bloody scalp. He also saw that the savage had a long and prominent scar on the left side of his face.

Such was the fate of the father of Captain Samuel Brady. Only the year before, his younger brother, James, had also been killed by Indians. The young man, with three or four companions, had stood their guns against a tree. An Indian suddenly fired, at which the others fled. Brady, however, seized a gun, and shot the savage, only to find himself left to contend alone against a host of enemies. Two other guns he also fired at his foes with fatal effect, but while reaching for the fourth gun was knocked senseless. He was tomahawked, scalped, and left for dead. Coming to conciousness, the plucky fellow managed to crawl to a settler's cabin. He lived three or four days, and then died from his wounds.

In conformity to the wild customs of the frontier, the elder brother took a solemn oath that the remainder of his life should be devoted to wreaking a dreadful vengeance on the race whose members had thus twice desolated the family circle.

In 1780 Brady was dispatched from Fort Pitt to the distant towns of the Sandusky on a scout. He chose for his companions a few men and four Chickasaw Indians. The season was wet. The streams were swollen beyond their banks. Owing to several mishaps, their provisions ran low. The chart of the country which Brady carried proved to be defective and misleading. In time, however, they reached the neighborhood of the Indian towns.

22

While stealing through the woods, the sound of human voices broke upon them. Leaving his comrades behind him, Brady slipped forward to make observations. Sitting beside the embers of a camp-fire he found two squaws. He turned back unnoticed, leaving them unharmed. Coming back to his companions, he detected by their sullen looks and gruff answers that something had happened. The young scout sat down unconcernedly to clean his rifle. For some time nothing was said. He then called on the men to hand him their ammunition pouches, in order to make an equal distribution of the powder on hand. Instead of obeying the command, the men flatly refused. They informed Brady that the faithless Chickasaws had deserted, taking with them all the provisions, and that instead of continuing the scout, they had resolved on flight.

To this startling announcement Brady replied by handing the speaker his powder-horn, and asked him to see how much powder it contained. There was not a grain left. Raising his gun to his shoulder, Brady announced that he had one load yet in the weapon and *that* he would use to maintain his authority. The men, awed into admiration for their young leader, yielded. Matters having been thus settled, Brady hid all of his company but one man in a ravine. He and his companion then started to the village, wading the river to an island opposite the town, where they lay during the night.

In the morning a dense fog covered the landscape. At noon it lifted. The astonished spies discovered a vast concourse of Indians, evidently just returned from an expedition against the frontiers, bringing with them a number of fine horses. The crowd was wild with hilarity over some races, by which they were testing the animals and celebrating the occasion. That night Brady, having accomplished the object of his journey, rejoined his men and commenced the return trip. Entirely destitute of provisions they nevertheless subsisted for a time on strawberries. Only one rifle-charge was left in the party.

The loaded gun was given to Brady. Discovering a deer-track, the scout followed it, and, coming within sight of the animal, attempted to fire. To his intense disappointment the gun failed to go off, and the deer fled. Brady picked the touch-hole of the weapon, and was starting in renewed pursuit of the game, when he discovered a party of Indians. They were led by a large and powerful savage on horseback, carrying in his arms a white child. The child's mother rode behind him on the horse. Ten warriors followed the leader.

Brady was a kind-hearted man. Moreover, he was young, and, therefore, gallant. From his concealment his quick eye perceived that the woman had been brutally mistreated. One of her arms was broken. Her face was a mass of bruises. Brady forgot himself. He raised his gun, and aiming carefully for fear of injury to the mother or her child, fired, the unerring bullet plunging into the heart of the savage. The Indians were paralyzed by fright and confusion.

Seizing his opportunity, Brady rushed forth, caught the child in one arm, the woman in the other, and disappeared in the brush amid a shower of balls. He was infinitely disgusted to find that his cowardly men had fled, allowing two prisoners to escape. Nevertheless he made his way with his two helpless companions to Fort McIntosh, and from there to Pittsburgh, where he received the congratulations of General Broadhead.

Brady's next service was a scout, with a man named Phouts, in the direction of the Susquehanna. Their start was made two hours before day. At evening they halted by a small creek and built a fire. While out hunting they discovered a deer-lick, and, as a consequence, brought into camp some excellent venison. The following day, a blue smoke, floating above the top of a distant forest, indicated an Indian camp. They approached cautiously and discovered, to their surprise, one old Indian sitting by the fire mending his moccasins. Phouts prepared to fire, but Brady prevented him from doing so, and the two men left unobserved.

A few hours later they came upon a well-defined Indian trail.

Brady noted the signs, and became convinced that a strong party of Indians had passed there the previous day. He at once detei mined to take the old savage captive, and return forthwith to Pittsburgh. Early in the morning they returned to the Indian's camp, and found the savage lying on his back by the fire. Brady crept forward toward the Indian, and when within a few feet, gave a whoop and jumped on the prostrate savage. A brief struggle ended in the old fellow being strongly tied.

On being assured that he would be taken to Pittsburgh unharmed, the captive politely pulled aside some bushes, and pointed out a most excellent canoe. The trio embarked, floating down the creek to the spot where they had encamped the previous night, and landed. Here they encamped until morning. Brady rose early and went up the creek to where they had left some venison hanging on a tree, which they wanted for breakfast.

Meanwhile, an interesting little occurrence took place in Brady's absence. The wily Indian complained to Phouts, who was a dull Dutchman, that his cords hurt him, and begged his guard to loosen them for a few moments. The Dutchman, charmed by the docile behavior and extreme humility of the prisoner, took off the cords entirely.

The old man sat meekly on the ground without a suspicious movement. At a moment when Phouts stooped to fix the fire, the Indian gave a lightning spring toward the Dutchman's gun, which was leaning against a tree, seized it, and fired at point-blank range. In the hurry his aim was bad, and the ball only took off a part of the Dutchman's bullet-pouch. Phouts rushed on the savage, and, with one blow from his tomahawk, clove asunder his skull. Brady, alarmed by the report, hurried back, elieved to find that nothing worse had happened. Their return to Pittsburgh was made without further incident.

Brady's genius for scouting was soon recognized, and he was constantly employed on the most perilous missions. On one occasion his bravery almost brought about a fatal result. He was taken captive by a band of Indians, near Beaver River. He and four companions had come upon an Indian camp. A fire was burning, and near by lay some tempting deer meat. Their hunger overcame their prudence, and the men, roasting the venison, were soon in the midst of a hearty meal.

It is said that one of the men stopped eating, and suggested that the meat might be poisoned. At that instant there was a report from a dozen rifles. Brady's four companions dropped dead. The Indians, recognizing him, had saved his life only to reserve him for the pleasure of torture. He was taken to their village, given the usual reception of blows and beatings, and was forced to run the gauntlet. The traditional stake, with a pile of fagots, was prepared. Previous to commencing the torture, he was stripped and a circle of Indians formed around him for a fantastic dance.

The torture fires were already blazing. He felt that his end was at hand, but still, with cool head and fearless eye, he calculated the chances of escape. When the dance was at its height, a squaw, carrying in her arms a young child, strode up to Brady and hit him a terrible blow with a war-club. She was about to repeat the outrage when Brady, gathering all his strength, sprang upon her, tore the child from her arms, and threw it clear over the circle of dancers into the flames beyond. The Indians, struck with horror, rushed, as by one thought, to rescue the child. This Brady had foreseen. In the midst of the confusion he dashed through the crowd, overturning every one in his way, and disappearing in a neighboring ravine.

Another story related of Brady places him in company with sixteen companions. The party was encamped for a night. Towards morning a gun was heard, and the scouts quickly withdrew to an elevated bluff. Beneath them they discovered six Indians standing around a fire. Brady ordered his men to lie down while he kept watch. At day-break he placed them side by side, with himself at the end of the line. At an opportune moment Brady touched, with his elbow, the man on his

left, who in turn communicated it to his neighbor, and so on
down the line. When the nudge reached the last man, he fired,
followed by all the others. Every Indian in the camp was
killed, with perhaps, a single exception.

Brady and two companions, passing along the northern shore
of the Ohio, once reached the neighborhood of a cabin occupied
by a man named Gray. Suddenly Brady detected the presence of Indians. In the moment of concealing himself Brady
saw Gray approaching carelessly on horseback. As the hunter
passed him Brady sprang out, dragged him off his horse,
and whispered, "I am Sam Brady. For heaven's sake, keep
quiet."

That this summary treatment saved Gray's life there can be
no doubt. The four men approached the site of the cabin and
discovered it to be a heap of embers. Of Gray's wife and children there was no trace. Gray, frantic with grief, begged his
companions to join him in pursuit of the abductors. To Brady
such an appeal was never made in vain. In two hours they
came upon the Indians, who were there in force. There, bound
hand and foot, sat Gray's wife and children.

The number of the savages so much exceeded that of Brady's
party that a night attack was the only hope for the rescue of
the captives: At an auspicious moment the four avengers stole
noiselessly into the camp and distributed themselves among the
sleepers. At a given signal from Brady each man tomahawked
the nearest Indians. The survivors, leaping to their feet,
bounded into the forest, leaving their captives in the hands of
the white men.

Probably the most famous of Brady's exploits is that known
as "Brady's Leap." He had been pursued by Indians for some
distance from Sandusky, and, at last, seemed to be hedged in
in all directions. It was a principle with the scout to never
surrender. Taking in the situation with a quick glance, he
bounded off toward a creek, at a point where it rushed through
a rocky gorge. From bank to bank was more than twenty-five

feet. On his way, Brady hurled two savages to the ground. The whole swarm were following him with wild yells, believing that when he reached the brink of the chasm, he must be forced to pause and become their captive. Rushing forward with the greatest impetuosity, Brady collected all his energies, and as his foot touched the verge of the precipice, he gave a terrific leap, catching the bushes on the steep, rocky cliff of the opposite bank, and quickly scrambling to his feet.

BRADY'S LEAP.

The Indians were dumfounded. It was not long, however, till they made their way around, and were again in pursuit of Brady. For his part, he had received a bullet in his leg as he jumped the chasm, and found himself unable to maintain his terrific speed. He made his way to a body of water, which still bears the name of "Brady's Lake." He unhesitatingly plunged in, diving to a spot covered by pond lilies. Here he found that he could keep his face under water by breathing through the hollow stem of a weed. The Indians followed his bloody track to the edge of the lake, and concluded that he had committed suicide. When their pursuit was abandoned Brady came out of the water and made his way home.

In 1786 Captain Brady married a Miss Drucilla Swearingen. Her father, a prominent soldier of the Revolution, objected to the match, but the beautiful young lady, enamored with the prowess and prestige of her lover, married him. The fond and lovely wife suffered greatly in mind during the absences of her brave husband on lengthy scouts. He was always a little lame from the wound received at the time of his famous leap. He also became quite deaf in his old age. This he attributed to his having remained so long under the water of the lake. His last years were spent at West Liberty, West Virginia, where he died.

CHAPTER IX.

THE DAYS OF DANIEL BOONE.

A BOOK of American pioneers would be incomplete without a sketch of Daniel Boone, the pioneer of Kentucky. It is not because he had such thrilling adventures, for the experiences of many of the borderers far surpassed those of Boone in wild heroism and wonderful feats. It is the character of Boone which impressed itself upon the minds of his contemporaries, and gives him such a prominent place in the history of the Ohio valley His grandfather came to this country from England. No fur ther reason need be sought for this move on the part of the old gentleman than the fact that he had nineteen children. He possessed peculiar qualifications for the population of a new country.

Our hero was born in Berks County, Pennsylvania, but his family removed at an early day to North Carolina. His education consisted in a short term at a school, opened by a wandering Irishman. The building was a square log structure, with a fire-place occupying one side of the room, and holding a log ten feet long. One day young Boone found himself at a spot where his schoolmaster had been observed to frequently stop. Under some vines he discovered, to his surprise, a bottle of whisky. That night Master Boone took some comrades into his confidence, and poured into the bottle a quantity of tartar-emetic.

Having set up the job, the boys waited on the following morning for the *dénouement*. During recess the boys, with many a poke in one another's ribs, observed the unsuspecting pedagogue going to the spot where the bottle was hidden. He reappeared in a few moments with his face red as fire. The school was called together more quickly than usual, and the urchins trembled on their puncheon seats. The first two scholars made wretched failures of their lessons, and received terrific thrashings. Boone's turn came next. The Irishman's face was as white as paper. Boone's head was buzzing with curiosity about the whisky bottle, and he too failed. The master began to whip his pupil when the medicine began to take fearful effect. Boone revenged himself for his beating by throwing the wretched man down, at which signal the whole school joined in a shout and ran off.

We have one other brief glimpse of Boone's boyhood. One evening he failed to return from a hunt. His father and neighbors set out to search for the missing lad, who was but fourteen years old. At the end of two days the father found the lad living in a temporary hovel of sods and branches. Numerous skins of wild animals decorated the place. A piece of venison was roasting at the fire. Here the boy was enjoying himself all alone.

When he arrived at manhood, Boone married Rebecca Bryan. The first explorers brought back glowing reports of Kentucky, and in 1769, Boone, fascinated by these stories, with five companions, started to view this inland paradise themselves. They built a cabin on Red River, to protect themselves from a tremendous rain, which fell steadily for two weeks. Here they remained almost stationary for six months. The vast droves of buffalo and shadowy herds of deer supplied the men with profitable employment and exciting pleasure.

On the 22d of December, 1769, Boone and Stuart resolved to explore the interior of the country. In all the six months of their residence in the lovely region, neither the figure or even a foot-print of a savage had been seen. After a few days' journey, the men discovered a lofty mountain, which they climbed, in order to obtain a view of the country. Standing on its top, their dark figures outlined against the sky, and visible for many miles, the hunters' eyes were gladdened with a view of the fairest landscape in the world. Sloping hills, alternated with lovely valleys; leafless forests, with wide extended plains. Far to the north rolled the peaceful Ohio, beyond which lay expanses of a country destined to be the seat of empire, the home of busy millions.

Coming down from the mountain, little suspecting any danger, the two hunters were startled by a terrific yell just to their right. At the same instant the bushes parted, and dark forms emerging quickly, surrounded them, and they were taken prisoners.

The captives were as yet ignorant of Indian customs. They knew not one word of the language. As the howling captors bound them and marched them off to the forest, Boone did not know but that it might be to his death. He had, however, the cold and self-possessed temper which has in all times characterized men of action and leadership, a disposition which knows no special joy nor disheartening depression. There was nothing to be done except to obey his savage guards.

Manners are an art. It has been said that there is a mode of conduct possible which will blind the shrewdest insight and foil the most expert observer. The popular notion of the art of manners assumes that it belongs solely to the refined, the elegant; that its home is in society, and its disciples the votaries of fashion. Yet the languid belle and the prancing dandy are by no means the only nor the real experts in manners. The shaggy backwoodsman, dressed in the skin of wild animals, speaking in a peculiar dialect of frontier phraseology, and passing his life in restless warfare with a hideous and blood-thirsty foe, practices the so-called parlor art with infinitely more zeal and success than the empty-headed throngs of fashionable society.

Boone, on this occasion, revealed his superior skill in this regard. Though his heart was full of apprehension, his demeanor indicated the most fearless indifference. He acted

BOONE RESCUES THE GALLOWAY SISTERS.

a part. He had a care for the tone of his voice, the poise of his head, the length of his step, the expression of his eye. He succeeded in what he was about. The Indians insensibly gave way to the influence of his manners. Reading in his eye no fear, and in his air no discontent, their vigilance insensibly relaxed. They and their captive could not exchange one single word. It was all pantomine, or manners.

On the seventh night after the capture, the Indians went to sleep. For three days Boone had been unbound. At night the bonds had heretofore been replaced. But what need was there to tie a man who was willing to stay with them anyhow.

Boone and his companion escaped. They did not kill any of their guards, nor did they attempt it. It was not a physical achievement, but a mental one. They made their way back to their cabin. The door was open. The rude furniture was broken in pieces. There was no fire in the fire-place. The stock of skins, the fruit of six months' toil, was gone. There was no clue to their companions. The whole thing was a mystery, and continued to be so. To the day of his death, Boone never knew whether the other men had stolen the stock and made off with it, or whether they had been killed by Indians, and the cabin plundered by the murderers.

There are some rare joys in the life in the wilderness. Such was the accidental meeting in the wilderness of Boone with his brother, who, with a companion, had also come up to Kentucky. There are many sorrows in a life in the wilderness. Such was that which befell Boone when, a few days later, he and Stuart were pursued by Indians, and Stuart was killed and scalped.

Only a week afterward, a still more distressing calamity happened. The companion of Boone's brother happened to remain away from the camp one night on a hunt. Finding, in a day or two, that he did not return, the two brothers began a search. In time they came upon the remains of the unfortunate man. While asleep by his fire, he was surrounded and attacked by a troop of famished wolves. The stock of his gun was shattered from the desperate use he had made of it in trying to beat back the animals. At last, his strength failing, the throng of brutes had borne him to the ground, and quickly stripped the flesh from his bones, which the Boones found scattered about. But for the gun, the remains would have been beyond identification.

Boone and his brother thus left alone soon found their ammunition supply running low. The brother returned to Carolina to procure a new stock of powder and ball, leaving Boone in complete solitude. " I was," he says, " left by myself, without bread, salt, or sugar, without the company of my fellow-creatures, or even a horse or dog." On the 27th of July, 1770, his brother returned. He brought with him two good horses, with heavy packs of the much-needed supplies. Not till March, '71, did they think of returning. During all this time they maintained ceaseless vigilance, never making a permanent camp. During his brother's absence, Boone had frequently slept in a canebrake, without fire, and heard the yell of the Indians around him.

At the date last named Daniel rejoined his family after an absence of three years, during which he had tasted neither bread nor salt. He came home fired with the fever for removing to the new country. He sold out his property, loaded some horses and milch cows with the necessary baggage, and, amid prophecies of their destruction, started back to the wilderness with his wife and children.

His clear statements of the advantages of the region induced five other families and forty well armed men to accompany him. The party felt great confidence in its strength. Pride goeth before destruction. The party of immigrants were attacked by Indians near Cumberland Mountain, and six of their number killed, among whom, to the infinite sorrow of the great pioneer, was Boone's eldest son. This reception so startled the party that they beat a hasty retreat to the settlements on Clinch River, forty miles to their rear, where they remained for several years.

In 1774 and 1775 Daniel Boone was engaged in the border conflicts of the time. Only one incident of his part in these struggles has been preserved. He was taken prisoner one night by the Indians. He had just extinguished his camp-fire, wrapped himself in his blanket, and lain down to sleep, being, as was his custom, on a lone hunt, when he suddenly felt himself seized in the darkness by a number of hands.

Resistance was useless. He was bound with strips of buffalo hide, and carried to the Indian camp. The squaws immediately began to search their prisoner for valuables, and they soon drew forth a flask of strong whisky. Boone looked on with secret joy as he saw the bottle passed around from mouth to mouth. He earnestly wished that the bottle was ten times its size, and that every drop might stretch a brave dead-drunk on the ground. He felt, to his sorrow, that there was not enough liquor to intoxicate the company.

At that moment a gun was heard in the distance. The braves jumped up, held a short talk with the squaws, pointing frequently to Boone, and then seizing their guns, hurried away in the darkness to see what the firing of the gun meant. The squaws sat down cross-legged around the fire, and took frequent drinks from the bottle until, one by one, they sprawled out on the ground, and went sound asleep.

It was the time for action. With the frontiersman's ingenuity and pluck, Boone rolled over and over toward the fire, held his feet and then his hands in the blaze, in spite of the torture, until his bonds were burnt asunder. He sprang to his feet, and, though severely burned, snatched up his rifle for escape. He says, that at that moment he was on the point of tomahawking the drunken squaws, but on second thought reflected that to kill such defenseless wretches would be murder, and he desisted. Devoting his tomahawk to less bloody work, he walked to an ash sapling, and chopped out three large chips to mark the spot. He concealed himself in a canebrake, and, in a day or two, made his way home.

Many years afterward a gentleman laid out and purchased a tract of several thousand acres, and, by chance, took as one of the corners of his survey "an ash marked by three distinct notches of the tomahawk." Another series of years rolled by, the ash had grown until the bark had completely covered the marks. The land became involved in litigation. It was impossible to find the boundary tree.

Daniel Boone, who at that time was living in Missouri, was sent for to identify the spot. He had almost forgotten the incident we have related, but, after talking the matter over, remembered it. He returned to Kentucky, and, in company with several witnesses, went to the locality where he had been a prisoner twenty years before. Waiting until the moon rose, so as to reproduce, as far as possible, his surroundings on the night of his capture, Boone started through the woods, eying each tree attentively, and at last stopped before a large ash, averring positively that it was the tree.

His companions examined the trunk closely. Not a mark was to be seen in the bark. The men were skeptical, but Boone took an ax and cut off a strip of the bark. Still nothing was to be seen. He then scraped and cut with his butcher-knife, until he did come to a place where the tree had been scarred a long time before. The astonished men then went to work, scraped the whole trunk carefully until three hacks, as plain as three notches ever were, could be seen. On the strength of this remarkable testimony the gentleman who had sent for Boone won his lawsuit.

In the spring of 1775 Boone and some companions were employed to guard a company of surveyors through Kentucky. The party had two battles with the Indians, losing eleven of their number. These attacks suggested the necessity of building a small fort, lest the Indians should little by little destroy the whole party. For two weeks the men worked with unremitting toil in the construction of a block-house on the Kentucky River, to which the name of Boonesborough was eventually given. Beside the block-house several cabins were built, and the whole surrounded by a palisade.

When the work was done it looked so strong, so secure; it was such a snug retreat from all the dangers of the forest, that Boone resolved to bring his family there. He returned to the settlement on the Clinch River, and at once started with Mrs. Boone and her daughters for the new fort in Kentucky. The women of Boone's family were the first white women who ever looked upon the Kentucky River. A few months prior to the founding of Boonesborough James Harrod had erected a block-house at Harrodsburg. These two places soon became famous as the only refuge from the savages south of the Ohio.

Boone's family had a lonely life. Yet the excitement in which they lived, growing out of constant danger from wild animals and Indians, took the place of companionship. Three more families soon came to make their home in the fort. After a few months' residence, the women of the place were accustomed to venture outside of the palisade for short distances.

One July day, Jemima Boone, with two girls named Calloway, growing weary of the cramped quarters of the palisade, took a canoe, and crossed the Kentucky River to a point where the overhanging trees formed a dense and pleasant shade. The cool retreat afforded an agreeable relief from the heat of a July day. These pioneer girls had few pleasures, and the little diversion was all the more enjoyed.

While floating lazily in the water, sometimes splashing with their paddles, five Indians hid themselves near by. The girls were unconscious of any impending danger, until they discovered that their boat, propelled by an unseen force, was moving into a leafy nook out of sight of the fort. Looking for the cause, they discovered in front of them the head of an Indian. He was swimming with all his might with the tying rope of the boat in his teeth. The girls screamed at the top of their voices. They were heard at the fort. The men were scattered through the forest, busy with their usual occupations.

Before any thing could be done to rescue the girls, the Indians had seized them and started off through the forest at the top of their speed. It was nearly two hours before word of the horrible mishap could be sent to the men of the fort and a party of sufficient strength made up to attempt a rescue. Those hours seemed ages. The women at the fort wrung their hands in agony, while the one man who happened to be there hurried off to find help. When Boone at last got started with eight companions, the Indians were several miles in advance.

Darkness came on, but the pursuers caught no glimpse of the chase. All through the night the white men, with a skill which we of the present day can neither explain nor understand, followed the trail of the savages. Some time during the following night the ruffians were discovered. They were attacked and driven off before they had time to kill their fair prisoners. Two of the Indians were killed, while Boone's party was uninjured. The poor girls were overjoyed at their rescue, and the glad welcome which they received at the fort on their return may well be imagined.

The wandering band of Indians who had captured the three girls was a precursor of a host of warriors who were on their way to destroy the white settlements. Two hundred braves surrounded Boonesborough, and for two days attempted to capture the place. They retreated only to renew the attempt a few days later. Now and then some defender of the fort was killed, so that the garrison was depleted to fifteen men. The Indians fought with great boldness. Under cover of night, they stole up to the gates of the fort, and attempted to hew them down with their tomahawks. The arrival of a hundred men, under Colonel Bowman, coming to the relief of Boonesborough, Harrodsburg, and Logan's Fort, suddenly put an end to the siege.

The wants of the little community could not be supplied without some exposure and risk. The dangers of hunting were great. Behind each tree or log might lurk a savage. A still greater danger was the procurement of salt. In January, 1778,

Boone took thirty men to the Blue Lick, to make salt for all the different stations in Kentucky.

It is related that one day he had wandered some distance from his party, and was suddenly confronted by two stalwart Indians. Boone threw himself behind a tree, and cautiously exposed a small portion of his body, to attract their aim. An Indian fired, and Boone dropped as if killed. To make the second savage throw away his shot, Boone repeated the trick, and while the two Indians were hurriedly attempting to reload, rushed out and deliberately shot the foremost savage. He then advanced upon the other Indian.

The white man relied on his knife, the Indian on his tomahawk. Boone planted his foot on the corpse of the dead savage, and awaited the attack with resolute eye and compressed lips. His antagonist advanced, and with the well-known, quick, circular movement, was about to bury his hatchet in the white man's brain. At the instant, when the Indian's arm was lifted, Boone, quick as lightning, plunged his knife into his exposed side. There was a spurt of hot blood which crimsoned the hand upon the knife handle, a convulsive, despairing groan. The hatchet descended, but slipped from the nerveless grasp and stuck in the ground. The Indian threw his hands to his side in vain attempt to stop the crimson tide, bestowed one look of unutterable malignity and hopelessness upon the man who still stood confronting him with the bloody hand and knife yet held aloft, then fell to rise no more.

On the 7th of February Boone, while out hunting, discovered a war party of a hundred Indians approaching him. He took to flight, but being then a man beyond the prime of life, and somewhat stiff from exposure, he was unable to contend with the swift braves who pursued him. He was captured and taken back to the lick, where he found his whole party of twenty-seven men prisoners like himself.

At this point we note a significant fact. The Indians neither tortured their prisoners nor offered to put them to death.

The conflict with the white man was a recent thing with the tribes so far west. Boone and his companions were taken to the Indian town of Chillicothe. As usual, Boone's mild and patient character made its impression upon the savages. While his courage excited the admiration of the fiercest brave, his gentleness touched the heart of the humblest squaw. His knowledge of human nature also helped him. Sometimes he was invited to engage in shooting matches with the Indians. On such occasions he usually took care to plant his bullets a little wider from the mark than the Indians, lest he should excite their animosity by beating them.

In the spring Boone was taken to Detroit. Here Governor Hamilton himself offered £100 for his ransom, but so strong was the affection of the Indians for their prisoner that they refused to consider it. Several English gentlemen, touched with sympathy for the misfortunes of the old pioneer, made pressing offers of money and other articles; but old Boone, with sturdy independence, refused to receive benefits which he could never return. In this incident we discover the character of Boone's reputation. It was in the midst of the Revolutionary War. Yet the Englishmen recognized Boone as a noncombatant. The Indians themselves knew that he was not an Indian fighter. He was simply and truly a pioneer.

Boone was taken back to Chillicothe, only to be terrified by the preparation of a great war-party for an attack on Boonesborough. His anxiety on account of his wife and children became intolerable. He resolved, at every risk, to attempt an escape so as to warn them of the impending danger. Early one morning he started from Chillicothe, directing his course toward Boonesborough. He traversed the one hundred and sixty miles in four days, during which time he ate but one meal and slept none.

Just at sunset he came in sight of the fort. The gates were open. Some women were leisurely milking the cows on a pleasant stretch of turf some distance from them. A little further off a man was chopping wood. The whole place looked to the returned captive like a bit of Acadia. Every thing wore an air of peace and quiet, as if danger were the farthest thing from the minds of the little company of pioneers. Boone, hoarse, haggard, disfigured by Indian paint and costume, his eyes glaring wildly from their sunken sockets, shouted to the people to come into the fort. At the apparition waving its arms in the twilight, the people made haste to follow its advice, fleeing wildly to the gates as if it were a wild man.

A moment later old Boone was recognized. A shout of welcome went up. Receiving the greetings of his friends, he told them in a few short words of their danger, ordered every person outside the gates to be called in, and preparation to be made for an Indian attack. This done, he looked anxiously around for his family. A hard disappointment awaited him. Wife and daughters, giving him up for dead, had returned to North Carolina, taking all his property with them. Swallowing his chagrin, Boone, after a rest, went to work with a will to repair and strengthen the fort. Traces of lurking Indians could be seen in the surrounding woods, spies, no doubt, upon the fort. Their reports must have been bad, as the Indian invasion was not forthcoming.

In the previous September, Simon Kenton had abandoned his cabin at Washington, Kentucky, and seeing a white man who told him that a settlement had already been made in the interior at a place called Boonesborough, had repaired to this place. He was overjoyed to find a substantial fort, and was greeted by Boone himself.

Kenton was a valuable accession to the place. It was on the failure of the Indian invasion to materialize that Boone resolved on his expedition against the Indian village at Paint Creek. We have elsewhere mentioned the fact of Boone's retreat, on finding that his advance was discovered, and have related the adventures of Kenton, who resolved to go on with his friend Montgomery.

Boone's reason for retreat was the conviction that the whole Indian force were now on their way to Boonesborough, and that the condition of the fort and of his own party was extremely critical. He hurried back, and fell in with the trail of a great Indian war-party headed directly towards Boonesborough. Making a wide detour to avoid the savages, and traveling night and day, he and his men reached the fort on the evening of the seventh day, in advance of the Indians.

On the following morning, five hundred warriors appeared before the fort. They were commanded by British officers. The ensuing siege was, in fact, an obscure chapter in the Revolutionary War. A demand for surrender was made, accompanied by the significant and cruel hint that, if hostilities ensued, the handful of British officers would hardly be able to restrain the Indians from massacring the members of the garrison should they be taken prisoners. Boone asked two days to consider. The request, strange to say, was granted.

The intervening time was busily employed in strengthening the fort. Every man resolved to die in its defense rather than surrender. When Boone informed the British commander of his decision, the latter said that he meant no harm to the settlers, and that if nine of the principal men would come out of the fort and treat with him, he and his Indians would at once go away. For some unexplained reason, Boone assented to this proposal, and, with eight picked men, emerged from the fort, and was soon surrounded by throngs of hideous braves. Some sort of "a treaty" was pretended to be patched up.

Boone and his friends prepared to return, when the British commander said that it was an invariable custom of the Indians at the close of a treaty for two warriors to take hold of either hand of each white man. The Indians at once proceeded to act on the hint. The white men, who were not surprised by the movement, flung off their assailants, and started for the fort. The men at the latter place, who were looking on with deep anxiety, instantly fired upon the Indians, under cover of which the nine men reached the fort and barred the gates. Only one of their number had been wounded in this scrimmage.

A siege of nine days followed. Every attack by the Indians resulted in the loss of many of their braves, while the whites suffered but little. The fort stood sixty yards from the river bank. The enemy, foiled in their other efforts, commenced to dig a mine from the river bank into the fort. One morning Boone's quick eye detected the discoloration of the river from the fresh earth thrown into it, and instantly divined the state of affairs. A deep trench was cut by the garrison under the palisade and then in front of the fort so as to intersect the approaching mine. This stratagem forced the Indians to abandon their attempt. At last, foiled in every effort, the savages withdrew. This was the last siege Boonesborough ever sustained. It occurred in the summer of 1778.

In the fall of this year, Boone, who was piqued at the facility with which his family had given him up for lost, returned to North Carolina. He was detained here by family troubles until 1780, when he again returned to Boonesborough with his wife and daughters.

Shortly after his return, Boone and his brother went to Blue Licks, where he had been taken captive, and were surprised by Indians. The brother was killed and scalped. Boone fled, urged on by a relentless pursuit. The Indians had with them a remarkable dog, which tracked Boone incessantly, and prevented his concealing himself. The situation was critical. Every twist and turn he made was detected by his pursuers, who were guided by the dog. At last Boone calmly paused, and waited till the animal should come in sight. It was a hazardous thing to stop with the Indians so near. In a moment the dog came bounding toward him, with a great red tongue lolling from his mouth, and uttering loud and mournful bays. At that moment Boone fired, and killed the brute. Then, under cover of the forest and approaching night, he made his escape.

Somewhere about this time in Boone's career, he, with a few

companions, was surprised in the woods by a large party of
Indians. The whites were eating their breakfast, and the savages sat down near by without hostile demonstrations, and pretended to prepare their own meal, acting as if they were completely ignorant of the presence of Boone. The latter cautioned
his men in an undertone to be prepared for a fight at any
moment. Boone then walked toward the Indian chief unarmed,
and intently gnawing the meat from a bone. The savage, who
was also eating, licked his greasy fingers, and rose to greet
Boone. The latter asked to see a knife, with which the Indian
was cutting his meat. Boone took the long knife, and with a
dexterous juggle, affected to swallow it, concealing it at the
same time in his sleeve.

The Indians looked on with wide-eyed astonishment, while
Boone struck his stomach, pronouncing the knife very good. In
a few moments he went through another contortion, and apparently vomited forth the knife, which he wiped on his sleeve and
returned to the Indian. The latter took it cautiously between
his thumb and forefinger, and flung it into the bushes, as if the
thing were contaminating. The whole party of savages then
instantly broke and ran, regarding Boone, no doubt, as the
devil himself.

Kentucky was filling up rapidly with settlers. Numerous
other stations besides Boonesborough and Harrodsburg afforded
refuge from savages. For a year or two the country was free
from Indian hostilities. The settlers, busy with their farms,
began to hope that the wars with the savages were over. In
1782, however, the tempest of destruction broke forth again.
Numerous isolated outrages were committed by Indians.

In the spring, twenty-five savages sneaked up to Estill's
station, entered a cabin somewhat apart from the rest, and after
outraging a woman and her two daughters, brutally murdered
them. A few moments later some women of the settlement discovered the tragedy which had been enacted. The men of the
place were nearly all absent, searching for this very band of

Indians. Word was with difficulty conveyed to Captain Estill, who commanded the squad of pioneers. On receiving the information, instant pursuit was resolved on. Five men, anxious about their families, returned to the station. Ten more were soon left behind on account of their jaded horses.

The party, reduced to twenty-five men, pushed on, and overtook the Indians, whose number was exactly the same. The battle, which is memorable in the annals of pioneer warfare, took place at a small stream, on the opposite banks of which the combatants were posted. For an hour the loss on both sides was equal. The Indians fought with the pertinacity and coolness of the whites themselves. It seemed, as the battle continued, that nothing remained except to fight until all the men on each side were killed. Estill resolved on a stratagem. Six men were ordered to attempt a flank movement. They were, however, utterly destroyed in the effort. The Indians now pressed their foes hard. Estill, himself, became engaged in a terrible hand-to-hand struggle with the Wyandot chief. Each man made furious exertions to overpower his adversary. The friends of each dared not fire for fear of wounding the wrong man.

At last, a mishap of the most serious character occurred. Estill had in the year before broken his arm. In this combat, the bones, imperfectly knitted, came apart. As the arm gave way, Estill gave a cry of despair, and the next instant the Indian sunk a knife into his heart. The triumph of the savage was short. Just as he shook the gory scalp in air, a rifle ball laid him in the lowly dust beside his fallen foe. The whites fled, bearing wild reports of the numbers of the Indians to the agitated settlements. Panic and defeat seemed about to overwhelm the pioneers. Band after band met the fate of Estill's company.

In August came the famous attack of Simon Girty, on Bryant's station, on the southern bank of the Elkhorn, between Maysville and Lexington, Kentucky. The garrison of the place was about to march to the relief of Hoy's station. Just as the gates were thrown open, a volley of rifle-balls rattled against the sides of the fort. No weakening of the garrison was to be thought of; instead, preparations for a siege had to be made at once. Their greatest peril in case of a siege arose from a scarcity of water. The spring on which they depended was some distance away from the fort. In a neighboring wood, signs of an ambush could be detected.

A council was held in the fort, and it was suggested that all the women get buckets, and go down to the spring after water, as if no ambush was suspected. The Indians, believing themselves undiscovered, would hardly attack a party of squaws, when by waiting longer, some of the fighting part of the garrison might be ambuscaded at the spring. This plan was adopted. Only one thing was wanting. This was the women's consent. Sharp words were indulged in. They did not see why the men could not go after the water. At last, some of the stronger and more sensible women took a practical view of the situation, and seizing their buckets, started boldly to the spring. The others followed with fear and trembling. On they went, defenseless and frightened, to within a short distance of the deadly ambush, where five hundred Indians lay concealed.

The buckets were filled with assumed deliberation, and the trembling procession of females started back to the fort. As they crossed the wide, open space their steps quickened, until every woman was in a dead run for the gates. Though pale with fear, they reached the fort without having been molested. As had been surmised, the Indians withheld their attack in the belief that some of the men of the fort could be caught at the spring before long.

Meanwhile an Indian decoy party had appeared on the opposite side of the fort. Thirteen men went out and attacked them, a maneuver which at once brought the whole Indian force upon the opposite side of the fort, which they believed to be unprotected. Heavy volleys of rifle-shots poured into them at point-blank range, destroyed their delusion, and the Indians fled to the woods. A regular battle was now begun.

At two o'clock a diversion occurred. Two messengers had carried the news of the attack to Lexington, near which a company, on its way to Hoy's station, was met, and its course changed to Bryant's station. At two o'clock in the afternoon this re-enforcement reached the vicinity of the fort. The Indians, discovering their approach, attempted to cut them off. The horsemen spurred on through clouds of dust, and made their way into the fort. Those on foot were not so fortunate. Finding themselves about to be destroyed, they took to a corn-field and attempted to escape. Some succeeded, but several were cut down in their flight. In the evening Girty called on the place to surrender. A man named Reynolds replied from the fort with taunts and insults, which put Girty in a terrible rage.

In the morning the men looked out through the palisades toward the spot where the Indians had encamped the night before, and were astonished to find the place entirely deserted. The enemy was in full retreat. Re-enforcements also began to pour into the fort, among them a strong company under Daniel Boone, from Boonesborough. Each little party which arrived had a leader, and among the multitude of counselors arose a discussion, which ended in a unanimous resolve not to wait for General Logan, who with a strong force was marching to Bryant's, but to commence pursuit of the Indians at once.

On the afternoon of the 18th of August, 1782, began the fatal march. The trail of the Indians was very plain. Here and there the enemy had chopped bits out of the trees. These signs made Boone and a few others cautious, as they indicated no anxiety to conceal retreat, but rather the reverse. At the Lower Blue Licks the whites, on the following day, came in sight of the enemy. The pursuers were gathered on the southern bank of the Licking River. On the opposite side a small group of savages could be seen standing on the top of a ridge. They coolly stared at the whites, and then disappeared.

A hurried consulation was held as to what should be done. The men were now a long way from any point of support. The country was wild and lonely, well adapted for ambuscades. The enemy was largely superior in strength to the whites. Boone advised a return or, at least, a halt, until Logan's force could come up with them. The discussion continued, when suddenly Hugh McGary, whose fierce and impetuous temper chafed at delay or deliberation when Indians were so near, gave a loud yell for "all who are not cowards" to follow him. At the same instant he spurred his horse into the stream.

The example was contagious. Calm deliberation was at an end, and the whole company crowded pell-mell after him. Through the river and up the opposite ridge they rushed in confused tumult. They hurried along the trail about a mile, burning with the reckless zeal which the rash McGary had inspired. Suddenly a party of Indians confronted them and fired. The place was inauspicious for the whites. They were on open ground, while the foe occupied a ravine, filled with a dense growth of trees and bushes. This ravine flanked the ridge from which the whites fought.

A severe battle at once began. The lagging settlers hurried to the front to the support of their companions. As soon as the Indians saw the whites well bunched together, a strong party of several hundred warriors started to throw themselves in their rear and cut off retreat. The movement was easy and on the point of success. The whites, seeing their peril, broke and ran back toward the river. The scene was awful. The battle of Blue Licks was really a slaughter. The Indians fell upon the fugitives, outnumbering them ten to one, and tomahawking them not singly, but by dozens.

At the moment of the retreat, Boone, who was in the front of the fight, and had already seen his son and many neighbors killed, found himself and a few friends surrounded by savages, and retreat hopelessly cut off. Thoroughly acquainted with the ground, he spurred forward boldly into the ravine which the

Indians had occupied, finding it, as he expected, almost deserted. By a roundabout course he reached the Licking, crossed it at a remote point, and reached the settlements in safety.

At the ford the Indians plunged into the water, falling upon and scalping their unhappy victims, and then letting the corpses float away, leaving behind a crimson trail in the blue water. There was no selfishness among the whites. Those who were able boldly helped their companions. Young Reynolds, who had given Girty the insult from the walls of the fort, was mounted on a fine horse. Half-way to the ford he overtook Captain Patterson, a man infirm from former wounds, and in his flight on foot in good way to be killed. With kingly generosity Reynolds sprang to the ground, placed his protesting friend in the saddle, and continued his own flight on foot. He saved his friend, but was taken prisoner.

He was at first guarded by three Indians, but the excitement of the pursuit was so fascinating that two of the savages turned their prisoner over to the third one, and eagerly ran on to take part in the fray. Reynolds marched quietly on, under the eye of his captor, who carried a tomahawk and loaded rifle. But when the Indian stooped down for a moment to tie his moccasin, Reynolds leaped on him, stunning him with terrific blows from his fists, and instantly disappeared in a thicket, making his way home in safety.

The survivors of the battle of Blue Licks spread terror among the sorrowing settlements. Sixty of the picked men of Kentucky had been slain, and a number taken captives. It was a time when every man was worth much to the new community. On the second day after the slaughter General Logan, with four hundred and fifty men, visited the fatal spot, and interred the swollen and disfigured bodies of the dead. Blue Licks was the most unlucky spot Boone ever knew. Here he had been taken captive, and kept so for many months. Here, too, his brother had been killed before his eyes, while he himself barely escaped with his life. And here, at last, his son Israel, together with sixty of his neighbors and friends, had fallen in the battle we have just described. He subsequently took part in an expedition against the Indian towns of Ohio, but without results.

Here Boone's adventures close. We have no record that he ever figured in any subsequent fight with the Indians. He remained for some years a quiet farmer. As the years rolled on and his old friends, one by one, passed away, he became lonely, and, to some extent, unhappy. The country in which he had been a pioneer grew and developed into a splendid State of fertile farms and thrifty towns. Political questions succeeded the old agitations of the border wars.

But in all this Boone took no part. He wandered around— in the present, but not of it. In 1792 he dictated a brief and rather dry sketch of his life to some young man who could write. The young scribe palmed off some cheap rhetoric on the old man, who, no doubt, regarded it as thrilling eloquence. He was never so happy as when some one would take the book, in which his name appeared "in print," and read it to him. He never wearied of it. Innumerable times the dull book was read over to him, and he never failed to listen with intense interest, rubbing his hands and exclaiming, "All that's true—every word of it—not a lie in it!" He never spoke of himself unless questioned, but this published account of his life was the Delilah of his imagination.

The last years of Boone were strikingly like those of Simon Kenton, George Rogers Clark, and many others of the earliest settlers. The brave and heroic race of pioneers seemed to have no capacity for adapting themselves to the new and changed conditions of life which surrounded them. Their rigid and unyielding disposition, which refused to yield to circumstances, but viewed the advancing tide of civilization with sullen and morose regrets, has in it something of the very nature of the red men, in fighting whom they passed their lives.

Boone became embarrassed and involved in lawsuits, lost all his property, and, at last, heartsore and unhappy, took his way to Missouri. Here, in the wilderness, he once more found comparative peace. He hunted and trapped, selling his furs at St. Louis, till he had laid up a considerable sum.

One day he reappeared at Boonesborough. He spent no time in reminiscence or pleasure, but with an expression on his face which indicated that he had some important task to perform, which would never let him rest until it was accomplished, sought out all his creditors, took their word for the amount which was owing to them, and paid them all off in full. This done, the honest old man shouldered his gun, and trudged back to Missouri. His face wore a brighter look than for some time. He took long hunting and trapping expeditions to the north-west, to the sources of the Missouri River. On one occasion he was on the Osage River, and was taken dangerously ill. His only companion was a negro lad. One pleasant day he managed to crawl out of his cabin, and marked out the spot where he wished the boy to bury him. He did not die, however, but lived to meet with further reverses.

The title which he had acquired through the Spanish government to certain Missouri lands was declared invalid, and at the age of seventy-six the venerable pioneer again found himself without one acre in all the boundless domain which he had explored. He, however, maintained his sweetness of temper, and in 1812, petitioned the Legislature of Kentucky to use its influence with Congress for the confirmation of his Spanish title to ten thousand acres of land. The request was granted, but Congress hesitated, and, after long delay, confirmed in him the title to one thousand acres of land, unmarketable at two cents an acre. Before this tardy and insufficient act of justice was done, his faithful wife, who had followed him through so many years of adventure, passed away. From that time he lived with his son, passing his days in meditative rambles through the forests. At the advanced age of eighty-two years he went on a hunting expedition of more than two hundred miles.

In 1819 a distinguished artist visited Boone at his dwelling near the Missouri, for the purpose of taking his portrait, and found him in a "small, rude cabin, indisposed, and reclining on his bed. A slice from the loin of a buck, twisted about the ramrod of his rifle, within reach of him as he lay, was roasting before the fire. Several other cabins, arranged in the form of a parallelogram, were occupied by the descendants of the pioneer. Here he lived in the midst of his posterity. His withered energies and locks of snow indicated that the sources of existence were nearly exhausted."

He died September 26, 1820, at the home of his son-in-law, in Flanders, Calloway County, Missouri, being then eighty-seven years old.

Daniel Boone is the most honored of all the pioneers of the Ohio valley. This is as it should be. The gentleness and humanity which pervaded his life stand out in marked contrast with the fierceness and brutality which characterized so many of the borderers. He was a true pioneer.

Governor Morehead, in a memorial address on the life and services of Daniel Boone, has said : "His life is a forcible example of the powerful influence a single absorbing passion exerted over the destiny of an individual. Possessing no other acquirements than a very common education, he was enabled, nevertheless, to maintain through a long and useful career, a conspicuous rank among the most distinguished of his contemporaries. He united, in an eminent degree, the qualities of shrewdness, caution, courage, and uncommon muscular strength. He was seldom taken by surprise, he never shrank from danger, nor cowered beneath the pressure of exposure and fatigue. His manners were simple and unobtrusive—exempt from the rudeness characteristic of the backwoodsman. In his person there was nothing remarkably striking. He was five feet ten inches in height, and of robust and powerful proportions. His countenance was mild and contemplative. His ordinary habits were those of a hunter. He died as he lived, in a cabin, and perhaps his trusty rifle was the most valuable of all his chattels."

CAPTURE OF THE BOONE AND GALLOWAY GIRLS.

24

CHAPTER X.

THE CRUELTIES OF GIRTY.

OR the traitor there has been erected in every age and country a pillar of historic infamy. By whatever name he is known, apostate, renegade, turncoat, or Tory, mankind have for him one universal expression of contempt. His name, of all historic characters, is buried the deepest in the mire. He becomes a by-word, a hissing, a reproach among the nations of the earth. For him no curse is bitter enough, no oblivion black enough. He lives in the midst of the fiercest passions which darken the human heart. He is a hater and the hated. The rage which he excites among the followers of the cause which he has deserted is only equaled by the disgust and secret loathing which he inspires among the partisans of the cause which he has joined.

Of all enmities, that of the apostate is most bitter. Of all hatreds, that of the renegade is most bloody. Within him rage storms of wrath, without him storm tempests of calumny. When the occasion for his shame has passed, and he is no longer useful to the ranks of which he became the dishonored recruit, he is sent without the camp. He is spurned as a viper. He is shunned as a leper. He is despised as a devil.

Another man fights and falls in the cause of wrong, yet to him mankind accords the laurels of heroism. Upon his tomb the historian inscribes the legend, "He was mistaken, but he was great." From that time on his error is forgotten. His name is inscribed among those of the heroes and the martyrs. The philosopher moralizes upon his career. He points out the fact that the dead was in the grasp of immutable laws; that he was not his own master; that ancestry, birth, place, temperament, surroundings, fortune, accident, and circumstances are the powers which have controlled him, in whose Titanic grasp he was but a puppet. This is the charity of history. This is the kindness of philosophy. This is the imperial task to which the human mind of after ages devotes herself, the task of preserving and immortalizing Truth, Heroism, and Honor, whereever found.

Not so with the renegade. He is the abhorrence of all future generations. He may have fallen fighting in the ranks of the brave and true. No matter. Above his grave rises the black shaft of shame. He may have made fearful sacrifices. He may have deserted one cause and joined another from an honest intellectual conviction. It is nothing. For him men have but epithets of shame, sneers of derision. He is disowned and dishonored. For him there is no charity. His virtues pass into oblivion. His solitary crime of apostasy becomes overshadowing and colossal. Philosophy refuses to inquire into the origin and reasons of his infamy. He, too, may have been a puppet, moved by invisible wires from remote agencies. Yet for his sin there is no atonement, no mercy-seat. His name is inscribed with those of Benedict Arnold and Brutus, of Julian and Judas Iscariot.

Concerning such characters the real truth is never known. The whirlwinds of abuse which overwhelm their lives throw dust in the eyes of the historian. He sees only a vast mass of slanders, invectives, reproaches, and vilifications. There seems to have been no good in the man. Passion, it may be, has exaggerated his vices. Enmity may have lied about his virtues. But the exact truth can never be obtained. He may have been worse than he seems; he may have been better than he seems. Concerning these things it is impossible to judge

To the ranks of traitors of which we have been speaking belongs Simon Girty, the Renegade, or the White Savage. It is not impossible that he has been slandered. We can not tell. The story of his life is certainly a black one.

Among all the Tories of the Revolution Simon Girty was the most notorious. He was born in north-western Pennsylvania. His father was an Irishman. "The old man was beastly intemperate. A jug of whisky was the extent of his ambition. Grog was his song, and grog would he have. His sottishness turned his wife's affection. Ready for seduction, she yielded her heart to a neighboring rustic, who, to remove all obstacles to their wishes, knocked old Girty on the head, and bore off the trophy of his prowess."

The murdered man had been an Indian trader. He left four boys, Thomas, Simon, George, and James. During the Old French war the three younger boys were taken captive by the Indians. Inheriting the nature of savages, their surroundings only developed them. Each was adopted into an Indian tribe. Each became a blood-thirsty ruffian, and during long careers of violence inflicted every cruelty upon the persons and families of the white settlers.

Of the three brothers Simon became the most notorious, as he was the most wicked. At the close of Pontiac's war, Girty was delivered to Bouquet as a hostage for the good behavior of the Senecas, of which tribe he was a member. The savage propensities of the young ruffian were so strong that he escaped from his civilized companions, and sought again the wild and wicked life of the wigwams. Strangely enough his appetite for barbarism was at this time forced to remain unsatisfied. The Senecas, being bound by the condition in the treaty of peace, deliberately took Mr. Girty by force, and dragged him back to Pittsburgh.

Of course, when Dunmore's war broke out in 1774, Girty's natural taste for scenes of violence led him to take an active part. Here he met Simon Kenton, for whose life he afterwards

interceded with the Wyandots. Here, too, he met Colonel Crawford, at whose hospitable cabin on the Youghiogheny he was a
frequent guest. In attempting to account for his subsequent
treachery and desertion, the border writers mention several
incidents, which tradition reports as having transpired about
this time.

One story goes that he aspired to the hand of one of Colonel
Crawford's daughters. The refusal, with which his advances
were met, poisoned his malignant heart with a sleepless longing for revenge. This account is supposed to furnish some
reason for Girty's awful inhumanity to Colonel Crawford some
years later.

Another story runs to the effect that Girty and another
scout, having rendered some two or three months' service in the
militia, without receiving their pay, repaired to the head-
quarters of General Lewis, and insolently demanded that the
arrears of salary be made up. The military discipline of the
time seems to have been a little singular, for General Lewis not
only received the application with a storm of curses, but proceeded to exercise himself in bloodying the heads of the two
scouts with several severe blows from his cane. Strangely
enough this style of reception and military etiquette displeased
the untutored scouts. Girty picked himself up, and shaking his
fist at the general, with a fearful oath, threateningly said, " *Sir,
for this your quarters shall swim in blood.*"

On the 22d of February, 1775, a day which, at that time,
was not yet celebrated as the birthday of the Father of his
country, Girty became a commissioned officer in the militia at
Pittsburgh. In accordance with English laws, he took the
necessary oaths of allegiance to the king and his abhorrence
of papacy.

Here, again, the ingenious border writers find a reason for
Girty's faithlessness. They say he aspired to a captaincy, but
was only made an orderly-sergeant. This affront his sensitive
soul could by no means endure. He remained, however, in the

service at Fort Pitt until the early part of 1778. That his real sympathies, if such his inclinations might be called, were with the Indians, among whom he had been raised, and not with the struggling cause of the colonial patriots, is natural, and easy to believe.

A savage seeks the society of savages, just as surely as a gentleman seeks that of gentlemen. Accordingly we find Girty, together with a pair of precious scoundrels, McKee and Elliott, and twelve followers, one day making up their packs and deserting from Fort Pitt. The news spread far and wide over the agitated frontiers. Wherever the ruffians went, they spread lies about the defeat of the American forces, the triumph of the British, and the intention of the colonists to avenge their defeat by the murder of every Indian in the Ohio valley. The settlers trembled for the safety of their families. The mischief which the white scoundrels might work among credulous and excitable savages was incalculable. Their evil designs were looked upon as a matter of certainty.

Nor did the fears of the settlers exaggerate the real dangers of the situation. The Indians were made to believe that George Washington was killed, and that the members of Congress were hung in the very chambers where they had been accustomed to deliberate. As poor Heckewelder said, speaking of the renegade's visit to Gnadenhutten: "It was enough to break the hearts of the missionaries."

Girty started for Detroit. On the way he was captured by the Wyandots. Some Senecas demanded that he be delivered up to them, on the ground that he was an adopted member of their tribe, and had taken arms against them. In fact, Girty's national allegiance was a little mixed. Was he a traitor to the Senecas, or to the Americans, or to both, or to neither? For this enigma, the Wyandot chief had a solution. "He is our prisoner." Such logic won the day. By shrewd explanations that he was now devoted to their cause Girty procured himself to be set at liberty, and proceeded to Detroit. Here the commandant, Hamilton, gave him a hearty reception. He was at once employed by the British upon a salary to incite the Indians to warfare upon the unprotected settlers of the border.

Girty was now in his element. To the instinctive ferocity of his own nature, he added the relentless zeal of the renegade. His name became a household word of terror all along the border, from Pittsburgh to Louisville. About it hung every association of cruelty and fiendishness. Dressed and painted like an Indian, he seemed, as he really was, the very incarnation of fierceness and brutality. Inheriting from his Irish ancestry a capacity for rude eloquence, with which the children of the Emerald Isle are often gifted, his terrible voice rose high and commanding above all the hideous clamor and savage din of every Indian council-house. Convulsed with fury, a human volcano in eruption, he awed the savages themselves by the resistless torrents of his rage, and excited their admiration and emulation by his infinite thirst for blood and infernal schemes of vengeance.

The picture of the man, as it is preserved for us in the tales of the borders, represents him as a monstrosity in human form. We can fairly hear him yet, as he stalked through the village, or galloped through the forest, filling the air with an awful din and roar of oaths and curses. He it was who inspired and directed the many attacks on the settlers of the Ohio valley. It was the diabolical brain of Girty which tormented the Christian Indians of the Moravian settlements, drove them from spot to spot, and placed them in that ambiguous position which the pioneers mistook for treachery or hostility, and which resulted in the slaughter of more than ninety of their number.

One, among many instances of his cruelty toward them, must be related. Shortly after the massacre at Gnadenhutten, Heckewelder, Zeisberger, and two other missionaries were ordered by Girty to meet him on the lower Sandusky. Here they were hospitably received by some traders. The traders told them that Girty had commanded them to proceed to

Detroit forthwith.   But exhausted by their toilsome journey
on foot, the missionaries availed themselves of the kind invitation of the traders to remain at this point for a week or two.

Here, for the first time, they learned of the awful tragedy
on the Muskingum.   Their minds were greatly uneasy, not only
by reason of the fearful news, but also from an apprehension
that Girty might return from a terrible expedition against the
frontiers and find his orders disobeyed with regard to their
being taken to Detroit.

The two missionaries were quartered in different houses,
separated by some distance.   Between them lay the restless
and filthy town of the Wyandots.   For the missionaries to pass
through the village and visit one another was an undertaking
of considerable danger.   Nevertheless, it was attempted a time
or two.   One day, when the Indian village seemed all quiet,
Heckewelder ventured to cross it to the house where his friends
were lodged.   He reached the place in safety.

While engaged in conversation, the missionaries were horrified and startled by two scalp-yells from different directions.   Two
war-parties were just returning.   Heckewelder at once started
from the house, which stood on a lofty ridge of ground, to make
his way back to his quarters.   The elevated ground prevented
the people of the village from hearing the scalp-yell of the war-
party approaching from the rear of the house in which Heckewelder was talking.   The savages all ran in the opposite direction to meet the other party.   Heckewelder followed in their
rear, and passed the deserted village in safety.

But the missionaries' troubles were not ended.   Girty returned, and behaved like a madman on learning that they were
there.   "He flew at the Frenchman," says Heckewelder, "who
was in the room adjoining ours, most furiously, striking him,
and threatening to split his head in two, for disobeying the
orders he had given him.   He swore the most horrid oaths
respecting us, and continued in that way until after midnight.
His oaths were all to the purport that he would never leave the

house until he split our heads in two with his tomahawk, and
made our brains stick to the walls of the rooms in which we
were! I omit the names he called us by and the words he
made use of while swearing, as also the place he would go to if
he did not fulfill all which he had sworn he would do to us.
He had somewhere procured liquor, and would, as we were told
by those who were near him, at every drink renew his oaths,
which he repeated until he fell asleep.

"Never before did any of us hear the like oaths, or know any
one to rave like him. He appeared like a host of evil spirits.
He would sometimes come up to the bolted door between us and
him, threatening to chop it in pieces to get at us. No Indian
we ever saw drunk would have been a match for him. How
we should escape the clutches of this white beast in human
form no one could foresee."

The poor missionaries passed a miserable night, within the
sound of the fearful ravings of the monster. When morning
dawned they were fortunately enabled to leave the place in a
boat which was going to Detroit.

The wicked and devilish part which Girty played in the execution of Colonel Crawford is given in another chapter, as is
also the incident of a different character, in which he attempted
to save Kenton's life. Toward the close of the Revolutionary
War a thread of romance is twisted like a skein of gold through
the dark web of Girty's career.

In March 1779 a family of emigrants named Malott embarked
on the Monongahela in two flat-bottomed boats for a voyage to
Kentucky. Mrs. Malott and her five children, with Captain
Reynolds, were in the rear boat. Mrs. Reynolds, several children, and a Mrs. Hardin were in the forward boat. Some forty
miles below Wheeling the little fleet, in which there were also
some canoes, was attacked by Indians.

Several of the voyagers were killed, and no less than nineteen of them taken prisoner to the squalid villages of the Delawares and the Wyandots. Among these was Catharine Malott,

then fifteen years old.   Some three years afterward, when Mrs. Malott had obtained her liberty at Detroit, she seems to have employed Girty to trace her children.   He found Catharine, a very pretty girl, adopted into an Indian family.   The people being very proud of her, refused to give her up.   Girty's influence, and a well-timed promise, which was never intended to be kept, that she should be returned after visiting her mother in Detroit, secured her release.

Once at Detroit, Girty married her.   During the next seven years Girty, softened somewhat by his new relations, remained comparatively quiet, leading the life of an Indian trader.   For awhile he was tolerably quiet.   In time, however, he became a hard drinker, and was separated from his family.

When the Indians of the west, after some years of comparative quiet, following the close of the Revolutionary War, combined in one last and furious effort to drive the white man from the territory of their fathers, an attempt which was met by the memorable and unfortunate expedition of General Harmar in 1790, by the no less tragic campaign of St. Clair in 1791, and finally, by the triumphant and overwhelming blow inflicted by General Wayne in 1794, Simon Girty again became prominent among the savages.   At every council his voice was lifted in the support of bitter, relentless, and continued war.   He was present, animating the Indian forces by his reckless courage, at each important battle of these campaigns.   One incident early in 1791 has been preserved.

A party of hunters from Cincinnati were startled by the discharge of fire-arms from the neighborhood of Dunlap's Station.   This was a settlement on the Great Miami River, eight miles from Hamilton.   Here the settlers had erected several block-houses, connected by a stockade, fronting southward on the river at a point where the water is deep.   The hunters beat a hasty retreat for Cincinnati, seventeen miles away.   No one doubted that the station had been attacked by Indians.

Before daylight seventy men left Cincinnati for the relief

of the station. On arriving at the fort, they learned that the Indians had withdrawn. One man had been killed by a shot fired through a crack between the logs. Not far from the fort they found the body of Abner Hunt. It was mangled, the brains beaten out, and two war-clubs laid across the breast. Hunt had been out with three companions named Wallace, Sloan, and Cunningham, exploring the country. Cunningham was killed on the spot by an ambuscade of Indians; Hunt was captured only to be subsequently put to death. Wallace took to flight. Two fleet Indians pursued. In his flight Wallace had the misfortune to be tripped and thrown by the loosening of his leggins. He pluckily tied them up, and escaped in spite of the mishap. Sloan and Wallace carried the news of the Indians' approach to the fort.

Before sunrise on the 10th of January, the women of the fort, while milking the cows, raised an alarm cry that the Indians were upon them. Before the fight was begun, Simon Girty strode forward toward the fort, driving Abner Hunt before him by means of a rope, with which the prisoner was bound. Within speaking distance of the fort was a large stump. This Girty compelled Hunt to mount and to urge the surrender of the fort in the most earnest manner. Lieutenant Kingsbury, in command at the station, replied that he would not surrender if he were surrounded by five hundred devils and persuaded to do so by Demosthenes himself. An Indian shot at him, and struck off the white plume from his hat. Girty, to revenge himself for this disappointment, drove poor Hunt back to a spot on the plain, which, though out of range of the guns, was in full view of the garrison. Here he proceeded to torture the unhappy wretch, and finally put him to death.

This scene over, the Indians began a desperate attack. They fired from behind stumps, trees, and logs. A pile of brush near the stockade was soon in flames. The Indians then rushed forward with fire-brands to burn the block-houses, but they were driven back by a whirlwind of bullets. All day long the attack was continued. Night brought no relief. The entire number in the fort was about thirty men, and as many women and children. Girty conducted the attack with great boldness and ingenuity. But the stubborn resistance of the defenders of the station successfully met him at every point. Both men and women teased the savages by momentarily exposing themselves above the pickets and inviting a shot.

That night, at ten o'clock, John S. Wallace attempted to leave the fort, in order to make his way to Cincinnati and procure relief. So vigilant were the besiegers, that he was unable to pass through their lines. For three hours he continued his attempts. Driven back each time, he next turned his attention to the river. The night was very dark. There were no indications of the presence of savages on the opposite bank.

About three o'clock in the morning, Mr. Wallace and a soldier named William Wiseman got into a canoe, and silently paddled across the river. They then made their way on foot through the river bottoms for a couple of miles. An attempt to cross the river on the floating ice proved unsuccessful. At the spot where New Baltimore stands, they at last did get across, and early in the day met the relief party from Cincinnati, of which we have already spoken.

Another battle in which Girty was known to be engaged was that which resulted in St. Clair's defeat, twenty-three miles north of Greenville, Ohio. During the rout of the American army, Girty captured a white woman. A Wyandot squaw at once demanded that the female captive be given to her, in accordance with the Indian custom. Girty refused, and became furious. The decline of his influence, a thing which has been experienced by every renegade, is shown by the fact that the warriors came up and forced Girty to give up the captive.

After this we hear of Girty establishing a trading-house on the site of the present town of St. Mary's, Mercer County, Ohio. Girty was also present at the famous battle of Fallen Timbers, in 1794, after which he moved to Malden, Canada. He was perpetually haunted by the fear of falling into the hands of the Americans. In 1796, when Detroit was upon the point of a final surrender by the British, he happened to be in the city. Some boat loads of American troops were coming in sight. Girty would not wait for the ferry-boat, but excitedly plunged his horse into the Detroit River, and made for the Canada shore, pouring out volleys of curses upon the Americans all the way.

In 1813 a Mr. Workman, of Ohio, stopped at a hotel kept by a Frenchman, in Malden. Sitting in the bar-room in a corner by the glowing fire-place was a blind and gray-headed old man. He was about five feet, ten inches in height, broad across the chest, and of powerful and muscular build. He was then nearly seventy years old. The old man was none other than the notorious Simon Girty. He had been blind for four years, and was afflicted with rheumatism and other intolerable diseases, a perfect sot, a complete human wreck. He lingered on through two more years of misery, and, at last, died without a friend and without a hope.

CHAPTER XI.

THE DOOM OF CRAWFORD.

MONG the many unfortunate military enterprises undertaken on the western border during the Revolutionary War, none is more notable than that against Sandusky, under Colonel William Crawford. Cornwallis had surrendered. The war with England was at an end. The patriotic minds of the colonies, inspired by the magnificent destiny dawning upon their country, were already busy with the great problems of self-government. On the western frontiers, however, the murderous forays of the Indians raged with unprecedented violence. The settlers continued to be roused at midnight in their lonely cabins by the blood-curdling war-cry. Children continued to be snatched away into captivity by dark hands thrust out from behind clumps of bushes and fallen logs. The corpses of the near and dear still continued to be found in lonely ravines or open fields.

The center of the Indian power was at Sandusky. In 1782 a permission for the organization of a great volunteer expedition against the Indians of the west was about all the government could do. This, however, was enough. Far and wide through the settlements along the Monongahela, the Youghiogheny, and the Ohio went the thrilling word that the expedition was to start on the 20th of May.

The popular heart, inspired by the successes of the Revolution, was now fired with enthusiasm and zeal for an attack on the deadly enemies of the west. In many an isolated cabin there was a lively stir of preparation. With troubled forebodings many a mother heard the resolutions of brave sons to join the march to the front. Maidens, parting from their lovers, sat in the shadow of their first sorrow. Children, whose tongues had scarcely learned to lisp the dreaded syllable of war, sobbed in solitude at the absence of the stalwart forms they loved.

The scene at Mingo Bottom, the rendezvous for the expedition, was truly American. For ten days beforehand the borderers came riding in, equipped in homely fashion for the campaign. The pioneer soldier was a curiosity. His buckskin hunting-shirt was belted at the waist. Through the belt was thrust the cruel tomahawk, the glittering scalping-knife, and the string of his ammunition-pouch. His hat of felt or fur was not infrequently decorated with tossing plumes, or the tails of animals. Over his shoulder he carried his rifle. Perhaps in his bosom was thrust some memento, a handkerchief or a scarf from some admiring maiden.

When at last the grim and motley assemblage was complete, its first task was to elect officers. William Crawford received two hundred and thirty-five out of the four hundred and sixty-five votes cast, and was declared colonel in command of the expedition. He had had considerable military experience, and was fitted by nature to be a soldier and a leader. He was ambitious, cool, and brave. Familiar with border warfare, the expedition in hand was adapted to the highest qualities of his genius. Yet he accepted the command with reluctance. Before his tender farewell to his family, the prudent father made his will.

His associate officers were the very flower of the border. Among them was David Williamson, second in command; John McClelland, field major; Dr. John Knight, surgeon; John Slover, Jonathan Zane, of whom we have heard before, guides of the expedition; and an officer of the regular army, who gave his name as John Rose, who volunteered for the purpose of acting as aid-de-camp to the commanding officer.

Concerning this latter gentleman more will be said hereafter. For the present it is sufficient to say that, early in the Revolution, he had applied to the American army for a commission. Though fine looking, of elegant manners, and, as was supected, of noble birth, speaking the French language, and highly gifted, his request was refused. He had studied medicine, he said, and sympathizing with the colonists, had left the Old World, against the protest of his friends, to join his fortunes with theirs. Upon the details of his history and life, the young stranger preserved the most profound silence. He had, at last, received a commission as surgeon; but, after two or three years of service, discovering a jealousy on the part of some young American officers, he had resigned. In spite of the mystery that surrounded him, he was a great favorite. It was not long before the wild borderers, assembled at Mingo Bottom, absolutely idolized the young officer, who volunteered from lack of other service.

On the 25th of May the expedition set out for Sandusky, one hundred and fifty miles away. Though not an Indian had been seen, the greatest precautions were taken against ambuscades and surprises. Their route led them through the desolate and fire-blasted settlements of the Moravians on the Muskingum.

David Williamson, the officer second in command of the expedition, was familiar with this spot. He it was who had commanded the gang of murderers, by whose bloody hands the inncocent Moravian Indians had been put to death. Yet, when he found himself once more near the scene of this appalling massacre, there is no record, no evidence that his heart was moved with one sensation of regret, with a single throb of pity. Such is the brutalizing influence of war upon the warrior.

The march was designed to be hasty. The plan was to surprise the savages. Day after day they advanced, without finding the print of a single moccasin or hearing the crack of a single hostile rifle. It was not the advance of an army with banners, to the music of the fife and drum. It was the insidious movement, swift and silent, of a mighty serpent, winding stealthily through the sunless forests toward the unsuspecting towns of the Indians. Now and then an incident happened which attracted the attention of the men. Some of the volunteers lost their horses, and were compelled to return to the settlements. This the borderers regarded as a bad sign. "Perhaps the rest of us will not go back at all!" said one of the men.

On another day, a fox got into the lines. The men at once surrounded it on all sides, but in spite of their utmost efforts to capture it, the animal escaped. In every considerable company of men there will be some who are positively and blindly superstitious. In addition to these there will be a larger number of credulous and talkative persons who, when informed that a certain thing is an omen or sign, at once take it up as a matter of fact. So it came to be whispered through the camp that the escape of the fox was a bad omen. " If the whole army," said they, "is unable to kill a fox, under such circumstances, what success can be expected against Indians ?"

The army at last emerged from the forests, which they had traversed, into the rolling prairies of Ohio. " To most of the volunteers," says the historian of this expedition, "the sight of the plains was a novel one. The high, coarse grass, the islands of timber, the gradually undulating surface, were all objects of surprise. Birds of strange plumage flew over them, prairie hens rose before them, sailing away and slowly dropping into the grass on either hand. Sand-hill cranes blew their shrill pipes, startled by the sudden apparition. Prairie owls, on cumbrous wings, fluttered away in the distance, and the noisy bittern was heard along the streamlets. Wild geese were frightened from their nests, and, occasionally, in widening circles far above them, soared the imperial eagle."

At length the destination of the expedition, into which the entire western border had concentrated its energy and valor, was almost reached. On the morning of the 4th of June the

25

men were awake and ready for the march before the brightness
of the sunrise had illuminated the landscape. Throughout the
whole camp there was a bustle of unusual excitement. Through
their long march scarcely an Indian had been seen. The men
felt themselves to be approaching a crisis. Their nerves were
strung at the highest tension. Guns were examined, and fresh
charges put in. Packs were readjusted, and saddle girths carefully tightened. The army were encamped near the site of the
present village of Wyandot in the county of that name in the
State of Ohio.

The march was begun just as the flaming disk of day
appeared above the horizon. The direction taken was nearly
north-west. Six miles' travel brought them to the mouth of
the Little Sandusky. The spot was a familiar one to Slover.
He had been taken captive by the Miami Indians when only
eight years of age, spending the next six years of his life with
that tribe.

Three Indian trails led from the spot of which we are now
speaking. One south-east, through the Plains, to Owl Creek,
now the Vernon River, leading thence to Walhomding. This
was the route taken by the Moravian missionaries and their
converts at the time of their exile from the settlements on the
Muskingum to the barren plains of Sandusky. A second trail
led to the south, up the east side of the Little Sandusky. The
third ran to the south-west, toward the Shawanese town upon
Mad River. Besides these, there was also a fourth trace, leading north along the east side of the river, through the woods.

This latter was the one which Crawford took. The army
moved cautiously, for Slover assured Crawford that the Wyandot town was near at hand. Following the turn of the river,
the army marched rapidly in a westerly direction. There was
an opening in the woods, towards which the men pressed on
eagerly. Just before them lay the Wyandot town, the goal of
the expedition.

Yet, though a hostile army was now within full view of

the place, there was no sign of life in the village. The shrill war-cry, the screams of the squaws, the barking of the dogs, were all wanting. Were the inhabitants of the place asleep, or was the village enchanted? As the invaders drew nearer, they found, to their surprise, that the Wyandot town was without an inhabitant. All was a solitude. The empty huts were silent and deserted. Grass was growing in the doorways. The ashes of the camp-fires seemed to have been beaten by many a rain since the hot coals had glowed in their midst.

The army was astonished. Some mistake had been made. Where, then, was Sandusky, the principal town of the Wyandots, to attack which the volunteers had traveled one hundred and sixty miles? A halt was called. It was one o'clock in the afternoon, the officers of the army were hastily called together for a council of war, to consider the strange aspect of affairs.

Leaving the officers of the volunteer army in anxious consultation, let us briefly sketch the state of affairs among the Indians. The reverses experienced by them early in the year, together with the Gnadenhutten massacre, had roused the Indians to the highest activity and watchfulness. Every white settlement on the frontier was placed under the surveillance of invisible spies. When the cabins of the pioneers began to be pervaded by an unusual stir in preparation for the expedition against Sandusky, fleet runners, unbeknown to the white men, bore the startling news to the villages of their tribes.

When the assemblage of volunteers took place at Mingo Bottom, every movement was observed by subtle scouts, and the tidings reported to their chiefs. That a great expedition was forming was evident. Its destination, however, was unknown. In every forest through which the army had passed lurked unseen savages, watching their course. Meanwhile, runners were dispatched to every village, bearing the news that the Indians must concentrate all their forces to successfully resist this invasion. Messengers were also dispatched to Detroit, begging the British commandant to send instant and powerful aid to his Indian allies. The old Wyandot town had been deserted some time before this. Its people had removed to a point on the river eight miles below the old town. Its location was five miles below the present town of Upper Sandusky, just where the Kilbourne road crosses the river.

That the destination of Crawford and his men was to be the Sandusky towns seemed clear to the Indians. In this they were confirmed by Crawford's encampment on the night of the 3d of June. Eighteen miles down the river from that camp was the chief Wyandot town, where the warriors were prepared to march at any instant. Eleven miles in another direction stood the village of Captain Pipe, the war chief of the Delawares. Here, too, the savages stood all night long plumed and ready for battle.

On the morning of the 4th of June the Delaware war-chief moved forward with his two hundred braves to an appointed rendezvous with the Wyandot braves. From the village of the latter the squaws and children were carefully removed and concealed in a deep ravine. The traders in the town hastily packed their goods and started for Detroit.

Besides the Wyandots, whose numbers exceeded those of the Delawares, the combined forces of which already surpassed the volunteer army, there was also moving to the Indian rendezvous, two other re-enforcements. From the Shawanese town, forty miles away, were coming two hundred braves of that tribe. They were not expected to arrive until the next day. From the north was coming powerful succor of a different sort. The commandant of Detroit had dispatched to the scene of action Butler's Mounted Rangers, with three pieces of artillery.

It was impossible for this re-enforcement to reach the rendezvous before the 5th of June. Far in advance of the Rangers, however, mounted on the swiftest horse in the company, rode Matthew Elliott at the top of his speed. He it was who was to have command of all the allied forces. He reached his command about noon of the fourth. Second in command to him was his fellow-ruffian and Tory, Simon Girty. Such were the preparations made for the destruction of Crawford's army.

The council of war, held on the site of the deserted Wyandot town, resulted in an advance in search of the real Sandusky, which Slover rightly believed to be eight miles farther down the river. The army had proceeded some three or four miles when some of the men expressed an earnest desire to return home, for the reason that there remained only five days' provisions. Crawford again called a halt. His officers were at once summoned for another council. Jonathan Zane urged an immediate retreat. He was of the opinion that the Indians would in the end bring an overwhelming force against them. The failure to discover any Indians as yet convinced him that they were concentrated at some point not far away for a determined resistance. In this view Crawford coincided. It was, however, at last, resolved to continue the advance during the afternoon, and, in case of continued failure to meet the enemy, that a retreat should be commenced during the night.

In front of the army rode a party of scouts. The country was rolling prairie, flecked with island-groves of thickly growing trees. At one of these green oases the scouts reined in their panting horses. One mile to the east of them lay the Sandusky River, its winding course marked out upon the landscape by a fringe of forest trees. Midway between the grove and the river ran the trail leading to the Wyandot town. South-west of the grove, not very far off, was a cranberry marsh, impassable to horsemen. This swamp the scouts had passed without discovering it. After a few moments' pause, this advance guard put spurs to their horses, and galloped on over the prairie. Having left the grove about a mile to the rear, the scouts suddenly discovered a large body of Indians running directly toward them—they were in sight of the Indian rendezvous. One of their number, riding their fleetest horse, at once galloped back to inform Crawford of the enemy's whereabouts. The rest retired slowly as the savages advanced.

Just as the Americans had finished their council of war the breathless scout dashed in, bearing the news of the discovery of the Indians. In a moment the lagging army took fire with enthusiasm, and started forward at the top of their speed. They found that the Indians had already reached the island grove and taken possession of it. Crawford's military eye at once discerned this to be a strategic point. By a rapid charge the Indians were driven, and the Americans, in turn, took possession of the cover.

The firing began at four o'clock in the afternoon. The Indians, led by Elliott and Girty, were concealed by the thick, high grass of the open prairie. They would creep forward, unseen, close to the trees, and fire upon the Americans from their concealment. Some of the borderers climbed the trees, and from their bushy tops took deadly aim at the heads of the enemy moving about in the grass. Great execution was done in this way. One man said afterward, "I do not know how many Indians I killed, but I never saw the same head again above the grass after I shot at it." The battle raged with fury. Every tree and log in the grove blazed with the incessant flashes of the American rifles. Not a foe was visible on either side. Yet every point in the surrounding prairie gave forth continuous explosions, and, over all floated a bank of white smoke.

The afternoon was exceedingly sultry. Not a breath of air was stirring. The river was a mile away. No spring or stream of water was to be found in the grove. The soldiers were attacked by the intolerable torment of thirst. In this emergency one of the men, John Sherrard, distinguished himself. In the excitement of the conflict he had rendered his gun useless by ramming a ball into the barrel without having put in a charge of powder. He said "I will not be idle." He went in search of water. He found a place where a tree had been torn up by the roots. In the cavity left in the ground had collected a pool of stagnant water. Pushing aside the green scum, he filled his canteen and hat, and ran to carry the water to his thirsty comrades. During the afternoon he made twenty trips of this kind.

For a while the issue of the battle was doubtful. Toward sunset the fire of the savages weakened. Their caution about exposure increased. They had evidently suffered. At dark they had withdrawn beyond the range of the American rifles. The Americans, being left in possession of the field, were the victors. To guard against a night surprise, each party resorted to the same device. They built a line of huge camp-fires, and then fell back from them for some distance. By this means any approaching foe would be revealed. The loss of the American army was five killed and nineteen wounded. The battle-field was three miles north, and half a mile east of the spot now occupied by the court-house in Upper Sandusky.

At sunrise on the beautiful morning of the 5th of June, occasional shots at long range began to be exchanged between the contending forces. As the day advanced the enemy's firing continued to be slack and irregular. As to the cause of this feebleness the Americans were fatally mistaken. They regarded it as an indication of depression occasioned by the defeat of the previous day. In fact, however, the Wyandots and Delawares were abundantly satisfied with simply being able to hold the Americans in check until the arrival of the band of braves from the Shawanese village, and of the redoubtable Butler's Rangers. Every hour brought these re-enforcements, of which the Americans were totally ignorant, nearer to the field of battle.

Crawford would gladly have attacked the foe early in the day, but the volunteers seemed in a poor condition for the undertaking. Many of the men were sick from the fatigues of the march. Others were suffering from the combined effects of the heat and of the poisonous water which they had been compelled to drink. Besides these there were nineteen wounded. Fifteen or twenty more were required to nurse the sick. These subtractions from the little army so weakened its strength for the time being that it was thought best to withhold the attack until nightfall. The morning was spent in comparative repose. The volunteers were confident of an easy victory. The men lay in the shade, already chatting gayly of the success of the expedition. Some even talked of the welcome they would receive on their return. A change, however, was to come over the spirit of the idlers in the grove.

An hour or two after noon a sentinel stationed in a copse north-east of the grove discovered a small speck at a great distance in the prairie. As his eager eye watched the apparition it grew larger. A few moments later he perceived it to be a body of mounted men. Pausing yet a moment, it became plain that these troops were white men. The sentinel stood no longer, but dashed toward his commander with information of the discovery. The grove at once became the scene of animation and excitement. The loungers sprang from their mossy couches and buckled on their fierce equipment for battle. Horses were saddled, the wounded were carried to the rear. While the volunteers were thus making their active preparations for a battle, the officers were grouped in a hurried council of war. The notion of an attack was at once abandoned, in the presence of the civilized foe. A defensive policy was all that remained. It was no longer a question of the destruction of the Indian towns; it was a question of the destruction of the army.

While deliberating upon the critical situation, another scout came running in with the news of the approach of other re-enforcements to the enemy. The officers looked with anxious gaze in the direction indicated; there they beheld, in full career over the open prairie, the painted warriors of the Shawanese, with fluttering plumes and fantastic decorations, coming to the help of their brethren.

Let us take a survey of the situation. Crawford and his men were still encamped in the small grove. To the north of them, in the direction of their town, were encamped the Wyandots, supported by the newly arrived Butler's Rangers. To the south of the grove, and a little to the west of the trail along which the army had come, were posted the Delawares. This position they had assumed during the battle of the previous day. Posted as they were, in the rear of Crawford, they endangered his retreat. The Shawanese, as if by previous arrangement, encamped to the south-east of the grove. The trail along which the army must pass in case of retreat was thus made to run between the two camps of the Shawanese and the Delawares—a maneuver of great skill.

As the council of war continued, small squads of Indians were discovered pouring in from all quarters as re-enforcements. But one course was open to the Americans. That was retreat. Orders were given for a retrograde movement, to commence at nine o'clock that night. The dead were buried. For the seven dangerously wounded, litters were made. The army was to march in four divisions, keeping the wounded in the center. As soon as it was dark the sentinels were called in, and the body formed for the march, with Crawford at the head.

At the moment of starting, the enemy, having discovered the intentions of the Americans, opened a hot fire. Some of the men became alarmed. The arrangements for a regular retreat were, in the excitement and panic of the moment, forgotten. The men in the foremost ranks started to run, and, the example being contagious, the whole army was soon in full flight. The seven men in the litters were left behind. Of these, five were helped upon comrades' horses. Two unfortunate men were left to the insatiate vengeance of the savages. The first division, under Major McClelland, was soon engaged with the Delawares and Shawanese. McClelland fell from his horse, dangerously wounded, at the first fire. Calling to John Orr, who was on foot, the wounded captain bade the man take his horse, and make his escape, which he did. In the darkness and confusion McClelland was believed by the few who saw him fall, either to have been killed outright, or to have been trampled to death under the hoofs of the

oncoming horses. In fact, he was reserved for a more dreadful fate.

The enemy, on their part, fearful lest Crawford's movements
formed some kind of maneuver, and not a flight, hesitated in
their pursuit. Meanwhile, the rear divisions, seeing McClelland's party furiously attacked by the Delawares, bore off to the
south-west to avoid the Indians, leaving their struggling companions to their left. At an earlier point in the narrative mention has been made of a vast cranberry swamp, lying west of
the trail followed by the army in its advance. Into this swamp,
owing to the darkness, some of the Americans unfortunately
blundered. Many of the men were compelled to leave their
horses hopelessly mired in the bog. To add to their danger,
the Americans were attacked in the rear by the enemy, suffering considerable loss. The remainder skirted the morass on
the west, clear around, to a point nearly opposite that of their
entrance to the swamp.

A little before daylight they again found themselves on the
trail, having, in their march, described a half circle around the
swamp, of which the center was the present town of Upper
Sandusky. The men of McClelland's division had fought their
way along the diameter of the circle, and, in a badly demoralized condition, reunited with their friends at the deserted Wyandot village. At this point a halt was made. Straggling
parties came up with the others, until nearly three hundred of
the volunteers were once more together.

An investigation was made, to find who were missing. To
the great sorrow of the entire army, Colonel Crawford was
nowhere to be found. Nothing was known of him. Whether
killed, captured, or escaped was a matter of conjecture. Dr.
John Knight and John Slover, together with the brave McClelland, were also missing. The command of the army now
devolved upon Williamson, who, seconded by the brilliant military genius of Rose, made the most powerful exertions to rally
the broken army for a regular retreat.

Even in the midst of such tragic scenes as these occur incidents calculated to provoke a smile. One of the volunteers discovered a brass kettle, left in a deserted Indian sugar-camp. In spite of his peril, the prize was too great for his prudence. He dismounted from his horse, seized a huge bowlder, and pounded the utensil flat for transportation. Through all the exciting scenes of the retreat, this article kept its place on Vance's saddle.

John Sherrard, the man who had carried water to his comrades during the battle, had, in the confusion of the flight from the grove, become separated from his companions. In company with Daniel Harbaugh, he followed the track of the army as best he could. Riding through the forest soon after sunrise on the 6th, Harbaugh, less agile than his companion, was shot by an Indian. Sherrard, sickened at the death of his companion, nevertheless removed the saddle and bridle from the dead man's horse and substituted them for his own, which were inferior. He had proceeded but a short distance, when he recklessly resolved to return for a pack of provisions which he had left tied to his own saddle. Securing this, he resumed his journey, and overtook the retreating army.

At two o'clock in the afternoon of the 6th of June, the retreating army, by that time somewhat rallied from the demoralization of the night, were attacked from the rear by a large force of the enemy. The volunteers succeeded in beating off the foe, an achievement in which they were aided by a terrible thunder-storm which broke over the combatants. When the rain ceased the foe renewed the attack, and at night the two armies slept within sight of each other. In the morning shots were again exchanged near the spot where the village of Crestline now stands. Thenceforth the retreat of the broken and dispirited army was continued without interruption.

It is not to be supposed that the volunteers all reached home at once. For days they continued to straggle back. Some of the men became completely bewildered. Nicholas Dawson had become separated from his companions, and was endeavoring to make his way home when he was discovered by two other volunteers. Dawson at that time was *traveling in exactly the wrong direction, going back toward Sandusky.* The men attempted to convince him of his error, but he pertinaciously insisted that he was right. At last the men told him that he would certainly be captured by the savages and tortured to death if he proceeded in his present course, and that as it would be better for him to die from a painless and sudden gun-shot wound than from the merciless barbarities of the savages, they would kill him out of friendship. This argument proved successful. Dawson turned about reluctantly, and, with the others, reached home in safety.

Philip Smith and a young man named Rankin had also become separated from the army, owing to the loss of their horses. They had their guns, but were afraid to use them to procure game for fear of attracting the attention of the Indians. By chance they came across an Indian pony, which Smith undertook to dispatch with his tomahawk. The animal, however, proved to be an expert dodger. Rankin at last blindfolded it, and thus enabled Smith to deal a fatal blow. On the flesh of the pony they subsisted for some time.

On the third night of their retreat two volunteers on horses fell in with them. While proceeding along the banks of a stream they were ambuscaded by four savages. Smith was in the act of stooping to get a drink from the river. The two men on horseback were shot dead. Smith seized a gun and ran up the bank after his companion, Rankin, who had also taken to flight. The latter mistook Smith for a enemy, and three times attempted to shoot him. He succeeded, however, in dodging, until he came near enough to be recognized. Escaping from these Indians, the wanderers came upon a camp, evidently just deserted. A white man, freshly scalped, lay on the ground. As they looked at him, he took his hand and rubbed his bloody head. He had been scalped while alive, but, of course, death was near. Over the camp fire hung a pot of boiling hominy. This the famished wanderers feared to eat lest it should be poisoned. They, at last, reached home naked, footsore, and famished. To acquaintances they were unrecognizable. The loved ones of their families, however, knew the wanderers at once.

Many were the cabins of the frontier in which were weeping of women and wailing of children for the brave ones which returned not. Sherrard made his home with the widowed mother of James Paull, who had also accompanied the expedition. Concerning her boy nothing could be learned. At the moment of retreat from the grove, Sherrard noticed that the young man was sound asleep. He gave the sleeper a shake, and shouted, "Up, James! let 's be off. They 're all starting, and we 'll be left." He had seen the young man spring to his feet, but at that moment lost sight of him in the darkness, and of his fate could tell nothing. The poor widow bore her mighty sorrow alone, and never ceased to look for the return of her boy.

Sherrard had another distressing scene to go through with. As soon as he had obtained a little rest, he started to return the pack-saddle of Daniel Harbaugh, which he had taken from his dead companion's horse, to his widow. The story of her husband's death was heart-breaking to the sorrowing woman. She, however, *knew* that he was dead. Though stricken with grief she was not doomed to be haunted forever after by a fearful uncertainty.

Among those who could learn nothing definite concerning their loved relatives, was Hannah Crawford, wife of the colonel in command of the expedition. For a long time she suffered from hope deferred until the heart grew sick indeed. When at last she heard the awful truth, which will be hereafter related in these pages, she was of all the sorrowing ones of the stricken frontier the most to be commiserated.

As has been stated, to the genius and exertions of John Rose, aid-de-camp to Colonel Crawford, more than to any thing else was due the fact that so many of the expedition escaped destruction. Without detailing his further splendid services to the colonies, we here give his own explanation of the mystery which surrounded him. Just before leaving America, he wrote to his friend, General Irvine, his true history. His name, he said, was not *John Rose*, but *Gustavus H. de Rosenthal*, of Lavonia, Russia, a baron of the empire. He had had a duel, brought on by a blow inflicted by his enemy upon an aged uncle. In the encounter, which took place in an apartment in the royal palace at St. Petersburg, he had killed his antagonist. He at once fled to America to draw his sword in behalf of the colonies. At the close of the Revolution he received from the emperor a pardon, as a result of which he returned to his native land.

It yet remains for us to detail the remarkable adventures, or perchance the tragic doom, of those men who, either at the moment of retreat from the grove, or subsequently in the confusion and entanglement in the cranberry marsh, became at once separated from their companions and found themselves alone in the midst of an enemy's country, separated from the nearest white settlement by a wilderness one hundred and sixty miles in width, infested by swarms of hostile Indians, who were certain to scour the woods in every direction in search of stragglers from the retreating and broken army.

Among those who had the misfortune to lose their horses in the mire of the cranberry marsh were John Slover, the guide, and James Paull. These, with five others, being pursued by savages, fled in a northerly direction. After pursuing this course all night they turned, for some unaccountable reason, toward the south-west. About ten o'clock in the forenoon they halted to eat. Each man had a scrap of pork. From this they proposed to make a sumptuous breakfast.

Hardly had the poor fellows seated themselves on the ground when a file of Indian warriors was discovered coming along a neighboring trail which the volunteers had not observed.

The latter ran off, leaving their baggage and provisions, but were not discovered. Their loss of provisions, scanty though the supply was, was a most serious mishap. At last they resolved to return and secure them, which was accomplished successfully. At twelve o'clock they perceived another party of Indians approaching, but by skulking in the grass and bushes of the prairie, they again escaped discovery.

The progress of the party was slow, one of the men having burnt his foot, and the other being attacked with rheumatism, contracted from exposure to the rain storm which has been previously mentioned. When at last they struck woodland, they turned due east in their line of march. On the 7th of June, the man with the rheumatism was left behind in a swamp. "Waiting for him some time," says Slover, in his narrative, "I saw him coming within one hundred yards, as I sat on the body of an old tree mending my moccasins; but taking my eye from him I saw him no more. He had not observed our tracks, but had gone a different way. We whistled on our chargers, and afterwards halloed for him, but in vain." This man afterwards reached his home in safety. The terrible adventures which he escaped by thus missing his way will be hereafter related.

The man with the burned foot was James Paull. On the afternoon of the 5th, in making their hurried preparations for retreat, he, with many others, was engaged in baking bread. In this task some of the men, for want of a better baking-pan, made use of a spade which had been picked up in the desolated settlement of the Moravians. When the last loaf had been turned out, the hot spade was thrown down, and Paull had stepped on it with his bare foot, burning himself badly.

Passing through what is now Wayne county, about nine o'clock on the 8th of June, the party was ambuscaded by a band of Shawanese. With tireless pertinacity, these red detectives of the wilderness had all the while been on the trail of the fugitives. Two of the white men were shot dead. Paull, notwithstanding his burnt foot, ran for his life, and escaped.

Slover and the other two men were taken captives. By a remarkable coincidence, one of the captors had been in the party which had captured Slover in the mountains of Virginia when but a boy. The Indian, however, had nothing but curses for his old acquaintance. Sick at heart, the three prisoners started for the Shawanese towns, on Mad River, in what is now Logan county, Ohio.

On the third day after their capture they came in sight of a small Indian village. Slover had hoped that his old captor might treat him with some clemency. On his entrance to the village this hope was dashed in pieces. The inhabitants of the place, crazy with joy over the great victory at Sandusky, were delighted to find that the fun was not yet over. They at once began the enjoyment of abusing the captives. The three white men were beaten with clubs, chastised with lashes, and buffeted by the vile mob from one side of the village to the other.

This treatment was not the most ominous circumstance. The rabble seized one of Slover's companions, the oldest man in the party, and stripped him naked. Two of them at once began the task of *painting the unfortunate man black.* As the artists progressed with their work a dense throng of hideous squaws and screaming children surrounded them, watching every stroke of the brush with intense interest. The captive, alarmed at the proceeding, began to surmise that it was an indication that he was to be burnt. He broke down in tears, and called to Slover, asking him what it meant. With devilish temper, the Indians warned Slover not to tell the man any thing.

The three men were next told that they were to run the gauntlet to the council-house, which was about a thousand feet away. Foremost in the dreadful race ran the man who had been painted black. Upon him were concentrated the chief efforts of the savages. Many fired powder into his flesh as he passed them. Stunned, bruised, and bleeding from the assaults of his enemies, the poor man was unable to reach the goal as soon as Slover and his companion. When he did so, his body had been gashed in a dozen places with tomahawks. Here and there large holes had been burnt in the flesh. A gun wad,

SLOVER'S COMPANION RUNNING THE GAUNTLET.

fired into his neck, had inflicted a painful wound, from which the blood streamed in large quantities.

Shattered as he was, through exertions nerved by despair

26

itself, he reached the council-house. Exultant with hope, he stretched out his hand to lay hold of the door. But for him there was no rest, no mercy. While his hand was still extended in the belief that he had secured temporary safety, a dozen slimy hands jerked him back from the door, whose refuge mocked him. Again and again, he fought to tear himself loose from their grasp. But a few steps would he run, till again he was seized and hurled back.

Though growing weaker at every moment, and frantic with despair, the instinct of self-preservation still remained to him, and he sought to wrest from his tormentors a club or tomahawk. Perceiving his purpose, the savages would hold out to him their weapons, and then, as his eager fingers were about to clutch the object, would snatch it away with hideous laughter, and deal the wretch another blow. Sometimes they would allow him to run from them a considerable distance, only to make his recapture the occasion for a pretended punishment and renewed beatings.

There is a limit to human endurance. There is a point, beyond which the will, electric, exalted, sublime, can no longer sustain one. That point was reached. The captive fell to the ground. As the showers of blows were rained upon him, he no longer fought back with the ferocity of a tiger and the courage of a madman. He only feebly tried to screen his face and head with his lacerated arms. At last even this frail defense gave way. The blows of the club and the tomahawk fell upon the body of the prostrate man, and met with neither resistance nor retaliation. Now and then a sob, a gasp, a quiver was to be heard escaping from his lips. Finally, even these last, faint flutterings of life disappeared. The spirit had departed, leaving the shapeless mass, which had been its splendid home, to be tossed by cruel hands to hungry dogs.

That evening Slover, with an anguish in his heart which no pen can describe, looked on not only this scene, but also on three other black and mangled bodies. As they lay in all their mutilation, the scout could recognize in one the remains of William Harrison, the son-in-law of Colonel Crawford. Removing his eye to the second corpse, he saw in it young William Crawford, the youthful nephew of the commander. The third corpse was that of Major John McClelland. These three brave men had furnished a gorge of infernal revelry for the beastly savages. The heads and limbs were impaled on lofty poles in the center of the town. The trunks became food for dogs.

Harrison was one of the most noted men in the Ohio valley. He was a lawyer of polished education and lofty intellect. He had rendered distinguished services to the colonies.

The surviving companion of Slover was shortly sent away to another town. Of his fate we have no account. There is no reason to suppose that it was different from that of the brave men which we have described. That night a great council was held in the village. Slover was placed in the center of the room, and there subjected to every question which the Indian intellect could invent.

The council lasted fifteen days. In it were represented a dozen different tribes. Here in this assembly all the pride, all the exultation, all the savage joy to which the destruction of Crawford's army had given rise found expression. No rhetoric was bombastic enough for the vanity of the orators; no congratulations were complimentary enough for the pride of the warriors.

In the midst of the council was received a message from the commandant at Detroit. Of this communication the key-note was clear to the dullest ear. It bade the Indians to take no more prisoners. The exhortation was received with a mighty uproar of applause. The council resolved to follow the advice. Henceforth they were to take no more prisoners, but kill outright every unfortunate who fell into their hands. This was not all. In the enthusiasm of the moment they determined that if any tribe not represented at the council took any captives, the others would go upon the war-path, take away the captives, and put them to death.

During these days Slover suffered more from the villainous white men in the village, who were continually instigating the savage mind to cruelty, than from the Indians themselves. Simon Girty was there. This abominable liar almost drove the inhabitants of the place insane by telling them that he had asked Slover how he liked to live there, and that he had answered that he intended at the first opportunity to take a scalp and escape.

Another white man came to him and told him that his home had been in Virginia; that he had three brothers there, and wanted to get away. Slover was too old a scout to say any thing to the treacherous villain. This prudence, however, did not save him. The fellow went off and reported in the village that Slover had consented to go with him.

There was another white man in the place. He lived two miles from the town, in a house built of squared logs, with a shingle roof. He dressed in a gorgeous uniform of gold-laced clothes. He spoke but little in the council. When he did it had a marked effect. He did not question Slover, but during all the time he seemed to be oblivious of the latter's presence in the town. He never spoke to him. This man was in the employ of the British Government. He was the counterpart of Girty and Elliott. His name was Alexander McKee.

On the morning after the close of the council Slover was sitting before the door of the cabin where he had been kept. A file of forty Indian warriors suddenly came up and surrounded the cabin. Their captain was a white man. It was George Girty, a brother of Simon. These Indians took Slover, and put a rope around his neck. They stripped him naked. His arms were bound behind him, and he was painted black from head to foot. During this operation Girty stood before him, hurling at him a storm of curses. Slover was then taken to a town five miles away. Being a stranger, the inhabitants of the place had prepared a reception for him. The emblem of their hospitality was the war club; their method of expressing it was falling upon Slover, and beating him half to death.

Two miles away was another town. It was not far from the site of what is now West Liberty, Logan County, Ohio. Only one-half of the council house had a roof. Slover noticed this. In the center of that part of the structure which had no covering was a huge post, sixteen feet in height. About four feet from the post were three large piles of firewood. Slover was taken to the post. One rope was passed around his neck, another about his waist, and a third about his feet. These were tightly bound to the post. This done, a large savage, carrying a torch, stuck it into the dry wood, which quickly leaped into flame.

At this moment a wind began to roar through the forest, swaying the trees in a frightful manner. The dust in the streets of the village was caught up and whirled along in mighty clouds. Terrific thunder-peals seemed to split asunder the sky-dome. The crowd around the stake withdrew their fascinated gaze from the dreadful drama being there enacted, and looked with apprehension at the darkening landscape and the ragged storm-line which was rapidly approaching. Huge drops of rain began to fall. With screams and pushings the crowd scrambled for the sheltered part of the council-house. Here and there an old squaw or an aged warrior stood stolidly where they were, as if to express their contempt for the others, while the floods of water which now descended drenched them to the skin.

The fire was quickly extinguished. The rain lasted about twenty minutes. When it was over, and the sun reappeared in an azure sky from which the clouds were rapidly clearing, the Indians stood still for some minutes, awe-stricken and silent.

At last the spell was broken. The crowd before so still became noisy and turbulent. A dispute arose. Some wanted to proceed with the torture, the prevailing part insisted on saving the prisoner until the next morning. Slover was untied.

Even though the respite was short, his spirits rose. Making him sit down the Indians began a war dance around him.

At eleven o'clock at night Half Moon asked Slover if he was sleepy, The captive answered " Yes." Three Indians were appointed for his guard. Taking him to a block-house, they tied his arms around the wrists and above the elbows so tightly that the cord cut deep into the flesh. To his neck was fastened a rope, the other end of which was tied to a beam in the house. It was long enough to permit him to lie down on a couch, which consisted of a board.

Slover, overcome with anxiety at the fate prepared for him, waited nervously hour after hour for his guards to go to sleep. But they too, though from different motives, were full of excited interest concerning the festivities of the morrow. Not till an hour before daybreak did they weary in their animated conversation. At that hour two of them lay down and went to sleep. The third copper-colored gentleman came over and questioned Slover as to how he would like "eating fire." The prisoner was giving up his last earthly hope for a chance to escape, when to his great joy the third Indian rolled over and began to snore.

The scout instantly set to work. Turning on his right side he managed little by little, with infinite effort and skill, to slip the cords from his left arm. At that moment his heart sank within him. One of the warriors rose and stirred the fire. Slover expected to have his bonds examined, and thought all was over. But the sleepy savage lay down and again became unconscious.

There was no time to be lost. It was within a few minutes of daybreak. The people of the village were likely to rise early in preparation for the sports of the day. Some old squaws might already be stirring in the lodges. Slover made frantic efforts to loosen the rope from his neck. He tried to gnaw it, but might as well have bitten a bar of iron as to chew the cursed buffalo hide. He tugged at it till his fingers bled. But all in vain. At last, just at daybreak, he discovered, to his joy, that it was a slip-knot. He pulled the noose apart, slipped it over his head, lightly stepped over the sleeping warriors, and left the cabin.

He sped through the town, passing a squaw and five children who were asleep under a tree, and jumped into a cornfield. Here he untied his right arm, which had swollen till it had turned black. Collecting his thoughts, he remembered to have seen some horses on his way to the cornfield. He started back, snatched up an old quilt hanging on a fence, quickly caught one of the horses by the mane, threw the rope, with which he had himself been tied, around the horse's neck for a halter, sprang astride the animal and galloped away.

His course lay to the north-east. On he dashed, without a pause or a backward look. His horse was strong and swift. He had only the quilt for a saddle, and the rope halter for a bridle. *He was entirely naked.* As his horse plunged through the forest, the branches of the trees lacerated his bare body until he was covered with blood from head to foot. Yet of this he was unconscious. He felt not the strokes and bruises. He noticed not the torn flesh, nor the flowing blood. He only knew that he was flying, flying from fiends and flames to liberty and life; flying from torture and the stake to home and friends. Fifty miles away lay the blue Scioto. For his horse he had no mercy, but mindful of the keen and swift pursuers, who were already swarming after him, devising in their hellish hearts new and fearful vengeance, he urged the animal on, hour after hour, at its topmost speed.

At eleven o'clock in the morning he reached the Scioto. At three o'clock in the afternoon he had left the river twenty-five miles behind him. At this point his horse failed. All its splendid powers had been expended in the noble race. Seventy-five miles had been accomplished in eleven hours. It could go no further. Slover instantly sprang from the animal, and started ahead running on foot.

The sun set in the west, but still he ran. Stars came out
in the blue canopy of night. It was the hour of repose for all
mankind. Yet for the fugitive there was neither rest nor relief.
Once he relaxed into a walk. At that moment *he heard halloo-
ing behind him.* It may have been the phantom of his fevered
imagination, the offspring of a brain heated with surges of boiling blood. No matter. The fugitive sprang forward as if every
tree in the forest was a savage, and every wandering star-beam
the glint of a rifle.

Not until daybreak did Slover resume a walk. In his hand
he carried a crooked stick. Was it a weapon, a means of defense
against his pursuers? No, and yes. No, because it was as
worthless as a shadow as a physical weapon. Yes, because by
it he carefully replaced the weeds bent by his feet, in order to
hide his trail. Once he sat down.

That moment exhausted nature entered a protest. He vomited. Feeling somewhat better, he again proceeded. The high
excitement of the previous day was no longer present to sustain him. He became painfully conscious of his wounds. Poisoned nettles irritated his flesh. Thorns and briers stuck in his
legs. Swarms of flies hovered about the festering sores. Millions of mosquitoes feasted on him, lingering, hurrying, or pausing with their victim. Sleep was impossible. His only defense
was the piece of quilt, and a handful of bushes which he carried.

On the third day about three o'clock he found some rasp-
berries. This was the first food he had eaten since the morning before his escape. He was not hungry, but extremely weak.
Yet he had strength enough to swim the Muskingum at a point
where it was two hundred yards wide. On the fourth day he
found two small crawfish, and ate them. The next night he
came within five miles of Wheeling. During the whole time he
had not slept one moment. When opposite Wheeling he saw a
man on the other side of the river, and called to him. The
stranger, however, was not disposed to venture over at the bidding of such a wild and suspicious looking character as Slover.

At length, by earnest persuasion, and by naming various persons in the expedition, known to the stranger, the latter came to Slover's help. The trials of the fugitive were over. In a few days he was able to make his way home. Such were the powers of endurance and recuperation of the iron frames of the pioneers.

Such were Slover's adventures. What had become of James Paull? He, as will be remembered, had made his escape into the woods at the moment of Slover's capture. He was pursued by two Indians. Lamed by his burnt foot, every step gave him intolerable pain. In spite of this he outran his pursuers, seeing which they fired at him. Coming to a steep bank of a creek, he fearlessly leaped over, gun in hand. At this moment the savages lost sight of him, and either abandoned the chase or passed another way. In the descent of the precipice Paull had torn his burnt foot in a horrible manner. To enable him to proceed at all he was forced to tear a strip from his ragged pantaloons, and bind it around the injured member.

Paull was an experienced woodsman. To hide his trail he walked on fallen logs, traveled in circles, and, climbing trees, would crawl out to the extremity of their branches, and let himself drop. At night he slept in a hollow log. In the morning the unhappy man found his foot swollen to the size of a water bucket. He had no provisions, and was afraid to fire his gun. Nevertheless, he gathered enough wild berries to sustain life.

The second night he crawled into a crevice in a rock, making himself a bed of leaves. The next morning he saw a deer. At that moment the pangs of hunger overcame his prudence. He shot the animal. But he had no knife; he had to cut open the skin with his gun-flint, and tear off the flesh with his fingers. This he ate raw, as a fire was not to be thought of. Continuing his journey, he crossed the Muskingum, and came upon an abandoned Indian camp. Some empty kegs were lying around. In one of them he ventured to kindle a little fire and cook some veni-

son.   When he lay down to sleep the smoke protected him from
the gnats and mosquitoes.

In two days he reached the Ohio River at a point above
Wheeling.   Building himself a rude raft, bound together with
withes of bark, he crossed the Ohio, and for the first time felt
himself out of danger.   In the river bottom he found a number
of horses.   He at once set to work, with an ingenuity of which
only the most skillful pioneer is capable, to manufacture a rude
halter out of the bark of trees.

This done, he attempted to capture a horse—a much more
difficult task.   The animals were both smart and wild.   They
would graze quietly, apparently without noticing his approach,
until his hand had almost grasped the mane of one of their
number.   At that moment, with a wild snort and a lofty kick,
they would turn and gallop out of his reach.

After great trouble Paull succeeded in capturing an old mare,
the worst in the lot.   On this animal he continued his journey,
finally reaching a fort near Short creek.   Here the inhabitants,
alarmed by the news of the destruction of Crawford's army,
had collected, in anxious expectation of an Indian invasion.
Here too, he found some of the volunteers who, like himself, had
escaped from the clutches of the savages.   Resting for a day,
he procured a horse that was a horse, and proceeded to a settlement where he had some relatives.

For some time he was detained here by his foot, of which
the terrible inflammation threatened him with the loss of the
member.   In time, however, he made his way back to the humble home of his widowed mother, who, ignorant of her boy's
fate, had nevertheless continued to watch for his return.

In after years Paull became a prominent man in Virginia.
He took an active part in the Indian campaigns toward the close
of the century.   His descendants are numerous and of high
standing.   Personally he was a man of splendid physique,
formed like a king, and bearing the head of a philosopher.   He
was generous to a fault, and possessed a heart of unflinching

courage. He died on the ninth day of July, 1841, at his home in Fayette County, Virginia, aged nearly eighty-one years.

Of all the men in the army the returned volunteers could tell the least of the fate of Colonel Crawford and Doctor Knight. The explanation of this is to be found in the account which follows. It will be remembered that as the army was formed in line of march in the deep darkness of the grove near Sandusky, at nine o'clock of the evening of June the 5th, waiting for the word of command to commence their perilous retreat, a furious assault was made by the enemy. This precipitated matters. The volunteers, without waiting for command, broke ranks and galloped away in the greatest confusion.

At the moment of flight Colonel Crawford missed his son, John Crawford, his son-in-law, William Harrison, and his nephew, William Crawford. Alarmed at their absence, he commenced to search for them in the darkness, and shouted aloud their names. He ran hither and thither among the trees in frantic endeavor to find the missing men. At this moment Doctor Knight came up, and declared that the young men must be ahead of them, as the grove was then nearly deserted. Crawford answered that he was positive they were not in front, and begged Knight not to leave him. The doctor promised him he would not, and joined in the anxious search.

By this time the grove was rapidly filling up with the enemy. Knight and Crawford were now joined by an old man and a lad, both on horseback. The four endeavored to make their escape, in their course overtaking the volunteers who were entangled in the cranberry marsh. They traveled fifteen or twenty yards apart, guiding themselves by the north star. The old man frequently lagged behind, and never failed when he did so to call out for the others to wait. While crossing a stream the old man made his usual halloo from the rear. He was about to be reprimanded for the act, when an Indian yell was heard not far from him. After that the old man was not heard to call again, and no more was seen of him.

At sunrise, Crawford and his companions, whose progress had been slow and circuitous, found themselves only eight miles from the battle-field. The horses of Crawford and the young man already jaded, now gave out, and had to be abandoned. At two o'clock in the afternoon the travelers fell in with Captain Biggs, who had carried Lieutenant Ashley from the field of action dangerously wounded.

On the next morning, journeying through what is now Crawford county, they found a deer which was freshly killed. The meat was joyously cut up, and bound in packs for transportation. A mile farther on they were startled by the smoke of a camp-fire. Leaving the wounded man with the lad, the others cautiously approached the fire. No one was found near it. While roasting their venison one of the volunteers came up. He was the man who had killed the deer. Hearing the others approach, he mistook them for Indians, and ran off. From that time he also was a member of the little company with Crawford.

In their journey, somewhat against the judgment of Knight and Biggs, they followed the trail of the army. Crawford and the doctor, who had loaned his horse to Ashley, proceeded on foot about two hundred yards in advance of the others. Biggs and the wounded officer were placed in the center on horses, and the two young men followed on foot. While advancing along the south bank of the Sandusky, at a point just east of the present town of Leesville, three Indians started up within twenty steps from Knight and Crawford. Knight sprang behind a tree and was about to fire. Crawford shouted to him not to do so.

While hesitating, one of the Indians, a Delaware, who had often seen Knight, ran up and took him by the hand, calling him "doctor." Biggs fired on seeing the Indians, but missed his aim. "They then told us to call these people," says Knight, "and make them come there, else they would go and kill them;" which the colonel did, but the four got off, and escaped for that time.

Crawford and Knight were at once led captive to the camp

of the Delawares. This was on Friday afternoon. On Sunday evening, five Indians came into camp. They carried in their hands two small and bloody objects. It was dusk. This made it difficult to discern what they were. Crawford stooped and looked closely. Turning, deathly sick, to Dr. Knight, he said, "They are the scalps of Captain Biggs and Lieutenant Ashley."

Besides Crawford and Knight, there were other prisoners in the camp. Altogether there were eleven. The Indians soon discovered, to their joy, that Crawford was the commander of the American army—the "Big Captain." This information was immediately carried to Captain Pipe.

The startling and important news at once became the occcasion for a grave council of the chiefs of the Delaware nation. All other captives might be easily disposed of by the braves in any village. Not so with the American "chief." For him there must be devised no common fate. Captain Pipe presided over the assembly which discussed the grave question. There was complete unanimity of opinion. From the great and terrible chief, who, in years gone by had been the greatest rival of the noble White Eyes, who, on the latter's death, became the most prominent man of all the Delawares, and who, by his solitary prestige and influence, had won his people from a policy of neutrality, and made them of all the Indian allies of the British the bitterest and the bloodiest, down to the youngest brave, who, by the taking of some scalp in the recent battles, had earned a warrior's privilege of admission to the council-hall— every voice pronounced in favor of DEATH BY FIRE.

The Delawares, however, were subject to the sway of the Wyandots. Among the latter the burning of prisoners was no longer practiced; nor did the Delawares dare to inflict the death penalty in that manner upon so great a captive, without first obtaining permission from the Half King of the Wyandots. How could his consent be obtained? This was the question which agitated the council. At last the oldest and wisest chiefs devised a stratagem. A runner, bearing a belt of wampum, was

despatched to the Half King of the Wyandots, with the following message : " Uncle ! We, your nephews, salute you in a spirit
of kindness, love, and respect.   Uncle ! We have a project in
view which we ardently wish to accomplish, and *can* accomplish, if our uncle will not overrule us !   By returning the
wampum, we will have your *pledged word !*"

The Half King was puzzled.   He questioned the messenger,
but the latter, carefully trained, professed ignorance.   At last
the Half King, supposing the project to be some secret foray
against the white settlements, returned the wampum to the
bearer, with the word, " Say to my nephews, they have my
pledge."   Crawford's doom was fixed.

On Monday morning, the 10th of June, the prisoners were
informed that they must go to Sandusky.   Crawford, learning
that Simon Girty who, as will be remembered, was an old
friend, was at Sandusky, urged strongly to be taken to that
place at once.   While the other prisoners halted for the night
at the deserted Wyandot town, Crawford, under two guards,
was taken to Sandusky, arriving there in the night.   He
demanded to be at once taken to Girty's lodge.   Here, sitting
in the dim light of a smoldering camp-fire, he made his appeal,
long and earnest, to the renegade, to save him.   He offered
Girty one thousand dollars to save his life.

The ruffian moodily stirred the ashes, and said nothing.   At
last, being urged by Crawford for an answer, he turned, and
with a look which, to any other than a despairing man would
have told that he was lying, promised, in a cold, indifferent tone,
to do what was asked.   He also told the colonel that William
Harrison and young William Crawford had been captured by
the Shawanese, but pardoned.   The falsity of this statement we
already know from what Slover had witnessed.

Knight and his nine companions, on the morning of the
11th, were met by Captain Pipe at the old Wyandot town.   The
latter, with his own hands, proceeded to *paint the faces of all the
prisoners black*.   While thus engaged, he told Knight in very

good English, that he was to be taken to the Shawanese towns to see his friends. The ominous import of these smooth words was at once read by Knight. During the morning Colonel Crawford was also brought to this place. Pipe, who had not seen him the night before, with whom he was well acquainted, received him with pretended kindness, joked about his making a good Indian, but nevertheless *painted him black.*

The whole party now started toward the Wyandot town. Crawford and Knight were kept somewhat in the rear. Presently a savage shouted back some unintelligible words. Their guards hurried them forward. They now understood what the maneuver meant. Lying by the roadside were the corpses, pale and gory, of four of their companions. They had been scalped and tomahawked.

The suspicion of Knight was confirmed as to their real destination, when, instead of proceeding to the Wyandot village, their guards struck into another trail leading to the north-west. Coming to a small creek, Crawford and Knight were removed to a little distance, while the others were seated around the foot of the tree. At the place where they halted they had found a number of squaws and Indian boys. In a moment Crawford and Knight were horrified to see these fall upon the five prisoners and tomahawk them all. A squaw cut off the head of one man and kicked it around in great glee as a football.

Saddened at this awful scene, and wrapped in the blackest gloom concerning their own fate, the two prisoners, now left alone, resumed their march. On their way they met Simon Girty, but he had no word of kindness. Waiting until Knight came up, the latter went toward him reaching out his hand, but the ruffian bade him be gone, calling him a "damned rascal." Three quarters of a mile from the village of Tymochtee another halt was made. The reason of this and the awful occurrences which transpired will appear when we return to the story of the unfortunate Crawford. For the present we proceed to relate the incidents which afterwards befell Knight, "who for over two hours before leaving the place drank to the dregs, it may be premised, a cup of inexpressible horror."

After nightfall Knight was taken on to Tymochtee, where he lay bound all night. The next morning he was placed in charge of an Indian named Tutelu, who at once started with him for the Shawanese towns, forty miles away. The prisoner was on foot. Behind him strode his savage guard, wielding an enormous lash, with which he urged the prisoner forward. Knight, pretending to think that he was to become an Indian, asked Tutelu if they were not to live together as brothers, in one house, when they reached the town. The Indian, human as he was, was touched by the flattery, and answered "Yes." At night the captive was bound and laid down to rest, but the vigilant guard closed not his eyes. At daybreak he untied his captive.

Tutelu rose and began to replenish the fire. A swarm of mosquitoes was bothering them, and Knight asked the savage if he should make a smoke behind him. He answered "Yes." The doctor stooped and picked up the end of a small stick which had been burnt till it was but eighteen inches long. For the purpose which he contemplated it was altogether too small. Yet it was the best to be had. He then took up another little stick, taking a coal between them, and went behind the Indian. Instantly dropping the coal, he struck the savage on the head with all his force, so that he fell forward with both his hands in the fire. The Indian scrambled to his feet, badly burned, and ran off, howling in the most fearful manner. Knight followed at the top of his speed to shoot him, but in drawing back the hammer of the Indian's gun, he broke the mainspring, and was forced to abandon the chase.

Tutelu never stopped running, it is presumed, till he reached the Shawanese towns. He arrived there, finding Slover, who was then still a captive. The Indian had a wound four inches long in his head. He also had another thing in his head. It was a story. With pompous manner and swelling words he related that his prisoner, the doctor, was a big, strong, tall man, that, being promised by Knight that he would not go away, he had untied him.

According to Tutelu, while he was kindling the fire, the doctor had snatched up the gun behind him and struck him; Tutelu had made a slash at Knight with his knife, cutting off his fingers and inflicting two stabs. As soon as his relation was over, Slover stepped into the group and told the Delawares that Tutelu had lied, that he knew the doctor, and he was a weak, little man. The Indians laughed heartily, and told Tutelu that they believed his whole story was false.

After abandoning his chase, Knight returned to the fire. He equipped himself for a journey home with the blanket, moccasins, gun, and ammunition of the Indian. He was not far from the spot now occupied by Kenton, Hardin county, Ohio. In his journey the only food he could find was green gooseberries. These, however, he was unable to eat on account of a wound in his jaw, which had been inflicted by an Indian out of pure malice. He tried every way possible to fix his gun, but failing, finally threw it away. His medical knowledge proved of some value to him. After his jaw got better, and he began to eat gooseberries, mandrakes, raw black birds, and terrapin, these delicacies gave him dyspepsia. Unlike most of the borderers, he was a delicate man, unused to hardships. To cure the trouble spoken of, he would gather and eat a little wild ginger. On the morning of the 4th of July he reached Fort Pitt.

Sadly let us turn back to the scene where Crawford was halted on the afternoon of the 11th of June, three-quarters of a mile from Tymochtee. When he arrived he found a large fire burning. As it was a hot summer day his suspicions were at once aroused. A hundred Indians were lying about on the ground. The picture, if transferred to canvas, would be one of utter inactivity and laziness.

As the approaching party suddenly appeared in sight, an electric shock would not have more quickly and completely

27

transformed the scene of idleness to one of intense activity and animation. A dozen warriors ran forward and seized Crawford. They tore his clothes from him with eager hands. He was made to sit down on the ground. Surrounded by a howling mob, he at once became the object of showers of dirt, stones, and sticks. While some were engaged in this sport, others quickly fixed in the ground a large stake, some fifteen feet long, which had been previously prepared. Others still ran quickly to and fro, piling up around the stake great heaps of light, dry hickory wood, which had also been split and prepared for the occasion. The wood was arranged loosely, with large apertures, through which the draft might more quickly carry the sputtering blaze.

Crawford had taken in the entire scene at a glance. He called to Girty, who was in the crowd, and asked if he was to be burnt. The brute, who had not made the least exertion to save his old friend, yelled back, " of course." The wretched man was seized and his hands bound behind him. A rope was fastened to the stake, and the other end passed around his body. It was long enough to permit him to walk around the stake several times.

It was four o'clock. The afternoon sun was already casting somber shades through the forest. Over head patches of the azure sky, as calm and peaceful as eternity, could be seen by the doomed man. From the top of a lofty tree a little bird caroled forth its woodland song, happy, innocent, and free. But in the dark assemblage beneath the trees every malignant countenance was lit up by the wild insanity, the everlasting unrest, of sin, of wickedness, of hell.

Willing hands applied a torch to the heaps of wood. The crackling flames leaped quickly through the open spaces. As the wood began to kindle, Captain Pipe arose, and addressed the crowd briefly, but earnestly, in his own dark language, making all the while the most terrible gestures at the heroic man, who stood calmly at the stake confronting his doom. As the speaker finished, an unearthly yell burst from the hoarse throats of his auditors. Heedless of the small flames which were already shooting upward through the wood, they leaped within the circle, and fell upon the unfortunate Crawford.

A hundred yards away stood Doctor Knight, an unwilling spectator, filled with an anguish which it is impossible to conceive. The throng about Crawford was so dense for the time being that his friend could not tell what was being done. He could only see uplifted hands rising and falling above the heads of the crowd, and hear its angry roar. In a moment the throng fell back. Knight could then see that they had cut off Crawford's ears, and beaten him black and blue.

Though compelled by the circle of flames which now leaped up and walled in the unfortunate man, to remain at a little distance, the tormentors were by no means through. Warriors shot burning blasts of powder into his quivering flesh. Indian boys snatched blazing hickory poles, and held them against his body. As, wild with pain, he ran around and around the stake, to avoid one party of tormentors, he was confronted at every point by others, with burning fagots and redhot irons. The squaws threw quantities of burning coals against him, which, falling on the ground at his feet, left him a path of fire to tread.

In the extremity of his agony, a scream from the maddened man rang out through the forest, "Girty! Girty! shoot me through the heart! Quick!! For God's sake, do not refuse me!" And it is on record that to this appeal the monster made answer with a laugh. Crawford turned then in his supplications from man to God. Leaning against the stake, enduring all the torments which malice could invent, with manly fortitude and heroic calmness, in low, earnest tones he poured out his supplications to the Almighty.

How long the awful scene continued, we do not know. Dr. Knight says two hours. But this is, probably, much too long. That the time should have seemed to him almost endless, is not surprising.   At last nature seemed to be able to endure no more.   Crawford fainted, and fell on his stomach.   An old hag, with the countenance of a devil, threw a quantity of coals and ashes on the back of the prostrate man.   With a deep groan, he again arose, probably in a delirium, and began to walk slowly around the stake.   He was as black as coal from head to foot, save where the burnt flesh had broken off, from which spots ran reddened rivulets.

The end came at last.   Tradition says that the spirit of the dying man took its flight just as the western sun threw its setting beams across the landscape.

Such was THE DOOM OF CRAWFORD.   Far and wide through the settlements of the white man spread a melancholy gloom as the story passed from lip to lip.   Heart-rending was the anguish in a lonely cabin upon the banks of the Youghiogheny, where the widow wept without hope.

CHAPTER XII.

THE ROMANCE OF RED EAGLE.

AR to the south, within sound of the restless roar of the Gulf of Mexico, in a country of remarkable fertility, threaded by numberless creeks and rivers, the white man found a great Indian confederacy. This moist region was called, for want of a better name, the Creek Country. In the process of time, the Indians who inhabited it came to be called the Creeks. This nation, thus so unceremoniously christened by the whites, was, in fact, composed of many tribes of Indians. Long before La Salle had paddled his weary way down the Mississippi, the Muscogees, whose original home, according to their traditions, had been in the country of Mexico, had, after long wanderings as far north as the Ohio, finally settled in the region which we know by the names of Alabama and Mississippi. The Muscogees were warriors. They at once began a series of conquests, and, like Rome, adopted the policy of incorporating the conquered tribes with themselves.

When the first bold explorers threaded their way through the tropical forests and the network of lagoons to the towns of this confederacy, they found a people who, in the darkness of their native barbarism, were in a crude way working out for themselves the problem of civilization. They had fixed rules governing marriage and divorce. They lived in houses. They wore clothes. Each town had a separate local government. It had public buildings and pleasure houses. They had fixed

FLIGHT OF THE INDIANS AFTER THE MASSACRE.

maxims and methods of government. They had, moreover, a system of social caste. There were certain families who constituted a hereditary nobility. Of these, the family of the Wind ranked first. To it belonged the right of chieftaincy. It was, so to speak, the royal family. Inferior to the family of the Wind was the family of the Bear; and next in rank was that of the Deer. These three castes managed to absorb all the positions of rank and profit.

At the time of the war of which we are about to write, they had, in addition to their unaided achievements, derived great benefit from intercourse with the white men. Many of them had intermarried. The upper classes had learned to read and write. Many half-breed children had been sent to northern schools for education. The system of a community of property, which is the very core of barbarism, was giving way to the system of individual property. They owned in their own right, horses, houses, looms, farms, and farming implements. They had learned, not merely to trade, but even to manufacture cloth and other articles. All this, too, they had achieved in spite of their fertile soil and the genial climate. History shows that nature prodigal of her gifts, enervates, while a sterile country and vigorous climate stimulate and sharpen the intellect and energies of men.

The Creeks were treated by the United States Government with justice and fairness. There was no reasonable cause for complaint on either side.

About 1780 there was born in the Creek nation a child destined to be known among his own people as Red Eagle. To the whites he was known as William Weatherford. His mother was a princess; that is, she belonged to the family of the Wind. He was the nephew of Alexander McGillivray, a man of mixed blood, whose genius, shrewdness, and abilities won for him the leading place in the Creek nation. He styled himself Emperor Alexander. One author speaks of him "as a man of towering intellect and vast information, who ruled the Creek country for a quarter of a century." Another writer says: "He was a man of the highest intellectual abilities, and of wonderful talents for intrigue and diplomacy. A more wily Talleyrand never trod the red war-paths of the frontiers, or quaffed the deceptive black drink at sham councils."

When Charles Weatherford, a shrewd and wily Scotch trader, married the sister of the Emperor Alexander McGillivray, he attained at once a rank and influence among the Creeks which few men of the purest Muscogee blood possessed. The Scotchman, while serving the nation, managed to accumulate almost boundless wealth. He lived like a king in his splendid mansion on the banks of the Alabama. Here he had every luxury which money could procure. Troops of negro slaves ministered to himself and to his guests. His table abounded in the rarest tropical fruits, choice game from distant forests, and sparkling liquors, cobweby with age.

From the spacious verandas which surrounded his palatial home, one looked out over a tropical landscape of surpassing loveliness. The grounds immediately surrounding the house were filled with noble forest trees, from whose branches hung graceful festoons of southern vines and mosses. Magnolia blossoms showered their fragrance upon the summer air. Wild orange-trees, bearing the emblems of every season of the year, were scattered here and there. Roses and honeysuckles, in wild and negligent profusion, wound their clinging arms in fond embrace about the nearest object of support. Near the house Weatherford kept the finest race-track in America. To indulge his favorite sport, he imported blooded stock from the most famous stables of Europe.

Amid these surroundings was born Red Eagle. The son of the wealthiest man in the nation, and by inheritance a chief of the ruling family, he had the best of tutors, and no pains nor expense were spared in his education. He grew up a spoiled child of fortune. He cared nothing for books. His tastes were the offspring of the wild ancestry of his Indian mother. He was fond of every athletic sport. He was a splendid swimmer, a tireless walker, and an unequaled hunter with the bow and the rifle. He was a natural master. From no meeting for athletic sports among the Creek towns was Red Eagle ever absent. No young man in all the nation could approach him in a foot-race. In games of ball, a sport conducted with such violence that broken limbs and even death were not infrequent, he was the acknowledged king.

While but a child, he displayed the rarest graces of horsemanship. No colt was too unruly, no stallion too high-mettled for this adventurous youth to mount and dash in mad career across the country. Such was his perfection as a rider that he seemed almost a part of the animal he rode. An old Indian woman, who knew the young chief in his boyhood, telling of his daring, his skill, his grace as a horseman, said : "The squaws would quit hoeing corn and smile and gaze upon him as he rode by the corn-patch."

These things made Red Eagle the idol of his people. In the wars with the Choctaws and Chickasaws, even before he reached manhood, he displayed the most tireless activity and reckless courage. His name was greeted with enthusiasm as that of the coming chief in every house in the nation. Besides this, he possessed great personal beauty. His figure was symmetrical and imposing, and his countenance that of a born king. He possessed intellectual ability of the highest order. His mind, ignoring trifles, grappled with the most important subjects which agitated his country.

To all these gifts was added that of eloquence. Red Eagle was the greatest orator that ever lived among the Creeks. It was his ambition from boyhood to become distinguished in council. Lazy and indifferent about his general education, he gave the most persistent attention to the study of declamation and oratory. As he reached maturity, his eloquent voice soon reigned without a rival in the council-hall. His imagination was rich, bold, and vivid ; his manner impressive in the highest degree. When unimportant questions were being discussed, Red Eagle looked on with indifference. His lips were sealed. But when great themes agitated the council, Red Eagle, with

TECUMSEH ENTERING THE COUNCIL.

his unapproachable power of statement, his wealth of imagery, his burning zeal, took the lead in the debate, and bore down all opposition. His very vices endeared him to the popular heart. Reared in wealth and idleness, the young chief was, it is said, given to many excesses.

Such was the man, longing for some great popular cause in which to employ his wealth of talents and influence, whom Tecumseh found when, in 1811, he had arrived, from the far north, in the Creek country, accompanied by thirty warriors. The great chief who dwelt by the waters of the Miami had journeyed all the way to the mighty confederacy of the south for two purposes. As an agent of the British, he was to incite the southern tribes to join in the approaching war with the Americans. For himself, he came to forin a great offensive and defensive alliance of all the Indians of America against the white man.

On the day when, with great pomp, he entered the council-hall of the Creeks, he called on the red men to abandon the plows and looms and arms of the whites, to burn the garments they had been induced to wear, to trample under foot and forget the lessons and customs which they had been taught by their white foes. He told them that the white men, by teaching them to till the ground, were seeking to weaken and degrade their martial spirit, so that the conquest of their country might be more easy. Then, with impressive gesture and accent, he warned them that, as the whites already held the negroes in bondage, their purpose was, as soon they became strong enough, to reduce the Indians to slavery.

A prophet accompanied Tecumseh, whose business it was to practice upon the superstition of the people. He told them that the Great Spirit commanded the red man to make war upon the white man. To prove that this message was from the Great Spirit, the prophet promised them a miracle. Whoever fought in the war should come out of it unharmed, while the Americans would be destroyed in impassable morasses with which the Great Spirit would surround them. Besides these methods, Tecumseh employed another. He went among the people, and electioneered with the warriors in person.

In this way a large part, perhaps a majority, of the Creeks became ready and impatient for a war with the whites. A strong and influential minority, however, refused to yield to Tecumseh's arguments. Among these was Big Warrior. Although Tecumseh was his honored guest, he obstinately refused to forsake his allegiance. It is said that Tecumseh at last grew so angry with Big Warrior, that he threatened, when he reached Detroit, to stamp his foot on the ground and shake down all the houses in Tookabatcha, and that a few months afterwards an earthquake made the Creeks believe that this threat had been carried out. The wealthier Creeks, who were, of course, a minority, having accumulated property, which is the greatest of all conservative forces in society, were strongly opposed to the war.   They saw in it nothing to gain, and every thing to lose.

Among his converts, Tecumseh readily discovered that of all men in the nation Red Eagle was the man for his purpose. His great talents seemed to be lying idle, waiting for some employment worthy of their owner.   He was wealthy, and had nothing to gain by commerce with the whites.   He was born to fortune, and consequently held his possessions in light esteem.   Of wild and undisciplined passions, and full of a lofty patriotism and love of state affairs, he had nursed in his heart for many years a bitter jealousy and overmastering hostility towards the whites.   He hated the restraint of law and civilization.   He loved the license and wild liberty of savage life. As his tastes led him to the sports of the forest, he looked with concern on the encroachments of the white men.   Moreover, he seemed to fear that an attempt would be made to reduce his people to slavery like that of the negroes.

So, after listening to the wily Tecumseh, Red Eagle, who saw in his plans a gratification for his own fierce love for war and a new field for fame, threw himself heart and soul into the enterprise of the northern chieftain.   Re-enforced by Red Eagle, Tecumseh found new methods of working upon the Creeks.   He directed his prophet to "inspire" some Creeks with prophetic powers.

A shrewd and unscrupulous half-breed named Francis, was shut up alone in a cabin for ten days, during which time the prophet howled and danced around the building in the most fantastic manner.   When the ten days were accomplished, he brought Francis forth, telling the people that he was now blind, but would soon receive his sight back so improved that he could see what was to happen in the future.   Francis allowed himself to be led around, pretending to stumble over obstacles like a blind man.   Suddenly he affirmed that he had received his sight, with the improved quality of

prophecy. He, with others inspired in a similar manner, worked
night and day, practicing all sorts of conjurations in behalf of
the war-party. Public feeling among the Creeks was roused
to the highest pitch of excitement. The strife of factions
became very bitter. The two parties indulged in crimination
and recrimination. The Creeks were ready for civil war.

A spark soon fell in the tinder box. Some Creeks, returning with Tecumseh to Canada, assaulted a settlement and murdered seven families. Under the treaty between the Creeks
and the United States, the murderers were required to be punished. The chiefs of the peace party at once organized bands
of warriors for this purpose. The murderers were pursued to
their retreats among the most distant tribes, hounded down
by the relentless avengers, shot, stabbed, or tomahawked in
open fight or by secret stealth wherever found, until the last
criminal paid for his fault with the penalty of death.

This vengeance widened the schism in the Creek nation.
The war party retaliated by committing a number of outrages
upon the white men. Big Warrior was aroused. He asked for
a council with the chiefs of the war party. The request was
haughtily refused. Next he sent word to them, saying, that if
the miracles which they talked about should also be wrought
before the chiefs of the peace party, then the latter would
also believe. To this the war Creeks responded by murdering a
party of emigrants, by sacking a plantation, and by destroying
the property of some of the peaceful Creeks themselves.

About this time a friendly half-breed named McNac was
attacked in his home and had his cattle stolen. He saved himself for awhile by hiding in the swamp, but was unluckily captured by High Head Jim. McNac lied. He said he belonged
to the war-party. He found out that a plot was laid to kill
Big Warrior, Captain Isaacs, Mad Dragon's son, and all the
chiefs of the peace party. This done, High Head Jim said
war was at once to be waged upon the whites. McNac escaped
and warned the intended victims. Meanwhile marauding parties

of increasing size roamed over the country, plundering plantations of whites and peace Indians alike. The settlers resolved
on self-defense. An army of two hundred volunteers went out
to whip a marauding party of the Creeks. The battle fought
is known as the battle of Burnt Corn. The white men were
ingloriously whipped.

At this point in the war Red Eagle wavered. He discovered that he had failed to carry with him the entire Creek
nation. Among the minority who sternly opposed him were
many of his friends and relatives. He had met them face to
face in the bloody battle of Burnt Corn. His ambition had led
him to seek a war with the whites. In fact, it had involved
him in a civil war.

There was yet another motive. He was rich, young, handsome, and a widower. He had a sweetheart, Lucy Cornells, a
young girl of mixed blood, the rarest beauty of the Creek
nation. Upon her Red Eagle had lavished all the wealth of
his passionate affections. In his nature there was much of
romance and sentiment. In debate he was the sternest of the
stern. In love he was the tenderest of the tender. He now
found that among the Creeks against whom he was about
to wage cruel and bloody civil war was the family of his
sweetheart.

On the discovery by McNac of the plot for the assassination, the peace Indians and half-breeds were struck with con-
sternation. Among throngs of others, Lucy Cornells's father fled
with his family to take refuge in Fort Mims. Against this very
fort Red Eagle was already plotting a campaign. What were
all the affairs of state, the triumphs in debate, the glory of the
battle-field to Red Eagle, who was as chivalrous as he was
brave, if thereby he must lose the affection of the girl he
loved? More than this, how could he imperil her life, which
was dearer to him than his own, by a siege and probably massacre, where she had sought refuge from his own arms.

These things perplexed Red Eagle. He kept his own

counsel, and resolved to seek the advice of his relatives, who belonged to the peace party. He secretly made his way to their homes. He told them that he was in love. A man in love has no reason, no judgment. He is like a diver at the bottom of the ocean. All around him is strange, mysterious, and unreal. All his past life is forgotten. All his plans and hopes for the future are driven from his mind. He even forgets his own identity. Those who are most nearly and dearly related to him seem to him but phantoms. With them he has no real, tangible connection. All thought, all memory, all consciousness are absorbed and concentrated into a single notion, one overmastering feeling. It is the fact that he is countless fathoms deep beneath the surface where others float. If any emergency befalls, if for any reason he needs help, all he can do is to make the signal of distress to friends above him. This was what Red Eagle did. From the depths of the ocean he pulled the signal rope.

His friends, like all friends, were ready with advice. They told him to go back, to remove as secretly as possible his family, his negroes, and as much of his live stock as he could, to their plantations, which were in the district of the peace party; that he should follow them there, and remain quietly at home until the troubles of the nation were over. Red Eagle accepted this advice. He was like one who is mesmerized. All that is necessary to make the subject do any particular thing is simply to crook the finger. No matter how ridiculous it may be he will not refuse to obey. He went back to his home.

But it was now too late for him to retreat. His infidelity had been suspected. In his absence his children and negroes had been seized, and were held as hostages for his fidelity. He was told that if he deserted the cause of the war-party, his children should at once be put to death.

Red Eagle was now overwhelmed by the very storm which he had stirred. He had evoked the Genii from their prison, and the spirits would not down at his bidding. For him there remained but one thing. It was to lead his men to battle. So there was preparation for war. The Creek braves painted themselves in gaudy colors, and concentrated in large numbers. The white men, on their part, hastily constructed small forts, or repaired fortifications which were already in existence. Of these, of which there were more than twenty among the settlements, Fort Mims was the largest and strongest. It was located near the Alabama River, and a few miles above its junction with the Tombigbee. Samuel Mims and his neighbors had constructed

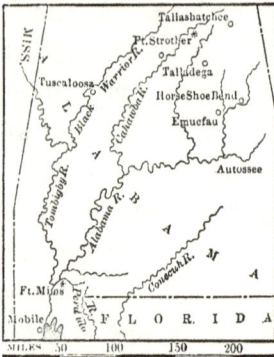

REGION OF THE CREEK WAR.

the fortification, and to that place the people of the surrounding country—men, women, and children, white, black, red, and yellow—fled for safety.

General Claiborne, with a small force of volunteers and regulars, was the military commander of the whites. To Fort Mims he dispatched Major Beasley, with one hundred and seventy-five men. These, with the militia already there, gave the post a garrison of two hundred and forty-five men. Beasley was ordered to construct a second stockade around the first, and two additional block-houses, an order which was but partially carried out.

Altogether there were about five hundred and fifty people in the fort whose lives were committed to the care of Major Beasley. He, however, neglected the proper precautions. He forgot the great responsibility resting on his shoulders. His raw troops, instead of being disciplined by daily drills and military routine, passed their time in playing cards and drinking. The new line of picketing was left unfinished, as were also the new block-houses. He was even deaf to the plainest warnings of danger. A negro, who had been captured by Red Eagle, escaped, and making his way to Fort Mims with infinite peril, told the commandant that an overwhelming force of

Indians were on their way to attack it. Beasley sent out some scouts, but they, as they discovered no Indians in the immediate neighborhood of the fort, returned and told the negro he was a liar. On another day, two negroes, who had been out guarding some cattle, came running to the fort in the greatest terror. They declared that they had seen a large body of Indians. A party of horsemen at once sallied forth to the spot where the negroes averred they had seen the savages. They found the forest silent, and apparently unoccupied. Red Eagle's men had disappeared like phantoms. So the brave horsemen rode back to the fort and denounced the negroes as liars. One of them was at once tied to a whipping-post and flogged, for giving a false alarm. The other was saved for awhile by the interference of his master. It is a historical fact that when the attack, which we are about to describe, was made upon the fort, this negro was standing tied, waiting for his whipping.

When the negro who had been whipped went forth to attend to his cattle, he again saw the Indians, but fearing to return to the fort and give the alarm, lest he should be whipped, he ran away. Such was the work of the commander's folly.

Red Eagle was a soldier—a strategist. Of him, Andrew Jackson afterwards said: "This man is fit to command great armies." The negroes had told the truth. The Indians were hovering near the fort. They had been there for several days, watching their opportunity. Of all this the defenders of the fort were sweetly oblivious. The gates stood open day and night. The wind had blown a heap of sand against the bottom of the gates. This fact, trifling to a careless observer, was really important. The gates could not be closed until the accumulating sand should be shoveled away. This would take time. The gates could not be closed in a hurry. Red Eagle observed the pile of sand, although the commander of the fort did not. The Indian strategist said: "We will wait until the sand is heaped a little higher." The wind was busy while the soldiers slept. The sand heap grew.

28

On the morning when the runaway negro had a second time seen Indians Red Eagle lay within a few hundred yards of the fort at the head of a thousand warriors. He was like a wild animal watching for its prey, only waiting the proper moment to spring forth. The morning hours passed as usual at the fort. No guards were posted. The men occupied themselves with idle games and disorderly fun. All seemed opportune. Why did not the tiger spring forth from the forest? The dinner-bell rang in the fort. There was a confused uproar of men, women, and children crowding their way with noisy fun toward the tables of the barracks. There was time for all to be quietly seated at the meal.

At that moment Red Eagle rose and gave the signal for advance. A line of Indians started forward with the speed of the wind, yet as silent as cats, toward the open gates. They were within ninety feet of them before any one in the fort discovered the enemy. A few men who happened to be near the gates started to close them. They gave the heavy, wooden portals a sudden pull, but they remained fixed in their place. The sand heaps blown up by the sportive wind were to cost hundreds of lives. In their fright and despair the men tugged furiously and frantically at the gates. They tried to kick the sand away. It was no use. They could not budge the gates. The Indians rushed in with resistless momentum, hurling the little group of white men back from their pathway with the force of an express train.

The alarm-cry was now heard in every quarter of the fort. Women screamed. Men upset the dinner tables in their frantic haste. Every one seized the nearest weapon, gun, tomahawk, or club, and rushed forth to expel the foe. Luckily there was a second line of picketing, partly completed, back of the gate, which prevented the Indians from making their way at once into the body of the fort. The garrison, in wild confusion, at once commenced a hand-to-hand conflict. Among the first to fall, mortally wounded, was Major Beasley, the careless commandant. He refused to be carried to the interior of the fort preferring to remain where he was, to animate and direct his troops, and by courage to atone for his negligence. He remained in command of his troops until death overtook him.

The battle was terrible. The men fought like demons. Upon their success in driving the Indians from the fort depended, as they knew, not only their own lives, but those of the women and children who had been placed in their care. It was a fight in which the antagonists sought to club, chop, and hack each other to death. They siezed one another's throat with a vise-like gripe, of which the invincible tenacity relaxed only with death itself. For two hours the conflict raged with stubborn violence. The very women of the fort, horrified by the fate which seemed to await them, armed themselves with such weapons as they could procure, and with wild screams and nervous fury, mingled in the bloody fray.

In spite of the utmost endeavors of the white men; in spite of the barricade of corpses behind which they fought; in spite of the wounds and flowing blood, the savages gained ground. Outnumbering the garrison three to one, they beat back their foes, overpowering them at point after point. As the Indians advanced into the interior of the fort they fired the buildings. The whites, driven back farther and farther, were forced for their last refuge to a small inclosure called the bastion. Above the din of the conflict arose in every quarter the warning cry of " To the bastion !" In a moment the inclosure was packed so full of people that no one could move, much less fight. The wails of women mingled with the roar of the flames and the hoarse shouts of the blackened soldiery grew feebler and feebler.

At this point, Red Eagle rose to the height of heroism. He called upon his warriors to desist. Dismounting from his splen-did horse, he placed himself in front of the howling murderers, and sought by imperious commands and earnest appeals to stop the carnage. But for the second time in his life he found that

he had let loose a storm which he could not control. As he
now labored to save the lives of the remaining whites, his followers, with fierce suspicion, told him that not long before he
had attempted to desert from the cause, and if he made further
efforts in behalf of their enemies that he himself was the first
man who should be put to death. Foiled in his best intentions,
Red Eagle mounted and rode away from the scene of the massacre to calm the raging torrent of his thoughts in solitude.

The persons remaining in the fort were put to death, making
more than five hundred people who perished in the massacre.
About twenty of the occupants of the fort succeeded in chopping a hole through the outer picketing. Their adventures were
various. Dr. Thomas G. Holmes wandered five days in swamps
and cane-brakes. At last he fired his gun for help. Some white
men who were near were so frightened that they themselves
took to the swamp and remained for two days. Holmes was
finally saved. Lieutenant Chamblies was twice wounded in his
flight, but succeeded in concealing himself in a pile of logs.
Toward night the lieutenant was horrified to discover a band
of Indians surrounding the log-pile and setting fire to it. He
remained in his position till he was terribly burned, but was
rejoiced to see the Indians leave just as he was forced to crawl
from his hiding-place.

Zachariah McGirth had left Fort Mims on the morning of
the massacre, leaving behind him his wife and children. Having gone but a few miles he heard the roar of battle at the fort,
and started back, filled with anxiety concerning his family.
Late at night he made his way into the fort, and began an
agonizing search among the bodies of the slain for the corpses
of his wife and children. By the help of a torch and the glow
from the embers of the block-houses, he sought everywhere,
turning over and examining the bloody and mangled remains.

After several hours spent in the sickening task, he was
forced to conclude that his family were among those who had
been consumed in the buildings. As a matter of fact, a young

Indian, recognizing in McGirth's wife a former friend, had rescued her and her children. He told his fellow-warriors that he wished to make them slaves. McGirth, ignorant of all this, caring no longer for life, became the most reckless scout and Indian fighter in the American army. Several months afterward his family were restored to him; it was as if they had arisen from the dead.

Two days after the massacre of Fort Mims, the prophet Francis, at the head of a band of warriors, assaulted a house and killed twelve persons. A Mrs. Merrill, in the house with an infant in her arms, had been scalped and left for dead. Hours afterward she revived, and attempted to crawl to Fort Sinquefield, two miles away, which she succeeded in doing. At the time, her husband was serving as a volunteer in the army. He heard of the butchery, receiving information of his wife's supposed death. Before the wife had recovered sufficiently to communicate with her husband, he too, was reported as killed in battle. In fact, he was sent by mistake with the wounded volunteers from Tennessee to that State.

Years passed by. Mrs. Merrill married again. Late one evening, an emigrant family on their way to Texas asked for a night's lodging at her house. Scarcely had the guests been comfortably seated, when the husband of the emigrant family and the hostess recognized each other. Each had married, supposing the other dead. In this complication what was to be done? They talked far into the night. Both were happy in their present relations. They at last resolved, not, perhaps, without a shade of regret, to forget the past and live for the future as they were.

Misfortunes come not as single spies, but in battalions. The dead at Fort Mims were brought to Fort Sinquefield for burial. The people in the fort, unarmed and absorbed in their sorrow, went outside the stockade to a little valley fifty yards away to bury the bodies of their friends. At this moment, Francis, who was shadowing the place, attempted to throw his party of war-

riors between the white people and the gates. The men succeeded in reaching the fort, but the women and children were
unfortunately cut off.

Their condition seemed hopeless. A thrill of horror shot
through the hearts of the men at the fort. But life is full of
strange coincidences. A young man named Isaac Haden, a hunter, who kept a large pack of hounds trained to chase and seize
any living object upon which their master might set them,
appeared at this critical moment returning from a hunt. His

THE DOG CHARGE.

quick eye caught the situation. With a cry to his hounds he
dashed forward on his horse against the host of Indians. The
watchers at the fort and the helpless women without paused in
breathless anxiety to witness the strange maneuver. In a
moment every one of the sixty ferocious hounds had his fangs
fastened in the throat of a savage. The Indians were overwhelmed by the strange assault. In the few precious moments
the imperiled ones were rescued. Young Haden had his noble
horse shot from under him, and had five bullet-holes through
his clothes. A Mrs. Phillips was the only one who lost her life.

The news of the massacre of Fort Mims spread like wild-fire through the south. The entire white population on the Creek frontiers was in danger of instant destruction. To obtain help from the government at Washington, was impossible. It would take a month to send the news, and another one for the soldiers to reach the field of action. In this crisis the warm-hearted south-ern States impul-sively called for vol-unteers to save their friends and neighbors.

General Andrew Jackson, lying sick and enfeebled on his bed of pain, an-nounced that he would start to the front as soon as he could be helped into a saddle. He was yet a sick man, pale and emaciated, when, under the inspiration of his lofty will, he

ANDREW JACKSON.

started to meet the army of volunteers which had been raised for him. Arrived there, he found one thousand raw troops, completely without provision for the expedition into the Indian country. Nevertheless, with or without food, he determined to march. In a single day the army constructed a supply post, called Fort Deposit, on Thompson's creek. During the march southward the men seem to have subsisted almost entirely upon the zeal and enthusiasm of Jackson's eloquent addresses, which were issued to the men several times a day.

During the night of the 2d of November Jackson prepared to assault the Indian town of Tallushatchee. The two wings of the army encircled the town on either side.   At sunrise two companies were thrown forward into the circle.   This at once brought on the battle.   It raged with great fury.   That victory belonged to the Americans was very soon evident.   But the Indians refused to fly or accept quarter.   Again and again, parties of braves, and even single warriors were urged to throw down their arms and submit.   But with a heroism which rivaled that of Leonidas and his three hundred Spartans, every offer of mercy was rejected.   Every warrior fought the overwhelming hosts which surrounded him as long as he could stand or sit.   Even in the agonies of death the Creek braves would shoot malignant and unforgiving glances at their conquering foe, and feebly attempt to hurl a tomahawk at the nearest white man. They forced the Americans to turn the battle into a butchery. Every brave in the village was killed, the total falling not short of two hundred.   History presents no more complete destruction of any fighting force.

Still no provisions reached the army.   With unflinching boldness Jackson continued his march to the south.   He built another post, Fort Strother, for the reception of provisions.   It was literally an empty mockery.   There were no provisions. Here word reached Jackson that some friendly Indians were besieged at Talladega.   The ingenuity of the messenger who brought the news, in effecting his escape from the beleaguered town, has not been equaled among all the marvelous exploits heretofore recited in these pages.   He was a boy.   He had covered himself with the skin of a large hog, and had wandered about on all fours, as if hunting for roots.   At times, when he came near to hostile Indians, he would lie down comfortably in a mud puddle.   In this way he had escaped detection.

Once more Jackson marched his army into the presence of an enemy, without supplies.   The battle of Talladega was similar in plan to its predecessor, and about as successful.   Two hundred and ninety-nine Indian warriors were counted dead upon the ground.

More extensive operations were absolutely impossible until food could be procured by Jackson for his starving men. While his army lay idle at Fort Strother, Red Eagle's superb genius for war was active in other parts of the field. There was danger of famine among the white settlers, unless the crops could be gathered from the fields. To do this it was necessary, temporarily at least, to rid the country of hostile prowlers. In this way came about the celebrated "Canoe Fight." A force of seventy-two men, under Captain Sam Dale, undertook to rid a particular section of the country of Indians. Dale was marching his command along the south-east bank of the Alabama River, when, dissatisfied at finding no traces of Indians, he determined to cross the river. The job was by no means a small one. Only two little canoes were to be had. The river was a quarter of a mile wide.

At last, however, only twelve men, together with Dale, remained on the east bank of the river. While waiting their turn for transportation, the little company was startled by a volley of bullets from a large force of Indians. Dale's men concealed themselves in the dense undergrowth of the river bank, and behind trees. The situation was dangerous. Should the savages suspect, from the infrequency of the fire, the smallness of their numbers, they would quickly rush down and overpower them.

Escape to the other side was the one thing to be desired. For this purpose, however, they had only one canoe, the other being across the river. This boat would hold but six men, and the movement would involve a separation of the company. The Indians on shore, seeing the canoe crossing the river, would at once suspect the smallness of the force opposed to them, and would quickly overpower those who were left behind.

Dale signaled to his men on the other side for assistance. Eight of them started to cross the river, but discovering the immense strength of the Indian force, hastily put back to shore. A new danger now assailed the little band. A large canoe, containing eleven warriors, was discovered putting out from the bank and making its way down to a point opposite Dale's posi- tion. In a few moments they attempted to land.

Dale's party, attacked from front and rear, fought in both directions. Two of the warriors in the canoe attempted to swim ashore. One was shot through the top of the head. The other reached the shore and was met by Austill. At the moment of the encounter Austill slipped and fell into the water. The sav- age cast one keen glance at the little force, and then made his escape. Dale at once saw that it was but a matter of a few minutes before the whole Indian force, informed of the weak- ness of his company, would be upon them.

In this emergency Dale announced a desperate resolution. He called for volunteers to man the little canoe which they had, and attack the Indian canoe party. For this perilous attempt three men, James Smith, Jeremiah Austill, and a large negro named Cæsar, offered their services. With them Dale sprang into the canoe. The negro acted as steersman, while the white men plied the paddles. When half-way toward the hostile canoe with its nine occupants, Dale's men found to their dismay that their powder was wet and their guns useless.

By strange fortune the Indians in the canoe had exhausted their ammunition. There remained nothing but a hand to hand fight between four men on the one hand and nine on the other. The negro threw the little canoe alongside of the larger, and held it firmly there. The Indians sprang to their feet, prepared with knives and clubs to resist the assault. At the moment of contact Dale leaped into the larger canoe. While Austill and Smith beat the Indians with clubbed guns, Dale, with incon- ceivable quickness, gave the one nearest him a powerful shove, throwing him backwards against his neighbor, he in turn falling upon the third Indian, and so on, until every savage in the boat had lost his balance, and all were floundering together in the bottom. Dale seized the advantage, clubbing out the brains of savage after savage, and throwing their corpses into the river.

The last Indian was an old friend of Dale. The latter hesitated, and was about to lower his weapon, when the savage attempted to grapple with him. Dale was too quick. Stepping back, with a single blow he killed his antagonist. In less than two minutes from the time the boats came alongside of each other every one of the nine Indians was a corpse, floating down with the current toward the vast and lonely gulf. Of the white men, Austill alone was wounded.

With swift strokes of the paddles the two canoes were brought back to the

RED EAGLE'S LEAP.

shore, the remaining men taken on board, and an escape made to the opposite side of the river amid a heavy fire from the Indians.

On the 23d of December, 1813, Red Eagle, with a large force of Indians, awaited at Holy Ground an assault from General Claiborne. The spot was admirably chosen for defense. It was a high bluff, surrounded on the land side by marshes and ravines, on the eastern side of the Alabama River, just below what is now Powell's Ferry, in Lowndes county, Alabama. To the natural strength of the place was added that of heavy log fortifications.

The assault by the Americans was a comparative failure, as the Indians escaped by hundreds. Red Eagle, the last to leave the place, was almost on the point of being captured. Mounted on a gray horse of magnificent speed and endurance, he galloped rapidly toward a point where the bluff was but fifteen feet high. Over this perpendicular precipice wildly dashed the gallant rider and his noble steed. They both disappeared beneath the waves of the river, but in a few moments Red Eagle was seen, far out in the current of the river, to emerge from the depths, still on his horse which bravely bore him to the opposite shore.

During the time of the incidents which we have been relating, General Jackson had a series of troubles with his army, which developed the incomparable metal of the man, and have been admired and laughed at by several generations of men. While detained at Fort Strother, a mutinous spirit developed itself among the men, who, on account of the lack of provisions, threatened to disband. One morning Jackson was informed that the militia regiment intended to march home in a body. Jackson at once placed himself at the head of the volunteers and confronted the militia, telling them that they could march home only by cutting their way through his lines. This was more than the militia-men had counted on. They yielded.

But the volunteers were scarcely less discontented than the militia. That night they themselves resolved to go home. In the morning Jackson reversed the plan of the previous day. He placed the militia in front of the volunteers, and told them that their way home lay through the ranks. The joke was so rich that, for the time being, the trouble blew over.

Great was the distress from want of food. A soldier passed General Jackson and saw that he was eating something. He mutinously demanded that he should have a share of it. " Willingly," replied Jackson, and thrusting his hand into his pocket, offered the man some acorns. For some days they had been his only food.

At last, however, Jackson was left without any supporters. The entire army resolved that, if provisions did not come within two days, they would go home. They, however, promised that if the provision train was met they would return. On the appointed day the men marched away. Jackson went aftei them, and begged for volunteers to remain with him. To this appeal one hundred and nine men responded.

Twelve miles from the fort the army met the provision train. The men were furnished ample supplies of food. But with mouths and stomachs full of meat they determined, in spite of their promise, to return home. Jackson's rage was terrible. His left arm was still in a sling. He was more emaciated than when he had left his sick-bed. Snatching a musket from a man, he planted himself in front of the column of mutineers and broke forth into a wild storm of vituperation. He told them that they could march home only over his dead body, and that the man who first advanced toward him should be shot dead. Raising his gun to his shoulder, he waited. The troops who would have fought an army were conquered by the will of a single man. The mutineers returned to their camp.

But the troops shortly devised another expedient. Through a pretended flaw in their contract of enlistment, they claimed that their term had expired. On the afternoon of December 9th, they commenced strapping up their knapsacks. Jackson at once called on all good soldiers to assist him. The militia were drawn up behind a line of cannon confronting the mutineers. The artillery-men held lighted matches in their hands. Jackson then addressed his rebellious soldiery, and demanded from them an explicit answer, whether they would remain peaceably with the army, then, and there. He took out his watch to count the seconds which still remained for the men to answer. If they refused, at a signal the cannon and musketry of the militia-line would leap into flame, and hurl leaden storms of death and destruction into the ranks of the mutineers. The latter made their choice. They decided to remain. A fourth time Jackson had won a battle against his own troops.

At last Jackson received four thousand fresh recruits from Tennessee. Red Eagle and his army were concentrated in a sort of peninsula, called the Horseshoe, formed by a bend of the Tallapoosa River. The bend inclosed a hundred acres of ground, and at its narrowest part was about three hundred yards wide. Across this narrow place Red Eagle had constructed a strong fortification, which was designed to resist even artillery-fire. Within the inclosure the houses were further protected by embankments of earth. At the bank of the river floated one hundred canoes, as a possible means of retreat. The perfection of these preparations have caused certain writers to imagine that some white engineer had planned them. In fact, they were the conceptions of Red Eagle's brain.

On the 27th of March, 1814, Jackson found himself in front of this remarkable redoubt with two thousand soldiers. General Coffee, with seven hundred cavalry and a force of friendly Indians, were thrown across the river to occupy the opposite side of the bend in the rear of the fortification, and cut off retreat. By ten o'clock Coffee occupied this position. Jackson commenced a heavy attack with artillery and musketry upon the front of the breastworks, making but little impression. Coffee, without especial direction from his commander, resolved to throw a part of his men across the river in canoes, and by attacking the Indians in the rear, effect a diversion in favor of Jackson.

After an hour or so of ineffectual fighting, Jackson resolved to storm the works. The men were formed in solid column. This column was a projectile which was expected to force a breach where the cannon had failed. At the given word the long line of men started forward to hurl themselves against the fortification. In spite of the heavy fire from the enemy, which mowed down their ranks, the Tennesseeans hurried forward, reached the breastworks, thrust their rifles into the port-holes, and fired at the yelling savages within, or swarmed up and over the barricade. On the top of the breastworks there was many a fierce hand-to-hand en-

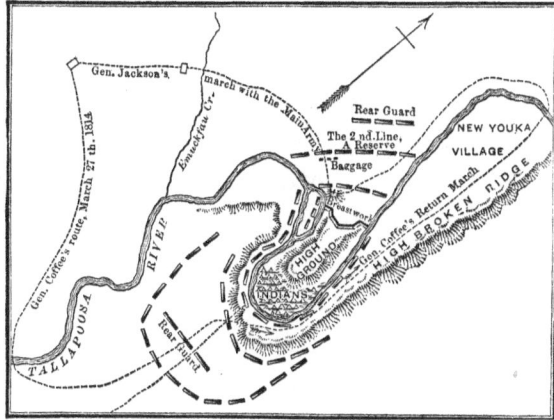

PLAN OF THE BATTLE OF THE HORSESHOE.

counter—the whites fighting to force their way into the fort, the savages struggling to hurl them back.

In a short time the number of Indians upon the parapet was seen to grow fewer and fewer. Every time an Indian fell his place was taken by two white men. Presently Jackson's troops began to leap down into the inclosure. The works were taken. But the defenders of the place were not conquered. To do that there was only one way. That way was BUTCHERY. It was a repetition of Tallushatchee. No savage would surrender. Again and again Jackson offered quarter, but the brave Creeks only riddled the messengers with bullets. At last, Red Eagle's men, beaten at every point, fled to the fleet of canoes to escape by water. Some did escape, but the majority fell beneath the unerring fire from Coffee's command. One old Indian, terribly wounded, jumped into the river, caught hold of a root in the bottom to keep himself down, and by breathing through the long joint of a cane, one end of which was in his mouth and the other above the water, remained hidden until nightfall, when he rose from his watery bed and made his way into the forest.

In the morning sixteen warriors were found concealed in a brush heap. They were surrounded by two hundred men, and called upon to surrender. They not only refused, but made insulting and defiant gestures. Of them, it might be said, that they were killed, but not conquered.

Five hundred and fifty-seven dead warriors were found in the fort. Besides this uncounted numbers had been killed in the river. The power of the Creek nation was crushed.

It was but a little while till the Creek leaders sent their messengers to Jackson, humbly begging for peace. To these overtures there was one reply: "Bring Red Eagle here, bound hand and foot; then we will talk of peace." It was Jackson's purpose to hang the Indian commander as a punishment for the massacre of Fort Mims.

Sad-faced messengers bore the dreadful news to Red Eagle. Peace there could be only on condition of the sacrifice of his life. His friends urged him to leave the country. To all such suggestions Red Eagle made no reply, but simply flashed one look of indignation from his proud and scornful eye. Many hours he sat alone in his wigwam, lost in thought. Sometimes he would walk to the door and look out upon the landscape with a sigh. Then he would return and resume his reverie. He counseled with no one. What was passing in his mind his broken-spirited followers did not suspect. He neither slept nor ate.

At last Red Eagle seemed to have come to some conclusion. Long before dawn one morning, without vouchsafing a single explanation, he mounted his splendid gray horse, and rode away through the forest in solitude and silence. An observer might have seen his lips tightly compressed. From his eye shone a strange light. He alone knew his destination.

He took his course toward the camp of Andrew Jackson. When within a few miles of the camp, a noble deer bounded across his path. Quick as thought Red Eagle fired, bringing down the game. He then reloaded his rifle. That load was for the heart of Big Warrior, in case he should offer any insult

to Red Eagle in the American camp. Laying the deer behind
him on his horse, he rode on. He came within sight of an
American sentinel, and calmly inquired for General Jackson's
head-quarters. He rode up to the door of the tent pointed out
to him. Andrew Jackson came forward, and in a spasm of rage
demanded of him how he dared to approach him when such a
penalty hung over him. To this Red Eagle replied:

"General Jackson, I am afraid of no man. I am a Creek
warrior. For myself I ask no favor. I come to beg mercy for
the women and children of my people, who are now starving in
the woods without an ear of corn. You may kill me if you
wish. I am done fighting. Of my warriors but a few live.
The rest have been killed. If I could fight you longer I would,
but save the women and children. They have never harmed
you. As for me, do with me as you please."

These words were delivered with a pathos and eloquence
which can not be described. A crowd had gathered around to
witness the strange scene. As once before in history, here was
a man found willing to die for his people. And as on that other
occasion, from which over the centuries there comes floating to
our ears the cries of the mob, "Crucify him, crucify him," so
here the crowd broke out into loud cries of "Kill him, kill him."

The hero recognizes the hero. There is an affinity between
high-born souls. Andrew Jackson rebuked the crowd. He
invited his distinguished prisoner into his quarters. After a
conversation, Jackson repeated the terms of peace which had
been offered, and then said, "You are at liberty to leave if
you wish. No opposition shall be made. But if I capture
you hereafter, you will be hung." To this Red Eagle replied
with burning words. He said that he accepted the terms of
peace. That no matter what fate awaited himself, his people
would at least be made happier by it.

The war was ended, but Red Eagle was not hung. Andrew
Jackson, instead of offering him punishment afforded him protection. His life was saved from the conspiracies of the friendly
29

Indians in Jackson's camp by the very guards with which his captor had surrounded him. In time he was left free to return to his old home and plantation. But there he found himself surrounded by hosts of implacable enemies, who sought his life. He went to Fort Claiborne, and placed himself under the protection of the commanding officer. But here, too, were men in whose breasts rankled the poisoned stings of civil war. He was obliged to leave the fort at night and in secret. He made his way to Jackson's camp, and in time was taken by the American general to his home in Tennessee, where he remained as a guest for nearly a year.

As time rolled on the hostilites of war died away. Red Eagle returned to his plantation. Again he accumulated property, again he was waited on by troops of slaves, and dispensed magnificent hospitality to his friends. His spirit was unbroken by misfortune, and his commanding genius again asserted itself in the councils of the Creeks. He died at his home on the 9th of March, 1824. Through the intermarriage of his children with the whites Red Eagle's descendants show few traces of their Indian blood. The dark eye, the erect form, and perhaps a slight tinge in the cheek are all that remain as badges of their noble lineage.

CHAPTER XIII.

THE TRUE STORY OF THE PROPHET.

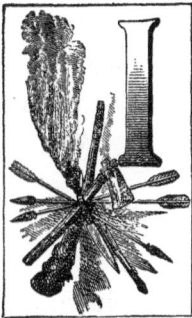

IN 1805, Penagashega, or "The Change of Feathers," the prophet of the Shawanese tribe was gathered to his fathers. As soon as the news of the great prophet's death reached a certain Shawanese Indian by the name of Laulewasickaw, the latter rolled his eyes piously towards heaven and fell on his face. How long he remained in this position we know not, but when he arose his actions were singular in the extreme. He shunned his former companions, bearing an important and mysterious air, the very personification of solemnity. He proceeded to engage in long and severe fasts. He resorted to hollow trees and desolate caverns, and there kept up protracted vigils.

At last, tired of this sort of thing or having continued it long enough to suit his purposes, he returned to his village, and with mock humility and a dramatic display of great piety, announced that the spirit of prophecy had entered into him, and that he would no longer be known as Penagashega, but as Tenshacutawan. This startling announcement certainly so overwhelms the reader with astonishment and admiration, that we at once hurry to satisfy the curiosity thus aroused by an explanation of the causes and meaning of this move on the part of our friend, whom we will henceforth know simply as "The Prophet."

According to his own story, the Prophet was descended from

a great Creek warrior, his grandfather. On a certain occasion, this esteemed ancestor, then a young and handsome man, had left the villages of his tribe, and gone with the leading men to the city of Charleston to hold a council with the English governor.

At some of the interviews which took place, the governor's daughter, a young lady of great beauty and spirit, contrived to be present. She had conceived a violent admiration for the Indian character, and had determined to bestow herself upon some lord of the forest. She took occasion one evening to inform her father of this wish, and begged him to select for her a suitable husband from the noble array of chiefs then in Charleston. Ridicule, argument, entreaties, and tears were of no avail to shake the resolute girl in her purpose.

On the following morning, the governor, pale from loss of sleep, inquired of the Indians which of their number was the most expert hunter. Of course the entire company pointed out the modest young warrior who was destined to become the grandfather of the Prophet, and to hand down to his descendant that characteristic modesty which was so conspicuously absent from the latter. After further interviews with his daughter, the governor announced to the council of Creeks that his daughter was disposed to marry one of their number. Significantly pointing toward the illustrious individual of whom we have spoken, he announced that his own consent was already given.

The chiefs were naturally incredulous. Their doubts, however, were dispelled by the earnestness of the governor and the evident anxiety of the young lady. Satisfied on this point, the Creeks at once began to labor with the young chief. Their arguments, re-enforced by his native gallantry, soon won the day, and the young warrior announced his satisfaction with the arrangement, and proceeded to give the young lady a hearty embrace, to which she seemed perfectly agreeable. He was immediately conducted to another apartment, where he was disrobed of the Indian costume by a train of black servants and clad in a new suit. The marriage ceremony was at once performed.

The Creeks returned to their homes, but the young warrior remained in Charleston with his wife. In time there were born to him two daughters and a son. At the birth of the latter, the old governor caused a round of thirty guns to be fired. At the age of eight years, the boy's father died, and he was taken charge of by the governor. The Creeks frequently visited him, and he in turn from time to time was permitted to make long stays among the people of his father. Gradually, he adopted their dress, customs, and language. There came a time when he refused to return to the whites, and ever afterward lived among the Indians. "This," says the Prophet, "was my father."

However truly our friend the Prophet foretold the future, it is certain that he lied about the past. His father and mother were, in all probability, of the purest Shawanese blood. This tribe was the most restless of all the American Indians. Tradition says that they are the descendants of the famous Eries. At different times we find them living on the Susquehanna River; at the Suwanee River in Florida, giving their name to it; on the Cumberland, in Kentucky; in the Wyoming valley, in Pennsylvania, and on the Wabash in Indiana. The Prophet's family removed from Florida to the north side of the Ohio River about the middle of the eighteenth century.

The Prophet was the youngest of six sons. He passed his boyhood like any other young Indian, in the wigwams and hunting-grounds of his people. He was more distinguished for intrigue and craft than for skill as a hunter or bravery as a warrior. He was a great braggart, telling no end of yarns of his great achievements. Possessing a shrewd insight into character, and never missing an opportunity to impress upon his people his vast importance and ability, he, in spite of his laziness and natural cowardice, managed to maintain a fairly creditable position in his tribe. But for his older brother, or as some will have it his twin, known everywhere as Tecumseh, or The Shooting Star, he would probably have remained in obscurity.

Tecumseh was born about 1768, after his parents had removed to Ohio. His father's death occurring when he was but six years old, he was placed under the charge of his eldest brother, Cheeseekau. The latter was a brave man, of noble character. His chief occupation and care was the proper training of the young Tecumseh, who was early recognized as the hope of the family. It was Cheeseekau who taught the fatherless boy to hunt, who led him to battle, who instructed him in all the athletic exercises, and who, by constant and zealous labor, imbued his mind with a love for truth, a ready generosity, a manly courage in battle, and a dignified fortitude in suffering. It was Cheeseekau who taught him, while but a boy, to use the bow and arrow with a skill which far exceeded that possessed by any other Indian boy of the tribe. It was this same elder brother who drilled him in the art of eloquence, and who wrought into his mind the idea which afterwards became the inspiration of the great chieftain—the idea of the salvation of his people from the white man.

TECUMSEH.

There were other children of this interesting family. Of these we have time to mention only Tecumseh's sister, Tecumapease. She was sensible, kind-hearted, and intelligent. Between her and her brother there existed the warmest affection. She was always his favorite. The first fruits of the chase belonged to Tecumapease. The choicest presents of the white man to Tecumseh became trophies for his sister.

Educated by the care of his elder brother, and cherished by the affection of a noble sister, Tecumseh grew to manhood. His ruling passion, even in his earlier years, is said to have been war. Among his companions he was easily the leader. Mimic combats and sham battles were his favorite sports. While his brother, the Prophet, remained at home engaged in idle and disreputable intrigues, Tecumseh followed the hunters in their chase and the war-parties on their way to battle.

As may be imagined, the Indian warfare which raged during all his earlier years made a profound impression on his mind. In childhood he sat around the camp-fires, and with earnest look and fascinated attention heard the stories of the Indian conflicts of the Revolutionary War. The battle of Point Pleasant, the murder of Cornstalk, the siege of Wheeling, the innumerable combats which took place around the block-houses of Kentucky, and along the course of the Ohio, the genius of Brant, the massacre of the Moravian Indians, the terrible defeat of Crawford—these were the things which formed the subjects of excited discussions around the camp-fires, where were faithfully reported, with vivid description and animated gesture, the details of every combat. These were the things upon which the youthful imagination of Tecumseh was nourished.

In his lonely chase he revolved in his mind the things which he had heard. With clenched fist and determined countenance, he brooded over the wrongs of the white man to his people. There came to him, too, stories of the great Pontiac and his wonderful conspiracy—the plan a ruin, and its creator an outcast before Tecumseh had drawn the breath of life.

The years passed by, and the terrible warfare with the white man raged without abatement. In this, as a matter of course, Tecumseh took a part. He is said to have fled in fright during the first battle at which he was present. The same story is related of Frederick the Great. Certain it is that Tecumseh never again was guilty of any such weakness. At another time he participated in an attack on a boat descending the Ohio River.

After the battle a captive was burned to death. Tecumseh had never seen any thing of the kind before. He broke forth into a storm of denunciation at the fiendish practice. From that time forth no prisoners were burned by any war party of which Tecumseh was a member.

When he was nineteen years of age Tecumseh and Cheeseekau took a long journey to the south. This the elder brother believed would tend to enlarge the understanding of his pupil, and enrich his expanding mind with general ideas. Their travels reached as far as the Creek country. There they found the Cherokees engaged in a war with the whites.

The two brothers from the hunting grounds of the north at once enlisted in the struggle. In an attack on a certain fort Cheeseekau led the charge. Just before the attack he told his followers that in the conflict he would be shot in the forehead and killed. The thing turned out as he had prophesied. He fell, pierced by a bullet midway between the eyes. As he sank, mortally wounded, upon the battle-field, he exclaimed with his expiring breath, "Happy am I to thus fall in battle, and not die in a wigwam like an old squaw." The Indians, panic-stricken at the fall of their leader, as well as at the fulfillment of the prophecy, fled in all directions.

Tecumseh seems to have suddenly become a man. The death of his brother threw him at once on his own resources. The band of warriors who had followed Cheeseekau all the way from the north, chose Tecumseh as their leader. To show himself worthy of this honor Tecumseh took ten men and went to the nearest white settlement, attacked and killed all the men, and took the women and children prisoners. He remained two years in the south, learning many languages, and becoming acquainted with many chiefs. During most of this time he was engaged in the warfare with the white man. No expedition or foray was thought complete without Tecumseh. His military genius won him great renown. One night Tecumseh, with a dozen warriors, was encamped on the Alabama River. All of the men had lain down for the night except Tecumseh, who was dressing some meat by the fire. At that moment the camp was attacked by thirty white men. With a shrill cry Tecumseh roused every warrior to his feet. Their leader at their head, the Indians rushed furiously toward a certain point in the circle formed by their foes. Two white men were killed outright, and the others, giving way before the impetuous charge, suffered Tecumseh and his band to break through, and make their way to their boats.

At the end of two years the young Tecumseh, now renowned for his martial feats, returned to his own people. He arrived in time to take part in the defeat of General St. Clair. In the war during 1794, when General Wayne led his triumphant expedition into the heart of the Indian country, Tecumseh became quite prominent for a young chief. He joined in an Indian attack on Fort Recovery. Ninety riflemen and fifty dragoons, having just escorted a supply train to the fort, were returning to the main army. Upon these the Indians precipitated themselves with great fury. Numbers of the white men were killed, and the rest fled toward the fort, and many succeeded in reaching it. The Indians then attacked the fort, but after two days withdrew without having effected their object.

Tecumseh was also present at the battle of Fallen Timbers, a name which it took from the fact that the battle-field was covered with fallen forest trees, wrecked by some tornado. All the world knows that in this battle Mad Anthony Wayne crushed the Indian powers of the Ohio valley. One incident shows that Tecumseh was still young. In the excitement of the fray he rammed a bullet into his gun without first inserting a charge of powder, thus losing the use of the weapon. Driven to the rear by the advancing enemy, he obtained a fowling-piece, which he used with considerable effect. As the Indians began to fly he exerted all his influence and every effort to rally them, and twice succeeded in making a stand with a handful of Shawanese. At last he, with the others, was compelled to retreat.

Tecumseh did not attend the peace council at Greenville. He remained at home in his wigwam, sullen and angry. In the following year he gathered about him a band of followers, calling himself its chief. This new tribe was migratory, like all the Shawanese. One crop of corn was raised on the shores of the great Miami, another was raised near the Whitewater River. In 1798, the Delawares, residing on White River, in Indiana, invited Tecumseh and his tribe to come and dwell with them. This invitation was accepted, and for several years Tecumseh kept his head-quarters at that place.

Numberless incidents are related of Tecumseh about this time. He was a great hunter, partly as a matter of sport, and partly because it enabled him to give the highly prized venison to the sick and poor of his tribe. One day a crowd of young Shawanese wagered him that each of them could kill as many deer in a three days' hunt as he. Tecumseh quietly accepted the challenge, and the hunters made their preparations that evening for a start before daylight. The three days ran by, and the crowd of boasters once more assembled around the camp-fire of their village. The largest number of deer-skins brought in by any one brave was twelve. Tecumseh brought with him thirty.

In 1803, Captain Herrod, who lived sixteen miles north-west of Chillicothe, while felling a tree in the forest, was shot by an unknown foe. Herrod was greatly beloved, and the whole valley of the Scioto was thrown into a panic. Bands of white men, suspecting the murder to have been the work of an Indian, organized for revenge. Wawillaway, an old Shawanese chief, and a great friend of the whites, was returning from one of the settlements where he had been trading his skins. At a spot in the forest, near the cabin of a hunter named Wolf, Wawillaway, a brave and intelligent Indian, and much respected by the whites, was confronted by Wolf and his hired man. The Indian shook hands with the men cordially, and was greeted in the same manner. The trio smoked the peace pipe, and violence on

DANIEL BOONE.

459

either side seemed not to be thought of. After a while Wolf proposed that they trade guns. While examining the Indian's weapon, the white man secretly removed the priming and then handed it back, saying he would not trade. Wolf's manner then changed, and he asked Wawillaway if the Indians had begun war. "No, no," said the chief, "the Indians and white men are now all brothers." The conversation then turned on the murder of Herrod, of which Wawillaway had not heard. Wolf charged that it was the work of the Indians. The chief replied that he might have been killed by some white enemy. He then shook hands, and turned to go, when Wolf fired from behind, inflicting a mortal wound. The brave Shawanese turned upon his assailants, killed one, and wounded the other. Exhausted by his efforts, and mortally wounded, he fell dead.

This occurrence operated to inflame the whole country, and a frontier war seemed imminent. A company of prominent citizens, in the hope of quieting matters, rode to Greenville, Ohio, in the Indian country, where they found Tecumseh with a large body of Indians. A council was held, and the whites candidly related all the circumstances connected with the murder of Wawillaway. After some hesitation, the Indians accepted the explanation, and declared their intention of abiding by the treaty of Greenville. This, however, was not enough. Tecumseh agreed to go to Chillicothe and exert his influence in behalf of peace. In the council held at that place Tecumseh fulfilled his promise in a speech of great power and eloquence, which effectually quieted the disturbance.

One incident connected with the murder of Wawillaway deserves mention. His two sons vowed vengeance upon Wolf. The latter fled to Kentucky, and employed an agent to negotiate with his enemies. After much debate and delay, the two Indians agreed, for the consideration of a horse and a new saddle, bridle, and gun apiece, to bury the hatchet. On an appointed day, the settlers from far and near came together to witness the fulfillment of this contract. In the midst of a hollow square stood Wolf, with his horses and their trappings. Opposite him stood the two young Indians. The latter lifted their hands toward heaven, calling on the Great Spirit to avenge the wrong which they had suffered, and at the same time to witness the sincerity of their forgiveness of their father's murderer. They took Wolf by the hand, and the three sat down together to smoke the calumet of peace. The two parties to this singular contract were good friends ever afterward.

It is to another class of events, however, that we must look to get glimpses of the motives and ideas of Tecumseh's interior life at this time. The early tendency of his mind to dwell upon the wrongs of the white man against his race expressed itself in a long study of the problem as to how the ruin of the red man and his impending extinction might be averted. Tecumseh did not talk much. He kept himself in the background. While the records of these years abound with the names of Blue Jacket, The Owl, and Turkey Foot, that of Tecumseh is not mentioned. There is evidence to show that his mind was actively employed on the great subject which we have mentioned.

Things were constantly occurring to give him food for thought. The Indian wars were over, but the outrages and wrongs continued. In 1801 William Henry Harrison was appointed governor of that portion of the North-west Territory known as Indiana. At the very first talk which the new governor had with his Indian constituency, the latter had no less than six murders by white men to complain of, the murderers having gone "unwhipt of justice." One of the cases bore heavily upon the minds of the Indians. Two warriors, a squaw, and some children had been hunting on Blue River, when their camp was discovered by three white men, who approached as friends, and were hospitably entertained. At an opportune moment the villainous visitors had murdered the whole party of Indians, made off with their property, and boasted of their feat in the white settlements without fear of punishment.

The able and interesting communications of Governor Harrison are full of details as to the irritation between the whites and the Indians. Besides these open outrages, the poor Indians suffered in many ways. Six thousand gallons of whisky were sold each year to the Indians upon the Wabash, who scarcely numbered six hundred warriors. "Every horror is produced," says Governor Harrison, "among these unhappy people by their intercourse with the whites. This is so certain that I can at once tell, upon looking at an Indian whom I chance to meet, whether he belongs to a neighboring or more distant tribe. The latter is generally well clothed, healthy, and vigorous, the former half naked, filthy, and enfeebled by intoxication; and many of them without arms, excepting a knife, which they carry for the most villainous purposes."

Among the many murders committed was one at a tavern, where a white man and an Indian, who were drinking together, got into a quarrel. Another white man took the Indian away to a distant house to keep him till he sobered off. The man with whom he had quarreled procured a cudgel, proceeded to the house, forced open the door of the room where the Indian lay, and beat him to death with a club. The murderer was arrested, tried, made no attempt at defense, and yet the jury of white men, although the facts of the murder were proved without contradiction or question, brought in a verdict in five minutes of "not guilty," simply on the ground that the victim was an Indian.

It is not to be forgotten that agents of the British Government continually circulated among the Indians, promising help from England in case they would make war upon the whites. This was also an important factor in the problem which was being worked out by Tecumseh. From childhood he had been taught to regard the great Pontiac as the foremost of all the Indian leaders of the past, and he did not fail to see that as Pontiac's scheme hinged upon the assistance of France, so his own plans might be confidently formed with regard to help from England.

The assumption of prophetic powers by Tecumseh's brother, the Prophet, in 1805, was in some way intimately connected with Tecumseh's plans. The chief, assisted by the smaller cunning of his brother, and thoroughly understanding the Indian character, saw that for the purpose of laying hold of the hearts and minds of the Indians; of uniting scattered and broken tribes in the execution of a single great enterprise; of the revival of the spirit of his people, among whom the effects of Wayne's victory in the battle of Fallen Timbers were still painfully manifest, and of the rallying of a wide and enthusiastic following, the Indians could be approached in no way so successfully as through their superstitions. Speaking strictly, Tecumseh's brother was an Indian Mohammed.

So the Prophet changed his name. He preached that he was the Anointed of the Great Spirit to reform the manners of the red men. All the innovations in dress and habits which they had learned from the white men must be abandoned. Calling together a large assembly in northern Ohio of Indians from many tribes, he, in the presence of this company, made an official announcement of his doctrines. He denounced witchcraft and drunkenness. He said that he had been carried up into the clouds, and had been shown the dwelling-place of the devil. Here he had seen the multitudes of those who had died drunkards in their eternal home. From the mouth of every one of them proceeded flames of fire.

When he was questioned as to whether he was not a drunkard himself, he admitted the truth, but said that the fright from his vision prevented him from drinking any more. He attacked the practice of Indian women marrying white men, and also the growing tendency toward individual property. He proclaimed celestial rewards for all who would become his followers, and boldly laid claim to the power of foretelling future events, curing sickness, preventing death on the battle-field, and working all sorts of miracles.

The Prophet was a first-rate orator, though wanting in the

TECUMSEH AS A DEER HUNTER.

courage and truthfulness of his brother. President Jefferson wrote of him as follows :

" The Wabash Prophet is more rogue than fool, if to be a rogue is not the greatest of all follies. He rose to notice while I was in the administration, and became of course a proper subject for me. The inquiry was made with diligence. His declared object was the reformation of his red brethren and their return to their pristine manners of living. He pretended to be in constant communication with the Great Spirit; that he was instructed by him to make known to the Indians that they were created by him, distinct from the whites, of different natures, for different purposes, and placed under different circumstances adapted to their nature and destinies; that they must return from all the ways of the whites to the habits and opinions of their forefathers; they must not eat the flesh of hogs, of bullocks, of sheep, etc., the deer and the buffalo having been created for their food. They must not bake bread of wheat, but of Indian corn; they must not wear linen nor woolen, but must dress like their fathers, in the skins and furs of animals; they must not drink ardent spirits, and I do not remember whether he extended his inhibitions to the gun and gunpowder in favor of the bow and arrow.

"I concluded from all this that he was a visionary, enveloped in their antiquities, and vainly endeavoring to lead back his brethren to the fancied beatitudes of their golden age. I thought there was little danger of his making many proselytes from the habits and comforts they had learned from the whites to the hardships and privations of savagism, and no great harm if he did. But his followers increased until the British thought him worth corrupting, and found him corruptible. I suppose his views were then changed, but his proceedings in consequence of them were after I left the administration, and are therefore unknown to me; nor have I ever been informed what were the particular acts on his part which produced an actual commencement of hostilities on ours. I have no doubt, however, that the

30

subsequent are but a chapter apart, like that of Henry and Lord Liverpool in the book of the kings of England."

At first the following of the Prophet was small, but superstition is always ready to take up with new leaders. The bolder the imposition, the more followers it finds. As the stories of the Prophet passed from mouth to mouth, the wonders ascribed to him grew with lightning rapidity. As the tales were borne to the far off shores of Lake Superior, miracles of the most prodigious proportions were related. Still such reports were not confined to distant tribes. The people in the very next wigwam to the Prophet's would affirm with dogged obstinacy, bold faces, and invincible positiveness the details of wonders which the Prophet had wrought, and which they themselves had witnessed. Perhaps an explanation for this may be found in the fact that, hearing others relate stories of the Prophet's miracles, which their credulous minds believed, they, in turn, not wishing to be behind the rest, thought it necessary to bear testimony to wonders themselves. In fact, the nearer they were to the Prophet, and the closer their relations with him, the keener would be their pique if they had had no stories to tell. So each of the Prophet's followers strove to surpass the rest in the tales which he could tell of supernatural occurrences.

All this sort of thing, it will be observed, has for its foundation a belief that miracles did occur; in short, in their possibility and reality as a general thing, the only question being as to the particular details. If such a belief in the possibility of the miracles, and in the fact that they really were occurring, had been absent from the Prophet's followers, it is evident that the above explanation would be incorrect. Some other reason would have to be found to account for the existence of the testimony to his miracles. Perhaps it would not be necessary to go farther in such a case than to say that the stories were lies. In the present instance, however, there can be no doubt that the followers of the Prophet believed him to be an actual miracle worker, the only question in their minds, if there was any at all, being as to what particular miracles he had wrought.

It is the invariable course of history for Superstition to go hand in hand with her sisters, Intolerance and Persecution. Such was the case with the Prophet. He instituted a persecution against witchcraft. An old woman was denounced as a witch by him, and she was called upon repeatedly to give up her charm and medicine-bag. She was put to the stake and burned. In her fearful agony, hoping for relief, she screamed out that her grandson had her charm. This accusation, instead of saving her, resulted in the young Indian, who was out hunting, being forthwith pursued and arrested. He confessed that he had borrowed the charm, and by means of it had flown through the air over Kentucky to the banks of the Mississippi, and back again, before bed-time. He insisted, however, that he had returned the charm to his grandmother, and was finally released.

On the following day an old chief named Teteboxti was accused of being a wizard. Knowing that his doom was fixed, the old man arrayed himself in his finest clothes, and confronted the grim circle of inquisitors in the council-house. The trial was speedy. The sentence was passed. The old chief calmly assisted in the construction of his own funeral pile. Touched by his white hairs, the council became merciful. They voted to tomahawk him and burn his body afterwards. This was done. Many others met the same fate.

When Governor Harrison heard of the witchcraft delusion and the far-reaching influence of the Prophet, he was justly alarmed. No one knew better than he the sway of superstition among ignorant minds. He knew that, although the Indians had been quiet for ten years, and could be roused by the call of no ordinary leader, nevertheless deceived by a mask of religion, they might once more plunge the frontiers into bloody war. He wrote them a most earnest letter, urging them to drive out the Prophet, and boldly asserting that the latter was a fraud. He told the Indians that the pretender could work no miracles. "Ask of him to cause the sun to stand still, the moon to alter its course, the rivers to cease to flow, or the dead to rise from their graves."

The Prophet took the governor at his word. He announced that on a certain day he would cause darkness to cover the sun. By some means he had learned that a total eclipse of the sun would occur on a certain day. The reports of the prophecy spread to a thousand villages.

On the appointed day a vast assemblage of Indians from far and near gathered to witness the miracle. They were arranged in a great circle. Painted Ottawas, wild Ojibwas, fierce Dacotahs, ugly Kickapoos, and curious Illinois, as well as numbers from nearer tribes, were there. Over the multitude hung a deathlike silence. The rattling tongues of the squaws were hushed, and the cheeks of the boldest warriors were blanched with unnatural pallor.

An hour before noon the Prophet, dressed with dazzling magnificence, came out of his wigwam, and strode with slow and stately steps toward the center of the circle. A slight buzz of apprehension went through the assembly. A few Indian youths ran from one point to another, carrying messages and perfecting details. At last all was ready. The Prophet rose. Extending his right arm and turning his face toward the heavens, he pronounced an unintelligible incantation. As he proceeded a disc of darkness was observed to be slowly appearing upon the edge of the sun. The eyes of the vast assemblage were turned from the Prophet toward the phenomenon. As the moments progressed the dark spot enlarged. There was a perceptible diminution of light.

An hour went by. The Prophet still continued his diablarie. The landscape, before so sunny, took on somber hues of brown. The air was close and still. It grew darker and darker. The multitude was thrilled with awe. They clung closely to one another. Not a few believed that the end of the world was at hand. The deep shadows, the darkened air, the increasing obscurity, which at sunset would have attracted no attention, occurring in the middle of the day, with the sun in high heaven, seemed portentous and awful. The Prophet alone remained calm and unmoved. At the moment of total eclipse, he cried out in a loud voice, "Behold! did I not prophesy truly?"

The reports of this miracle gave a wonderful impulse to the cause of the Prophet. Tecumseh now appeared on the scene. He took care to lend the aid of his powerful name and influence to the Prophet by an ostentatious reverence. The latter returned the compliment by pointing out Tecumseh as the leader chosen by the Great Spirit to save the red man. Thus these two brothers acted well their parts. With Tecumseh to do the heavy tragedy, and the Prophet to shift the scenes and throw on the red lights, the drama proceeded well. The Indians were fired with fanaticism and military enthusiasm.

The whites were alarmed. The ever-increasing throng of savages about Tecumseh and his brother seemed ready to break out into violence. At a council in Ohio, Tecumseh made a three hours' speech. He reviewed all the treaties with the white men, and undertook to prove their nullity. Every appeal which could rouse the passions of his followers and stir their hearts with bitterness and hostility was made. The orator hurled a bold defiance against the enemies of his people. The Indians who were present, excited by his fiery eloquence, were unable to keep their seats.

While Tecumseh's influence was rising at home, the fame of the Prophet was spreading abroad. In a village of the Ojibwas, on Lake Superior, was an unfortunate captive named John Tanner. He afterwards escaped, and related that one day a strange Indian arrived in the village. For days he preserved the most mysterious silence. Then he told them that he was a messenger from the great Shawanese Prophet. On a certain day the Indians assembled in their council-house. In the midst of the room stood an object in form and size something like a prostrate man. Over it was thrown a blanket. The stranger carried four strings of beads, said to be made from the flesh of the Prophet. Each Indian in the assembly took hold of these beads, and by this act adopted the new religion. They also, though with reluctance, gave up their medicine-bags.

The more fanatical of the Indians went to dwell with the Prophet. In this movement we see a new proof that the laws of society, whether civilized or barbarous, are the same. This great religious uprising among the Indians, and the war which followed it, were parallel to such religious wars as those of Mohammed and of many another leader. Religion, the very genius of which is peace, has more often than any thing else been the cloak of the great soldier.

The Indians, followers of Tecumseh and the Prophet, who had taken up their residence on the banks of the Wabash, at a village called "The Prophet's Town," soon began to mingle warlike exercises with their religious devotions. The great plan to which Tecumseh had devoted all his genius and energies was nothing less than a mighty confederation of the Indian tribes of the continent, who were to unite and drive the white men beyond the Alleghanies.

As the great scheme had taken shape in his mind its form became less and less that of a mere temporary alliance, such as the immortal Pontiac had sought; and more and more that of a "great and permanent confederation, an empire of red men, of which Tecumseh should be the leader and emperor." For four years he traveled incessantly in the propagation of his enterprise. Now he visited the farthest extremities of Lake Superior. At another time he traversed the unknown regions beyond the Mississippi. Again he labored with the Creeks, securing Red Eagle as his most illustrious convert.

The United States Government was alarmed. It was reported in the spring of 1810 that Tecumseh controlled more than sixteen hundred warriors. It was evident that the exposed settlements in Indiana were in danger. Shortly, faithful scouts reported that Tecumseh's following numbered three thousand warriors.

Many messages, threatening on the part of Governor Harrison, deceitful or defiant on the part of Tecumseh, passed back and forth. There were frequent councils. The Indian chief, with forty braves, visited Vincennes to have a talk with Governor Harrison. After much singular dancing and conjuring, Tecumseh began the council. He demanded that the "Seventeen Fires," as he called the United States, give up the lands which they claimed by virtue of treaties with separate tribes. He boldly announced that he intended to go to war unless this was done. To these demands Governor Harrison replied with definite refusals. Tecumseh became so angry, that the peace talk came near ending in a free fight. An adjournment to the following day operated to quiet matters somewhat.

This council was held on the 12th of August, 1810. It broke up, leaving the Indians irritated and defiant and the white people of Vincennes alarmed and apprehensive. As the year progressed, evidences of Indian hostility became more frequent. Horses were stolen. Here and there murders were committed. The Indians, in the spring of 1811, captured a boat filled with salt. It had been sent up the Wabash for distribution among all the tribes. In the previous year the Prophet had refused to take any salt, sending an insulting message to Governor Harrison. This year he was wiser. He took all the salt, including not only his own, but that which belonged to a dozen other tribes. At a council held afterward, Tecumseh hissed out to General Harrison that he was hard to please, and that he was angry at one time because the Indians took no salt and another year because they did take it.

The good people at Vincennes lived in the shadow of a constant fear. They knew that Tecumseh might, at any time, launch his fleet of light canoes at the Prophet's town and, gliding down on the swift current of the Wabash, suddenly and silently attack Vincennes before a single word of warning could

reach and rouse their victims.   Meanwhile reports continued to
come in of Tecumseh's intrigues among distant tribes.

The last council with Tecumseh was held at Vincennes on
the 27th of July, 1811.   The chieftain, accompanied by a retinue of one hundred and seventy-five well-armed Indians, took
his position on one side of an arbor prepared for the council,
while Governor Harrison, with seventy soldiers, occupied a
position opposite.   Tecumseh's speech when called upon to surrender a number of Indians, who had murdered some whites,
was artful and ingenious.   He preached a regular sermon to the
white men, on the duty of the forgiveness of injuries.   He also
begged that nothing be done with the Indians during his absence,
which was about to transpire, on a journey to the South.   He
assured Harrison that his only object was to prevail on all the
tribes to unite in the bonds of peace.

We now know how different was his real mission.   Every
effort was made by frequent changes of garb, and skillful
maneuverings to impress Tecumseh with the military strength of
Vincennes.   A Pottawatomie, called the Deaf Chief, was present at the council, but unable to hear the proceedings.   In the
evening he was informed as to what had taken place, and going
up to General Harrison, told him that he would have confronted
Tecumseh with proofs of his hostility had he understood the
latter's pretensions of friendliness.

This incident was related to Tecumseh, who quietly informed
his brother that the Deaf Chief must be put out of the way.
The latter heard of the threat.   He calmly repaired to his tent,
arrayed himself in the full costume of the warrior, sprang into
his canoe, and paddled his solitary way to Tecumseh's camp.
Arriving in the presence of the great chief, the Indian reproached
him bitterly for the threat of assassination, and dared him to
an open combat.   To every taunt and insult Tecumseh returned
majestic indifference.   With a war-whoop of defiance, the Indian
again betook himself to his canoe.   A little later a sharp crack
from a rifle was heard from the bushes along the shore.   The

boatman might have been seen to fall heavily backwards, and the canoe without a helmsman bearing the corpse of its owner drifted on into the night.

In August, the governor again sent a demand for the surrender of some murderers, to which the Indians replied with the usual insulting refusal. Under strict orders to preserve peace if possible, Governor Harrison resolved to confront the Indians with a strong military force before Tecumseh should return. In order to stop the outrages of which reports were brought in every day, and in compliance with loud demands from the citizens of Vincennes and other settlements, the governor resolved to erect a fort on the Wabash, and break up the large and dangerous assemblage of hostile Indians at the Prophet's town.

On the 26th of September, 1811, Governor Harrison marched out of Vincennes at the head of nine hundred troops. Six days afterward the army encamped on the eastern bank of the Wabash, at a point two miles above the present bustling city of Terre Haute. Here the men were employed in the construction of a log fort, named by the soldiers Fort Harrison.

FORT HARRISON.

Evidence accumulated to show that the host of Indians at the Prophet's town, instead of submitting on the approach of the army, were preparing to risk a battle. This was expressly contrary to Tecumseh's orders. It seems probable that the Prophet, jealous of his brother's sudden fame, was all the more anxious for a battle in the latter's absence.   His town, which was the objective point of the invaders, was the center and capital of the new religious fanaticism. Here the Great Spirit was supposed to dwell.   Here were performed the strange and mysterious rites with which the new worship was carried on.   Hideous dances, midnight orgies, self-inflicted tortures, and the dark ceremonies of Indian magic occupied the frenzied savages.

To the thousands of converts, who had everywhere adopted the religion of the Prophet, this sacred town was as Jerusalem to the Jews, and Mecca to the Mohammedans.   Its fortifications were believed to be impregnable, and here a thousand braves, the flower of a hundred warlike tribes, worked into a frantic frenzy, alike by the fervor of fanaticism, the promptings of patriotism, the fever of hatred, and the undying love of warfare, prepared to give battle to the invading army.

Leaving a small garrison at Fort Harrison, the troops advanced along the south-east bank of the Wabash.   After passing Big Raccoon Creek it was determined to cross the Wabash, in order to avoid the woody shores on the south-east side.   This was effected at a point near the site of the present town of Montezuma, Parke county, Indiana.

On the 6th of November the army came in sight of the Prophet's town.   Small bodies of Indians, armed and painted for battle, could be seen scurrying hither and thither across the country.   As the army continued to advance every effort was made to communicate with these savages, and assure them of the peaceful intentions of the whites.   While this fact is well authenticated, it must be confessed that an army of a thousand men approaching within a mile of their principal town, and which had already constructed and garrisoned two forts, was not calculated to cause the savages to regard the invaders' intentions as purely peaceful.   In fact the thing now wears the appearance of a huge joke.   However, toward evening three chiefs advanced, representing that the Prophet on his part, also, contemplated nothing but peace, and that his heart was over-flowing with love for his white brethren. Thus the Indian answered one joke with another. He also asked that the white men refrain from hostilities until the following day, when a peace talk could be had.

The army encamped for the night about three quarters of a mile from the Prophet's town, on the now famous Tippecanoe Battle Ground, seven miles north-east of the present city of Lafayette. The place was a beautiful spot of timber-land, about ten feet higher than the marshy prairie in front, which stretched away toward the Prophet's town, and perhaps twice that height above the prairie in the rear. Here the army encamped.

Meanwhile the Indians were by no means idle. All night long the chiefs sat in council. A dozen different plans for the attack were proposed. At one time it was decided to meet the whites in council on the next day, agree to their proposals, and withdraw, leaving behind two Winnebagoes, who were to rush forward and assassinate the governor. This was to be the signal for battle. Later in the night, which was dark and rainy, the plan was changed. The Prophet, mixing some mysterious hell-broth, pretended to read in it the fact that one-half of Harri-son's army was dead, and the other half crazy. Encouraged by this assurance the whole body of warriors, at four o'clock in the morning, began to creep across the miry prairie toward the American camp.

Early though it was, General Harrison had risen, and was pulling on his boots before a camp-fire. The drummer was just being roused to wake the men. Suddenly a shot was heard, followed by a wild yell from multitudes of savage throats. The men, who had slept in rank with their clothes on and arms in hand, sprang to their feet. A number of Indians made their way into the heart of the camp before they could be arrested. The place was dark except as it was illuminated by the glow of the smoldering camp-fires. The men hurried to put these out as quickly as possible, to prevent the enemy from having so good a mark. They soon rallied from the surprise, and began to fight with great courage.

In the confusion of the moment the large white horse of Governor Harrison could not be found, and the American commander was forced to mount a borrowed plug of a different color. This circumstance no doubt saved his life. One of his aids, who also rode a white horse, fell, pierced by a dozen balls, in the very beginning of the attack. There can be no doubt that he was mistaken for his chief.

Harrison took a most active part in the battle, riding from point to point, rallying and encouraging his men. Not so with the Prophet. Selecting for himself an elevated position, he chanted a wild war-song. Though invisible in the darkness, his shrill and piercing voice could be distinctly heard above the din of the battle in every part of the field. Here, like an evil genius, he presided over the destinies of the battle until his braves, wounded and dying, were being driven back from the point of attack.

The American troops which were encamped around the edge of the spot of woodland, succeeded in keeping the Indians out of the camp until it became sufficiently light for a general charge, which resulted in the complete rout of the Indians. During the battle many instances of heroism occurred. Captain Warrick was shot through the body. His wound was dressed, and though it was evident he could live but a few hours, his great physical strength was unexhausted. He insisted on going back to head his company. This was but one of many such occurrences.

When the Indians fled, the whites found thirty-seven of their own number killed, and a hundred and fifty-one wounded. Twenty-five of the latter afterwards died from their wounds. During the day the shattered army was employed in strengthening their position. Their only food was broiled horseflesh. On the following day they advanced to the Prophet's town.

No defiant war-whoop greeted them. The place was desolate and deserted. It had been abandoned in a panic. The Indians, more civilized than the wild tribes of the plains which we know to-day, had left behind all their household furniture, many fire-arms, great quantities of corn, numbers of hogs and chickens. The only human being in the village was an old chief, with a broken leg. He had been left behind by his people, and was unable to escape. The whites ministered to his wants and left him. Taking the provisions for their own use, the entire village was destroyed. The Prophet's influence was forever broken.

Tecumseh was already on his way home. His trip had been successful. Red Eagle and the Creeks were preparing for war. The Cherokees, the Osages, the Seminoles, were all ready to take up the hatchet. The great confederacy seemed almost an accomplished fact. Confident and happy, Tecumseh hurried back to the Prophet's town. He was ignorant of what had happened. As he and his party approached they gave the salute-yell. Instead of a wild chorus of replies from the direction of the village, all was wrapped in utter silence.

Anxious and alarmed, he hurried forward. He caught sight of the spot where the village had been. Not a cabin was to be seen. He rubbed his eyes and looked again, to see if it was not a dream, a nightmare. Not so. The village had disappeared. Only heaps of ashes marked its site. All its fortifications, all the stores of food and ammunition, and the collection of arms, the fruit of years of weary toil, were gone. Tecumseh saw at once what had happened. He was overwhelmed with sorrow. Just at the moment of apparent triumph he found the very foundation of the fabric dissolved in thin air. Guided by some stragglers Tecumseh hurried to the camp, twenty miles away, where the disgraced Prophet awaited with fear and trembling his brother's return. Great and terrible was Tecumseh's rage. He seized the unfortunate impostor by the hair, and threatened to kill him. The battle had been fought in direct opposition to his orders.

All had been staked, and all was lost. The Prophet's influence was utterly gone. He was the object of contempt and abuse. The very boys yelled at him as he sneaked through a village. Yet, because he was Tecumseh's brother, he was saved from further punishment. Tecumseh wrote to General Harrison that he desired to go to Washington. The request was granted, but he was required to go alone. This wounded the spirit of the disappointed man. The would-be emperor refused to go without a retinue. Filled with unutterable fury, he joined the English army in Canada. When invited to take part in a peace-council, he said: "No! I have taken sides with the king, and I will suffer my bones to bleach on this shore before I will recross that stream to take part in any council of neutrality."

Tecumseh took an active part in the war, and before long found himself at the head of seven hundred warriors. Nearly all the leading chiefs followed his lead and went over to the British side. Fort Dearborn, then a lonely post on the spot where Chicago, the "Wonder of the West," now handles the commerce of a continent, was evacuated by its occupants. The departing garrison and the families of the fort were assaulted by savages, and nearly all killed. Tecumseh also devised two sieges to be conducted by Indians.

Fort Wayne was a wooden fortification, garrisoned by seventy men. Early in September word reached General Harrison, at Cincinnati, that this post was besieged and in great peril. Five men, headed by Logan, an Indian chief of wide fame, undertook to communicate with the garrison. At the moment of their arrival the besiegers were gathered on two sides of the fort, in an attempt to take the place by stratagem. The messengers reached the very walls of the place without opposition, and came suddenly upon four Indian chiefs, with a flag of truce, who were attempting to lure the officers of the fort into a peace-talk outside the fortification, where they might be assassinated. The alarmed chiefs made off, while the five scouts entered the fort.

The situation was found to be full of distress. As soon as a letter could be written the bold men sallied forth, and dashed through the lines of the astonished besiegers, to carry the news to General Harrison. The defenders of Fort Wayne deposed their commander, and elected Lieutenant Curtis as his successor. Troops failing to arrive, the Indians demanded the surrender of the place, and this being refused, made a heavy attack. They had two cannon, which burst at the first fire, being made of wood and hooped with iron, by some scalawag English traders. The garrison fought well. The Indians were repulsed with heavy loss. General Harrison at last arrived in the vicinity, and failing to ambush him, the Indians withdrew.

Captain Zachary Taylor, afterwards President of the United States, was the commandant of Fort Harrison. His force numbered about thirty-five effective men. On the 3d of September a lot of Indians with their women and children appeared before the fort, and begged for admission, under pretense of holding a council. Failing in this, they continued to linger around, and at midnight the garrison was aroused by an alarm of fire. One of the block-houses at the corner of the fortification, containing the provisions of the garrison, was in flames. Several barrels of whisky took fire, and the whole structure was so quickly ablaze that no efforts to extinguish the flames could avail. A strong force of Indians poured volleys of balls into the fort, and were evidently preparing to force an entrance through the gap left by the destruction of the block-house.

The men prevented the spread of the flames as well as they could, while their captain, sick with bilious fever, tore down a log structure, and braving the bullets of the savages, constructed a hasty barricade opposite the gap. Behind this the men fought bravely, repulsing every assault. So inevitable did the destruction of the garrison seem, that two men attempted to escape through the gap left by the fire. One was killed; the other concealed himself, and was re-admitted to the fort in the morning. The loss of their provisions threatened the handful of

men with starvation. A wagon-train from Vincennes coming to
their relief was attacked, and nearly the whole escort killed.
In time a stronger force made its way to the little outpost.
The Indians, to revenge themselves for their disappointment,
attacked a settlement at Pigeon Roost, on a branch of White
River, in Clarke county, Indiana, and massacred twenty-one
men, women, and children.

In the progress of the war, a Shawanese chief named Logan
proved to be a most valuable scout for the Americans. He was,
however, suspected of treachery. Deeply hurt, he, with Captain Johnny and Bright Horn, his inseparable companions,
started out to prove his fidelity. They were surprised by some
hostile Indians, and captured. Logan pretended to be deserting to the British, and succeeded in retaining his arms. One
of the guards, noticing something in Captain Johnny's mouth,
looked inquiringly toward him. The latter coolly said, "Me
chaw heap tobac." The tobacco was a bullet. While some of
their captors were searching the woods for black haws, Logan
and his companions attacked the remainder. Five Indians were
killed. Logan received a mortal wound. He made his way
back to the American camp. He lingered two days in the
greatest agony. The men, understanding that he had fallen to
vindicate his honor, bestowed every attention possible. The
faithful chief passed away with a smile of triumph on his face,
satisfied that he had answered his accusers, though at the cost
of his life. His mother was Tecumapease, the only sister of
Tecumseh.

Among the many tragic occurrences of the Indian warfare
in 1812, none was more fearful than the battle and massacre of
Raisin. Frenchtown was on the river Raisin, only eighteen
miles from Malden, Canada, where the British had their entire
force. A cry for help came from the place, and in the dead of
winter six hundred men marched from the Maumee to this place.
A sharp battle resulted in the evacuation of Frenchtown by
the British. Two hundred and fifty more Americans were then

GENERAL HARRISON'S CAVALRY HORSES STAMPEDED.

BATLE OF TIPPECANOE-WHERE JO DAVIESS FELL.

sent forward to re-enforce the first army. On the morning of
January 22, 1813, two thousand British and Indians attacked
the Americans. A bloody battle resulted in the surrender of
the entire American force. The English commander left the
wounded in the place, taking the rest to Malden. On the following morning two hundred Indians, painted black and red,
entered the place, and barbarously massacred the helpless
wounded. Many were burnt alive in the buildings in which
they lay. Nearly three hundred perished in the battle and the
massacre together. The whole town was filled with corpses.
Tecumseh was in the Wabash region at the time, raising
re-enforcements.

In April Tecumseh appeared before Fort Meigs, on the Maumee River, where General Harrison had his head-quarters. The
English erected three batteries. To match this, Harrison constructed an earth embankment, twelve feet high, in which the
cannon-balls buried themselves harmlessly. General Clay at
last approached to the relief of the fort with eight hundred
men. A battle ensued in the attempt to throw themselves into
the fort. The activity of Tecumseh's warriors defeated the
effort, less than two hundred out of the whole number reaching
the fort. The English commander allowed his Indian allies to
tomahawk such of the prisoners as they pleased, more than
twenty being brutally murdered. Tecumseh had been in
another part of the battle-field. Discovering what was going
on, he rode at full speed to the spot, dismounted, and with
drawn tomahawk beat his men off from the prisoners, and
cursed the English commander for his crime. The latter said
he could not control the Indians, but Tecumseh answered,
"Begone! You are unfit to command; go and put on the dress
of a squaw."

Tecumseh was an unruly ally. He despised Proctor, the
English commander with whom he operated. One day, provisions being scarce, salt beef was given the English soldiers, while
the Indians received only horse-flesh. Angered at the outrage,

Tecumseh strode to Proctor's tent and demanded an explanation. Seeing the English general about to treat the complaint with indifference, Tecumseh significantly struck the hilt of the commander's sword, touching at the same time the handle of his tomahawk, and said, "You are Proctor—I am Tecumseh." This hint at a mode of settling the difficulty, brought Proctor to terms at once.

Tecumseh's last grudge against Proctor was the retreat of the English from Malden after Commodore Perry's victory on Lake Erie. Tecumseh urged a battle with every argument and taunt. "We must compare our father's conduct to a fat dog that carries its tail on its back, but when affrighted, it drops it between its legs and runs off." Tecumseh, disgusted at the retreat, would have deserted the English cause but for the fact that he had induced other tribes to join it. Proctor pretended from time to time that he would halt and give battle. When the retreat commenced, Tecumseh said, "We are now going to follow the British, and I am sure that we shall never return." At last, on the 5th of October, Proctor was forced to halt and oppose the pursuing Americans in the battle of the Thames. Just before the engagement, Tecumseh said to the group of chiefs about him; "Brother warriors, we are now about to enter into an engagement, from which I shall never come out—my body will remain on the field of battle." Unbuckling his sword and handing it to a chief he said, "When my son becomes a noted warrior, and able to wield a sword give this to him."

As the battle advanced, the victory of the Americans became apparent. The Indians fought well, until they suddenly missed the loud, commanding battle-cry of Tecumseh. There was a pause, a shudder, and then all incontinently fled. The great chieftain had fallen, pierced by a pistol ball. The discussion as to who killed Tecumseh became a singularly heated one in subsequent political campaigns, the chief recommendation for office in that day being skill as an Indian fighter. The preponderance of evidence seems to indicate that Colonel Richard M. Johnson was the slayer of the famous chief.

Tecumseh never allowed his portrait to be painted. He is described as a perfect Apollo in form, his face oval, his nose straight and handsome, and his mouth regular and beautiful. His eyes singularly enough, were "hazel, clear, and pleasant in conversation, but like balls of fire when excited by anger or enthusiasm." His bearing was that of a noble and lofty spirit, a true "King of the Woods," as the English called him. He was temperate in his habits, loving truth and honor better than life. His mind was of a high order. He possessed a genius which must have made him eminent in any age or country. Like Powhatan, Pontiac, and Brant, his illustrious predecessors, he had failed; yet like them he was great in defeat. He was the first great chieftain who prohibited the massacre of prisoners. He died at forty-four, in the very prime of life.

The Prophet survived his brother twenty-two years. He, with the remnant of his tribe, removed to the Indian Territory, where, shorn of his power and influence, he still continued in a small way to exercise his "supernatural" gifts for the delusion and mystification of a few ignorant dupes. He had only one eye, and possessed a countenance of which every line revealed craft and deceptiveness. In 1823, Isaac Harvey, a Quaker missionary at Wapakoneta, one day visited a sick Indian, a consumptive. Entering the cabin, he found the sick man lying face downwards, his bared back cut in several places, and faint from loss of blood. Standing over him was the Prophet, with a bloody knife in his hands. He explained that the sick man was bewitched, and that the gashes in his back were to let out the demon. The good Quaker put the fraud out of the room, and dressed the sick man's wounds. Nor did his work stop here. At great personal risk he continued to fight the belief in witchcraft, and to oppose the Prophet's delusions, until the lunacy was banished entirely from the Shawanese tribe. The impostor himself alone continued the pretense of belief in it.

CHAPTER XIV.

THE SORROWS OF THE SEMINOLES.

M I a negro, a slave? My skin is dark, but not black. I am an Indian—a Seminole. The white man shall not make me black. I will make the white man red with blood, and then blacken him in the sun and rain, where the wolf shall smell of his bones, and the buzzard shall live upon his flesh." Where, when, and by whom was expression given to this dark sentiment? The speaker was Osceola, a young Seminole warrior. The scene, a trader's cabin, at a settlement in Florida. Osceola had sought to buy a keg of powder. He had been refused on the ground that the United States forbade the sale of ammunition or fire-arms to the Seminoles. The time of this affront was the early part of the year 1835. Who was Osceola, what his race, and what the occasion for this collision between its members and the white man?

About the middle of the last century a great chief arose among the Creeks, named Secoffee. He had ambition, genius, eloquence, the gift of leadership, and the spirit of rebellion. He revolted from the confederacy of the Creeks, and drawing after him a third part of the tribe, took his way to the heart of Florida. The Creeks attempted, by terrible wars, to conquer the rebels, and force them to return to their old allegiance. Failing in this, they sought revenge by branding the runaways with the name of "The Seminoles," a name originally a badge of disgrace, signifying simply "The Runaways." The insult failed, as well as the armies of the Creeks, to accomplish its purpose. Long since has the humiliating meaning been forgotten among men, who remember only the sad but beautiful name, Seminole.

Fugitives themselves, the Seminoles always afforded refuge and safety to the negroes of Georgia, who likewise fled from the bondage of their masters. This practice brought on a small war between the Georgians and the Seminoles, which eventually resulted in the purchase of Florida from Spain. The United States thus found itself with a red elephant on its hands. The whites along the frontier hated their Indian neighbors. They longed to get their greedy hands upon their property.

Adventurers, speculators, and pioneers kept up an incessant din, demanding that the Indians of Florida be confined to certain limits, and that the rest of the country be thrown open to settlers. The whites wanted the country, so they said. This was sufficient reason in the opinion of the government and of the age to rob the Indians of their lands. Inasmuch as at the present day vast expanses of Florida remain a wilderness, untrodden by the foot of man, undeveloped and unexplored, the folly, the falsehood, and the wickedness of the clamor for the spoliation of the Seminoles is apparent to every candid mind. Nevertheless, the government, by intrigue and stratagem, on the 18th of September, 1824, took the step which was ultimately to desolate the peninsula to which mankind have given the name "The Land of Flowers." A considerable portion of the Seminole chiefs were induced to sign a treaty by which they bound themselves to withdraw with their people to a certain designated reservation. This treaty was to afford a pretext in case of its violation for the destruction of the Seminoles.

It brought nothing but trouble. The Indians, unsettled and driven from the old homes, failed to quiet down in any new ones. Angry and furious, they roamed the peninsula at will, from end to end. Of course, this brought on collisions and outrages. Moreover, the old question of the negroes among the Seminoles gave increasing difficulty. The whites claimed that the Indians robbed their cornfields, burned their houses, and killed their cattle. The southerners were passionate. No one knew at what moment an Indian war might break out.

So in 1833 the government induced a party of chiefs to visit another unexplored wilderness, now comprising the State of Arkansas, with a view to the removal of the entire Seminole nation to that place. By some manipulation the United States succeeded in inducing a number of the chiefs to sign what is known as the treaty of "Payne's Landing," whereby they agreed to make the removal to Arkansas, provided an investigating band should make a favorable report concerning the country. The latter, under the seductive arts of the Indian agents, signed a treaty whereby they admitted that the country was satisfactory, and binding the Seminoles absolutely to the removal.

When these chiefs returned from Arkansas, and told their people what had been done, a universal dissatisfaction arose. The authority of the commissioners was denied. Indeed, more than half of them deliberately swore they had never signed the treaty, and that their names had been forged. There was widespread agitation. In every wigwam was heard the sound of dispute; in every council-house the roar of argument. The negro slaves belonging to the Seminoles banded together and boldly refused to follow their masters into exile, to a country where subsistence was only to be obtained by hard labor. As if by common impulse the Seminoles began to accumulate ammunition and weapons. The government retaliated by forbidding the sale of these articles to Indians or negroes. In response to a refusal to sell even powder, Osceola, a young warrior, not even a chief, uttered the terrible threat which stands at the opening of this chapter.

As the months went by, this high-spirited brave became one of the leaders of the war-party of the Seminoles. The old chiefs of the nation were timid and conservative. They inclined to a compliance with the demands of the United States. With the ringing voice of command, Osceola swore that the first Indian who commenced the sale or disposal of his property, preparatory to removal, should be put to death. It was not long before this threat was carried out. Charley Mathlar, an old chief, had driven his cattle to one of the army posts, and there, in conformity with the treaty, received from the government agent the money for them. He was returning home from this trip, carrying in his hands a handkerchief, in which was tied up the gold and silver thus obtained.

Osceola, mindful of his threat, posted himself with a band of braves in the forest beside the path, along which the old chief must come. As the latter approached, his enemies fired. Covering his face with his hands, he fell prostrate, receiving the blows from the braves without a word. With imperious tone Osceola said that the gold and silver was made of the red man's blood. Forbidding his followers to touch the accursed thing, he took it with his own hands and threw it in every direction.

Osceola was not satisfied. He determined to obtain revenge for the murder of Charley Mathlar, to which, as he said, the white man had driven him. With sixty followers he concealed himself in a dense forest, in the neighborhood of Fort King. General Thompson and Lieutenant Smith were taking an afternoon walk. As they approached the ambush they were fired upon and killed.

The fierce appetite for war and blood, which sometimes sleeps, but never is utterly eradicated from the savage heart, had during the long years of comparative peace and of agricultural pursuits slumbered inactive in the breasts of the Seminoles. As the deed of blood was accomplished, this old appetite was roused, like some sleeping animal, to rage and fury in the bosoms of the Indians. With fierce, exultant cries they leaped forth from their concealment, scalped the fallen men, in whose bodies were no less than thirty-seven balls, and to satisfy the craving appetites of all, as well as to prove to their companions their participation in the murder, cut the scalps into sixty small pieces, and distributed them to every member of the party.

Near by was the sutler's store, from which provisions were supplied to the fort. It was just the hour for the evening meal. Through the windows, open for the fresh sea breeze, which during certain hours in the day makes Florida delightful beyond any climate in the world, the savages discovered four gentlemen aud one boy seated at the table. They fired through the open doors and windows, killing every inmate of the house. The scalps of the slain were cut up and distributed as before. With greedy hands the store was rifled. Then the torch was applied, and the band rode away, leaving the buildings in flames.

Horrible as was this occurrence, which stands as the opening of the Florida war, a war of which the histories are few and the events but little known, which is passed over lightly by every historian of our country, who is more careful for its fame than for the truth, it must be remembered that the Seminoles were frantic with agitation and insane with grief, both at the sorrows they had suffered and at the exile which confronted them. They had been driven from the villages which they and their fathers had inhabited for three quarters of a century; they had been quarreled with and hated by their neighbors, who for forty years had sought only their destruction or exile, and the robbery of their lands. Houseless and homeless, they had roamed restlessly through the peninsula, angry with themselves and embittered by hatred for their enemies. Their braves had been arrested and placed in irons; their hunting parties had been robbed and murdered.

The territorial legislature, in a petition to congress, had accused them of the violation of a treaty, into which their chiefs had been entrapped, and to which the nation at large had never agreed. Guilty of much, they had, nevertheless, been charged with murders which they did not commit, and slandered for outrages of which they were innocent. Their exile was demanded on the strength of a treaty alleged to have been made with the exploring party sent to Arkansas, which the chiefs themselves repudiated as a forgery. Their most trusted leaders had been corrupted with money, and their hereditary chiefs had been bribed with presents. The suffering Seminoles, unlike the Indians of other portions of the country, could not retreat from the aggressions of the white men farther into the wilderness. Nature had hemmed them in by sea and gulf. For them there were but two alternatives, exile or war.

The Indians were by no means idle. One hundred troops were marching from Fort Brooke to the help of Fort King, where the above outrages were committed. They were discovered passing through an immense swamp. The Indians, two hundred in number, commanded by Jumper and Alligator, posted themselves on the west side of the road. Every warrior was protected or concealed amid the broad leaves of the high palmettos. On the other side of the road was a deep pond. Just as the troops arrived at this point, where they were, so to speak, between the devil and the deep water, the ambushed Indians fired. Alligator says, "The soldiers shouted and whooped, and the officers shook their swords and swore."

They seem to have done no more effective fighting. A cannon was loaded and fired a time or two, but the balls hissed harmlessly through the air, and fell with dull thuds far back in the swamp. Almost every white man was killed on the spot. Six got away, and endeavored to build a log barricade or pen, behind which they would be safe. The negroes, who formed powerful and ferocious allies of the Seminoles, attacked the rude rampart. When they clambered over the logs, only three men were found alive in the pen. Two of these were killed outright. The third snatched a rifle from the hands of his enemies, and with a terrific blow brained his opponent. He swiftly leaped over the logs, and started down the road at full speed. Two Indians on horseback gave chase, and, firing from a distance, killed him. Every man but two in the command was killed. The Indians lost only three warriors.

The whole Seminole country seemed to burst into flames at once. Sixteen plantations in East Florida, upon each of which were employed over a hundred negroes, together with sugar mills, cotton gins, storehouses, and fine residences, were completely destroyed during the month of January, 1836. The wealthiest people fled through the swamps for their lives, destitute of the common necessaries of life. None could tell at what moment or in what manner they would be assailed, and subjected to the most cruel and brutal death. "In some instances the lives of mothers were spared, that they might see their children cut in pieces, and their limbs used as weapons to assail the living."

A Frenchman, traveling in Florida in 1851, heard the story of the destruction of one of these planter's homes, from his guide, and published it in Paris. Though no date was given, the affair doubtless occurred early in the war. The guide had been a member of a company of volunteers, who were encamped on the shores of the St. John's River. One day a negro was observed swimming the river. He directed his course to the camp. As he touched the shore he ran toward the soldiers, all dripping with the water, explaining in agitated tones that the Indians were attacking the house of Mr. Montgomery, his master, and begging for help.

A party of men hastily prepared to accompany the slave to the threatened mansion, which was some little distance above, on the opposite side of the St. John's. The place was found to be well defended, and in no immediate danger, as the Indians had been gone for some hours. Montgomery, however, expressed great fears for the safety of his neighbor, Motte, who lived some miles farther up the river. Leaving a guard at Montgomery's, the men started on to Motte's.

When within a short distance of the house, which was spacious and elegant, the soldiers discovered smoke and flames beginning to issue from the windows. No Indians were in sight. Hurrying forward, the men entered the burning building. The

INDIAN VILLAGE IN WINTER.

492

owner seemed to be absent, yet he could not have been gone long. The rooms, with their elegant furniture, which one after another were being reached by the flames, gave evidence of recent occupation.

Pushing on into the parlor, the soldiers discovered the scene of an awful tragedy. Four mutilated corpses, yet warm with life, were lying on the floor. One was that of an old man, Mr. Motte himself. He was on the floor, partially leaning against the wall. He had been scalped, and the blood still trickled down his pallid features, and reddened all his snow-white beard. Right by him lay the mangled form of his youngest daughter. A few feet off were the two other beautiful daughters lying, scalped and lifeless. There had been a struggle; the old man still grasped his gun, and the oldest daughter still held in her jeweled hand a large pistol. The apartment, with its handsome fittings, was already full of fire. The floor and walls were in a blaze; the garments of the dead were burning.

Swift hands snatched the corpses from the flames, and bore them out for interment. Just as they were about to leave the doomed house, which was now filled with a frightful roar from the flames, the soldiers heard a shriek. The next moment, an old lady, scalped and bloody, but yet living, the mother of the girls, sprung toward them. She was tenderly transported to a place of safety, and survived for a year or so.

In the yard the men found the body of the colored gardener. One man stopped to water his horse. He heard a low cry from the marsh. Advancing cautiously, he found a poor mulatto girl, half-dead with fright. She had been lying in the swamp for hours. From her the story of the tragedy was learned. She had gone to get some water for the house, when Indians were discovered climbing the garden wall. The family were at the time out in the garden gathering flowers. They had time to reach the house and barricade the doors. The colored gardener sought to join them, but was killed on the way. The mulatto girl being too far away to reach the house,

fled to the marsh. Here she endured agony, but it was not
the agony of death. She saw the Indians surround the house.
She heard their demand for surrender, and the refusal of the
inmates. She saw the doors battered down, heard the shots,
the shrieks, the moans. Then there had been a silence. For
an hour or two the Indians remained in the house, ransacking it. At last they came forth with their plunder, fired the
house, and disappeared in the hammock. For many years the
ruined mansion bore the name of the House of Blood.

Two months after the massacre of Major Dade's command,
General Gaines, who with a considerable force from New
Orleans had reached the scene of hostilities, came upon the
spot where the awful tragedy had been enacted. Here was a
cart amid a lot of broken and scattered boxes. The two oxen
were lying dead, their yokes still on them. A little farther on
were the offensive remains of some horses. Next the men
came upon a little triangular breastwork of logs. A soldier
counted the corpses, by that time almost skeletons, lying within
the triangle. There were thirty of them. They were lying in
a regular row, parallel to each other, behind the barricade, their
heads next to the logs over which they had fired, and their
bodies stretched out on the ground. They had been shot dead
in their ranks, and lay in death as they had fought in life.

A little farther on, other bodies were found lying along the
road. Behind every tree, log, or even bush, to which the men
had resorted for cover, was one or more corpses. At one spot,
two hundred yards down the road, lay a cluster of bodies in
regular ranks, like the others. This had been the advance
guard. The soldiers were overwhelmed with horror. If such
was the beginning, what would be the end of the war ?

Their apprehensions were indeed justified. The very first
movement in the war was a terrible blunder. General Gaines,
finding no supplies at Fort King, resolved to withdraw to Fort
Brooke, on Tampa Bay. On the way, while crossing a river,
an immense force of warriors attacked him. A rude breastwork

of logs was hastily thrown up, and a runner dispatched to Fort Drane, ordering General Clinch to hurry forward with all his troops and supplies, and take the Indians, numbering more than fifteen hundred braves, in the rear, while Gaines attacked them in the front.

While the army, pinched with hunger and annoyed by the Indians, remained quiet in their fortified camp awaiting Clinch, an old negro named Cæsar came up to the lines, and shouted "that the Indians were tired of fighting, and wished to come in and shake hands." In pursuance of arrangements made with this embassador, a large number of warriors without their arms, assembled under a flag of truce about five hundred yards from the camp. Midway between the hostile armies three chiefs met a like number of American officers, and arranged a temporary cessation of hostilities. The Indians were to withdraw to the south side of the Withlacoochie, and remain there until a permanent peace was concluded. At that moment, General Clinch, from Fort Drane came in sight, and supposing the assemblage of Indians to be a hostile one, instantly charged upon them, inflicting great slaughter. So the conference broke up, and the Indians, freshly enraged, fled to their towns, swearing new oaths of vengeance.

On the twenty-second day of February Major-General Scott arrived in Florida, assuming command of the American forces. From the first all his efforts met with embarrassment and failure. His troops almost starved before rations could be had. In attempting a forward movement, large numbers of his provision wagons and horses were swept away in fording a river. Such provision as was rescued was exposed to a tremendous rain of many days, and ruined. The stormy weather delayed the movement of troops, and the exposure caused large numbers of the men, unused to the climate, to be attacked with malignant fevers. The cannon mired in bottomless bogs. Generals Gaines and Clinch refused to co-operate with Scott, and a bitter quarrel broke out between the commanders.

Assailed by these overwhelming difficulties, the army was compelled to straggle back to Fort Drane to escape starvations They arrived there famished and fever-stricken, only to find that General Gaines, who had not been expected in that part of the country, had deliberately appropriated nineteen thousand rations to his own use. Nevertheless General Scott, misled by dishonest scouts, utterly ignorant of the geography of a country which consisted of dense and impassable jungles, into which the light of day never penetrated, and of endless swamps, interspersed with bottomless bayous and salt lagoons, managed to send out numerous detachments in all directions to search for the enemy, whose whereabouts was utterly unknown. The Indians, thoroughly familiar with the country, led these detachments on wild and fatiguing chases only to disappear from view entirely, and fall upon the worn soldiery as they attempted to make their way back to their commander. Meanwhile the heated season coming on, together with scanty water from poisonous pools, made the condition of the men still more intolerable. In short, the campaign was an utter and ruinous failure.

About the first of June, General Call assumed command of the army. He, however, though having several engagements with the enemy, met with no better success than his predecessor. His principal undertaking was to send a strong detachment against the enemy, which were supposed to be posted in large numbers in the great Wahoo swamp.

After a journey of incomparable difficulty, the men wading much of the time up to their armpits in mire and water, the enemy was met in great strength. In endeavoring to dislodge them from a vast morass, the men themselves became entangled in its deceitful depths. The loss was heavy, although the engagement was accounted a victory. At night, however, it was deemed impossible to remain or to risk another engagement. The horses were dying for want of food. The ammunition was exhausted. The supplies, too, were gone. They had been lost in the difficulties of the advance. There remained nothing to be done except a disastrous and painful retreat. On the 27th of November, 1836, General Call was succeeded by General Jessup. The latter pushed the campaign with vigor. As the summer approached the Indians themselves, who had been accustomed to subsist on agricultural productions, were compelled to sue for peace. They again agreed to withdraw to Arkansas, and hostilities, for the time being, ceased.

By agreement large numbers of the Seminoles assembled in a camp near Fort Brooke, preparatory to an embarkation on government vessels for transportation to Arkansas. The old chief Micanopy had been largely instrumental in this consent to the exile of his people. He was encamped with hundreds of his followers at Fort Brooke, ready to bid a last farewell to the country he loved, and seek a new home in the barren wilderness west of the Mississippi. On the night of the 4th of June two dark forms made their way through the sleeping Indian camp toward the wigwam of old Micanopy. They were Osceola and Coacooche, the young and ferocious chiefs of the war-party. With noiseless tread they entered the rude apartment, unsheathed their glittering knives and roused the old chief from his slumbers. With whispered words they told him that he was a traitor to his people, that as they had sworn to kill the first Indian who should prepare to remove from Florida, and had fulfilled their oath by the slaughter of Charley Mathlar, so now they had sworn to take the life of Micanopy as that of a traitor, unless he at once consented to arouse the sleeping camp and lead the people before the break of day in a flight to the south, where they would be beyond the reach of the American army, and thus again foil the schemes of the enemies of the Seminoles to drive them into cruel exile.

The old man heard the whispered threats of the dark conspirators. He was timid and irresolute. He doubted himself whether he was not, as they hissed through their teeth in the darkness, a traitor to his people. He still hesitated. Osceola uplifted his right hand, from which the bright blade glistened
32

in the starlight, to plunge the dagger into the chieftain's heart. Agitated beyond measure, the old man gave his consent to their demand. Dark messengers passed swiftly and noiselessly from tent to tent, rousing the occupants, and conveying the order of their chief to prepare for instant flight. Not a question was asked. In a quarter of an hour, every one of the seven hundred Indians was proceeding through the forest without so much noise as would come from the breaking of a twig or the rustle of a dried palmetto leaf.

At sunrise, General Jessup, proud and pleased at the apparent termination of the war, rose to give orders for the embarkation of the exiles. In a half an hour he repaired to the spot where the Indian camp had been pitched. To his dismay and astonishment, he found only a few bare poles from the wigwams. The whole Indian assemblage had fled, and were many miles away, beyond the reach of successful pursuit. On that day General Jessup, the third commander-in-chief of the Florida army, tendered his resignation. He continued in actual command, however, until the 15th of May, 1838.

To General Hernandez the commander-in-chief intrusted the military operations of a campaign in East Florida, along the Atlantic coast. On the 9th of September, 1837, Hernandez succeeded in capturing King Philip, a noted Seminole chief of intelligence and influence, and the father of Coacoochee. The chieftain, finding himself in the toils of his enemies, sent word to his distinguished son, earnestly requesting him to come and confer with his father. Coacoochee was brave. Moreover, he had a special mission to perform for Osceola. Placing a large white plume in his hat, he boldly visited the camp of Hernandez, accompanied by Blue Snake, another chief.

On being shown into the presence of the American general, Coacoochee presented him with a handsome peace pipe, from the great Osceola, accompanied by a request for a conference. To this proposition Hernandez acceded, and Coacoochee departed with a message to Osceola, to the effect that he might have a council with the American general. On the appointed day, Coa-coochee returned to General Hernandez with information that Osceola, with a hundred warriors, was on his way to St. Augustine, for the appointed peace talk. Hernandez, with a design in his mind which, whether inspired by his commander or originated by himself, bears the ear-marks of a deep and damnable treachery, eager to get the game in his trap, hurried forward to meet Osceola. Seven miles southwest of St. Augustine, he met the distinguished Indian chieftain, and entered into a conference.

He at once commenced to question Osceola closely as to the purposes and plans of the Indians. While the conversation was progressing, the council was quickly and quietly surrounded by an overwhelming force of American soldiers. With quick intuition, Osceola read the sinister purposes of his enemy. As the questions were put to him he looked nervously about him at the surrounding military, gave a few vague and uneasy replies, and then lapsed into silence. Overcome by uncontrollable emotion, he turned to Coa-Hajo, and said, " I feel choked; you must speak for me."

Seeing that his purposes were discovered, Hernandez gave a signal, and in a moment Osceola and his little band of braves were made prisoners without a struggle. The date of this infamy was October 22, 1837. Osceola and his companions were at once placed in irons and thrown into the dungeon of the castle of St. Marco, at St. Augustine.

Notwithstanding the treachery by which he had been betrayed, Osceola communicated with Hernandez, and proposed to send a message to his people and their chiefs, recommending them to come in and consent to an exile to Arkansas. This proposition was agreed to. The messengers were sent. A council was held, and the scheme promised well. It however met with a sudden interruption. Coacoochee and his friend Talmus Hadjo were immured in another of the dark and mysterious dungeons in the castle of St. Marco, at St. Augustine, the most ancient military work in the United States.

While Osceola in one part of the old structure was planning for a submission by his people to exile, Coacoochee and his

friend weary with studying the arms of Spain, which were carved on the walls of their prison cell, and growing more languid and sickly day by day from the confinement, resolved to escape, or die in the effort. They occupied an apartment about eighteen feet square, with walls of stone, and a lofty ceiling. The only window through which they received light and air, and consequently the only chance for escape, was a small embrasure eighteen feet from the floor. From this aperture to the bottom of the ditch on the outside, was more than fifty feet. The two prisoners examined the hole attentively, and saw that it was exceedingly small, but believed that they might possibly squeeze through it.

All their preparations had to be carried on in complete silence, as a sentinel stood constantly at the door of the cell. With deft fingers the prisoners tore into strips a few forage bags which formed their bed, and wove them into a rude rope. The first thing was to reach the embrasure. Again and again Coacoochee stood on the shoulders of his companion and strained himself to the utmost to reach the sill. All in vain; the window remained two feet above his fingers.

At last the prisoners managed to secrete a knife. Standing on the shoulders of his companion, Coacoochee gradually worked it into a crevice in the rock as high up as he could reach. When the blade and half of the short, heavy handle had been inserted the other part of the handle remained a stout and serviceable peg, by means of which the athletic Indian raised himself to the embrasure. He found it small, but believed that if he and his companion could get rid of their flesh they might get through. They at once feigned sickness, and procured through their guards some roots, of which they knew the effect. For three weeks the prisoners abstained almost entirely from food, taking large quantities of the medicinal root, and at the end of the time were little more than skin and bone.

On a certain night, when there would be no moon, they resolved to attempt their escape. During the evening the keeper came in frequently, annoying the prisoners so much that they almost resolved to seize and gag him. They more prudently pretended to be asleep, and at last the keeper came no more. Taking one end of the rope in his hand, Coacoochee once more climbed up to the embrasure. Here he made fast the rope, letting one end hang down inside for his friend, who was to follow, and dangling the other end down toward the ditch. With great difficulty the Indian forced his body through the aperture. Great strips of skin were torn from him. But with a capacity for the endurance of physical suffering which only an Indian could have, he resolutely persisted. He lay hold of the rope on the outside with his hands, and descended head foremost till he had dragged his feet through the embrasure, and at last leaped to the ground.

Though terribly wounded he was unconscious of the pain, and turned all his thoughts to the arrival of his comrade. At length he heard the struggle of his companion far above him. There was a low gasp of despair. The man had forced his head and shoulders into the hole and was caught fast, being unable to move either backward or forward. Coacoochee called to him in the lowest possible tone to keep calm and rest for a moment, then to force out all his breath and at the same instant endeavor to move an inch or so. For a few moments Coacoochee could hear his friend following this advice, when suddenly he was alarmed to find him tumbling head foremost down the whole distance. Extricating himself with a sudden jerk, the rope had broken.

As he lay on the ground a confused and bloody mass, Coacoochee thought him dead. Nevertheless, in spite of the danger of discovery, he dragged his companion to a pool of water, which revived him. The poor fellow was so lame that he could not walk a step. It was almost dawn. In a short time their escape would be discovered. Although himself weak from emaciation and wounds, Coacoochee placed his friend on his back, and started to the nearest woods. Before long he caught sight of a mule, which he captured. The two Indians mounted. Forcing the animal to its highest speed, and guiding it solely by seizing its ears, Coacoochee and his friend hurried across the country with which they were so familiar. After five days they arrived among their people.

Coacoochee's emaciation and wounds spoke eloquently of what he had endured. Nevertheless he rested not until he had told them the story of the treachery by which he and Osceola had been betrayed, and of their confinement in loathsome cells. Alarmed and suspicious, the other chiefs at once abandoned all idea of further conference or communication with the Americans.

Poor Osceola, the master-spirit of the war, who had risen from the ranks of the humblest warriors by dint of his lofty genius, had at least twice confronted not only the Americans, but all of the leading chiefs of his own people, and, overcoming the latter, had resisted the demands of the enemies of the Seminoles for their exile from Florida; who had hurled the united nation against the Americans for two years, foiling all their efforts and defeating all their armies, languished and pined in his lonely cell at St. Augustine. The high independence of feeling, which had never before known restraint, became enfeebled, and sunk as the chances of escape passed away. His proud spirit was broken by defeat and imprisonment. For greater security he was removed from St. Augustine to Fort Moultrie, Charleston Harbor. This removal plunged him into a melancholy which never left him. Hope was gone, and the conviction that he was forever banished from his native land weighed and wore upon his spirits until nature became exhausted. He declined to see visitors, and, refusing all sustenance, sat alone in his dark dungeon brooding, brooding over the mighty sorrows of his people and the overwhelming disasters which had befallen him.

One morning, when his keeper came to the cell, he called to Osceola, but the young chieftain did not reply. He called again, louder and more sharply, but no answer came save the mocking echo from the stone walls of the dungeon. Suspicious and alarmed, the man procured help and opened the door of the dungeon.　Groping around by the light of a tallow candle to the spot where lay a heap of mouldy straw, which formed the bed of the prisoner, there they found him cold and unresponsive in death.　At the age of thirty-three years the young, the brilliant, the great Osceola, a brave and generous enemy, a proud and manly man, the noblest offspring of his suffering people, died thus of a broken heart.

In December, 1837, Colonel Zachary Taylor, at the head of a thousand men advanced one hundred and fifty miles into the enemy's country, through an unexplored wilderness of jungles and bayous, crossing a dozen streams every day, over which there were no bridges, and traveling without guides in the face of a numerous and powerful foe. Toward the latter part of the month they came up with

ZACHARY TAYLOR.

a large body of warriors, commanded by Alligator.　The Indians were encamped on the hard sandy beach on the north side of the great Lake Okeechobee.　Between the whites and the Indians lay a morass three quarters of a mile wide, covered with a thick growth of saw-grass five feet high and three feet deep in mud and water.　The swamp extended on either side as far as the eye could reach.　It was totally impassable for horses, and nearly so for men.

The soldiers dismounted, and relieving themselves of all unnecessary weight, prepared to cross the morass and give battle to the enemy. In spots where the mire was deep enough for a man to sink out of sight in its treacherous depths, the Indians had cut down the grass, so as to lure the troops into the fatal trap. Notwithstanding these difficulties, the Americans gave battle, and after several hours of hard fighting came out victorious. At nightfall it was necessary to commence the inevitable retreat, which no victory, however complete, could prevent; for in this remarkable war the impossibility of transporting provisions for more than a few days through the aqueous wilderness embarrassed and crippled the American army from first to last. In order to retrace their steps through the swamp in the darkness, and transport one hundred and twelve wounded men, rude litters were constructed, and a small foot-way built across the swamp. Colonel Taylor brought back his command without further loss, and on the 15th of May, 1838, succeeded General Jessup as commander-in-chief.

We may not trace the irregular, laborious, and indecisive warfare of the ensuing year. In May, 1839, the Indians again agreed to a cessation of hostilities, and to confine themselves to a designated part of the peninsula. Many of the settlers, supposing the war was at an end, returned to their homes.

The throngs of unemployed and starving people, who had fled to the crowded villages for safety, again ventured on their plantations. Their hopes, however, were soon scattered to the winds. In July the Indians, irrepressible and invincible, again began their outrages. Colonel Harney, with twenty-six dragoons and three traders, had proceeded to Charlotte's Harbor, to establish a trading post in pursuance of the agreement with the Indians. They were encamped, with a large supply of Indian goods, in a pine barren on the Coloosahatchee river. At dawn on the 22d of July, they were attacked by a band of warriors commanded by Bow Legs. The men were overpowered in their beds, and, embarrassed by their mosquito-bars, were unable to make any effectual resistance. Twenty-four were killed, and two captured. Colonel Harney and two companions escaped, and, after living for days on crabs and oysters, made their way home.

And so the war was renewed. As before, the Indians were driven from swamp to swamp, from jungle to jungle, and from bayous to lagoons, leading the exhausted, famished, and fever-stricken troops hither and yon in fruitless chases over a region of country embracing more than 45,000 square miles.

The territorial legislature saw, as every one saw, that the Indians, hemmed in by the sea and unable to fly, would fight until the last brave was exterminated. This war would cost the lives of four or five white men to every Indian that was killed. So the legislature resolved upon an expedient. They sent to Havana, and purchased at an enormous expense the most famous kennel of blood-hounds in the world. With these animals, which had been trained to the pursuit of fugitive slaves, it was purposed to hunt out the Indians, and by this means track, overpower, and kill. Five experienced Spaniards accompanied the troop of blood-hounds. They were attached to each column of troops, attended by their keepers. The animals were fed liberally upon bloody meat, to supply which young calves accompanied each detachment, and then, being put upon the Indian trail, started forward in the horrible and fiendish pursuit. Such were the means adopted in the nineteenth century to drive a people from the land which was their own.

The Spanish Indians inhabiting the southern extremity of the peninsula, finding themselves encroached upon more and more by their brethren from the north, who, amid hardships which it is impossible to imagine, much more to describe, were gradually being beaten back by the whites, now began to take a hand in the war. They pillaged certain unfortunate vessels which were wrecked upon their coast, and murdered the seamen. They even attacked the little settlements on the islands along the western coast. Indian Key was a small island about twenty miles from the main-land. Here, among others, lived Doctor Perrine. a scientific man of high literary attainments, who, inspired by an enthusiasm for scientific research, had, with his family, made this spot his home, in order to carry forward an investigation of the botanical species of Florida.

On the 7th of August, 1840, about two o'clock in the morning, the Perrines, in common with the other people of the island, were awakened from their sleep by Indian yells, and a number of shots fired. At that moment the glass in their windows was crushed by missiles from without. Mrs. Perrine and her three children hurried down stairs to a room from which a trap-door led to the cellar. The cellar was used for bathing, the tide filling it twice a day. Doctor Perrine saw his family safely down into this place, and then returned to the piazza to find out what was the matter. Mrs. Perrine and her daughters passed through the water and crawled into a small place about three feet high and ten feet long, constructed of plank and rocks, through which the tide had access to the cellar. No sooner were they secreted in this hole than they heard the doctor talking with the Indians in Spanish, and telling them that he was a physician. At this the Indians ran off with a shout, joining the others in the work of pillaging, firing other houses on the island, and massacring the inhabitants. Doctor Perrine then shut the trap-door, and placed a heavy chest over it, determined if possible, to conceal the retreat of his family and brave the worst himself.

At daylight the Indians returned. They commenced battering in the doors and windows. The doctor fled to the cupola, which was entered by a heavy trap-door. The Indians swarmed through the rooms in search of the occupants. They turned over beds, broke open closets, and tried every door without success. At last they concentrated their efforts on the heavy door leading to the cupola. For a time it resisted their efforts. At last it gave way beneath their terrific assaults, and with wild yells the Indians rushed up into the cupola and massacred the unfortunate man who had retreated to that spot. All this the family heard from their concealment in the cellar.

At last the savages were heard to descend the steps and commence smashing the crockery, glass, and doors of the house, taking savage joy in the mere act of destruction. Trunks and chests of clothing were dragged out of the house and loaded into boats. Two Indians came around the house to the place where the plank covered the spot in which Mrs. Perrine and her children were concealed. One of them lifted a board and looked in, but fortunately the family were crouched at the farther end of the hole, and escaped discovery in the darkness.

In a little while the unhappy people detected a smell of smoke. It grew stronger and stronger. They could hear the roar of the flames in the dwelling above. In a half an hour the rafters gave way, and the whole flaming structure fell with a terrific crash into the cellar. The smoke became intolerable. The planks above them took fire. To avoid suffocation they plastered their heads with mud, and threw the water constantly over their faces as well as upon the planks, in a vain attempt to extinguish the flames.

From the spot where the family were concealed, by chance there led a turtle-crawl. Henry Perrine, a lad, in spite of his mother's entreaties, began to scream with the agonies of suffocation. Discovering the turtle-crawl through an opening between the posts, he proceeded to push the posts aside, and declaring that he would rather be killed by the savages than burnt to death, attempted to get out. The aperture, however, was too small. With his fingers and nails he tore away the mud into which the palmetto post was sunk, and by the most strenuous efforts pulled it out of its socket. The boy instantly passed into the turtle-crawl and out into the open air.

Mrs. Perrine and her two daughters, fearful to follow the boy, yet unable to remain where they were, dug away another post and passed under a wharf which was constructed at the spot. On this structure three cords of wood were burning. The floor over their heads was almost consumed, and the coals dropped through upon them as they passed. As they reached the shore the whole structure fell in. Had they been a moment later they would have been buried in a grave of fire.

Mrs. Perrine at once caught sight of a launch, and beckoning to her son, who was crouching near by, they waded out to it and sprang aboard. The launch was grounded. The boy and the largest girl at once jumped into the water up to their necks, and managed slowly to push the launch off the shoal. With a paddle and two poles they proceeded about a mile, when they were picked up by a schooner, to which a number of the inhabitants of the place had already fled for refuge. The launch in which they had made their escape was one which the Indians had been loading with plunder. In a few days the unhappy family were transported to St. Augustine.

The Seminoles were certainly the most tantalizing of all the American Indians. The entire territory of Florida was divided up among their chiefs, each of whom operated in his own respective section. Sometimes the blow was one of open violence, sometimes of secret stealth, and not infrequently it was an exasperating prank. Of course the whole country was tired of the war. The officers bit eagerly at every hint at submission by the Indians.

In November, 1840, after infinite pains, Halleck-Tustenuggee and Tiger Tail were induced to come to Fort King. They remained three or four days. They pretended the utmost humility, and from their words one would have thought the whole Indian force was about to surrender. They ate very heartily of the provisions of the fort, and several times a day would request the commander to make some one of their band, who appeared to have straggled into the fort by accident, a present of food. These stragglers would at once disappear with the supplies; no doubt carrying them to a hidden camp, where many a chuckle was indulged in at the expense of the Americans.

The officers of the fort innocently believed that peace was

at hand. One morning they found that their artful guests had fled. The whole thing was a trick to secure a few days of high living! The next move of these scamps was more tragic. Fifteen soldiers were escorting Mrs. Montgomery from Micanopy to a point eight miles distant, when they were attacked by Indians. Mrs. Montgomery was killed by a ball in her breast. The handful of men fought hand to hand, but were overpowered and slain. Considerable plunder fell into the hands of the greedy savages. Strange as it may seem, Cosa-Tustenuggee was frightened at this atrocity, for " *conscience doth make cowards of us all.*" He came in soon after and surrendered to the whites, consenting to exile.

All attempts to track these marauding parties seemed futile. The trail was lost in the nearest marsh, and the clue could not be regained. The Indians made their homes in the center of immense hummocks or jungles. Here, unseen and unsuspected, their squaws cultivated considerable patches of land, and to these retreats they fled for concealment after some outrage.

Halleck-Tustenuggee's operations, as we have seen, filled the country north, west, and south of St. Augustine with perpetual alarm. In March, 1841, he appeared in the neighborhood of Fort Brooks, on the Oklawaha River. A soldier came out for a hunt, and was shot. The Indians danced and yelled over his body, hoping to tease the garrison into coming out of the fort for an attack. The garrison, believing that a long expected provision train was being attacked, sallied forth, resolving to die in battle rather than of starvation. The valor of the men availed to beat off the Indians with heavy loss, a circumstance which gave their chief food for thought.

Waxehadjo was a chief, whose face was as ugly as his name, who carried on his bloody warfare near Tampa, on the West Florida coast. One day word was brought to Fort Brooke, at Tampa, of the murder of a mail carrier on the road to Fort Cross. A party of mounted soldiers at once started in pursuit of the murderers. The pursuers came upon them early in the morning. The chief and two Indians were sitting by a camp-fire, having just breakfasted on the provisions in the poor mail man's pouch. In the midst of the coals on which the meal had been cooked they had placed the gory head of the murdered victim, where the soldiers were horrified to see it. The two common Indians succeeded in escaping. The chief took refuge in a pool. The white men discovered his hiding place by some bubbles coming up through the water. Several rifles were fired, and a soldier wading in found him grasping the grass in the bottom, in the last agonies of death. His body was nailed to a tree, " as a warning to his companions." Had an Indian done as much to the body of a white enemy, it would have been spoken of as " horrid brutality."

All ordinary methods of scouting failing, the Americans or-ganized " canoe bands," which threaded the inland waters of Florida to their innermost recesses to track out the Indians. This plan, which is another illustration of the fact that genius for warfare is really a genius for adaptation to the peculiar cir-cumstances of the war, was, in a measure, successful. The ordinary movement of troops was entirely inadequate to deal with the problem. " Marches of weeks and months, through deep sand and muddy water, burdened with a knapsack and musket, exposed to a vertical sun and drenching rains, brought the troops no nearer the enemy, who, with his rifle and a few companions, watched their weary progress from day to day, intercepting detachments at every point, with a fleetness, unex-ampled, eluding and misleading by their intimate knowledge of the country. Hardly could the troops reach their destination, before the section of the country which they had just left would be alarmed by the inroads of the Indians."

In January, 1841, four hundred men set out from Tampa toward the Kissimmee River. On the way the men built Fort Carroll, and encamped later at Fort Gardner. The whole coun-try was found to be overflowed. Finding it impossible to pro-ceed with their plan, it was resolved to attempt an interview with the great Coacoochee, or Wild Cat, who was believed to inhabit an island in Lake Tohopekaliga. Micco, an aged Indian, friendly to the Americans, undertook to hunt up the chief, and try to arrange for a council. As a special reason for believing that this might be secured, the whites had in their camp the daughter of Coacoochee, who had been captured in a skirmish. The chief himself had been committing a new outrage, having killed and robbed a party of strolling actors near St. Augustine, and was concealed with unusual care.

Micco at last returned, saying that Coacoochee was hid in a cypress swamp, four days' journey from the camp, but that he had consented to come in and have a talk. On the appointed day he was seen approaching the camp, accompanied by seven trusty warriors. A curious sight presented itself. From the plunder of the theatrical party the Indians had rigged themselves out in all the gaudy finery of the stage. Coacoochee was dressed in the toga of imperial purple, which cloaked the noble form of Julius Cæsar. Another wore the hideous costume of Richard III. Horatio in modest garb walked swiftly by the side of Falstaff. Scarlet vests and glittering spangles were distributed freely among the singular company.

At the sound of her father's voice Coacoochee's daughter sprang past the guard at the door of her tent, and ran to his open arms. With the instinct of a savage she gave him at once a handful of broken cartridges and bullets, which she had picked up around the camp. The young chief won the confidence of the whites by his noble and open bearing and eloquent tongue. " The white man comes ; he grows pale and sick here, while his red brother thrives in the land the Great Spirit has given him. Why may we not live here in peace ? The white men are as thick as the leaves in the hummock. They come upon us thicker every day. They may shoot us ; they may drive our children night and day ; they may chain our hands and feet, but the red man's heart will be always free." Yet he ended by promising to assemble his people at Tampa, and take them into exile.

Coacoochee was perhaps sincere in his professions. For many months he claimed to be working to induce his tribe to emigrate. But the patience of the whites was exhausted. On the 21st of May, 1842, he came to Fort Pierce, as he had been accustomed to do to request supplies of whisky and food. His arrest, previously decided upon, was put into execution. He was at first taken to New Orleans, but was returned in chains to Tampa Bay.

Meanwhile the war proceeded somewhat more favorably for the Americans, but with the usual number of romantic incidents. In June an expedition of forty trained scouts set out to surprise the camp of Halleck-Tustenuggee. The men, after a fatiguing journey, arrived at the edge of a swamp, six miles wide, on the opposite side of which the Indians were supposed to be encamped. It was the hour of midnight. The horses were hastily picketed, and every useless burden left on the margin of the morass. To the dense shades of the cypress swamp was added the darkness of a moonless night. Guided by stalwart negroes, unable to see their hands before them, marching through the water four feet deep, the force of two hundred men started across the swamp.

At daybreak a halt was called. Just forty-six men were present. The rest were struggling through the swamps, or had ceased all struggles forever. The men crawled stealthily toward the cluster of indian huts, which was in sight. A gun was fired when close to the lodges to rouse the occupants, but the breathless watchers were chagrined to discover not a sign of life. The dull rumble of the explosion died away among the cypress-trees, but no war-whoop met the ears of the white men, and no savages attempted to escape. Not a human being occupied the huts. The men could only express their chagrin and disappointment, after all their fruitless toil, by setting fire to the sheds. The weary march back, through the shades of death, was all that remained for them.

Another band of scouts scoured the Wahoo swamp. Four

33

large corn-fields with growing crops were found hidden in the recesses of the vast morass. While destroying these, early one morning, an Indian was discovered approaching in a canoe. Perceiving the white men, he instantly put about and using his paddle with wonderful effect, made every effort to escape. Finding himself unable to avoid his pursuers, he sprang from his canoe and disappeared in the swamp. Several shots were fired at him, and he was believed to have fallen. The soldiers jumped from their boats into four feet of water, and searched the swamp in all directions. His canoe floated idly on the stagnant water, and the spot where the Indian had jumped was marked by the break in the heavy green scum, but the savage himself was nowhere to be seen. Months afterward this man was captured. He said that the soldiers on this occasion had passed right by him while he lay concealed in the water, covering his face with a leaf of a pond lily.

Coacoochee reached Tampa Bay early in July, 1841. On the morning of the 4th he and his warriors, loaded with chains, were brought up on the deck of the transport, which was anchored in the harbor, for a council with Colonel Worth, who had become commander-in-chief of the Florida army. The council was a dramatic occasion. The spirit of the Indians was utterly broken by their misfortunes. Colonel Worth spoke firmly but kindly to his great captive, giving him to understand that the war must end, and that unless Coacoochee induced his tribe to emigrate within a certain time to Arkansas that he and his warriors should be hung. At the close of his speech there was a long silence.

At last a clanking of chains announced that Coacoochee was struggling to his feet to reply. In eloquent words he reviewed his life and the misfortunes of his people, and at last came to the practical question of the moment. "You say I must end the war! Look at these irons! Can I go to my warriors? Coacoochee chained? No; do not ask me to see them. I never wish to tread upon my land unless I am free. If I can go to them *unchained*, they will follow me in; but I fear they will not obey me when I talk to them in irons. They will say my heart is weak; that I am afraid. Could I go free they will surrender and emigrate."

Of course this was impossible. Once more Colonel Worth assured him that unless his people would come in by an appointed day, the setting sun would witness his execution. The vessel lay two miles from the shore. The prisoners were surrounded day and night by strong guards. Escape was impossible. So Coacoochee accepted the terms.

Five trusty messengers were released to carry his talk to his people. To them he said: "If your hearts are bad, let me see them now; take them in your hands and let me know that they are false; but do not, like dogs, bite me as soon as you turn your backs. Say to my band that my feet are chained, yet I send them my word as true from the heart as if I were with them. The great white chief says when my band comes in, I shall again walk free. He has given you forty days to do this business in. Take these sticks; here are thirty-nine, one for each day; *this*, much larger than the rest, with blood upon it, is the fortieth. When the others are thrown away, and this only remains, say to my people that with the setting sun Coacoochee hangs like a dog, with none but white men to hear his last words."

The voice of the speaker had sunk almost to a whisper. The awed bystanders heard some broken words, by which he sent a remembrance to his wife and child. With this the scene ended. The chains were taken from the five messengers, and they stepped over the side of the vessel into a row-boat. The chief, whose fate they held in their hands, stood immovable, following them with his eyes as far as they could be seen. During the days that followed the lines of anxiety in his face deepened perceptibly. He would sit all day with his eyes turned landward, looking eagerly for the appearance of his people. When the sun set each day far across the lonely gulf, without the arrival of any Indians, he sighed heavily, and sank into deeper melancholy.

Coacoochee's people were loyal to him. In time they began to gather on the low shores of Tampa Bay. The chief's spirits revived. At last the full number of his band were present. When the news was announced the whole bearing of the man changed. From the humble and gloomy captive, he altered suddenly into the proud and haughty chief. "Take off my irons," he cried, "that I may once more meet my warriors like a man." This, though hazardous, was done, that the promise of Colonel Worth might be fulfilled. Coacoochee dressed himself in his grandest attire. His breast glittered with silver ornaments. A red sash was bound around his waist. Three ostrich plumes ornamented his crimson turban. Impatiently springing into the boat, he started for the shore. As his foot touched the soil, he drew his manly form to its utmost height, waved his arms, and uttered a terrific whoop.

Though Coacoochee's tribe had thus submitted, the work was but begun. His wide influence was yet to be exerted over other bands and chiefs. Eighty miles south of Tampa Bay, the Americans had pitched a camp on Pease Creek, for the purpose of having a basis for an invasion of the Big Cypress Swamp and the Everglades. To this camp Sole-Micco, a friendly Indian, one day came for refuge. Four months previous he had gone to carry a friendly talk to Hospetarke. Just before his arrival among the latter's band, a council had been held which had decreed that the bearer of any message from the whites should be put to death.

Sole-Micco was suspected, but swore that he was hunting for his mother, who was believed to reside somewhere in Big Swamp. The prophet of the tribe announced that he would find out whether the story was true. He built ten fires in a circle, divided his time between praying and dancing, got out his supplies of roots, snake skins, and young alligators, examined the palm of the Indian, and at last announced that the latter had lied. Had not Sole-Micco had some relatives in the band who prepared to fight in his behalf, he would have been killed.

When Sole-Micco reported to Coacoochee the hostility of this band and the vicious influence of the prophet, the chief feared lest he might render other bands unmanageable. He at once sent his younger brother to the band with a peace-talk. Hospetarke agreed to come into the camp on Pease Creek and hold a council. For a week the old rascal kept sending word to the camp each day that he was coming, but was very old, very sick, and very tired, and required whisky, food, and tobacco to give him strength to make the journey. His statements must have been true, as he could only travel two or three miles a day without sending in for more supplies. While he was advancing at a snail's pace, Coacoochee was also on his way to Pease Creek. The latter arriving, was suffered to go alone to the old Indian's camp and bring him in.

It was evident that the old chief was simply playing a game, and that he must be met with a counter-stratagem. A council was appointed to be held in the cabin of the vessel which had brought Colonel Worth and Coacoochee down the coast. The Indians assembled in the apartment at the appointed hour, and were secretly surrounded by soldiers. At a given signal the doors were closed and every Indian was made a prisoner. Wild and fierce was the storm of abuse which raged when the Indians discovered the treachery. At this moment Coacoochee, in order that he might not be believed to have a share in the conspiracy, came into the cabin with a whisky bottle in his hand, pretending to be drunk. He railed at the white men for betraying his friends, while he was enjoying his bottle, and succeeded in diverting all suspicion from himself. The warriors selected a few messengers to bring in their women and children, and the whole band was then taken to Tampa Bay in chains.

The assemblage of Indians at Tampa Bay became restless. Coacoochee had exhausted his ingenuity in the way of ballplays, dances and games, to content the Indians and occupy their minds while the plans for securing the submission of others were being executed. The assemblage was becoming impatient and explosive. Numbers of troops guarded the camp at every point. At night a space of two miles' square was lit up by lines of beacon fires, so that the movements of every person in the camp were distinctly visible. Coacoochee was anxious to bring the long delay to a close. The eleventh day of October was set as the day for sailing.

As soon as the announcement was made, the camp became the scene of strange activities. Young and old, little and big, set to work pounding corn for the journey. The fabulous stories which had so long been current were revived. A dozen times a day Coacoochee, who had been to New Orleans and back, was called upon to reassure his people that when at sea, beyond the sight of land, they were *not* to be cast overboard.

The departure from their native land into exile was a sorrowful experience. Yet the interests and feelings of the multitude, packed into the little vessel, were widely different. First there were the Seminoles, of whom we have heard much. Then there were the negroes. These latter were isolated by a barbarism, a savagery peculiar to themselves. They were mostly runaways, or captives taken by the Indians from their masters in Georgia and Alabama. They had their own sorrows, which it does not fall within the scope of this book to detail. If the records of the time are to be believed, they were far more blood-thirsty, more fiercely brutal, more utterly inhuman, than the Indians themselves. They gloried in the war because peace meant to them simply slavery, while war meant wild and hideous license. "Ten resolute negroes," it is said, "with a knowledge of the country, were sufficient to desolate the frontier from one end to the other."

Besides these two unhappy peoples there were also a small number of Mickasukie Indians. These were the original occupants of Florida. They regarded with equal bitterness and hatred the negroes, the Seminoles, and the whites. To them

RESCUE OF LUCY CORNELL BY RED EAGLE.

they were all alike, invaders and enemies. Halleck Tustenug-
gee was their chief. In camp they had obstinately refused
rations, when issued with those of the Seminoles or negroes.
Even when packed on board the filthy vessel they refused to
share the society of the unhappy wretches about them, but
shut themselves off in one corner of the ship in the solitude
of sorrow.

Thus, loaded with people of such different varieties of
wretchedness, the vessel moved slowly down the bay. In the
dense throng now and then a convulsive sob escaped from the
negroes or the squaws, but in general the crowd preserved a
profound silence. Hour after hour they watched the receding
shores with fixed and melancholy gaze until twilight hid them
from their view. In the morning no land was in sight. With
the departure of Coacoochee the most dangerous and the most
noble of all the Indian chiefs was removed from Florida.

The war in Florida continued to rage for a year or two
longer. Little by little the genius of Colonel Worth availed to
detach separate bands of Indians from the rest, obtain their submission, and transport them to Arkansas. The American troops
who had become rather scouts than soldiers, threaded their way
to the darkest and most inaccessible spots in Florida, hunted the
Indians from their hiding places, captured the warriors, and
humiliated their chiefs. Of all the Indians in the territory at
the beginning of the war only one hundred and twenty, capable
of bearing arms, remained at its close. The policy of the United
States in this war has always been regarded as a blot on her
fame. Such a policy has never been pursued toward any other
tribe of Indians. The Sorrows of the Seminoles did not end
with their exile to Arkansas. It is safe to say that they will
not do so until the last unhappy descendant of the tribe which
produced Osceola and Coacoochee shall have passed to the happy
hunting grounds.

CHAPTER XV.

BLACK HAWK'S HUMILIATION.

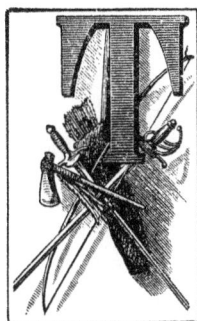

THE Sac Indians have a curious account of creation. According to their story, the gods in the beginning created the earth and every species of bird, beast, and fish. They next created a man. But this creature, as may easily be believed, was shortly discovered to be both cruel and foolish. To improve him the gods put into him the heart of the best beast they had created. This, however, failed to improve its perverse owner. So the Almighty took a piece of himself, of which he made a heart for the man, who at once became wise and gentle. The earth, meanwhile, brought forth fruits in abundance. Besides man it was inhabited by innumerable giants and gods.

It seems, according to this tale, that another tribe of gods, who had their home under the seas, had a fuss with the gods of the earth. The former pooled their issues with the giants for the purpose of destroying their common enemy. A council was held, at which, after much debate, it was decided that the allies were still too weak to attack Wesukkah, the chief god of the earth. So they conceived a stratagem. A great feast was to be prepared on the earth, to which Wesukkah should be invited. At an opportune moment his enemies would then fall upon him and put him to death. But Wesukkah was wide awake. No sooner had the council decided on this plan than Wesukkah's younger brother appeared in the midst of the assembly. He was at once inquired of, "Where is thy brother

Wesukkah?" to which he replied, "I know not; am I my
brother's keeper?" The conspirators, seeing their plan was discovered, instantly slew the young god.

Wesukkah was deeply grieved at the fate of his brother.
The gods who dwell above the clouds, hearing his noisy lamenta-
tions, came down and offered to help him destroy his enemies.
Frightened at their danger, the gods from under the sea had run
off, leaving their friends, the giants, alone upon earth. The
battle-field between Wesukkah and the giants was a flame of
fire. The giants fought bravely, but were utterly destroyed,
not one of their number being left alive.

The gods under the sea, frightened at the fate of their allies,
instantly besought their friends for help. The call was not unheeded. Through the influence of the deities of the thunder
and the wind, the god of the cold, with his dreadful armies of
frost, snow, hail and ice, came from the north, and smote the
whole earth. Every river, lake, and sea was converted into solid
ice. For many days enormous hailstones, the size of a man's
head, smote the inhabitants of the earth. When the storm
ceased, all of them, both men, beasts, and gods, save a few
choice ones of each kind, which Wesukkah had covered with
the hollow of his hand, were found to have perished.

In the process of time, the gods of the sea ventured to peep
out from their hiding-place, and seeing Wesukkah almost entirely
alone upon the earth, thought that now their enemy might indeed
be conquered. Every attempt failed, and the gods of the sea,
finding themselves unable to secure the earth for their own
habitation, gnashed their teeth, and resolved to destroy it altogether. They besought the god of thunder for aid, and he,
calling together all his clouds, commanded them to pour water
upon the earth. This order they obeyed, and the flood continued until the whole surface of the earth, including the highest
mountains, was covered with water.

Wesukkah, however, saw the deluge coming, and took some
air to make himself a boat. Into this he went, taking with him

a few of every sort of living creature, including man. The air boat floated safely on the top of the flood. After a good while, Wesukkah commanded a fish to go down into the waters, and bring up some earth from the bottom. After great difficulty, the fish returned with a mouthful of dirt, out of which Wesukkah, spreading it forth on the surface of the water, formed this earth. Tired with their long confinement, he and the creatures that were with him in his air boat came forth and inhabited it.

Though the Sacs have such a specific account of creation, they have neglected to preserve their subsequent history with any thing like detail. All we know is, that they and the Foxes once inhabited the shores of the St. Lawrence. Being attacked by the Iroquois, they fled to the western shores of Lake Michigan, and thence to the valley of the Mississippi. Elsewhere we have related the story of the assassination of the great Pontiac in an Illinois village. This murder was the cause of one of the most terrible Indian wars known to history. The Sacs and Foxes from the north, together with a large number of Pontiacean tribes, invaded the fertile plains of the Illinois, overran the country, destroyed the villages, and almost utterly annihilated the great Illinois confederacy, of which the Kaskaskias, the Peorias, the Miamis, and the Meas were but individual tribes.

Having subjugated and massacred the inhabitants of the fair region to which the name of the ruined confederacy is still given, the Sacs and Foxes determined to remain in the delightful country. Their principal village was constructed on the east side of Rock River, near its junction with the Mississippi. Of this region a traveler said, more than a century ago, " It is healthy and amazingly fruitful. The grape, the plum, the gooseberry, and various other native fruits abound. The wild honeysuckle gives its perfume to the air, and a thousand indigenous flowers mingle their diversified hues with the verdure of the plain."

As usual, the difficulties of the United States with these tribes grew out of a treaty. It was made in 1804, and in it it was agreed by the Indians to give up about all their territory east of the Mississippi, for a small annuity. The origin of this treaty was claimed by the Indians to be as follows : In 1804 some of the Sacs went down to St. Louis to try to secure the release of one of their friends, who was under arrest for murder. The party was absent a long time. When they returned they were dressed in fine clothes, and each man possessed a silver medal. They related to their tribe that after having requested the Americans to release their friend, the governor told them that he wanted some land. Papers were drawn up and eagerly signed by the Indians, thinking that the safety of their friend was secured. They were supplied with a great deal of whisky, and were so drunk during their stay that they could only remember that their friend, instead of being restored to them, was called out before them and shot dead by a file of soldiers. This is the account which the great chieftain of the Sacs afterward gave of the treaty.

When the war of 1812 broke out, Black Hawk, a rising young warrior of the tribe, yielding to the solicitations of Tecumseh and the omnipresent Simon Girty, resolved to join the British army, taking with him five hundred braves. Black Hawk soon wearied of the war and returned home. On his way he visited an old man, the father of a boy which Black Hawk had adopted. The old Indian, lying at the point of death, feebly related the following story :

After Black Hawk's departure to the war, he, with a few others, repaired to a white settlement on Salt River, to pass the winter. He and his boy had pitched their wigwam near a small fort, of which the occupants seemed friendly. One evening the young hunter did not return to the lodge. In the morning the old man and his squaw, with hearts full of apprehension, started on a search for the wanderer. They followed his tracks through the snow till a deer trail was reached. Pursuing this for some distance, they found a dressed deer which he had killed, hanging to a tree. At this point also, were the tracks of white men. The snow was greatly disturbed, as if the spot had been the scene of a struggle. In one place they discovered a stain of blood on the white surface. The tracks of the men turned toward the fort. Not far distant the boy was found lying dead—shot, stabbed, and scalped. Black Hawk had been much attached to this boy, and was deeply angered at the outrage. Rejoining his warriors, he told them the story, and the whole body resolved to return to the war.

When Tecumseh fell dead in the battle of the Thames, Black Hawk was fighting by his side. We have seen how Brant had fought under the great Pontiac years before he himself came into fame. It is not extravagant to say that the mind and career of Brant were powerfully influenced by the character and fame of the mighty leader whom he thus supported. Tecumseh himself, though born after Pontiac had been buried in his forest grave, was, even more than Brant, a pupil of the great conspirator. The far-reaching influence of Pontiac, which did not die with its author, may therefore be traced in Black Hawk. It may be said that Black Hawk was but an echo of Tecumseh, and thus indirectly of Pontiac himself. "The evil that men do lives after them."

Few incidents are related of Black Hawk from the time of the close of the war of 1812 to the year 1832, when he became famous. About 1820 a young Sac killed an Indian of the Iowa tribe. In imitation of the whites, these tribes had arranged to surrender the murderer, to be dealt with by the friends of the murdered man. A party of Sacs, with Black Hawk at their head, prepared for the diplomatic journey to the Iowas, which the occasion demanded. At the moment of departure they discovered that the young man who had committed the murder was ill. He would nevertheless have accompanied them had not his brother interfered. The latter, with high generosity, insisted that his brother was too sick to travel, and that he would go and die in his place.

After a journey of seven days the party arrived within sight of the Iowa village. The young brave went calmly forward, singing his death-song, and seated himself in the midst of the lodges. A deputation of chiefs came out from the village, with whom Black Hawk held a short talk, explaining that the young warrior, who had surrendered himself to them, had, on account of his brother's sickness, taken his place, and had come to die in his stead. The talk ended. The Iowas, with impassive countenances, returned to the village. Black Hawk and his companions took a last look at their doomed friend, about whom a crowd, armed with sticks and stones, was already gathering, and sadly turned their faces homeward.

That evening, while in camp, the rapid gallop of a horse was heard. The dusky company seized their arms, with every ear attent and every eye strained to pierce the darkness. The horse came nearer and nearer. Suddenly the rider reined in and leaped from his saddle, right into their midst. It was the young brave who had been left behind. The Iowas had at first threatened him. But when his generosity and self-sacrifice became known there was a sudden revulsion of feeling among these simple children of the forest. Nature taught them to instinctively recognize and worship the hero. It is civilization and life in cities, greed and selfishness, which blunt this fine instinct, and teach men to ignore and sneer at heroism. The Iowas had not only released their prisoner, but sent him back to his people with a present of two fine horses.

A year or two after this touching incident Black Hawk and the band of warriors, who with admiring devotion followed the footsteps of their leader everywhere, were encamped on the Two Rivers on a hunting expedition. One day some white settlers met him in the forest, and accused him of having killed some of their hogs. Black Hawk understood their language but imperfectly. At last, gathering the idea, he indignantly denied the charge. The white ruffians forthwith jumped on him, snatched away his gun and rendered it useless by firing it in the air, and proceeded to beat him most unmercifully with sticks. They then returned the gun, kicked him, and told him to leave the neighborhood. From this outrage Black Hawk never recovered. The humiliation of his proud spirit was insufferable.

In the summer of 1823 the United States urged upon the Sacs and Foxes the necessity of a removal, in accordance with the treaty of 1804, of which we have spoken, to the west bank of the Mississippi. This caused a division in the tribe. Keokuk, the great peace chief of the Sacs, whose ascendancy and influence was rapidly overshadowing that of Black Hawk, favored the removal, and with a majority of the tribe withdrew to the Iowa River. Black Hawk, of course, took the opposite side to that of his rival, in which position he found not a few supporters.

The site of their village at the mouth of Rock River was, as has been said, one of the most delightful spots in the northwest. Besides its natural advantages and the beauty of the scenery, the place was endeared to every heart by associations. For unnumbered years the dead of every family had been buried under the shadow of the stately forest trees. Every sorrow of the past was a tie which bound their hearts to the place. Every joy which they had experienced was associated in memory with this home. To leave the one seemed to be giving up the other. So Black Hawk entered a violent remonstrance against the proceedings of the whites, and refused to stir. He even went further. When a white man undertook to sell whisky to his people Black Hawk, with two or three companions, went to the house and rolled out the barrels. He then broke in the heads, and spilled the liquor on the ground.

The difficulties increased with time. Black Hawk and his people, returning from their winter hunt, found their lodges occupied by white settlers, who claimed to have bought the land. To this Black Hawk replied, that his reason taught him that land could not be sold. In this remark of an ignorant savage, who spoke purely from instinct, there is food for reflection. If we open the works of the English philosopher, Mill, we find him, after an elaborate induction, arriving at the same conclusion.   The theory of our law says that the owner of land is entitled to the possession of it, and any one who enters thereon without his permission, does so without right, and is a trespasser. If this be true, he inquires, why then might not a small minority, say a million men, of enormous wealth, buy up every foot of land on the globe, and as to them every other man, woman, and child become trespassers, wrong-doers in the eye of the law, legally liable to be driven off the globe?   The hand of the philosopher reaches down from the heights and

BLACK HAWK.

grasps that of the savage extended upward from the depths.

But Black Hawk had another argument.   He said that even if his land could be sold, it never had been.   To these arguments, one or the other of which every fair man will say was true, the United States had but a single reply.   That reply consisted of one word—"MOVE!"   The squaws had planted their corn, and it was beginning to grow.   The white men deliberately plowed it up.   Black Hawk told the settlers that they must get off of his land.   At this the governor of Illinois pronounced the territory to be in a state of "actual invasion."   Seven hundred troops started up the river to "remove the Indians, dead or alive, to the west side of the Mississippi."

A council was held at Fort Armstrong. Black Hawk was present. He heard the demands of the white man. After listening patiently, he rose and made the usual reply, that his lands could not be and never had been sold. At the close of his speech, General Gaines inquired "Who is Black Hawk? Is he a chief? By what right does he appear in council?" To this insult, which meant that the United States refused to recognize any other chief among the Sacs than Keokuk, who was present to witness the humiliation of his rival, no reply was made. With quivering features, Black Hawk arose, gathered his blanket around him, and stalked in silence from the council-hall. On the following morning he was again in his seat. When the council opened he arose, and with biting emphasis said: "My father, you inquired yesterday 'Who is Black Hawk? Why does he sit among the chiefs?' I will tell you who I am. I am a Sac. My father was a Sac. I am a warrior. So was my father. Ask those young men who have followed me to battle, and they will tell you who Black Hawk is. Provoke our people to war, and you will learn who Black Hawk is."

Matters were at a dead lock concerning the removal of the Indians. Seven hundred militia-men were on the ground. On the 25th of June, being in the year 1831, sixteen hundred mounted re-enforcements arrived. This was the key to the lock. That night Black Hawk and his braves, with their women and children, fled from the village which their fathers had built, without the firing of a gun. In the morning they were seen on the west bank of the Mississippi. Above them floated a white flag. This occurrence was heralded through the country as "a great victory over General Black Hawk."

New troubles awaited the exiles. It was too late in the season for them to plant corn and beans a second time. This, however, did not do away with the necessity for them. One night some of the warriors, heartsick at the cries of the women and children for food, crossed the river, as Black Hawk says,

34

" to steal roasting-ears from their own fields." They were fired upon by the whites, and foiled in their efforts. This was rubbing salt in fresh wounds.

The condition of the Indians was miserable. The Winnebagoes, occupying what is now the state of Wisconsin, seeing the distresses of their friends, invited Black Hawk, in the Spring of 1832, to bring his people to their country, and raise a crop of beans and corn. The old chief, overwhelmed with trouble, fearful lest his followers would desert to Keokuk, of whose prosperity and fortune he was intensely jealous, found himself looked to by his people to extricate them from their troubles. He had never been a man of great resources, and, besides this, was now overtaken by age and disappointment. Not knowing what better to do, he accepted the invitation, placed his women and children in canoes, and with his warriors armed and mounted, started up the Mississippi.

Having, in the early part of April, reached a point opposite their old home at the mouth of Rock River, they, perhaps rashly, but certainly without any wicked or hostile intent, crossed to the east side of the Mississippi, with the avowed purpose of ascending Rock River to the villages of the Winnebagoes. They had proceeded up Rock River but a short distance when General Atkinson, the commandant at Fort Armstrong, sent a messenger after Black Hawk, ordering him to return. The old chief refused to obey, explaining that he was going to visit the Winnebagoes on their invitation, and raise a crop of corn with them. A second messenger brought a repetition of the order, with a threat that unless they obeyed peaceably they would be pursued and forced to return. At this point Black Hawk also found that the Winnebagoes did not desire his presence in their country if it would involve them in hostilities with the United States. He resolved, therefore, that if pursued he would return peaceably to the western side of the Mississippi. With true Indian dilatoriness, he stopped to compliment some visiting chiefs with a dog feast. He was engaged in the preparation for this, when he was informed that a large army had approached within eight miles of his camp.

Three young Indians were at once sent out with a flag of truce, to ask for a council and arrange for a peaceable retreat. These messengers were deliberately taken prisoners by the whites. Finding that they did not return, Black Hawk sent out five others to learn what was the matter. These were pursued by twenty horsemen, and two of them killed. At the time of the army's approach, Black Hawk had with him only forty warriors, whom he concealed in ambush. The rest were ten miles away. When the troops approached, the Indians fired, and the soldiers fled in a panic. In the reports of this defeat, the Indian force was gravely asserted to have exceeded fifteen hundred men. All the blankets, provisions, and camp equipage of the Americans fell into Black Hawk's hands.

The old chief, elated by his victory, and encouraged by re-enforcements, as well as enraged at the murder of the bearers of his flags of truce, resolved to fight rather than retreat beyond the Mississippi. A bloody border war followed. Farm houses were attacked, horses stolen, and settlers murdered as usual. In the early engagements of the war, the Indians had the advantage. When the whole force of the American army, exceeding twenty-five hundred men, became available for the conflict, the tide began to turn. Black Hawk and his people commenced a retreat toward the Wisconsin River. The army was in full pursuit. The members of Black Hawk's band were reduced to a diet of roots and horseflesh. Many of them died of actual starvation, and their corpses were found by their pursuers strewn along the pathway of their flight. Reaching the Wisconsin River, the women and children were embarked upon hastily constructed rafts, for a descent toward the Mississippi. On the voyage these helpless people were attacked by troops stationed on shore, some killed, some drowned, and some captured. Of those who escaped to the woods, the majority perished from starvation.

Meanwhile Black Hawk and the rest of his band struck out

directly across the country toward the Mississippi. Many,
weakened by hunger, succumbed to the hardships of the way.
A part of the women and children were embarked in canoes as
soon as the river was reached. Some of these vessels upset in
the river, and their occupants sank beneath the waves. On the
1st of August, while the remainder of the Indians were waiting
for transportation, they were overtaken and attacked by the
troops. Black Hawk again sent forward a messenger with a
flag of truce, who was fired upon and killed. Not less than one
hundred and fifty Indians, nearly half the entire force, were
killed in the action. Black Hawk, with the remainder, jumped
into the river, attempting to swim to the opposite shore.

During the battle a young squaw with a child in her arms
was shot in the breast, and fell covering the child with her body.
When the soldiers came up, they heard the cries of the child,
and, running to the spot, removed it from beneath the corpse
of its mother. One arm of the infant was amputated, and the
child afterwards recovered. Among the women who sprang into
the river was a squaw with an infant wrapped in a blanket,
which she carried in her teeth. The mother seized the tail of
a horse which was swimming across, and in this way reached
the opposite shore in safety.

Though Black Hawk escaped alive from this battle, he did
not long avoid the toils of his enemies. His followers deserted
him one by one, and he was at last betrayed and captured,
through the treachery of two Winnebagoes. He was at once
removed to Jefferson Barracks, below St. Louis, and there confined and forced to wear a ball and chain. The winter was
gloomy enough to the old chief.

Among those who had been captured with him was a young
warrior or chief named Naopope. An artist visited the Indians
in prison, and sought to paint the likeness of Naopope. "Paint
me as I am," thundered Cromwell, when an artist sought to hide
the hideous warts and blemishes, which disfigured the countenance of the Protector of England. "Make me so, and show

me as I am to the great father," cried Naopope to his portrait painter, seizing the ball and chain that were fastened to his leg, and raising them on high. When the artist refused to do this the Indian distorted his face with incessant grimaces, and prevented his picture from being taken. Such was the unconquerable spirit of this poor manacled captive in the dungeon of Jefferson Barracks.

In the following spring Black Hawk was taken to Washington City. When confronted by President Jackson, the old Indian bluntly remarked, "I am a man and you are only another." God and the savage are no respecters of persons. When told that he would be liberated, Black Hawk said: "Brother, I have come on my own part and in behalf of my companions to bid you farewell. Our great father has at length been pleased to permit us to return to our hunting grounds. We have buried the tomahawk, and the sound of the rifle will hereafter only bring death to the deer and the buffalo. Brother, you have treated the red men very kindly. Your squaws have made them presents, and you have given them plenty to eat and drink. The memory of your friendship will remain till the Great Spirit says it is time for Black Hawk to sing his death-song. Brother, your houses are as numerous as the leaves upon the trees, and your young warriors like the sands upon the shore of the big lake that rolls before us. The red man has but few houses and few warriors, but the red man has a heart that throbs as warmly as the heart of his white brother. The Great Spirit has given us our hunting grounds, and the skin of the deer which we kill there is his favorite, for its color is white, and this is the emblem of peace. This hunting-dress and these feathers of the eagle are white. Accept them, my brother; I have given one like this to the White Otter. Accept of it as a memorial of Black Hawk. When he is far away this will serve to remind you of him. May the Great Spirit bless you and your children. Farewell."

Black Hawk and his companions were taken to Baltimore,

Philadelphia, New York, and all the eastern cities before their return. Everywhere great multitudes thronged to see the great "General Black Hawk." Extensive military displays were made to impress the savages with the power of the United States. The crowning feature of Black Hawk's humiliation was, however, yet to come. He was to be formally liberated, but was also to be degraded and removed from his office of chief of the Sacs, among whom henceforth his life-long enemy and rival, Keokuk, was to be alone acknowledged as chief. The spot where the ceremony was to be performed was Fort Armstrong, on the site of the old Sac village. "This was the favorite island of the Indians—in former years abundant in fruits and flowers, and from time immemorial the fancied abode of a good spirit, who watched over their village and protected their hunting grounds. No spot could have been selected calculated to awaken so many painful associations in the mind of Black Hawk as Rock Island. For half a century it had been the witness of his power and influence; it was now to become the scene of his disgrace and reluctant submission to a rival."

On arriving at Fort Armstrong, runners were sent out summoning the Indians from far and wide to attend the strange ceremony. They came by scores and hundreds, both from the Sacs and all the neighboring tribes, who remembered the fame of Black Hawk, and were now curious to witness his infamy. Chief of all the arrivals was that of the princely Keokuk. He ascended the Mississippi reclining in two canoes, lashed side by side, and covered with a canopy. Handsome decorations covered the vessels. Near the chief sat his three wives. Following him came a long line of canoes, filled with his people. Each brave was painted in the most elaborate style, and equipped with all the panoply of war. At high noon the great Keokuk, with stately step and lofty bearing, disembarked amid the rattle of scores of Indian drums, and the shouts and songs of his people. It was indeed a triumph.

The afternoon and evening were devoted to games and

dances. From all the gay assembly Black Hawk alone remained apart in solitude. He might have been seen, crouched in the corner of his room in the fort, his face buried in his hands, and his soul given over to grief and gloom.

On the following day the grand council was assembled. Keokuk and a hundred gaudily attired warriors were given the posts of honor. Presently Black Hawk and his son, unattended, entered the room with an air of profound dejection, and timidly took an obscure seat. They had protested strongly against this unnecessary ceremony of disgrace, and came filled with the deepest mortification. For a time profound silence reigned. Then Major Garland arose and made

KEOKUK.

a lengthy speech. He concluded by saying, that he wished it distinctly understood by all persons, that hereafter their great father, the President, would receive and acknowledge Keokuk alone as the chief of the Sac and Fox nation; that Black Hawk must listen and conform to his counsels, and that the band of Black Hawk must be henceforth merged in that of Keokuk.

There was a moment of silence, in which the features of the

old chief were seen to twitch with uncontrollable emotion. Then, springing to his feet, he exclaimed, in a voice trembling with futile rage: "I am a man—an old man. I will not conform to the counsels of any one. I will act for myself—no one shall govern me. I am old—my hair is gray—I once gave counsels to my young men. Am I now to conform to others? I shall soon go to the Great Spirit, when I shall be at rest. What I said to our great father at Washington, I say again—I will always listen to him. I am done." This speech was the cry of defeat, the lament of the fallen chieftain.

Major Garland attempted to make explanations, to the effect that he had only *requested* him to listen to the counsels of Keokuk. To this he made no reply, but, drawing his blanket around him, sat in moody silence. At last Keokuk rose, came to him, and talked for awhile in a low tone. The words of the wily Keokuk were not without their effect. Before the council ended Black Hawk rose and said that it was his wish, if his speech had been put upon paper, that a line might be drawn through it. He did not mean what he said. This was the last drop of gall in the cup of bitterness.

During the remainder of his life Black Hawk, with a few old braves, who, having followed him in prosperity, did not desert him in adversity, lived at a point on a small stream called Devil Creek, isolated from his tribe. It was the attempt of the fallen chief to hide his disgrace. He never ceased to recall his happy life on Rock River. "I liked my towns, my cornfields, and the home of my people," he would say to the white men who visited him. "I fought for it. I did wrong, perhaps; but that is past—let it be forgotten. The country which was mine is now yours. Keep it as we did—it will produce you good crops." He attributed all his misfortunes to Keokuk, and never ceased to regret that he had been led into armed resistance to the United States. He died in 1838, being about seventy-two years old. His old age was given over to sorrowful melancholy. Death was indeed to him a welcome guest.

CHAPTER XVI.

THE HISTORY OF KIT CARSON.

HE genius for pioneering is born in a man, just as the genius for debate or for war. It runs in families, and is handed down from father to son. It is that strange spirit of unrest which dissatisfies some men with their civilized surroundings, and impels them toward the wilderness. There they are happy, fighting the savage, shooting the buffalo, and struggling with nature in her fiercest aspect. When the tide of emigration sets in their direction, and society assumes a somewhat settled state, these bold men give a pull at their throat bands as if suffocated, and resolutely set their faces toward the west, to seek out a location where the spice of adventure and danger gives a wild variety to life.

Such was the Carson family, of Kentucky, to whom was born, on December 24, 1809, their son Christopher, or, as he is widely known, " Kit." At this time Kentucky society began to assume a state, wild and rough, we would think, but to the Carsons dull and monotonous. Affrays with Indians happened only once in a year or two. In 1810, none of Mr. Carson's neighbors had been scalped since Kit was born. When he went out for a hunt, he could no longer hope to be treed all night by a bear. All this was a bore; and it bore on his mind so that, when Kit was a year old, the family sold out their scraggy farm, said good-bye to their nearest neighbors, five miles off, and with hearts lighter than for several years, set out for what is now central Missouri. Here they found no end of exciting adventure. They and a few neighbors lived together in a rough log fort, in order to be safe from the Indians. In laying out and working their farms outside the log inclosure, it was necessary for a part of them to act as guards, posted at the extremities of the fields, to give instant warning of the approach of redskins, and signal a retreat to the fort.

Amid such scenes were passed the boyhood days of Kit Carson. When he reached the age of sixteen, his father, good man, being determined that his son Kit should not lead such a roving life as he himself had led, apprenticed Christopher to a harness-maker. But the master could make no harness strong enough to hitch the soaring spirit of Kit Carson to a trade. The restless love of freedom and appetite for adventure which belonged to the father, were intensified in the son, and in 1826 he broke away from the restraint, by joining a party whose journey took them eight hundred miles across the plains, to Santa Fé, New Mexico.

Though young, and destitute of the necessary equipment, not even owning a gun, nor being able, by the utmost exertions as teamster and guide, to do more than earn the food he ate, his purpose was made up to be a hunter and trapper. In April, 1829, he was selected as a member of a party of forty men, under the leadership of Ewing Young, organized at Taos, New Mexico, for the double purpose of chastising a tribe of Indians, who had been on the war-path and driven a party of Young's trappers out of the country, and also for pursuing the lucrative occupation of trapping beaver. The real purpose of the expedition was carefully concealed from the Mexican authorities, and after a brisk and secret advance, they came suddenly upon the band of Navajoe braves, which had massacred their friends. Preparations for the fight were quickly made on both sides. Part of the whites advanced stealthily, to lie in ambush behind some rock which lay a little to the side and nearly midway between the main combatants. Not seeing this movement, the

Indians charged on the remainder of the party, and, as they came in front of the ambush, were suddenly assailed by a murderous cross-fire. Fifteen braves fell heavily from their horses, killed by the first fire; the remainder, pursued by the trappers, fled in all directions.

After this fight it was decided that the party should divide, only eighteen of them continuing to the valley of the Sacramento in California. Of this detachment Carson was a member. Learning from some friendly Indians that the country through which their path lay, and which had never before been explored by white men, was destitute, alike, of game and water, the meat of three deer was prepared to take with them, and the skins of the animals were converted into water tanks. A week was passed with this meager supply of water for eighteen men and a large number of horses. For food an old mare was killed on the fifth day and devoured with great gusto. About the seventh day they reached the dry bed of one of those singular rivers, which suddenly sink out of sight and reappear at the distance of hundreds of miles after an underground course, probably, through quicksand. The channel is usually defined on the surface, and, though dry, delicious water is easily had by scooping a hole of a few feet in the sand. After this their path lay through a beautiful country, abounding in water and forage, elk, deer, and antelope of the finest varieties. The men were elated with what seemed a good omen of the success which awaited them in their trapping.

When at last the Sacramento River was reached the men began to keep a sharp lookout for "signs" of beaver. The presence of them in great abundance caused a thrill of joy to the trappers. The significance of this word "signs" is very great as the trappers use it. The cunning beaver can seldom be seen on the bank or in the river, for he has no great means of defense when attacked, and relies on his exquisite sight and hearing to warn him of danger in time for retreat. The marks he leaves behind him, however, are to the expert eye as legible as the words on this page. The beaver's unequaled industry in felling large trees, cutting twigs, peeling off the tender cuticle of the willow bushes, digging away the banks, and carrying the earth on his shovel-shaped tail to his dam, and the innumerable footprints which he leaves, are a part of these "signs." The little twig, half denuded of its bark, floating down stream, unnoticed by any but the keen-eyed trapper, reveals to him by its freshness the proximity of the prize more than the great dam, which to a greenhorn would seem a splendid indication of its builder's presence, because the dam is probably an old and abandoned one.

The beaver's dam, a wonderful structure, is built by him to provide him with food in the winter when every thing above the water is dry and sapless. "He chooses a place favorable for obtaining food, and also where his labors will be assisted by natural formations or accidents in the river's course. Having carefully selected his location, he and his fellows set to work to fell giant trees. While one party is cutting the hard wood on one side of the tree with their sharp teeth, another works on the opposite side, the incision on the side on which they want the tree to fall being made, with the skill of the true forester, much lower than the other, which is made to slant downward to the first. By this sort of craft the largest trees are made to fall into and across the stream. When it has fallen the leaves and small branches are at once woven into a close network, adapted to catching floating *débris*, and to receiving the earth which they throw on by the tail load. Several trees are felled in this way, till as many are down as is desired. Then comes the mud-work, in which Mr. Beaver is an artist. A large gang march to the bank, load each others' tails, and swim, with their cargoes elevated above the water, to the dumping-spot, where they at once mould it to its place."

Their houses they have previously built on the banks. They consist of large and airy subterranean rooms, above the water-mark. In these houses, trappers say, they live in pairs, and much resemble human beings in the arrangement and management of their household affairs, Madame Beaver having the ruling voice in domestic and internal arrangements, while the outside work of building dams and providing food is the more especial business of Monsieur. To this end he builds his dam, the deep water preserving fresh and tender the leaves and shrubs on which his family must subsist during the winter. Some say he goes so far as to bundle up small branches of trees and willows, which he stows away in the muddy bottom of the river. Trapper yarns have it that beaver society is regularly organized, there being chiefs, some of whom roll in wealth and have troops of slaves ready to do instant service, such as bring a fresh bundle of green twigs for dinner from the river bottom.

The signs having been discovered, the trappers selected a comfortable location for their camp, and part of them started out to set traps, while the remainder kept guard and did the cooking. The trap is much like the ordinary steel trap used for catching foxes or wolves, only somewhat smaller. It is baited with a peculiar animal substance of strong scent, which draws the beaver from his hiding-place, and so excites his appetite as to induce him before long to reach in his paw, when in an instant he is a prisoner. The traps, when visited, are emptied and reset. The game is killed and skinned, the pelts dried and cured in camp, and packed in bales for loading on the mules. The Sacramento region proved to be a splendid field for operations, and great was the success.

While in camp here the party were applied to by the priest of the mission of San Räfael for help in capturing some Indians belonging to his mission, who had stolen some of his property and deserted to a hostile Indian village, which refused to give them up. Carson and a dozen companions, ready for any fun, offered their services, and attacked the Indian village, killing one-third of its population, capturing the deserters, and with them the stolen property. For this they refused all compensation, but the priest secured them a good purchaser for their furs.

One night, when unsuspicious of danger, the camp lost sixty of their horses, which were driven off by a party of redskins. Carson was ordered to pick a dozen companions, and with the remaining thirteen horses give chase. After a break-neck ride of a hundred miles toward the mountains, they suddenly came upon the savages, who were sitting around their camp-fires feasting on six of the horses, which they had killed for that purpose. Enraged beyond measure at the sight, the trappers charged the camp with a yell, killing eight savages in the twinkling of an eye, while the rest escaped. When Carson returned with all the horses except the six which had been killed, he was voted a hero. Yet he was only twenty years old, and this was his first expedition. Here it was, too, that he laid the foundation of his fame as a hunter, in which regard he afterward acquired a reputation unequaled by any man in the Rocky Mountains. His companions say he was exceedingly modest, and of a refined and gentle nature, which contrasted strangely with his wild profession. He was only five feet and a half high, agile but rather slight in build, possessing a gray eye and light brown hair. He talked little, and was remarkably cautious in exposing himself, always sleeping where the glare of the camp-fire did not fall on him, and carefully loading gun and pistols before retiring.

In September the party, well laden with valuable furs, turned their faces homeward. On their way, passing through a Mexican town, the men, in true trapper style, feeling the object of the trip largely accomplished, succumbed to the seductive influences of the whisky on sale there, as well as to the winsome familiarities of the Mexican maiden. Carson, however, carefully avoided such indulgences, and exerted himself to get the party out of town.

On the day after leaving the place, while the trappers' heads were still heavy and aching from the debauch, Carson discovered a band of five hundred Indians approaching. The men were at the moment in camp. The Indians halted, made friendly signs, and in a few moments two of their number came into the trappers' camp, eying things with great curiosity. Shortly a few more braves sauntered in, and then still more, until enough were present to overwhelm the little band of whites if a struggle ensued. At this moment Mr. Young discovered that the Indians, instead of being unarmed, had their weapons concealed in their garments. It was evidently their intention to massacre the entire party, and make off with the booty. Young whispered his discovery with blanched lips to Carson.

The moment was critical. But in these trying moments Carson's genius never failed to equal the emergency. Quickly calling his men to his side, he ordered each man to cover a savage with his gun. Taken completely by surprise, the intruders began to retreat from the row of deadly rifles. "Leave the camp!" said Carson, in a clear-cut tone. "If you refuse, each one of us will kill our man, even if we at last are killed ourselves." The effect was electric. Death, with blood-shot eyeballs, stared them out of countenance, and with a bound the red murderers cleared the camp.

A week or two after this, the trappers ran across a band of Indians which had annoyed them on their outbound trip. The "*lex talionis*" of Moses and the Israelites is the only possible law for the wanderers in any wilderness. Stealing quickly upon the group of huts, the whites were upon their foes almost as soon as discovered. A noble warrior sank to rise no more at each crack of the trappers' rifles, and in a few moments the rout became complete. A very nice herd of horses and mules, the only thing of value in the village, was captured by this stroke.

That night the trappers settled down around their camp-fire for a comfortable sleep, after the day's exertion. Some mention was made about the probability of a return of the redskins, and two of the most vigilant were appointed to keep watch, one before midnight, the other after. Shortly after the change of sentry at midnight, the man on watch became aware of a dark body moving in the darkness over the prairie in the direc-

TRADING WITH THE INDIANS.

544

tion of the camp. It was but the work of a moment to arouse the men, who, with rifles grasped and pistols cocked, were instantly on the alert. Carson slipped out to reconnoitre, and returning reported a large herd of horses driven by a few Indians, who had probably stolen them. Without any over-nice honesty, a volley of rifle-balls was directed toward the astonished Indians, who fled in great precipitation, leaving their property, the second capture of the day, to the trappers. On the following morning the best of the herd were selected for use; two of the fattest animals were killed for food, and the remainder turned loose on the prairie, to rejoice once more in the wild liberty of their sires.

In April, 1830, just a year after its departure, the expedition found itself once more among the group of huts which was dignified by the name of Taos. The proceeds of the trip were twenty-four thousand dollars, which soon found its way into the pockets of the men, and then found its way out again, for the trapper after his trip is like the sailor home from his voyage. It was the chief care of each man to get on a profound, inglorious, and terrible drunk, which only ended with his money. On this occasion Carson yielded somewhat to the demoralizing atmosphere, but it was his first and last spree. Nature seemed to have made him a gentleman in spite of his rough surroundings. Refinement is a quality of the mind. Wealth and luxury only sharpen the outline of vulgarity. The frontier cabin of the trapper, where a woman was seldom seen, and the softening influence of children was unknown; over which the great and jagged Rockies flung the chilly shadows of an early sunset, and where the brutal savages, instead of turning toward the light of civilization, rather drew the pioneer down into their own gloom and brutality—this frontier cabin only served to throw into bolder relief the character of the GENTLEMAN.

It was in the autumn of 1830 that Kit Carson enlisted for his second trapping expedition. He was greatly sought after for this purpose by the organizers of trapping parties. The party joined by Carson passed the winter in quarters on

Salmon River, and began their real work with the season of 1831, along Snake River, on which are the famous Shoshonee Falls, more than one third higher than Niagara. Meeting another party of trappers, Carson learned that Captain Gaunt, an old mountaineer, with a small company, were ten days' journey to the south. He and four companions resolved, for a change, to join Gaunt, and after a rapid journey were cordially welcomed by him.

The time for going into winter quarters was at hand. This was always looked forward to with interest, as it marked a great change in the trapper's mode of life. No longer did he gallop with free rein over the flower-embroidered prairie; no longer select his spot for the evening camp-fire, and, while the game, brought down by his own expert hand, was steaming over the coals, and flinging its savory odor upon the breeze, busy himself with baiting and setting his traps at the water's edge; and after a dash in the cooling current, feast upon the tempting meal; then with his saddle for a pillow, his blanket for a bed, and the star-fretted sky for a canopy, sink to sleep, as the dying embers threw their fitful flashes more and more dimly into the surrounding forest.

All this was changed. His home, when in winter quarters, was a conical tent of dressed buffalo skins, supported on a framework of light poles, spread out in a circle at the bottom, and crossed near the top, where they were held by being thrust through the opening in the buffalo skins. These were sewed tightly into the shape of a cone, except one straight seam, which was fastened by a lacing to within four or five feet of the ground. The opening thus left was the door, over which a buffalo skin was tightly stretched. The bottom of the tent was securely fastened to the ground by wooden pins. In the center of this tent, which is about eighteen feet in diameter, and fifteen feet high, he had his fire, the smoke from which, in theory, was to escape by the opening above, but, in fact, filled the apartment.

In here the men passed their days and nights, except when

they went out to attend to their horses. Early in the winter the snow fell to the depth of six feet, and removed not till the spring. Water for the shaggy Indian ponies had to be obtained from the river through a hole chopped in the ice. These hardy beasts had no shelter except such as was afforded by an over-hanging rock, and some forest trees. To obtain food for them was a serious task. It had to be done by cutting down cotton-wood trees, and gathering the bark and branches for fodder. But the ponies stood it as well as the men, who thought them-selves comfortable and happy in their warm buffalo tent. Here they slept and smoked, told stories and cooked meals, dressed their skins, or ornamented their saddles.

Not a small part of their time did they spend over that magic annihilator of time and surroundings—a pack of cards! The man who held the ace of trumps never failed to be regarded as a marvelously lucky fellow, and the fellow with two bowers and a queen, as little short of a hero! We may smile at these little details of the trapper's life, but it is more fitting that a tear should fall, for these are the men, some of whom are known to world-wide fame, as the hero of this chapter, but many of whom are unknown to history, and will be nameless for evermore—these are the men, " who," as reads our title-page, " by their valor and war-craft, beat back the savages from the borders of civilization, and gave the American forests to the plow and the sickle." All honor, then, to the brave pioneer, the fruit of whose toils and triumphs he beheld from afar off, while we alone have lived to enter into the land of promise!

One cold January night, some Crow Indians succeeded in stealing nine horses from the camp. A dozen men, with Carson, of course, at their head, started in pursuit. At the end of forty miles their horses, weak from insufficient food, made a halt necessary, and they turned into a clump of woods. Here they unexpectedly found their enemies. Making fast their horses, and examining their guns, Carson directed the men to make a detour, so as to approach the savages from the direction in which they least expected danger—that in which they traveled. To get close enough to reconnoiter, it was necessary to perform a large part of this journey crawling through the deep snow on hands and knees. In this way they were able to discover two rude forts, in which a large force of Indians were performing the war-dance. The nine horses were tied outside.

To insure success the trappers, in spite of the bitter cold, lay concealed till the dance ended, and the last sleepy redskin snored solemnly in the darkness. Carson then slipped forward, cut the halters, and by means of snow-balls drove the horses away without noise. Having secured them, a division of opinion was found as to whether they should make an attack. Carson and two others strongly urged it, as otherwise they would be pursued, and probably have to fight anyhow under less favorable circumstances. The advice of Carson was followed, and they again neared the sleeping foe. A dog in the camp barked, and the warriors, springing to their feet, became marks for the deadly rifles of the pioneers. Those who survived the first fire hurriedly ran to the other fort. A desperate sortie was repulsed with the loss of several more. At daybreak the pioneers withdrew, mounted their horses, and by night rejoined their comrades at quarters on the Arkansas River.

In the spring they *cached* their furs, and broke camp. Three weeks later, while on the South Platte, Carson and one companion were sent by Captain Gaunt in pursuit of two men who had deserted the party. Suspecting their design, Kit made for the furs in *cache* at the old camp. Three hundred pounds, belonging equally to the entire party, were missing, and the deserters, probably killed by the Indians, were never heard of afterward. Failing to recover the furs, Carson and his companion felt that a return to Gaunt's party was unwise and impracticable. They therefore repaired the old log fortification which had surrounded their buffalo tent the winter before, and, without venturing out of it much, managed to keep well supplied with game. Here the two men lived for a month, one of them always on guard, anxiously looking for relief, which came at last. Gaunt had entirely given them up, fearing that they had attempted to return to him and had been killed by the Indians of the region, who were on the war-path.

The journey to rejoin the main body of Gaunt's party proved exceedingly dangerous, even for the band of twenty-one veteran trappers. On several occasions a stampede occurred, by which they lost a horse or two. The stampede is accomplished by the Indians turning loose some wild horses, which are trained to dash at full speed through the camp of the white men. All the picketed horses, being greatly excited, attempt to follow, more or less succeeding in breaking loose, and rushing with their wild companions into an Indian lair, much as greenies fall a prey to the seductive wiles of the confidence man.

One morning Carson took a trio of companions to cross a range and look for beaver. Their outward path was by a precipitous way directly across the mountain. But in the afternoon as they turned home a longer walk was found more practicable for the descent. As they were leisurely riding back to the camp there suddenly appeared in their path, directly in front of them, four powerful and splendidly mounted Indians, decked out in fantastic plumes and gayly colored paint, indicating unmistakably that they were on the war-path. The emergency demanded an immediate decision as to the best course to pursue. In all likelihood these warriors were only the advance guard of a large war party ambushed behind the rocks. To advance was dangerous, yet to retreat was to be pursued and almost certainly overtaken and killed. The three other men turned to Carson, who without a word dug his spurs deep into the sides of his mustang, and, closely followed by the others, dashed at full speed upon the astonished braves. In a moment sixty splendid warriors were discovered in ambush near the trail. Thick and fast flew their bullets. Kit and his three friends, throwing themselves as much as possible to the other side of their horses, dashed on without returning a shot. They were running the gauntlet. In three minutes they would either be safe or for ever silent.

At one point the copper-faced devils were within sixty feet of them. But in their surprise at the boldness of the trappers, their aim was unsteady, and in a few moments Carson had reached the camp, alive and unhurt. Two of his companions had received severe wounds, and on the following day, when the march was resumed, it was necessary to take two poles, let the ends rest on two trusty horses, and swing a buffalo robe in the center as a litter for the wounded men.

When they reached Gaunt the hunt for beaver was found to have been unsuccessful, and the ill luck continued. Tired of going empty-handed, Kit Carson resolved to strike out and try it alone. Two companions volunteered to join him, in spite of the greatly increased danger of trapping with such a small party. After several months of great success, attained by the superior skill of Carson, they returned to Taos, and disposed of their furs at advantageous prices.

The humdrum life in the mud huts of Taos was dull enough to poor Kit, with his fierce love of adventure, and thrusting away all notion of settling down after his two years of absence, he soon arranged to join a trading party. They had been out some weeks when they met another party of traders, commanded by Mr. Robidaux. Right gladly did they grasp each other's hands and interchange stories of their luck. The snow began to fall soon after the meeting, and the men took the hint to go into winter quarters. For the purposes of companionship and security the two parties arranged to encamp together.

Again Carson began that wonderful life in the buffalo lodge of which we have spoken. Again, as the storm raged without, the men lay around the fire in their warm but wind-shaken tent, and with many a yarn and jest drowned out the dreary roar of the tempest. On these occasions Carson was much less of a talker than the other fellows. He joined heartily in the laugh, but except when the talk took a practical turn, as to what would have been the safest way to deal with the redskins on some occasion, or how a trapper who was lost, and without a gun, might manage, he rarely spoke. It was rather his forte to furnish the theme of conversation by some daring exploit of his own.

Among Mr. Robidaux's company was a keen and shrewd California Indian, who was valued for his skill rather than esteemed for his trustworthiness. One morning six of the finest horses, worth two hundred dollars apiece, were missing, and this fellow as well. Illy able to thus lose the entire profits of his expedition, Robidaux asked Carson to attempt a reprisal. Kit, though prudent when only his own interests were at stake, shrank from no danger to help a friend. To help him on his perilous mission Carson determined to select a first class brave from a village of friendly Utahs near by. His choice was soon made, and the Utah seemed proud of the honor. Both were splendidly mounted, and quickly striking the trail of the flying thief, they dashed on their errand of vengeance. No man could follow a trail or read its characteristics more rapidly than Kit Carson, although still the youngest man of his party, being yet only twenty-three years old—"the boy," as the old trappers affectionately called him.

Hardly for a moment was the rein drawn for the first hundred miles, and Kit felt confident of overtaking the treacherous rascal within two or three days. After a few hours' halt the first night, they were preparing to start again, when Carson's Indian companion affirmed that his horse had broken down and he could go no farther. That the noble animal was sick was evident, but Kit strongly suspected that it had been purposely made so. Should he turn back? The savage he pursued was an experienced and dangerous fighter, armed to the teeth, and no doubt desperate. Thinking only of his friend, the heroic fellow left his companion, and flew along the trail alone. Alone in the wilderness! Around him stretched the illimitable plains; bounded, to the eye, only by the gloomy Rockies, which from

afar could be seen lying in eternal and majestic repose. Not a
sound broke the stillness of the morning but the rapid thud,
thud of his horse's hoofs as they rose and fell in the snowy
trail, with the regularity of a machine. Sometimes a thought

CARSON KILLING THE HORSE-THIEF.

of the brave mother whom he had left years before in the little
Missouri clearing would force itself upward as his gallant steed
bore him on to what might be death.

He had left his companion about thirty miles to the rear
when he discovered the chase. The pace of pursuer and pur-

sued became terrific. A spectator seeing those two figures, and wondering at the singular sight, would have seen the one behind gradually gaining on the other. Seeing this, the Indian began to make for some rocks behind which he could fire at his pursuer as he approached, and reload without exposure. The plan was good. It had almost succeeded. But behind him was the Hero of the Rockies. Without pausing an instant in his tremendous career, Carson unslung his rifle, and with the aim that never missed, shot his enemy through the heart, just as he turned behind the cover. At the same instant the other's gun went off, but in a wild direction. When Carson returned to the winter camp with the stolen horses he was greeted with a cheer. Not alone in that camp was the exploit talked over on many an evening; but borne in some mysterious manner through the wilderness, the story of the deed was the favorite theme around a hundred camp fires.

Carson seemed to bear a charmed life. As on a previous occasion, he had left the main party and with three picked companions had undertaken a separate expedition. One night the little party had made their evening halt. They had been without meat for some days. Kit picked up his rifle and started out to look around. About a mile from the camp he was elated with the sight of some magnificent elk. Gaining the cover of some low, scraggy pine trees, he succeeded, by great care, in getting within gunshot of the prize. Without dwelling on his aim, he sped a bullet after the largest and fattest buck in the herd, and with one bound the noble creature fell dead with a fearful wound through his heart and lungs.

Scarcely had the echoing ring of the shot died away, when Carson heard a terrific roar coming directly from the woods behind him. Turning instantly to discover its source, Carson saw two immense grizzly bears bounding towards him, their eyes blazing with anger, their white teeth glistening with rage and hunger, their forearms hung with huge bony claws with which to tear and mangle his flesh. Flinging down his empty rifle, for which he would have given worlds, if the little leaden bullet in the heart of the elk had never left its barrel, he fairly flew over the ground in his race for the nearest tree. It was a goal for which life was the stake. He had just grasped a limb

CARSON ATTACKED BY GRIZZLIES.

and swung upward as the infuriated beasts brushed its trunk. It would be but a moment, however, till they would commence to climb the tree, an art in which they would succeed quite as well as Kit. Providentially a bear has a tender nose. With his glittering hunting knife Carson hacked off a serviceable little club. When Messrs. Bruin began to ascend the trunk, in order to secure the evening meal, into which their imaginations had already transformed poor Kit, they received the compliment of smart raps on their lovely noses. With a mingled roar of rage and pain they quickly descended, only, as the agony wore off, to renew their ambitious toil.

This drama of the gentlemen Bruin ascending, getting their snouts tickled, and letting go in their dreadful anguish, held the boards for several hours. They felt greatly injured. First, Carson had beaten them in the race, and they were conscience-smitten over a life of previous indulgence in the pleasures of the table, which had impaired their condition as racers. Then he had beaten them at their own pet game of climbing trees, and finally his undue familiarity with their noses was offensive. Again and again they tried to tear him out of the tree; again and again he drew the claret with his club. At last, in their disappointment and grief they sat down and had a regular cry, after which they gloomily slunk off into the forest, at a little time after which our hero felt safe in descending from his roost. It was well into the night when he reached his alarmed companions. The story had to take the place of a supper. Long before morning the body of the noble elk had become the prey of the ignoble wolves.

In July Carson, for the first time, attended the summer rendezvous on Green River, at which all the traders and trappers out in the mountains met for purposes of trade and barter. It was a characteristic scene in the pioneer's life. Not a trader's pack was opened until all the parties known to be in the mountains had arrived. The lodges were struck in convenient spots, and around the roaring camp-fires the lonely trapper passed the happiest part of the year. The rendezvous was a sort of a fair. There were annually gathered together two or three hundred white men, and not a few Indians. It was the time for the exchange of yarns and experiences, for gambling and horse racing, for quarrels and fights, as well as for barter.

Among the crowd was a swaggering, bullying Frenchman, named Shunan, who had whipped two men under his size in one day, and boasted that he " could lick all the Americans in the mountains." He had rather cowed the men, and as no one else seemed disposed to stop his insults, Carson quietly determined

ENCOUNTER BETWEEN CARSON AND SHUNAN.

to make it his own affair. Stepping up to the bully, who was twice his size, he said, in the presence of a crowd: " Shunan, there are a dozen men here who can whip you. Keep your mouth shut, or I will be under the necessity of killing you. According to the trapper code, both men went hurriedly to their lodges, and, mounting their horses, prepared to fight. The crowd embraced every one on the ground. Shunan had his rifle; Carson, in the hurry, had picked up only a single-barreled horse pistol. The two men rode rapidly toward each other, until their horses' heads almost touched. Suddenly reining up, Carson said, " Are you looking for me ? " " No," was the lying answer of the man, as he lifted his rifle to shoot. But, before he could fire, Carson had lodged a ball in Shunan's right fore-arm, disabling his antagonist and saving himself.

Such is the code of the frontier. Where men have no law they become legislators themselves; where they have no judge, or jury, or executioner, they quickly fill all these functions themselves. Such is the demand of the mind for law and judg-ment, and such are its resources when thrown upon itself. These things are right. They are the beginnings of the mighty struggle for law, a struggle which, in proportion to its success, means the crushing out of barbarism, cruelty, violence, and injustice, and the uplifting of civilization and order, humanity and righteousness.

Two months after the breaking up of the rendezvous, Car-son's party suffered the usual theft of their horses by Indians, and as inevitably Kit and a dozen men started out in pursuit. On overtaking them the redskins made signs of friendship, and protested their innocent intentions. Each party laid down their arms, and marched to a point midway between, for a conference. The trappers stated promptly that " peace talk " must be pre-ceded by the surrender of their horses. With much evasion, the Indians' chief offered to return five of the poorest horses, as all he could do. On hearing this, the trappers broke and ran for their guns. Kit and a man named Markhead, being in the lead, on the return, selected the two advance Indians for adversaries. Carson was about to fire at his man, when he suddenly saw Markhead examining the lock of his gun, while his foe had a rifle leveled at him. True to his nature, Kit fired at Markhead's adversary, killing him, thus saving Markhead, but at imminent risk to himself. His own adversary took advantage of his opportunity to fire, but inflicted only a dangerous wound on Carson's shoulder. As their leader fell, several of the trappers sprang forward to bear him bleeding from the field.

As darkness came on, the fighting ceased, and the men gathered in their camp. The cold was intense, but no fire could be lighted, as it would reveal their whereabouts to the savages. Disheartened by the misfortune of Carson, whose life-blood ebbed in crimson tide upon the spotless snow, they determined to retreat, and for the first time in his life Carson returned to his command without the horses of which he had gone in search.

The fall hunt, this year, was unsuccessful, and Carson's party divided on Big Snake River, Kit's company of five men starting to Fort Hall. The country through which they traveled was barren, and their provisions were soon exhausted. For days they subsisted on a root which they found in small quantities. At last this disappeared. Then they bled their mules and drank the blood. This weakened the animals till it could be carried no further. The horrors of starvation confronted them. When they went supperless to sleep, the famished men in their dreams beheld the greatest abundance of game and food, but could not quite partake of it. Now the sleeper would behold a herd of elk; just as he had almost come within gunshot, the animals would mockingly bound away. Now, hungered from a long hunt, he sat by the fire watching the steaming mess in the camp kettle, when, just as it was ready for his watering mouth, the kettle turned over, and its savory contents were lost. Now he was putting to his mouth a rare bit of buffalo liver, when the cry of "Indians" made him jump for his gun, and snatched him away from the untasted morsel.

In their extremity, a band of impoverished but friendly Indians were met, who, without any hope of recompense, divided their own too meager supplies with the famished whites, and by this kind help from the poorest of the poor, Carson was enabled to conduct his party to the hospitable fort. Here the exhausted men recuperated rapidly, and in two weeks were eager to ascertain the truth of the stories of wonderful buffalo herds two hundred miles to the northeast, which were heard by them in their enforced inactivity.

Every thing being in readiness, Carson and his men started out from their haven of safety, and two days brought them in sight of what the novice would at first view have thought a distant forest, but from which, at a great distance, could be heard a dull and thunderous roar. A nearer approach revealed a bellowing multitude of buffalo, so great that no man could number them. In every part of the vast herd were going on deadly combats between rival beasts. Over the combatants rose a dense cloud of dust, through which could be caught glimpses of the bloody conflict. Without delaying to watch the wonderful sight, the trappers rapidly skirted the herds, and directed their course toward a narrow valley or ravine, in which were to be had timber for the poles on which to dry the meat, and water for the horses. Long before day they were up, and a part of them had commenced driving one of the detached herds toward this valley. The stupid but timid buffalo headed for the fatal trap at a full gallop.

Meanwhile the other men had carefully posted themselves at the other outlets of the valley. In a little while the " surround" was complete. Then with a yell each man dashed in and closed on the game. Desperately did the powerful creatures dash from side to side in frantic effort to escape. Some, in fact, broke through the *corral*, but in spite of this the slaughter was immense. Many of the buffalo, bewildered by the attacks on every side, almost stood still in the agony of their terror, and waited for their executioner. In less than ten minutes fifty of them had fallen to rise no more. Poles were then planted in the ground and strung with ropes of hide, on which the strips of meat were hung for curing in the sun. When sufficiently dried it was packed in bales. When all their horses were loaded, the slow march back to the fort was begun.

Unknown to the trappers, their train had a constant escort from their sworn enemies, the Blackfeet Indians. No attack was made, however. At the fort the horses were placed in a fenced inclosure for protection, and a sentry placed on watch. One night the fellow on guard, perhaps a little the worse for liquor, saw two men approach the bars, let them down, and deliberately commence driving every horse out into the prairie. It never occurred to Mr. Guard that the Indians would come except in force, and his intelligent mind never doubted that the two men were his comrades, who had orders to take the horses outside for better pasturage. Thanking his lucky stars for the relief, he said nothing to his industrious friends, but curled down in a fence corner and went to sleep. In the morning it was found that the Blackfeet had, without firing a gun or losing a brave, run off every horse and mule belonging to the fort, and left the enraged trappers without an animal on which to make pursuit. It came near terminating even more seriously for poor Simmonds, the sentry. Several of the trappers in their rage threatened to kill him, and, by way of emphasis, put a few rifle shots through his fur hat as it rested on his own precious head.

This little trick of their Blackfeet friends was not forgotten, when, in the following spring, a strong body of the trappers found themselves in proximity to the chief village of the nation. Kit Carson and a friend or two, after a careful reconnoiter, reported that there were signs of a hurried removal to be seen. Every heart in the company beat high with the excitement of approaching revenge, the darkest passion of human nature. Forty-three picked men, under the command of Carson, were detailed for the fight; the remaining fifty-five were to guard the valuable stores of the party, and advance slowly as a reserve. With a wild yell the trappers charged the village, killing a dozen braves in an instant. But the Indians were the children of a noble tribe, brave, strong, skillful, and well equipped. They quickly rallied, and commenced a bloody struggle, which lasted over three hours, an unusual time for Indian warfare. Every man was concealed behind trees, rocks, or whatever could afford protection. Sometimes the same rock would afford cover for an Indian and a trapper. Neither could leave the place without being killed. For an hour the two men would seek to kill each other. At last, in a moment of negligence or unskillfulness, one of them would bite the dust.

The trappers retained the advantage gained at the outset until the prolonged combat began to exhaust their ammunition. The sagacious redskins at once divined the cause of the slackened fire, and charged on their foes. The hand to hand engagement is the one in which individual skill and heroism develops its noblest examples. The trappers, by the use of their reddened knives and smoking pistols, again and again drove back their assailants, but at last were driven to a stubborn retreat. In executing this movement, the horse of a mountaineer named Cotton, who was at the extreme right of the field of battle, stumbled and fell, pinning his rider to the earth. Carson's keen eye, which incessantly swept the entire field, perceived the accident at the same time that a half dozen dusky warriors bounded forward to scalp the unfortunate man. Springing from his horse, with a rallying cry to his now scattered men, Carson ran toward his friend, and, taking aim as he ran, shot the foremost savage down. The trappers now came running from all directions at their commander's call, and the remaining five braves started for cover. Only two of them ever reached it. Cotton, with a little help, extricated himself from the painful situation in which his accident left him.

Seing that Cotton was all right, Carson turned to look for his horse, and found that he had run away. It was no time or place to remain on foot. The savages might overtake him at any moment. Ready for any emergency, Kit mounted behind one of his comrades, and in this position waited till his runaway horse could be recaptured. When the reserve came up with its precious supplies of ammunition, the trappers prepared to make a final and crushing attack on the Indians. This last struggle

36

resulted in the disastrous defeat of the tribe, and so broke its power and spirit that for years the trappers and hunters pursued their occupation without molestation from the humbled Blackfeet.

At the summer rendezvous Kit arranged to join a couple of traders who had planned an expedition into the Navajoe country. This tribe had attained a sort of red man's civilization, a thing which is perfectly possible. All civilizations are not alike. The Chinese civilization is the oldest on the globe, yet among the lower classes a rat is a great dainty at the dinner table; from twelve to twenty persons of all ages and either sex sleep huddled together in a single small room; a few cents constitute a day's wages. India has her cities and commerce; her religions older far than Christianity; her temples of marble, ivory, and gold, the architecture of which is unequaled on the globe; but in India are found fanatics who have held their right arms upward for twenty years, until the joints have become solid bone, covered with shriveled parchment, and the extended members can not be lowered. There is, too, a civilization in Russia, a civilization of fashion, aristocracy, and wealth, of colleges, of railroads, of libraries, and palaces. In Russia it was that her ruler employed the idle laborers in constructing, at untold cost, a magnificent winter palace made entirely of ice, and destined to melt away as the summer sun flung his radiance across its crystal towers; and it was the czar of all the Russias who by the stroke of his pen peacefully emancipated twenty million serfs. Yet in this same country, where the body is free, the mind is in chains. Torture and the executioner's ax paralyze not merely the tongue but the intellect as well. Worse than these penalties are those by which wise and good men, valuable members of society, are sent to the terrible mines of Siberia. There in the darkness alike of day and night they spend the remainder of their lives. College professors, scientists, and editors, treated worse than the blackest felons, toil on in these fearful abodes of torture, losing eyesight, hair, teeth, strength, intelligence, until at last they drop their fetters and leap into the skeleton arms of Death. Yet Russia is civilized.

So we say that though an Indian civilization might possess many elements strange and grotesque in our eyes, still it was a

THE RESCUE OF COTTON.

possibility. The Navajoes had something approaching it. They were wealthy, and fond of their possessions. Their customs were somewhat settled. They knew the art of weaving beautiful blankets, and manufacturing many other articles which commanded high prices. Carson and his fellow traders found a ready market among them for their merchandise, and returned from their trip with large herds of splendid horses and mules, loaded down with valuable blankets and furs.

For the next year or two Carson went ahead with his life of hunting and trapping. His character is in marked contrast with those of his companions. Carson was a kind-hearted, even-tempered, and intensely practical man. Though a sparing talker, he was one of those geniuses who perform every thing they undertake with skill, rapidity, and success. He had a remarkably smooth, well-balanced, and symmetrical nature, which was rare for a trapper, who was generally a dare-devil, crack-brained fellow, utterly reckless, erratic, and without stability of purpose. So far from making trapping and hunting his life-work, he had ordinarily followed a dozen different callings— now making Sunday-school speeches in the Eastern cities; now selling patent medicine in the malarial districts of the Middle States; now preaching to the Indians; and now a New Mexican desperado and cut-throat.

This was just about the career of Williams, an old fellow who was with Carson at this time. He had translated the Bible into two Indian dialects. His irregular genius showed itself in an incident in a Mexican town. He was at the time a trader or shopkeeper there. One day some of his customers complained of his prices, and undertook to jew him down. Williams flew into a terrible rage. He blasphemed and abused them in the most horrible manner. Finally, springing on them like a tiger, he kicked them all out of his little booth or lodge; and, as if disgusted with the whole community, commenced throwing his goods and merchandise, helter-skelter, into the street, nor did he stop till his booth was entirely dismantled. Then with horrid curses, and his eyes ablaze with insane fury, he seized his rifle, and shaking the dust of the place from his feet, he angrily took himself off to the mountains.

Another one of these eccentric characters, one who stood high in the trapper profession, was a fellow named Mitchell.

He had at one time acquired the notion of some wonderful gold mines being hidden away in the mountains of northern Texas. With the purpose of discovering them, he joined the Comanche nation, became one of their braves, married a pretty Indian squaw, and for some years was one of their leaders in battle, and a terror to their foes. Becoming convinced that the gold mines were myths, he made to his Comanche friends some plausible excuse for a temporary absence, and left them forever.

Some years after that period of Carson's life of which we are now speaking, Mitchell made a trading trip into Kansas. It was the first time in many years that he had been in the States. Kansas was just in the convulsion of political passion which preceded the civil war. The free-soilers and pro-slavery men were carrying on a guerrilla warfare, each trying to drive the other out of the state. Farm-houses were burned; men were fired upon from thickets as they passed along the road; corpses were found in the forest with knives sticking in their hearts. All this seemed natural enough to Mitchell, with his frontier notions, but his trip was a business one. In his lonely life in the mountains, Mitchell had remained ignorant of all political issues. With the instinctive caution of the frontiersman, as well as from the natural reserve which he felt when among civilized (!) men, he avoided all conversation on political questions. Patriotism and suspicion at once spotted him as a dangerous man, and caused him to be avoided or treated with indifference and marked reserve. Once he was seen reading a newspaper with great interest. It was a fragment of an old New Orleans paper, bitterly pro-slavery. He was observed to put it carefully in his pocket. That night a masked company of free-soilers told him to leave town in six hours, or he would be killed. He left. The article he had been reading related to a new way of making hats, in which silk was substituted for beaver fur, and prophesying that the latter would be entirely supplanted!

On another occasion he went into a store to buy a lot of powder and ball to take back with him. The storekeeper looked suspiciously at him, and asked him where he came from. "None of yer business," said Mitchell. "What do you want with ammunition?" "To load my gun. What d'ye s'pose; did you think I wanted ter make bread of it?" This was enough for the storekeeper. With a triumphant glance at the bystanders he said, "I understand what you free-soilers want with ammunition, you dogs; you want to kill us. We want all we have ourselves." All this to the poor mountaineer, who considered every white man his "brother," was insupportable. Hastily finishing his business, he gave up a long contemplated trip to the eastern cities, and started back to New Mexico. A friend fell in with him on his return trip, and asked where he had been.

"After being away for twenty years, I thought I would like to see the whites once more. But what I saw in Kansas disgusted me so I could go no further. They do nothing but get up war-parties against each other. I would rather be in an Indian country than in civilized Kansas."

We have already hinted at a fact which, though its origin was thousands of miles away, in Europe, reached in its effect the lonely mountains of New Mexico, and robbed Kit Carson and his friends of their occupation. The increasing scarcity and high prices of the beaver fur had induced the hat manufacturers of Europe to look for a substitute. It was found in silk, which, though not so durable, presented an equally beautiful appearance in the "plug" hat. Thus the market for beaver fur was seriously affected. The prices fell with the demand, and the lonely mountaineer, like Othello, found "his occupation gone."

This fact, sad enough for the poor trappers, is repeated at every step in the progress of civilization. Human invention is constantly destroying old trades and occupations. It makes a reaping machine, and both the men who use and the men who manufacture the "cradle" are thrown out of employment. It builds a railroad, and all the innkeepers, who had their clean little hostelries distributed along the roads, so that, after each day's journey, the tired traveler might find lodging and refreshment for " man and beast," find their inns deserted and their business gone. It invents a loom, by which, with one boy to fill the shuttles, the work of twenty hand-weavers is done, and better done. It constructs an automatic air brake for the express train, and the brakesmen are discharged; the engineer does their work, and does it better. All this presents a great problem. In order to live, men must have work. Every year an increasing multitude complain, and not without reason, that there is less labor to do than formerly, and that their hands, though willing, can find no task. Idle classes are dangerous. They are brought into the world without asking their consent, and being here they demand, and rightly, too, that they shall have an opportunity to earn money and procure food. All this, we say, presents a great and serious question. So it was, when their trade was taken away, the trappers were grieved and angry. They felt like striking back, but whom should they hit? Deep in their sullen hearts they cursed the inventor of the silk hat. He was a dog, a devil, a brute !

Kit to some extent shared these feelings, but he cheerfully sought another occupation. There was a trading-post called Bent's Fort. Here he was offered the position of hunter to the fort. It was the duty of the hunter to provide the daily supply of game, summer and winter, for the table of the fort. If he had bad luck in his hunting, the fellows at the fort were sure to be cross. If his provision lacked variety, they were likely to speak of it. Carson's great skill with his gun caused him to be sought after for this position. He accepted it, and held it for eight consecutive years. It is said that, during all these years, " not a single word of disagreement passed between him and his employers." This fact is a monument to Kit's expertness as a hunter.

If any thing in the world will bring on a fuss, it is an insufficient meal. Kit's boarders were unfailingly provided for. He never returned empty handed. On these expeditions Kit

was mounted on his magnificent horse, "Apache." They knew
and loved each other. Neither horse nor rider had an equal, as
hunters, in the Rocky Mountains. During these years Kit's
fame spread over the entire West. He was called the "Monarch

CARSON AND HIS FAVORITE HORSE, "APACHE."

of the Prairies, the "Nestor of New Mexico;" but the name he
was most pleased with was, the "Hero of the Rockies." Among
the lodges of the Arrapahoes, Cheyennes, and Comanches, Kit
was an honored guest on many occasions. One reason for his
remaining so quiet for eight years is found in his marriage with

an Indian girl, of whom he was passionately fond. It was his misfortune to lose his dusky bride by death, when they had only been married two years. To an infant daughter, however, were transferred the entire wealth of his affections. When of suitable age, he sent her to St. Louis, to receive every advantage which education could bestow. During this time Carson guided many emigrants across the Sierra Nevada Mountains, patiently helping their toiling ox-teams along the rocky roads.

In 1842, Carson made a trip to the States. For the first time in sixteen years, he looked upon the home of his childhood. But Time had swept his unsparing hand over the place. The old log cabin, in the door of which Kit's mother had stood sixteen years before, waving her hand to her boy as he rode proudly away that sunny morning, was now a crumbling ruin. No light gleamed from its cheerless window. No loving arms were clasped convulsively around the wanderer's neck.

The father and mother slept the sleep that knows no waking, beneath the foot of a lonely forest tree, and within hearing of the ceaseless murmur of the Missouri River. Brothers and sisters, too, were gone; some dead; some, impelled by the same restless spirit which made its home in the heart of Carson, were scattered abroad in the wildernesses of the West. None left! Staggered at this desolation, Carson sat down in the shadows of a double darkness—the darkness of the night without, and of the night within. And as the night-bird, wandering from its mate, uttered its lonely cry in the gloom of the forest, the strong man, sensible of his utter loneliness, gave way to the melancholy of the hour, and wept in the solitude as only men can weep.

Shaking off these sad memories, Kit went to St. Louis, where he spent ten days. It was his first visit to a great city. The roar of the streets and bustle of excited throngs contrasted strangely with his life in the mountains. But he was no " greeny," ready to bite at the traps of the city sharpers. He visited the places of interest, investigated the methods of doing business, and availed himself of his opportunities for acquiring information.

But this trip had one momentous result. Carson became acquainted with Lieutenant John C. Fremont, who was just proceeding on his first journey of exploration. Fremont was greatly in need of an experienced pioneer to guide his party through the mountains, as well as give them the benefit of his experience as to means of subsistence and defense against Indians. Opportunely meeting Carson, he employed him, and thus Kit was introduced into a work which has made his name a household word throughout the republic. The object of the expedition was to survey the South Pass, in what we know as Wyoming Territory, and obtain the altitude of the highest peaks. Up to this time, America was profoundly ignorant of the West.

The success of the expedition was complete. Carson had proven invaluable, for his hunting and trapping career had made him familiar with the entire West, from Mexico on the south to British America on the north. In the following year, Fremont made his second exploring expedition, on behalf of the United States Government. As before, he made Carson his right-hand man. His object this time was to push his investigations westward from the Rockies to the Sierra Nevadas, there connect his work with the Pacific coast surveys, which had already been made, and thus lay a foundation for a survey and map of the entire West.

This party had many thrilling adventures. After leaving the Rockies, and traveling many days across the barren plains, their provisions began to give out. The journey was longer, and game scarcer, than they expected. Before them lay the snowy Sierras; to attempt to cross them in the enfeebled condition of the party was perilous in the extreme. Behind, lay the plains they had just traversed; to retrace their steps was to starve long before they reached a point where supplies could be had. So it was that the only record of Fremont's second expedition came near being the horrible hieroglyphics of bleaching skeletons, which are so often left by explorers, the fearful meaning of which is so readily understood.

To attempt a crossing of the mountains was urged by Carson as the only alternative. It was resolved upon. Snow-shoes for the entire party were indispensable to traversing the whitened expanse, into the depths of which a man unshod would sink out of sight forever. Kit swiftly instructed the men how to make them, and then, with an advance party, pushed on to explore the route, and see if it was practicable to break a path for the animals. The distance was three leagues. Carson said if they could make that, the green valley of the Sacramento, with its splendid game and abounding forage, would open before the weary wanderers. It was a labor of fifteen days to beat and pack the snow with mallets for the passage of the mules. But in this time, most of the animals had died. In the extremity of the situation, the famished beasts ate each other's tails and tore the leather from the pack saddles to devour it. At last, Sutter's Fort was reached, with its hospitable welcome and its abundant table. Carson cautioned the men to eat sparingly, but they could not be restrained. Partly from the terrible strain which they had endured, partly from too sudden indulgence, two of the party lost their reason and became raving maniacs.

On the return trip, just at they were going to camp one evening, a man and boy ran up. The strangers hastily related that they belonged to a Mexican trading party. They, with four others, had been left in charge of the horses, and in the absence of the main party, these six, two of whom were women, were attacked by Indians. The two speakers, Fuentes and the boy, Pablo, had managed to get away. Anguish riven, the one by the unknown fate of his wife, the other by that of his father and mother, they implored the help of the explorers. Only two men volunteered their assistance, Kit Carson and his fellow mountaineer, Godey. The lips of sorrow never appealed in vain to the brave but unselfish Carson.

There were thirty Indians in the attacking party. Carson and Godey, accompanied by Fuentes, determined to attempt a rescue of the unfortunate captives. Quickly striking the trail of the marauders, they commenced their pursuit. At the end of twenty miles the horse Fuentes rode broke down. To procure another was impossible. Leaving the unfortunate man behind, Carson and his companion dashed on their errand of kindness. It was two men against thirty. But fear was a stranger to the bold hearts. All day they rode. Night came on. Still they rested not. Much of the time they led their horses, and followed the trail in the darkness by feeling. The tracks grew fresher. A few hours only separated them from the chase. To be fresh for the fray they dismounted, and wrapped in their blankets, wet with heavy dew, they tried to sleep. But the cold, wet atmosphere rendered sleep impossible. No fire could be lighted. At early dawn they perceived a neighboring ravine. There they thought safe to build a small fire and warm themselves. The horses were again mounted.

The sun was still on his upward journey when they discovered their enemies, thirty in all, engaged in their usual feast of horse-flesh. The stolen animals, which were yet alive, were picketed at a short distance. The two mountaineers determined to crawl in among the horses, and then be guided by events. The strange figures of the crawling men frightened a colt, and stirred up a commotion in the herd. The Indians, ever quick to read the signal of danger in the conduct of their animals, sprang for their weapons. As the savages came in range the trappers fired. Two braves bit the dust. The remainder, astonished at the conduct of Carson and Godey, suddenly seemed to believe that the two were a decoy, supported by a large party, which sought by stratagem to lure them into giving battle.

As Kit had foreseen, the Indians at once fled, leaving their camp to the victors. Here the terrible scene presented itself of the mangled bodies of the two men, pierced with a hundred arrows. The women were found a little further off. Their naked bodies each had a sharpened stake driven through it into the ground. With sad hearts at the comparative failure of their errand, the trappers interred the bodies, collected the horses, and took themselves back to their more selfish companions. The property was restored to the strangers; the sad story of the victims told to the wifeless husband and the lonely boy. Bowed down with grief, yet overflowing with gratitude, they offered all their horses as a gift to Carson and Godey. Hastily wiping away a tear with his shaggy sleeve, Kit refused to accept any thing, and instead, thrust a small sum of money into the boy's hand. Camp was broken. The men mounted, and with a farewell to the strangers, the party rode away, leaving them alone in the forest in the shadow of their mighty grief.

In the spring of 1845 Kit, being out of employment, resolved to be a farmer. He determined to settle down, fell trees, grub stumps, plow the glebe, sow seed, and gather crops; to become acquainted with corn husking, potato hoeing, and butter making; to learn the mystery of weaning calves, killing hogs, and stringing dried pumpkin. It was a strange calling, that of the patient farmer, for the impetuous Kit to select. But as men approach middle life they become more and more conservative. Carson and a mountaineer named Owens purchased an eligible tract of land on which to make a farm. Kit furnished the money, and laid in a stock of wooden plows, Mexican axes, farm carts, and other utensils. With a company of hired hands he built temporary huts, and chopped away at the trees in fine style. True, they were a little green at the business. The fences were rather clumsy, the fields rather stumpy. The farm-house, which Kit insisted on having built, was very large and barny, while the barn was small and badly located. Still things moved on fairly, and Kit might some day have made a farmer. He tried to persuade himself he was contented. But when Fremont sent him word of a third expedition Carson just took twenty-four hours to sell out the whole place for a third of what it had cost, get out his rifle, saddle his horse, and start to join Fremont.

The third expedition thus joined by Carson had many adventures. One night, through carelessness in keeping watch, some treacherous Klamath Indians stole in the camp and cleft the skulls of three of the sleepers before they were discovered. In retaliation Carson, at the head of a war party, burned their village and killed twenty braves. The war with Mexico, which was declared at that time, served to complicate the fortunes of the explorers. Carson was detailed to take dispatches to Washington City. On his way overland he met General Kearney, who was under orders to proceed with his command to the scene of hostilities in California. Kearney at once determined to forward the dispatches by another messenger, and have Carson return with him as a guide.

Kit gave up his important trip to the capital with great secret reluctance, but it was smothered in his own breast. He saw how much he was needed. To serve others was always his first impulse; to consider himself, his last. Without a murmur he turned back to the wilderness. It was not long before Kearney's command came in conflict with the Mexican forces. His men, being nearly all on foot, suffered severely. In the first regular battle Carson and a squad of twenty-five of the mounted men headed a charge on the enemy. Just before reaching the foe Kit's horse stumbled and fell, throwing its rider under the feet of the advancing column, which dashed on right over him. This accident, though fraught with great danger, in all probability saved his life. Every man in the front squad of twenty-five was killed except Kit.

The Mexicans continued to harass Kearney, at last managing to surround him on a small hill, on which Kearney and his command were virtually besieged. At the close of the day's engagement, which found them in this perilous situation, a council of war was held. Three messengers had been previously dispatched to San Diego with a call for re-enforcements. Each of them had been made captive by the Mexicans before reaching their destination. To attempt to break through the besieging lines meant, in view of their own shattered condition and the superior numbers of the enemy, certain destruction of the command. To remain where they were for more than a short time was impossible. The situation was gloomy in the extreme. After all had expressed their opinions and no plan had been suggested, Carson rose and said: "General, I will volunteer to undertake to creep through the Mexican lines, push on to San Diego, and bring you succor."

The effect of the simple words was electric. Lieutenant Beale, a brave young naval officer, offered to join Carson. Kearney gratefully accepted the generous offer. Making farewells, which not improbably might be their last, Carson and Beale slipped out under cover of the darkness, determined to render up their lives rather than abandon the attempt. Crawling stealthily on hands and knees, over rocks and through thorny underbrush, stopping every few moments to listen, the brave men slowly made their way into the hostile camp. In spite of great care, their heavy shoes would sometimes strike a rock, and it was found necessary to remove them and thrust them into their belts.

The Mexican pickets were found to be arranged in three rows, the sentinels in the second row being opposite the spaces in the first, and the third opposite the spaces in the second. Carson at once decided to take a diagonal course through the lines. Even this path took them within a short distance of the watchful sentinels. The gleam of the bayonet in the starlight shot through the overhanging branches; yet, with Carson's marvelous skill, the fruit of a lifetime of Indian warfare, they reached the third line of pickets. In five minutes they would have been safe. Though neither spoke, each *felt* the increased confidence of the other. But, hush! Kit, who was in the lead, with his quick ear caught the sound of crunching twigs, and a heavy footfall approaching. Pushing Beale with his foot, as a signal to follow his example, Carson threw himself perfectly flat on the ground, and awaited developments. The sounds grew louder.

Presently, the dim figure of a sentinel on horseback revealed itself to the piercing eye of the pioneer.

On came the Mexican. The two Americans lay right in his path. Beale said afterwards : "I looked on myself as a corpse." When within six feet of Carson, the Mexican dismounted leisurely, drew out a cigaretto and a bit of paper, which, by the help of flint and steel, he proceeded to ignite. The blaze of the paper distinctly revealed the two prostrate forms. In relating the story, Carson, who never exaggerated, said : "I heard every heart-beat of Beale, as we lay there, and they sounded to me like the strokes of a maul." But the Mexican, when the paper blazed, was intent on lighting his cigaretto. He did not raise his eyes The yellow flame lit up his sinister countenance. He leisurely drew three or four puffs, then, with a quick motion, flung the little torch on the ground, where it flickered for a moment and went out. With a grunt of satisfaction, he re-adjusted his accouterments, mounted his horse, which, with finer instinct than his master, was already snorting slightly at the figures in the grass, and shortly disappeared among the trees.

Not till the Mexican was well out of the way, did Carson stir. Then he commenced his onward progress. Feeling that danger was now behind and not before them, they hurried forward. The Mexican camp was left far to the rear, and the disfigured heroes rose and warmly clasped each other's hands in the moment of thankfulness for their escape. To put on their shoes was their first thought. But, misery of miseries, these had not been thought of in the perilous journey of two miles on hands and knees, and both pairs were missing. To push on barefooted was the only alternative. Carson had no guide but the stars, no map but his knowledge of the country. Yet, to avoid all beaten trails, along which the enemy swarmed, and to select a circuitous route to San Diego, over rocks and through thickets, was easy work. The loss of their shoes was a terrible misfortune. The country was covered with a thick growth of the prickly pear, which, at every step, lacerated their bleeding feet with poison-tipped needles. All night and all the next day, without food or rest, sustained only by mental excitement and the thought of the little body of suffering troops which was folded in the fatal coils of the Mexican serpent, they proceeded. Another night closed in around them; yet they seemed insensible to fatigue and pain. Toward midnight, the outlines of San Diego were marked upon the horizon. Hurrying on, the poor fellows made their way at once to the bed-room of Commodore Stockton, and told him the situation of their comrades. Their condition was pitiable—clothing in rags, feet bleeding terribly and swollen to twice their natural size, mind and body exhausted to the last extremity. Their noble mission accomplished, poor Beale fainted away, only to wake a gibbering maniac. It was two years before reason fully re-asserted her sway. Carson, however, would neither eat nor sleep until the relief column was on its way. Then he, too, hardened, though he was, by exposure and frontier life, broke down, and for a month was prostrated by his fearful exertion. Kearney and his command were saved.

Carson subsequently made two trips to Washington City, bearing dispatches to the government. At this time, he was appointed Indian agent for New Mexico, as a reward for his services in the war. Not being identified with any political party, he lacked the backing, which, far more than merit or service to his country, was required to obtain an office. The United States Senate refused to confirm the appointment of the honest and heroic pioneer.

For the second time in his life Kit resolved to settle down as a farmer. This time he bought a place at Rayado. The location was beautiful; the valley rich in soil and teeming with noble game. Kit's second wife, whom he had married some years before, was a highly connected Mexican lady. He was attached to his children beyond any thing else on earth. He built himself a comfortable mansion; his farm was managed by experienced hands. In spite of all the terrible experiences, which lay like packs of wolves in the thicket of his memory, Carson was

37

a happy man. The claims upon his skill as an Indian fighter and his kindness to every suffering heart continued to reach him in his happy valley. Thence he was frequently called to guide United States troops, or attempt a rescue of some unfortunate captive. Perhaps he felt a more tender regret at leaving home than formerly; perhaps the effect which his death might have on the happiness of his little family circle sometimes occurred to him, but he was as quick to respond as ever.

The Apaches at this time almost rendered life a burden in Northern Mexico. They are small in stature, but a marvel of symmetry in proportion, perfect in health, unequaled in athletic skill and performance. The Apache's limbs are straight, his muscles hard as iron, and his frame as elastic as rubber. Treachery glistens in his coal-black eye, and the instinct of the murderer is hidden in his heart. On one occasion word was brought of the killing of a Mr. White, and the capture of his wife and child. A detachment of troops undertook the rescue. Carson was riding some distance in advance when he sighted the redskins and their weeping captive on the opposite bank of a stream. Carson yelled for the men to advance at double quick, for he saw no time was to be lost. But for some reason the officer in command was jealous of Kit, and coolly halted his men. During that short halt Carson saw the tomahawk sink into the skull of Mrs. White and her little girl.

Carson's adventurous disposition, instead of courting physical danger, began to manifest itself in bold speculations, in which he had great success. Nor was it remarkable. The same disposition of genius, placed in different surroundings, will manifest itself in a way externally different, but really the same. It is said that Jay Gould, with his vast organizing power, would equal Napoleon if placed in Napoleon's situation.

Kit's fame was a great burden to him. When in San Francisco, he was lionized, passed free to theaters, on railroads, invited to countless entertainments. This was embarrassing to the quiet mountaineer. Once at Fort Laramie a fellow, who was but a specimen from a large class, came in, eagerly seeking to have the great Kit Carson pointed out to him. The bystanders directed him to Kit. For a moment the stranger looked at the small, mild-eyed, soft-mannered man before him in dumb astonishment. He had looked for a large, fierce desperado to correspond with the great feats of Kit he had heard of. In a moment astonishment gave way to a knowing look, as he said, "See here, feller, what's this yer givin' me? Yer not Kit Carson. Mind, I'm no greenhorn. Howsumever, I'll let yer off this wunst, ef yer'll pint out the genooine Kit."

Carson, with a face as grave as a parson, and an air of mock timidity, pointed to an enormous trader, with a tremendous mustache, dressed in a hunting shirt, buckskin leggins, and an enormous slouch hat. This personage satisfied the stranger's notion. Offering a "chaw of terbac" to Kit, who quietly declined it, he watched the big trader for an hour with the greatest interest, and then took himself off, well satisfied that he had seen the "genooine Kit." He, like the majority of people, looked to a large man for great deeds, one of the greatest delusions in the world, and one which is utterly refuted by history.

The popular reverence for large men and expansive stomachs, is shown by the United States Senate, of which it is said only a half dozen men fall below six feet, one inch, in height, and two hundred and twenty pounds in weight. The Chinese, we once heard a lecturer say, believe that the brains are in the abdomen, and estimate a man's ability by his waist band. When they wish to call a man an idiot they say, "Your stomach is no larger than my little finger," while their rarest compliment is, "Your stomach is three miles around!" It is possible the lecturer was only satirizing the popular worship of stomachs, which prevails in American politics.

One evening, as Kit returned to his comfortable farm at Rayado, leading his noble horse, which was laden with a blacktailed deer and some wild turkeys, a man informed him of a plot for robbery and murder, to prevent which Carson's assistance was wanted. A ruffian named Fox had been engaged at Taos in raising a band of desperadoes, who were ostensibly to serve as an escort through the Indian country of two English-men, Brevoort and Weatherhead, who were supposed to carry a large amount of money for investment in stock. The real object of the villains was to murder the strangers and capture the money. By some means a hint of the plot was dropped and brought to. Carson, who followed up the clue, satisfied him-self of its truth, and became convinced that the crime was to be consummated in a lonely canon near Cimaron River. One hour's preparation sufficed to place him at the head of thirty finely mounted dragoons. Selecting a short route, known only to himself, Carson required of his men the highest possible speed. It was the only hope, and was successful. The chase was over-taken. Fox was arrested before he could strike a blow. The astonished Englishmen were informed of their danger. The gang of desperadoes were ordered to leave camp. Messrs. Bre-voort and Weatherhead afterward presented Kit with a superb pair of silver-mounted revolvers as a token of their gratitude.

The following summer Kit went to St. Louis on a trading trip. On his return he brought with him a large stock of goods. One day, as the train wended its way over the green prairies, a village of Cheyennes was discovered by the party. One of their braves had been flogged for some misdemeanor by a party of whites a few days before, and the tribe was ablaze with wrath. Carson knew nothing of the grievance, but quickly perceived that an attack was contemplated. Orders were given for each man to be on the alert, and the village was left twenty miles to the rear, when small parties of warriors of twos and threes began to come in sight. These had on their war-paint and feathers. As they approached Carson spoke to them in a friendly way, and to show he was not afraid, went into camp, and invited the Indians to come in and have a smoke.

No sooner had the pipe gone round than the Indians began to talk vigorously among themselves. It must not be forgotten that several years before, while hunter at Bent's fort, Carson had been a great friend of the Cheyennes. His appearance had greatly changed, and he was not recognized. Every word of the visitors was understood by him. Supposing they were not understood, they were coolly perfecting a plot to massacre the whites. Suddenly Kit stepped forward, told them his name, how he had once been a friend, and had to his knowledge never wronged their tribe. Now they rewarded him with a plan to kill him. He closed by ordering them to leave the camp or they would be shot. Nonplused at the turn affairs had taken, with a threat of return, they hastily left.

The train moved on. Each man walked beside his mule, a whip in one hand and a rifle in the other. Carson plainly told the men they were in great peril, but inspired them with his own courage. He scanned the horizon incessantly, but saw nothing more dangerous than a hungry wolf or a wandering antelope. Evening came. The wagons were arranged in a circle, inside of which the mules were tethered. Grass was cut and fed to them. The men gathered some driftwood, and built their camp fire also in the guarded ring. Carson felt that the responsibility of saving his men rested with him. In the party was one of those Mexican runners, a young man who, with a message in his head, can run with little fatigue seventy miles in a day. Calling the boy outside the wagons, when the supper was over, Carson pointed out the direction of Rayado, and told him he must leave many miles behind him by sunrise. The lad bent his dark intelligent face upon his master, and resolved to make every exertion to fulfill his command. Obtaining a few rations of provisions, which he bound about his waist, he received from Kit full instructions as to the dangerous places in the journey. He was to proceed with the utmost speed to Rayado, and start out a relief party. Making his bow, he started swiftly on his errand. Kit watched the agile figure, as it sped over the prairie in the dim moonlight, until it was but a speck on the horizon.

The camp was not disturbed that night. The following morning five Indians appeared. Carson called to them, told them he had the night before dispatched a fleet messenger to Rayado, and that if his party was massacred, his friends, the soldiers, would surely inflict swift and terrible vengeance on the Cheyennes. The Indians said they would look for his moccasin tracks and see if the story was true. Carson saw that this was a turning point in his favor. An hour later the whole village of Cheyennes passed in sight, evidently making for safety as fast as possible. They had found the moccasin tracks, and saw the chase had been gone too long to be overtaken. The train proceeded without interruption, until they met a body of troops, who had started at once on the arrival of the Mexican runner. Under this strong escort the remainder of the trip was happily completed.

In 1853, Kit was again appointed and this time confirmed as Indian agent, a position he graced and honored as no other living American would have done. His great knowledge of Indian character was a splendid equipment. Sometimes around their council fires he distributed the bounty of the government, and instructed them in the primary lessons of civilization. Sometimes it was at his own home that he received them as friends, and earnestly advised them to let whisky alone. Again at the head of a column of United States troops he filled the faithless hearts of the Apaches with a fear of justice if not a love of kindness. In one hand he offered the olive branch; in the other, he held his loaded rifle.

Kit at last permanently quieted the Utahs and Apaches. Thenceforward he devoted himself to the works of peace among his Indian *protéges.* The fierce passion for war was supplanted in their breasts by a love of comfort and domestic life; the tomahawk and the scalping knife grew rusty and forgotten, while the sinewy hand which had wielded them learned to grasp the plow and the sickle. Kit, too, felt that in the remainder of his life war and adventure would have no place. He was mistaken.

The flames of the civil war were already filling the heavens with the red light of doom. Carson was destined to serve his country as a soldier. A lover of the Union, he was made Colonel of the First New Mexico Volunteers. The Indians, always ready to seize a pretext for making war on the government, cast in their lot with the Confederacy. Far away on the plains and in the mountains of New Mexico, where the roar of Gettysburg was silent, and the story of bloody Chickamauga was unknown, there took place terrible struggles between combatants who knew not the ideas for which they fought. The red man fought to be fighting the whites. The brave New Mexican fought the Indian much as he had fought him all his life. The shock of the civil war hurled these ancient foes upon the frontier of civilization against each other. But while the ideas were not present with them as they were among the ranks on many a historic field of conflict, the battle was none the less bloody and the suffering none the less severe.

The campaigns conducted by Carson were splendidly managed. On the sixth day of January, 1864, he started out with a force of four hundred men, only twenty of whom were mounted, upon the famous expedition which forever crushed the power of the Navajoes. By maneuvering with a skill of which Carson alone was capable in an Indian war, he succeeded in entrapping the bulk of the Navajoe Nation in the Canon de Chelly, one of the largest on the globe. It is forty miles long, with perpendicular walls of rock, fifteen hundred feet high. Carson quickly divided his command, sending one detachment to enter at the east end, while he planted himself at the mouth. Far down in the gloomy depths, the narrow bit of sky looking like a blue ribbon above them, the column cautiously picked its way. Scattering bands of Indians, who saw the doom of their companions, posted themselves along the rocks and crags to annoy the troops, but their efforts were ineffectual. Sometimes a volley was fired from below, at the pigmy warriors on the dizzy height, but generally they reserved themselves for the larger game

which was in the trap. On the second day, Carson attacked
the whole force of Indians as they attempted in vain to break
out of the deadly chasm. They were terribly punished, and
were at last forced to surrender.

By this splendid strategy, between five and ten thousand
Indians surrendered to Carson, the largest capture ever made in
Indian warfare; and this was achieved by four hundred soldiers,
with scarcely the loss of a man. The entire war presents no finer
piece of generalship. The majority of the captives were placed
on a reservation in Arkansas, but were subsequently permitted
to return to their old hunting-grounds, where they are living in
happiness and peace.

In the official report to the War Department, is the following:

"You have, doubtless, seen the last of the Navajoe war, a
war that has continued, with but few intermissions, for the last
one hundred and eighty years, and which during that time has
been marked by every shade of atrocity, brutality, and ferocity
which can be imagined. I beg to congratulate you on the prospect that this formidable band of robbers and murderers has
been at last made to succumb. To Colonel Kit Carson, in command of the expedition, whose courage and perseverance excited
all to great energy and inspired great resolution, the credit is
mainly due."

For his gallant services, " Colonel Kit Carson " was pro-
moted to the rank of brigadier-general.

After the close of the war, Kit, as we will continue to call
him, found himself in failing health, the result of an accident
in 1860. He was descending a steep mountain, leading his
horse, when the animal slipped and fell on him, inflicting internal
injury. In spite of sickness, he labored unceasingly to promote
the welfare of the Indians. On the 27th of April, 1868, his
wife died suddenly, leaving seven children. This threw him
into the deepest dejection. In a few days, he found himself too
weak to ride horseback, his lifelong pleasure. Then he took
short walks around his yard. Then it was noticed that even

this was too much for him; he no longer left his room. Silent and thoughtful, the hero would sit in his arm-chair all day long. Sometimes, a smile would break over his face; again, the look would be one of intense concentration. Perhaps he was, in fancy, living over his life as a trapper, as hunter to Bent's Fort, or as guide for Fremont and rescuer of Kearney's command.

One morning, Kit Carson was too weak to leave his bed. The next, the 23d of May, 1868, he refused all nourishment. Towards evening, a film coated the kindly eye, and the hand responded more and more feebly to the will. It was evening. The great sun had thrown its latest radiance upon the lowly couch, and was sinking behind the lonely Rockies, over which he had so often wandered. Suddenly he called out in a clear voice, " Doctor, Compadre, adios !" It was the end.

One of Nature's noblemen had passed away.

CHAPTER XVII.

HEROES OF THE LONE STAR STATE.

NELSON LEE, THE TEXAN RANGER.

URING the revolutionary struggles of the Lone Star republic, Texas was a great magnet, toward which were irresistibly attracted, from every portion of the Union, men of physical courage and restless appetite for adventure. This race of men, collected from all parts of the country, had much in common. By a principle of natural selection, they were all kindred spirits. War, adventure, scouting, Indian fighting were their pleasures. What to other men was tragedy, was to them comedy. When taken prisoners by the Mexicans, they drew the black beans, which doomed them to military execution within ten minutes, with the same light, airy demeanor with which they would have thrown dice for drinks or flirted with a Mexican maid. Strange, wild fellows they were, often of gigantic stature, shaggy as lions, and not less brave. Such were the men who, in the wars between Texas and Mexico, and later, between the United States and Mexico, formed those historic bands of scouts known as "Texan Rangers."

Among the restless fellows who were drawn to Texas by the very troubles which drove other people from the State was Nelson Lee, a young man born and raised near Watertown, New York. He had volunteered for the Black Hawk war, but his company was scourged by small-pox while on their way to the front, and before the men recovered, poor old Black Hawk had been captured and deposed from his chieftaincy. Disappointed in this, young Lee took up a seafaring life. Tiring of this, he, in 1839, resolved to abandon the sea, and cast his fortunes among the fierce Texans. The state at that time, as will be remembered, was an independent republic, but a bloody border warfare raged incessantly with Mexico. Perhaps less with the notion of reconquering Texas than with annoying her people and gathering plunder, Mexican bandits were continually crossing the border and falling upon some remote and unsuspecting settlement like destroying devils, and then retreating as rapidly as they advanced. Of course, the Texans retaliated in the bloodiest manner.

For the purpose of protecting the settlers from these raids, as well as punishing the Mexicans, there came into existence bands of scouts, or bushwhackers, employed by the Texas government at a dollar a day, and known as the "Texan Rangers." Lee, finding no other employment so congenial or so profitable, soon enlisted in one of these companies, under Captain Cameron. The Ranger was usually dressed in buckskin, with a cap made from the fur of a wild-cat. Three or four revolvers and as many bowie knives were thrust through his belt, and a short rifle was thrown across his arm. The most important part of his equipment was a horse of great speed and endurance, on which a journey of eighty miles could be readily made between sunrise and sunset.

Lee's first taste of Ranger warfare was a fight with a band of Comanche Indians, who worried the settlements quite as much as the Mexicans. He was green at the business, but won the respect of his companions by his boldness, even if he did little execution. When, after a two hours' fight, the Indians took to flight, they left behind a deep impression on the mind of the young Ranger. A month or two afterward Lee and fifteen companions, under command of Ben McCullough, were sent out on a scout. Falling in with the trail of seven hundred Comanches,

the little party of spies remained a respectful distance and shadowed their movements. The Rangers were compelled to behold
from afar the sack and burning of the village of Lindville.
Meanwhile a call had been sent for re-enforcements, and the
scouts, who never let the enemy get out of their sight, were
joined by recruits, the fighting force numbering three hundred

THE RANGERS PURSUING THE COMANCHES.

men. The object of an attack was not merely to punish the
Indians, but to rescue seven white women, who had been taken
captive. These latter were rightly conjectured to be in the rear
of the camp with the old men. One detachment was to move
around to the rear and release the women if possible, while the
men fought from the front.

The first company arrived within view of their victims. The
Indians observed them at the same instant. In a moment the

red devils could be seen running toward the foot of a tree where sat the seven captive women. The Rangers heard despairing shrieks and saw the waving of white arms in the air, in the frenzy of supplication. Above the heads of the crowd could be seen tomahawks rising and falling. Horrified at the sight, the men rode at full speed into the Indian camp. The murderers had fled, leaving behind the corpses of five of their prisoners. In their hurry they failed to dispatch the two remaining women. These were rescued by the Rangers with tender gallantry.

While this was taking place Lee, fighting with the other detachment, received a bullet in his left arm, causing him to drop his bridle rein. His spirited horse sprang forward, directly in the midst of the Indians. Perceiving their comrade's danger, the Rangers threw themselves upon the Indians, and in a hand to hand conflict almost exterminated their foes. A little later Lee joined a company of Rangers, under the famous Jack Hays, at San Antonio.

In the intervals between scouting expeditions against the Mexicans, the Rangers occupied themselves with hunting and watching for Indian trails. One morning, while eating breakfast in their camp, on a short point of land at the intersection of Walker's Creek and the Guadaloupe River, the men discovered two Indians on the top of a high hill, near where they were encamped. It was evident that the men were in a trap. Hays called them together, and in a few ringing words explained the peril, then ordered them to follow him. He took his way directly up the hill toward the Indians, who were still watching the Rangers' movements with eager scrutiny. When half-way up the ascent, the savages suddenly disappeared. The same instant Hays wheeled his horse sharply to the right, and, followed by his men, swept around the side of the mountain at the top of his speed.

The Indian camp, containing two hundred warriors, was taken completely by surprise. They fought boldly, but at a disadvantage. At the first charge of the Rangers one of them, known as Big Sam Taylor, received an arrow through his cheek and neck. Failing to withdraw it he broke it off, and fought through the entire engagement with the cruel shaft thrust through his flesh. Later in the fight, when the dead Indians were heaped thickly upon the ground, Hays discovered a wounded chief, and resolved to take him captive. As the white man approached, he perceived a quick movement on the part of the Indian, and jumped aside. At the same instant an arrow sped from the bow of a fallen red man, and, missing Hays, buried itself in the throbbing heart of a Ranger named Mott. Even when assailed by several of his enemies, the stern old warrior, in spite of his broken leg, fought like a lion, beating off his foes again and again, until a pistol ball ended his struggles. When the battle was over, the Rangers found three of their men dead and four wounded. Of the Indians ninety corpses lay on the ground in the majesty of death.

On the way back to San Antonio after this fight, Lee dismounted with the rest one evening on the bank of a small stream. As his feet struck the ground, he heard a loud rattle in the grass, and instantly felt a fearful pain in his right leg. He was bitten by a rattlesnake. A Spaniard in the party sprang forward, killed the monster snake, and quickly cutting pieces of flesh from its wriggling body, applied them to the wound. Lee says he could feel them draw. The prompt treatment saved his life.

Arriving near San Antonio, the Rangers were enraged to find the town in the possession of a band of Mexican guerrillas. Entering the place at night, the Rangers surrounded a house where large numbers of the enemy were enjoying themselves in a grand fandango. A horrible fight ensued, which freed the town from the band of ruffians.

On one occasion, Lee left his magnificent horse, the Black Prince, at the town of Seguin. After an absence of some days he returned, to find that Indians had taken nearly every horse in the village, including the noble animal which he loved better than his life. Lee and a party of friends, mounted on mules, set out to make a reprisal. They traveled nearly all day, without success, when a black speck was discovered far away on the prairie. It attracted attention, and every eye was strained to watch the object. It grew larger. It came nearer. In time it could be seen to move. A little later, it assumed the outline of an animal. Two men declared that it was a horse. This conjecture proved correct. The animal, without rein or rider, was coming toward them at the top of its speed. In a little while the Black Prince, with mane and tail flying, eyes ablaze, nostrils distended, his black coat covered with flecks of white foam, dashed into the camp and, panting for breath, stopped by his owner's side. He had broken from his captors and traveled more than a hundred miles to rejoin his master.

One day Lee met Hays in San Antonio, and learned that Christolphe Rublo, in boyhood a vicious vagabond, in manhood a desperate villain, had been in the town as a spy for the Mexicans. He was suspected to have gone to the mission of San Juan, nine miles down the river. A band of twenty Rangers galloped to the place. The great gates swung open, and Lee and the rest entered. Rublo concealed himself behind the gates and attempted to escape, but fell into a ditch and was captured. He was taken to San Antonio, the people of which demanded the execution of the ruffian.

Jack Hays, however, declared that Lee and his fellow Rangers should conduct the prisoner to the town of Seguin, which was entitled to deal with him as its citizens wished, on account of Rublo's outrages upon them. The dispute over this question well-nigh involved the fiery Texans in a fight.

In the afternoon, Rublo and his fellow-villain, called the Ranchero, were brought out, placed upon horses, and marched from the town between files of shaggy Rangers. The arguments of the San Antonio people, that they would be in great danger if the Rangers left them to take the two prisoners to

Seguin, contained great truth. In this emergency the fertile mind of Hays devised a stratagem.

After leaving San Antonio and following the road toward Seguin till after nightfall, Lee and a companion named Escue, in whose special charge the two prisoners were, gradually fell to the rear of the Rangers, and then, under cover of darkness, turned sharply to the right, abandoning all roads and trails, and, with their two captives, struck out into the open plain. Meanwhile, the main body of Rangers wheeled about and marched back to San Antonio. Lee and his companion wrapped themselves and their prisoners in dark buffalo skins to avoid observation by the Mexican horsemen who were scouring the country, and hurried across the plain through a blinding rain.

Sometime after midnight a halt was called. Lee took Rublo from his pony, bound him hand and foot, and, with cocked pistol in hand, sat down by his side. The desperado knew that, unless he escaped, the outraged citizens of Seguin would, on the next day, take his life. Lee says that, for his part, he was perfectly well aware that, if Rublo should escape from him, the same citizens of Seguin would take his own life for permitting the escape. With this understanding, let us proceed.

Escue, who had charge of the Ranchero, selected a spot for passing the night some rods distant from Lee. His prisoner covered himself up with buffalo skins, and apparently fell into a deep sleep. Escue tied the halter of his horse to his ankle, believing this would keep him awake. In spite of this he went to sleep. The cunning Ranchero slipped out of his bonds, carefully arranged his hat among the buffalo skins, so that to the casual eye he was seen to be still lying there, took the halter off of Escue's horse and tied it to the limb of a tree, mounted and rode away.

In the morning Lee discovered a band of Mexicans approaching. The moment was critical. Escue's own horse was gone. The one left by the Ranchero was a broken down animal, useless for escape. The pony on which Rublo was mounted was a good one. Lee instantly made up his mind. He drew his revolver, shot his prisoner through the heart, yelled to Escue to mount the pony from which the lifeless desperado had fallen, and the two men began their flight, in which they were successful.

Lee and Escue brought word to San Antonio of the approach of the Mexicans. The Rangers fought a hard battle on the banks of Salado Creek. This invasion of the Mexicans, under General Woll, raised a popular clamor for a counter expedition against Mexico.

In the fall of 1842 the government of Texas gave a reluctant consent for the expedition. Twelve or fifteen hundred men, "renegades, refugees from justice, adventurers of all sorts, ready for any enterprise that afforded a reasonable prospect of excitement and plunder, dare-devils, afraid of nothing under the sun," assembled at San Antonio. General Somerville, who was placed in command, proved to be incompetent. He delayed marching for two months. Great numbers of the recruits deserted. When, finally, the Rio Grande was reached, various reasons induced Somerville to order a retreat of the expedition. Three hundred men, of which Lee was one, refused to obey. Somerville and the rest returned to their homes, but these bold fellows determined to push on into the enemy's country.

On the 23d of December, 1842, about two o'clock in the morning, the three hundred Rangers entered the town of Mier, and commenced a street fight in the darkness with the Mexican troops. Some of the Rangers, with crowbars and picks, were busily engaged in breaking openings through the stone walls of the buildings, and thus making their way toward the square, where the Mexicans were posted. The fight lasted many hours. In this battle Big Foot Wallace, whose adventures we detail hereafter, had a narrow escape. In one of the charges he followed a party of retreating Mexicans too far. They suddenly turned upon him, and in a flash surrounded him, rendering escape apparently impossible. He made a lunge at an opening

38

in the circle of enemies, threw one man down, and, receiving a bayonet-thrust through his left arm, succeeded in escaping.

At two o'clock in the afternoon there was a cessation of hostilities. The Mexicans sent out a flag of truce. For reasons never fully understood a surrender was made by the Texans. . Both Lee and Wallace agree that this was a mistake.

At the moment of the surrender, Lee, with ten companions, occupied a house at some distance from the main body. Noticing that the firing had ceased, Lee slipped out into the street to a point where he commanded a view of the Square, and discovered the Texans marching up and laying down their arms. Hurrying back to his comrades, he explained the situation in a few short words, announced his determination to die rather than be taken to a Mexican prison, and suiting the act to the word, leaped through a back window. He found himself in a large garden, and discovering a clump of high weeds, he crawled into their midst, remaining there till nightfall.

As soon as he felt safe in so doing, he left his hiding-place, stealthily made his way out of the town, and in half an hour found himself alone in the darkness on the banks of the rushing Rio Grande. Arranging his clothes in a bundle, and carrying his rifle, he plunged into the river. For a long time he swam. It seemed impossible to reach the opposite shore. Just as his strength was about to give way completely, Lee discovered the outline of the land. Putting forth all remaining strength, he managed to reach it only to find a perpendicular bluff, affording him not the slightest point of support. After a few faint and ineffectual struggles to clamber out of the water, he fell back into the waves, and floated hopelessly and helplessly down the tide.

At last he came within reach of a tree, which had been blown down and extended over the water. By means of this he clambered on to the shore, only to find himself in the midst of the prickly pear, of which the needle-like thorns lacerated his bleeding feet and limbs at every step. Exercising all the time in order to resist the cold of a stiff norther, he passed a miserable night.

In the morning, the unhappy man discovered a column of smoke apparently rising from a camp fire about a mile away. He at once made his way to the spot, crawling through the grass, and discovered two Mexican herdsmen, one a youth, the other a man of forty years.

Lee had pluck, and knew the Mexican character thoroughly. The two herdsmen were eating their breakfast. Near by stood their guns and ammunition. With an unloaded revolver in one hand, and a bowie knife in the other, the Ranger sprang out of the bushes and shouted for the Mexicans to surrender. The terrified herdsmen at once fell on their knees with a prayer for mercy.

Having compelled the youth to bind the man hand and foot, and having secured their guns and ammunition, Lee calmly proceeded to devour the breakfast which the herdsmen had prepared for themselves. Refreshed by the food, he proceeded to talk the situation over with his friends, and told them, that if they would guide him to a certain trail, he would set them free. The bargain was struck. After a three days' journey, during which time he did not suffer himself to sleep a moment, Lee found himself in a region where he no longer needed a guide. He took one of the Mexicans' guns, placed it at the foot of a tree with a lot of ammunition, called their attention particularly to the spot, and then ordered them to proceed as before. When the party had marched five miles from the spot where the gun had been left, Lee turned his prisoners loose, telling them that the gun and ammunition were to enable them to kill game on their way back. Lee made his way home without trouble.

Lee took an active part in the war of the United States with Mexico. His adventures during this war we will not here relate. He subsequently engaged in the cattle business, and in 1855 joined with a company of men in an enterprise, the object of which was to purchase a large drove of mules and drive them overland to the San Francisco market.

Among the articles which Lee purchased as an equipment for this trip was an enormous silver watch. It contained an alarm of remarkable noise and duration, which could be regulated to go off at any moment, and while ringing the alarm, the watch would actually move across a table.

The company was made up and commenced its march, large purchases of mules being made from time to time, and the easy journeys day by day gradually carrying them far beyond the boundaries of the settlements. On the evening of the 2d of April they were encamped in a beautiful valley. The hunters brought in some capital game, and a neighboring stream furnished lovely trout. After an abundant meal the men one by one went to sleep. Lee was on watch till midnight, when he was relieved. At that hour there were no indications of danger. The only sound which disturbed the profound silence of nature, was the irregular tinkle of the horses' bells.

Lee had been asleep but a short time when he was roused by a fearful shriek. He sprang to his feet, only to discover that the camp was full of painted Indians, who were killing the white men one after another. Lee had taken but a swift glance at the scene of horror, lit up by the dull glow of the dying camp-fire, when a lasso was thrown over his head, and he was jerked violently to the ground. A moment later several Indians sprang upon him and bound him. Three others besides Lee, named Thomas Martin, Stewart, and Aikens, escaped the massacre, and were bound similarly to Lee.

In removing Lee's clothing, one of the Indians discovered the silver watch which we have mentioned. The savage was delighted at the bright toy. While regarding it with the greatest curiosity, the minute-hand reached half-past three. At that instant the alarm went off. The savage was dumfounded as the thing roared and rattled for two minutes. Frightened beyond measure, he held the thing at arm's length, seemingly too much paralyzed by fear to let it drop, and looked away from it with an expression of sickly horror on his face. The other Indians quickly gathered about him. When the alarm ceased they began an unintelligible jabber. The first Indian pointed repeatedly to Lee, and finally the crowd of savages came toward him, and offered him the watch, with various gestures indicating that they wanted to hear it go off again.

The Ranger saw his advantage. His hands were unbound. He took the watch and, with many ceremonies and great solemnity, regulated it, so that in a few moments it went off again. After this the Indians had a long consultation. From their frequent gestures toward the sky, Lee divined that they regarded it as something supernatural and himself as some sort of a prophet.

When morning broke, the chief put the watch carefully away, and the Indians gave their attention once more to the white men's camp. The corpses of the poor fellows who had been murdered in their sleep were horribly mutilated. Some had arms and hands chopped off; some were disemboweled; some had their tongues drawn out and sharp sticks thrust through them. Toward the four men who were yet alive, the Indians behaved frightfully, flourishing tomahawks about their heads and pressing the blades of glittering knives against their throats as if unable to resist the fierce passion for murder.

At last the four prisoners were blindfolded and bound on the backs of mules. These animals were unbridled, and were left to follow the bell-mare at their own sweet will. At times the mules would knock their blindfolded riders against trees, inflicting fearful wounds. Each accident of this sort made the whole party of Indians yell with delight.

As evening approached, the hideous Comanches selected a camping-ground. A supper was made from horse-flesh. When the Indians had satisfied their own hunger, they tossed chunks of frying meat at the prisoners. These fiery bits, on which the fat was often ablaze, instead of being caught in their mouths, fell on the naked legs of the white men, burning them severaly. The prisoners were put to bed in a peculiar fashion. They were laid on their backs on the ground, their hands and feet extended as widely as possible, and fastened stiffly with buffalo thongs to four stakes conveniently driven in the ground. To say that they were unable to move hand or foot is to speak the literal truth. For several days they continued on their journey, butted against trees by the rascally mules, burnt with hot horse-flesh, and staked out at night in the fashion indicated.

Lee kept his thoughts busy, reflecting how he might take advantage of the incident of the watch. By the time he reached the Indian village he had matured in his own mind a unique system of theology, which he determined to teach the Indians if possible. The sun, as the Indians already believed, was God. The watch, in Lee's new theology, was the brother of the sun, and on most intimate terms with him. The revolution of the hands each day, Lee determined to make the Indians believe had a mysterious and sympathetic connection with the movement of the sun. Finally, it remained to convince the savages that Lee himself was the Great Spirit of the watch, and that if any thing happened either to him or to it, it would also destroy the sun.

Lee was taken to the house of the chief. Ordinarily a prisoner was the chief object of attention in the village. But on this occasion the watch was the favorite by heavy odds. A council was called. The watch was brought forth. After long and vociferous speeches the Indian sages pointed significantly to Lee and to the watch, desiring him to make it sound the alarm. Lee, pious fraud as he was, kneeled down, put up his hands toward the sun, as if in the attitude of prayer, then worked with the watch, pretending to persuade it to go, and finally rose to his feet, shook his head solemnly, and pointed to the sun as if to indicate that the celestial being prevented the watch from going off.

Later in the day Lee, who was rapidly rising in importance in popular opinion, was taken by a strong guard to a spot outside of the village, where a large crowd had already assembled. Here he found his friends Martin, Stewart, and Aikens, each drawn up and tied to pairs of posts, planted three feet apart. Some terrible ceremony was taking place. The Indians formed in a circle about the wretched men and deliberately scalped Stewart and Martin. Then they took sharp arrow-heads and made gashes in the bodies of the two men. This " they continued until every inch of the bodies of the unhappy men was haggled and hacked and scarified and covered with clotted blood." The two men screamed out in their agony, begging that they might be put to death. Lee and Aikens, sickened beyond measure, shut their eyes to keep out the horrid sight. The Indians did not neglect to pull their hair and flourish knives and hatchets about their heads as if to impress them that the fate of Stewart and Martin would shortly be theirs.

After two hours of torture the ring of warriors stopped dancing, formed closely about Stewart and Martin, and, at an appointed signal, a score of tomahawks were buried in the brain of each prisoner. When the scene of slaughter was ended, Lee and Aikens were separated.

From this time on he longed only for death. One day his bonds were removed. Hoping only to exasperate his captors into killing him outright, he picked up a club and tried to kill the nearest Indian. Instead of attaining the desired result, he found the savages only laughed at him. Not a day passed that the Indians did not beseech Lee to make the watch go off. Through all these requests he maintained a sullen and obstinate refusal.

One day Aikens was unexpectedly brought into the tent where Lee was kept, and the two men had a talk. Aikens, who was thoroughly familiar with Indian character and customs, told Lee that he himself was shortly to be put to death, but that he believed that Lee might yet escape through the instrumentality of the watch, if, instead of being sullen and stubborn, he would comply with the Indians' wishes, and exert himself to win their favor.

Lee took the advice. In time he was adopted into the tribe. He had long since lost sight of Aikens, and indeed never learned his fate. Little by little, Lee won their confidence, and acquired more and more liberty. He was allowed no weapons, but was permitted to walk about the village.

One day, Lee was suddenly ordered to mount a big mule, and follow Big Wolf, the chief. A band of warriors accompanied them. They traveled all day. At evening, Lee hastened to cook Big Wolf's supper. He had, indeed, for a long time, been his servant. During this whole period, the chief never took a mouthful of food until after Lee had tasted it, a precaution against poison.

At the close of the second day, they reached the village of the great chief, Spotted Leopard. Lee took an instinctive dislike to this chief and his people. Among the latter, however, was one who was his friend. She was Kianceta, the Weasel. Of her Lee speaks with enthusiam. She was of slender and beautiful figure, graceful and dignified. Her weird costume, with its gay embroidery and bead work, was partly obscured by her coal black hair, which fell in luxuriant profusion half-way to the ground.

But Kianceta's spirit was even fairer than her form. "She sympathized with the poor captive, when others laughed at him. She sat down by his side and looked up sorrowfully into his face, when the young savages of the village beat him with stones and sticks. A hundred times she stood between him and those who threatened harm; gave him corn when others had it not; attended him when sick, casting red-hot stones into a trough of water to make him a steam bath, and wrapping him with thick buffalo skins, until his cold was broken up and his health restored."

In spite of the charms of Kianceta, Lee furtively watched

his chances for escape. A half mile from the village was a
dark, wooded ravine, which if he could reach Lee believed
escape to be possible. After many nights passed in planning,
he resolved on the attempt. With the knife which he was at

SPOTTED LEOPARD, THE COMANCHE CHIEF.

this time permitted to carry he cut up some strips of venison
to serve him as food in his flight, and concealed the bundle of
them in a log. One midnight, when the village was asleep, and
Spotted Leopard snored loudly, on his royal couch, Lee slipped
quietly from the tent, made his way quietly to the log where

his venison was hidden, secured the precious pack and started to leave the village. He had reached the outer row of wigwams, when he was startled by the growl of a big dog, which confronted him, showing his white teeth.

In a moment the bark was caught up and answered by another cur at the farther end of the village. Others still disturbed the midnight air with fierce barks and lugubrious howls. On they came, one after another, with growls and snarls, to the spot where poor Lee stood, half dead with fright. It was but a moment from the time when the first dog discovered him until he found himself surrounded on all sides by barking curs.

Another danger also appeared. The village was roused by the unusual disturbance among the dogs, and sleepy warriors could be heard, one after another, from their wigwams, cursing the dogs, and telling them to lie down. Lee no longer thought of flight, but only of avoiding discovery. He crawled back to his tent and lay down, bitterly disappointed at his failure.

Still he did not give up. Days and weeks rolled by before he matured another plan. Although he was ordered not to go beyond the boundaries of the village, he disregarded the command, and ventured out from day to day, each time going a little farther. At first he was often told to go back. Then his disobedience was less and less noticed. Finally no one interfered with him at all.

One evening, just at dark, he started off in a slow, careless walk toward the ravine. He had gone a considerable distance when three warriors suddenly confronted him. He pretended to be cutting a stick from some bushes on which to cook his master's meat. The trick was too thin. The suspicions of the Indians were aroused. They seized him roughly by the arm and marched him back to the village. They reported the occurrence to Spotted Leopard. A long and earnest consultation was had, at the close of which the chief came out, seized Lee, and jerked him forcibly into the wigwam. After binding the runaway, hand and foot, the Indian rolled up his leggins and deliberately slashed a sharp knife across the muscle on the front of his leg just below the knee. This surgical operation was designed to cripple Lee, so escape would be impossible. The white man was kept tied for two weeks. Every day Spotted Leopard would seize his leg and work it back and forth, breaking open the wound anew. Eventually the limb healed, but was permanently stiff.

From time to time, Lee accompanied Spotted Leopard and his people on long hunts around the head-waters of the Guadaloupe. Once they had a fierce battle with the Apaches. Lee prayed that the Comanches might be whipped, but in this he was disappointed. On another occasion, they were visited by a friendly tribe, with a chief named Rolling Thunder. This Indian was naturally reverent. He was more fond of worshiping the sun on his knees than of dancing the war-dance. Such a character is unusual among the Indians. Lee was called out to give an exhibition with his watch, which he did, with marked effect, the pious Rolling Thunder ascribing every thing wonderful to some supernatural power.

Another party of Indians, on another occasion, encamped near them. In the afternoon Lee noticed an unusual stir among Spotted Leopard's people, which ended in the whole party's moving down toward the neighboring camp of the strangers. Lee felt something unusual was going to happen. Breathless with suspense, he listened. Presently a human voice rang out through the air in one awful scream of agony. At intervals it was repeated, growing feebler and feebler. An hour or two later, some Indians came after Lee, and took him through the strangers' camp. Scattered around he saw torn fragments of the uniform of a United States soldier. A few steps farther on, Lee saw the remains of the soldier. A stick had been thrust under his heel cords, and he had been hung up head downward, until at last, bleeding from many wounds, he gave up the ghost. No doubt he had been captured near some army post.

One day Lee discovered three white women captives of another band of the same tribe. It was months before he could speak to them. At last, on the occasion of a great feast and dance he was enabled to do so. They were English by birth. A Mormon missionary had induced them to leave their home, and, with a party of two hundred others, come to America. After a long voyage from England, they had landed at Indianola, on Matagorda Bay. From that point, their way lay overland to the Great Salt Lake. On the journey through the mountains many of the teams gave out. The party became separated. The Indians became troublesome, and finally captured large numbers, among whom were these three women. Lee felt a burning interest in this story of the misfortunes of these poor creatures, compared to which his own, inasmuch as he was at best an adventurer, were trifling.

After their capture the men were massacred. Mrs. Haskin's infant child was seized by an Indian, a hole cut under its chin, and then hung on the sharp limb of a tree, and left until death should relieve it. The three women were the common drudges of the camp. The elder, the mother of the others, becoming too feeble to work, was, soon after Lee met her, put to death by torture.

The pious Rolling Thunder made visits of increasing frequency to Spotted Leopard, which resulted at last in a change of masters for Lee. The chief use which Rolling Thunder made of his new captive was to make him describe the wonders of the world and of civilization.

Before long he invited Lee to choose a wife. To this the white man assented, and, after a careful inspection of the entire tribe, chose a young and slender squaw, rather dirty but good-looking, known as the Sleek Otter. The marriage resulted happily, and Lee received increased privileges.

During Lee's residence with this tribe two young warriors, who had a fierce quarrel of long standing, which the council had again and again attempted to settle, determined to fight, the matter to the death. Both men were athletic and powerful. They met in the center of a ring, and their left arms, as far up as the elbow, were lashed together with buffalo hide so firmly that there was no possibility of the men breaking away from each other. In the right hand of each was placed a hunting knife with a sharp blade nine inches long. The brothers of the combatants stood at a little distance, similarly armed.

At a given signal the two men raised their bright blades in air, then brought them down suddenly. In an instant they were again uplifted, no longer bright, but crimsoned with blood. For a minute the knives rose and fell incessantly, the men struggling with fury. "At length a mortal thrust by one was followed by a fierce blow from the other, gashing through the side of the neck, from which the purple tide of life spouted up in a wide, high arch, when both fell lifeless to the ground." Had either survived, the brother of the other would have at once put him to death.

Lee took many trips with Rolling Thunder, but on no occasion did the chief sleep alone with him in the tent. At last they took a three days' journey together without a companion toward a village, three days' journey to the north. While at this place the chief got drunk, and on the way home was exceedingly thirsty. After a long search a little pool of water was discovered. He ordered Lee to get him a drink in his hunting horn. The latter being unable to do this without scooping up considerable mud, the thirsty Indian sprang from his horse, threw down his rifle, and lying flat on the ground, drank eagerly from the pool. On the spur of the moment, as Lee's eye caught sight of a hatchet hanging on the Indian's saddle, a fearful thought burst upon him. In a moment the idea was put into execution. Snatching the hatchet, he bent over, and deliberately buried it in the Indian's head.

It was the work of a moment to seize the dead chief's gun and knife, mount his horse, and, leading the mule which he had himself ridden, dash away across the country. It was a lonely journey through a lonely wilderness, across rocky ridges, and along dark ravines. Late at night he paused for the first time. His only resource in the way of food was to kill the mule. Building a small fire he prepared himself a meal from the meat. Though refreshed by eating, a new horror presented itself. The blood and smell of the animal was scented by wild beasts, which crashed through the forest with horrid cries throughout the night.

At the end of fifty-six days' travel, Lee fell in with some Mexican traders, and, more dead than alive, was kindly cared for. When he had sufficiently recovered he left Texas, having had enough of life as a Ranger.

CHAPTER XVIII.

HEROES OF THE LONE STAR STATE, CONTINUED.

DAVID CROCKETT.

HE man whose name stands at the head of this chapter deserves a place in any sketch, however brief, of the heroes of the Lone Star State. This is not on account of his life, but of his death. Although nearly his entire career was passed elsewhere, he did for Texas all that a man could do—he gave his life for her. He was the most original character produced upon the American frontiers, as well as by all odds the most famous one.

David Crockett was born in a wretched cabin in East Tennessee, in the year 1786. His father was one of the worst specimens of frontier life. He kept a tavern, which consisted of nothing more than a tumbling cabin, with one room and an earthen floor. Its only accommodations consisted of a great jug of vile whisky. The old man, furthermore, was mean. When the boy was only twelve years old, the father hired him to a Dutchman to go on foot with him for four hundred miles and drive a herd of cattle. The trip was hard even for a man. Many a night the wretched boy, weary, supperless, spattered with mud, and drenched with rain, would lie on the ground without shelter or covering. The journey terminated in Virginia, where the Dutchman lived.

As for the boy, it remained to make his way back home

through the wilderness, four hundred miles in extent. He ob-tained permission to follow an emigrant's wagon, but quickly tiring of their slow progress, struck out alone into the wilder-ness, and soon left the emigrants far behind. We neither know how he obtained food, how he crossed the rivers, nor how he defended himself from wild beasts. We only know that it was winter when he started and spring when he reached his jour-ney's end.

The home to which he returned was miserable enough. The father was an intemperate old dog, and frequently would take a stout hickory stick and chase David for a mile or two, threat-ening each moment to kill him. The boy had a marvelous knack for avoiding his pursuer, and simply shouted and laughed at his father's drunken failures. Crockett naturally drifted away from such a home and engaged in many wild trips over the country to the eastern cities, once even arranging to go to London. This he failed to carry out.

He married an Irish girl in his neighborhood when quite young, and, after the birth of two children, he packed his little belongings on one shaky old horse, placed his wife and children on its mate, and struck across the country to penetrate two hun-dred and fifty miles further into the western wilderness. This was not his only move. Apparently from innate vagrancy, he would no sooner gather a crop than he would abandon his crum-bling shanty, and remove to some other location.

When the Creek war broke out in 1811, such a restless woodsman as Crockett was eager to engage in the conflict. He had many thrilling adventures during the war which we may not here recount. The sufferings of the army for want of food, which were shared by Crockett, have been briefly related else-where. During the war his wife died, but, with ready adapta-tion to circumstances, he quickly married a widow whom he met. A few months after his marriage, intent on another change of location, he and three neighbors set out on an explor-ing tour in central Alabama.

One morning when the explorers awoke, they discovered that their horses were gone. Crockett at once set out on foot, through forest, bog, and ravine, across creeks and over hills, to follow them. It is almost impossible to believe, yet true, that before nightfall he had traversed fifty miles. He stopped that night at a settler's cabin, but awoke in the morning to find himself so lame from his great walk that he could scarcely move. Though suffering greatly, he left the cabin and hobbled along a few miles, hoping that exercise would improve him.

While proceeding in this way, consumed with fever and tottering with weakness, he fell, overcome by deathly sickness. A happy fortune prevented him from being left here to die or be devoured by wild beasts. Some Indians, coming through the forest, saw the prostrate form of the poor, sick, white man, and quickly attempted to minister to his wants. One of them had a watermelon, from which he cut a slice for the refreshment of the sufferer. Then, taking him in their arms, they carried him to the cabin of a white man, two miles distant. With true frontier kindness, the people of the place received him, put him to bed, and prepared such herbs and other primitive medicines as their resources afforded.

The next day, as the delirium was beginning to settle down in dense clouds upon the mind of the patient, two white men, having been informed by the Indians that one of their countrymen was lying sick at the place, came to the cabin. They proved to be acquaintances of Crockett. The latter was able to recognize them, and in his delirium begged and besought them to take him to his three companions whom he had left at the camp. He was placed upon a sort of litter, and they carried him all the way, fifty miles, to the spot where his companions were waiting.

At the end of the journey his fever had risen to a fearful height. It was evident that a long spell of sickness was before him. All that could be done was to find the cabin of some

39

kind pioneer woman, and there leave Crockett, unaided by medical skill, to fight, single-handed, the battle of life and death. He received the kindest attention. His pallet occupied the corner on the earthen floor of the cabin. After weeks of suffering he began to recover. Although emaciated and tottering with weakness, he employed a wagoner to carry him home. He arrived there to find that his family had given him up for dead.

In spite of this misadventure, Crockett, instead of settling down, removed with his family to a spot called Shoal Creek, in what is now Giles county, Tennessee. In a new country, cattle stealing is regarded as the worst of crimes, and is punished with instant death. This grows out of the fact that it is the crime to which society in such a region is most liable, and against which it has the least protection. Crockett, whose great force of character always asserted itself in every situation, became a self-appointed justice of the peace. Subsequently, he was legally appointed to the position.

Before the appointment, whenever Crockett made up his mind that a fellow ought to be punished, he had simply ordered the young men who were his self-appointed constables to catch the culprit. When he was brought before him there was a short, sharp trial, lasting not more than three minutes, and then the judge passed sentence, saying: " Take the thief, strip off his shirt, tie him to a tree, and give him a good flogging. Then burn down his cabin and drive him out of the country." From this judgment no appeal would lie. When Crockett was legally appointed justice, he was greatly troubled in mind to learn that they required written warrants. In spite of this difficulty, he got along pretty well, and as he says, " My judgments stuck like wax."

David Crockett would probably never have been known to fame had he not entered politics. He was a famous hunter, and popular; on this account, some of the rough settlers suggested that he become a candidate for the legislature. He was ambitious, and took fire at the suggestion. In, June, 1821, he began his campaign. He says: "It was a brand-fire new business to me. It now became necessary that I should tell the people something about the government and an eternal sight of other things, that I know'd nothing more about than I did about Latin and law, and such things as that. I know'd so little about it, that if any one had told me that General Jackson was the government I should have believed it, for I had never read even a newspaper in my life."

About this time there was a great squirrel hunt on Duck River, which Crockett resolved to attend. The people were to divide into two parties, and hunt for two days. Then they were to assemble, count the scalps, and the party which had killed the less number of squirrels was to pay for a big dinner and country frolic. Owing to Crockett's marvelous skill, his party killed the most squirrels.

As the dinner proceeded and whisky began to flow like water, Crockett was called out to make a speech as a candidate, to be followed by his opponent. Crockett was, he says, "As ignorant of the business as an outlandish negro. I got up and told the people I reckoned they knowed what I had come for, but if not I could tell them. I had come for their votes, and if they did n't watch mighty close I would get them too. But the worst of all was that I could not tell them any thing about the government. I choked up as bad as if my mouth had been jamm'd and cramm'd chock full of dry mush." However, he managed to tell a story or two, and then seeing the people in a good humor took care to remark that he was "as dry as a powder horn, and that it was time for us all to wet our whistles a little." He then went off to a liquor stand, taking nearly the whole crowd with him, and leaving his competitor to speak to about six men.

Crockett was elected to the legislature, as a matter of course. When he went to the State Capital he felt that the most important thing for him to do was to learn the meaning of the words *government* and *judiciary*. Having learned these points by a great deal of adroit questioning, he felt quite well equipped. He became the fun maker of the legislature. While he liked to raise a laugh at others, he would not stand a laugh at himself. One day a legislator referred to him as "the gentleman from the cane." That evening Crockett invited the man pleasantly to take a walk with him, and when they reached a lonely spot announced that he brought his companion there for the purpose of whipping him within an inch of his life. The man pleaded so hard, however, that Crockett let him off.

After the adjournment of the legislature, Crockett again determined to move further west. He and a companion struck out into a new region on the Obion River. Here he killed deer and elk almost without number. He built a cabin and planted a crop of corn. During the summer he killed no less than ten bears. In the fall he returned for his family and brought them to his new quarters.

His physical endurance was wonderful. In the winter, about Christmas, he was trying to cross a slough by getting on a log and poling across. Somehow he fell into the water, which was ten feet deep. The weather was extremely cold. Getting out on the bank, which was covered with a deep snow, he removed his clothes and hung them on a tree to dry. He then attempted to warm himself by running, but found his legs taken with the cramp, so that he could not make a step six inches long. It was late in the evening before he dragged himself back to his cabin, a feat accomplished with infinite suffering. Yet he relates that he wrapped himself in bear skin, and lying down upon the floor with his feet to the fire, passed the night with comfort and awoke in the morning without feeling any ill effects whatever from his exposure.

During the continuation of the same storm which was raging at the time of the above incident the meat gave out in the cabin, and the men set out in the blinding sleet to hunt game. Crockett, with three dogs, one of which was pretty old, started in a direction where he thought he might find a bear. Every hour the storm grew more furious. The bushes, with which the forest was filled, became so thick with ice that he could no longer force his way through. He had seated himself on a log to rest, when he heard his dogs set up a terrible barking. He followed them as best he could, but no game was in sight, and he concluded the dogs were only making mischief. "Just at that moment," says he, "looking on before my dogs, I saw the biggest bear that ever was seen in America. At that distance he looked like a big, black bull." He hurried forward to find his dogs engaged in a life and death conflict with the bear. It required three bullets to kill him.

The storm had not abated at all. Crockett hurried back through the icy forest to his cabin, twelve miles away. He and the other two men, who had returned unsuccessful from their hunt, taking four pack horses, set out at once, in spite of fatigue and tempest, to secure the game, an enterprise in which they succeeded. In this way the cabin was furnished with an abundant supply of splendid meat.

It soon occurred to Crockett to again offer himself for the legislature. On a certain day he appeared at a great political gathering, and began his own peculiar method of electioneering. Having mounted a stump, he began to banter his opponent, Dr. Butler. He took care to assure his audience that though he was very poor, he proposed to furnish his supporters all the whisky they could drink. "When I goes electioneering, I goes fixed for the purpose. I've got a suit of deer leather clothes with two big pockets. I puts a bottle of whisky in one, and a twist of tobacco in t'other, and starts out. Then if I meets a friend, why I pulls out my bottle and gives him a drink. He'll be mighty apt, before he drinks, to throw away his tobacco. So, when he is done, I pulls my twist out of t'other pocket, and gives him a chaw. I never likes to leave a man worse off than I found him."

Dr. Butler, Crockett's opponent, lived in a frame house. In

the front room the middle of the floor was covered with a piece of carpet. One day the doctor called to some men, passing, to come in and take a drink. The whisky sat on a table in the center of the room. The men came in and, of course, had never seen a carpet before. They walked cautiously around on the bare part of the floor without daring to put their feet upon the carpet.

Soon afterward, they were heard inquiring of Crockett's friends how he lived. On learning that he lived in a log cabin of one room, without any glass for the window, and with earth alone for the floor, they declared that he was the fellow for them. "Why," said one of them, "when Butler called us into his house to take a drink, he spread down one of his best bed quilts for us to walk on. He's too proud for us." Crockett was elected to the legislature, and served two years.

The bear hunter soon found himself a famous man. Without changing his mode of life, he announced himself as a candidate for Congress, and though unable to read, and barely able to sign his name, was elected by nearly three thousand majority. On his way to Washington City, he reached Raleigh, North Carolina, on a cold, wet evening. Entering the tavern and elbowing his way through the crowd toward the fire, some fellow gave him a shove, and said with an oath, "Who are you?" Crockett roared out, "I am that same David Crockett, fresh from the back woods, half horse, half alligator, a little touched with the snapping turtle. I can wade the Mississippi, leap the Ohio, ride upon a streak of lightning, and slip without a scratch down a honey locust. I can whip my weight in wild cats, and if any gentleman pleases for a ten-dollar bill he can throw in a panther. I can hug a bear too close for comfort, and eat any man opposed to General Jackson." They made room for Crockett around the fire!

When the bear hunter got to Washington, he was invited to dine with President Adams, at a state dinner. The newspapers of the time gave what purported to be Crockett's own account of that dinner. " I went to dinner, and I walked all around the long table looking for something that I liked. At last I took my seat beside a fat goose, and I helped myself to as much of it as I wanted. I had n't took three bites when I saw a man away up the table talking French to a woman on t' other side. He dodged his head and she dodged hers, and then they got to drinking wine across the table. When I looked back again, my plate was gone, goose and all. I seed a white man walking off with it. I says, Hello mister, bring back my plate. He fetched it back in a hurry, but when he set it down before me, how do you think it was? Licked as clean as my hand. If it was n't I wish I may be shot. Says he, What will you have, sir? And says I, you may well say that after stealing my goose. I then filled my plate with bacon and greens, and whenever I looked up or down the table I held on to my plate with my left hand.

" When we were all done eating, I saw a man coming along carrying a great glass thing, with a glass handle below, something like a candlestick. It was stuck full of little glass cups with something in them that looked good to eat. Says I, Mister, bring that thing here—thinks I, let's taste 'em. I found they were mighty sweet and good, so I took six of them."

Crockett found that his constituency were so much annoyed by this story that he obtained certificates of his good behavior at the table from three New York 'congressmen. This done, he felt better. Crockett passed two terms in Congress. The third time he stood for election he was beaten. But after two years of retirement was elected for another term. During this last term he made a tour of the eastern cities, attracting great attention.

In Boston he made a speech full of force and rude eloquence, surprising in the knowledge which it displayed, when one considers the man, explaining why he had become opposed to the policy of President Jackson. The fifth time Crockett was a candidate for Congress, he made tremendous efforts. He appeared at the political meetings in his old costume as a bear hunter, with his rifle on his shoulder, and accompanied by his three famous bear dogs. He made funny speeches and gave away whisky like water. **But all in vain.** His constituency could

COLONEL DAVID CROCKETT.

not forgive him for going back on Andrew Jackson. He was beaten. He was terribly crushed by the defeat. Bear hunting and pioneer life had lost their charm. To drown his sorrow, he determined to join the adventurers who were thronging to the state of Texas.

His head-quarters were at San Antonio. Early in the month of February, 1836, Santa Anna, at the head of a large Mexican army, appeared before the town. The defenders of the place, seeing that they were being surrounded, withdrew to the fortress of Alamo, just outside the town of San Antonio. Crockett and a few followers constituted a most important part of the garrison, which consisted of only one hundred and fifty bold and desperate men. Over the battlements they unfurled an immense flag of thirteen stripes, and with a large, white star of five points surrounded by the letters of the word " TEXAS."

The Alamo, at that time, consisted of a chapel, seventy-five feet long, sixty-two feet wide, and twenty-two and a half feet high, surrounded by walls of solid masonry four feet thick. The upper part of the walls were arranged for fourteen mounted cannon. Besides this building were two long and narrow barracks of similar construction, the walls being of solid rock. The singular structure was built by Roman Catholic missionaries from Spain, about the middle of the last century, and was occupied by them for many years. Here, long years before, the tireless priests had sought, by processions, chants, mystical emblems, and beautiful ceremonies, to win the hearts of the Indians, and induce them to adopt the true religion. These efforts were not unsuccessful. The good fathers found the savages far more disposed to virtue and more susceptible to religious impressions than the Spanish soldiers, their own countrymen, attached to the mission, who were gamblers and roustabouts of the worst sort.

For several days the enemy devoted themselves to ravaging the surrounding country and picking off the defenders of the fortress by their sharp-shooters. On the morning of the 6th of March, just at dawn, the garrison, already weakened and shattered by a bombardment which had lasted for two days, were roused by the single blast of a bugle in the enemy's camp. At that moment, Santa Anna's entire army of three thousand men, divided into three columns a certain number of men in each of which carried axes and scaling ladders, moved forward at a double-quick to storm the fortress simultaneously at different points. The cannon from the fortress rendered but little service. The gates were battered down and the enemy swarmed over the walls. The outer wall was abandoned, and the garrison took refuge in the heavy buildings already described. All this passed within a few minutes after the bugle sounded.

"The early loss of the outer wall, so thinly manned, was inevitable; and it was not until the garrison became more concentrated, that the main struggle began. They were more compact as to space, but not as to unity, for there was no communication between the buildings, nor often between rooms. There was now no retreat from point to point; each group of defenders had to fight and die in the den in which it was brought to bay. The struggle was made up of a series of separate and desperate combats, often hand to hand, between squads of the garrison and bodies of the invaders. From without, the Mexicans concentrated the fire of all their cannon upon the openings in the walls. Within was the roar of the musketry, the cries and curses of the maddened men, the deadly stabs given and received, the floors flowing with blood and encumbered with heaps of corpses.

The contest was too unequal. Little by little the separate squads of Texans were butchered in the rooms in which they had taken refuge. Only six men of the entire garrison remained alive. Of these David Crockett was one. He stood in the corner of the room like a lion at bay. Twenty Mexicans lay dead at his feet. His few comrades, too, had fallen, and lay in death, their hands still clenching the hair and throats of their enemies. As the Mexicans poured in upon him, the brave man still fought, his eyes flashing fire, his shattered rifle in his right hand, and in his left a gleaming bowie-knife dripping with blood. His face was covered with blood from a gash in his forehead.

He was seized, disarmed, and, with five other prisoners, also captured alive in different portions of the fortress, taken to the spot where Santa Anna was standing. The Mexican commander cried out, "Kill them! kill them on the spot!" Instantly a dozen swords were uplifted. Crockett, at that moment, sprang like a tiger at the throat of Santa Anna, but, before he could reach him, a fatal thrust pierced his heart, and he fell without a word. There still remained, however, upon his brow the frown of indignation, and his lip was curled with a smile of defiance and scorn.

THE FIGHTING PARSON.

Andrew Jackson Potter was born in Chariton county, Missouri, April 3, 1830. His parents were from Kentucky, and settled finally in what is now called Gentry county, where he spent his childhood days. His father died in 1840. The boy was nimble, fearless, self-reliant, and at an early age earned a distinction as rider at horse races. "Andy's horse always won."

At the beginning of the Mexican war he entered the army, but was rejected because he was under size. In a few days he was employed as teamster in a wagon train of army supplies destined for Santa Fe. About the fifth night after leaving Fort Leavenworth the caravan was attacked by the Indians. One man was killed by a ball which passed through Potter's clothes.

A day or two afterward two Indians traveled with the teams all afternoon. In the evening three others of friendly bearing appeared. The next day, two or three small groups fell in with the train. Suddenly a band of Cheyenne warriors with drawn bows surrounded the train. The drivers, terror-stricken, huddled together behind the wagons. Potter stole toward a pony grazing at the road-side intending to mount the animal and fly when the killing commenced. The capture ended, however, by the savages loading themselves with merchandise from the wagons, and leaving the train to proceed without other damage.

A month afterward a more serious attack was made on them. While the teamsters were eating supper, the war whoop and a shower of arrows signaled them to arms. The train-master had drilled his men, fifty in number, armed with flint-locks, to form for the defensive in two divisions, the first to deliver their fire when ordered, and while they reloaded, the other company to fire. By this method the savages were given a hot reception, and in an hour or so, withdrew across the river, leaving a number of ponies and pools of blood as evidence of their loss. At the first volley fired Potter dropped, as his comrades thought dead. But the old blunderbuss of a gun had merely kicked him over. The sight and danger of savages soon lost their terror, and hunting excursions were indulged in by the less cautious of the company.

On one occasion Potter found himself alone. While leisurely letting his mule graze he discovered a number of Indians stealing along to cut him off from the teams. Quick as thought, leaping from a prostrate position, he was on the mule and slashing his spurs into its sides. He thrashed the frightened brute wildly with his fists. In his insane haste to mount, he failed to catch the reins, which had been lengthened to let the mule graze. It happened that the animal was headed toward the wagons, and the rider had nothing to do but to kick and pound, and the mule nothing to do but run. And they were at it, each to the last extent of strength. The rider had been trained to race, and had always won. The mule was being trained at a fearful rate. They sped through brush and rocks and logs. Every leap seemed unto death. Potter, yet daring danger at every step, swept on and on. Arrows grazed him every moment. The savages, yelling, were at his very heels. They had been leveling their lances for a mile, preparing to hurl them at him. He was barely beyond their reach. A few yards to his right, they were abreast of him! A moment more, dead or safe! A

gully momentarily hindered those who were in the act of striking him down. A turn in the trail, and he was in the camp.

Potter abandoned ox-driving in April, 1851, and took the
position of interpreter, guide, property man, and generalissimo
of a company of Mormons. His outfit was a musket, knife,
revolver, and mule. The first night the Mexicans stole the
mule. The Mormons turned pale at the rage of their guide.
Mounted on a borrowed horse, he galloped away at early
dawn to recover his property. He made an exhaustive search
through the region before he found four greasers surrounding
the animal and trying to "rope it." He dashed into their
midst with his "pepper-box" revolver and shot one dead. The
other three made at him with their knives. For ten minutes
he was the busiest man alive, but kept their blades out of his
body, if not his clothes. Well-nigh dead with exhaustion from
the terrible struggle, he at length wounded two and the other
fled. His Mormon employés saw the fight from a distance,
and greeted the victor with a triumphant reception.

As a Mormon escort, Potter was not happy, so he took a
number of men and made his way to the mines of Arizona,
where they gathered a quantity of precious metal. But game
was scarce, and the Apaches were harassing. With seven
picked men Potter made a journey of a thousand miles, to San
Antonio, Texas. He was now of age, with an iron constitution,
and a frame of the finest and most powerful build. His splendid muscles, compacted by a hardy frontier life, were perfect.
His courage was superb; yet under this cover of brawn and in
this gnarled and knotty creature, throbbed a heart of womanly
tenderness. Frank, peaceable, kind-hearted, generous, brave, he
was universally popular.

At a Methodist camp-meeting he became a Christian. It
was from midnight to noon with him in an instant. His Christianity was of the "Andrew Jackson" type, through and through,
and well adapted to the purposes of the locality. A religious
old gentleman had a tract of timber land which was being taken

by a saw-mill man in spite of all the remonstrances, threats, and persuasions that could be made. One day the injured neighbor came out and related his grievance to Potter. The job suited him. He was a peace-maker. The two called on the trespassing bully. Potter stated the case in his quiet way, and said, " Pay for what you have taken and stop." It was done.

This little incident is a hint at a marvelous faculty which he possessed when aroused or enraged. He spoke in a low tone, which gave each word the emphasis of a sledge-hammer. His look, manner, and tone at such a time would instantly assuage the fury of the fiercest ruffian. In Texas, they said, " Potter's man always whips." The Church people, especially, gave him a liberal share of the various burdens.

On a stormy evening he was called to see a pugnacious old Dutchman who had come home drunk, beaten his wife horribly, and driven his family out in the storm. This was in Potter's line. He went, pleased that so much of his border experience was available in religious work. The old Dutchwoman was found sitting by a fodder stack in the rain, bruised and crying. The cabin door was barred. With one kick, Potter smashed it in. He dealt the old man a terrific blow, which sent him headlong into the fire, then jerked him out, jumped astride him, and commenced to pound and exhort the old sinner with amazing vigor. The response from the prostrate congregation was so faint and slow, that he was tempted to close the exercises. With a minute's respite and a sup of water, the congregation called for its gun. A quiet " No," from the parson satisfied the audience that prayer could not be answered. Another intermission, a little more bathing and camphor, enabled the congregation to yell for its knife. A gesture with the fist at the congregation stopped this. When Potter left the house the Dutchman was subdued enough.

In 1861 Potter visited the scenes of his childhood in Missouri. In the family where he visited was a man who abused his wife most cruelly. Guiltily suspecting that Potter might interfere, he swore that he would knife the parson if he came in his way. This was a case after Potter's own heart. He told the fellow that he must never repeat this work. The man whipped out his knife, seized his gun, and was about to fire, when Potter quietly approached, took the weapon out of his hands, and pounded him in the stomach with the muzzle. The ruffian stood pitiable and unresisting, saying, "You have my arms, I can not fight." "Take your gun," said Potter, thrusting it at him, "and ask that woman's forgiveness, or you will never need a gun or knife again." It was done.

When the war broke out, Potter enlisted in a cavalry regiment. He was a favorite among the soldiers. Long before his commission was issued he was, by common consent, made chaplain. Among the cavalrymen was a six-foot Texan, of powerful build, overbearing, and quarrelsome. He was a desperate character. No one cared to resist any bearable imposition from him. He became the terror of the camp.

Texan justice is swift. The Fighting Parson resolved to take the matter in hand. A crowd gathered around as he walked toward the bully and shouted, "You are a liar. Now resent it." The stalwart Texan rushed at his antagonist to stamp him in the dust. A hundred soldiers who knew little of the parson, drew their knives to protect him. He pushed the ruffian in the breast, saying, "Coward, stop!" The Texan was cowed into a wilted puppy.

A slanderous statement was made in a Brownsville paper about Wood's regiment, while they were in camp at that place. The chaplain sought out the editor who had thus defied the troops. The sermon was short, but the congregation grew pale and trembling as it proceeded. The announcement at the close, that the exercises would be resumed in half an hour, when the preacher and a squad of soldiers would pitch the press and audience into the Rio Grande, to be washed of their vileness, completed the conversion of the congregation, and it started through a back window pell-mell for a new field of usefulness.

Colonel Debray's regiment, of which Potter was chaplain, was ordered to Navasota, in 1864, to join in the campaign against General Banks. On reaching their destination, the commissary refused to honor the colonel's order for supplies. After two or three failures the parson went. "Who are you?" growled the officer. "A white man," said a quiet, deep voice. There was unburnt powder in the tone. The commissary glanced at his customer. "What do you want?" said the officer. "Corn," said Potter, "and we'll have it or arrest you." "Don't try that," said the commissary; "we will settle this with six shooters." "I am ready," said Potter. The corn was instantly furnished.

With this incident our incomplete sketch of the Fighting Parson must terminate. He is, no doubt, the greatest living representative of a class of men who have been found ever on our frontiers; brave in beating back the savages; dauntless in rebuking the border ruffians; zealous and successful in planting the seeds of law and order, of civilization and religion, in the wild soil of the pioneer heart. The greater part of this man's career, his encounters with ruffians at revival meetings, his sermons in desperate neighborhoods, with a pair of huge revolvers lying before him on his pulpit, his eloquent addresses, his pure religious zeal, lie outside of the scope of this work. He is still living in Boerne, Western Texas, ardently engaged in his sacred calling. The days of fights are long since over. At the age of fifty-three, he is enabled to devote all his energies to the gospel of peace.

www.ingramcontent.com/pod-product-compliance
Lightning Source LLC
Chambersburg PA
CBHW022111080426
42734CB00006B/84